EXHIBIT 5-6 STOCK MARKET CAPITALIZATION DEVELOPED COUNTRIES,

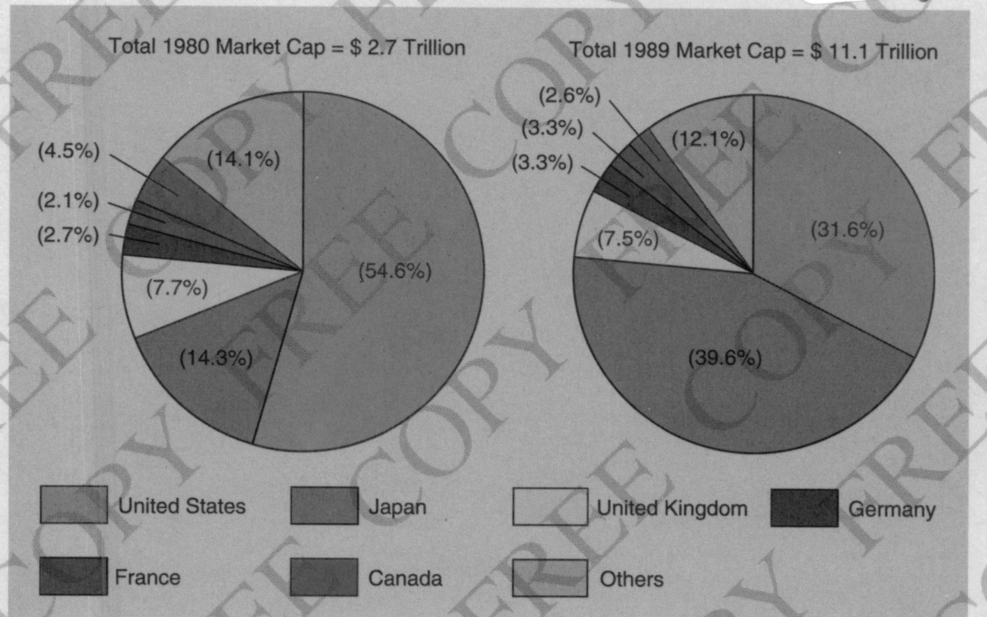

Source: Calculations and graphic based on data from International Finance Corporation, *Emerging Stock Markets Factbook,* 1990.

EXHIBIT 5-7 STOCK MARKET CAPITALIZATION EMERGING MARKETS 1980 AND 1989

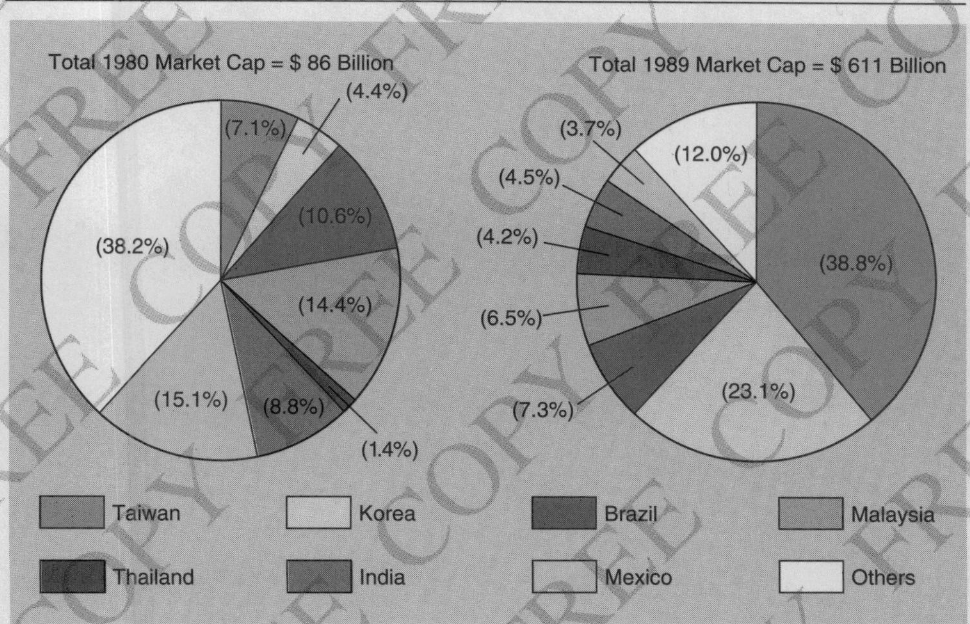

Source: Calculations and graphic based on data from International Finance Corporation, *Emerging Stock Markets Factbook,* 1990.

FINANCIAL INSTITUTIONS AND MARKETS

A Global Perspective

McGraw-Hill Series in Finance

Consulting Editor

Charles A. D'Ambrosio, *University of Washington*

Archer and Kerr: Readings and Cases in Corporate Finance
Blake: Financial Market Analysis
Brealey and Myers: Principles of Corporate Finance
Doherty: Corporate Risk Management: A Financial Exposition
Dubofsky: Options and Financial Futures: Valuation and Uses
Edmister: Financial Institutions: Markets and Management
Edwards and Ma: Futures and Options
Francis: Investments: Analysis and Management
Francis: Management of Investments
Fuller and Farrell: Modern Investments and Security Analysis
Garbade: Securities Markets
Gibson: Option Valuation: Analyzing and Pricing Standardized Option Contracts
Johnson: Financial Institutions and Markets: A Global Perspective
Johnson and Slottje: Case Studies in Finance Using Lotus 1-2-3
Johnson and Slottje: Case Studies in Finance Using Microsoft Excel
Kester and Luehrman: Case Problems in International Finance
Lang: Strategy for Personal Finance
Levi: International Finance: The Markets and Financial Management of Multinational Business
Martin, Petty, and Klock: Personal Financial Management
Schall and Haley: Introduction to Financial Management
Sharpe: Portfolio Theory and Capital Markets
Smith: Case Problems and Readings: A Supplement for Investments and Portfolio Management

FINANCIAL INSTITUTIONS AND MARKETS

A Global Perspective

Hazel J. Johnson

University of Louisville

McGraw-Hill, Inc.

New York St. Louis San Francisco Auckland Bogotá Caracas Lisbon
London Madrid Mexico Milan Montreal New Delhi Paris
San Juan Singapore Sydney Tokyo Toronto

FINANCIAL INSTITUTIONS AND MARKETS
A Global Perspective

1 2 3 4 5 6 7 8 9 0 DOW DOW 9 0 9 8 7 6 5 4 3

ISBN 0-07-032639-8

This book was set in Times Roman by The Clarinda Company.
The editors were Kenneth A. MacLeod, Peitr Bohen, and Bernadette Boylan;
the designer was Joan Greenfield;
the production supervisor was Louise Karam.
R. R. Donnelley & Sons Company was printer and binder.

Part-Opener Photo Credits
Part I Arlene Collins/Monkmeyer
Part II Steve Elmore/The Stock Market
Part III Jay Freis/The Image Bank
Part IV Joel Gordon
Part V Jaye R. Phillips/The Picture Cube
Part VI Hazel Hankin/Stock, Boston

Library of Congress Cataloging-in-Publication Data

Johnson, Hazel.
Financial institutions and markets: a global perspective / Hazel J. Johnson.
p. cm. — (McGraw-Hill series in finance)
Includes index.
ISBN 0-07-032639-8
1. Financial institutions—United States. 2. Financial institutions, International. I. Title. II. Series.
HG2491.J64 1993
332.1′5—dc20 92-35125

ABOUT THE AUTHOR

Dr. Hazel J. Johnson is a member of the finance faculty of the College of Business and Public Administration of the University of Louisville and a former member of the finance faculty of Georgetown University. Prior to earning her doctorate at the University of Florida, she worked as a C.P.A. and auditor for a national accounting firm, as a bank financial analyst, and as manager of internal audit for a national insurance company. Dr. Johnson's research has been published in the United States and abroad on topics including decision-making in the banking industry, international capital flows and investment trends, international comparisons of economic development, and the Latin American debt crisis. Other professional activities include serving as a professional banking school instructor and as a consultant for financial institutions. In addition, Dr. Johnson has published other books including *Dispelling the Myth of Globalization: The Case for Regionalization* (Praeger, 1991) and *The Bank Valuation Handbook: A Market-Based Approach to Valuing a Bank* (Probus, 1992). Forthcoming publications with Probus in 1993 include *Bank Keiretsu; Global Banking Trends;* and *A Guide to the Capital Budgeting Decision.*

FREE COPY

In loving memory of
Ida W. Kelly and Lucille V. Johnson

CONTENTS IN BRIEF

CONTENTS

PREFACE

Financial markets make it possible for resources to be devoted to productive uses for the benefit of society. These financial resources are made available for the short-term or for longer periods of time. Some of the most familiar financial institutions that help accomplish this allocation are commercial banks, mutual funds, pension funds, and insurance companies. This book describes financial institutions and markets in the United States. It also outlines the challenges faced by U.S. institutions—the consolidation of the banking industry, the savings and loan crisis, the strong competition among financial institutions as they diversify into new lines of business, and the regulatory environment that sometimes helps and sometimes hurts the process of advancement in the financial sector.

Of course, the United States is only one participant (albeit a major participant) in the financial market place. Increased competition among the United States and its trading partners means that the functions of U.S. markets cannot be fully understood unless analyzed in an international context. Accordingly, this book includes descriptions of the financial sectors of other countries, including Japan, the United Kingdom, Germany, Canada, and others. With this coverage, students can begin to appreciate the similarities or common themes throughout the world. They will also gain insight into the differences—many of which are tied to economic or political factors. Japan, for example, has become a leading financial market because of large trade surpluses (exports in excess of imports) in recent years. As its 12 members work to form a single European Market, the European Community is being reshaped into one unified financial market instead of 12 separate groups of laws and practices. History, economic circumstance, and political orientation have molded financial institutions and markets to varying degrees in different countries. The international material included in this book is integrated throughout the text with the country coverage indicated at the beginning of the chapters.

The book is organized into six parts:

		Chapters
I	Money and Capital Markets	1–9
II	Bank Regulation	10–12
III	Bank Management	13–15
IV	Banks Around the World	16–18
V	Nonbank Depository Institutions	19–20
VI	Contractual Nonbank Financial Institutions	21–24

Part 1 describes money or short-term markets (Chapter 3) and capital or long-term markets (Chapters 4 and 5), including derivative securities. It begins with a discussion of the process of financial intermediation (Chapter 1) and the characteristics of money (Chapter 2). The operation of foreign currency markets is covered in Chapter 6, and Euromarkets in Chapter 7. Interest rates are essentially compensation for providing short-term and long-term funds; foreign exchange rates have a significant impact on cross-border transactions. Chapters 8 and 9 discuss these issues.

Part II is devoted to bank regulation, first in the United States (Chapters 10 and 11) and then in other countries (Chapter 12). In the United States, the system of state and nationally chartered commercial banks is a byproduct of the country's historical development. The creation of the Federal Reserve System was the response to an unsatisfactory monetary system and the Federal Deposit Insurance Corporation (along with other banking reform) was intended to help restore order to a banking system that was seriously out of control. Today, the issue of U.S. bank regulation is not at all resolved, but the systems of other countries provide a useful frame of reference for further refinement of the U.S. system.

Part III addresses bank management. The profitability of a bank, or any financial intermediary, is tied to its assets and liabilities (Chapter 13). At the same time, an adequate level of liquid and low-yielding assets must be maintained to meet deposit withdrawal requests and loan demand, creating a trade-off between profitability and liquidity. The composition of investment and loan portfolios helps a bank to manage this profitability/liquidity trade-off (Chapter 14). Ultimately, the management of bank assets and liabilities is reflected in the bank's equity (Chapter 15). Since the viability of an institution is directly related to the size of this equity base, asset-liability management is a critical consideration.

Part IV compares commercial banks to noncommercial banks (Chapter 16) and U.S. commercial banks to those in other countries (Chapters 17 and 18). Within a given country, commercial banks help to facilitate the payments system and economic development. Noncommercial banks, such as the Bank for International Settlements, the International Monetary Fund, and the World Bank, promote the orderliness of markets and the proper allocation of capital in a worldwide context. Domestically, other countries' commercial banks serve many of the same functions as U.S. banks. However, the structure and scope of banking activities varies considerably. These differences often create competitive advantages for non-U.S. banks.

Part V contains material that describes other depository institutions. Savings and loan associations and mutual savings banks are often referred to as thrift institutions (Chapter 19). The thrift industry has been subject to considerable restructuring as failures and mergers have severely reduced the number of institutions. On the other hand, credit unions have been spared much of the disruption noted in the thrift industry, primarily because of a strong self-help tradition and favorable legal status (Chapter 20).

Besides depository institutions, investment companies or mutual funds (Chapter 21), pension funds (Chapter 22), insurance companies (Chapter 23), and finance companies (Chapter 24) are major forces in the financial market place. They receive funding from nondeposit sources, but still provide important intermediation functions as they channel resources for productive purposes. All four categories of institutions provide long-term financing for industry and important products for individuals. Investment companies purchase the short-term obligations of industrial firms, making it possible for industrial firms to bypass commercial banks. Investment companies even offer their own investors transactions accounts that compete with bank checking accounts. In fact, as the scope of activities of nondepository financial institutions broadens, differences between their services and traditional bank services continue to blur.

The evolution of financial services is far from complete. As long as there are economic development needs here and abroad, financial institutions will create improved products and innovations to meet those needs.

McGraw-Hill and the author would like to thank the following reviewers for their many helpful comments and suggestions: Dean Dudley, Eastern Illinois University; John M. Finkelstein, University of New Mexico; F. Douglas Foster, Duke University; John Helmuth, Rochester Institute of Technology; Gordon V. Karels, University of Nebraska–Lincoln; Robert W. McLeod, University of Alabama; John Olienyk, Colorado State University; Coleen C. Pantalone, Northeastern University; Tony Plath, University of North Carolina–Charlotte; Donald G. Simonson, University of New Mexico; Roger Stover, Iowa State University; Ernest Swift, Georgia State University; David A. Walker, Georgetown University; and Jill Wetmore, Saginaw Valley State University.

Hazel J. Johnson

FINANCIAL INSTITUTIONS AND MARKETS

A Global Perspective

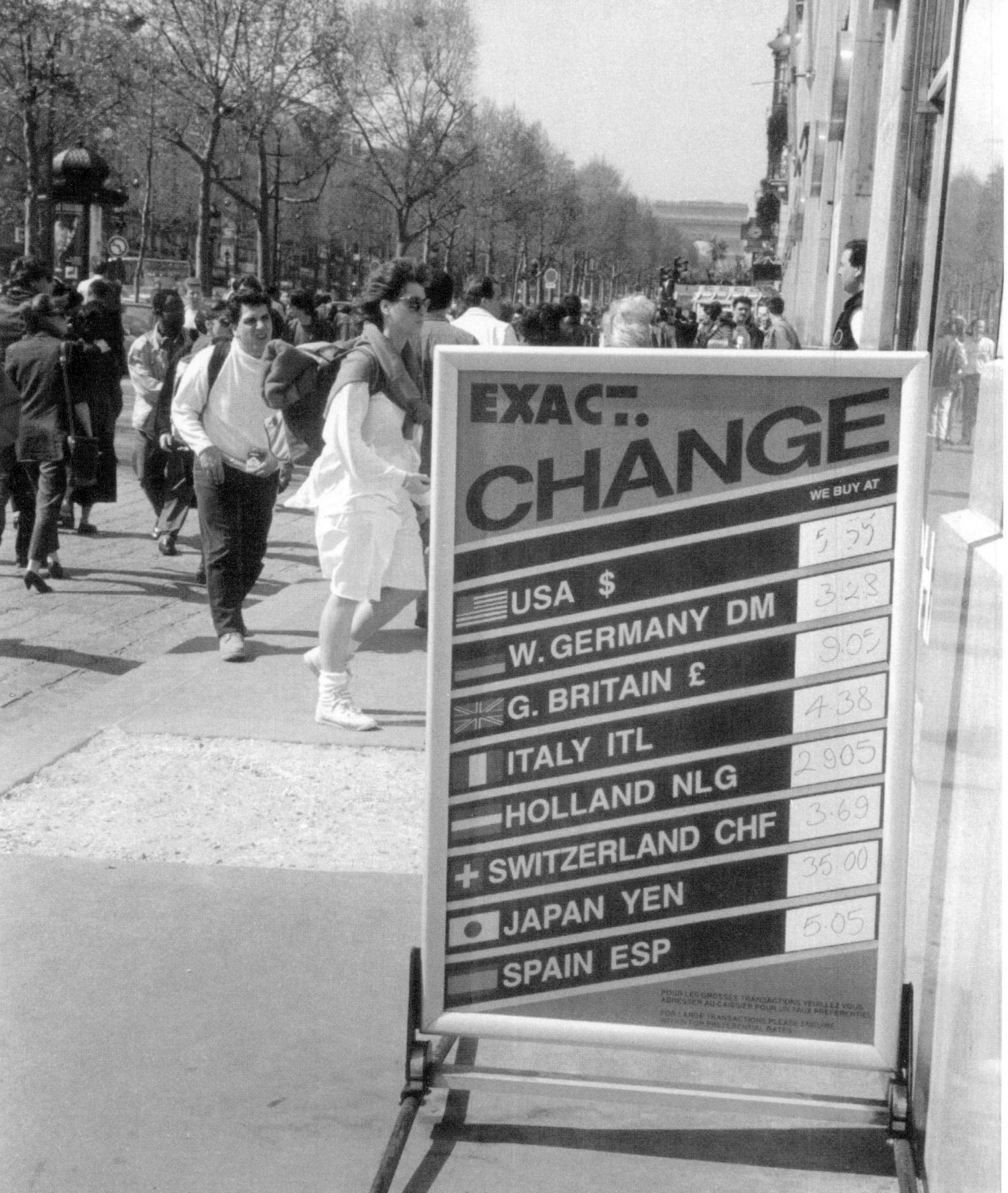
EXAC
CHANGE
WE BUY AT
5.55
USA $
3.28
W. GERMANY DM
9.05
G. BRITAIN £
4.38
ITALY ITL
2.905
HOLLAND NLG
3.69
SWITZERLAND CHF
35.00
JAPAN YEN
5.05
SPAIN ESP

PART ONE

MONEY AND CAPITAL MARKETS

CHAPTER 1

FINANCIAL INSTITUTIONS AND INTERMEDIATION

CHAPTER OUTLINE

CHAPTER OVERVIEW

This chapter:

- Analyzes the role of financial institutions in society
- Describes the process of financial intermediation
- Differentiates direct and indirect financing
- Outlines recent changes in the financial services industry in terms of domestic and international competition
- Describes financial markets

Financial institutions facilitate economic growth in modern society by performing essential intermediation and distribution functions. When they act as intermediaries, financial institutions channel funds to productive uses while providing investors with a variety of outlets for their savings. Securities brokers and dealers efficiently distribute securities that companies issue to finance productive undertakings. Smooth-running and well-developed financial markets facilitate this process. As efficient as the U.S. financial markets have become, they now face significant change in a time of new alignments in domestic markets and increased international competition.

THE ROLE OF FINANCIAL INSTITUTIONS

The term *financial institutions* describes a wide array of firms. The most familiar financial institution is probably a commercial bank. In fact, commercial banks are the oldest financial institutions in most countries, and they handle a significant portion of every country's financial assets. Financial institutions include:

Commercial banks
Savings and loan associations
Mutual savings banks
Credit unions
Insurance companies
Pension funds
Investment companies
Investment bankers
Securities brokers and dealers
Finance companies

Why do financial institutions exist, and why are they so diverse? In fact, they share common attributes. All have at least some contact with the general public; all accept money and provide services in return. The discussion of their development starts with a simple world that assumes the existence of money and works toward the complex system of financial markets today.

EXAMPLE OF A FINANCIAL TRANSACTION

Savings Units

First, assume a tiny economy, a world populated by only two people—person A and person B. Person A works throughout the year to obtain all necessities of life—food, shelter, and clothing. Person A now has \$100 of excess resources. Assuming no liabilities, person A has wealth of \$100, or W_0 = \$100. When income exceeds expenditures for the year, person A becomes a *surplus savings unit.*

Surplus savings unit (SSU):
An economic entity whose income for a particular period exceeds expenditures.

The amount of person A's wealth will stay the same without any productive application for the excess resources, that is, without investment opportunities.

Now consider person B, who also has worked successfully during the year to satisfy basic needs but without accumulating excess resources like person A. Person B's current wealth is zero. Hence, the summation of wealth of the two citizens of this small economy is \$100.

Person B, however, has come up with a 1-year project that promises to return 20 percent on investment. Yet, with no funds available for investment, B will be unable to take advantage of the lucrative opportunity. All other things being equal, the wealth of this society 1 year from now, W_1, will be identical to its current wealth, as noted in Exhibit 1-1.

Direct Financing

The clear solution to this dilemma is for person A to lend person B the funds necessary for the project. If this happens, person B becomes a *deficit savings unit.*

Deficit savings unit (DSU):
An economic unit whose current income is less than current expenditures.

EXHIBIT 1-1 A TWO-PERSON WORLD

	W_0	W_1
Without direct financing		
Person		
A	$100	$100
B	0	0
Economy	$100	$100
	W_0	W_1
With direct financing		
Person		
A	$100	$110
B	0	10
Economy	$100	$120

When the ultimate user of funds—a DSU or an entrepreneur—obtains necessary resources from an investor or SSU, the process is called *direct financing.*

Direct financing:
The provision of funds for investment to the ultimate user of the funds (DSU) by an ultimate investor (SSU).

This arrangement makes it possible for a person with an idea or an opportunity to undertake a worthwhile project what would, otherwise, have been forgone. The benefits of direct financing reach beyond one individual, however. They are an important source of growth in an economy.

If we assume that person A is willing to provide financing in the amount of $100 at an agreed-upon rate of 10 percent (probably documented in a promissory note signed by person B), A earns $10; total wealth 1 year from now will be $110 [$100 (1.10) = $110], or W_1 = $110, as also shown in Exhibit 1-1. Person B's wealth also increases. After repayment of principal and interest, B's wealth will have increased to $10 [$100(1.20) − $110 = $10]. On an aggregate basis then, the wealth of the economy grows to $120, increasing by the 20 percent return on B's project. In the absence of financing, this growth would not have occurred. Notice that the economy grows by the rate of return available from investment and that this rate of return is shared, in negotiated proportions, between SSUs and DSUs.

Direct financing works only when *mutual* agreement on all terms of the arrangement is possible. In this example person A had confidence in the proposed project and did not object to the required holding period. Person B agreed to the 10 percent interest rate.

FINANCIAL INTERMEDIATION

An Expanded Example

Direct financing in a world of more than a handful of people can be an inefficient way to allocate capital. Suppose there are 100 SSUs and 100 DSUs, all of them as interested in financing their projects at favorable terms as the original person B. If each DSU investigates a direct financing arrangement with each ultimate investor, search and information costs become unreasonable (up to 10,000 searches, with 100 DSUs each investigating 100 SSUs). If each of the ultimate investors also looks for the "right" investment, information costs will mount even faster.

Enter a financial intermediary, a commercial bank, as shown in Exhibit 1-2. The bank, not the individuals, can analyze each of the projects proposed by the entrepreneurs (B_1

EXHIBIT 1-2 EXPANDED WORLD WITH FINANCIAL INTERMEDIATION AND INDIRECT FINANCING

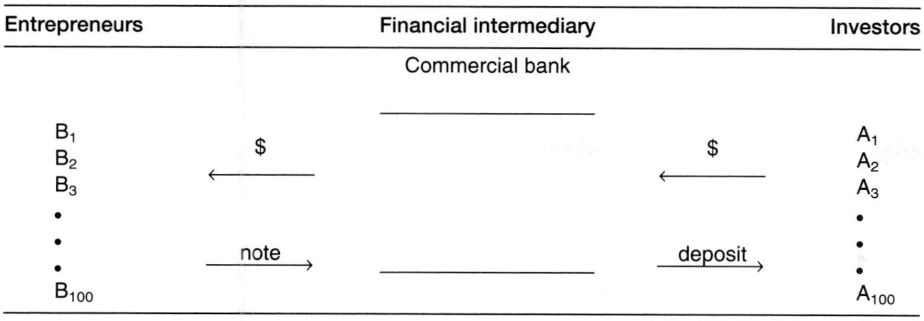

Entrepreneurs		Financial intermediary		Investors
		Commercial bank		
B_1 B_2 B_3 • • • B_{100}	$ ← note →		$ ← deposit →	A_1 A_2 A_3 • • • A_{100}

through B_{100}). Because no more than 100 "feasibility studies" are required, information costs are reduced. In fact, the bank may be able to offer the ultimate investors (A_1 through A_{100}) a wider range of financial opportunities than would have been available through direct financing. This is *indirect financing.*

Indirect financing:
The process by which entrepreneurs obtain money for investment from a financial intermediary who, in turn, has accumulated the funds from ultimate investors.

Exhibit 1-2 illustrates how investment dollars flow from SSUs through the intermediary to the entrepreneurs, producing essentially the same net result as with direct financing. The distinction is that the commercial bank holds promissory notes. The ultimate investor now holds a bank deposit, a different financial instrument. The promissory note is a *primary security;* the deposit is a *secondary security.*

Primary security:
A financial claim issued by the ultimate user of the funds, the DSU.

Secondary security:
A financial claim issued by a financial intermediary.

Change in the financial instrument held by ultimate investors is the essence of *financial intermediation.*

Financial intermediation:
The process of facilitating the flow of funds from surplus savings units (SSUs) to deficit savings units (DSUs), with primary securities (issued by DSUs) held by financial institutions and secondary securities (issued by financial institutions) held by SSUs.

Forms of Financial Intermediation

Indirect financing through financial intermediaries, like direct financing, facilitates economic growth by allowing capital to be channeled to investment projects. The effect of indirect financing is a significant change in the type of securities held by the investing public. The type of intermediation, or change, that occurs may be described in four broad categories:

1. *Denomination intermediation.* A number of relatively small investments may be pooled together to finance projects that require large amounts of capital.
2. *Maturity intermediation.* Deposits and other secondary securities may have short terms to maturity and may, in fact, be payable to the investor upon demand, while fi-

nancing made available to DSUs has a maturity more appropriate for the project involved (frequently longer-term).

3. *Risk intermediation.* The SSUs do not bear direct risk of default (nonpayment of principal or interest) by DSUs. The secondary securities issued to the SSU are backed by the financial strength of the intermediary (and, in the case of federally insured deposits, by the federal government).
4. *Information intermediation.* The SSUs do not need to research all projects in which they ultimately invest. Investors instead rely on the management skill and financial position of the intermediary.

Other Financial Intermediaries—Briefly

Banks are but one of several financial institutions that perform intermediation functions and serve an industrial economy. Other financial intermediaries are savings and loan associations, mutual savings banks, credit unions, investment companies, pension funds, insurance companies, and finance companies.

Depository Institutions *Commercial banks, savings and loan associations, mutual savings banks, and credit unions* are *depository institutions.* That is, they all issue secondary securities in the form of the customer's deposit, money that can be withdrawn upon demand or according to terms of the deposit agreement. Mutual savings and loan associations, mutual savings banks, and credit unions technically issue ownership shares, not deposits.

Savings and loan associations (S&Ls) were established to provide real estate finance by accepting small savers' deposits and investing in residential mortgages. To this traditional function have been added consumer and commercial loans. Savings and loan associations now also accept checking and large-denomination deposits.

Mutual savings banks were also originally geared to the small investor. These institutions made mortgage loans and accepted primarily savings deposits. Their activities have grown in ways similar to S&Ls.

Like S&Ls and mutual savings banks, *credit unions* provide a savings vehicle for the small investor. They invest these funds in small consumer loans for purposes other than residential housing. Members of credit unions share some form of common bond, frequently employment or occupation. As credit unions have evolved, they, too, have begun to offer a full range of consumer services.

Nondepository Financial Institutions *Investment companies, pension funds, insurance companies,* and *finance companies* are financial intermediaries that are *not* depository institutions. Thus, the secondary securities that they issue are different. *Investment companies* (for example, Fidelity Mutual Funds) pool money in small denominations to make large purchases of corporate and government securities. To this extent, they are similar to commercial banks, but investment companies issue ownership shares, not deposits, to their investors. The rate of return from an investment company share depends on the rate of return of the securities in which the company invests, with no guarantee or insurance for the investor.

Pension funds offer the secondary security of deferred income. Contributors to pension funds receive the promise of lump-sum or periodic payments at or during retirement from employment. Contributions into pension funds are made by both employers and employees. Pension funds are major providers of money for industrial expansion.

Insurance companies promise protection from a variety of specified risks in exchange for investor funds. This promised protection is documented in an insurance policy. The two major types of insurance companies are life insurers and property and casualty insurers. Life insurers protect investors from death and disability during the term of the policy.

(Some life insurance policies also include a savings component.) Property and casualty insurers protect against all other risks—automobile insurance is an example. Like pension funds, insurance companies invest policyholder funds in loans to and securities of commercial enterprises.

Finance companies cater to both consumers and businesses. In this sense, they offer services that are similar to those of commercial banks, although finance companies generally make riskier loans than banks—that is, there is often a higher probability of nonrepayment of loans that finance companies make. As a result, finance company loan rates are higher than bank loan rates. Another difference is that finance companies do not accept deposits but issue securities similar to those of nonfinancial firms.

These financial intermediaries, together with commercial banks, control a large share of the financial assets of the economy. While the secondary security varies, depending on the institution, the process of intermediation is much the same.

AN ANALYSIS OF FINANCIAL INTERMEDIATION

This section provides an introductory analysis of intermediation by examining one transaction in which a commercial bank acts as intermediary, with a variety of changes in the financial position of all parties.

The Balance Sheet

This example illustrates the flow of funds in financial intermediation by tracing a $10,000 deposit made by an investor A through the balance sheet of a commercial bank to the balance sheet of an entrepreneur B. Exhibit 1-3 shows that investor A has cash on hand (a liquid asset) in the amount of $10,000. When A deposits the money in the bank, A's liquid asset is reclassified as cash in bank, and the bank's vault cash (asset) and deposits (liability) accounts both increase by $10,000.

The bank then makes a loan of $10,000 to a third party, entrepreneur B. After the loan is made, the bank's $10,000 addition to vault cash is reclassified as loans. On B's balance sheet, cash in bank (asset) and notes payable (liability) accounts both increase by $10,000. Without the intermediary—that is, if A had provided direct loan financing to

EXHIBIT 1-3 BALANCE SHEET IMPACT OF FINANCIAL INTERMEDIATION

	A	Commercial bank	B
Before transaction			
Assets			
Cash on hand	10,000		
Liabilities			
After deposit			
Assets			
Cash in bank	10,000		
Vault cash		+10,000	
Liabilities			
Deposits		+10,000	
After loan			
Assets			
Cash in bank	10,000		+10,000
Loans		+10,000	
Liabilities			
Deposits		+10,000	
Notes payable			+10,000

B—A's and B's balance sheets would have changed in exactly the same *amount,* but the asset held by A would have been a promissory note executed by B, not a bank deposit.

Income and Expense

To analyze the compensation to each of the parties in the intermediation process, assume first that these balances are unchanged for 1 year. Also assume that the bank pays interest on deposits at 8 percent and charges 11 percent interest on loans and that B's investment project has a rate of return of 20 percent.

According to Exhibit 1-4, A earns $800 (8 percent of the $10,000), which the bank is obligated to pay because of its contractual commitment. Once the bank enters into this contract with A, the liability of the bank to A is not affected by the bank's investment decision. Yet because interest expense for the bank (interest *income* for A) begins accruing im–mediately on deposit, it is in the bank's best interest to put the $10,000 to productive use as soon as possible. Assuming that the bank makes the loan to B on the day of A's deposit, the bank's interest income from the loan to B (interest *expense* for B) begins accruing right away. Likewise, B promptly invests the loan proceeds in the proposed project.

At the end of the year, the bank's (pretax) net interest earnings are $300—the $1100 loan income less the $800 deposit interest expense payable to A. The earnings of B before taxes are $900—$2000 in project revenues less $1100 in interest expense. The total amount earned depends on the return on B's investment, assumed here to be 20 percent, or $2000. That $2000 is distributed among the three participants in the intermediation process: $800 + $300 + $900.

What is important in terms of financial intermediation is the nature of the bank's earnings. They depend on the *spread,* or the difference between the bank's cost of money (the deposit rate in this example) and its investment rate of return (the loan rate). In the case of commercial banks, the spread is referred to as *net interest margin.*

Net Interest Margin:
The difference between the average rate earned on earning assets and the average rate paid on interest-bearing liabilities.

The spread or net interest margin is a basic measure of profitability for the financial intermediary and is the institution's compensation for lending risks—for example, the risk of nonrepayment. The intermediary incurs additional expense in the form of information gathering and customer service that also must be covered by the spread. Moreover, it cannot lend all its assets long-term. To ensure that customers can withdraw cash on demand, the bank must invest some deposits (its liabilities) in assets that can be quickly converted to cash. These more liquid assets do not earn as high a rate of return as loans to entrepreneurs and other clients, which reduces the intermediary's profitability. (See Exhibit 1-5.)

The example shows how a financial intermediary facilitates the productive investment function of the economy—this is the reason for being. It performs services that transform the financial instruments available to the public so that they have more appealing denomination, maturity, and risk characteristics. It is a source of information that the public

EXHIBIT 1-4 COMPENSATION TO PARTICIPANTS IN FINANCIAL INTERMEDIATION

	A	Bank	B
Bank deposit interest	800	(800)	
Bank loan interest		1100	(1100)
Project return			2000
Net returns	800	300	900

Ernst Baltensperger's bank theory overview classifies models in three basic categories:* (1) those that assume that the bank is a price setter in deposit and credit markets, (2) those that apply portfolio theory and rely heavily on the assumption of risk aversion, and (3) those that emphasize the real resource cost of providing banking services. Many of these models do not address the issue of scale, that is, the bank's optimal size.

Baltensperger's synthesis of the earlier work develops a model addressing both the bank's asset mix and scale. The bank's expected profit is specified as:

$$E(\pi) = rE - iD - C - L$$

where $E(\pi)$ = the bank's expected profit
r = rate of return on earning assets
E = dollar amount of earning assets
i = rate of interest paid on deposits
D = dollar amount of deposits
C = dollar production cost (especially labor cost) of providing real resource banking services (such as check clearing, credit evaluation, safekeeping, and bookkeeping)
L = opportunity cost of holding liquid assets

The bank's deposits D are assumed to equal earning assets E plus reserves R. Baltensperger shows that the bank will maximize expected profit with respect to R and D (and thus E) by investing in earning assets until marginal revenue exactly equals the sum of marginal production and liquidity costs. To finance these investments, deposits should expand until marginal revenue and costs become equal.

This model could be applied beyond commercial banking. Because a number of financial institutions offer deposit and loan services, Baltensperger's framework can be useful in analyzing the general case of financial intermediaries.

*Baltensperger, Ernst. "Alternative Approaches to the Theory of the Banking Firm," *Journal of Monetary Economics,* vol. 6 (1980), pp. 1–37.

needs to evaluate investment instruments. For these services it earns money itself—the spread reduced by the cost of doing business (information processing and customer service).

DIRECT FINANCING

Not all financial institutions are intermediaries, that is, not all change the security held by the ultimate investor. Other financial institutions that are not intermediaries perform vital roles in the distribution of primary securities. *Investment bankers* and *securities brokers and dealers* sell to the public the same debt and equity securities issued by nonfinancial firms. *Investment bankers* advise corporations on the terms and conditions of issuing securities, including the proper timing, pricing, and maturity. Securities issued in this way include stocks, bonds, and commercial paper. As compensation for their security issuing services, investment bankers receive fee income. They also underwrite securities or assume the risk of selling the entire issue. Compensation for this service is the spread, or the difference between the price the investment bank pays to the issuing firm and the price at which it sells the security to the investing public.

While not engaging in intermediation, *securities brokers and dealers* perform a vital function by placing new securities issues in the hands of investors. After stocks and bonds have been issued, investors may resell securities (to other investors) through brokers in a number of markets. The existence of smoothly functioning markets, which let investors convert stock or bond holdings into cash or more liquid assets, facilitates the sale of additional securities whenever they are offered.

FINANCIAL MARKETS

The *financial markets* of the United States, where securities transactions take place, are efficient and well organized, with a variety of institutions to help capital flow throughout the economy. Until recently, virtually all financial markets had physical locations, such as in New York or Chicago. With the advent of technological change, some are now computer or telephone networks performing the same functions. The over-the-counter (OTC) market for stocks, National Association of Securities Dealers Automated Quotation System (NASDAQ), and the foreign currency markets that operate 24 hours a day are examples.

Primary and Secondary Markets

Financial markets may be classified in one of two fundamental categories, *primary* and *secondary markets.*

Primary markets:
Markets that bring surplus savings units together with deficit savings units in the process of financing productive activities. Securities are sold for the first time in primary markets.

When a company, for example, International Business Machines (IBM), wants to raise equity capital, it issues securities in addition to those outstanding and now held by investors. It does this through a transaction in the primary markets, and the aggregate number and value of securities in the economy increases. Thus, IBM thereby receives a capital infusion for investment in presumably profitable projects that facilitate economic growth.

Secondary markets:
Markets in which already existing securities change hands. In effect, securities are transferred from one surplus savings unit to another.

Examples of U.S. secondary markets are the New York Stock Exchange, the American Stock Exchange, and the over-the-counter market. Of course, in secondary-market transactions the firm that originally issued the securities does not receive additional financing. Without strong secondary markets for existing securities, investors would be less inclined to purchase them in the primary market in the first place (that is, less inclined to provide corporate financing). Active secondary markets let investors buy or sell securities with minimal expense. Secondary markets also give borrowing firms such as IBM (deficit savings units) valuable information about market conditions for new issues of securities, including rates of return that the market is likely to demand of a new issue.

Money and Capital Markets

Beyond the primary-secondary market distinction, financial markets may be classified in terms of the time to maturity of the securities traded. Short-term securities (with 1 year or less to maturity) are traded in *money markets.* Money markets help investors and borrowers manage liquid assets that they do not want to tie up for long periods. United States Treasury bills, commercial paper, and negotiable bank certificates of deposit are examples of instruments that are traded in these markets. Long-term securities (those with more than 1 year to maturity or with perpetual life) are traded in *capital markets.* These securities help finance industrial projects that enhance economic development, such as high-technology manufacturing facilities. Stocks, bonds, and mortgages are traded in capital markets.

Competition and deregulation (fewer government constraints) have brought major changes to the financial services industry. The industry continues to evolve to meet both domestic and foreign challenges.

FINANCIAL SERVICES: A CHANGING INDUSTRY

All financial intermediaries originally operated in market niches in which they tended to specialize. Historically, for example, commercial banks have been an important part of the economy's payments system and a major source of short-term finance for industry. Banks now offer consumer, real estate, and longer-term commercial services. Over time, many institutions diversified into other activities so that functions may now overlap.

Competition in financial services has blurred the difference between many formerly distinct institutions. For example, all depository institutions along with life insurance companies now provide mortgage finance. All depository institutions, investment companies, and securities brokers and dealers offer accounts that are checking accounts for all intents and purposes. Investment companies offer rates of return to small investors that are often more attractive than rates available at depository institutions.

Changing Market Niches

While the U.S. financial system continues to be one of the world's most advanced, the effect of the blurring of niches has been a decline in the importance of commercial banks and other depository institutions. Exhibit 1-6 shows the change. In 1964, depository institutions had 58 percent of the total financial assets held by financial institutions. By 1989, their share had dropped to 49 percent. The primary beneficiaries of this shift have been investment companies and pension funds. The competitive rates of return available through investment companies have clearly attracted ultimate investors, particularly small investors, away from depository institutions. At the same time, the significant growth in assets under management at both investment companies and pension funds has given corporations alternatives to bank loans. Thus, banks face threats to both their deposit base and loan portfolio.

The savings and loan industry has been perhaps the hardest hit by these changes. From 1960 through 1989 the number of S&Ls declined from 4098 to fewer than 3000. The income on long-term, fixed-rate mortgage loans was insufficient to cover the cost of maintaining their deposit base as money market interest rates rose dramatically during the 1970s. During the 1980s the riskier investments that S&Ls were permitted only served to worsen the situation. Failures have now reached record levels, and the cost of this industry shakeout has been estimated as high as $500 billion.

Banks are affected as well. They have lost much of their low-cost deposits and top-tier corporate loan business. At the heart of this effect is a change in the interest rate environment that has produced a trend toward direct financing of corporate America. Major corporate clients have found it more economical to borrow short-term funds in the commercial paper market directly from the investing public rather than to borrow from a bank. Commercial paper lets large, creditworthy firms borrow for periods of up to 270 days.

EXHIBIT 1-6 SHARE OF FINANCIAL ASSETS HELD BY FINANCIAL INSTITUTIONS, 1964–1989

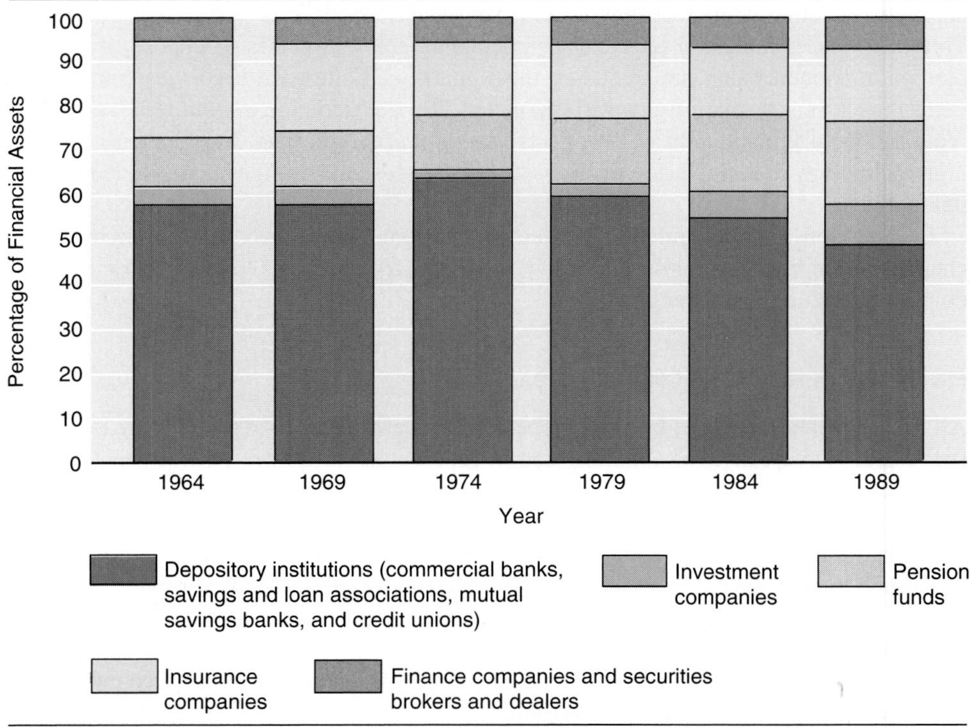

Source: Calculations and graphic based on Board of Governors of the Federal Reserve System, *Flow of Funds Accounts; Financial Assets and Liabilities,* various issues.

Exhibit 1-7 shows that the commercial paper rate has been only slightly higher than the Treasury bill rate (the lowest short-term rate available) since 1975, while the prime rate (charged to such large bank borrowers) has been significantly higher.

As Exhibit 1-8 shows, the amount of commercial paper outstanding represented less than 5 percent of the amount of domestic bank loans in 1964. This percentage has in-

EXHIBIT 1-7 INTEREST RATES: T-BILL, COMMERCIAL PAPER, AND PRIME, 1964–1989

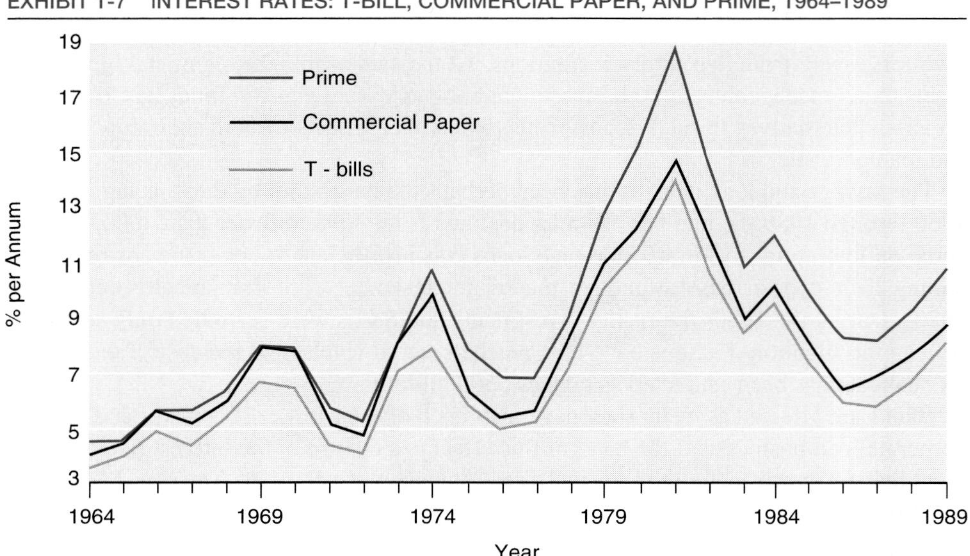

Source: Based on data from United States Department of Commerce, Bureau of Economic Analysis, *Business Statistics 1961–1988* and *Survey of Current Business, April 1991.*

EXHIBIT 1-8 COMMERCIAL PAPER AS A PERCENTAGE OF DOMESTIC BANK LOANS, 1964–1989

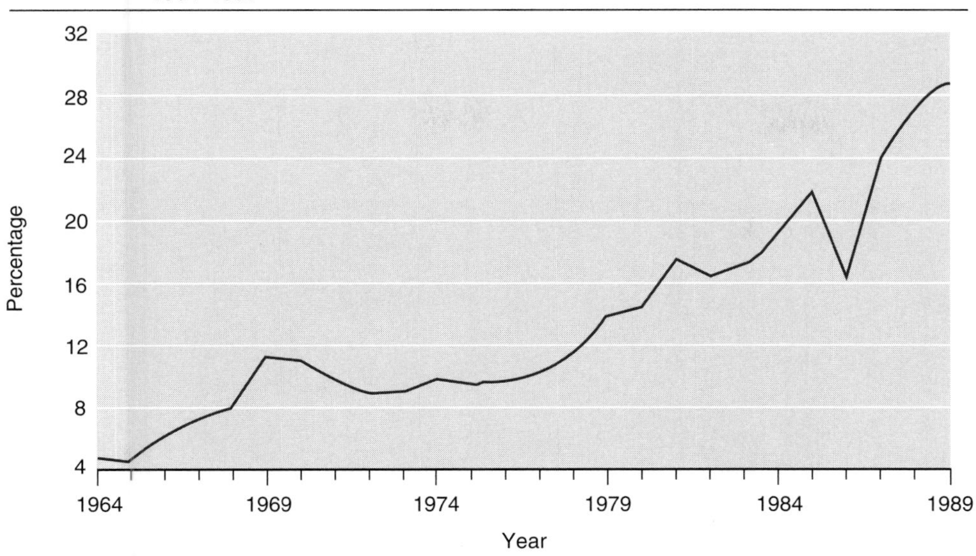

Source: Calculations and graphic based on Board of Governors of the Federal Reserve System, *Flow of Funds Accounts; Financial Assets and Liabilities,* various issues.

creased steadily, until in 1989 commercial paper totaled almost 29 percent of the dollar value of outstanding bank loans, a trend that has contributed to a decline in commercial bank market share.

The loss of a low-cost deposit base, the flight of major corporate clients, the expansion of other financial institutions into once-traditional banking services, and the inability of commercial banks to expand into other profitable activities all create tremendous pressure on banks. In fact, these pressures are undoubtedly at the root of the highest rate of bank failures since the Great Depression of the 1930s. Exhibit 1-9 shows that since the end of World War II (1945), annual commercial bank failures numbered fewer than 20 per year. During the 1980s this number rose to over 200.

EXHIBIT 1-9 COMMERCIAL BANK FAILURES, 1934–1989

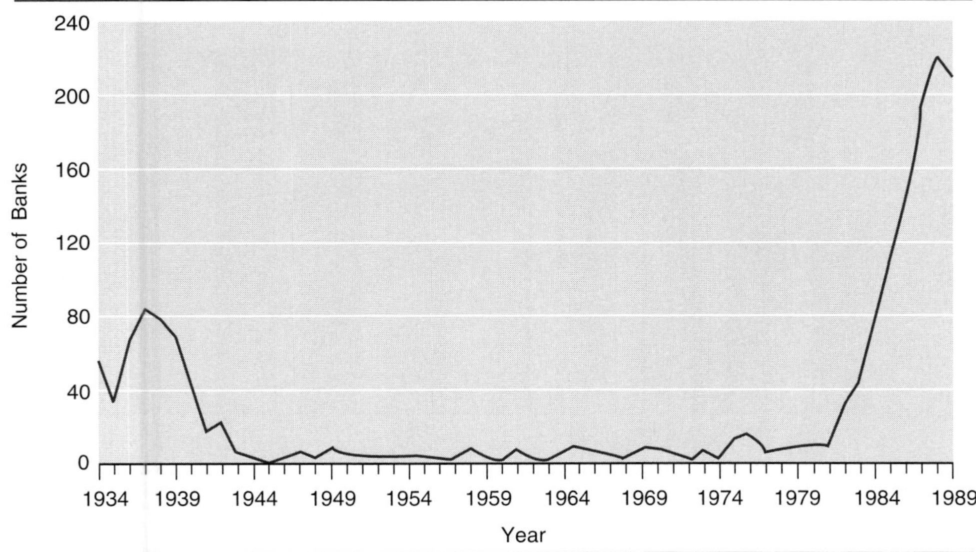

Source: Based on data from Federal Deposit Insurance Corporation, *1988 Annual Report* and *FDIC Quarterly Banking Profile* (4Q 1988 and 4Q 1989).

EXHIBIT 1-10 FOREIGN BANK LOANS AS A PERCENTAGE OF DOMESTIC BANK LOANS, 1964–1989

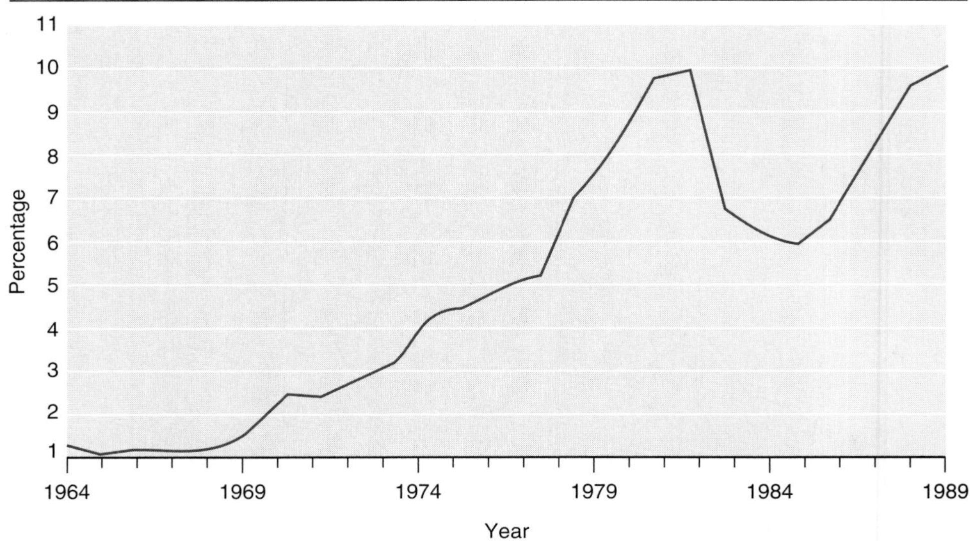

Source: Calculations and graphic based on Board of Governors of the Federal Reserve System, *Flow of Funds Accounts; Financial Assets and Liabilities,* various issues.

A More Global Industry

The whole question of the ability of financial institutions to compete is of central importance as global markets develop. Domestic commercial banks compete at home not only with other domestic financial institutions but also increasingly with foreign banks. Exhibit 1-10 indicates that foreign bank loans during the 1960s represented less than 2 percent

EXHIBIT 1-11 ASSETS OF FOREIGN BANKS IN THE UNITED STATES AS A PERCENTAGE OF TOTAL BANK ASSETS, 1980–1989

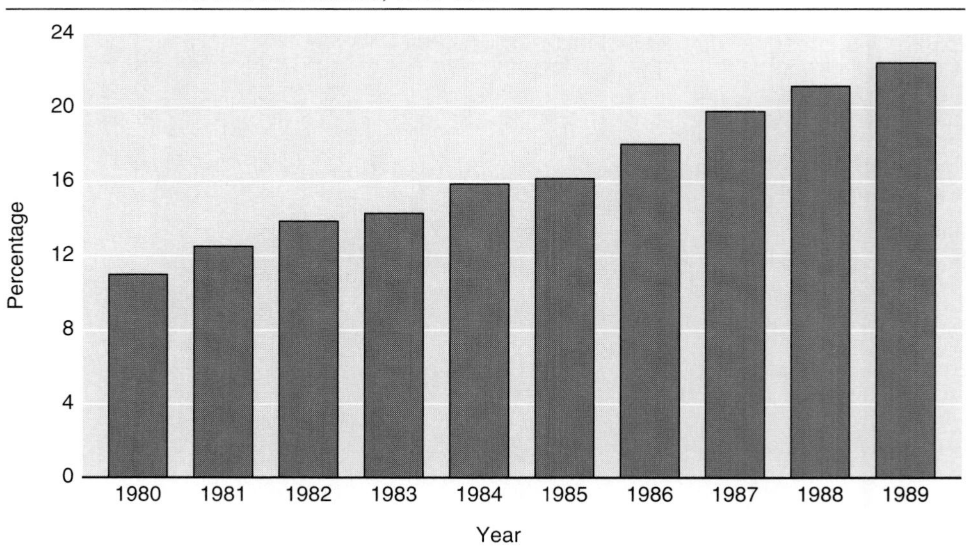

Source: Calculations and graphic based on Task Force on the International Competitiveness of U.S. Financial Institutions, *Report of the Subcommittee on Financial Institutions Supervision, Regulations, and Insurance,* U.S. Government Printing Office, October 1990, and Barth, James R., R. Dan Brumbaugh, Jr., and Robert E. Litan, *Banking Industry in Turmoil: A Report on the Condition of the U.S. Banking Industry and the Bank Insurance Fund,* U.S. Government Printing Office, December 1990.

of the amount of domestic bank loans. Twenty-five years later, the percentage was closer to 10 percent.

In terms of total assets, the foreign presence is even more obvious. As shown in Exhibit 1-11, total assets of foreign banks exceeded 10 percent of all banking assets in the United States as early as 1980. By 1989, the figure exceeded 22 percent.

One reason for the growing foreign bank activity appears to be differential treatment of banks by U.S. laws and regulations. Foreign banks can engage in securities underwriting and hold substantial equity (ownership) positions in corporations, activities generally prohibited to U.S. banks. These facts point up the issue that competitiveness involves not only economic circumstances and rates of return on investment but also the political environment in which financial institutions operate—whether domestic or international.

SUMMARY

Financial institutions continue to evolve. Although the provider may change, the needed services remain fairly constant. Liquidity and capital investment funds must be channeled from surplus savings units to deficit savings units. Depository institutions (commercial banks, savings and loan associations, mutual savings banks, and credit unions) are now competing with other institutions for market share. Traditional banking services can be obtained now from any number of financial institutions—including investment companies, insurance companies, and pension funds—and finance companies. One consequence is that savings and loan associations and commercial banks have failed at alarming rates.

Competition between domestic and foreign institutions is becoming much keener. From a relatively small foreign presence less than three decades ago, international interests now control as much as 22 percent of U.S. banking assets. The economies of the world clearly are becoming more integrated. If anything is a constant in the changing financial services industry, it may be the continuing trend toward integration of institutions, markets, and economies.

KEY TERMS

barter system
capital market
deficit savings unit
denomination intermediation
direct financing
financial institutions
financial intermediation
financial markets
indirect financing
information intermediation
maturity intermediation
money market
net interest margin
primary markets
primary security
risk intermediation
secondary markets
secondary security
surplus savings unit

END-OF-CHAPTER QUESTIONS

1. What is the difference between a surplus savings economic unit and a deficit savings unit?
2. How do financial intermediaries affect transactions between surplus savings units and deficit savings units?
3. The government and business sectors of the U.S. economy are both deficit savings sectors. Do you think there is a difference in the nature of the two sectors' expenditures?
4. Describe the four types of financial intermediation.
5. **a.** Why have nonfinancial corporations begun to depend more on direct (versus indirect) financing?
   b. What financial instrument has made shor-term direct financing more feasible?
   c. What financial institutions help nonfinancial corporations engage in direct financing?

6. In what way are commercial banks, savings and loan associations, mutual savings banks, and credit unions different from other financial institutions?

7. All financial intermediaries issue secondary securities. What is the nature of the secondary securities of:

a. Investment companies

b. Pension funds

c. Insurance companies

d. Finance companies

8. What is a financial intermediary's spread?

9. All other things being equal, what impact does an increase in deposit interest rates have on a bank's net interest margin (spread)?

10. What happens to a bank's spread if an increase in bank deposit rates is "passed on" to the bank's loan customers?

11. Differentiate primary and secondary financial markets.

12. Why should the financial managers of corporations be concerned with activity in secondary financial markets?

13. What is the difference between money and capital markets?

14. How should the New York Stock Exchange be classified—primary or secondary market, money or capital market?

15. What financial institutions have offered alternatives for small depositors that have seriously eroded commercial bank market share?

16. Describe the recent trend in commercial bank failures.

17. Since 1964, how has the mix of domestic versus foreign bank loans changed in the United States?

SELECTED REFERENCES

Baltensperger, Ernst. "Alternative Approaches to the Theory of the Banking Firm," *Journal of Monetary Economics,* vol. 6 (1980), pp. 1–17.

Barth, James R., R. Dan Brumbaugh, Jr., and Robert E. Litan. *Banking Industry in Turmoil: A Report on the Condition of the U.S. Banking Industry and the Bank Insurance Fund,* U.S. Government Printing Office, Washington, D.C., December 1990.

Board of Governors of the Federal Reserve System. *Flow of Funds Accounts; Financial Assets and Liabilities,* Washington, D.C.

Federal Deposit Insurance Corporation. *1988 Annual Report* and *1989 Annual Report,* Washington D.C.

Federal Deposit Insurance Corporation. *FDIC Quarterly Banking Profile,* Washington D.C.

Selgin, George A. "Commercial Banks as Pure Intermediaries: Between 'Old' and 'New' Views," *Southern Economic Journal,* vol. 56, no. 1 (1989), pp. 80–86.

Task Force on the International Competitiveness of U.S. Financial Institutions. *Report of the Subcommittee on Financial Institutions Supervision, Regulation, and Insurance,* U.S. Government Printing Office, Washington, D.C., October 1990.

U.S. Department of Commerce, Bureau of Economic Analysis. *Business Statistics 1961–1988,* Washington, D.C.

U.S. Department of Commerce, Bureau of Economic Analysis *Survey of Current Business, April 1991,* Washington, D.C.

Walsh, Carl E., and Peter R. Hartley. "Financial Intermediation, Monetary Policy, and Equilibrium Business Cycles," *Federal Reserve Bank of San Francisco Economic Review,* issue 4 (Fall 1988), pp. 19–28.

CHAPTER 2

MONEY

CHAPTER OUTLINE

THE FUNCTIONS OF MONEY

MONETARY SYSTEMS
- Barter System
- Full-Bodied Money
- Paper Money

MONETARY STANDARDS

THE ADOPTION OF MONETARY STANDARDS
- Bretton Woods, 1944
- The Smithsonian Agreement, 1971
- The Snake in the Tunnel

EXPANSION OF THE MONEY SUPPLY BY BANKS
- Bank Reserves
- Money Supply Expansion
- Defining the Money Supply

INTERNATIONAL COMPARISONS:
- IMF members (exchange rate arrangements)

CHAPTER OVERVIEW

This chapter:

- Discusses the characteristics of money
- Traces the development of money to the present day
- Establishes the link between the banking system and the money supply
- Defines the current specifications of money supply and recent changes in its composition

At the heart of any financial system is its money. Money is the common bond that ties financial institutions in the United States to each other and to institutions in other countries. Money functions as a medium of exchange, a unit of account, a store of value, and a standard for deferred payments. Monetary systems have evolved over time from barter economies through gold and silver coin to paper money, which dominates now both because of the scarcity of precious metal and because it can accommodate a sophisticated society's need for a flexible money supply.

Today methods of payment go beyond currency and coin. For example, bank checking accounts, credit union share draft accounts, and money market fund shares are all forms of money. As a result, the money supply is now affected by a wide circle of financial institutions. This chapter describes money and introduces the topics of currency exchange rates and money creation by financial institutions.

THE FUNCTIONS OF MONEY

Money lets people satisfy individual needs by allowing access to goods and services produced by other members of society according to their particular aptitude or occupation. Most people, for example, buy food by exchanging cash for specific items sold in stores. The store, in turn, buys these items through a similar exchange with a distributor. The distributor, too, relies on other sources, eventually traceable to a company or individual actually producing food. This chain of events is repeated in the delivery of any number of products. In this way, people can work in a specialized field or profession but still satisfy their need for life's necessities. Such specialization enhances individual productivity and productiveness of society as a whole. Money serves four functions that make this arrangement possible:

- Medium of exchange
- Unit of account
- Store of value
- Standard for deferred payments

In the case of acceptance of money in exchange for goods and services, money functions as a *medium of exchange.*

Medium of exchange:
The function of money that permits its universal exchange for other commodities.

As a medium of exchange, money must take a tangible form, as either currency or, perhaps, a bank check.

Second, money is a *unit of account*—an abstract, intangible concept, in the same sense that length is not tangible.

Unit of account:
The function of money that results in the pricing of other commodities in terms of units of an economy's money.

Effectively, this means that money describes the price or relative value of items that are bought and sold. The price of an object has to do with the appropriate *amount* of money to purchase it, not the value of the money itself. For this reason, we can say that money is a standard of value for all other goods and services in the economy. A unit of account need not have a physical quality. When a person buys a newspaper in San Francisco for $1, the unit of account (the abstract concept) is $1 and the medium of exchange (the tangible item) is U.S. coins or paper currency. When a person uses a credit card to buy a sweater in New York for $50, the unit of account is $50 and the medium of exchange is a credit card draft (the tangible sales slip that documents the sale).

Throughout history a country's medium of exchange and unit of account generally have been incorporated into the same monetary instrument. A graphic example of what happens when medium of exchange and unit of account diverge may be found in Germany in the early 1920s, as shown in Exhibit 2-1.

The third function of money is as a *store of value.*

EXHIBIT 2-1 THE POST–WORLD WAR I MONETARY DISTRESS OF GERMANY

After World War I, the German economy underwent a period of hyperinflation that simultaneously affected the money supply, the general level of prices, and the foreign exchange rate of the German mark. From December 1918 to June 1923, currency in circulation increased from 33.1 billion marks to 17.4 trillion marks, representing an average annual increase of 284 percent. The average annual increase in wholesale prices for the 2-year period ended June 1923 was 3725 percent. The average annual devaluation of the mark (relative to the U.S. dollar) during the same 2-year period was 3884 percent.

Wages and prices were stated in terms of a commodity, for example, the number of marks that were necessary to purchase a specified quantity of wheat, milk, or butter, at the time of payment. In 1922, a state bond issue, denominated in rye, was sold. In 1923, a German firm issued a loan denominated for 200,000 kilograms of flax. When the instrument matured, the lender received interest and principal in the number of marks necessary to purchase the stated amounts of rye or flax.

Such examples of separation of the functions of medium of exchange and unit of account are rare. This unfortunate period in German history underscores the need for money to also act as a store of value.

Sources: Kindleberger, Charles P., *A Financial History of Western Europe*, George Allen & Unwin, London, 1984, pp. 312–313, and Struthers, J., and H. Speight, *Money: Institutions, Theory and Policy*, 1986, p. 7.

Store of value:
The function of money that prevents its value from declining over time.

To serve an economy's needs effectively, money must retain its purchasing power so that it can be used after it is earned. If money were not a store of value, people would be forced to invest all cash proceeds immediately in assets that *did* retain value. Inflation threatens the store of value function because each unit of money buys fewer goods and services as time passes. That is, \$1 received today will not be enough to buy \$1's worth of goods 1 year from now.[1]

As both a unit of account and a store of value, money can function as a *standard for deferred payments.*

Standard for deferred payments:
The function of money that allows future commitments to be denominated in financial terms rather than in terms of other nonmonetary commodities.

This function allows financial transactions (such as bank deposits and bond issues) today, with future payments specified in monetary terms.

MONETARY SYSTEMS

Monetary systems are the general mechanisms for exchange of goods and services. There are three types of monetary systems incorporating, at various levels of efficiency, all the functions of money described above. In ascending order of efficiency, these are:

[1] Inflation and price changes are described in Chapter 8.

- Barter
- Full-bodied money
- Paper money

Barter System

A *barter system* restricts ultimate users to the exchange of commodities, an arrangement that requires a *double coincidence of want.*

Double coincidence of want:
The situation in which each of two parties seeks to obtain the product or commodity that the other possesses, making it possible for them to engage in barter.

That is, a farmer who has produced 10 bales of hay and needs 5 yards of material for clothing must first find an individual who both needs hay *and* possesses the cloth. Assuming the farmer's success in finding this match, the next obstacle to overcome is mutual agreement on price. In terms of hay, what is the price of cloth? In terms of cloth, what is the price of hay? This dilemma is not uncommon in Russia and other Eastern European countries that frequently engage in barter in order to obtain Western goods.

The search for double coincidence of want and negotiation of relative prices is repeated whenever a producer needs anything other than the commodity produced. Search and information costs in a purely barter economy quickly become prohibitive, restricting the free flow of goods and services by which we tend to characterize more developed economic systems.[2] The denomination of commodities in terms of money results in more efficiency. The double coincidence of want is no longer necessary, and the farmer can sell hay to anyone who needs it, later exchanging the money for other commodities. (See Exhibit 2-2.)

Full-Bodied Money

The first systems of modern *full-bodied* money used coins made of precious metals, usually gold or silver.

[2] Even if these conditions *are* met, the total number of prices in a system with n commodities is $n(n-1)/2$, the total of all possible combinations of n items. When one of the commodities is modern money, the number of prices is reduced to $n-1$. Every other commodity is denominated in terms of money.

EXHIBIT 2-2 BARTER SYSTEMS OF THE WORLD

In primitive chiefdoms and kingdoms the only mode of transaction was the barter system. This was because there were no organized political and economic institutions to impart legal tender status to standard commodities that could then serve as money. Consequently, a number of commodities were adopted as exchange media in Africa, America, Asia, Australia and Europe. Cattle represented one of the oldest commodities used as money. Cattle were used widely by the Romans as a means for striking a bargain. The Latin word *pecunia* (money) is derived from *pecus* (cattle). Salt also served as money in ancient Rome. Salary is derived from the Latin word *salarium* (salt). The American Red Indians used the feathers of rare birds as money and the Arabs used dates and tea. Other commodities which were also widely used as money in primitive Europe included oil, wheat, furs and wine.

Source: Onoh, J. K., *Money and Banking in Africa,* Longman Group Limited, London, 1982, p. 1.

Full-bodied money:
Money (medium of exchange) with an intrinsic value that is equal to its value as a unit of account. Many commodities have been used as full-bodied money, but the most common have been precious metals.

These systems existed as early as 560 B.C. during the era of Croesus, King of Lydia, an ancient kingdom in what is now Turkey. The first coins were made of electrum, an alloy of gold and silver. Full-bodied metallic coins were used in the United States from 1792 until 1965, when the government discontinued the use of silver in newly minted dimes and quarters. By 1970, no precious metal was used in U.S. coins that circulated as money.[3]

While metallic coins performed all the functions of money, the system presented some problems. People would melt down the coins to hoard the precious metals, and the weight of the coins made large transactions cumbersome. Coin counterfeiting and shortages of gold in the nineteenth century also threatened the full-bodied money system.

Paper Money

Early goldsmiths have been credited with the creation of *paper money.* When they served as custodians of gold for their customers, they issued receipts for the gold held in safekeeping. To redeem their property, patrons exchanged these receipts for their gold. As the receipts were fully collateralized by gold, they began to circulate themselves as money. Goldsmiths, thus, became the world's first bankers.

Until the early 1930s, most paper money (by then issued primarily by sovereign governments) remained convertible into gold. For many years thereafter, only the U.S. dollar was convertible into gold. Finally, in 1971, the United States suspended gold convertibility of the dollar.

MONETARY STANDARDS

The *monetary standard* of a country is the specific physical form of money the country adopts. In general, the form is either:

- Commodity standard
- Noncommodity (paper) standard

Historically, the most important commodity standards have been:

- Gold coin
- Gold bullion
- Gold exchange
- Silver

In the case of adoption of a *gold coin* standard, mints freely accept gold from the public and manufacture coins as prescribed by law. Gold coin is legal tender—that is, must be accepted as payment.

The *gold bullion* standard requires that paper money (bank or government liabilities) be convertible into gold bullion. A number of countries switched to this standard after World War I (1918) in an effort to conserve their gold reserves. A gold bullion (bar) contains considerably more gold than a coin, making conversion an expensive exercise in paper money terms, thereby discouraging gold conversions. At the same time, the conver-

[3] Precious-metal coins may still be used as investments and collector's items.

sion feature still standardized the payment settlements, facilitating trade between countries using the gold bullion standard.

A *gold exchange* standard does not obligate the adopting country to convert its currency into gold in any form. Instead, the paper money is legal tender and convertible into drafts (similar to checks) that are payable in the currency of a country that *has* adopted either the gold coin or gold bullion standard. Countries on a gold exchange standard maintain reserves of the gold-bullion-standard currency and purchase these reserves with gold in the foreign country on the gold bullion standard. The use of "gold drafts" in this case eliminates the expense of shipping and handling gold bullion.

The principles of operating on a *silver standard* would be similar to operating on a gold standard. While some countries have successively adopted a silver standard, a gold standard, or both standards (bimetallism), the silver standard has become progressively less attractive as the market value of silver has declined compared to gold.

Most of the countries of the world have adopted a *paper (noncommodity)* standard. A noncommodity standard is either an *inconvertible* paper standard or a *controlled* paper standard. As one would guess, a country adopting an *inconvertible* paper standard does not permit currency conversion into either gold or silver. Unlimited conversion into foreign currencies is possible, however, as long as the countries in question do not restrict such conversion. A *controlled* paper standard allows limited conversion into gold or silver. The controlled paper standard historically has discouraged international trade, fostered inflation, and encouraged illegal foreign currency exchange (black market) activities.

THE ADOPTION OF MONETARY STANDARDS

Today's monetary standards are the result of both national and international economic developments. Progression to the current, international monetary system has at times not been smooth, and the pattern of adopted standards has changed dramatically over the past century. By 1933, after the Great Depression and accompanying banking crises here and abroad, many countries no longer used a gold coin or gold bullion standard. Remaining on a gold standard were the United States and the so-called gold block of France, Belgium, the Netherlands, Switzerland, and Italy.

Bretton Woods, 1944

Before the end of World War II, the 1944 Bretton Woods Articles of Agreement established the International Monetary Fund (IMF), whose current membership is 152 countries. (Nonmembers include Switzerland, an associate member, and all the former communist bloc countries except for China, Hungary, Poland, Romania, Vietnam, and the former Yugoslavia.) The original IMF charter required members to (1) agree with the IMF upon a currency exchange rate (the official par value of a country's currency) and (2) take appropriate action to maintain the value of their currencies within a narrow band around that par value (1 percent or below), called a "tunnel."[4]

Member countries were to maintain these parities in terms of gold or in terms of the U.S. dollar. Even though par values were expressed in terms of gold, all currencies were effectively pegged to the U.S. dollar, with 1 ounce of gold equivalent to U.S.$35. This agreement ended reliance on a gold bullion standard for all countries, except the United States, and established a *gold exchange standard.*[5]

Gold convertibility of the U.S. dollar proved to be unsustainable. Between 1947 and

[4] Foreign currency markets and exchange rates are discussed in Chapters 6 and 9.

[5] In the case of the exchange of non-U.S. currencies for *other* non-U.S. currencies, a more appropriate designation is *inconvertible paper standard.*

1956, short-term holdings of U.S. dollars by foreign entities rose from $4.8 billion to $13 billion. Given U.S. gold reserves then valued at $22 billion, these relatively large foreign holdings of dollars were not seen as a serious threat until European banks (especially in England and Switzerland) began to trade U.S. dollars in what came to be known as Eurodollar markets. In 1958, an alarming $2.3 billion in gold was drained from U.S. reserves. Despite measures taken by the U.S. government to halt the outflow, this trend continued throughout the 1960s.

In the late 1960s, speculators, anticipating a decline in the value of the dollar because of this gold drain, borrowed dollars in the Eurodollar market and quickly sold them for other relatively more valuable currencies.[6] This dollar selling put downward pressure on the value of the dollar and upward pressure on the value of other currencies. Monetary officials in other countries were forced to sell their own currencies and buy dollars in order to try to maintain the parities (relative currency values) mandated by the Bretton Woods charter. Foreign official coffers were soon flooded with U.S. dollars. At the same time, U.S. corporate treasurers, also fearful of devaluation, converted massive amounts of liquid assets (denominated in U.S. dollars) into other currencies. The U.S. gold reserves were severely strained.

The Smithsonian Agreement, 1971

In August 1971 the United States suspended gold convertibility of the dollar. In December of the same year the G-10 countries[7] met and negotiated the Smithsonian Agreement, which placed the G-10 countries on an *inconvertible paper standard,* the "dollar standard." Nine currencies were revalued relative to the U.S. dollar, making them convertible into the dollar, with the dollar not convertible into gold. With the exception of Canada, the countries agreed to revaluations from 7.5 to 16.9 percent above the par values that had been stipulated prior to the Smithsonian meeting, and the 1 percent band around par value (the tunnel) became 2.25 percent. The Canadian dollar was allowed to float; that is, it was not pegged to the U.S. dollar. Although this agreement effectively reduced the value of the dollar relative to other currencies, the change was expressed in terms of an increase in the price of gold from $35 an ounce to $38. The official explanation was that the dollar had depreciated in terms of gold, not in terms of the other currencies.

The Snake in the Tunnel

At the same time, the European Community (EC), which had been created by the 1957 Treaty of Rome, sought a closer coordination of its currency values (monetary integration) than the Smithsonian Agreement provided. In accordance with recommendations of the 1970 Werner Report, an official EC report, the EC in 1971 established a maximum band around par values that was half the size of the Smithsonian band—the colorfully named "snake in the tunnel."

Meanwhile, confidence in the Smithsonian Agreement faltered. The United States, following 3 years of large trade surpluses, posted substantial trade deficits in 1971 and 1972.[8] As the market value of the dollar fell in light of these deficits, central banks in

[6] If the U.S. dollar should decline in value, a speculator needs less foreign currency to purchase the U.S. dollars necessary to repay the loan. The speculator realizes profit equal to the change in foreign currency value of the dollar.

[7] The "Group of Ten" (G-10) are Belgium, Canada, France, Germany, Italy, Japan, the Netherlands, Sweden, the United Kingdom, and the United States. Switzerland is an associate member.

[8] From 1968 to 1970, the U.S. trade surplus (excess of exports over imports) grew from $1.4 billion to $3.8 billion. This situation reversed in 1971 and 1972 with trade deficits (excess of imports over exports) of $0.9 billion and $5.2 billion, respectively.

EXHIBIT 2-3 EXCHANGE RATE ARRANGEMENTS (AS OF DECEMBER 31, 1990)

Currency Pegged to		
U.S. dollar	**French franc**	**Other currency**
Afghanistan	Benin	Bhutan (Indian rupee)
Angola	Burkina Faso	Kiribati (Australian dollar)
Antigua & Barbuda	Cameroon	Lesotho (South African rand)
The Bahamas	Central African Republic	Swaziland (South African rand)
Barbados	Chad	Tonga (Australian dollar)
Belize	Comoros	The former Yugoslavia
Djibouti	Congo	(Deutsche mark)
Dominica	Côte d'Ivoire	
Dominican Republic	Equatorial Guinea	
Ethiopia	Gabon	
Grenada	Mali	
Guyana	Niger	
Haiti	Senegal	
Iraq	Togo	
Liberia		
Oman		
Panama		
St. Kitts & Nevis		
St. Lucia		
St. Vincent and the Grenadines		
Sudan		
Suriname		
Syrian Arab Republic		
Trinidad and Tobago		
Republic of Yemen		

SDR*	Other basket of currencies	
Burundi	Algeria	Malta
I.R. of Iran	Austria	Mauritius
Libya	Bangladesh	Morocco
Myanmar	Botswana	Nepal
Rwanda	Bulgaria	Norway
Seychelles	Cape Verde	Papua New Guinea
	Cyprus	Poland
	Czechoslovakia	Romania
	Fiji	Sao Tome & Principe
	Finland	Solomon Islands
	Hungary	Sweden
	Iceland	Tanzania
	Israel	Thailand
	Jordan	Uganda
	Kenya	Vanuatu
	Kuwait	Western Samoa
	Malawi	Zimbabwe
	Malaysia	

other countries were forced to intervene in currency markets to maintain the parities agreed upon. This meant buying the U.S. dollar and selling their own and other foreign currencies. The governments of Germany and Japan, in particular, accumulated large reserves of U.S. dollars. The general consensus was that the 1971 U.S. dollar devaluation was not sufficient to avoid the need for this kind of market intervention. In the United States, sentiments grew that the special role of the dollar was no longer appropriate and that the currency should be allowed to float.

Limited Flexibility (in terms of a single currency or basket of currencies)	
Single currency†	**Basket of currencies**‡
Bahrain	Belgium
Qatar	Denmark
Saudi Arabia	France
United Arab Emirates	Germany
	Ireland
	Italy
	Luxembourg
	Netherlands
	Spain
	United Kingdom

More Flexibility		
Adjusted to set of indicators§	**Other managed float**	**Independent float**
Chile	P.R. of China	Argentina
Colombia	Costa Rica	Australia
Madagascar	Ecuador	Bolivia
Mozambique	Egypt	Brazil
Zambia	Greece	Canada
	Guinea	El Salvador
	Guinea-Bissau	The Gambia
	Honduras	Ghana
	India	Guatemala
	Indonesia	Jamaica
	Korea	Japan
	P.D. Rep. Lao	Lebanon
	Mauritania	Maldives
	Mexico	Namibia
	Nicaragua	New Zealand
	Pakistan	Nigeria
	Portugal	Paraguay
	Singapore	Peru
	Somalia	Philippines
	Sri Lanka	Sierra Leone
	Tunisia	South Africa
	Turkey	United States
	Vietnam	Uruguay
		Venezuela
		Zaire

*An SDR is a *special drawing right,* an instrument created by the International Monetary Fund (IMF). An SDR is denominated in the currencies of 16 countries with exports in excess of 1 percent of the world total. As of year-end 1990, the SDR was valued at U.S. $1.4227.

†Flexibility is in terms of the U.S. dollar.

‡Arrangement is part of the European Monetary System.

§Exchange rates are adjusted frequently according to indicators determined by the respective countries.

Source: International Financial Statistics. International Monetary Fund, May 1991.

In March 1973, after a number of monetary crises, the G-10 countries and Switzerland, Denmark, Luxembourg, and Ireland met and abandoned the dollar standard. France, Germany, Belgium, the Netherlands, Luxembourg, Sweden, and a comember of the snake, Norway, agreed to a joint float. Currencies of the United States, Canada, the United Kingdom, Japan, Switzerland, and Ireland were allowed to float. While membership of the snake has varied, depending upon individual national economic conditions, the monetary relationships established in March 1973 remain essentially unchanged today. (See Exhibit 2-3.)

EXPANSION OF THE MONEY SUPPLY BY BANKS

Within the global monetary system, financial institutions help meet capital investment needs by providing liquidity and expanding the money supply.[9] This may best be seen in the case of banks by returning to history's first bankers, the goldsmiths. As long as the goldsmiths' total receipts issued (their liabilities) equaled the value of the gold they held in safekeeping (their assets), these receipts, even though they circulated as money, did not increase the money supply. In banking terms, receipts were deposits, and the gold was held against future redemption requests or withdrawals. With time, this basic safekeeping system developed to allow issuance of receipts that were not completely backed by gold, which had the effect of increasing the money supply.

Bank Reserves

Gold initially was a reserve asset, representing 100 percent of the goldsmith's liabilities (deposits).

Reserve assets:
Assets (cash and other liquid instruments) held for the satisfaction of future requests for cash (withdrawals) that are related to specific liabilities (deposits).

When the receipts themselves came to be used as money, redemption requests became less frequent and more predictable. In fact, the amount of gold actually needed to satisfy withdrawals was considerably less than total outstanding receipts. In other words, *required* reserves were less than 100 percent of deposits. The goldsmiths could conceivably lend any *excess reserves* or, alternatively, issue gold receipts that were not backed by gold (earning interest on the loans, in either case).

Excess reserves:
The amount by which actual reserve assets exceed required reserves.

When excess reserves are loaned, the money supply increases. This is, in fact, at the heart of our modern banking system.

Money Supply Expansion

Banking practice and regulation expressly permit maintenance of *fractional reserves;* banks are not required to keep reserve assets to match 100 percent of deposits. The fractional reserve requirement means that a deposit of liquid assets into the banking system expands the money supply by an amount that is more than the amount of the deposit. This deposit has a magnifying effect.

To see this, assume that required reserves for each institution in the system are 20 percent of deposits. Let the variable r represent this required reserve percentage. Assume further that a person with $100 in cash decides to put the $100 in a demand deposit account at bank A on January 2.

Demand deposit:
Depository institution account that may be withdrawn upon demand via check or other means.

[9] This section discusses the role of private financial institutions in money supply changes. Chapters 11 and 12 describe government monetary policy.

Date		Bank		
1-2		Bank A		
	Reserves	100	Deposits	100
1-3		Bank A		
	Reserves	20	Deposits	100
	Loans	80		
		Bank B		
	Reserves	80	Deposits	80
1-4		Bank A		
	Reserves	20	Deposits	100
	Loans	80		
		Bank B		
	Reserves	16	Deposits	80
	Loans	64		
		Bank C		
	Reserves	64	Deposits	64
1-5		Bank A		
	Reserves	20	Deposits	100
	Loans	80		
		Bank B		
	Reserves	16	Deposits	80
	Loans	64		
		Bank C		
	Reserves	12.80	Deposits	64
	Loans	51.20		
		Bank D		
	Reserves	51.20	Deposits	51.20

Look at Exhibit 2-4; notice that, immediately after the deposit of \$100 in cash, assets and liabilities of bank A increase by the amount of the deposit. With a 20 percent reserve requirement, at the close of business on January 2, Bank A has \$80 in excess reserves, \$100 − r(\$100), or \$100 (1 − r).

The following day, January 3, bank A lends that \$80 to another of its customers by crediting that customer's demand deposit account by \$80 and recording a loan in the same amount. That same day, the customer writes an \$80 check to a vendor who presents the check to bank A for payment and deposits the cash into an account at bank B. The accounting entries on the books of both banks are as follows:

	Debit	Credit
Bank A		
1. Loans	80	
Deposits		80
2. Deposits	80	
Reserves		80
Bank B		
Reserves	80	
Deposits		80

At the close of business on January 3, these transactions have left bank A with no excess reserves, because reserves are now exactly 20 percent of deposits. Bank B, however, has $64 in excess reserves, $80 (1 − *r*). On January 4, bank B lends its excess reserves, and the process begins again. By the end of the day, bank C has $51.20 in excess reserves, $64 (1 − *r*). At the close of business on January 5, bank C's excess reserves are similarly invested in loans. This continues until no bank in the system has excess reserves. Note that each deposit D creates excess reserves of $D\,(1 - r)$.

The effect of the initial $100 cash deposit on the money supply is the change in deposits in the entire banking system or the total of the changes in each institution's deposits.

$$\begin{aligned} D_t &= D_A + D_B + D_C + D_D + \cdots + D_n \\ &= 100 + 100\,(1 - r) + 100\,(1 - r)^2 + 100\,(1 - r)^3 + \cdots + 100(1-r)^n \qquad (1) \\ &= 100\,[1 + (1 - r) + (1 - r)^2 + (1 - r)^3 + \cdots (1 - r)^n] \end{aligned}$$

where D_t = total change in deposits or the effect on money supply
D_i = increase in deposits at bank i
100 = the amount of the original infusion of liquidity
r = required reserve percentage

The total effect on money supply reduces to the following relationship.[10]

$$D_t = L/r \qquad (2)$$

where L is the amount of the liquidity infusion ($100 in the example above).

With a 20 percent reserve requirement, a $100 cash deposit into the banking system eventually increases the money supply by $500. This happens whenever cash is converted into banking system deposits. It also happens when government expenditures exceed government receipts—that is, when the government spends more for goods and services than it collects in taxes and other revenues—or when a government agency purchases more government securities on the open market than it sells.

This is not restricted to American depositors with U.S. dollars. The money supply also expands when a check drawn on a non-dollar-denominated account is deposited in a U.S. bank. Such a transaction is roughly equivalent to the sale of foreign currency for U.S. dollars, which dollars are then deposited into the banking system. Suppose, for example, that a Japanese customer opens an account in a U.S. bank with a check drawn on a Japanese bank and denominated in Japanese yen. The U.S. bank presents the check to the Japanese bank and receives credit; the yen must be converted into dollars and credited to the customer's U.S. account. These dollars are a liquidity infusion into the banking system as much as a domestic cash deposit.

When transactions such as these occur in the opposite direction, the money supply *contracts*. The amount of the contraction is a multiple of the amount of the transaction, just as the bank deposit is, where the multiple equals the inverse of the reserve requirement. Reduction of the money supply results when deposits are converted to cash (and *not* redeposited), when government receipts exceed expenditures, when a government agency sells more government securities than it purchases, and when U.S. dollar–denominated deposits are transferred to bank accounts denominated in other currencies.

[10] The bracketed term in Equation 1 is a geometric series in which each successive term increases by the multiplicative factor q that, in this case, has the value $1 - r$. The value of this term converges to

$$\begin{aligned} [1 - (q^{\infty})]/(1 - q) &= [1 - (1-r)^{\infty}]/[1 - (1 - r)] \\ &= (1 - 0)/(1 - 1 + r) \\ &= 1/r \end{aligned}$$

Deposits of commercial banks are an integral part of the money supply because they serve all the necessary functions of money—medium of exchange, unit of account, store of value, and standard for deferred payments. Other financial institutions offer accounts with features that are virtually identical to commercial bank demand deposits, including negotiable order of withdrawal, (N.O.W.) accounts, share draft accounts in credit unions, and brokerage firm transactions accounts. The definition of money includes these and other liquid financial instruments.

The three main classifications of money are M_1, M_2, and M_3, with the most liquid being M_1.

M_1:

Currency and coin in circulation, demand deposits in commercial banks, transactions accounts at other depository institutions, and traveler's checks.

M_2:

Classification M_1 plus savings accounts, money market deposit accounts at depository institutions, certificates of deposit and repurchase agreements in amounts under $100,000, overnight repurchase agreements of commercial banks, overnight Eurodollars issued to U.S. residents (excluding financial institutions), and retail money market fund balances.

M_3:

Classification M_2 plus certificates of deposit and repurchase agreements in denominations greater than $100,000, institutional money market fund balances, and term Eurodollars issued to U.S. residents (excluding financial institutions).

Exhibit 2-5 illustrates the growth in each of the money supply aggregates from 1964 through 1989. The broadest measure, M_3, grew from $425 billion in 1964 to $4 trillion in 1989. In 1964, cash and transactions accounts, M_1, represented 37 percent of total money supply. Twenty-five years later, this figure was only 20 percent.

EXHIBIT 2-5 MONEY SUPPLY, 1964–1989

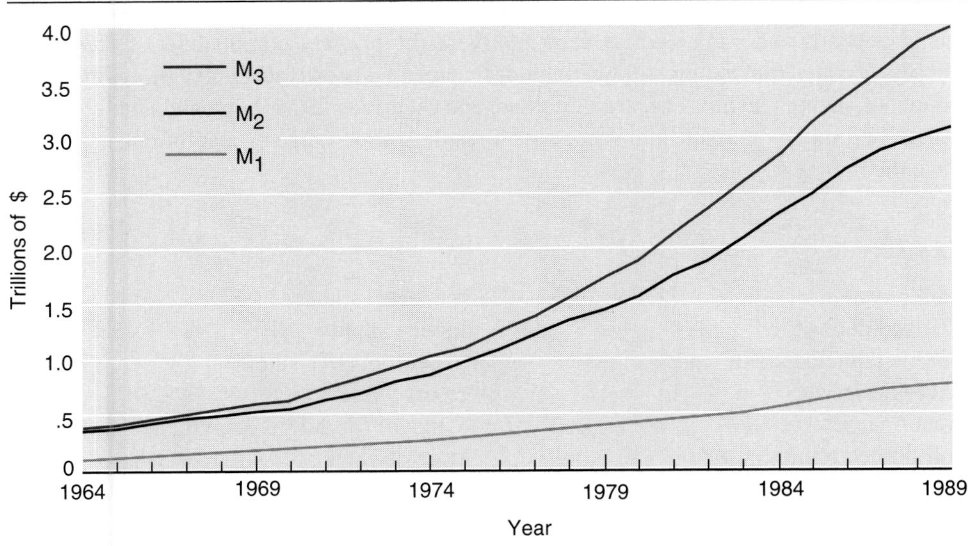

Source: United States Department of Commerce, Bureau of Economic Analysis, *Business Statistics 1961–1988* and *Survey of Current Business, April 1991.*

The largest segment of the money supply in 1989 was the less liquid assets in M_2, primarily composed of small time deposits, money market deposit accounts, savings accounts, and retail money market fund balances—accounts controlled by individuals. This amount grew from $253 billion in 1964 to $2.3 trillion in 1989, without much change in the percentage M_2 represents of M_3. At the same time, large-denomination deposits and institutional money market fund balances ($M_3 - M_2$) increased from $15 billion in 1964 (4 percent of M_3) to $858 billion in 1989 (21 percent of M_3).

The increase in M_3 has come at the expense of the more liquid M_1 segment (37 percent of M_3 in 1964 but only 20 percent by 1989). Basically, it is a sign of substantial growth in interest–rate–sensitive instruments, which represents a corresponding loss for commercial banks in traditional demand deposit accounts. To some extent, the factors that led to these changes in the money supply have affected all the financial institutions and markets that are the subject of this text.

SUMMARY

Money links financial institutions to each other and to the customers that they serve. It is a medium of exchange, a unit of account, a store of value, and a standard for deferred payments. In a less developed economy, the method of exchanging goods and services, the monetary system, may be based on barter. In more advanced economies, the monetary system is full-bodied money or paper money. Paper money has the advantage of being easier to transport and more convenient for large transactions.

Monetary standards describe the physical attributes of money with the two primary classifications being commodity and noncommodity (paper) standards. Commodity standards usually involve gold. Gold coin, as full-bodied money, has value in its own right. The gold bullion standard uses paper money that is convertible into gold. The gold exchange standard uses paper money that may be exchanged for another currency that, in turn, may be converted into gold. Silver standards have similar definitions but have been less common.

Today monetary standards that have been adopted are primarily noncommodity (paper) standards. An inconvertible paper standard allows conversion into other currencies but not into gold or silver. A controlled paper standard does not even allow conversion into other currencies. Most countries have adopted the inconvertible paper standard.

At one time, commercial banks were the only private financial institutions that issued money. In addition to currency and coin (issued by government monetary authorities), demand deposits and bank savings accounts were the primary components of the money supply. Today, the money supply includes demand deposit accounts; transactions accounts of savings institutions, credit unions, and securities firms; large and small time deposits; and money market fund shares. As a result, a wide range of institutions now influence the money supply.

KEY TERMS

barter system
demand deposit
double coincidence of want
excess reserves
fractional reserves
full-bodied money
medium of exchange
monetary standard
money supply
paper money system
reserve assets
standard for deferred payments
store of value
unit of account

END-OF-CHAPTER QUESTIONS

1. What are the primary functions of money?
2. Explain the advantages of a modern monetary system over a barter system.
3. What is full-bodied money?
4. Differentiate among gold coin, gold bullion, and gold exchange monetary standards.
5. Why do you suppose that the Bretton Woods arrangement was agreed to in the year 1944?
6. Describe the actions of the European Community (EC) with respect to the 1971 Smithsonian Agreement.
7. What problems for a country can be caused by wild fluctuations in the foreign exchange rate of its currency?
8. What events led to the suspension of gold convertibility of the U.S. dollar?
9. Explain expansion of the money supply in connection with the maintenance of fractional bank reserves.
10. The money supply is an important element in a country's economic development. What impact would an inadequate money supply have on the economy?

END-OF-CHAPTER PROBLEMS

1. Suppose that a country operates under a barter system. If 5 yards of textile material have the same value as 10 bales of hay, what is the price of (a) 1 yard of textile material? and (b) 1 bale of hay?
2. Suppose that a foreign currency speculator borrows $100,000 and converts them into British pounds (£) when the exchange rate is $1.85 = £1 ($1 = £0.5405) and repays the dollar loan when the exchange rate is $1.90 = £1 ($1 = £0.5263). Ignoring interest on the loan, did the speculator profit from this transaction? If so, by how much?
3. If the money supply increases by $600 million after a liquidity infusion of $72 million, what is the implied reserve requirement?
4. Refer to the *Federal Reserve Bulletin* or the *Survey of Current Business.* Determine (a) the dollar amount of change in M_1, M_2, and M_3 during the most recent 12-month period and (b) the percentage change in each.

SELECTED REFERENCES

Kaufman, Hugo M. *Germany's International Monetary Policy and the European Monetary System,* Columbia University Press, New York, 1985.

Kindleberger, Charles P. *A Financial History of Western Europe,* George Allen & Unwin Ltd., London, 1984.

Mullineux, Andrew. *International Banking and Financial Systems: A Comparison,* Graham & Trotman Ltd., London, 1987.

Onoh, J. K. *Money and Banking in Africa,* Longman Group Limited, London, 1982.

Struthers, J., and H. Speight. *Money; Institutions, Theory and Policy.* Longman Group Limited, London, 1986.

CHAPTER 3

MONEY MARKETS

CHAPTER OUTLINE

CHAPTER OVERVIEW

This chapter:

- Defines money markets
- Explains the roles of money market participants
- Describes financial instruments traded in money markets and analyzes their pricing
- Examines recent trends in U.S. money markets

Smoothly functioning financial markets allow financial institutions to perform distribution and intermediation functions efficiently and effectively. Financial markets are either *money* or *capital* markets, depending on the maturity of the specific financial instruments that are traded. This chapter discusses money markets, which are markets for short-term loans, and the next two chapters describe capital markets.

U.S. money markets are based on a foundation of *Treasury bills,* (T-bills), which are U.S. government liabilities of less than 1 year in original maturity. Treasury bills are auctioned in the primary market and traded in an active secondary market created by government securities dealers. A number of other financial instruments have evolved to complement the T-bill market. Commercial banks and other depository institutions participate in markets for *federal funds* and *repurchase agreements,* both of which constitute short-term agreements to borrow and lend. *Negotiable certificates of deposit,* issued by banks and savings and loans, are widely held as liquid assets by nonfinancial corporations, personal trusts, pension funds, state and local governments, and others. *Commercial paper* (short-term liabilities of corporations) is another vehicle for short-term financing that has grown rapidly in recent years; finance companies, nonfinancial corporations, and bank holding companies use commercial paper. *Banker's acceptances* (bank liabilities) accommodate financing needs associated primarily with international trade.

These markets, or markets like them, are found in virtually every industrialized country. In some countries, interbank transactions form the core of the money markets—Japan and Hong Kong are examples. In other countries, institutions with no equivalent in the United States play vital roles in the smooth operation of money markets. Japanese *Tanshi* companies and British *discount houses* perform what would be considered quasi-governmental functions in the United States.

While the configuration of money markets may vary from one country to another, whatever their format, money markets are the mechanism allowing a variety of participants to meet a wide range of liquidity objectives in any economy.

This chapter first discusses the nature of money markets and the participants in them. Next are descriptions of specific money market instruments, including concepts of instrument pricing and the relative significance of the various instruments within national boundaries of the United States and other countries. Outside the United States, the markets of the United Kingdom, Japan, Hong Kong, and Singapore, which are among the world's largest, form the basis for some international comparisons.[1] Finally, money market trends are examined.

WHAT IS A MONEY MARKET?

The maturity of financial instruments that are traded is one way to differentiate markets. If the securities traded are short-term instruments, the market is called a *money market.* When maturities exceed 1 year, the market is considered a *capital market* (the subject of Chapters 4 and 5).

Another differentiation is whether the securities are new (offered in the *primary* market) or already existing (traded in the *secondary* market). When U.S. T-bills are sold to the public for the first time, the sale takes place in a primary money market. When investors buy or sell already existing T-bills through dealers, these transactions occur in a secondary money market. A counterpart in the capital market would be an initial public offering of common stock—a primary capital market transaction—while the

[1]At the end of 1990, deposit or commercial banks in these countries held foreign assets, primarily cross-border claims on other banks, in the following amounts (in billions of dollars):

United Kingdom	1069.0
Japan	950.6
United States	654.3
Hong Kong	463.8
Singapore	346.7

subsequent exchange of stock through stockbrokers occurs in the secondary capital market.

Treasury bills are issued only in maturities of under 1 year, while common stock has no maturity date, which makes common stock a long-term financial instrument.

Money market:
A market in which financial instruments with maturities up to 1 year are bought and sold.

Money markets enable market participants to borrow or lend liquid assets and thereby meet needs for cash or investment of cash.

Liquid assets:
Assets that may be converted into cash quickly, without significant loss of value.

Investing excess liquid assets—that is, lending—reduces the opportunity cost of holding cash or cash equivalents. Borrowing short-term funds eliminates disruption that would be caused by temporary cash flow deficits.

Opportunity cost of holding cash:
That rate of return that could be earned if the next best alternative to cash were held by an investor, that is, that rate of return that is forgone when an investor holds cash.

The federal government uses the money market to effectuate certain phases of government monetary policy, such as adjustments to the money supply. It does this through the Federal Reserve Board, which establishes government objectives with respect to the money supply, interest rates, and credit availability. Monetary policy is discussed in Chapters 11 and 12.

MONEY MARKET PARTICIPANTS

The United States

The major money market participants are:

- The U.S. Treasury
- The Federal Reserve System
- Government securities dealers
- Commercial banks

The *U.S. Treasury* issues the T-bills and other securities that are the foundation of the money market. Short-term issues enable the government to raise money to meet necessary expenditures between receipts of tax revenue. The Treasury also arranges for the refinancing of maturing issues.

The *Federal Reserve System* historically holds over 75 percent of its financial assets in the form of U.S. government securities (6 percent of the total outstanding in 1991), and its role in the operation of money markets is a crucial one. The Federal Reserve (Fed) as the fiscal agent for the Treasury accepts bids for and distributes all government securities in the primary market. If it appears that the money supply should be contracted to guard against inflation, the Federal Reserve will enter the secondary money market and sell government securities, increasing the amount of securities held by the private sector and decreasing the money supply. If the economy appears to need stimulation in the face of potential stagnation, the Fed purchases securities, thereby increasing the money supply. The Federal Reserve frequently uses repurchase agreements (repos) and reverse repos to effect these adjustments. Its ultimate responsibility for the money supply makes the Federal Reserve the single most influential participant in U.S. money markets.

Government securities dealers make markets in Treasury securities by buying large blocks of securities from the Federal Reserve in the primary market and distributing them to customers. The dealers hold inventories of securities that facilitate secondary trading by their customers. Dealers also buy and sell for their own accounts, further helping support an active and liquid market.

In the United States, *commercial banks* are major money market participants. In 1991 they provided 79 percent of negotiable certificates of deposit (CDs) and 69 percent of federal funds and repurchase agreements.[2] Bank holding companies are issuers of approximately 4 percent of commercial paper outstanding. Banks extend lines of credit supporting the commercial paper of nonfinancial firms, making the paper safer and more appealing to investors. As a group, banks hold a larger percentage of U.S. government securities than any other group of financial institutions (approximately 12 percent in 1991). Fractional reserve requirements give commercial banks significant influence on the expansion and contraction of the overall money supply whenever liquidity changes occur in the economy.

The United Kingdom and Japan

In many other countries the money market functions of commercial banks, government entities, and securities dealers parallel those of their U.S. counterparts. Such markets may vary in degree of development, but the basic functions take place in a comparable fashion. Two financial systems, however, have institutions for which there are no U.S. parallels. In the United Kingdom, *discount houses* act as intermediaries between the government and the commercial (clearing) banks. These private firms absorb the entire weekly U.K. Treasury bill offering, can borrow from the Bank of England (the United Kingdom's central bank), are active dealers in short-term government securities, and make a secondary market with merchant banks in negotiable CDs and acceptances.

In the United States, commercial banks may borrow directly from the Federal Reserve. British clearing banks must make their liquidity adjustments through the discount houses; they may not borrow directly from the Bank of England. It is this function of U.K. discount houses that distinguishes them from any U.S. financial institution. The Bank of England carries out its monetary policy largely by purchase and sale of Treasury and commercial bills through the intermediary discount houses. Only recently, in the "big bang" of 1986, did banks gain the right to operate in the government securities market as U.S. banks do. The U.K. discount house model is also used in Singapore.

Another unique set of financial firms is the *Tanshi houses* of Japan. The Japanese government has licensed these six private companies in perpetuity to act as intermediaries in all money markets except the *gensaki* (repurchase agreement) market. Like discount houses, these nonbank firms may borrow from the central bank (the Bank of Japan), which frequently carries out its monetary policy through the *Tanshi.* They are the primary means through which large banks maintain reserve requirements. Because of their close relationship with the Bank of Japan, these nongovernmental companies essentially supervise bill-discount and call money markets, important components of Japan's money markets.

MONEY MARKET INSTRUMENTS

In the United States, the most widely traded money market instruments are:

- U.S. Treasury bills
- Federal funds

[2]Savings and loan associations and mutual savings banks accounted for 20 percent of negotiable CDs and 11 percent of federal funds and repurchase agreements.

- Repurchase agreements
- Negotiable certificates of deposit
- Commercial paper
- Banker's acceptances

Of these, the last three are traded in physical form, while the remaining instruments are kept track of in book-entry form (electronic record keeping) with written confirmations.

Money market instruments share certain qualities that make them useful for wholesale (large) transactions:

- *Liquidity,* which describes the ability to convert an asset into cash with relative ease while not significantly depressing its price in the process, is perhaps the most important quality.
- *Default risk,* which is the risk of nonpayment of principal or interest, must be minimal in order for the security to be considered a safe haven for excess liquidity.
- *Short time to maturity,* given that adverse price movements attributable to interest rate changes are smaller for shorter-term assets, helps ensure that interest rate changes will not affect the security's market value materially.

Treasury Securities

Treasury securities are obligations of the U.S. government. They are issued to cover government budget deficits (excess of expenditures over revenues) and to refinance maturing government debt. The most common are *bills, notes,* and *bonds.* Treasury bills have original maturities of 1 year or less, while notes are for 1 to 10 years, and bonds have maturities greater than 10 years.

Treasury bills (T-bills):
Short-term obligations of the U.S. Treasury Department with original maturities of 1 year or less.

Treasury bills and other Treasury securities (with less than 1 year of remaining life) are the most important instruments in U.S. money markets. Exhibit 3-1 shows that, in 1989, these short-term instruments represented over 30 percent of all money market instruments

EXHIBIT 3-1 MONEY MARKET INSTRUMENTS OUTSTANDING UNITED STATES (MARCH 31, 1989)

	Amount*		%†
Treasury securities			
Treasury bills	$417.0		
Others‡	264.5	$681.5	31.4
Federal funds and repurchase agreements §		367.6	16.9
Negotiable certificates of deposit		575.9	26.5
Commercial paper		486.8	22.4
Bankers' acceptances		61.6	2.8
		$2,173.4	100.0

*Billions of dollars.
†Percentage of total money market instruments outstanding.
‡Treasury notes with less than 1 year to maturity remaining.
§Federal Reserve statistics do not separate federal funds and repurchase agreements.
Source: Board of Governors of the Federal Reserve System, *Flow of Funds Accounts; Financial Assets and Liabilities Outstanding,* and Department of the Treasury, *Monthly Statement of the Public Debt of the United States.*

outstanding, a larger share than any other single instrument. In the primary Treasury bill market, the minimum denomination is $10,000, and multiples of $5000, $10,000, $100,000, and $1,000,000 are sold. Original maturities are 3 months, 6 months, or 1 year.

The Primary Market

The Bidding Process The Treasury Department auctions an announced quantity of new bills each week through Federal Reserve district banks and their branches. Bids may be submitted by government securities firms (for clients or for their own accounts), individuals, or financial and nonfinancial corporations. Submitted bids are either *competitive* or *noncompetitive. Competitive* bids specify the desired quantity of bills and the lowest interest rate the buyer is willing to accept. Large investors usually submit competitive bids, which make up the bulk of the aggregate dollar value of total bids. Treasury rules prohibit any single bidder from obtaining more than 35 percent of any new issue, however. *Noncompetitive* bids are limited to $1 million or less and state only the quantity of bills desired. A noncompetitive bidder accepts the weighted average interest rate of the winning competitive bids. Historically, noncompetitive bids have constituted 10 to 25 percent of the total.

The day of the auction, Federal Reserve banks and branches accept bids until 1:00 P.M. Eastern time, when all bids are forwarded to the Treasury. Noncompetitive bids receive their quantity allocations first, but at then-unspecified rates. Then competitive bids are considered. The bidder with the lowest interest rate receives the next allocation, followed by the bidder with the second-lowest interest rate. The process continues until all bills have been allocated. The Treasury computes the weighted average interest rate of the winning competitive bids and uses this rate to price all noncompetitive bids.

T-Bill Pricing and Delivery Treasury bills are sold at a *discount* price.

Discount pricing:

Setting the price of a financial instrument at the face value less the amount of interest that will be earned through the maturity date.

Interest earned is the difference between the price paid to purchase the instrument and the amount received upon maturity. A T-bill price is face value (for example, $10,000) less applicable discount according to the given rate of interest. The discount is based on a 360-day year and the number of days between date of purchase and maturity date and is quoted per $100 of face value. Once the interest rate is set through the auction, the price is determined by this formula:

$$\begin{aligned} P &= 100 - \text{discount} \\ &= 100 - 100\,(k)\,(N/360) \\ &= 100\,[1 - k\,(N/360)] \end{aligned} \tag{1}$$

where P = price per $100 of face value
k = appropriate interest rate
N = number of days to maturity

At an interest rate of 8 percent for 3-month bills (91 days to maturity), the Treasury bill price would be $97.9778 per $100 face value. Rounded to three decimals, the cost to purchase $1 million in bills is $979,780 ($97.978 × 10,000 = $979,780), and, upon maturity, the interest earned totals $20,220.

Treasury bill purchases are recorded in a *book-entry system.* Physical securities are never delivered. Instead, a record of transactions is maintained electronically by the Treasury and the Federal Reserve system. This arrangement significantly reduces transaction costs by eliminating the need to handle, ship, or store physical documents.

Once the Treasury auction is complete, settlement (that is, payment and delivery) is accomplished through a *tiered custodial system.*

Tiered custodial system:
System that segments ownership records of T-bills. The Treasury records ownership by the relevant Federal Reserve bank. The particular Federal Reserve bank records ownership for a depository institution. Only the depository institution maintains records of ultimate ownership.

Treasury Department records reflect liabilities to the specific Federal Reserve banks from which it receives winning bids (competitive and noncompetitive). In turn, Federal Reserve banks record the ownership of securities (Reserve Bank liabilities) for each financial institution (commercial bank or other depository institution) that submits a winning bid. Each financial institution also segregates its records of Treasury bill holdings (assets) into those held (1) for its own account, (2) for depository institutions with no Federal Reserve account, (3) for brokers and dealers, and (4) for ultimate investors. The Treasury makes payments of interest and principal through this tiered custodial system as well.

The Secondary Market

The United States The secondary market in Treasury bills is a vast and exceedingly efficient telecommunications network, whose major participants are *primary government securities dealers,* approximately forty financial institutions so designated by the Federal Reserve. These banks, brokerage firms, and bond houses buy and sell Treasury bills for their own and their customers' accounts. Customers include depository institutions, insurance companies, pension funds, nonfinancial firms, and state and local governments.

Government dealers help to maintain an orderly market mechanism through trades of Treasury bills for their own accounts. They earn profits based on the difference between the price at which they are willing to purchase Treasury bills, the *bid price,* and the price at which they will sell them, the *asked price.* The efficiency of the market is evidenced by narrow *bid-asked spreads,* typically ranging from 2 to 4 *basis points.*

Bid-asked spread:
Dealer profit in a T-bill transaction; the difference between the purchase and sales prices that a dealer will accept.

Basis point:
One-hundredth of 1 percent.

Thus, the customary spread is approximately \$50 to \$100 per \$1 million of 3-month bills.[3] (See Exhibit 3-2.)

As the core of the U.S. money market, the U.S. Treasury bill market attracts both domestic and international investors. The Treasury has sold 3-month maturities since 1929 and 6-month and 1-year maturities since the late 1950s.

[3] Calculation of the dollar amount of a 2-basis-point spread on a \$1 million, 91-day Treasury bill is comparable to calculation of the discount.

$$\begin{aligned}\text{Spread} &= 1{,}000{,}000\,[\,k(N/360)]\\ &= 1{,}000{,}000\,[.0002\,(91/360)]\\ &= 50.56\end{aligned}$$

EXHIBIT 3-2 THE CASE OF SALOMON BROTHERS: SCANDAL IN THE GOVERNMENT SECURITIES MARKET

During the 1960s and 1970s, there were only five primary government securities dealers, and the industry was essentially self-regulating, as these dealers were exempt from federal oversight. Since 1981, the number of primary dealers has grown to forty, but the industry remains highly concentrated with Salomon Brothers historically commanding the most significant role.

Because of the importance of a handful of primary dealers, there have long been suspicions that the bidding process was not as competitive as it should be. In some cases, such suspicions seemed credible; for example, in a 1979 auction of $3.3 billion in Treasury securities, all primary dealers bid exactly the same price.

More recently, Salomon Brothers' activity in the market violated the Treasury Department rule with respect to purchases by a single dealer for its own account. On several occasions, the firm gained control of more than 35 percent of new issues by using customers' accounts, sometimes with their knowledge and consent and sometimes without. The motive for this behavior is excess profits that may be generated by "cornering the market":

- The firm places a bid for 35 percent of the issue at a price sufficiently high to ensure acceptance by the Treasury Department (primary market).
- Simultaneously, the firm places orders on behalf of its largest clients at a similarly high price (primary market).
- The Treasury accepts the bids.
- The firm then purchases the customers' securities at cost, thus controlling a significant share of the total new issue (secondary market).
- When other bond dealers wish to purchase the securities, the firm can charge a monopolylike premium over cost and earn excess profits.

An investigation led to disclosure of Salomon's role in such market manipulation. One particularly graphic example of misconduct was a May 1991 auction in which Salomon gained control of 94 percent of an $11 billion issue. Criminal charges and civil lawsuits have been brought against the firm, and there are calls for regulatory reform of the industry.

Nevertheless, the market is so large that even this scandal has had relatively little impact on market stability. (In 1991, Salomon Brothers owned less than 2 percent of all Treasury securities outstanding.) The most significant outcome of the scandal is likely to be reform in the primary market for Treasury securities that includes a larger number of participants and greater accountability.

The United Kingdom In Europe, T-bills have an even longer history than in the United States, with the United Kingdom (location of the world's largest money market) first issuing Treasury bills in 1877. All U.K. bills have original maturities of 91 days and are bought and sold through discount houses, the financial institutions that act as intermediaries between British clearing (commercial) banks and the Bank of England, the central bank.

Since the "big bang" of 1986, regulatory changes empowered domestic and foreign banks to operate as primary dealers in the medium- and long-term government securities market, the *gilt-edged* market.

Gilt-edged market:
The market for medium- and long-term government securities in the United Kingdom.

With this new status, banks may now also bid on, but not act as primary dealers for, Treasury bills in the primary market. The right to bid on Treasury bills is probably less significant than the new bank powers in the gilt-edged market because the government has issued a substantially larger volume of medium- to long-term obligations (not short-term bills) in the last few years. As a result, Treasury bills do not play as significant a role in U.K. money markets as they do in the United States.

Asia The U.S. government sells Treasury securities through a *bid,* or *tender,* system.

Bid, or tender, system:
A predetermined quantity of securities is offered for sale and sold, or "tendered," to the highest bidders.

An alternative method of selling government securities has been through the *tap* system.

Tap system:
The government sells only those securities that the public requests.

Singapore made government securities available on a tap basis beginning in 1923, but the Singapore money market did not expand dramatically until three discount houses began operation in 1972 (an earlier discount house operated from 1964 to 1968), and Treasury bill sales were converted to the tender system in 1973. These factors and government initiatives to develop secondary markets in other money market instruments helped double the size of the money market in the 5 years that followed.

While many countries' money markets have developed around Treasury bills, others have evolved using other dominant liquid assets. Hong Kong, as a British colony (until 1997 when the People's Republic of China resumes power), has neither a central bank nor an indigenous government securities market. Thus, *call money,* the equivalent of U.S. federal funds, forms the core of the money markets of Hong Kong. Japan also has had a long tradition of a market in call money.[4]

Federal Funds

Federal funds are not formal securities. They are immediately available funds that are loaned or borrowed among financial institutions.

Immediately available funds:
Funds on deposit in a commercial bank or other depository institution that may be withdrawn with no delay.

Federal funds:
Immediately available short-term funds transferred (loaned or borrowed) between financial institutions, usually for a period of 1 day.

U.S. banks and (since 1980) other depository institutions that are federally insured (or eligible to apply for federal insurance) are required to maintain *reserves,* that is, liquid assets to back deposit liabilities at levels specified by the Federal Reserve. These reserves may consist of vault cash or deposits at a Federal Reserve bank. As deposits at Federal Reserve banks earn no interest, banks have an incentive to redeploy any excess reserves. The federal funds market developed as a way to do this.

[4]Recall that Japan, Hong Kong, and Singapore represent three of the five most significant international money markets.

The Market The federal funds market began in the 1920s when banks with excess reserves loaned the excess to banks that needed reserves at a "Fed funds" rate close to the rate that financial institutions pay to borrow directly from the Federal Reserve. The institution that borrows federal funds records a liability, *federal funds purchased.* The lending institution records an asset, *federal funds sold.* Federal Reserve rulings in 1928 and 1930 exempted federal funds purchased, including those created by book-entry or wire transfer, from reserve requirements. Given that banks could borrow from the Federal Reserve at a rate lower than the federal funds rate, the market was initially not very active. In the 1950s and 1960s, however, interest rates rose, short-term credit became difficult to obtain, and the demand for federal funds increased significantly. The market expanded so much that by 1970 roughly 60 percent of Federal Reserve member banks were active participants.

Federal funds transactions take two forms. If both institutions have Federal Reserve bank accounts, they may instruct the Federal Reserve to transfer funds from the account of the lender to the account of the borrower over Fedwire, the wire-transfer system of the Federal Reserve. Either party may initiate a transaction. Alternatively, an institution (respondent) may maintain an account with an institution acting as a federal funds broker (correspondent). In this case, the respondent bank informs the correspondent of its desire to sell federal funds, at which point the correspondent reclassifies the respondent's balance from demand deposits to federal funds purchased. The correspondent frequently resells the funds to a third party in the market.

Duration The duration of a federal funds transaction is usually 1 day—*overnight.* When both banks have Federal Reserve accounts, on the following day the Federal Reserve bank debits the account of the borrower (reduces the balance of the borrower's reserve bank account) and credits the account of the lender (increases the balance of the lender's account) for the principal amount of the transaction plus interest earned. If the transaction was brokered, the correspondent debits federal funds purchased in the amount of the transaction and interest expense for the interest to be paid, crediting the respondent's account.

Banks may also negotiate *term federal funds* loans, usually for a period of 90 days or less. An institution may choose this arrangement if it expects liquidity needs to persist longer than overnight, or if it anticipates a rise in interest rates in the near future. *Continuing contract federal funds* are, in effect, a continuous rollover of overnight federal funds at the rate that applies each day. This can evolve into a longer-term arrangement with a variable interest rate.[5]

Terms Most federal funds borrowings are unsecured. In fact, most are supported only by oral agreements made by telephone. This procedure is possible because the parties have long-standing business relationships or because the broker has no doubt about the institution's creditworthiness.

When federal funds are explicitly secured, the borrower places securities in the possession (custody account) of the lender. At the time the loan is repaid, custody of the securities is returned to the borrower. Title to the securities never changes, however.

Japan The U.S. federal funds market has a counterpart in several other countries. The *call money market* in Japan has operated since the turn of the century.

Call money:
Loaned funds that are repayable upon the request of either party.

[5]Because either party may withdraw from the contract, this arrangement may also be short-term.

All transactions go through one of nine *Tanshi* companies licensed by the Japanese Ministry of Finance. The term of a call money loan can range from a half-day to 7 days. *Half-day* money is borrowed at 9:00 A.M. and repaid at 1:00 P.M. or borrowed at 1:00 P.M. and repaid at 3:00 P.M. *Unconditional* money is repaid the following day. *Fixed maturity* money is repaid in 2 to 7 days.

Unlike U.S. federal funds, until 1985 any call loan other than half-day money had to be collateralized by government securities or high-quality corporate debt instruments. To accommodate foreign bank branches in Tokyo that possessed far fewer high-quality Japanese debt securities than Japanese banks, the government eliminated this requirement. Since the early 1970s other money market instruments have emerged, causing the call money market to become less significant in terms of total market volume.

Hong Kong In Hong Kong, the *interbank market* participants are licensed Hong Kong banks and authorized brokers.

Interbank market:
Money market transactions (short-term exchange of liquid assets) between banks with no intermediary.

Overnight call and other short-term deposits are the common vehicles, and collateral is rarely required. The larger Hong Kong banks had long conducted short-term transactions of this nature, but it was not until the late 1950s that the market became active. A comparable interbank market was the only way to adjust liquidity in Singapore until discount houses were established.

The United Kingdom Discount houses in the United Kingdom have traditionally served to provide short-term credit in the U.K. banking system by entering into call money arrangements with individual banks. Banks with surplus funds lent them to discount houses, and banks in need of liquidity called in their discount house loans. More recently, however, a parallel set of money markets has developed, one of which is the interbank market. Late in the 1960s clearing banks began to establish subsidiaries (nonclearing banks) to operate in the interbank market. Transactions generated by these and other institutions have since become dominant in the *sterling money markets.*

Sterling money market:
Short-term market for funds denominated in British pounds.

Thus, while the call money markets of Hong Kong, Singapore, Japan, and the United Kingdom have common features, the markets have developed in somewhat different ways. The call money market of Hong Kong has functioned in much the same way as the U.S. federal funds market, without any institutional intermediary. Singapore money markets did not become active until discount houses began operations and government securities were offered on a tender basis. Japan has maintained vigorous call money markets with the *Tanshi* houses as intermediaries since the turn of the century. Beginning in 1986, British call money markets with discount house intermediaries have had less impact because of deregulation and the growth of parallel, interbank markets.

Repurchase Agreements

The United States Repurchase agreements (repos) are agreements to sell securities and, later, to reverse the sale.

Repurchase agreement (repo):
An agreement between buyer and seller in the sale of securities to reverse the transaction in the future at a specified date and price.

These transactions commonly involve Treasury securities, but they may also involve government agency securities.

Government agency securities:
Securities issued by an agency of the U.S. federal government, with implicit backing of the federal government.

Repurchase agreements are essentially collateralized loans. A financial institution with large holdings of Treasury securities sells some portion of them for a predetermined period of time to obtain liquidity and promises to repurchase the securities at the end of that period. Of course, on the other side of the transaction is an institution with excess liquidity. The amount of the transaction is relatively large, and the interest rate is below the federal funds rate. The lower rate is justified, because the transaction is collateralized by government securities.

Repurchase agreements are typically as short term in nature as federal funds (or call money). Overnight, term, or continuing basis repurchase agreements are all negotiated. Unlike collateralized federal funds transactions, in which title to the securities does not change, in a repurchase agreement title *does transfer* to the purchaser.

In the United States, government securities dealers frequently engage in repurchase agreements for their own account to manage liquidity and to capitalize on anticipated changes in interest rates. If a dealer sells securities to a bank in one of these arrangements, the bank is said to have entered into a *reverse repo.* In fact, whichever party initially sells the securities enters a repo agreement, and the initial purchaser enters a reverse repo—one is simply the mirror image of the other. These transactions are commonly designated from the perspective of the securities dealer: If the dealer is the initial seller, the transaction is a repo; if the dealer is the initial purchaser, it is a reverse repo.

Repurchase agreements are useful to state and local governments because the time pattern of revenue receipts is frequently not the same as that for expenditures. Repurchase agreements have offered a safe, short-term outlet at close-to-market rates for temporary excess cash. In 1985, however, the market was shaken by the bankruptcies of two government securities dealers: ESM Government Securities and Bevill, Bresler, and Schulman. Improprieties in operating and auditing procedures led to losses of over $500 million for the customers of these firms. As a direct result, the state-insured thrift institution insurance system in Ohio collapsed and numerous municipalities lost operating revenues. These experiences were attributable to dealer violation of the repurchase agreements. Simply stated, dealers used securities more than once as collateral for loans to conceal operating losses.

Repurchase agreements are generally safe as long as participants observe certain guidelines:

- Execute clear and complete "master" repurchase agreements covering all terms of the transactions.
- Research the financial strength of the other party involved.
- Obtain control of the securities to be used as collateral.
- Evaluate the underlying securities to ascertain adequacy of the collateral.

Japan A Japanese counterpart to the repurchase agreement is the Japanese *gensaki.* While term repurchase agreements rarely exceed 30 days in the United States, the most common maturities in Japan are 30 to 60 days. Further, in the United States, nonfinancial corporations hold less than 25 percent of repurchase agreements. Nonfinancial corporations in Japan contribute over 60 percent to *gensaki* lending, exemplifying the close relationship between Japanese financial institutions and their corporate clients.

Negotiable Certificates of Deposit

Banks have issued certificates of deposit for many years, but it was not until the 1960s, when they were first issued in negotiable form, that certificates of deposit with original maturities of 6 months or less assumed a significant role in money markets.

Negotiable certificate of deposit (CD):
A financial instrument issued by a bank documenting a deposit, with principal and interest repayable to the bearer at a specified future date.

Note that a negotiable certificate of deposit is a bearer instrument and a term (not demand) deposit. In the 1950s, nonnegotiable, large-denomination CDs were unattractive because significant interest penalties were levied upon early withdrawal.[6] At that time, too, bank demand deposits paid no interest. As corporate treasurers became more sophisticated cash managers and sought alternatives to demand deposits as outlets for liquidity, the result was a severe reduction in demand deposit balances held by corporations.

The Birth of Negotiable CDs Here and Abroad The negotiable CD was the banks' response to this deposit drain. In 1961, what is now Citibank issued the first negotiable CDs in amounts greater than $100,000. Although subject to interest rate ceilings as specified by a Federal Reserve limitation called Regulation Q, the negotiable CD offered an alternative to non-interest-bearing demand deposits. Its enthusiastic reception helped banks regain a good measure of the funding that had been lost. (See Exhibit 3-3.)

Banks were able to increase the rate paid on negotiable CDs to attract more deposits as the need arose. This innovation brought widespread adoption of *bank liability management,* which enables banks to attract funds by offering higher interest rates and thereby changing their deposit base.[7] The interest rate ceiling was not a binding constraint until 1966, when Treasury bill interest rates rose to the point that they exceeded the maximum

[6]This is still true for many small-denomination nonnegotiable certificates, such as those held by individual bank customers.

[7]See Chapter 13 for discussion of liability management.

EXHIBIT 3-3 WALTER WRISTON AND THE NEGOTIABLE CD

In 1960, the first "Banker's Certificate" was offered by the overseas division of First National City Bank. The $1 million certificate was issued to Union Bank of Switzerland and was described as "marketable." In fact, Union Bank found that there was no market for the new instrument.

Walter Wriston, head of the overseas division, suggested to Discount Corporation, a government securities dealer, that it start a market in the new certificates. Discount Corporation was willing to do so *if* First National City provided the dealer with a $10 million unsecured loan (no collateral) to finance the operation. First National City overlooked its long-standing rule of not lending to securities dealers on an unsecured basis, and the market for banker's certificates was born.

On February 20, 1961, First National City announced the new banker's certificate to be sold in units of not less than $1 million with Discount Corporation agreeing to make a market. Walter Wriston would go on to become president and later chairman of the nation's largest bank, now called Citibank. The new certificate would become the most important money market instrument in the United States after the T-bill.

Source: Cleveland, Harold, and Thomas Huertas. *Citibank 1812–1970,* Harvard University Press, Cambridge, Massachusetts, 1985.

rate that could be paid on negotiable CDs. This meant that investors would not purchase more of the CDs as they matured, placing the banks in a "credit crunch." The banks reacted by offering competitively priced CDs *offshore* (that is, overseas) where Regulation Q was not applicable. So began the Eurodollar market.[8]

In 1970, Regulation Q interest rate ceilings were lifted for CDs over $100,000. By 1972 certificates of deposit represented approximately 40 percent of all bank deposits. Negotiable CDs are now second only to Treasury bills in terms of their importance in U.S. money markets. The negotiable CD is a major contribution by depository institutions to money markets in the United States and abroad.

When U.S. banks went offshore in 1966, they selected London as the location for offering dollar-denominated negotiable CDs. The instrument was readily accepted there—so much so that in 1968 the first sterling-denominated negotiable CDs were introduced. Negotiable CDs in domestic currency were first sold in Singapore in 1975 and in Hong Kong in 1977.

The first yen-denominated negotiable CDs were sold in 1979, when they could be sold only in minimum denominations of ¥500 million. This relatively high minimum was established to prevent undue competition with the *gensaki* (repurchase agreement) market. With the liberalization of the Japanese markets, however, the minimum was subsequently reduced to ¥300 million in 1984 and to ¥100 million in 1985. The relatively slower pace of financial innovation is typical of Japan, where the government has traditionally exercised tight control over the country's financial system.

CD Pricing The clear appeal of these instruments vis-à-vis other time deposits is their negotiability. Once issued, negotiable CDs may be sold through brokers, generally in round lots of $1 million. While the CD is originally issued at face value, its price in the secondary market depends on prevailing rates and the remaining time to maturity. Pricing is most easily analyzed in the context of the time value of money. Consider first three basic relationships:

$$\mathrm{FV}_n = \mathrm{PV}\,(1 + k)^n \tag{2a}$$

$$\mathrm{PV} = \mathrm{FV}_n/(1 + k)^n \tag{2b}$$

$$k = (\mathrm{FV}_n/\mathrm{PV})^{1/n} - 1 \tag{2c}$$

where FV_n = future value of an investment
PV = present value of an investment
k = rate of return
n = number of periods the investment is held

Equation 2a means that the value of an investment at some future time is a function of the initial investment, the rate of return being earned, and the length of time the investment is held. Equation 2b is a variation of Equation 2a and represents the current value of an investment with one specified future payoff. Equation 2c computes the rate of return for an investment when the price is given and the future payoff is specified.

To illustrate the pricing of a negotiable CD, assume that on day 0 a CD is issued at 8 percent with a maturity of 182 days (6 months). The original investor I_1 presumably will hold this CD for 182/365 of a year, so that the payoff of principal and interest on day 182 will be $103,912.09, according to Equation 2a:

$$\mathrm{FV}_{182} = 100{,}000\,(1 + .08)^{182/365}$$

[8]See Chapter 7.

But suppose I_1 decides to sell the CD to another investor I_2 on day 92, when 90 days remain to maturity and CDs of this risk classification are yielding 7.5 percent. Applying Equation 2b, the price of the CD on day 92, P_{92}, is $102,075.50:

$$P_{92} = 103{,}912.09/[(1 + .075)^{90/365}]$$

This is exactly the price that will yield investor I_2 a rate of return of 7.5 percent:

$$k = (103{,}912.09/102{,}075.50)^{365/90} - 1$$

Equation 2b can be adapted to generalize the price of a negotiable CD:

$$P_t = [P_0(1 + k_0)^{N/365}]/(1 + k_t)^{(N-t)/365}] \tag{3}$$

where P_t = price at time t
P_0 = face value of CD
k_0 = interest rate at time of issuance
N = original days to maturity
k_t = interest rate at time of sale in the secondary market

Commercial Paper

History of Issuance Another financial instrument that has significantly enhanced the alternatives for short-term liquidity adjustments is commercial paper. Commercial paper dates back to the beginning of trade in colonial America, even before banks were organized. The first form of commercial paper was bills of exchange.

Bill of exchange:
An order written by the seller of goods instructing the purchaser to pay the seller (or the bearer of the bill) a specified amount on a specified future date.

Bills of exchange essentially provide short-term loans to purchasers for a period of time between the sale of goods and the date of payment. They were used to smooth seasonal cash flow fluctuations. Bills of exchange could be *discounted* prior to the specified future date when the seller accepted the face amount of the bill less interest.

Bill discounting:
Receiving payment on a bill of exchange prior to the bill's maturity by surrendering the bill for face value less applicable interest for the time remaining to maturity.

The modern version of this instrument is called *commercial paper,* which is issued in large denominations, primarily by the most creditworthy firms.

Commercial paper:
Unsecured promissory notes, issued by corporations, with an original maturity of 270 days or less.

Commercial paper is a convenient way to raise short-term funds, because registration with the Securities and Exchange Commission (SEC) is not necessary, as it is in the case of issuing other securities for sale to the public. In order to be exempt from SEC registration, the issue must have an original maturity of 270 days or less and be intended for current transactions. The most common maturities of commercial paper are between 20 and

45 days. Like bills of exchange and Treasury bills, most commercial paper is issued on a discounted basis.

Generally, dealers distributed commercial paper to ultimate investors until 1920, when General Motors Acceptance Corporation (GMAC) began direct marketing of paper with maturities specifically tailored to ultimate investors. Within 10 years, other finance companies had followed suit.

Nonfinancial corporations began to rely on commercial paper during the credit crunch of 1966, when banks had difficulty attracting funds because regulated CD rates were not competitive with market interest rates. Many corporations that had previously relied on short-term bank loans issued commercial paper with lines of credit from their banks as backing.

A subsequent tight money environment in 1969 prompted bank holding companies to issue commercial paper in more than usual amounts, using the proceeds to buy loans from their subsidiary banks.[9] As a means to finance new bank loans, this method worked reasonably well until 1970, when the Federal Reserve imposed reserve requirements on commercial paper used in this manner. The effect at that time was to curtail issuance by bank holding companies. Currently, however, bank holding companies make extensive use of commercial paper to finance other activities, such as leasing, consumer, and mortgage finance.

Growth and Marketability The amount of commercial paper outstanding increased dramatically in the early 1980s, when short-term bank loans became prohibitively expensive, and commercial paper represented a much less costly source of funds. In 1980, for example, the difference between the prime bank loan rate and the commercial paper rate exceeded 6.5 percent. Although the spread has since narrowed, commercial paper remains an important segment of U.S. money markets. Nonfinancial corporations, finance companies, and bank holding companies accounted for almost 85 percent of total issues outstanding in 1991.

Because commercial paper is unsecured, the credit rating of the issuing company is a critical factor in the marketability of the issues. Three credit-rating firms rate the issues—Standard & Poor's Corporation (S&P), Moody's Investors Service, and Fitch Investor Service. Standard & Poor's designates investment-grade (high-quality) commercial paper as A-1 (highest investment grade), A-2 (high investment grade), and A-3 (good investment grade). Moody's comparable ratings are P-1, P-2, and P-3, while Fitch rates better-quality paper F-1, F-2, or F-3. Over 70 percent of the commercial paper rated by these firms receives the highest rating, and 98 percent receives the highest two ratings, which gives some indication of the importance of creditworthiness for successful marketing.

Banks play a vital role in these high average ratings. In most instances, issuing firms have backup lines of credit that cover 100 percent of the issue. When the credit of the issuing firm does not justify one of the top ratings, the firm may obtain a *letter of credit* from a bank with a top credit rating.

Letter of credit:

A letter issued by a bank or other firm indicating that a firm has arranged to obtain financing up to a specified amount.

A letter of credit backing the commercial paper in effect substitutes the credit rating of the bank for the credit rating of the issuer. This is called a *support arrangement,* and the

[9]Bank holding companies are corporations whose primary function is ownership of a bank (or banks) and other financial institutions. See also Chapter 17.

commercial paper is called "commercial paper supported by letter of credit" or a "documented discount note." Supporting firms besides banks might be insurance companies and parent companies (in the case of subsidiaries).

In many cases, while commercial paper has become a substitute for bank loans and eliminated a major source of bank revenues, such support arrangements have helped to lessen the negative impact because they result in fee income to banks.

Secondary Markets

The United States Compared to the market for Treasury bills and negotiable CDs, the secondary market for commercial paper is not as extensive. Dealers and direct issuers will redeem an issue prior to maturity if the investor is in dire need of funds, but early redemption is not encouraged. Of course, given that original maturities are so short, early redemption is generally not necessary.

Other Countries Commercial paper markets outside the United States are in various stages of development. In the United Kingdom, bill-brokers originally facilitated discounting of bills of exchange by working through banks and wealthy individuals. Discount houses perform this function now by accepting call money from clearing banks, buying bills at discount, and rediscounting them at the Bank of England. Perhaps because of this long tradition of bill discounting, the sterling commercial paper market was not authorized until 1986. As the 1986 legislation effectively exempts firms issuing commercial paper from preparing a prospectus (as is true in the United States), it removes a significant impediment to development of the market.

In Hong Kong, where the call money market has traditionally played a critical domestic role, commercial paper has been introduced only recently. The first major issues did not appear until 1979.

Introduction of discount houses in Singapore in 1972 facilitated discounting of bills of exchange. Bills of exchange that have been approved by the Monetary Authority of Singapore (the equivalent of a central bank) may also be held as liquid assets by commercial banks. The commercial paper market started formally in 1984.

Japanese bills of exchange with maturities of from 1 to 4 months have long been discounted by banks, but until 1971 the activity was considered part of the call money market. Individual promissory notes have relatively small denominations, so they are packaged in larger aggregates and attached to a bank's accommodation bill with a face value equal to the sum of the accompanying promissory notes. The banks then trade these accommodation bills among themselves, with *Tanshi* companies acting as brokers.

A domestic commercial paper market has been slow to evolve in Japan, despite the fact that Japanese companies issue commercial paper in the United States and in Euromarkets. In 1982 Japanese banking laws were revised to permit the establishment of a domestic market, but the Ministry of Finance formulated no regulations until 1987. These regulations classified commercial paper in the same category as commercial bills of exchange and designated banks and *Tanshi* companies as participants.

Banker's Acceptances

Banker's acceptances are a subset of bills of exchange that are guaranteed by "accepting" banks.

Banker's acceptance:

A time draft (postdated instrument) payable to a seller of goods, with payment guaranteed by a bank.

In these instruments, the credit of the bank substitutes for the credit of the purchaser, and the seller is ensured payment. Further, unlike an open trade credit arrangement (in which the seller provides credit for a period of time), the seller need not wait for payment. A banker's acceptance is immediately negotiable; the seller can either receive discounted payment at the accepting bank or hold the draft until the date of maturity. Banker's acceptances are particularly important in international trade. Maturities are 1, 3, or 6 months. Average maturity is 3 months.

Creating a Banker's Acceptance Creation of a banker's acceptance typically begins when an importer arranges a letter of credit through a bank, which then notifies an exporter (or the exporter's bank) that, once specific conditions have been satisfied, the exporter is entitled to draw (write) a draft on the importer's bank in the amount of the transaction. The conditions may include attaching documents to the draft verifying the shipment of goods.

Once the conditions have been satisfied, the exporter presents the documented draft to the importer's bank (perhaps through the exporter's bank). The importer's bank "accepts" the draft, and at that point the draft becomes a money market instrument. Payment to the exporter on the date of maturity is guaranteed, or, if the exporter decides to discount the draft immediately, payment is guaranteed to the holder of the acceptance.

Should the exporter decide to discount the acceptance, the importer's bank now has two alternatives. It can hold the acceptance in its portfolio until maturity, at which time the importer repays the bank. In the interim, a loan is recorded, as "customer's liability on acceptance outstanding." The accounting entry is:

	Debit	Credit
Customer's liability on acceptance O/S	X	
Cash		X

The second alternative is to sell the acceptance, in which case a liability, called "acceptance liability outstanding" is created. In this case, the entry is:

	Debit	Credit
Cash	X	
Acceptance liability O/S		X

There are other variations of acceptance creation. The draft may be drawn on the exporter's bank, especially if the importer's bank is relatively small. Alternatively, the importer's bank may arrange for a larger bank to accept the draft and provide the third bank a guarantee against loss. Some acceptances do not involve the shipment of goods at all. Drafts drawn for working capital, for example, are referred to as *finance bills.*

In all cases, the accepting bank charges a commission that is a function of the time to maturity and the creditworthiness of the borrower. If the acceptance is held in the portfolio of the accepting bank, the bank also earns interest equivalent to the discount. Generally, the borrower absorbs these costs.

The Market

The United States In the secondary market, investors find bankers' acceptances attractive because they are liquid and, although unsecured, have a historically low default rate. Investors include money market mutual funds, bank trust departments, state and local governments, insurance companies, pension funds, and commercial banks. Approximately thirty dealers and twelve brokers operate in the highly liquid U.S. market for banker's acceptances.

From the perspective of accepting banks, acceptance financing is comparable to CD financing. The bank has an obligation to pay the holder of the acceptance, just as it has an obligation to pay the holder of a CD. Likewise, funds obtained in the sale of the acceptance finance the customer's loan, just as funds obtained in the CD market finance other loans. Because of these similarities, the discount rate on acceptances is consistently within 10 basis points of the interest rate on CDs. For example, if the CD rate is 8.00 percent, the banker's acceptance discount rate will fall between 7.90 and 8.10 percent.

Banker's acceptance liabilities are not subject to reserve requirements as long as they qualify as one of three kinds of *eligible acceptance:*

- Domestic trade
- U.S. imports and exports
- Third country

Acceptances that finance *domestic* trade have historically been a small portion of the total market. Before the 1960s, acceptances to finance *U.S. imports and exports* were the most common, although currently they comprise less than half of all acceptance liabilities. The most common eligible category is now *third-country* acceptances, those that finance trade between countries outside the United States.

The growth of third-country acceptances was particularly strong during the 1970s, when non-U.S. borrowers found the U.S. acceptance market an attractive source of short-term financing. Most of these acceptances are *refinance bills* (working capital drafts). In these cases, the initial transactions between the two countries outside the United States are essentially the same as those described above. The refinance bill is created when the borrower's foreign bank holds the original draft drawn on it in its portfolio and draws another draft on a U.S. bank to replenish its funds. When the U.S. bank accepts this refinance bill, it then becomes a part of the U.S. acceptance market.

In recent years the U.S. acceptance market has not expanded as much as markets for other money market instruments, primarily because U.S. firms and their foreign counterparts have developed alternative sources of financing; commercial paper is an example. In the United States, banker's acceptances outstanding declined at an average annual rate of 2.1 percent between 1981 and 1991, while commercial paper increased at an annual rate of 13.3 percent. Elsewhere, the refinance bills of Japanese and other foreign banks have been replaced by borrowings in the Eurodollar markets.[10]

The United Kingdom and Japan Merchant banks are at the center of the U.K. banker's acceptance market (as distinguished from the discount house market).[11] While clearing banks maintain large branch networks of millions of individual depositors, merchant banks have made a niche for themselves by providing various financial services to businesses, including acceptance. But the acceptance business has experienced peaks and valleys as the government exerts and relaxes controls on other forms of lending.

The Japanese banker's acceptance market began in 1985, motivated by a desire to increase the demand for yen-denominated funds (very much in the interest of the United

[10]See Chapter 7 for a discussion of Eurodollar markets.
[11]Merchant banks are discussed in Chapter 5.

States because such an increase would help correct the then-overvalued dollar) and to give the Japanese government another instrument of monetary control. The growth of the market has been slower than anticipated, however, perhaps because of taxes imposed on banker's acceptances and the availability of other forms of short-term financing that are more competitively priced.

RECENT TRENDS

The 1970s were a period of financial innovation, driven partially by the high and volatile interest rates during the latter half of the decade. As a result, the expansion of private-sector money market instruments outpaced the growth in government debt.

During the 1970s, the amount of money market instruments outstanding consistently grew at double-digit rates. Total Treasury issues (including T-bills) grew from $226.6 billion in 1969 to $578.1 billion in 1979. This is a compound annual growth rate of 10 percent per year [($578.1 billion/$226.6 billion)$^{1/10}$ − 1 = 0.098]. Over the same period, private-sector (nongovernment) money market instruments grew at even higher rates. As shown in Exhibit 3-4, federal funds and repurchase agreements increased at the rate of 27.5 percent per year from 1969 through 1979. The relatively new negotiable CD enjoyed a comparably high growth rate of 23.9 percent. Banker's acceptances ranked next in terms of growth at 20 percent. The growth in commercial paper was lowest at 13 percent.

During the 1980s, the growth rate of private-sector money market instruments moderated, while government debt grew to over $2 trillion dollars by 1989, or at a 13 percent annual rate. Within the private sector, commercial paper showed the greatest percentage increase, 15.9 percent per year, higher than its 13 percent rate during the 1970s. Growth

EXHIBIT 3-4 GROWTH RATES OF FOUR TYPES OF MONEY MARKET INSTRUMENTS, 1969–1979, 1979–1989, AND 1989–1991

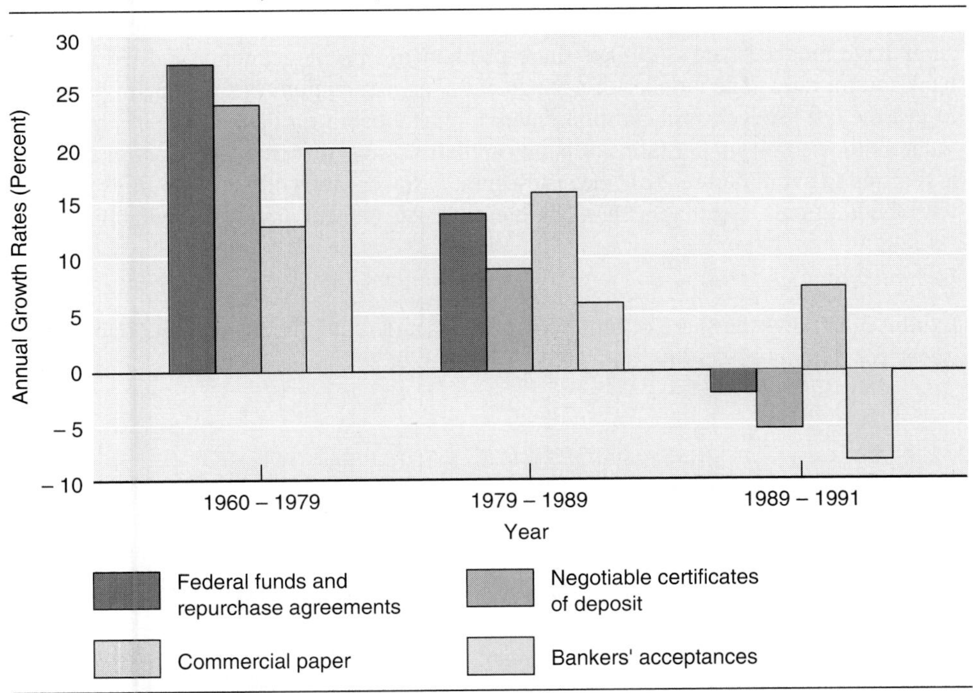

Source: Calculations and graphic based on data from Board of Governors of the Federal Reserve System, *Flow of Funds Accounts; Financial Assets and Liabilities Outstanding.*

in federal funds and repurchase agreements fell to 14.1 percent, roughly half the rate in the previous decade. Even so, federal funds and repos increased at a rate faster than the national debt.

It is notable that negotiable CDs and banker's acceptances outstanding increased at a much slower pace during the 1980s. The annual growth of negotiable CDs fell from 23.9 percent in the 1970s to 9.3 percent in the 1980s. For banker's acceptances, the growth rate of 20 percent fell to 6.1 percent during the 1980s.

From 1989 through 1991, growth in most private money market instruments was *negative* even as the U.S. government debt rose from $2.1 trillion to $2.6 trillion, an annual growth rate of 11.3 percent. Federal funds and repurchase agreements declined at an annual rate of 2 percent during the 2-year period. Negotiable CDs and banker's acceptances shrank by 5.2 and 8.0 percent, respectively.

On the other hand, commercial paper outstanding increased at an annual rate of 7.5 percent during the 2 years ended 1991. The amount of commercial paper issued by bank holding companies shrank. But the additional amounts issued by finance companies and nonfinancial corporations were large enough to more than offset the decline in bank holding company issuances.

Exhibit 3-5 shows the aggregate dollar amounts of these private-sector instruments in 1969, 1979, 1989, and 1991. Total instruments outstanding increased by a factor of 20 from 1969 ($74.6 billion) to 1989 ($1.49 trillion). Federal funds and repurchase agreements became a larger share of the total, while banker's acceptances dropped.

From 1969 to 1979, negotiable CDs grew to comprise almost half of private-sector money market instruments, while commercial paper dropped to less than 25 percent. Twelve years later, the commercial paper share had surpassed that of negotiable CDs.

These figures indicate that money markets have become less dependent on domestic commercial banks and the instruments that they issue. Given the financial sophistication of corporate managers and individuals, this trend is not likely to reverse.

The contraction in markets other than commercial paper from 1989 to 1991 is directly related to conditions in the banking and savings and loan industries. Competitive pressures have reduced banks' market share of financing in the economy and led to higher bank failure rates. The number of savings and loan associations has declined by one half in just the last few years. In addition, international concern for bank safety has caused regulators to push for higher ratios of bank capital to assets, that is, a larger buffer to absorb losses and to avoid failure. This means essentially lower ratios of bank liabilities to assets, with federal funds, negotiable CDs, and banker's acceptances among these liabilities.

Federal Funds and Repos

Exhibit 3-6 shows the share of total federal funds and repurchase agreement liabilities by issuer for 1969, 1979, 1989, and 1991. This market started as an exclusively interbank

EXHIBIT 3-5 MIX OF FOUR MONEY MARKET INSTRUMENTS, 1969–1991

	1969		1979		1989		1991	
	$*	%	$*	%	$*	%	$*	%
Federal funds and repos	8.7	11.7	98.6	20.5	367.6	24.7	352.9	23.7
Negotiable CDs	27.8	37.2	236.5	49.3	575.9	38.6	517.5	34.9
Commercial paper	32.6	43.7	110.9	23.1	486.8	32.6	562.3	37.9
Banker's acceptances	5.5	7.4	34.1	7.1	61.6	4.1	52.1	3.5
	74.6	100.0	480.1	100.0	1491.9	100.0	1484.8	100.0

*Billions of dollars.

Source: Calculations based on data from Board of Governors of the Federal Reserve System, *Flow of Funds Accounts; Financial Assets and Liabilities Outstanding.*

EXHIBIT 3-6 ISSUERS OF FEDERAL FUNDS AND REPURCHASE AGREEMENTS AS A PERCENTAGE OF TOTAL OUTSTANDING, 1969, 1979, 1989, AND 1991

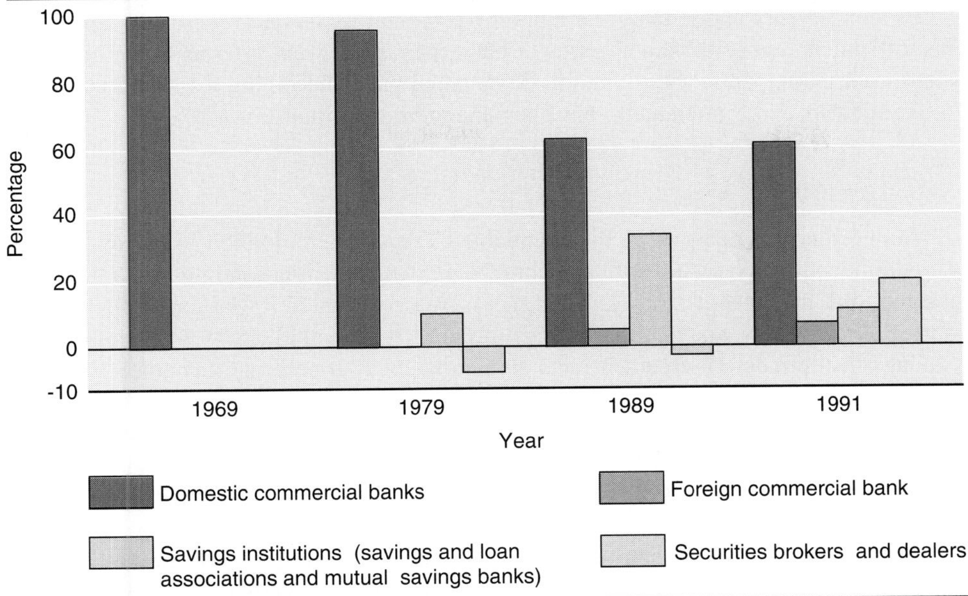

Source: Calculations and graphics based on data from Board of Governors of the Federal Reserve System, *Flow of Funds Accounts; Financial Assets and Liabilities Outstanding.*

market. Later, savings institutions (savings and loan associations and mutual savings banks) and securities brokers and dealers became more involved. As foreign banks entered the United States, they, too, have made their presence felt in the money markets.

In 1969, domestic commercial banks issued 100 percent of outstanding liabilities. Ten years later, their share of the market had declined somewhat to 95.6 percent. Savings institutions had begun to use this market to manage liquidity needs and had a 10.3 percent share. As of the end of 1979, brokers and dealers participated by providing net loans (assets of brokers and dealers rather than liabilities) of 5.9 percent of total liabilities outstanding.[12]

By 1989, savings institutions accounted for 33.8 percent of the market and foreign banks 5.5 percent. While the dollar amount of broker-dealer loans increased from $5.8 billion in 1979 to $7.9 billion in 1989, the market grew even faster so that the broker-dealer share actually declined (to a negative 2.1 percent). This effect is even more pronounced in the case of domestic commercial banks, whose net liabilities grew from $94.3 billion to $230.9 billion during the 10-year period but whose market share dropped to 62.8 from 95.6 percent.

Just 2 years later, commercial banks' liabilities had dropped to $215.4 billion, only 61 percent of the market. The market share of savings institutions dropped dramatically to 11.25 percent, going from $124.2 billion in 1989 to $39.7 billion in 1991. Foreign banks'

[12]Note that the 1979 dollar amounts (in billions) and percentages of liabilities outstanding are as follows:

Domestic commercial banks	$94.3	95.6%
Savings institutions	10.1	10.3
Brokers and dealers	−5.8	−5.9
	$98.6	100.0%

share of the market continued to increase to 7.5 percent by 1991. Broker-dealers were net borrowers with 20.2 percent of the total market.

In the 20 years ended 1989 the market for federal funds and repurchase agreements has expanded in absolute dollar terms. It has expanded as well in terms of the number of significant participants, with domestic commercial banks becoming less important, while broker-dealers and foreign banks have become more important.

Negotiable CDs

A similar trend has occurred in the negotiable CD market. As Exhibit 3-7 shows, domestic commercial banks issued 100 percent of the instruments outstanding in 1969. Despite the fact that their negotiable CD liabilities increased from $27.8 billion to $186 billion during the next 10 years, their percentage of the market declined to 78.7 percent by 1979. Savings institutions (13.4 percent) and foreign banks (7.9 percent) accounted for the remaining market.

In 1989 the $342 billion of domestic commercial bank CDs represented only 59.5 percent of the total. Savings institutions alone accounted for 30.7 percent of all negotiable CDs outstanding and the foreign bank–sector share advanced to 9.7 percent.

By 1991, a 2-year, $75 billion contraction in the negotiable CDs issued by savings and loan associations brought their share of the market down to 20.2 percent. Even though domestic commercial bank CDs fell by $12 billion, this decline was smaller than in the savings and loan industry, and the bank market increased to 63.9 percent of negotiable CDs outstanding. During the same period, the CDs issued by foreign banks grew by $26.5 billion and gave this sector a 15.9 percent market share, not much smaller than that

EXHIBIT 3-7 ISSUERS OF NEGOTIABLE CERTIFICATES OF DEPOSIT AS A PERCENTAGE OF TOTAL OUTSTANDING, 1969, 1979, 1989, AND 1991

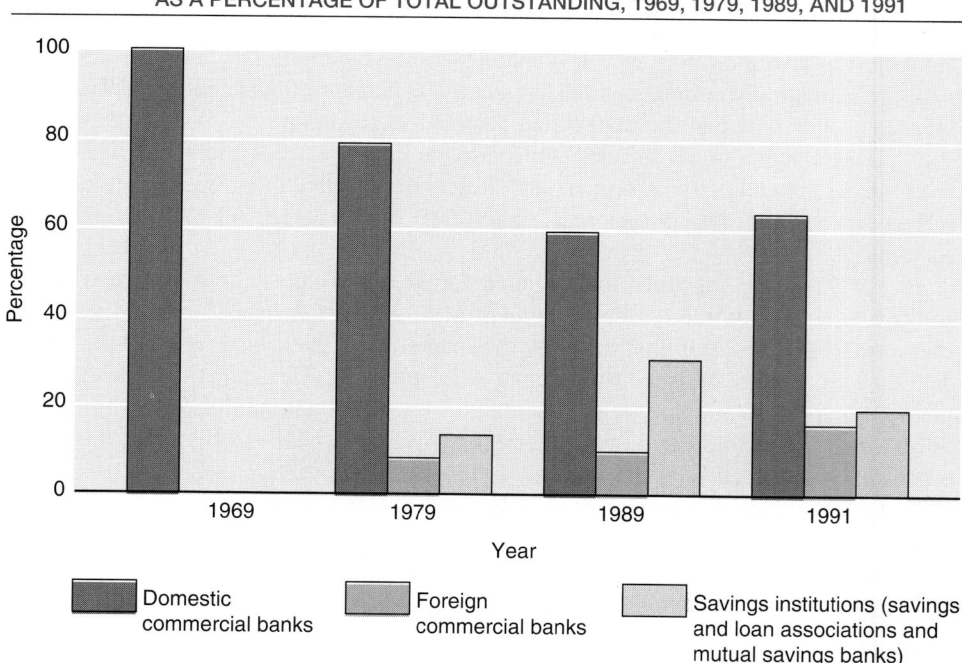

Source: Calculations and grapic based on data from Board of Governors of the Federal Reserve System, *Flow of Funds Accounts; Financial Assets and Liabilities Outstanding.*

of all domestic savings institutions. While the market has generally grown, the competition among participants for deposit funds has also increased.

COMMERCIAL PAPER

In the commercial paper market, finance companies have historically been the most significant issuers, accounting for over 70 percent of outstanding paper in 1969, as Exhibit 3-8 shows. The figure dropped to 54.7 percent in 1979 but was up again to almost 60 percent by 1989 and remained at this level in 1991.

Commercial bank holding companies issued less than 20 percent of the total outstanding commercial paper for the years indicated in Exhibit 3-8, and they have generally been less active in the market than nonfinancial corporations. In 1969 commercial banks had issuances totaling $4.3 billion (13.2 percent of the market) outstanding. By 1991, the total was $24.2 billion (4.3 percent of the market). During the same period, the commercial paper liabilities of nonfinancial corporations grew from $5.4 billion (16.5 percent of the market) to $119.9 billion (21.3 percent of the market). Nonfinancial corporations have found the commercial paper market an attractive alternative to short-term bank financing, which poses a serious challenge to bank lending activities.

International issues are also notable; foreign commercial paper played no role in the market in 1969 but came to command 15.5 percent of the total outstanding by 1991. While the dollar amount of bank paper increased by a factor of almost 5 during the 22 years ended 1991, foreign issues went from $4.6 billion (4.1 percent of the market) in 1979 to $87 billion (15.5 percent) in 1991, or an eighteen-fold dollar increase in just 12 years.

EXHIBIT 3-8 ISSUERS OF COMMERCIAL PAPER AS A PERCENTAGE OF TOTAL OUTSTANDING, 1969, 1979, 1989, AND 1991

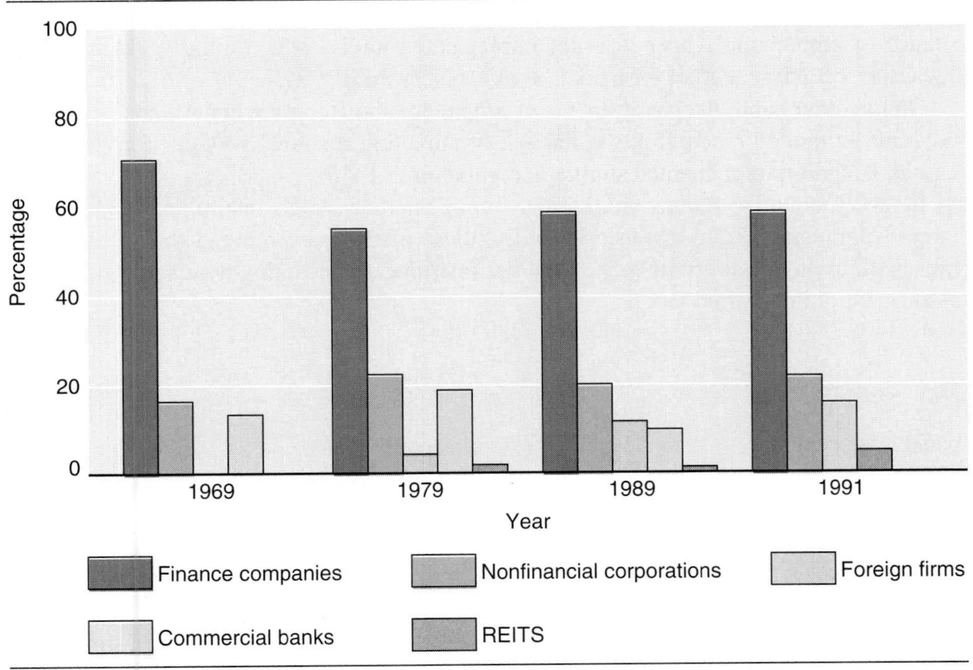

Source: Calculations and graphic based on data from Board of Governors of the Federal Reserve System, *Flow of Funds Accounts; Financial Assets and Liabilities Outstanding.*

Commercial banks are now much less dominant than they once were in the markets for federal funds, negotiable CDs, and commercial paper. At the same time, the presence of foreign firms is being felt in the United States.

SUMMARY

The short-term, or money, markets in the United States are centered first around Treasury bills, with negotiable CDs, federal funds and repurchase agreements, commercial paper, and banker's acceptances also important. Commercial banks, savings institutions, finance companies, government securities dealers, and foreign firms are the private-sector entities that are the most significant participants. The U.S. Treasury and the Federal Reserve are the biggest governmental participants.

In the United States participants generally conduct transactions directly with each other, with the exception of primary transactions in the T-bill market. In Japan, private *Tanshi* houses oversee all transactions except *gensaki* (repurchase agreements). In the United Kingdom, discount houses have traditionally served a similar purpose. Only recently have parallel money markets begun to develop that do not require the intervention of discount houses.

The money markets of the United States, the United Kingdom, Japan, Hong Kong, and Singapore are among the world's largest. While T-bills have been the most important money market instrument in the United States, call money (the equivalent of federal funds) dominates in other countries, most notably Japan and Hong Kong. Negotiable CDs were introduced in the United States in 1961. In 1968, the United Kingdom had also introduced a sterling-denominated negotiable CD. During the mid-1970s Singapore and Hong Kong did so. A yen-denominated instrument was not created until 1979 and at first only in large denominations so as not to compete with the *gensaki* market.

The treatment of negotiable CDs in Japan is a good example of that country's approach to financial market regulation. Japanese corporations issued commercial paper in the United States during the early 1980s because the 1982 Japanese law permitting the issuance of commercial paper was not implemented until 1987. Similarly, there was no Japanese secondary market for banker's acceptances until 1985.

On the other hand, the governments of Singapore and Hong Kong have encouraged innovation in money markets in the interest of attracting financial services activities. The United Kingdom implemented similar deregulation in 1986.

In every country, money markets are dominated by large institutions engaging in large-denomination transactions. Generally, these markets are moving toward deregulation, with a wider variety of money market instruments becoming available to a greater assortment of institutions.

KEY TERMS

banker's acceptance
basis point
bid-asked spread
bill discounting
bill of exchange
book-entry system
call money
commercial paper
competitive bid
discount house
discount pricing
federal funds
gilt-edged market
government agency securities
government securities dealer
immediately available funds
interbank market
letter of credit

liquid assets
money market
negotiable certificate of deposit
noncompetitive bid
opportunity cost of holding cash
repurchase agreement
sterling money markets
Tanshi company
tender system
tiered custodial system
Treasury bills

END-OF-CHAPTER QUESTIONS

1. What is the difference between money and capital markets?
2. Describe the U.S. federal funds market and its equivalent in other countries.
3. Describe recent trends with respect to participants in the markets for:
   a. Federal funds and repurchase agreements.
   b. Negotiable certificates of deposit.
   c. Commercial paper.
4. a. What is a repurchase agreement?
   b. What precautionary measures should be taken when entering repurchase agreements?
5. a. What is a discount house?
   b. In which countries (described in this chapter) may they be found?
   c. What is their function?
6. What contributions to money market operations do government securities dealers make?
7. Commercial paper is an unsecured financial instrument. How is it possible that the commercial paper of a firm with less than a top credit rating can be given a top rating?
8. a. Differentiate a banker's acceptance for U.S. imports and exports and a third-country acceptance.
   b. Under what circumstances would an acceptance be considered a refinance bill?
9. Discuss the role of the Federal Reserve as a money market participant.
10. In the primary market for Treasury securities, what is the difference between a tender system and a tap system?
11. Present evidence to support the statement that U.S. money markets are becoming more internationalized.
12. a. How have negotiable CDs given commercial banks more flexibility?
    b. Why has the amount of negotiable CDs decreased in recent years despite the added flexibility that they give banks?
13. Obtain a recent edition of the *Wall Street Journal.*
    a. What is the prime interest rate?
    b. Compare the prime interest rate with the commercial paper rate. What is the implication of this difference?

END OF CHAPTER PROBLEMS

1. Say that a noncompetitive bid for $1 million in 6-month (182-day) bills is submitted in a Treasury auction. If the weighted average interest rate of winning competitive bids is 7.75 percent, what is the total purchase price associated with this bid?
2. Suppose that you buy a $1 million negotiable CD with an 8.5 percent interest rate that matures in 3 months (91 days). Assume further that you decide to sell this CD when there are 30 days left to maturity and the going interest rate is 9 percent.
   a. For what price will you be able to sell it?
   b. What rate of return will you earn?
   c. Show that the party to whom you sell the CD will earn 9 percent.
3. An individual places a noncompetitive bid for 30-day T-bills with a $1 million face value through a commercial bank and the weighted average rate that applies is 7 percent.
   a. Show the T-accounts and their balances reflecting this transaction on the books of the commercial bank and the applicable Federal Reserve bank.

b. Now assume the commercial bank enters a successful competitive bid of its own for $4 million in T-bills and that the rate is 6.9 percent. How is this transaction reflected in the T-accounts of the commercial bank and the Federal Reserve bank?

4. An exporter presents a $500,000 draft to a commercial bank for payment due in 30 days. The draft is "accepted" and discounted, and the exporter is paid. If the discount rate is 6 percent, how much will the exporter be paid? Show the entry on the books of the bank that corresponds to this transaction.

5. If a government securities dealer asks a 6.96 percent discount on T-bills and bids a 7 percent discount, how much profit will be made on a purchase and sale of $2 million in T-bills with 30 days left to maturity?

SELECTED REFERENCES

Adams, T. F. M., and Iwao Hoshii. *A Financial History of the New Japan,* Kodansha International Ltd., Tokyo, 1972.

Bronte, Stephen. *Japanese Finance: Markets and Institutions,* Euromoney Publications, London, 1982.

Clarke, William M. *How the City Works; An Introduction to Its Financial Markets,* Waterlow Publishers, London, 1986.

Cook, Timothy Q., and Timothy D. Rowe, Editors. *Instruments of the Money Market,* Federal Reserve Bank of Richmond, Richmond, Virginia, 1986.

Falkena, H. B., L. J. Fourie, and W. J. Kok, Editors. *The Mechanics of the South African Financial System,* Macmillan South Africa Ltd., Johannesburg, 1984.

Feldman, Robert Alan. *Japanese Financial Markets; Deficits, Dilemmas, and Deregulation,* MIT Press, London, 1986.

Fisher, Anne B. "Who's Hurt by Salomon's Greed?" *Fortune,* vol. 124, no. 7 (September 23, 1991), p. 71.

Fraser, Donald R., and Peter S. Rose, Editors. *Financial Institutions and Markets in a Changing World,* 3d edition, Business Publications, Inc., Plano, Texas, 1987.

Galen, Michele. "Salomon: Honesty Is the Gutsiest Policy," *Business Week,* no. 3231 (September 16, 1991), pp. 100–101.

Grady, John, and Martin Weale. *British Banking, 1960–85,* Macmillan Press Ltd., London, 1986.

Havrilesky, Thomas M., and Robert Schweitzer, Editors. *Contemporary Developments in Financial Institutions and Markets,* 2d edition, Harlan Davidson, Inc., Arlington Heights, Illinois, 1987.

Henderson, John, and Jonathan P. Scott. *Securitization,* New York Institute of Finance, New York, 1988.

Huat, Tan Chwee. *Financial Institutions in Singapore,* 2d edition, Singapore University Press, Singapore, 1981.

Lee, S. Y., and Y. C. Jao. *Financial Structures and Monetary Policies in Southeast Asia,* St. Martin's Press, New York, 1982.

McRae, Hamish, and Frances Cairncross. *Capital City; London as a Financial Centre,* Methuen London Ltd., London, 1984.

Mullineux, A. W. *U.K. Banking after Deregulation,* Croom Helm Ltd., London, 1987.

Mullineux, Andrew. *International Banking and Financial Systems: A Comparison,* Graham & Trotman Ltd., London, 1987.

Neufeld, E. P. *The Financial System of Canada,* St. Martin's Press, New York, 1972.

——— *Financial Institutions and Markets in Southeast Asia; A Study of Brunei, Indonesia, Malaysia, Philippines, Singapore and Thailand,* Macmillan Press Ltd., London, 1984.

——— *Financial Institutions and Markets in the Southwest Pacific; A Study of Australia, Fiji, New Zealand, and Papua New Guinea,* Macmillan Press Ltd., London, 1985.

Skully, Michael T., Editor. *Financial Institutions and Markets in the Far East; A Study of China, Hong Kong, Japan, South Korea, and Taiwan,* St. Martin's Press, New York, 1982.

Srodes, James. "Rude Awakening: The Salomon Scandal Will Finally Move Congress to Reform the Government Securities Market," *Financial World,* vol. 160, no. 19 (September 17, 1991), pp. 22–23.

Struthers, J., and H. Speight. *Money; Institutions, Theory and Policy,* Longman Group Ltd., London, 1986.

Viner, Aron. *Inside Japanese Financial Markets,* Dow Jones–Irwin, Homewood, Illinois, 1988.

Weiss, Gary, Leah Nathans-Spiro, Jeffrey M. Laderman, Michael MacNamee, and Dean Foust. "The Salomon Shocker: How Bad Will It Get?" *Business Week,* no. 3228 (August 26, 1991), pp. 54–57.

Wilson, J. S. G. *Banking Policy and Structure; A Comparative Analysis,* Croom Helm Ltd., London, 1986.

CHAPTER 4

CAPITAL MARKET INSTRUMENTS

CHAPTER OUTLINE

CHAPTER OVERVIEW

This chapter

- Defines capital markets
- Analyzes capital market instruments in the United States
- Outlines developments in secondary mortgage markets
- Describes the process of securitization

The process of long-term, productive investment that was outlined in Chapter 1 occurs in capital markets, where long-term financial instruments are traded. It is the long-term nature of the instrument that differentiates capital markets from money markets.

Capital markets:
Markets in which financial instruments with maturities greater than 1 year are bought and sold.

Corporations secure financing through capital markets by selling long-term claims on their firms, whether in the form of bonds (liabilities) or stock (equity). Governments go to capital markets for operating funds, and households use them for residential mortgage financing. This chapter describes the capital market instruments that are issued and traded within national boundaries.

Capital market instruments are classified in five categories:

- Government notes and bonds
- Municipal bonds
- Corporate bonds
- Corporate stock
- Mortgages

Exhibit 4-1 shows that there were over $12 trillion in U.S. capital market instruments in 1991. Corporate stock and mortgages are the largest categories, each with almost $4 trillion in securities outstanding. Government and corporate bonds follow with $2.2 trillion and $1.7 trillion, respectively. Municipal bonds are the smallest category, with $712 billion. However, grouped together, bonds are the most important capital market instrument, representing 36.8 percent of the market. Stocks and mortgages follow, each representing roughly 32 percent of the total.

BONDS

Corporations and government entities issue bonds to raise funds for operations or for capital projects. The buyer of the bond has a claim on the issuer, who owes the buyer a specified amount in the future as well as (usually) interest payments in the interim.

Bonds:
Contractual liabilities that obligate the issuer to pay a specified amount (the par, face, or maturity value) at a given date in the future (the maturity date), generally with periodic interest payments in the interim at a fixed rate (the coupon rate).

Bearer bonds are payable to whomever holds the securities; *registered bonds* are payable only to the owner specified in the issuer's records. Even though bonds have a definite term or life, investors often do not hold these instruments until they mature. Thus, the valuation of bonds prior to maturity is an important concept to understand.

Bond Valuation

The value of a bond is the present value of its future cash flows. Hence, the value or price is based on:

EXHIBIT 4-1 U.S. CAPITAL MARKET INSTRUMENTS OUTSTANDING, 1991

	Amount*	%†
Government securities:		
Treasury notes and bonds (with remaining maturities greater than 1 year)	1,767.8	14.3
Federally sponsored agencies	396.9	3.2
Municipal bonds	711.8	5.8
Corporate bonds	1,673.1	13.5
Corporate stock	3,907.2	31.7
Mortgages	3,883.7	31.5
	12,340.5	100.0

*Billions of dollars.
†Percentage of total capital market instruments outstanding.
Source: Board of Governors of the Federal Reserve System, *Flow of Funds Accounts: Financial Assets and Liabilities,* and Department of the Treasury. *Monthly Statement of the Public Debt of the United States.*

- Interest payments
- Maturity value
- The investor's minimum required rate of return

The cash flows of a bond are an *annuity of interest payments* during the life of the bond plus a single future payoff of the *maturity value.* These future cash flows are determined at the time that the bond is issued. The *required rate of return* is an investor's opportunity cost, that is, the rate of return on the next best investment opportunity. This rate is driven by financial market conditions and, therefore, may change. A bond pricing formula values both the interest payments and the maturity value.

$$P_0 = I\left\{\sum_{t=1}^{n}\left[1/(1+k)^t\right]\right\} + M\left[1/(1+k)^n\right] \tag{1}$$

where P_0 = the current price of a bond
I = the amount of interest received each period: (maturity value × coupon rate)/(number of payments per year)
n = the number of periods before the bond matures
k = the investor's required rate of return per period
M = bond maturity or face value

Consider a bond with a face value of \$1000, a coupon rate of 8 percent paid semiannually, and 5 years to maturity. Suppose that an investor wants to earn 10 percent at a minimum. This bond pays \$80 per year in interest (\$1000 × 0.08), but the interest is paid semiannually, or two payments a year, at \$40 each. The required rate of return per 6-month period is 5 percent (10%/2). The number of 6-month periods before the bond matures is 10 (5 years × 2 periods per year). Applying Equation 1, the maximum price that the investor would pay for one of these bonds is \$922.78.[1]

$$\begin{aligned}P_0 &= 40\left\{\sum_{t=1}^{10}\left[1/(1.05)^t\right]\right\} + 1000\left[1/(1.05)^{10}\right]\\ &= 40(\text{PVIFA}_{.05,\,10}) + 1000(\text{PVIF}_{.05,\,10})\\ &= 308.87 + 613.91\\ &= 922.78\end{aligned}$$

Bond Yields

An investor who wants to earn 10 percent should pay less than the \$1000 par value. This is because the bond pays only 8 percent of the \$1000 face value each year. If the investor pays only \$922.78, there will be a *capital gain* in addition to the interim interest payments.

Capital gain:
The difference between the price that is originally paid for a bond and the cash proceeds realized at the time of maturity (the face value) or at the time of sale.

The *capital gains yield* in this case will be sufficient to bring the total return to 10 percent.

[1]The acronyms PVIFA and PVIF are present value interest factors of an annuity and a single amount, respectively. See the time value of money tables in Appendix A.

Capital gains yield:
Capital gain as a percentage of the value of a bond at the beginning of the time period.

The rate of return to a bond investor is determined both by interest payments and the change in value of the bond.

$$k_b = \text{CY} + \text{CGY} \tag{2}$$

where k_b = rate of return to a bond investor
CY = current yield (interest payment as a percentage of bond value)
CGY = capital gains yield

On the 8 percent, 5-year, $1000 bond purchased for $922.78, the average annual capital gain is 1.6 percent.

$$\begin{aligned} \text{CGY} &= (\text{average return per period}) \times (\text{number of periods per year}) \\ &= [(\text{FV/PV})^{1/n} - 1] \times 2 \\ &= [(1000/922.78)^{1/10} - 1] \times 2 \\ &= 0.016 \end{aligned}$$

For the first 6 months the current yield is 4.3 percent (40/922.78), or approximately 8.6 percent for the year, for a total return of roughly 10.2 percent. As the maturity date approaches, the value of the bond approaches its face value (increases, in this case), which causes the current yield to fall.[2] On average, however, the total annual rate of return over the 5 years is 10 percent.

If this bond had a coupon rate of 12 percent, instead of 8 percent, its price according to Equation 1 would be greater than its par value, or $1077.22.

$$\begin{aligned} P_0 &= 60\left\{\sum_{t=1}^{10}\left[1/(1.05)^t\right]\right\} + 1000\left[1/(1.05)^{10}\right] \\ &= 60(\text{PVIFA}_{.05,\,10}) + 1000(\text{PVIF}_{.05,\,10}) \\ &= 1077.22 \end{aligned}$$

The average annual change in price is a negative 1.5 percent[3] (capital loss), while the current yield in the first year is approximately 11.1 percent [(60/1077.22) × 2]. This brings the total first year return to approximately 9.6 percent. Since the value of the bond approaches its par value (decreases, in this case) as the maturity date approaches, the current yield increases so that, again, the average annual rate of return is 10 percent.

If a bond is sold at a stated market price, the unknown in Equation 1 is k, the rate of return, rather than P_0, the price. The rate k is then the yield to maturity, which is an expected rate of return, instead of the required rate of return.

Yield to maturity (YTM):
The average annual rate of return to a bond investor who buys a bond today and holds it until it matures. The YTM is that rate of return that causes the market price to be exactly equal to the present value of the future cash flows (interest payments and maturity value).

[2]See Chapter 8 for a discussion of the behavior of bond prices.

[3]$\text{CGY} = [(1000/1077.22)^{1/10} - 1] \times 2$
$= -0.015$

The YTM measures *both* the current yield and the capital gains yield together. Because the pricing formula is complex, YTM must be found through a trial-and-error process, although a number of hand-held calculators are programmed to perform the necessary iterations. Manually, YTM is approximated using this formula:

$$\text{YTM} = [I + (M - P_0)/n] \,/\, [(M + 2P_0) \,/\, 3] \tag{3}$$

where I = annual interest payment
n = number of years to maturity
M = bond maturity or face value

Note that the two terms in the numerator of Equation 3 are the annual interest payment plus the average annual capital gain (or loss). The denominator is an approximate average investment in the bond. Applying Equation 3 to the 8 percent coupon bond in the example above, the YTM approximation is 10.06 percent, very close to the actual 10 percent YTM.

Some bonds have a *call provision* which may prevent investors from realizing the yield to maturity.

Call provision:
A feature of a bond that entitles the issuer to retire the bond before maturity.

Because a call is exercisable at the discretion of the issuer and deprives the investor of anticipated income, a *call premium* (the excess of the call price over par value) is often payable to the investor upon call. This is particularly true if the issuer calls the bond because current interest rates are significantly below the bond's coupon rate. If the issuer calls the bond in order to comply with sinking fund requirements (gradual bond retirement), the call premium is generally much lower. In any event, call premiums decline as the maturity date of the bond approaches. Often, bonds may not be called for several years after issuance; this period of time is referred to as *call protection.*

While most bonds traded in the United States conform to the model described above, there are some variations. Some bonds do not pay periodic interest but are discounted in much the same way as commercial paper. These bonds are called *deep-discount,* or *zero-coupon, bonds.* They have become more popular in recent years because of certain tax advantages that they offer particular borrowers, but they are still a relatively small part of the market. Other bonds carry a coupon rate that changes with market interest rates. These *variable-rate bonds* serve to protect investors from adverse bond price changes, but they also prevent investors from locking in high rates of interest for extended periods of time. Variable-rate bonds are less common in U.S. markets than in Eurobond markets.[4]

Types of Bonds

Government and private enterprises are active bond market participants. Exhibit 4-2 shows the rates of growth in the four categories of bonds for periods from 1969 to 1991. During the 10 years ended 1979, government agencies and corporations had the largest increases in bonds outstanding. Agency issues went from \$30.6 billion to \$135.5 billion, increasing an average of 16 percent a year. Corporate bonds started from a higher base of \$177.4 billion in 1969 and increased at the rate of 10.1 percent a year to reach \$464.9 billion by 1979. United States Treasury and municipal bonds grew at the lower annual rates

[4]Eurobond and other international markets are discussed in Chapters 6 and 7.

EXHIBIT 4-2 GROWTH RATE OF BONDS, 1969–1979, 1979–1989, 1989–1991

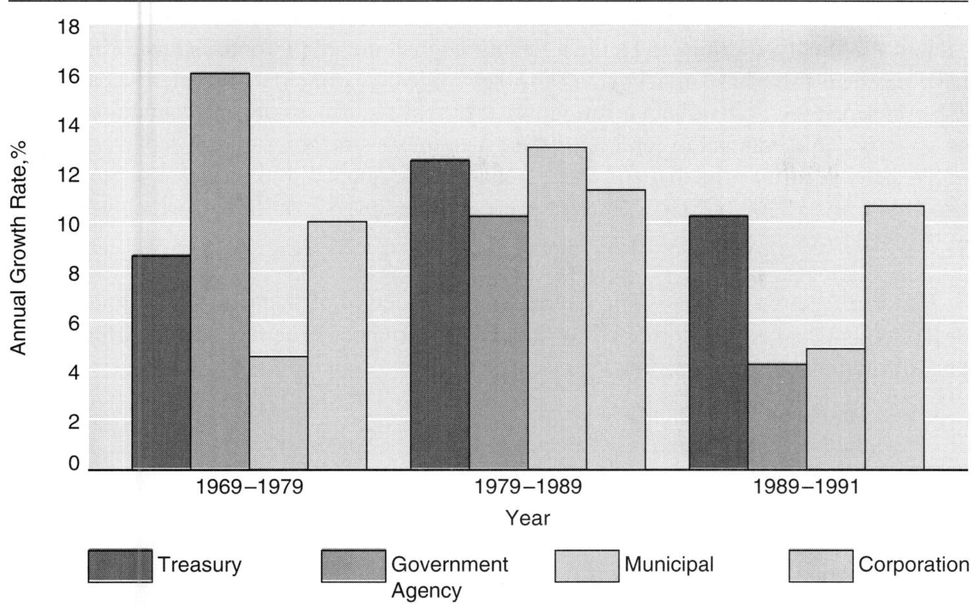

Source: Calculations and graphic based on data from Board of Governors of the Federal Reserve System, *Flow of Funds Accounts; Financial Assets and Liabilities,* various issues.

of 8.7 and 4.7 percent annually, respectively. By 1979, there were \$446.5 billion in Treasury bonds and \$193.3 billion in municipal bonds outstanding.

During the 10 years ended 1989, the growth of Treasury and municipal bonds outpaced the others. Treasury bond growth of 12.5 percent brought the total outstanding to \$1.5 trillion. Municipals grew slightly faster at a 12.8 percent annual rate to reach \$646.8 billion by 1989. Corporate and agency bonds increased at the average annual rate of 11.4 and 10.4 percent, respectively. By 1989, corporate long-term debt had reached \$1.4 trillion and government agency \$364 billion.

From 1989 to 1991, the growth of government agency and municipal bonds subsided to under 5 percent a year. Treasury and corporate bonds continued to grow at a rate of over 10 percent.

The strong growth in corporate bonds during the 1980s and early 1990s is not expected to continue. The amount of interest that a firm can pay on outstanding debt is limited by its operational cash flows. When the economy is soft and revenues fall, the fixed interest payments on debt can be difficult to meet. On the other hand, the federal government must issue debt to cover fiscal budget deficits (excess of expenditures over revenues). Since federal budget deficits have risen to the \$200 billion level or more in recent years, the increases in Treasury notes and bonds are less likely to moderate.

Treasury Notes and Bonds Chapter 3 described how the Federal Reserve auctions Treasury bills. The Fed also auctions Treasury notes and bonds in the primary market. The government securities dealers that make markets for Treasury bills also make markets for Treasury notes and bonds. Original maturities range from 1 to 10 years for notes and from 10 to 30 years for bonds. As is true with Treasury bills, note and bond prices are quoted as a percentage of \$100 of face value, with the fractional values expressed in thirty-seconds of a percent. A price of $99\frac{5}{32}$ can also be written as 99.5. Since $\frac{1}{32}$ is .03125 and $\frac{5}{32}$ is .15625, the price for a \$1000 bond that is quoted at 99.5 is \$991.56 ($P_0 = 10 \times 99.1562 = 991.56$).

The Treasury also issues 10-year notes and 20- and 30-year bonds to depository institutions in book-entry form under a program called Separate Trading of Registered Interest and Principal Securities (STRIPS). Securities that are sold in book-entry form do not have physical form but are accounted for electronically. Principal and interest payments are sold separately, effectively creating two different securities—a zero-coupon bond and an annuity. This innovation represents the government's response to the separate trading of Treasury security principal and interest that had developed in the private sector. In the late 1980s, over $300 billion of STRIPS were outstanding, $70 billion of which were held in stripped form.

Federal Agency Bonds The intermediation function of financial institutions that is described in Chapter 1 is supported by the U.S. government in certain sectors of the economy through federally sponsored agencies:

- Federal Home Loan Banks
- Federal National Mortgage Association
- Federal Home Loan Mortgage Corporation
- Farm Credit System
- Student Loan Marketing Association

The first three agencies channel funds into the mortgage market. The last two perform the same function in the agricultural sector and in higher education, respectively. All these agencies issue bonds.

In 1932 Congress created a *Federal Home Loan Bank* in each of twelve districts of the United States. These banks supervise federally chartered savings and loan associations and provide liquidity to member associations through their credit facility. The member associations in each district own their district bank, which, until 1989, was supervised by the Federal Home Loan Bank Board in Washington. The Financial Institutions Reform, Recovery, and Enforcement Act of 1989 (FIRREA), enacted in response to the failure of a large number of savings and loan associations, also created the Federal Housing Finance Board to supervise the district banks.[5]

The *Federal National Mortgage Association* (Fannie Mae), established in 1938 as a federal government agency, started the secondary market in federally insured mortgages. In 1968 the agency became a separate entity, now owned completely by private investors. The federal Department of Housing and Urban Development regulates the agency with respect to such matters as capital and financial disclosure. Since 1970, Fannie Mae has had the authority to purchase and sell conventional mortgages that are not insured by the government.

The *Federal Home Loan Mortgage Corporation* (Freddie Mac) is a more recent addition to the list of federal agencies. In 1970 Freddie Mac was introduced into the Federal Home Loan Bank System to develop a secondary market in conventional mortgages. The twelve Federal Home Loan District Banks and member S&L institutions are the agency's shareholders. The Federal Home Loan Bank Board supervised its operations until 1989, when the Reform, Recovery, and Enforcement Act reassigned oversight to the Department of Housing and Urban Development.

The *Farm Credit System* (including Farm Credit Banks and Banks for Cooperatives) dates back to 1917 when twelve Federal Land Banks were created. The Federal Intermediate Credit Banks and the Banks for Cooperatives originated in each district in 1923 and 1933, respectively. In addition, a Central Bank for Cooperatives helps to fund large loans or loans that involve more than one district. Farm cooperatives and credit institutions own these banks and the Farm Credit Administration (a federal agency) supervises them. In

[5]See Chapter 19 for a complete description of the changes in S&L regulation.

1977, the thirty-seven institutions issued the first debt obligation for which they were jointly responsible. Before then, each of the three systems issued debt for which it was individually responsible, but since 1979, all issuances have been joint obligations.

In 1985 the Farm Credit System was restructured to make the institutions more accountable to the U.S. secretary of treasury, the Federal Reserve Board, and the U.S. secretary of agriculture. Legislation in 1987 established the Farm Credit Insurance Corporation (to insure the obligations of the system banks) and required that minimum capital requirements be established for the banks.

Lenders under the Guaranteed Student Loan Program and individual investors own the stock of the *Student Loan Marketing Association* (Sallie Mae), created in 1970. The agency provides a secondary market for student loans that are guaranteed by the federal government and makes loans to institutions (called warehousing advances) so that they can offer more student loans. Unlike the other agencies, Sallie Mae has minimal supervision by the federal government.

The bonds issued by all these agencies are considered almost as safe as Treasury issues. Because of this, the yields on federal agency bonds are typically only 15 to 30 basis points above Treasury securities of similar maturity, a narrower spread than for high-quality corporate bonds. There are a number of reasons for this rate behavior:

- Agency issues hold a number of advantages for investors.

    Most interest income from government agency securities is exempt from state and local taxation, with the exception of Federal National Mortgage Association and Federal Home Loan Mortgage Corporation issues.

    Banks and savings and loan associations may use them as collateral when borrowing from the Federal Reserve.

    While banks are restricted in terms of the extent to which they can trade certain securities, they may trade agency securities without limitation. Savings and loan associations may use them to satisfy liquidity requirements.

- Federal agencies have lines of credit with the Treasury Department to use in the event that they have trouble meeting their obligations.
- Even without an explicit default guarantee, investors may feel that the federal government would not allow a federally sponsored agency to default on a debt obligation.

These factors combine to make federal agency bonds attractive investments.

Municipal Bonds Municipal bonds include all debt instruments issued by local, county, and state governments. Issuers use proceeds from the sale of municipal bonds to finance public utilities, school construction, roads, transportation systems, and industrial development. An appealing feature is that municipal bond interest payments to the holder are exempt from federal income taxation.

Municipal bonds are held by a wide spectrum of investors in the United States, with households and personal trusts holding 40 percent of outstanding municipals in 1991. Insurance companies, primarily property and casualty firms, held 18 percent. Commercial banks held 14 percent, mutual funds 14 percent, and money market funds 11 percent of outstanding issues.[6]

General obligation bonds are backed by the full faith and credit of the issuer. Taxpayer approval is usually required for issuance because the taxing authority of the government body is pledged for the repayment. *Revenue bonds* are backed only by cash flows from a specific project financed by the bond issue. If the income is not sufficient to ser-

[6]During the 1970s, commercial banks held close to 50 percent of municipal bonds but changes in the tax treatment of banks' municipal bond investments have reduced their participation. See also Chapter 14.

vice and retire the debt, tax revenues may not be allocated for this purpose. *Industrial revenue bonds* are issued by nonfinancial business concerns to help build the economic base of a political subdivision, that is, state or municipality. The political subdivision bears no liability for repayment.

To compare income from a tax-exempt municipal bond with that of a taxable bond, the *after-tax rate of interest* of a taxable bond must be identified.

$$k_{\mathrm{AT}} = k_{\mathrm{BT}}\,(1 - t) \tag{4}$$

where k_{AT} = after-tax rate of interest of a taxable bond
k_{BT} = before-tax rate of interest of a taxable bond
t = marginal tax rate of the bond investor

This after-tax rate is the appropriate rate to compare with the municipal bond yield.[7] All other things being equal, if the after-tax yield on a taxable bond is less than the yield of the municipal bond, the municipal bond is preferable.

Another way to analyze the interest from a tax-free bond is to determine the pretax rate for a taxable security that would cause an investor to be indifferent between the taxable bond and the municipal bond. This can be done by substituting the municipal bond yield for the after-tax rate in Equation 4 and solving for k_{BT}.

$$k_{\mathrm{M}}/(1 - t) = k_{\mathrm{BT}} \tag{5}$$

where k_M = municipal bond yield.

Corporate Bonds Corporate bonds include all bonds that are not either government bonds (Treasury or federal agency) or municipal bonds. Corporations use the money raised by selling bonds for long-term purposes. In the United States, nonfinancial corporations issued 60 percent of all corporate bonds that were outstanding in 1991. Finance companies and commercial banks accounted for 11 percent and 6.5 percent, respectively. Insurance companies (primarily life insurance companies) are the single largest investors in corporate bonds, holding 40 percent in 1991. Pension funds had the next largest holdings with 22.5 percent of the total outstanding. Foreign entities and households held 12 and 10 percent, respectively.

The wide variety of corporate bonds includes:

- Mortgage bonds
- Equipment trust certificates
- Debentures
- Subordinated debentures

Some bonds allow conversion into common stock, and some include warrants that can be exercised to buy common stock.

Firms issue *mortgage bonds* to finance specific projects. Once built or placed in operation, the project becomes collateral for the bond issue, making the issue *secured* debt. Utility companies are frequent issuers of mortgage bonds. Should the issuer default on the obligation, bondholders may legally take title to the project (collateral) in order to satisfy the debt.

Tangible property also collateralizes *equipment trust certificates.* In this case the prop-

[7]
$$\begin{aligned} k_{\mathrm{AT}} &= k_{\mathrm{BT}} - \text{tax} \\ &= k_{\mathrm{BT}} - k_{\mathrm{BT}}(t) \\ &= k_{\mathrm{BT}}(1 - t) \end{aligned}$$

erty is specific pieces of large equipment, usually the rolling stock of railroads (railcars) and airplanes. The collateral behind equipment trust certificates may be more readily marketable than that backing mortgage bonds in the event of a bond default.

Debentures are long-term liabilities that are supported not by collateral but only by the general creditworthiness of the issuer. For this reason, they are riskier from an investor's perspective. In case of bankruptcy, while the collateral behind mortgage bonds and equipment trust certificates can be sold to satisfy the obligations of the secured debt, holders of debentures are general creditors of the firm; they receive distributions only after the secured creditors have been paid.

Subordinated debentures are also unsecured, but they are junior in rights to debentures. In the event of liquidation, subordinated debenture holders receive a cash distribution only after more senior debt (both secured and unsecured) has been repaid. If debentures are subordinated to bank loans, for example, bank loans would have to be completely satisfied in a liquidation before the subordinated debenture holders receive any of the proceeds from asset sales.

Corporate bonds may sometimes be exchanged for other securities. *Convertible bonds* may be exchanged for a specific number of shares of common stock of the issuing firm. An investor will not elect to surrender the bond and convert, however, unless the market value of the stock to which the investor is entitled exceeds the market value of the bond. In the case of widely traded issues, the price of the bond fluctuates to keep its market value roughly equivalent to the value of the stock into which it may be converted.

Bonds are sometimes issued with *stock warrants* attached. Warrants are options to purchase common stock at a specified price up to a specified date. Should the bondholder decide to exercise the option and purchase stock, it is not necessary to surrender the underlying bond. Again, bondholders will exercise their warrants only if the market value of the stock exceeds the specified (exercise) price of the warrant.

Bonds are an important source of capital for the federal government, states and municipalities, and private corporations. In the United States, however, private-sector equity financing in the form of common stock has historically been a more important source of financing.

CORPORATE STOCK

The market value of common stock outstanding increased as fast as bonds during the 1980s and early 1990s. Exhibit 4-3 shows that the rate of increase of stock outstanding from 1969 to 1979 was just over 3 percent, much lower than the 10 percent annual increase in corporate bonds. From 1979 to 1989, however, the annual increase in stock outstanding was almost 11 percent. During the 2 years ended 1991, corporate stock increased at 9.7 percent per year. This relatively strong growth can be expected to continue because the high rate of debt financing during the 1980s cannot be sustained.

Holders of *corporate stock* have an ownership interest in the firm.

Corporate stock
Financial claims on a corporation held by the owners of the firm.

Stock is recorded in the equity section of the firm's balance sheet. Corporate stock takes two forms: preferred and common.

Preferred Stock

Preferred stock is a hybrid instrument that represents an equity interest but pays a fixed dividend (just as a bond pays a fixed interest payment).

EXHIBIT 4-3 GROWTH RATE OF CORPORATE STOCK, 1969–1979, 1979–1989, 1989–1991

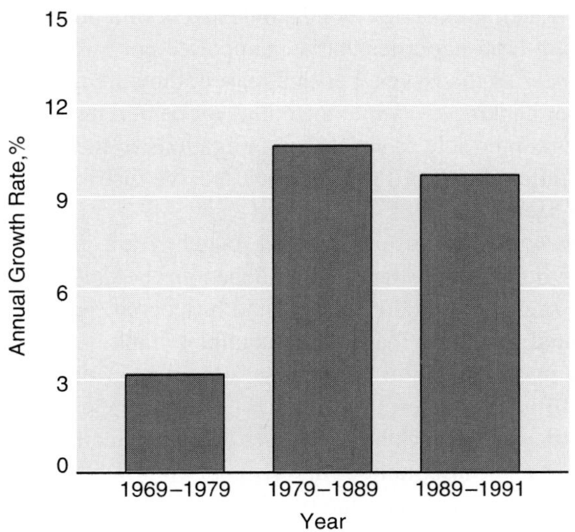

Source: Calculations and graphic are based on data from Board of Governors of the Federal Reserve System, *Flow of Funds Accounts; Financial Assets and Liabilities,* various issues.

Dividends:
Periodic cash flows paid to owners of corporate stock (frequently paid on a quarterly basis).

Often preferred stock is *cumulative;* that is, all preferred dividends (unpaid in the past and currently due) must be paid before common shareholders may receive any dividend payments. Like the value of a bond, the value of preferred stock depends on the future cash flows to which the investor is entitled. Because the dividend is fixed, a preferred stockholder is entitled to a perpetual stream of level cash flows.

$$P_0 = \sum_{t=1}^{\infty}\left[D/(1+k)^t\right] \tag{6}$$

where P_0 = price of a share of preferred stock today
D = fixed dividend per share
k = required rate of return

Equation 6 is a geometric series that converges to the valuation model for preferred stock: (See Exhibit 4-4.)

$$P_0 = D/k \tag{7}$$

With the observed market price of preferred stock and the dividend per share, which is known, an investor's *expected rate of return* can be determined by solving for k in Equation 7.

Expected rate of return *(k'):*
The rate that causes an asset's present value of future cash flows to equal its market price. The expected rate of return is determined by substituting all known (or estimated) values into the asset's valuation formula and solving for k.

The preferred stock valuation model is based on assumption of level dividends per share D, discounted at k, the required rate of return.

$$P_0 = D/(1 + k) + D/(1 + k)^2 + D/(1 + k)^3 + D/(1 + k)^\infty$$
$$= D/(1 + k)\{1 + [1/(1 + k)] + [1/(1 + k)^2] + [1/(1 + k)^\infty]$$

The bracketed quantity converges to

$$(1 - q^\infty)/(1 - q) \qquad \text{where } q = 1/(t + k)$$

Substituting for q, the bracketed quantity becomes

$$\{1 - [1/(1 + k)]^\infty\}/\{1 - [1/(1 + k)]\} = 1/[(1 + k - 1)/(1 + k)]$$
$$= 1/[k/(1 + k)]$$
$$= (1 + k)/k$$

Substituting for the bracketed quantity above and simplifying,

$$P_0 = [D/(1 + k)]\,[(1 + k)k]$$
$$= D/k$$

$$k' = D/P_0 \tag{8}$$

Notice that the expected return for a investor in preferred stock is its dividend yield only (comparable to the current yield of a bond).

Common Stock

Common stock is an equity interest with dividend payments that are not fixed and that vary, usually increasing over time. In the event of liquidation, common shareholders have the lowest priority in terms of any cash distribution.[8] Because of this, owners of common stock have what is called a *residual* claim on the firm.

Assuming that dividends increase at a constant rate, the value of a share of common stock is the value of a constantly growing stream of cash flows:

$$P_0 = D_0(1 + g)/(1 + k) + D_0(1 + g)^2/(1 + k)^2 + D_0(\ )(\ )^{n\infty} \tag{9}$$

where P_0 = the price of a share of common stock today
D_0 = the current dividend per share
g = the constant growth rate of dividends
k = the required rate of return, assuming $k < g$

Again, this relationship converges to (see Exhibit 4-5)

$$P_0 = D_1/(k - g) \tag{10}$$

where D_1 = dividend per share expected next period, or $D_0(1 + g)$.

[8]After subordinated debentures, the next priority is preferred stock. After preferred stock claims are satisfied, common stock cash distributions are made.

EXHIBIT 4-5 COMMON STOCK VALUATION MODEL

The common stock valuation model is based on dividends per share D, that grow at the constant rate of growth g, and are discounted at k, the required rate of return.

$$P_0 = D_0(1 + g)/ \ldots +(1 + k) + D_0(1 + g)^2/(1 + k)^2 + D_0(1 + g)^\infty/(1 + k)^\infty$$
$$= D_0(1+g)/ \ldots +(1 + k) \{1 + [(1 + g)/(1 + k)] + [(1 + g)^2/(1 + k)^2] + [(1 + g)^\infty/(1 + k)^\infty]$$

The bracketed quantity converges to

$$(1 - q^\infty)/(1 - q), \qquad \text{where } q = (1 + g)/(1 + k)$$

Substituting for q, the bracketed quantity becomes

$$\{1 - [(1 + g)/(1 + k)]^\infty\}/\{1 - [(1 + g)/(1 + k)]\} = 1/\{[(1 + k) - (1 + g)]/(1 + k)\}$$
$$= 1/[(k - g)/(1 + k)]$$
$$= (1 + k)/(k - g)$$

Substituting for the bracketed quantity above and simplifying,

$$P_0 = [D_0(1 + g)/(1 + k)]\,[(1 + k)/(k - g)]$$
$$= D_0(1 + g)/(k - g)$$

This model was developed by Myron Gordon and is commonly referred to as the Gordon Constant Growth Model.

Solving Equation 10 for k, the result is the expected return for a common shareholder when the price of the stock is known and a given growth rate has been estimated.

$$k' = D_1 / P_0 + g \tag{11}$$

Common stock return consists of the sum of dividend yield (D_1/P_0) and growth in the market price of the stock (capital gains yield). These components of return are comparable to the return components for bonds of current yield and capital gains.

Households and personal trusts represent the largest group of corporate stockholders in the United States, holding 54 percent of stock outstanding in 1991. Private pension funds and state and local government retirement funds are the next largest investors, with 19 and 8 percent, respectively. The foreign sector and mutual funds each held 6 percent of corporate stock outstanding. Mutual funds held 7 percent, the foreign sector 6 percent, and insurance companies 5 percent. Over time, the share of stock held by households has declined and the share of pension funds increased. From 1964 to 1991, the percentage of stock owned by households dropped from 85 to 54 percent. During the same period, the total pension fund share increased from 6 to 27 percent.

MORTGAGES

United States households generally obtain capital through mortgages. *Mortgages* are long-term loans that are secured by real property.

Mortgages:
Long-term liabilities collateralized by real property. Commonly, monthly payments are made that fully repay both principal and interest over the term of the loan.

Mortgages are issued to purchase real estate of four basic types:

- Homes
- Multifamily dwellings
- Commercial property
- Farms

Exhibit 4-6 shows that home mortgages (used to purchase one- to four-family dwellings) have grown consistently at annual rates of between 10 and 12 percent since 1969. Starting from a base of $280.2 billion in 1969, home mortgages increased to $2.7 trillion by 1991, or 70.5 percent of the total mortgages outstanding.

Mortgages for multifamily dwellings are a smaller part of the market, having grown at an annual rate of 9.8 percent from 1969 to 1979, 8.0 percent from 1979 to 1989, but only by 1.9 percent during the 2 years ended 1991. In 1991, mortgages for multifamily dwellings amounted to $303.5 billion, or 7.8 percent of total mortgages outstanding.

Commercial mortgages are used to finance real estate for business purposes, such as office buildings and shopping malls. These mortgages have consistently grown faster than multifamily-dwelling mortgages and even faster than home mortgages during the 1980s. However, the growth in excess of 11 percent per year slowed to 2.8 percent during the 2 years ended 1991. As of 1991, commercial mortgages amounted to $756.3 billion, or 19.5 percent of the total.

The growth in both multifamily and commercial mortgages has declined in recent years because of a soft real estate market in which many projects have high vacancy rates. This situation developed because of overbuilding during the 1980s. Strong growth

EXHIBIT 4-6 GROWTH RATE OF MORTGAGES

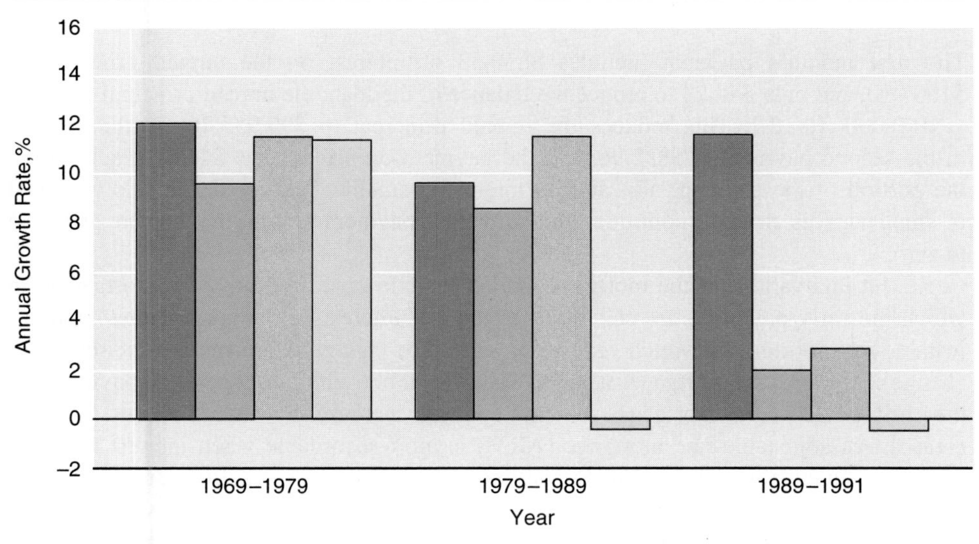

Source: Calculations and graphic based on data from Board of Governors of the Federal Reserve System, *Flow of Funds Accounts; Financial Assets and Liabilities,* various issues.

in multifamily and commercial mortgages will not resume until the oversupply of existing projects has been absorbed. By some estimates, this could be after the year 2000.

Farm mortgages are the smallest part of the market. Having increased at an 11.6 percent rate from 1969 through 1979, farm mortgages declined thereafter. An overexpansion similar to that in the commercial sector occurred, and the market is still correcting itself. As of 1991, farm mortgages stood at $83.7 billion, 2.2 percent of the total outstanding.

Mortgage Payments

Unlike corporate mortgage bond issuers who frequently pay only interest until the maturity date, households with mortgages most often pay equal monthly payments (an annuity) composed of both interest and partial principal repayment.

$$P = A(\text{PVIFA}_{k,n}) \tag{12}$$

where P = principal amount of the loan
A = monthly payment, amount of the annuity
k = periodic interest rate
n = number of periods in the term of the loan
$\text{PVIFA}_{k,n}$ = present value interest factor of an annuity, or $(1/k) - \{1/[k(1 + k)^n]\}$

The monthly payment is determined by the amount, the term, and the interest rate of the loan.

$$A = P/\text{PVIFA}_{k,n} \tag{12a}$$

For example, a 30-year mortgage loan for $100,000 with a 10 percent interest rate requires monthly payments of $877.57.

$$\begin{aligned} A &= 100{,}000/\{1/(.10 / 12) - 1/[(.10 / 12)(1 + .10 / 12)^{360}]\} \\ &= 100{,}000 / 113.9508193 \\ &= 877.57 \end{aligned}$$

The first month's payment includes $833.33 of interest on the unpaid principal of $100,000, and only $44.24 to reduce the balance of the loan, the unpaid principal [interest = 100,000(.10/12)]. This reduces the unpaid principal to $99,955.76, so the interest in the second payment is $832.96, and the payment on principal is $44.61. Each month the portion of the payment allocated to interest is smaller because the unpaid principal is smaller. This process continues until the last payment brings the unpaid principal to zero.

Recent innovations in the mortgage market include graduated payment mortgages (in which the early payments are calculated at rates of interest below market rates) and adjustable-rate mortgages (which require payments to change when market interest rates change). A graduated mortgage makes it easier for a household to afford the payments in the early years of the mortgage. As the payments increase, household income also increases. An adjustable-rate mortgage (ARM) is more affordable when interest rates are low, but payments increase when interest rates increase. An ARM helps ensure the lender of increasing interest income when interest rates rise, thereby shifting the exposure to interest rate risk from the lender to the borrower.

Households are the major borrowers in the mortgage market. In 1991, 73 percent of outstanding mortgages were generated by households. Unincorporated businesses accounted for 22 percent. Mortgage loans are offered by both commercial banks and thrift institutions. Commercial banks held 22 percent and savings and loan associations 16 percent of mortgage loans in 1991, while mutual savings banks held 4 percent. Life insurance companies held 7 percent of outstanding mortgages.

Individual mortgages are not well suited for trading in capital markets, largely because the amounts of specific loans are not uniform; they are tied to the market value of underlying property. Nor is information about the creditworthiness of individual borrowers readily available. Federally sponsored agencies, however, have developed secondary markets for mortgages through creation of mortgage pools.

Mortgage Pools

The Federal National Mortgage Association, the Federal Home Loan Mortgage Corporation, the Farmers Home Administration, and the Government National Mortgage Association (Ginnie Mae—a division of Housing and Urban Development) issue debt securities to the public with the proceeds used to invest in pools of mortgages.[9] In 1991, these mortgage pools held 27 percent of outstanding mortgages nationally; these are agency assets. Investors in these mortgage pool securities receive pass-through certificates (agency liabilities), which entitle them to interest and principal payments according to their share of the pool.

Pass-through certificates have an element of uncertainty for investors, however. If the mortgages in the pool, the underlying mortgages, are refinanced, perhaps because mortgage interest rates decline significantly, the actual term of a pass-through certificate will be shorter than the investor anticipated at the time of purchase. This means that total investment return may be significantly less than first estimated.

In 1982 the Federal Home Loan Mortgage Corporation introduced *collateralized mortgage obligations* (CMOs) to address this concern. The CMOs are divided into three groups, called *tranches,* A-1, A-2, and A-3. Holders of A-1 CMOs receive the customary pass-through of interest and principal payments, while A-2 and A-3 holders receive interest only. When A-1 principal is completely repaid, A-2 begins to receive distributions of principal. When A-2 is completely repaid, A-3 receives principal payments. These arrangements reduce some of the uncertainty as to the actual maturity date and rate of return, especially for A-1 investors. (See also the following section.)

This idea has been so well received that private firms now issue CMOs that are corporate bonds whose proceeds are invested in pass-through certificates. In 1991, CMO issuers held 10 percent of all agency securities.

In each case, individual loans are converted into marketable securities through "securitization," a growing trend in the United States.

SECURITIZATION

Pass-through certificates and CMOs are examples of *securitized* assets.

Securitization
The pooling of a group of loans with similar characteristics and the subsequent sale of interests in the pool to investors.

Securitization of mortgage loans in the United States is one of the best examples.

[9]Ginnie Mae securities are backed by the full faith and credit of the U.S. government.

Mortgage-Backed Securities

Mortgage-backed securities include:

- Pass-through certificates
- Mortgage-backed bonds
- Pay-through bonds
- Stripped mortgage-backed securities
- Real estate mortgage investment conduits

In 1970, Congress authorized the Government National Mortgage Association to guarantee securities that are backed by federally insured mortgage loans. The loans are held in trust, ownership certificates are issued, and payments of principal and interest are guaranteed by the issuer, an agency of the U.S. government. Mortgage-backed securities, called *Ginnie Maes,* are considered *pass-through certificates* because the entire cash flow from the loans is dedicated to payment of principal and interest to the investors. Ginnie Mae pass-through certificates are the most popular, but certificates issued by the Federal Home Loan Mortgage Corporation and the Federal National Mortgage Association are also widely held.

In 1977 Bank of America, a major commercial bank, began to issue pass-through certificates backed by conventional mortgage loans. Because these mortgage loans are not federally insured, Bank of America arranged private insurance. Private-sector pass-throughs are a relatively small segment of the market.

Mortgage-backed bonds are general obligations that must be paid from the general funds of the issuer. Unlike pass-through certificates, they are almost exactly comparable to other corporate bonds. A difference is that if the issuer defaults, the collateral for the bonds may be sold to satisfy bondholders' claims. This collateral is generally mortgage loans made by the bond issuer, but could include Treasury or government agency securities.

While mortgage-backed bonds are issued by both private firms and government agencies, private issues are more common. Private-sector issuers are savings and loan associations and mutual savings banks.

Collateralized mortgage obligations belong to the general classification of *pay-through* bonds. They are similar to pass-throughs in that the cash flows from the underlying mortgage pool are devoted exclusively to servicing the bonds. The difference is that they are issued in maturity classes to minimize the uncertainty of the timing of payments.

The original CMOs issued by the Federal Home Loan Mortgage Corporation were structured into three classes, or tranches—the first payable within 5 years, the second within 12 years, and the third within 20 years. The second and third classes receive only interest payments until the first is completely repaid; while the second is being repaid, the third receives interest only. Most CMOs now have four tranches. The fourth tranche is called a Z bond. The Z bonds pay neither interest nor principal (like zero coupon bonds) while the other classes are being repaid, but accrued interest is added to the principal balance in the interim. After the other tranches have been repaid, the Z bonds receive both interest and principal payments. This class is usually structured to be repaid within 25 to 30 years. (Because of prepayments of the underlying mortgages, all tranches are usually repaid before the stated maturity dates).

Approximately 80 percent of CMOs are backed by federal agency securities (issued by Federal Home Loan Mortgage Corporation, Federal National Mortgage Association, or Government National Mortgage Association). The Federal Home Loan Mortgage Corporation, originator of the CMO, is now responsible for only 20 percent of CMO issuances. Investment bankers, home builders, mortgage bankers, savings and loan associations, and insurance companies account for the remaining 80 percent. In 1991, outstanding CMOs totaled $151 billion.

Generally, *pass-through trusts* are not considered corporations; that is, the trust is not subject to income taxation. Accordingly, the income of such a trust is not taxed until distribution to investors. Before 1986, however, unless claims on the trust were structured as *stripped mortgage-backed securities* (STRIPS), the differential payouts to various classes of CMO investors caused the "trust" to be considered a corporation and therefore subject to income tax at both the corporate and the investor levels.

In order for the claims on the trust to qualify as stripped mortgage-backed securities, the trust must hold mortgages and pass through to a particular class of investors *fixed* percentages of interest and principal payments. For example, if there are two classes of trust certificates, the first might pay 25 percent of interest payments and 50 percent of the principal payments. The second would receive 75 percent of interest payments and the remaining 50 percent of principal. The first is a low-coupon bond (selling at a discount), the second a high-coupon bond (selling at a premium). The STRIPS may also convey interest only (IO STRIPS) or principal only (PO STRIPS). However the principal and interest are allocated, the key to qualification as STRIPS is that the percentages do not change over time.

The Tax Reform Act of 1986 created tax-exempt vehicles called *real estate mortgage conduits* (REMICs). The REMICS are trusts or corporations that hold fixed pools of mortgages or related assets and that issue claims including several classes of "regular" claims. Income to regular investors is similar to income to conventional bondholders. Amounts of interest and principal payments are fixed when the REMIC is established, although the timing of payments may be contingent upon prepayment experience. Income to regular investors is taxed at the time of accrual, rather than at the time of receipt.

The REMICs are permitted only one class of "residual" claims, defined as any claim for which principal payment amounts or interest rates are not specified. For example, payments to residual claims may be contingent upon reinvestment of income or upon prepayment experience. As long as conditions with respect to regular and residual claims are met, REMICs provide a tax-exempt structure through which CMOs may be issued. (See Exhibit 4-7.)

Other Forms of Securitization

While the bulk of securitization involves mortgages or mortgage-related instruments, other assets are also securitized. The Government National Mortgage Association has begun to issue pass-through certificates collateralized by mobile home loans. Salomon Brothers, a securities firm, has issued certificates of automobile receivables (CARs) and certificates of amortized revolving debt (CARDs). The CARs were collateralized by auto-

EXHIBIT 4-7 CMOS: LET THE BUYER BEWARE

Collaterialized mortgage obligations are one of the most complicated financial instruments offered today. Estimating cash flows can be so complicated that securities brokers must use computers to arrive at predictions, which are really no more than best guesses. Because CMOs trade so infrequently, a true market value is also difficult to determine. Potential CMO investors should inquire as to the effect of future interest rate changes on CMO cash flows, avoid CMO purchases of less than $25,000 (larger denominations are easier to sell), and select the simplest varieties.

Source: Willoughby, Jack, "Mortgage Follies; Collateralized Mortgage Obligations Offer High Yields, Along with Unpleasant Surprises," *Financial World,* vol. 160, no. 7 (April 2, 1991).

mobile loans made by Marine Midland Bank and placed in a trust to avoid imposition by the Fed of minimum reserve requirements on the certificates. A private company insures the certificates. General Motors Acceptance Corporation (the financial services affiliate of General Motors) has since begun to issue CARs. The first CARDs were collateralized by Bank One credit card receivables. There was no private insurance, but Bank One set aside loss reserves at a rate equal to twice the historical credit card default rate. The practice has since expanded.

Business loans have been securitized. Loans and receivables (assets) in this case serve as collateral for issue of commercial paper and corporate bonds (liabilities). The First National Bank of Wisconsin first issued securities backed by federally insured Small Business Administration (SBA) loans in 1986. A metals and mining firm, AMAX, securitized accounts receivable in 1982 by issuing commercial paper insured by a private company. Comdisco issued intermediate-term bonds backed by computer lease receivables in 1985. All these forms of securitization allow loans to be traded on the secondary market.

Advantages of Securitization

The growing variety of securitized assets indicates the advantages that the process of securitization offers. Selling mortgage loans to federal agencies lets savings and loan associations remove long-term assets from their books. As most of their deposits are short-term, sale of the mortgage loans helps S&Ls match the average maturity of their assets to those of their liabilities more closely. Holding pass-throughs and CMOs lets S&Ls diversify their mortgage-related assets; in the case of CMOs, the S&Ls also shorten the average time to maturity of these holdings.

Life insurance companies have longer-term liabilities. From their perspective, investment in long-term residential mortgage assets would be advantageous. But *individual* mortgage loans would not be cost-effective because of the cost of administration. By investing in mortgage-backed pass-throughs, life insurance firms have the benefit of mortgage loan equivalents while avoiding administrative expense.

Securitization enables borrowers to access a source of low-cost funds. When a firm's overall credit rating is lower than the credit rating of its receivables, securitizing the receivables can reduce the borrowers' rate of interest. Securitization also enables small and emerging companies to offer financing arrangements to their customers by selling on credit terms and then packaging the receivables for resale. For these and other reasons, securitization is likely to be an even more important component of capital market transactions in the future.

SUMMARY

Capital market instruments are long-term claims on governments, corporations, and households, and they are classified as bonds, stock, or mortgages. The U.S. Treasury issues bonds to finance the operations of the federal government. States and other political subdivisions issue municipal bonds to finance similar operations at the local level. Federal agencies issue bonds in order to purchase packages of mortgage loans and student loans from private lenders, thereby making more funds available for housing and education in the private sector. Corporations issue bonds and stock for long-term projects that will contribute to economic growth.

The value of capital market instruments is based on cash flows, required rate of interest, and timing of cash flows. Bonds and mortgages have a fixed term or time to maturity. Stock is a perpetual stream of payments. In each case, however, pricing formulas facilitate the valuation of these instruments. The formulas are also useful for computing an investor's expected return.

Capital market instruments total approximately $12 trillion. Mortgages and corporate stock represent the largest dollar value at $4 trillion each. Treasury and corporate bonds are next at over $1.5 trillion each. Together, federal agency and municipal bonds total about $1 trillion. In the last 10 years, there has been strong growth in bonds, stock, and mortgages.

The process of securitization has helped make this growth possible. Federal government agencies encouraged the process of securitization by purchasing pools of mortgage loans. Since then, the private sector has become actively involved as well. Now credit card, automobile, and business loans are packaged and sold, helping make fresh infusions of funds into the country's capital markets.

KEY TERMS

call provision
capital gains yield
collateralized mortgage obligations
common stock
debentures
equipment trust certificates
federal agency bonds
general obligation bonds
mortgage bonds
mortgage-backed bonds
mortgages
municipal bonds
pass-through certificates
preferred stock
real estate mortgage investment conduits
revenue bonds
securitization
stock warrants
stripped mortgage-backed securities
subordinated debentures
Treasury notes and bonds
yield to maturity

END-OF-CHAPTER QUESTIONS

1. List and define the major financial instruments of the U.S. capital markets.
2. What is the difference between a bond's yield to maturity and its current yield?
3. Differentiate between a debenture and a subordinated debenture.
4. How do federally sponsored agencies that operate in the secondary market for mortgages help make more mortgage loans available in the primary market?
5. With respect to municipal bonds, why should a revenue bond yield a higher return than a general obligation bond?
6. What are the differences between common stock and preferred stock?
7. Which is more volatile in price: a fixed-rate, zero-coupon bond or a variable-rate bond that pays periodic interest?
8. How does a CMO differ from a pass-through certificate?
9. Securitization helps financial institutions be more liquid by selling portions of their loan portfolio. Do consumers benefit from securitization?
10. Identify the advantages and disadvantages of adjustable–rate mortgages:
    - **a.** From the perspective of borrowers.
    - **b.** From the perspective of lenders.

END-OF-CHAPTER PROBLEMS

1. What is the maximum price that you should be willing to pay for a bond with 7 years to maturity, a $1000 par value, and an 8 percent coupon rate (paid semiannually) if your required rate of return is 12 percent?
2. If a 15-year zero-coupon bond is selling for $239.39, what is its yield to maturity?
3. If your marginal tax rate is 28 percent, what corporate bond yield would make you indifferent to a 7 percent municipal bond?

4. If a share of stock is selling for $40, its last dividend was $2, and the firm's growth rate is expected to be 15 percent, what rate of return do you expect shareholders to earn next year?

5. Suppose that a corporate bond is convertible into 20 shares of common stock.
   a. If the bond is currently selling at par ($1000), for what price should the stock be selling?
   b. If the stock were selling for $60 per share, for what price would you expect the bond to be selling?

6. An example in the chapter concerned an 8 percent coupon bond with a $1000 face value that paid interest semiannually and matured in 5 years. With a required rate of return of 10 percent, the value of the bond was $922.78. Now suppose that the bond paid interest annually instead of semiannually.
   a. Compute the new value.
   b. Why is this value different?

7. A preferred stock pays an annual dividend of $4, and the required rate of return is 13 percent.
   a. What is the most you would be willing to pay for a share of this stock?
   b. Now suppose that another preferred stock is selling for $25 and that the required return is again 13 percent. What annual dividend should this stock be paying?

8. A common stock that paid a $3.24 dividend last year is selling for $50. If the required return is 15 percent, what should be this stock's growth rate?

SELECTED REFERENCES

Cohen, Jerome B., Edward D. Zinbarg, and Arthur Zeikel. *Investment Analysis and Portfolio Management,* 5th edition, Richard D. Irwin, Inc., Homewood, Illinois, 1987.

Havrilesky, Thomas M., and Robert Schweitzer, Editors. *Contemporary Developments in Financial Institutions and Markets,* Harlan Davidson, Inc., Arlington Heights, Illinois, 1987.

Henderson, John, and Jonathan P. Scott. *Securitization,* New York Institute of Finance, New York, 1988.

Mayo, Herbert B. *Investments; An Introduction,* Dryden Press, New York, 1984.

U.S. Department of the Treasury. *Report of the Secretary of the Treasury on Government-Sponsored Enterprises,* Washington, D.C., April 1991.

CHAPTER 5

CAPITAL MARKETS, DERIVATIVE SECURITIES, AND INTERNATIONAL DIVERSIFICATION

CHAPTER OUTLINE

PRIMARY CAPITAL MARKETS
- Investment Banking
- Public Securities Issues
- Merchant Banking
- Commercial Banks and Investment Banking in Selected Countries
- Industry Finance in Selected Countries

SECONDARY CAPITAL MARKETS
- Organized Stock Exchanges
- The Over-the-Counter Market
- International Comparisons

DERIVATIVE SECURITIES
- Futures Contracts
- Options Contracts
- Swap Contracts

DIVERSIFICATION
- Expected Return of a Portfolio
- Portfolio Variance
- Correlations of Selected Stock Markets

INTERNATIONAL COMPARISONS:
- Brazil
- Canada
- France
- Germany
- India
- Japan
- Korea
- Malaysia
- Mexico
- Switzerland
- Taiwan
- Thailand
- United Kingdom

CHAPTER OVERVIEW

This chapter:

- Differentiates the functions of primary and secondary capital markets
- Describes the investment banking process
- Compares secondary markets in the United States
- Highlights changes in the relative size of stock markets in developed countries and emerging markets
- Introduces derivative securities
- Describes the concepts of capital asset portfolio diversification

When the stocks and bonds described in Chapter 4 are first issued, they are distributed to investors through primary markets. Investment bankers assist corporations in structuring the issues and take responsibility for selling the securities. Once issued, the securities are bought and sold in secondary markets, which are either organized exchanges or telecommunications networks. In terms of size, Japan and other Asian countries now boast the largest capital markets among developed and emerging markets.

The United States has been most active in introducing innovations in derivative securities—financial futures, options, and swaps. It is now possible to purchase derivative securities based on stocks, bonds, and stock indexes. Furthermore, swaps make it possible to restructure the cash flows of financial assets and liabilities.

These markets make it possible for investors to diversify their asset holdings beyond domestic investments and to improve risk/return tradeoffs. Continued expansion of international markets promises to make international diversification even easier.

PRIMARY CAPITAL MARKETS

As noted in Chapter 1, financial securities are offered for the first time in *primary markets.* For U.S. Treasury notes and bonds, initial issue is by periodic auctions through the Federal Reserve banks and member institutions (described in Chapter 3). For municipal bonds and corporate securities, primary markets operate in a different way, involving investment banks in this country and merchant banks outside the United States.

Investment Banking

Firms that facilitate the issue of stocks and bonds are called *investment banks.*

Investment banks:
Securities firms that are retained to advise issuing entities on stock and bond offerings and that take an active role in distribution of the securities to ultimate investors.

Investment bankers give advice as to the type of security that should be issued, the size and pricing of the offering, and even its timing. The client firm pays a fee for this service; the investment banker assumes some of the risk in selling the issue. This distribution activity is called *underwriting.*

Underwriting:
The initial distributing of securities by an entity other than the issuer, with the risk of price fluctuations borne to some extent by the distributor.

Usually investment banks take responsibility for selling the entire issue—the agreement between banker and issuer is a *firm commitment* in which the issuing firm is guaranteed a specific price and is relieved of the responsibility of marketing the securities. The two parties work together to establish the right price for the securities and then negotiate the *underwriter's discount,* the investment banker's compensation for risk taking and distribution. The issuing firm receives the issue price less the discount. If it turns out that the securities cannot be sold to the public for at least the discounted price, the investment banker absorbs a loss. When the issuing firm is not well known, the two parties may execute a *best efforts* agreement that allows sharing of the risk; the investment banker sells the securities at the best market price it can obtain.

Distribution of securities is commonly spread across several brokerage firms. The firm that negotiates with the issuing company is called the *originating house.* It and the other firms constitute the *syndicate.* Each member of the syndicate is responsible for the sale of a given share of the securities.

Before the securities can be offered to the public, the federal Securities and Exchange Commission (SEC) must approve the issue. The issuer and the investment bank prepare a preliminary prospectus providing financial and other data about the firm, the securities being offered for sale, and the intended use of the funds to be raised. The SEC is required to approve the adequacy of disclosure of the prospectus, not the merits of the particular issue. To alert prospective buyers that SEC approval is not final, the cover of the prospectus includes a statement to this effect in red lettering. The practice has led to the preliminary prospectus being nicknamed "red herring."

After any required modifications and subsequent SEC approval, the final prospectus is prepared (now without the red lettering) and distributed to prospective buyers. State and municipal bonds need not be registered with the SEC and are exempt from the prospectus requirement, but no corporate stock or bonds may be sold in the United States without an approved prospectus. The requirement for a prospectus is a common practice in most countries with developed securities markets.

Public Securities Issues

The 1980s saw considerable growth in the amount of new issues. As Exhibit 5-1 illustrates, total new issues of corporate securities and municipal bonds were $22 billion in 1963, with corporate bonds and municipal bonds each making up roughly half. Total volume had almost doubled in 10 years to $46 billion. By 1983 this volume had more than quadrupled to $196 billion, with $102 billion in new municipal bonds, almost $50 billion each in corporate bonds and common stock, and the rest in preferred stock. Five years later, the total of 1988 new securities issues had almost doubled once again, rising to $342 billion, with $172 billion in corporate bonds and $117 billion in municipals. This activity made investment banking one of the most lucrative financial services during the 1980s.

Merchant Banking

An institution with a major role in primary securities markets outside the United States is the *merchant bank.*

EXHIBIT 5-1 U.S. PUBLIC SECURITIES ISSUES, 1963–1988

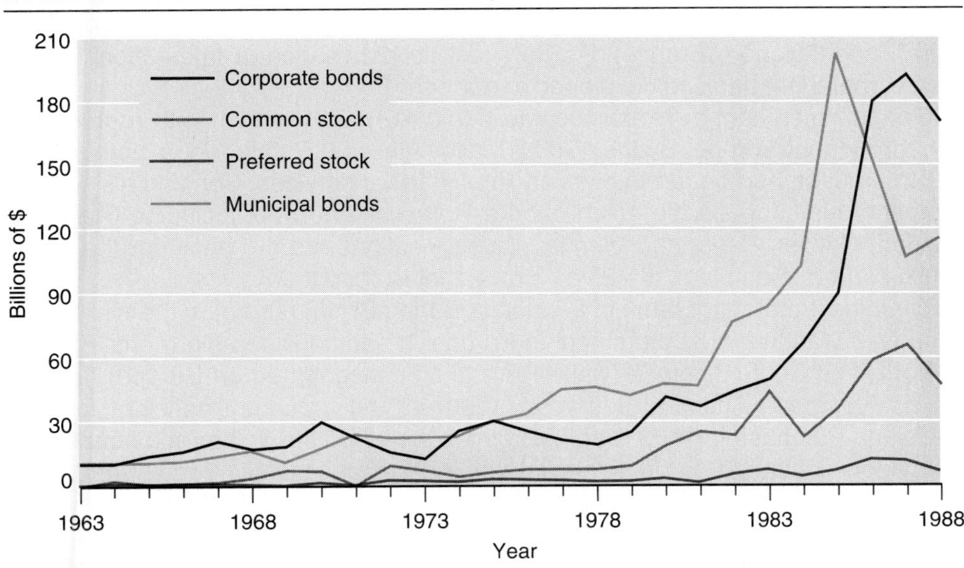

Source: Based on data from U.S. Department of Commerce, Bureau of Economic Analysis, *business Statistics 1961–1988.*

Merchant bank:
A bank that serves the needs of commercial enterprises by giving advice on financing alternatives and corporate mergers and by underwriting new issues, as well as accepting bills of exchange, providing foreign currency exchange facilities, and operating in the money markets.

Merchant banks operated in Italy as early as the fourteenth century. As the name implies, the first merchant bankers were European merchants who found that lending money and providing foreign exchange services made profitable and natural additions to their normal trading activities. Over time, England and northern Europe became centers for international trade, and London evolved as the hub of merchant banking, as it remains today. (See Exhibit 5-2.)

The London merchant banks are much smaller than clearing (commercial) banks, but both are licensed by the government. Unlike clearing bank operations, merchant bank operations are not financed by large numbers of small deposits, nor do merchant banks generally provide demand deposits or transactions accounts. They have little need therefore for extensive branch networks.

Merchant banks are primarily wholesale bankers; they lend funds in corporate and institutional markets. In recent years, they have focused more on primary market investment banking activities, where new issues are typically underwritten by a merchant bank or a stockbroker. Distinguishing characteristics of a merchant bank are that its staff is typically composed of a high proportion of professionals and that decisions are made quickly without recourse to bureaucratic chains of command, unlike the clearing banks with large numbers of employees to staff numerous branches and a hierarchy to manage them.

Merchant banks operate in a number of countries and reflect strong influence of the British model. In South Africa and Singapore, they are called merchant banks. In Australia they are referred to as *money market corporations* and in New Zealand as *unofficial*

EXHIBIT 5-2 MERCHANT BANKERS OF THE PAST

Italian merchants began the long tradition of merchant banking. One of the most famous of these was Cosimo de Medici, who in the mid-fifteenth century established a network of operations beyond Italy with offices in London, Bruges (Belgium), and Avignon (France). As Italy lost its dominance in international commerce, merchant banking developed in northern Europe.

German merchant bankers became particularly well known, with representation throughout Europe. By the 1700s, Mayer Amschel Rothschild, a clothing and coin merchant, had begun to diversify into financial services. Sending his sons to represent his interests, he established a Rothschild network including Frankfurt, London, Naples, Paris, and Vienna. These locations are the basis for the Rothschild corporate emblem, the Five Arrows, that is used today.

The oldest merchant bank in London is Baring Brothers; during the nineteenth century, it was the most prominent in Europe. It had considerable representation in North and South America (while Rothschild concentrated on Europe). In fact, when President Thomas Jefferson (1801–1809) sought financing for the Louisiana Purchase in 1803, Baring Brothers arranged the $15 million needed.

London continued to dominate international finance until World War I, with merchant banks playing a vital role. Much of the funding for the U.S. railway system was provided by London merchant banks. While New York, Tokyo, and other centers have grown in significance with respect to other aspects of international finance, London remains the world center of merchant banking.

money market corporations. Merchant banks in Hong Kong are called *deposit-taking companies. Diversified financial institutions* are South Korea's equivalent, while the Japanese variation is *securities houses.* Like their names, the licensing of and legal specifications for merchant banks vary from one country to another.

Commercial Banks and Investment Banking in Selected Countries

United States commercial banks have been prohibited, for the most part, from engaging in underwriting corporate securities domestically since passage of the Glass-Steagall Act in 1933. Banks have challenged this prohibition on the grounds that their nonbank competitors now offer services historically considered banking services, which erodes bank market share and profitability. This same sort of system also prevails in Japan. The Japanese securities system was patterned after the U.S. system, so Japanese banks are also not permitted to act as corporate securities underwriters.

Until the late 1980s, Canadian bankers operated under similar restrictions. Chartered (commercial) banks are now permitted to own securities firms. Some have bought securities firms, and others have started new companies.

The historical exclusion of banks from corporate underwriting is not observed in all countries; the most notable exceptions are Germany, Switzerland, and France.

In Germany, commercial banks are also referred to as "universal" banks. There are no restrictions on their security market activities, and there is no distinction between commercial and investment banks. German corporations rely more heavily than their U.S. counterparts on bank borrowing and the issuance of debt certificates that are not legally defined as securities. German nonfinancial firms meet less than .5 percent of their financing needs through equity issues, and government entities and commercial banks are the most important issuers of debt securities. In 1986, for example, private and public financial institutions were responsible for 64 percent of all bond issuances and the federal government for 24 percent, a total of 88 percent of 1986 issuances. In the United States, the corresponding percentages were 20 percent and 41 percent, respectively, for a total of 61 percent.

Swiss banks have a significant role in the primary securities market. Firm commitment agreements are typical, with the largest Swiss banks comprising the syndicate membership. Swiss firms with publicly traded stock are generally large and well known. Many companies are still privately held but issue debt in public markets.

In France, as in Germany, firms have historically used bank financing more than securities issuance. In recent years, though, the breadth of the French securities markets has increased markedly. For each new issue, the issuing firm's bank prepares and cosigns the prospectus after the terms have been set by the issuer, the originating house, and the Treasury Department.

Industry Finance in Selected Countries

Investment bankers (in the United States) and merchant or commercial banks (in other countries) help bring together investors and corporations in need of financing. The corporate mix of debt and equity varies considerably, depending upon a country's traditional reliance on particular sources of funds.

Exhibit 5-3 illustrates some of these differences. In the United States and the United Kingdom, for example, where capital markets have operated for relatively long periods of time, equity represents a substantial part of industrial financing. In Germany and France, where extensive bank borrowing has been the more traditional form of corporate funding, the equity percentages of total financing are not as high. In Japan, where until recently virtually all corporate funds were channeled through the banking system, equity levels are particularly low.

EXHIBIT 5-3 EQUITY VS. DEBT FINANCING OF CORPORATIONS IN SELECTED COUNTRIES*

		Debt %	
	Equity %	Short-term	Long-term
United States	57.4	18.3	24.3
Japan	19.2	56.7	24.1
United Kingdom	46.4	45.6	8.0
Germany	38.2	45.4	16.4
France†	28.7	55.2	16.1
Italy‡	32.2	44.6	23.2

*Balance sheet position as of 1986.
†As of 1985.
‡As of 1983.
Source: Bank of Japan, *Comparative Economic and Financial Statistics: Japan and Other Major Countries,* 1988, pp. 145–146.

Nevertheless, it is interesting that the countries with the largest market capitalizations are Japan and the United States—two countries that have maintained a distinct separation between commercial banking and investment banking. The exclusion of commercial banks from corporate underwriting possibly has served to encourage a robust, if specialized, securities industry. (See Exhibit 5-4.)

SECONDARY CAPITAL MARKETS

Once securities have been issued in the primary market, investors may sell or purchase them in *secondary markets.* In the United States, the secondary market for government

EXHIBIT 5-4 THE NIGERIAN PRIMARY CAPITAL MARKET

Nigeria has the largest population among the countries of sub-Saharan Africa and is a major producer of crude oil. Although Nigeria remains a poor country by Western standards, the oil revenues have helped spur the development of a stock market. However, unlike prices in primary markets in the United States, Nigerian securities prices are set by the government. The Securities and Exchange Commission (SEC) determines market prices of securities. The Capital Issues Commission (CIC), established in 1973, like its ad hoc predecessor, the Capital Issues Committee, attempts to set prices of publicly traded securities in order to protect the investors and to prevent price manipulation by market participants. The CIC's primary function is price-fixing in the primary market (an activity that some firms avoid by not offering their securities to the public), and it is not empowered to regulate the secondary market. The SEC, established in 1978, has the authority to require registration of *all* securities that ultimately may be held by investors other than those to whom they are originally sold and to supervise stock exchanges and securities firms.

Several factors are considered in setting the prices of equities. In general, the price is set so that the ratio of average annual earnings (over the preceding 5 years) to share price is 20 to 30 percent, depending upon the industry. Another measure that is determined by the government is the net asset value per share (assets *less* liabilities *divided* by number of outstanding shares). The lower of the prices implied by the earnings-price ratio and the net asset value per share, after adjustment for other relevant factors, becomes the price at which the stock may be sold.

Source: Nwankwo, G. O. *The Nigerian Financial System,* African Publishing Company, New York, 1980. Onoh, J. K., Editor. *The Foundations of Nigeria's Financial Infrastructure,* Croom Helm Ltd., London, 1980.

securities, which are traded through government securities dealers, is quite active and liquid. Municipal bonds are traded primarily over the counter (OTC) and generally less frequently than federal government bonds. The secondary market for mortgages has developed primarily because of government initiative.

Of the remaining securities, corporate bonds and stock are traded either on an *organized stock exchange* or *over the counter.*

Organized Stock Exchanges

An organized exchange is a physical place where stocks and bonds are traded.

Organized stock exchange:
A specific location where stocks (and some bonds) are traded by exchange members who specialize in particular securities. These specialists match buyers and sellers and maintain an orderly market by trading for their own account whenever there is an imbalance of buyers and sellers.

In order for a stock to be "listed" on an organized exchange, it must meet certain requirements. Listing requirements are most stringent on the New York Stock Exchange (NYSE). Among other things, a firm listed on the New York Stock Exchange must have at least 1 million shares held by the public with an aggregate value of at least $16 million. The American Stock Exchange (AMEX) lists generally smaller firms that are still of national interest. There are also regional exchanges, where securities of local firms trade. Over 90 percent of the securities listed on regional exchanges are also listed on either the NYSE or the AMEX. Regionals are the Midwest, Pacific, Boston, Philadelphia, and Cincinnati stock exchanges.

The NYSE, which has operated since 1792, is a private corporation with over 1000 members, who purchase "seats," or memberships. Over 1500 companies are listed. Shares sold on the NYSE have recently accounted for over 75 percent of total shares traded on organized exchanges.

As shown in Exhibit 5-5, the value of NYSE securities was almost $4 trillion in 1988, with $2.3 trillion in common stock and $1.6 trillion in bonds. The capitalization of AMEX was only $105 billion, with $81 billion in common stock. Regional exchanges are much smaller, with the Pacific Stock Exchange, the largest, having only an $8 billion capitalization in 1988.

The Over-the-Counter Market

The OTC market includes all securities transactions that are not conducted on an organized exchange. Dealers (as opposed to specialists) maintain market order. The National Association of Securities Dealers Automated Quotation system (NASDAQ) is a telecommunications network that connects dealers and provides instantaneous price information on over 4700 stocks. Because of the speed and efficiency of this market, NASDAQ has grown rapidly and now ranks third in size behind the Tokyo and New York stock exchanges.

Both organized exchanges and OTC markets are regulated by the SEC to prevent stock price manipulation, deception, and fraudulent practices. The National Association of Securities Dealers is a self-regulatory body that licenses brokers and dealers and sets standards for ethical behavior.

International Comparisons

The U.S. capital market has historically been the world's largest. As Exhibit 5-6 shows, as recently as 1980 the United States accounted for almost 55 percent of the value of se-

EXHIBIT 5-5 VALUE OF LISTED SECURITIES ON NATIONAL AND REGIONAL EXCHANGES, 1988

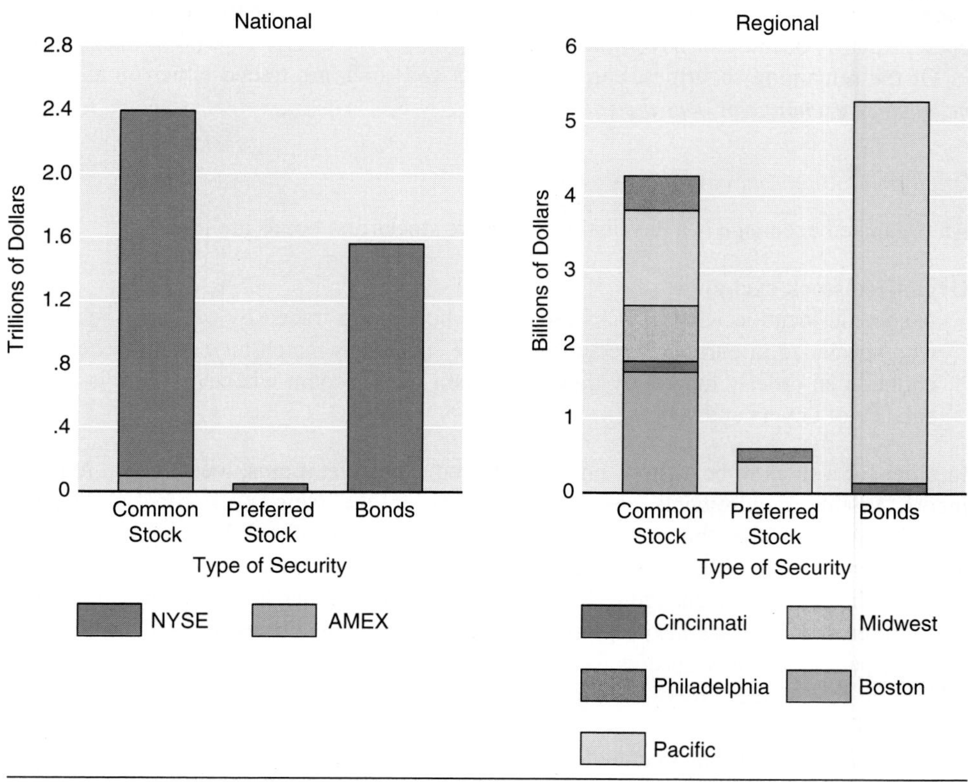

Source: Based on data from U.S. Securities and Exchange Commission; Fifty-fifth Annual Report 1989.

EXHIBIT 5-6 STOCK MARKET CAPITALIZATION DEVELOPED COUNTRIES, 1980 AND 1989

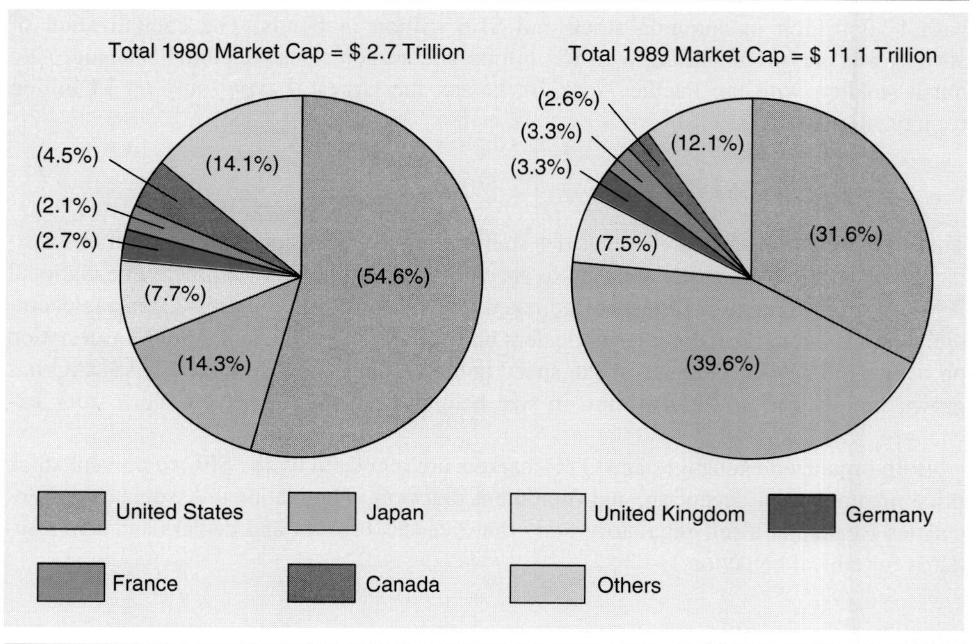

Source: Calculations and graphic based on data from International Finance Corporation, *Emerging Stock Markets Factbook,* 1990.

curities listed on the stock markets (stock market capitalization) of all developed countries. Japan was then a distant second (14 percent), and the United Kingdom was third (8 percent). Canada, Germany, and France followed with less than a 5 percent share each.

During the following 9 years, the stock market capitalization of developed countries rose from \$2.7 trillion in 1980 to \$11.1 trillion by 1989. The U.S. capitalization more than doubled from \$1.45 trillion to \$3.51 trillion, while the Japanese market outstripped even this impressive growth. In 1980, Japanese capitalization was \$380 billion. By 1989, it was up to \$4.39 trillion, more than a tenfold increase. This gave Japan almost a 40 percent share, exceeding the U.S. percentage of 32 percent of developed-country stock markets. The United Kingdom remained third (8 percent). France and Germany had moved slightly ahead of Canada.

Part of the phenomenal growth in the Japanese market is attributable to the appreciated value of the yen, but even in yen terms the market has grown substantially. Large Japanese trade surpluses during the 1980s contributed to this economic expansion.

The economic expansion of the Newly Industrialized Countries (NICs) of Asia has had a similar effect on their economies. Exhibit 5-7 shows the changes in stock market capitalization among emerging economies, particularly the growing dominance of South Korea and Taiwan in this group.[1] In 1980, when the total capitalization of emerging stock markets was \$86 billion, South Korea and Taiwan held less than a 12 percent combined share. The Mexican stock market was the largest, with 15 percent of the total. By 1989, emerging market capitalization stood at \$611 billion. As in the case of Japan, large trade surpluses spurred growth for Korea and Taiwan. Together their stock markets represented almost 62 percent of the 1989 total.

[1]Asian NICs are Singapore, Hong Kong, South Korea, and Taiwan. Hong Kong and Singapore are small city-states that are considered developed regions and are not counted among developing countries or emerging markets.

EXHIBIT 5-7 STOCK MARKET CAPITALIZATION EMERGING MARKETS 1980 AND 1989

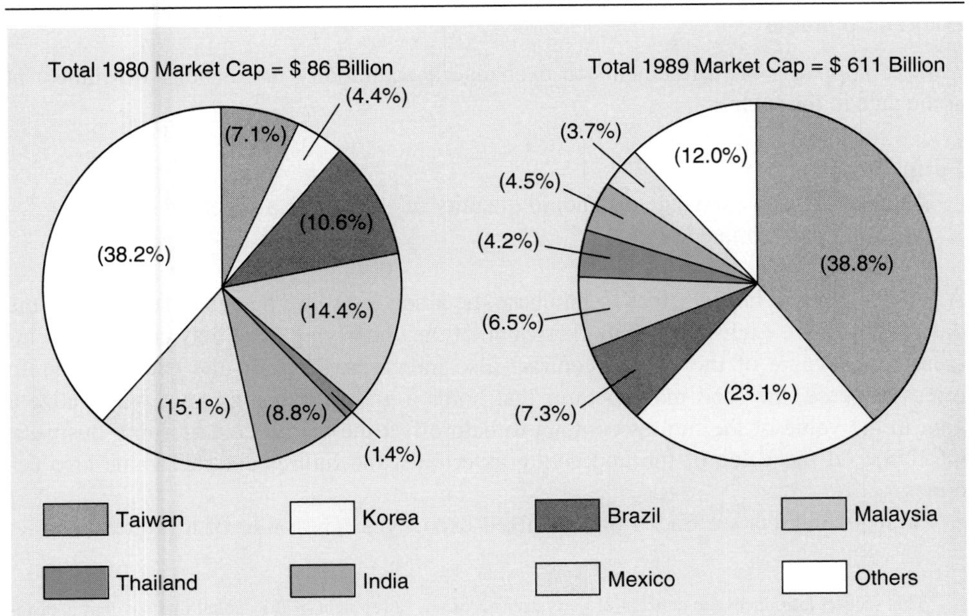

Source: Calculations and graphic based on data from International Finance Corporation, *Emerging Stock Markets Factbook,* 1990.

Taken together, these trends indicate that the balance of economic power has begun to shift. Whether in developed or emerging markets, the stock markets of the western hemisphere are being outpaced by their Asian counterparts. However, in terms of financial innovation, the United States still has few rivals. The growth in the market for derivative securities is one example of this innovation.

DERIVATIVE SECURITIES

Derivative securities are financial instruments that are based on other assets. In this one sense, they are similar to securitized assets. However, derivative securities, unlike securitized assets, are not obligations backed by the original issuer of the underlying security. Instead, derivative securities are contracts between two parties other than the original issuer of the underlying security. Derivative securities have evolved to help protect investors from certain risks:

- A manufacturer of cereal products is dependent on the grain market for inputs for its finished products. If the crops during a particular year are damaged by drought or other unfavorable conditions, the price of grain (and the manufacturer's cost of doing business) will increase.
- The owner of a large block of stock may fear that the stock's price will decline. If such a decline occurs, the investor will sustain large losses.
- A commercial bank may need to offer relatively long term, fixed-rate loans in order to be competitive with other financial institutions. If interest rates increase significantly, the bank will incur a significant opportunity cost in the form of lost interest income.

All of these are *financial risks* that derivative securities can help reduce. The food manufacturer can lock in the price of grain by buying a *futures* contract. The owner of the common stock can guard against losses by buying an *option* to sell the stock at a predetermined price. The commercial bank can enter into a *swap* contract to receive interest payments that vary with market conditions.[2]

Futures Contracts

Futures contracts are agreements to exchange a commodity or financial instrument at some date in the future.

Futures contract:
An agreement to exchange a standard quantity of an asset at a specified date in the future at a predetermined price.

A futures contract buyer agrees to purchase the asset; the seller agrees to sell. Before the date of the future exchange, the market value of the underlying asset may change. If it increases, the value of the futures contract also increases. Thus, in the event that grain prices increase, the food manufacturer that holds a grain futures contract will realize a gain in the value of the futures contract to help offset the higher cost of doing business. Of course, if the value of the underlying asset falls, the futures contract value also declines.

Futures contracts are traded on organized exchanges. The seller of a futures contract

[2]This section introduces the concept of derivative securities, a segment of the capital markets that is of increasing importance. The use of derivative securities to manage interest rate risk is discussed and illustrated in Chapter 15. The role of derivative securities in currency markets and foreign exchange risk management is described in Chapter 6.

can settle the obligation (open position) by delivering the underlying asset or by reentering the market and buying an offsetting contract through the exchange. Buyers may settle by taking delivery or by selling offsetting contracts. In fact, most open positions (95 percent) are settled by offsetting contracts.

Parties in a futures contract are generally anonymous, that is, not known to one another. Risk of default is minimized in this case because the exchange guarantees the other side of the transaction. To cover this guarantee provision, the exchange requires a *margin,* or cash deposit, of no more than 5 percent, by each party.

The exchange determines the adequacy of the margin each day by assessing the current value of the futures contract. Gains and losses in the value of the contract are then posted to each open position. Such daily revaluation of an open contract is called *marking to market.* If the margin (cash deposit) as a percentage of the value of the contract should fall below the minimum maintenance level, the exchange requires that the party place additional funds on deposit. The request for an additional deposit is a *margin call.*

The first futures contracts were based on commodities such as agricultural crops. Government securities were the first futures contracts offered for financial instruments, then sold on the leading commodity futures exchange, the Chicago Board of Trade (CBOT). Now other exchanges offer futures contracts, and the market has developed to include municipal bond futures (based on an index of municipals) and stock index futures (based on indexes such as the S&P 500). Unlike Treasury futures, there is no deliverable asset in the case of an index futures contract. Instead, the value of the contract is some multiple of the value of the index.

Exhibit 5-8 shows the standard denominations of a variety of futures contracts and their volume of trade during 1988. Information on U.K. and Japanese futures markets is also shown. While U.S. futures markets are the most active, foreign market trading is increasing.

Options Contracts

Another area of U.S. innovation in financial markets is the *option contract.*

Option contract:

An agreement that confers the right to buy or sell an asset at a set price through some future date. The right is exercisable at the discretion of the option buyer.

Like futures, options are traded on organized exchanges and guaranteed by the exchange on which they trade. Unlike futures purchasers, options purchasers are not *obligated* to take any action on or before the maturity date. If the option confers the right to purchase, it is a *call option.* A *put option* confers the right to sell. The option buyer will either *exercise* the option (if it is profitable to do so) or elect to *not exercise.*

The relationship between the price at which the option can be exercised, or the *strike price,* and the market price of the asset determines the profitability of exercising. The owner of a call option will exercise if the market price is sufficiently *above* the strike price. Exercising the call option enables the investor to purchase the asset below its current market value and resell at the higher market price. Conversely, the owner of a put option will exercise if the market price is sufficiently *below* the strike price, because the asset can be bought at the lower market price and immediately sold for the higher strike price. Thus, the owner of a large block of common stock can purchase a put option on the stock with a strike price at or near the current market price; should the market price decline in the future, the owner can exercise the option to sell at the higher strike price. When it is profitable to exercise an option, the option is *in the money.* When it is *out of the money,* exercising is unprofitable.

EXHIBIT 5-8 SAMPLE OF INTEREST RATE AND STOCK INDEX FUTURES CONTRACTS, CONTRACT SPECIFICATIONS, AND 1988 VOLUME FOR THE UNITED STATES, THE UNITED KINGDOM, AND JAPAN

Type	Face value of contract	Volume (000s of contracts)
	United States	
Chicago Board of Trade (CBOT)		
Interest rate		
U.S. Treasury bonds	\$100,000	70,308
U.S. Treasury notes	\$100,000	5,798
Municipal bond index	\$1,000 × index	1,274
30-day interest rate	\$5,000,000	19
Stock index		
Major market index (MMI)	Max \$250 × index	1,176
CBOE 250 index	\$500 × index	56
International Monetary Market (IMM) at Chicago Mercantile Exchange (CME)		
Interest rate		
U.S. Treasury bills	\$1,000,000	1,247
Stock index		
S&P 500	\$500 × index	11,354
New York Futures Exchange (NYFE)		
Stock index		
NYSE composite stock index	\$500 × index	1,669
Commodity Research Bureau (CRB) commodity price index	\$500 × index	206
	United Kingdom	
London International Financial Futures Exchange (LIFFE)		
Interest rate		
Gilt (government bond)	£50,000	5,662
U.S. Treasury bonds	\$100,000	2,052
German government bond	DM250,000	315
Yen bond	¥ 100,000,000	122
Stock index		
Financial Times stock index	£25 × index	470
	Japan	
Osaka Securities Exchange		
Stock index		
OSF 50	50 stocks	545
Nikkei 225 stock average	¥ 1000 × index	1,892
Tokyo Stock Exchange		
Interest rate		
10- and 20-year yen government bonds	¥ 100,000,000	17,460
Stock index		
Tokyo stock price index	¥ 10,000 × index	2,289

Source: International Monetary Fund, *International Capital Markets: Developments and Prospects,* April 1990.

An option buyer obtains the right to buy or sell by paying a fee, or premium, to an *option writer,* or seller. This premium depends on the current market price, the strike price, and volatility of the price of the asset. Volatility is an important factor because the market value of a relatively volatile asset is more likely to reach a given strike price than a less volatile asset, all other things being equal.

An option can be written so that the buyer can exercise either *any time up to* the expiration date or *only on* the expiration date. The first is an American option, the second a European option.

The four different roles market participants may play in the options market are to:

- Buy a call and obtain the right to buy the asset.
- Write (sell) a call and make a commitment to sell the asset, if the option is exercised.
- Buy a put and obtain the right to sell the asset.
- Write (sell) a put and make a commitment to buy the asset, if the option is exercised.

The buyer of an option will lose no more than the premium paid at the time of purchase. But the writer can lose much more. For example, consider Exhibit 5-9. Suppose that a common stock option has a strike price of $50 and that the option premium is $2.

The maximum loss for the call option buyer is $2 per share, plus brokerage fees. If brokerage fees are ignored, the option holder will not profit by exercising the option unless the market price exceeds the strike price plus the option premium. On the other hand, the option writer can gain no more than the $2 per share premium. If the market value of the stock *exceeds* the strike price (plus option premium), the option writer is exposed to *loss*. If the value of the stock continues to increase beyond the strike price,

EXHIBIT 5-9 OPTIONS TRADING, POTENTIAL GAINS AND LOSSES

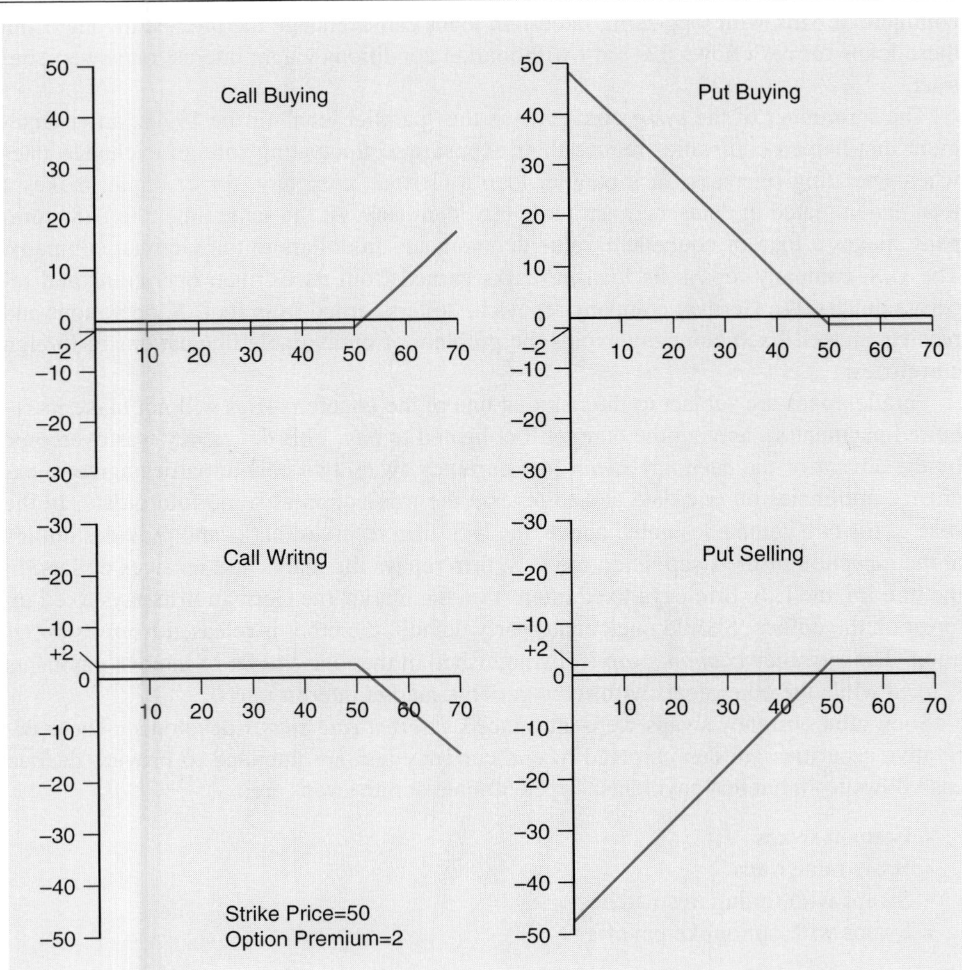

the option writer is exposed to potentially large (theoretically unbounded) losses if the stock must be purchased on the open market in order to satisfy the obligation (cover the position).

Similarly, the writer of a put option will sustain losses if the market price *declines* precipitously. As the market price falls, the put option writer faces purchase of the stock at the higher-than-market strike price (when the option buyer exercises), as the price at which it can be resold drops. This exposure makes option writing a speculative activity, and the exchanges require margins for option writers.

Besides stock options, there are also options contracts on fixed-income securities (interest rate options), stock indexes, and futures contracts. Exhibit 5-10 is a sample of interest rate and stock index options traded in the United States and the United Kingdom. Again, trading of these derivative securities is most active in the United States.

Swap Contracts

One of the fastest growing derivative securities is the *swap contract.*

Swap contract:
An agreement between two parties (counterparties) to exchange assets or a series of cash flows for a specified period of time at predetermined intervals.

The swap contract is used to manage foreign exchange risk or interest rate risk. Thus, the commercial bank with long-term, fixed-rate loans can exchange the interest income from these loans for cash flows that vary with market conditions via an interest rate swap contract.

The forerunner of the swap contract was the "parallel loan" of the 1970s, an arrangement that helped companies reduce their exposure to fluctuating foreign exchange rates when operating overseas. In a parallel loan a German company, for example, makes a loan denominated in deutsche marks to a U.S. company. At the same time, the U.S. company makes a loan of equivalent value denominated in dollars to the German company. The U.S. company repays its loan in marks earned from its German operations and receives dollars; the German company repays in dollars earned from its U.S. operations and receives marks. Each company avoids the problem of unfavorable fluctuations in foreign currencies.

Parallel loans are subject to the risk that one of the counterparties will not make its required payment(s), leaving the other still obligated to pay. This deficiency was overcome by the advent of the *currency swap.* In a currency swap, two counterparties agree to exchange currencies on one date and to reverse the transaction at some future date. In the case of the two companies noted above, the U.S. firm receives marks and provides dollars at the inception of the swap; later, the U.S. firm repays the marks and receives dollars. In the interim, the U.S. firm pays fixed interest on the marks; the German firm pays fixed interest on the dollars. Should one counterparty default, the other is released from its obligation. The *currency coupon swap* is distinguished in that one stream of interest payments is fixed while the other floats with some variable market interest rate.

Soon after currency swaps were introduced, *interest rate swaps* developed. These derivative securities are denominated in one currency and are intended to provide desired cash flows from interest payments. Types of interest rate swaps are:

- Coupon swaps
- Basis-rate swaps
- Swaps with timing mismatches
- Swaps with optionlike payoffs

EXHIBIT 5-10 SAMPLE OF INTEREST RATE AND STOCK INDEX OPTIONS CONTRACTS, CONTRACT SPECIFICATIONS, AND 1988 VOLUME FOR THE UNITED STATES AND THE UNITED KINGDOM

Type	Face value of contract	Volume (000s of contracts)
	United States	
Chicago Board of Trade (CBOT)		
Interest rate (futures options)		
U.S. Treasury bonds	$100,000	19,509
U.S. Treasury notes	$100,000	1,012
Municipal bond index	$100,000 × index	172
Chicago Board Options Exchange (CBOE)		
Interest rate		
U.S. Treasury notes and bonds	$100,000	140
Stock index		
S&P 100 index	$100 × index	57,434
S&P 500 index	$100 × index	4,817
International Monetary Market (IMM) at Chicago Mercantile Exchange (CME)		
Interest rate (futures options)		
U.S. Treasury bills	$1,000,000	1,374
Stock index		
S&P 500 index	$500 × index	734
New York Futures Exchange (NYFE)		
Stock index		
NYSE composite stock index	$500 × index	23
Commodity Research Bureau (CRB) price index	$500 × index	1
New York Stock Exchange (NYSE)		
Stock index		
NYSE composite index	$100 × index	781
American Stock Exchange (AMEX)		
Interest rate		
U.S. Treasury notes	$1,000,000	
U.S. Treasury bills	$100,000	37*
Stock index		
AMEX indexes†	$100 × index	7,001
Philadelphia Stock Exchange (PHLX)		
Stock index		
PHLX indexes‡	$100 × index	51
	United Kingdom	
London International Financial Futures Exchange (LIFFE)		
Interest rate (futures options)		
Gilt (government bond)	£50,000	1,150
U.S. Treasury bonds	$100,000	86
German government bond	DM250,000	315

*U.S. Treasury notes and bills combined.

† Includes AMEX major market index, AMEX institutional index, Amex computer technology index, and AMEX oil index.

‡ Includes PHLX value line index and PHLX national OTC index.

Source: International Monetary Fund, *International Capital Markets: Developments and Prospects,* April 1990.

Coupon swaps exchange a fixed-rate stream of interest payments for a variable-rate stream. No principal amounts change hands; instead a *notional principal* is agreed upon for a given length of time. One party agrees to pay a fixed rate of interest on the notional principal at specified intervals, perhaps monthly or quarterly. The counterparty agrees to pay a rate that floats with a published interest rate, or *basis,* perhaps the Treasury bill rate, the commercial paper rate, or the London Interbank Offered Rate (LIBOR). For example, the floating rate may be specified as "6-month LIBOR plus 1," meaning 1 percentage point above LIBOR for 6-month loans. Generally, the parties exchange only the difference between the two interest amounts.

The coupon swap is useful for companies with different objectives with respect to interest rates. For example, an industrial firm may have raised capital through a $50 million variable-rate loan but would rather have a predictable interest payment obligation for financial planning purposes. A financial institution, on the other hand, may prefer to have variable-rate liabilities (perhaps because its loans are primarily variable rate), but can raise funds competitively only through fixed-rate certificates of deposit (CDs) and other borrowings. Essentially, in a coupon swap between the two counterparties, the industrial firm agrees to pay to the financial institution a fixed rate of interest on the $50 million notional principal on a monthly basis; the financial institution uses these fixed payments to meet its CD obligations. In turn, the financial institution agrees to pay the variable rate to the industrial firm, again on a monthly basis; these payments satisfy the industrial firm's loan obligations. In practice, only the difference in the two interest payments is exchanged. For example, if the variable rate exceeds the fixed for a given month, the financial institution pays only the excess to the industrial firm; the industrial firm makes no payment.

In a *basis-rate swap,* both interest rates float, but the bases are different. For example, 6-month LIBOR may be swapped for 1-month LIBOR, or LIBOR may be swapped for the commercial paper rate. *Swaps with timing mismatches* involve counterparty payments according to different schedules. Perhaps one counterparty pays interest monthly while the other pays quarterly. A "zero" swap requires one party to pay at specified intervals throughout the term of the swap as described earlier. The other pays only at the end of the term, a "zero-coupon" arrangement.

Swaps with optionlike payoffs are similar to coupon swaps within specified ranges of market interest rate changes. Beyond these ranges, the terms of the swap change. For example, one party may agree to receive fixed-rate interest and pay floating-rate interest as long as the floating rate is within 2 percentage points of the current rate of 10 percent. If the market rate exceeds 12 percent, the party's obligation is then to pay the fixed rate of 12 percent. Likewise if the market rate falls below 8 percent, the party's obligation converts to a fixed rate of 8 percent. Alternatively, one party may agree to pay fixed-rate interest of 10 percent as long as the market rate remains within the plus-or-minus range of 2 percentage points. Should the market rate go beyond this range (above 12 or below 8 percent), the party pays a floating rate.

As these examples illustrate, swaps can be constructed in any number of ways. There are even *options on swaps,* or *swaptions.* The holder of a swaption has the right, but not the obligation, to enter into a swap contract on or before the exercise date. If the holder has the right to *receive* fixed interest payments, the instrument is a put swaption. On the other hand, if the holder has the right to *pay* fixed interest, it is a call swaption. As with other options, there is an up-front premium to pay in order to obtain the swaption.

The swap market began in order to solve problems of financial risk. In the earliest market activity, an intermediary brought the two counterparties together. Since the intermediary assumed no risk in the transaction, investment banks performed the matchmaking function quite well. As the market evolved, swap contracts became more standardized, and it was more important for the intermediary to be able to assume some of the risk, in much the same way, though not to the same extent, that organized exchanges assume risk in futures and options markets. For this reason, commercial banks are now significant intermediaries in the market for swaps—an efficient, high-volume business with relatively low margins (profits) for the banks.

A party can reverse, or "unwind," a swap position before the end of the term of the swap by canceling the agreement and delivering a final difference payment to the counterparty. Alternatively, the party can write a "mirror" contract to exactly offset the original swap in the secondary swap market. For example, the industrial firm mentioned earlier with a \$50 million variable loan originally entered a swap in which it paid fixed interest payments and received floating interest. To close this position, the firm could enter another swap contract in which it paid floating interest payments and received fixed interest. The secondary market is now so active that swap contracts for several hundred million dollars can be traded virtually 24 hours a day.

In general, derivative securities have evolved to satisfy particular needs. Specifically, futures, options, and swap contracts help investors reduce the risk associated with participation in financial markets.

DIVERSIFICATION

Financial risk may also be reduced through proper diversification of *asset portfolios* to help improve the risk/return trade-off.

Asset portfolio:
A combination of assets assembled to achieve certain investment objectives.

These assets can include cash, short-term debt instruments, bonds, and stock. *Diversification* of assets limits risk by spreading investments over a number of companies, industries, and/or countries.

Diversification:
The process of combining assets with the objective of reducing portfolio variability.

Portfolio *variability* is the extent to which the actual returns are different from *expected* returns. The sections below describe these basic concepts of portfolio diversification and examine the issue of international diversification.

Expected Return of a Portfolio

The rate of return of a portfolio depends on the return of each asset in the portfolio. The periodic rate of return of an asset is a combination of the current income and any change in the value of the asset. Current income is measured by either current yield in the case of debt securities or dividend yield in the case of preferred or common stock. Change in value is any capital gain or loss for the period.

Expected portfolio rate of return is the weighted average of the expected returns of the underlying assets.

$$\bar{k}_p = \sum_{i=1}^{n} w_i \bar{k}_i \tag{1}$$

where $\bar{k}_p$ = expected rate of return of the portfolio
w_i = proportion of the total dollar value of the portfolio that is represented by asset i, that is, the weight of asset i
$\bar{k}_i$ = expected rate of return of asset i
n = total number of assets in the portfolio

The expected return of each asset is a subjective determination that relies on probability distributions of future returns under certain circumstances. The subjective probabilities of these returns are then used to arrive at the expected return of the asset.

$$\bar{k}_p = \sum_{s=1}^{M} p_s k_{is} \tag{2}$$

where p_s = probability of state of nature s
k_{is} = rate of return of asset i in state of nature s
M = total number of states of nature

Another way to compute expected return is to use the historical average rate of return of an individual asset as a proxy for the future return. This approach is valid only if the average of past returns is believed to be an unbiased estimator of future returns.

Portfolio Variance

The variance of a portfolio is a function of the variability and covariability of the underlying assets.

$$\sigma_p^2 = \sum_{i=1}^{n} \sum_{j=1}^{n} w_i w_j \sigma_i \sigma_j r_{i,j} \tag{3}$$

where σ_p^2 = variance of return of the portfolio
σ_i = standard deviation of return of asset i
$r_{i,j}$ = correlation coefficient of the returns of assets i and j.

Notice that the variability of each underlying asset σ is only one of the determinants of portfolio variance. The weight of each underlying asset w also contributes to total portfolio variance.

Portfolio variance is not merely the weighted average of the individual variances. The *correlation coefficients* among the assets determine the degree to which diversification reduces overall portfolio risk.

Correlation coefficient:
A measure of the degree to which the returns of two assets move together.[3]

The value of a correlation coefficient can range from 1 to -1. A correlation coefficient of 1 means that the returns of two assets move in identical ways. If $r_{i,j} = 1$, combining assets i and j does nothing to reduce total variability of the portfolio vis-à-vis the individual assets. These assets i and j are perfectly positively correlated.

Conversely, a correlation coefficient of -1 means that returns of the two assets move in opposite directions. When one asset performs poorly, the other compensates by performing well. When the two are perfectly negatively correlated, or $r_{i,j} = -1$, a portfolio with *zero variance* can be constructed.

To see this relationship, consider Equation 3 in the case of a two-asset portfolio.

$$\sigma_p^2 = \sum_{i=1}^{2} \sum_{j=1}^{2} w_i w_j \sigma_i \sigma_j r_{i,j} \tag{4}$$

[3] $r_{i,j} = [\text{cov}(k_i, k_j)]/(\sigma_i \sigma_j)$ where cov (k_i, k_j) equals covariance of returns of assets i and j.

$$= w_1^2\sigma_1^2 + w_2^2\sigma_2^2 + 2w_1w_2\sigma_1\sigma_2r_{1,2}$$

The portfolio variance reduces to three terms.[4] The first two are variance terms, the third is a covariance term. For a two-asset portfolio, the standard deviation is the square root of Equation 4.

$$\sigma_p = [w_1^2\sigma_1^2 + w_2^2\sigma_2^2 + 2\, w_1w_2\, \sigma_1\sigma_2r_{1,2}]^{1/2} \tag{5}$$

Notice that if $r_{1,2} = 1$, the portfolio standard deviation is simply the weighted average of the standard deviations of the underlying assets.[5]

$$\sigma_p = w_1\sigma_1 + w_2\sigma_2 \tag{6}$$

In other words, there is no reduction in overall portfolio variability if perfectly positively correlated assets are combined.

On the other hand, if $r_{1,2} = -1$, portfolio variance is the *difference* of the weighted average standard deviations of individual assets.[6]

$$\sigma_p = w_1\sigma_1 - w_2\sigma_2 \tag{7}$$

In this case, a portfolio can be constructed to produce portfolio standard deviation of *zero,* that is, no variance and no risk. This is accomplished by setting σ_p equal to 0, substituting $1 - w_1$ for w_2, and solving for w_1.[7]

Virtually all investment securities reflect, to some extent, the impact of economywide influences. There are not likely to be any perfectly negatively correlated assets. Instead, within a given country, most asset returns will be mildly positively correlated.

This means that the theoretical *maximum* benefits of diversification, that is, zero portfolio variance, are not achievable. Yet as long as assets are not perfectly positively correlated, *some measure* of diversification benefit is possible. Outside national borders, it may even be possible to identify assets or groups of assets with mildly negative correlations.

Correlations of Selected Stock Markets

Exhibit 5-11 shows the correlation coefficients of ten stock markets for the 5 years ended 1989, comparing the three largest stock markets in the developed countries (Japan, the

[4] $\sigma_p^2 = w_1w_1\sigma_1\sigma_1r_{1,1} + w_1w_2\sigma_1\sigma_2r_{1,2} + w_2w_1\sigma_2\sigma_1r_{2,1} + w_2w_2\sigma_2\sigma_2r_{2,2}$

$= w_1^2\sigma_1^2\,(1) + 2w_1w_2\sigma_1\sigma_2r_{1,2} + w_2^2\sigma_2^2\,(1)$

$= w_1^2\sigma_1^2 + w_2^2\,\sigma_2^2 + 2w_1w_2\sigma_1\sigma_2r_{1,2}$

[5] $\sigma_p = [w_1^2\sigma_1^2 + w_2^2\,\sigma_2^2 + 2w_1w_2\sigma_1\sigma_2\,(1)]^{1/2}$

$= [(w_1\sigma_1 + w_2\sigma_2)^2]^{1/2}$

$= w_1\sigma_1 + w_2\sigma_2$

[6] $\sigma_p = [w_1^2\sigma_1^2 + w_2^2\sigma_2^2 + 2w_1w_2\sigma_1\sigma_2\,(-1)]^{1/2}$

$= [w_1^2\sigma_1^2 + w_2^2\sigma_2^2 - 2w_1w_2\sigma_1\sigma_2]^{1/2}$

$= [(w_1\sigma_1 - w_2\sigma_2)^2]^{1/2}$

$= w_1\sigma_1 - w_2\sigma_2$

[7] $\sigma_p = w_1\sigma_1 - w_2\sigma_2$

$= w_1\sigma_1 - (1 - w_1)\sigma_2$

$= w_1\sigma_1 - (1)\sigma_2 + w_1\sigma_2$

$= w_1\sigma_1 + w_1\sigma_2 - \sigma_2$

$= w_1(\sigma_1 + \sigma_2) - \sigma_2$

Setting $\sigma_p = 0$, $w_1 = \sigma_2/(\sigma_1 + \sigma_2)$

EXHIBIT 5-11 STOCK MARKET CORRELATION COEFFICIENTS FOR 5 YEARS ENDED 1989

	Japan	U.S.	U.K.	Taiwan	Korea	Brazil	Malaysia	Thailand	India	Mexico
Developed										
Japan	1.00									
U.S.	0.13	1.00								
U.K.	0.00	0.76	1.00							
Emerging										
Taiwan	0.05	0.09	0.18	1.00						
Korea	0.17	0.28	0.18	−0.20	1.00					
Brazil	0.05	0.03	0.02	0.02	0.18	1.00				
Malaysia	0.14	0.52	0.59	0.15	20.04	0.06	1.00			
Thailand	0.03	0.30	0.46	0.50	20.21	20.05	0.48	1.00		
India	20.04	20.03	20.06	20.05	20.03	20.04	20.03	20.04	1.00	
Mexico	0.14	0.34	0.36	0.41	0.12	20.10	0.38	0.43	0.02	1.00

Source: International Finance Corporation, *Emerging Stock Markets Factbook,* 1990.

United States, and the United Kingdom) with the seven emerging markets. Note that the three developed markets have positive correlations with a U.S./U.K. correlation of 0.76. The Japanese market shows much weaker correlations with the other two, suggesting that during the period there were potentially significant diversification benefits to be gained by combining investments in the U.S. or U.K. market with Japanese investments.

In some cases, the emerging markets showed high positive correlation with other markets. For example, the correlation of the Malaysian market with U.S. and U.K. markets was over 0.50. In other cases, however, negative correlations can be observed. For example, returns on the Indian stock market were negatively correlated with the returns of almost every other market included in the exhibit. The only exception is Mexico, with a small positive correlation of 0.02.

The Capital Asset Pricing Model (Exhibit 5-12) suggests that assets which have small positive and negative correlations with other assets can reduce the rate of return that is required of them, that is, make them attractive additions to asset portfolios. This brief review of correlation coefficients indicates how international financial markets present diversification opportunities.

EXHIBIT 5-12 THE THEORY OF PORTFOLIO DIVERSIFICATION AND ASSET PRICING

In pricing risky assets, the variance of an asset alone is not sufficient to estimate an appropriate required rate of return. Instead, the manner in which the asset returns covary with other assets is important. To determine optimal combinations of risk and return, this might suggest that an investor must analyze all possible asset combinations. However, the Capital Asset Pricing Model (CAPM) suggests that this is not necessary.

The assumptions of CAPM are:

1 All investors are single-period, risk-averse utility maximizers.
2 There are no taxes or transactions costs.
3 There exists a risk-free asset that earns a positive rate of return.
4 All investors have homogeneous expectations with respect to the expected returns and variances of all assets.
5 All investors may borrow or lend at the risk-free rate of return.

Under these assumptions, there is one portfolio that dominates the others. This portfolio is the market portfolio of risky assets. All investors will select this

(*continued on next page*)

portfolio in some combination with the risk-free asset, the exact combination depending on individual risk preferences. In the CAPM framework, the appropriate measure of risk for an individual asset is the way it covaries with the market portfolio, not its variance, nor the way that it covaries with any other asset. The β (beta) is the measure of covariance with the market portfolio. The Security Market Line (SML) suggests that the minimum-required rate of return for a risky asset is the risk-free rate plus a risk premium that is based on the asset's β.

$$k_i = k_{rf} + \beta_i (k_m - k_{rf})$$

where k_i = the minimum required rate of return for risky asset i
k_{rf} = risk-free rate of return
k_m = expected rate of return of the market portfolio
β_i = beta of asset i, the ratio of the covariance of k_i and k_m to the variance of market return, or cov $(k_i, k_m)/\sigma_m^2$
$\beta i(k_m - k_{rf})$ = risk premium for asset i

The correlation coefficient of asset i with the market portfolio r_{im} is also determined by its covariance with the market portfolio:

$$r_{im} = \text{cov}\ (k_i, k_m)/\sigma_i \sigma_m$$

Solve for the covariance

$$(r_{im})(\sigma_i \sigma_m) = \text{cov}\ (k_i, k_m)$$

and substitute this definition of covariance into the formula for β;

$$\beta_i = (r_{im})(\sigma_i \sigma_m)/\sigma_m^2$$
$$= (r_{im})(\sigma_i)/\sigma_m$$

Thus, the smaller the correlation coefficient of k_i with k_m, the smaller the β and the required risk premium.

CAPM has clear implications for domestic security markets. Also, in examining the stock markets of different countries, the small (sometimes negative) correlation coefficients that can be observed suggest that significant benefits may be obtainable through international portfolio diversification.

Fama, Eugene F. "Risk, Return, and Equilibrium: Some Clarifying Comments," *Journal of Finance,* vol. 23, March 1968, pp. 29–40.
Lintner, John. "Security Prices, Risk, and Maximal Gains from Diversification," *Journal of Finance,* vol. 20, December 1965, pp. 587–615.
Markowitz, Harry. "Portfolio Selection," *Journal of Finance,* vol. 7, March 1952, pp. 77–91.
Sharpe, William F. "Capital Asset Prices: A Theory of Market Equilibrium under Conditions of Risk," *Journal of Finance,* vol. 19, September 1964, pp. 425–442.

SUMMARY

Capital markets bring surplus savings units together with deficit savings units. Securities are sold for the first time in primary markets. In the United States, this process involves investment bankers that assume the risk of selling and distributing the stocks and bonds issued by corporations and government bodies. While commercial banks in other countries perform this function, U.S. commercial banks are largely precluded from doing so.

During the late 1980s U.S. state and local governments and corporations raised large sums of capital through public offerings of bonds. Nevertheless, U.S. corporations generally finance more of their assets with equity than corporations in other industrialized countries. In Germany and Japan, for example, bank loans have had a much larger role than equity in corporate finance.

Once issued, securities are traded among investors on secondary markets. In the United States, the New York Stock Exchange dominates all the others in terms of the value of traded securities.

Derivative securities are generally not issued by corporations and government bodies. They are, instead, agreements to exchange existing financial securities at some time in the future. Futures and options contracts are traded on organized exchanges, with the largest market in the United States. This market has now expanded vigorously to include contracts on stock indexes which have no underlying security. Swap contracts are also a growing part of U.S. capital markets. Derivative securities markets are also developing in other industrialized countries.

In fact, growth in Asian stock markets has been so strong in the last few years that the capitalization of the Japanese market now exceeds that of the United States. Growth in Pacific Rim economies promises to continue to challenge the dominance in world capital markets that the United States has enjoyed for half a century.

International financial markets will likely continue to grow because they offer diversification possibilities that are not readily available in domestic markets. Some of the larger emerging stock markets have particular potential because they have weak or negative correlations with the U.S. market. As national markets continue to liberalize policies governing foreign involvement, these benefits should be easier to realize.

KEY TERMS

asset portfolio
best efforts agreement
capital markets
common stock
correlation coefficient
derivative securities
diversification
firm commitment
futures contract
investment bank
margin call
marking to market
merchant bank
National Association of Securities Dealers
option contract
organized stock exchange
OTC market
primary capital markets
secondary capital markets
Securities and Exchange Commission
underwriter's discount
underwriting
underwriting syndicate

END-OF-CHAPTER QUESTIONS

1. In the United States, what is the difference between a commercial banker and an investment banker?
2. With respect to corporate finance,
   a. Discuss the relative importance of debt and equity for firms in the United States, Japan, and Germany.
   b. Explain some of the factors that have led to these differences.
3. Describe two types of services that investment bankers perform for their clients.
4. The SEC does not attest to the value of a new security issue. Why, then, does the SEC require that the issuer prepare a prospectus?
5. In financial circles, the 1980s is sometimes referred to as the "go-go 80s." Why do you suppose that this phrase was coined?

6. With respect to options, define:
   a. Strike price
   b. Option premium
7. In both secondary and derivative securities market trading, corporations and governments receive no additional funds for investment. Does this mean that the activity in both markets is irrelevant from a corporate financial management standpoint?
8. How does a commercial bank differ from a merchant bank?
9. How does the role of banks in securities markets differ in other countries as compared with the United States?
10. Why would an investment banker organize an underwriting syndicate if the banker could make more profit by handling the new security issue alone?
11. What do you believe has driven the large increases in stock market capitalization in Asian countries in recent years?
12. Referring to a recent edition of the *Wall Street Journal,* select a traded option quotation and identify the maturity date, the strike price, and the option premium.
13. When is it profitable for the buyer of a call option to exercise the option?
14. When is it profitable for the buyer of a put option to exercise the option?
15. What is the difference between a currency swap and an interest rate swap?
16. When might it be advisable to enter into a swap with optionlike payoffs?
17. Do you think that the reduced importance of U.S. markets in world finance can affect this country's standard of living? Why or why not?
18. As national financial markets become more open to cross-border investment, what impact might there be on the stock market correlations in Exhibit 5-11?
19. When constructing an asset portfolio, why is the variance of an individual asset not the most important measure of risk?
20. Describe the diversification benefits that may be derived when combining assets with a correlation coefficient of 1.
21. Referring to Exhibit 5-11, which emerging markets appear to have the most diversification benefits for an American investor?
22. Would you expect the correlations among various currencies to be stronger or weaker than the correlations among stock markets? Why or why not?
23. Suppose that two assets A and B have a perfect negative correlation, or $r_{AB} = -1$. The expected returns and standard deviations of return for these assets are as follows:

	A	B
Expected return	0.10	0.15
Standard deviation	0.02	0.07

   a. What combination of these assets will cause the portfolio variance to equal zero?
   b. What would be the expected return of this portfolio?

SELECTED REFERENCES

Brown, Keith C., and Donald J. Smith. "Forward Swaps, Swap Options, and the Management of Callable Debt," *New Developments in Commercial Banking,* Donald Chew, editor, Blackwell Publishers, Cambridge, Massachusetts, 1991, pp. 260–272.

Clarke, William M. *How the City of London Works; An Introduction to Its Financial Markets,* Waterlow Publishers, London, 1986.

Cohen, Jerome B., Edward D. Zinbarg, and Arthur Zeikel. *Investment Analysis and Portfolio Management,* 5th edition, Richard D. Irwin, Inc., Homewood, Illinois, 1987.

Comparative Economic and Financial Statistics; Japan and Other Major Countries, Bank of Japan, Tokyo, 1988.

Emerging Stock Markets Factbook 1990, International Finance Corporation, Washington, D.C., 1990.

Falkena, H. B., L. J. Fourie, and W. J. Kok, Editors. *The Mechanics of the South African Financial System; Financial Institutions, Instruments, and Markets,* Macmillan South Africa, Johannesburg, 1984.

Francke, Hans-Hermann, and Michael Hudson. *Banking and Finance in West Germany,* Croom Helm Ltd., London, 1984.

Havrilesky, Thomas M., and Robert Schweitzer, Editors. *Contemporary Developments in Financial Institutions and Markets,* Harlan Davidson, Inc., Arlington Heights, Illinois, 1987.

Mayo, Herbert B. *Investments; An Introduction,* Dryden Press, New York, 1984.

McRae, Hamish, and Frances Cairncross. *Capital City; London as a Financial Centre,* Methuen London Ltd., London, 1984.

Nwankwo, G. O. *The Nigerian Financial System,* Africana Publishing Company, New York, 1980.

Onoh, J. K., Editor. *The Foundations of Nigeria's Financial Infrastructure,* Croom Helm Ltd., London, 1980.

Rowley, Anthony. *Asian Stockmarkets; the Inside Story,* Far Eastern Economic Review, Hong Kong, 1987.

Skully, Michael T. *Merchant Banking in Australia,* Oxford University Press, Melbourne, 1987.

Smith, Clifford W., Charles W. Smithson, and L. MacDonald Wakeman. "The Evolving Market for Swaps," *New Dimensions in Commercial Banking,* Donald Chew, editor, Blackwell Publishers, Cambridge, Massachusetts, 1991, pp. 213–225.

U.S. Securities and Exchange Commission. *Internationalization of the Securities Markets; Report to the Senate Committee on Banking, Housing, and Urban Affairs and the House Committee on Energy and Commerce,* July 1987.

Viner, Aron. *Inside Japanese Financial Markets,* Dow Jones-Irwin, Homewood, Illinois, 1988.

CHAPTER 6

FOREIGN CURRENCY EXCHANGE MARKETS

CHAPTER OUTLINE

CHAPTER OVERVIEW

This chapter:

- Explains the need for foreign currency exchange
- Describes types of foreign currency transactions
- Discusses the operation of foreign exchange markets
- Illustrates methods of protecting against foreign exchange risk

Worldwide market reverberations following the U.S. market crash in October 1987 brought home the notion that the world's financial markets are, in fact, one global market. There is no doubt that trends toward financial market deregulation will lead to continuing market integration in the future. American businesspeople need to know much more about international markets in today's competitive environment.

The financial markets that operate across countries are varied in nature and in stage of development. The oldest are currency exchange markets, which operate virtually 24 hours a day because of overlapping time zones in the United States, Asia, and Europe. These efficient markets offer buyer and seller protection against unfavorable exchange rate fluctuations. Foreign exchange swaps, futures, and options are the newer instruments available besides more traditional forward contracts. This chapter describes the products available in and the operation of foreign exchange markets.[1]

FOREIGN CURRENCY EXCHANGE

Foreign currency exchange is fundamental to development of any other cross-border financial markets, and, in fact, foreign currency markets are the most advanced. They make it possible for people in two or more countries to do business together.

Exchange Rate Risk

Normally, a U.S. businessperson who buys a piece of equipment from, say, a German supplier must pay for the purchase in German currency, deutsche marks (DMs). At the time a contract is negotiated (December 31, for example), the cost of the equipment and the published exchange rate are both known, so the buyer can figure today's cost in U.S. dollars. If the cost of the equipment is DM1 million and the exchange rate is $1 = DM2.0020, each DM currently has a dollar value of $0.4995, bringing the total cost of the equipment to $499,500.

DM2.0020	=	$1
DM1	=	$0.4995
DM1,000,000	=	$499,500

Delivery of the equipment, however, is not scheduled until 3 months later (March 31), when payment is due. By that time, the exchange rate undoubtedly will have changed, and the dollar cost of the equipment may be lower or higher than originally anticipated.

Exchange rate risk:
The risk that changes in currency exchange rates may have an unfavorable impact on costs or revenues.

Suppose that the March 31 exchange rate is $1 = DM2.0833. Then the dollar value of the DM is $0.48, and the cost of the equipment falls to $480,000.

DM2.0833	=	$1
DM1	=	$0.4800
DM1,000,000	=	$480,000

In this case, the decline of the dollar value of the DM from $0.4995 to $0.4800 over the 3-month period would save the buyer $19,500 ($499,500 − $480,000). The favorable change in the exchange rate would cause the actual cost to be lower than first estimated.

If the March 31 exchange rate is, instead, $1 = DM1.9231, the equipment would cost more than originally anticipated.

DM1.9231	=	$1
DM1	=	$0.5200
DM1,000,000	=	$520,000

[1]Chapter 9 discusses the factors that influence the level of exchange rates and observed exchange rate patterns. Chapter 7 describes the exchange rate mechanism of the European Community.

The dollar value of the DM would increase from $0.4995 to $0.5200, and the equipment cost would increase by $20,500 ($520,000 − $499,500). Thus, the buyer will suffer economic loss if the dollar value of the DM increases over the 3-month period. The U.S. purchaser of the equipment cannot accurately predict the future exchange rate in the spot (immediate exchange) market, but it is possible to reduce the uncertainty of the future cost of the equipment. The businessperson may limit the downside risk of exchange rate movements through *foreign exchange hedging.*

Foreign exchange hedging:
Using financial contracts to protect against adverse changes in foreign exchange rates.

Contracts that may be used for hedging purposes are:

- Forward
- Swap
- Futures
- Options

Spot Market Exchange

An exchange of dollars for DMs or other currency takes place in the *spot exchange market.*

Spot foreign currency exchange market transaction:
The immediate exchange of currencies in the form of bank deposits, bank notes (money), or traveler's checks. Transactions are over the counter (immediate), unless they involve bank deposits, in which case both parties in the exchange have 2 days to deliver.

Spot transactions can be carried out through foreign exchange divisions of commercial banks or through nonbank foreign currency dealers. If a U.S. buyer decides to purchase DMs through a local bank, this amounts to letting dollars be transferred from the buyer's U.S. bank account to the dollar-denominated bank account of the DM seller. The DMs are transferred simultaneously into a DM account designated by the U.S. buyer either in Germany or in London. (If the DM account is in London, it is a Euromarket account, described in the next chapter.)

While the U.S. businessperson may deal with a local bank, that bank will not necessarily be the other side of the trade. Generally, only the head offices of money center banks or large regional banks make markets in foreign currency, trading for their own account and for their customers. The local bank is likely to contact one of these foreign currency dealers and ask for a price quotation. Quotations have two components—the *bid price* and the *asked price.*

Bid price:
The price that a dealer is willing to pay to purchase foreign currency.

Asked price:
The price at which a dealer will sell foreign currency.

The difference between the two prices is the dealer's profit margin.

If a bank gets a bid-asked quotation of 2.0060–2.0020 DM/$, the bid price of 2.0060

DM/$ means that the dealer will purchase DMs for $0.4985 each.[2] The asked price of 2.0020 DM/$ means that the dealer will sell at the rate of $0.4995 per DM, which yields a profit of $0.0010 per DM. This is the spot (immediate exchange) quotation. For a currency exchange several months in the future, depreciation or appreciation of the dollar value of the DM can significantly affect the prospective settlement price for any purchase.

Forward Exchange

To avoid this exposure to an increase in the dollar value of the DM, the U.S. businessperson can buy a *forward contract* (generally through a bank), thereby removing the uncertainty of currency fluctuations.

Forward foreign currency exchange contract:
An agreement between two parties to exchange foreign currencies at a predetermined rate on a specific date in the future. Two days before the specified date, the forward contract becomes a spot contract.

Forward contracts usually mature 30, 60, or 90 days or 6, 9, or 12 months from the date the contract is written. At the maturity date, currencies are transferred through bank deposits in the large interbank market.[3]

Forward Rate Determination While the advantage of a forward contract is that the purchaser can predetermine the exchange rate, a forward contract is not written at the current spot rate. A currency sells at a *premium* when the forward rate implies a dollar value of the foreign currency higher than the current spot rate. Conversely, the currency sells at a *discount* when the forward rate is lower in dollar terms than the spot rate.

Whether there will be a premium or a discount depends on relative interest rates in the two countries involved. Interest rates come into play because the bank that sells the forward contract will want to "cover" its position at the time the forward contract is written so that the bank is not exposed to adverse currency fluctuations. It does this by placing DMs on deposit when the forward contract is written.

A bank that agrees in December to sell DM1 million at the end of March will make a DM deposit in December that will grow to DM1 million in 3 months. Such a DM deposit is funded by borrowing dollars now and converting them to DMs. All these factors mean that the forward rate that the bank charges the customer will depend on the interest rate available on the DM deposit, the rate of interest on the dollar loan, and the bank's profit margin (which is ignored here in the interest of simplicity).

Exhibit 6-1 shows how the forward rate is determined. Note that the bank need not borrow the full DM1 million because it earns interest on its deposit during the 3-month period. Assuming that the interest rate available on a 3-month DM deposit is 8.5 percent, the bank will deposit DM979,811.57, the present value of DM1 million, at 8.5 percent for 3 months. In order to buy the DMs, the bank borrows the dollar equivalent on the spot market—DM979,811.57(0.4995 $/DM) = $489,415.88.

At an interest rate of 9.75 percent for the dollar loan, the bank's liability in 3 months will be $500,932.48. The bank must receive exactly this dollar amount from its customer in 3 months in exchange for the DM1 million in the maturing deposit. Setting the two amounts equal, the forward rate is 0.5009 $/DM, or DM1.9963 = $1.

[2]DM2.0060 = $1; DM1 = $1/2.0060 = $0.4985

[3]Specific instructions regarding the accounts to be credited are generally not given until time of delivery is close.

Given:

Businessperson wishes to buy DM1 million from bank in 3 months; spot rate = 2.0020 DM/\$; $k_{US} = 0.0975$; $k_{WG} = 0.0850$.

Procedure for bank to establish forward rate:

1 Determine the number of DMs necessary to deposit now in order to have DM1 million in 3 months.

$$\text{DM}1{,}000{,}000/(1.0850)^{.25} = \text{DM}979{,}811.57$$

2 Borrow the required dollars to finance this deposit.

$$\begin{aligned} \text{DM}2.0020 &= \$1 \\ \text{DM}1 &= \$0.4995 \\ \text{DM}979{,}811.57 &= \$489{,}415.88 \end{aligned}$$

3 Determine dollar liability in 3 months.

$$\$489{,}415.88(1.0975)^{.25} = \$500{,}932.48$$

4 Set dollar liability equal to DM proceeds in 3 months to determine appropriate forward exchange rate.

$$\begin{aligned} \text{DM}1{,}000{,}000 &= \$500{,}932.48 \\ \text{DM}1 &= \$0.5009 \text{ or} \\ \text{DM}1.9963 &= \$1 \end{aligned}$$

In general:

$$[X/(1 + k_{FC})^n] \text{ (spot rate) } [(1 + k_{US})^n] = X \text{ (forward rate)}$$

where X = foreign currency to be received

$X/(1 + k_{FC})^n$ = foreign currency borrowed

spot rate, forward rate = dollars per unit of foreign currency

k_{FC}, k_{US} = appropriate interest rates in foreign currency and dollars, respectively

Dividing both sides by X, the foreign currency to be received, and rearranging the terms produces the relationship

$$\text{(spot rate) } [(1 + k_{US})^n/(1 + k_{FC})^n] = \text{forward rate}$$

At this forward rate, the cost of the German equipment for the U.S. businessperson is \$500,900.

$$\begin{aligned} \text{DM}1 &= \$0.5009 \\ \text{DM}1{,}000{,}000 &= \$500{,}900 \end{aligned}$$

The cost is \$1400 higher than that implied by the current spot rate, but at least it is known with certainty in advance.

In this case, the forward dollar value of the DM (\$0.5009) is higher than the spot value (\$0.4995). The DM is selling at a forward premium; that is, its dollar forward value exceeds its dollar spot value. The dollar is selling at a forward discount; its DM forward value (DM1.9963) is less than its DM spot value (DM2.0020). These relationships are dictated by interest rate differentials. The relationship illustrated here among forward, spot, and interest rates is called *interest rate parity.*

Interest rate parity:
A concept indicating that interest rate differentials are reflected in the forward exchange rates of two currencies.

Referring again to Exhibit 6-1, note that the general equation reduces to

$$FR = SR(1 + k_{US})^n/(1 + k_{FC})^n \tag{1}$$

where FR = forward rate (dollars per unit of foreign currency)
SR = spot rate (dollars per unit of foreign currency)
k = appropriate interest rate
n = number of periods before contract maturity

If interest rates in the United States and a foreign country are the same, the forward rate will equal the spot rate (again ignoring any bank fees). If the U.S. interest rate exceeds the foreign interest rate, the forward dollar value of the foreign currency will exceed the spot dollar value; that is, the forward rate will be higher than the spot rate, as is the case in the dollar–deutsche mark example. The converse is true when the interest rate relationships are reversed.

As the term of a forward contract increases, the difference between actual forward rates and the forward rates determined by Equation 1 generally increases. Even so, the forward contract is a valuable means of reducing exchange rate risk because it removes uncertainty.

Other Forward Contracts Forward currency contracts can take forms other than the standard forward contract. Two alternative forms are:

- Option-date forward contracts
- Forward forward contracts

For firms that are not sure when a foreign currency transaction will occur, an *option-date forward contract* may be appropriate. These contracts are similar to standard forward contracts except that the maturity date of the contract is not a specific predetermined date. The contract gives the buyer the option to settle the transaction at any time within a specified period, which may be from the date of the agreement (spot) to some future date or between two future dates. The bank that writes (sells) the contract is exposed throughout the entire period, during which several spot rates may apply, so it sets the forward rate at the least favorable level for the contract buyer.

If both the transaction for which the currency is needed and the foreign currency cash flow are in the future, a *forward forward contract* may be appropriate, especially if the foreign currency is expected to appreciate in the future. Assume, for example, a U.S. businessperson intends to place an equipment order in Germany 2 months from now (end of February), with invoice payment due 1 month after that (end of March). If the mark appreciates in the meantime, the buyer still is exposed to a higher dollar cost for the equipment.

To cover this exchange exposure, the buyer could arrange forward contracts that will lock in the exchange rate only for the future 1 month of exposure between order placement date and invoice due date. This arrangement reduces the cost of the forward protection. To cover exposure for the month of March, the U.S. businessperson buys DM1 million 3 months forward (December 31 to March 31) and sells the same number of DMs 2 months forward (December 31 to February 28). The contracts will offset each other in January and February, with effectively no open DM position during these 2 months.

A bank determines the 2-month forward rate in much the same way as the 3-month rate. The difference is that the bank agrees to buy (not sell) DM1 million from the businessperson at the end of February. Exhibit 6-2 shows how the rate is determined. In this case, the bank borrows the present value of DM1 million since this is the amount of foreign currency that it will receive in 2 months. The DMs are converted into dollars, and the dollars are invested for 2 months.

A forward forward contract provides protection against adverse changes in exchange rates at less cost than a standard forward contract. The dollar value of a DM under the standard forward contract is \$0.5009. The spot value is \$0.4995, so the cost to the businessperson is \$0.0014 per DM, or a total of \$1400. Under the forward forward arrangement, the businessperson's cost is the difference between the 3-month rate at which DMs are bought (\$0.5009) and the 2-month rate at which they are sold (\$0.50045)—a difference of \$0.00045 per DM, which reduces total cost to \$450.

EXHIBIT 6-2 FORWARD FORWARD RATE DETERMINATION

The bank agrees to buy DMs from the businessperson at the end of February in exchange for dollars.

1 Since the bank will receive DMs at the end of February, it borrows the present value of the DMs and converts them to dollars.

$$\text{DM}1{,}000{,}000/(1.085)^{60/360} = \text{DM}986{,}495.35$$

2 At the spot rate of \$0.4995 per DM, the proceeds are \$492,754.43.

$$(0.4995\ \$/\text{DM})(\text{DM}986{,}495.35) = \$492{,}754.43$$

3 This dollar amount is deposited into a dollar account paying 9.75 percent that grows to \$500,454.53 in 2 months.

$$\$492{,}754.43\ [(1.0975)^{60/360}] = \$500{,}454.53$$

4 At the end of February, the bank will exchange this amount for the DM1 million from the corporate client and use the DM1 million to repay the 2-month DM loan. The projected \$500,454.53 balance is set equal to DM1,000,000.

$$\begin{aligned} \text{DM}1{,}000{,}000 &= \$500{,}454.535 \\ \text{DM}1 &= \$0.50045 \text{ or} \\ \text{DM}1.9982 &= \$1 \end{aligned}$$

The dollar value per DM is \$0.50045; that is, the 2-month forward exchange rate is DM1.9982 = \$1.

The businessperson buys DMs today at $0.4995, sells them 2 months forward at $0.50045, and buys them 3 months forward at $0.5009. The cost of the DM1 million equipment is the net of these.

Buy today	($499,500.00)
Sell 2 months forward	500,454.53
Buy 3 months forward	(500,900.00)
Net	($499,945.47)

This is less than $500 above the current cost of the equipment.

Currency Swaps

Another way to manage foreign exchange exposure is through *currency swaps,* which include both spot and forward transactions in one agreement. Like forward contracts, swaps are generally customized transactions.

Foreign currency swap:
An exchange of foreign currency in the spot market with a simultaneous agreement to reverse the transaction in the forward market. Both exchange rates and timing of the forward market transaction are specified at the time of the swap.

Multinational firms and banks use swaps to correct imbalances between their foreign currency assets and liabilities. A multinational firm, for example, may have a German subsidiary which has a temporary shortage of DMs that it expects to be corrected with cash inflows in 2 months. If, at the same time, the parent company has a dollar surplus, it can swap its dollars for DMs with a third party for 2 months and lend the marks to the subsidiary. At the end of the 2-month period, the subsidiary repays the DM loan to the parent, and the parent delivers the DMs to the third party in the swap transaction in exchange for dollars.

The Use of Swaps Commercial banks make extensive use of swaps. Those with international operations may make foreign currency loans, whose value will be influenced by exchange rate volatility. A U.S. bank can arrange financing for a German subsidiary of a U.S. firm that needs to borrow DM1 million for 3 months. If the bank funds the loan simply by buying marks on the spot market, there is a risk that the dollar value of the DM may decline (that is, that the DM may depreciate) in the interim, leaving the bank with a loan that is worth less in dollar terms.

As an example, assume the spot rate goes from the current DM2.0020 = $1 to DM2.2000 = $1 in 3 months. The face value of the loan then drops from $499,500 to $454,545, a $44,955 difference that represents a 31.4 percent annual loss $[(454{,}545/499{,}500)^4 - 1 = -0.314]$.

To protect the loan portfolio from exchange risk, the bank can swap the marks. The DM purchase to fund the loan may be made in the spot market, but the forward leg of the swap agreement locks in the price at which the bank can sell the DMs when its client repays the loan.

Another time an international bank faces exchange rate risk is when it accepts foreign currency deposits. An excess of DM deposits over DM loans exposes a bank to foreign currency loss if the dollar value of the foreign currency increases (that is, the foreign currency appreciates). If this happens, more dollars will be required to pay off the deposits in the future than are currently necessary. Assume (1) that excess deposits are accepted when the exchange rate is DM2.0020 = \$1, maturing in 3 months, and (2) that the mark appreciates to DM1.850 = \$1 (\$0.5405 per DM) during the 3 months until maturity. If the excess deposits are DM1 million, the net DM deposits will increase by the difference in the exchange rate times the excess amount, without any increase in bank assets, and the bank sustains a \$41,000 foreign currency loss that reduces bank capital [(\$0.4995 − \$0.5405)(1,000,000)].

To avoid this, the appropriate swap for the bank is to buy DMs in the spot market and sell them in the 3-month forward market so that the excess DM deposits are offset by additional DM assets. If the mark appreciates now, any appreciation will affect both assets and liabilities to the same extent.

If the imbalance is an excess of DM assets, perhaps DMs and short-term DM loans, the reverse is true. The bank should sell DMs in the spot market and repurchase them in the forward market.

Swap Rates Swap rates have a consistent relationship with spot and forward rates. To see this relationship, consider the combination of (1) buying a foreign currency in the spot market and (2) entering a swap arrangement to sell the currency now and repurchase it in the future. This is equivalent to buying a standard forward contract to purchase the currency in the future. Thus, the net of the spot purchase price and the swap rates (for spot sale and forward purchase) forms a floor below the forward purchase rate.

Spot (purchase) + swap (spot sale, forward purchase) = forward floor (purchase)

In the same sense, entering a swap to buy currency now (to sell it later) and immediately selling the proceeds of this swap purchase in the spot market is equivalent to a standard forward contract to sell. The forward selling rate should not exceed the net of the swap rates (for spot purchase and forward sale) and the spot selling rate. Thus, the net spot and swap rates form a ceiling for the forward exchange rate.

Spot (sale) + swap (spot purchase, forward sale) = forward ceiling (sale)

Foreign Exchange Futures

Foreign exchange futures contracts represent a more standardized method of protection from exchange rate risk than forward contracts or swaps, which are usually individualized transactions. Like forward contracts, *foreign exchange futures* are agreements to purchase or sell currency in the future.

Foreign currency exchange futures contract:
A contract, traded on organized exchanges in standard units, to exchange two currencies at some specified future date. The party purchasing the contract agrees to purchase foreign currency on the specified date. The party selling the contract agrees to sell the currency at that date.

Unlike forward contracts, futures are traded on an organized exchange. The units of underlying currency are standardized, and the time of delivery likewise is set at one of four particular dates (the third Wednesday of March, June, September, or December). With contracts traded on exchanges, of course, it is possible to buy or sell a futures contract at any time.[4]

The futures market can provide the same kind of protection from adverse exchange rate fluctuations that is available through the forward market. The U.S. buyer who needs

[4]Chapter 5 discusses the general operation of futures markets and specific contracts for interest rate and stock index futures.

DM1 million in 3 months to make an equipment purchase in Germany could buy futures contracts instead. Each exchange-traded DM futures contract is for DM125,000, so eight of them would be needed. Assume that it is currently the end of December and that the March futures contract is selling at the 3-month forward rate developed earlier—0.5009 \$/DM—for a total purchase price of \$500,900. Assume also that in the third week of March the spot rate is DM1.800 = \$1, or 0.5556 \$/DM. The futures buyer in this case can either accept delivery of the DM1 million at the spot rate or sell eight futures contracts to close the position and buy the DMs through a bank for settlement 2 days later (closer to the date that the currency will be needed). The economic effect is essentially the same in either case.

Exhibit 6-3 summarizes the gains and losses for spot versus futures market transactions. The spot market loss is \$56,100, and the futures market gain is \$54,700. The net loss is \$1400, the same cost of using the forward hedge illustrated earlier.

While the two methods appear to be interchangeable, these results are obtained because the 3-month forward rate on December 31 and the March futures price as of December 31 were identical. If this had not been the case, the results would have been dif-

EXHIBIT 6-3 FUTURES MARKET HEDGE

Dec. 31

U.S. businessperson orders equipment for delivery and payment in 3 months. Equipment will cost DM1 million. The spot rate is DM2.002 = \$1 (0.4995 \$/DM). The March futures contract is selling at DM1.9963 = \$1 (0.5009 \$/DM), the 3-month forward rate. The businessperson purchases eight contracts to cover the future foreign currency needs.

8 contracts × 125,000 DM/contract × 0.5009 \$/DM = \$500,900

March

The DM has appreciated to DM1.800 = \$1. The businessperson sells eight DM futures contracts, now selling at the spot rate, to settle the open position. The loss in the spot market is almost completely offset by the gain in the futures market.

Spot market	
Original estimate of equipment cost	
DM1,000,000 × 0.4995 \$/DM	\$499,500
Actual cost	
DM1,000,000 × 0.5556 \$/DM	(555,600)
Loss	(\$ 56,100)
Futures market	
Sale of eight DM contracts	
8 × DM125,000 × 0.5556 \$/DM	\$555,600
Purchase price of DM contracts	(500,900)
Gain	\$ 54,700

ferent. Moreover, expenses associated with the two methods are not necessarily equal. Forward contract charges (bank fees) tend to be less than futures contract costs (stockbroker commissions). Lastly, the margin required for a futures contract can create an opportunity cost while funds are on deposit.

At the same time, a futures contract provides more flexibility than the typical forward contract, because a futures contract may be disposed of at any time, while the forward contract is typically held until maturity. Futures contracts also are traded in relatively small denominations, so they may be more accessible for small investors and businesses than forward contracts.

Foreign Exchange Options

Foreign exchange options are relatively new vehicles to protect against adverse exchange rate fluctuations.

Foreign currency exchange option:
A contract that confers the right to buy or sell foreign currency at a specified price through some future date. This right is exercisable at the discretion of the option buyer.

Like futures, currency options are traded on organized exchanges and are guaranteed by the exchange on which they trade. Just as in the domestic options market, a foreign currency *call option* entitles the buyer to purchase the currency. The seller (writer) is obligated to sell. A foreign currency *put option* gives the buyer the right to sell the currency back to the writer.[5]

The purchase of an option is an appropriate choice when an international transaction depends on a contingency. If a U.S. company's plan to purchase German equipment for DM1 million depends on winning a competitive bid for a contract, its need for DMs would then be contingent on the outcome of the bidding. An options contract at a given strike price assures the U.S. company that it may purchase DMs at a known price, but does not obligate it to do so. For instance, with the spot rate at 0.4995 $/DM, the buyer may purchase call option contracts of DM62,500 each with a strike (exercise) price of 0.5150 $/DM for 0.0075 $/DM. Sixteen contracts (representing DM1 million) at $468.75 each would be needed for a total of $7500.[6]

Even if the company wins the competitive bid and orders the equipment, it would not necessarily exercise its call options. They would be exercised only if the spot rate were to rise higher than the strike price 0.5150 $/DM (DM1.9417 = $1), say, to 0.5556 $/DM. In this case, the DM1 million would then cost $522,500 [(DM1,000,000 × 0.515 $/DM) + $7,500]. This is less than the $555,600 cost that otherwise would have been paid on the spot market at that exchange rate (DM1,000,000 × 0.5556 $/DM). Of course, the $7500 call option premium must be paid in any event.

It is also possible to purchase an *option on a foreign currency exchange futures contract.* In this case, an option buyer has the right to buy or sell a currency futures contract. Futures option contracts are denominated in the same number of currency units as the corresponding futures contracts, and the market operates in much the same way as the regular options market. Futures options can be used to protect an actual asset or liability position against adverse currency fluctuations. For example, the firm that will need DM1 million only if it wins a contract may purchase options on currency futures contracts.

[5]Domestic options markets and instruments are discussed in Chapter 5.

[6] DM1,000,000/(62,500 DM/contract) = 16 contracts
(62,500 DM/contract) × (0.0075 $/DM) = $468.75/contract
(16 contracts) × $468.75/contract = $7500

With both regular or futures options, if favorable currency fluctuations occur instead of adverse ones, the options need not be exercised. The buyer can take advantage of the full benefit of the favorable exchange rate changes (net of the cost of the options).

THE OPERATION OF FOREIGN EXCHANGE MARKETS

Spot and Forward Markets

Spot currency transactions are conducted for the most part in special divisions of major commercial banks. Small banks and local offices of major banks typically maintain lines of credit with these larger banks or with their own head office for foreign exchange. An interesting feature of the market is that foreign currency trades almost always involve the U.S. dollar even if the desired trade is, say, deutsche marks for Swiss francs. In this case, the first transaction will be an exchange of DMs for dollars, followed by an exchange of dollars for Swiss francs. The U.S. dollar has assumed the role of an intermediary currency that is used to correct potential imbalances between supply and demand for any two other currencies. Because U.S. dollar markets are so firmly established, the transactions cost of trading in the dollar market is also lower than the cost of trading in nondollar markets.

Currency traders are often located in one large room at a bank, where each trader has access to several telephones, video screens, and news tapes. A trader generally specializes in one or a small number of currencies, communicating with other traders at banks around the world. Interbank transactions are in wholesale denominations of $1 million or more. An unusually large currency exchange may be facilitated by a broker working on a commission basis with several banks. Long-standing business relationships and preestablished lines of credit allow both sides of a trade to make firm commitments over the telephone.

The foreign exchange market operates 24 hours a day in different time zones around the world. When the New York market closes at 5 P.M., the San Francisco market is still open. At 8 P.M., New York time, the San Francisco market closes, and the Tokyo market opens. An hour later (9 P.M., New York time), the Hong Kong and Singapore markets open. At 3 A.M. Tokyo closes, but Frankfurt opens. An hour later (4 A.M., New York time), Hong Kong and Singapore close, and London opens. Continuous operation and almost instantaneous, firm commitments via telephone make the foreign exchange market one of the most efficient in the world.

The *forward* contracts market is also primarily an interbank market. Lines of credit between the participants may be exhausted while the forward position is open, but there is usually no cash deposit required. Large and creditworthy corporations can trade for themselves in the interbank market, but it is more common for such firms to have a bank operate as their agent.

Swap Market

Banks are also important participants in the currency *swap* market, making markets in swaps and carrying swap inventories. A bank's foreign currency swap activity is typically half that of its spot transactions business. Forward contracts occupy a distant third place, representing less than 5 percent of total volume.

In recent years, nonfinancial firms of different countries have begun to engage in swap arrangements in lieu of purchasing forward contracts. A U.S. firm that temporarily needs foreign currency, for example, may swap with a foreign firm operating in the United States and needing dollars temporarily. Such a foreign firm often can raise funds more easily at home (in its own domestic currency) than in the United States. Once a foreign firm has borrowed funds at home, it can then exchange the proceeds for dollars from the U.S. firm. The two parties agree to reverse the transaction at a future date.

Exhibit 6-4 shows the breakdown in outstanding swap agreements by currency in 1987 and 1988. The rise in total swap agreements from $182.8 billion to $316.8 billion helps illustrate the dimension of this market and growth in the use of these instruments. Note that the U.S. dollar dominated the market during these 2 years (representing over 40 percent of the total) but that the Japanese yen increased its share from 16.3 percent in 1987 to 20.7 percent in 1988. The German mark and the British pound follow in terms of market share, together making up less than 10 percent of outstanding swaps during 1987 and 1988. These four currencies are also among the most actively traded in other currency markets, including the futures and options markets.

Futures Market

Commodity futures for physical assets that help assure merchants and vendors of needed supplies are the precursors of financial futures contracts. The first *currency futures* contracts were not traded in the United States until 1975 when the Chicago Mercantile Exchange (CME) established the International Monetary Market (IMM), in which the most broadly traded currencies are represented. Currencies are also traded on the Midamerican Commodity Exchange in Chicago.

Futures markets in other countries have since opened. In 1980 the Sydney Futures Exchange established operations followed, 2 years later, by the London International Financial Futures Exchange (LIFFE). In 1984 the Singapore Monetary Exchange (SIMEX) commenced operations with a link to the Chicago Mercantile Exchange. The volume of trading on futures markets has shown significant growth at least partially because futures contracts offer a viable means of protecting investors from adverse changes in foreign currency values. The U.S. market is the most active. The United Kingdom and Singapore have the next highest trading volumes in foreign currency futures. (See Exhibit 6-5.)

EXHIBIT 6-4 OUTSTANDING SWAPS BY CURRENCY 1987 AND 1988

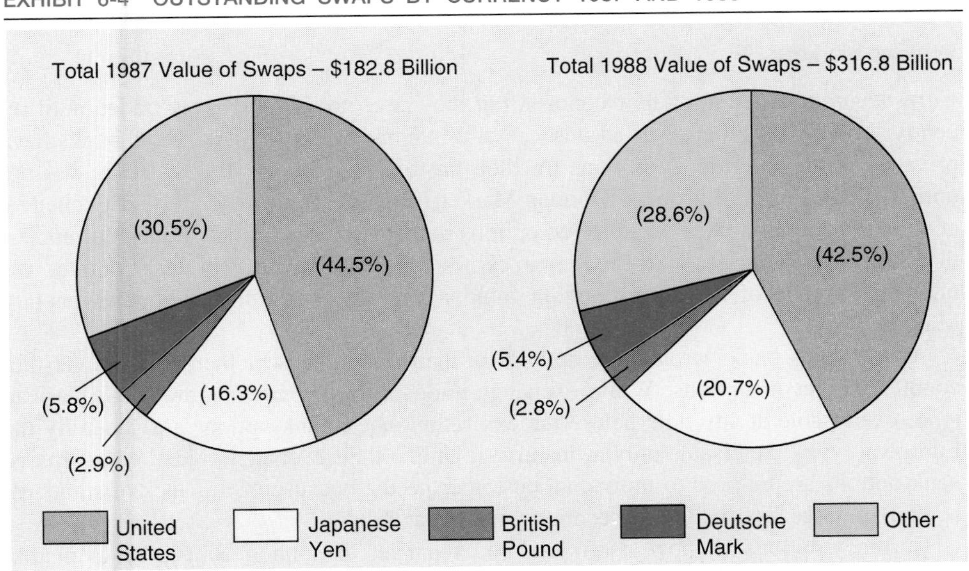

Source: Calculations and graphic based on data from International Monetary Fund, *International Capital Markets; Developments and Projects,* April 1990.

EXHIBIT 6-5 SAMPLE OF FOREIGN CURRENCY FUTURES CONTRACTS, CONTRACT SPECIFICATIONS, AND 1988 VOLUME FOR THE UNITED STATES, THE UNITED KINGDOM, AND SINGAPORE

Type	Face value of contract	Volume (000s of contracts)
	United States	
International Monetary Market (IMM) at Chicago Mercantile Exchange (CME)		
Eurodollar (3-month)*	$1,000,000	21,705
British pound*	£62,500	2,616
Canadian dollar	C$100,000	1,409
Deutsche mark*	DM125,000	5,662
Japanese yen*	¥ 12,500,000	6,433
Swiss franc	SFr125,000	5,283
French franc	FFr250,000	4
Australian dollar	A$100,000	76
	United Kingdom	
London International Financial Futures Exchange (LIFFE)		
Eurodollar (3-month)	$1,000,000	1,662
British pound (3-month)	£500,000	3,555
Japanese yen	¥ 12,500,000	3
Swiss franc	SFr125,000	3
British pound	£25,000	7
Deutsche mark	DM125,000	4
	Singapore	
Singapore International Monetary Exchange (SIMEX)		
Deutsche mark	DM125,000	98
Eurodollar	$1,000,000	1,881
Japanese yen	¥ 12,500,000	221
British pound	£62,500	3

*CME Eurodollar, British pound, deutsche mark, and Japanese yen are listed on a mutual link with SIMEX in Singapore.

Source: International Monetary Fund, *International Capital Markets; Developments and Prospects,* April 1990.

Options Market

Currency options are not a new concept, but they have not been actively traded until recently. In the 1920s there was an unsuccessful attempt to start a market, and banks have privately arranged currency options for their customers since the 1940s. But it was not until 1982, when the European Options Market in Amsterdam, the Montreal Exchange, and the Philadelphia Exchange offered options in the five most actively traded currencies, that the currency options market began in earnest. The denomination of each contract was one-half the size of the corresponding futures contract on the International Monetary Market.

At that point, banks wrote more options for their customers which created an over-the-counter market in options. While exchange-traded currency options are the American type (exercisable at any time before the expiration date), bank options are generally the European type (exercisable only at maturity). Unlike their exchange-traded counterparts, bank options are tailored to individual customer needs; because of this lack of standardization, they see relatively little secondary market activity.

Currency options are now also traded on exchanges in London, Singapore, Bangkok, Sydney, and Vancouver. In 1984 IMM offered the first *options* on deutsche mark *futures* contracts. Since that time, options on other major currency futures have been introduced.

EXHIBIT 6-6 SAMPLE OF FOREIGN CURRENCY OPTIONS CONTRACTS, CONTRACT SPECIFICATIONS, AND 1988 VOLUME FOR THE UNITED STATES, THE UNITED KINGDOM, AND SINGAPORE

Type	Face value of contract	Volume (000s of contracts)
United States		
International Monetary Market (IMM) at Chicago Mercantile Exchange (CME)		
(Options on futures)		
Eurodollar	$1,000,000	2,600
Pound sterling	£62,500	543
Deutsche mark	DM125,000	2,734
Swiss franc	SFr125,000	1,070
Japanese yen	¥ 12,500,000	2,945
Canadian dollar	C$100,000	314
Australian dollar	A$100,000	7
Philadelphia Stock Exchange (PHLX)		
Australian dollar	A$50,000	351
Canadian dollar	C$50,000	317
Deutsche mark	DM62,500	3,321
European Currency Unit (ECU)	ECU62,500	1
French franc	FFr250,000	252
Japanese yen	¥ 6,250,000	2,921
British pound	£31,250	1,283
Swiss franc	SFr62,500	1,067
United Kingdom		
London International Financial Futures Exchange (LIFFE)		
(options on futures)		
Eurodollar (3-month)	$1,000,000	77
British pound (3-month)	£500,000	446
Singapore		
Singapore International Monetary Exchange (SIMEX)		
Deutsche mark	DM125,000	12
Eurodollar	$1,000,000	11
Japanese yen	¥ 12,500,000	61

Source: International Monetary Fund, *International Capital Markets; Developments and Prospects,* April 1990.

The United States provides, again, the most active market in these derivative securities. (See Exhibit 6-6.)

SUMMARY

Foreign currency transactions are a requirement of international trade. Changes in exchange rates can adversely affect profits from such trade, however. Instruments that allow buyers and sellers to protect against unfavorable currency exchange fluctuations include forward, swap, futures, and options contracts. Forward contracts can be customized to fit individual needs with respect to timing and denomination. Special variations of the forward contract include option-date forward contracts and forward forward contracts. Forward exchange rates are affected by spot exchange rates and differential interest rates.

A currency swap is an exchange of currencies that is reversed at a future date. Spot, swap, and forward rates are interrelated because the standard forward contract is equivalent to the combination of a spot market transaction combined with a swap.

Foreign exchange futures and options contracts, unlike forwards and swaps, are traded on organized exchanges in several countries. Holding a futures contract requires some action in order to close out the position—either the specified exchange of currencies or taking an opposite position in order to cancel the first position. The owner of an options contract has the right, but not the obligation, to take further action.

All of these markets are very efficient, especially the spot market, which operates 24 hours a day. While the U.S. dollar has historically formed the core of foreign exchange markets, other currencies are gaining increased importance.

KEY TERMS

asked price
bid price
exchange rate risk
foreign currency swaps
foreign exchange futures
foreign exchange hedging
foreign exchange options
forward currency exchange contract
forward discount
forward exchange rate
forward forward exchange contract
forward premium
interest rate parity
option-date forward contract
spot currency exchange
spot exchange rate

END-OF-CHAPTER QUESTIONS

1. Differentiate among spot, forward, and futures contracts for foreign currency exchange.
2. What is a currency swap?
3. What are the determinants of a forward rate? When will a currency sell at a forward premium?
4. Under what circumstances might an option-date forward contract be more advisable than a standard forward?
5. Differentiate between an option on a foreign exchange futures contract and a foreign exchange option.
6. Look at a recent edition of the *Wall Street Journal.* Identify the foreign currency with the greatest number of open options on futures contracts (open interest) on the International Monetary Market (IMM).
7. Conceptually, what is the interrelationship between swap, spot, and forward market transactions?
8. Describe a scenario in which the writer of a deutsche mark call option (option holder has the right to buy deutsche marks) faces potentially unbounded losses.
9. Why do you suppose that the foreign currency divisions of major commercial banks are more active in swap contracts than in forward contracts?
10. Why might an industrial firm with foreign exchange exposure prefer to hedge with an option contract rather than a forward contract?

END-OF-CHAPTER PROBLEMS

1. What equilibrium 6-month forward rate is implied if the rates of interest on 6-month Swiss franc and U.S. dollar deposits are 7 and 5 percent, respectively? Assume the current spot rate is SFr1.6475 = $1.
2. Given your answer to *1,* assume now that a company wishes to purchase a SFr500,000, 6-month forward contract and that the bank selling the forward contract wants to build in a $500 fee into the forward rate. Under these circumstances, what is the appropriate forward rate?
3. Assume that the spot exchange rate for Japanese yen is ¥ 141.65 = $1 and that the 30-day forward rate is ¥141.85 = $1. In dollar terms, is the yen selling at a forward premium or discount? On an annual basis, what is the percentage premium or discount?
4. On March 31, your firm made a sale of equipment to a British customer for £187,500, but the company will not receive the pounds until the end of June.

a. What is the nature of the foreign exchange risk that the firm is exposed to?
b. If you decide to protect against this risk with options, what kind of option would you buy?
c. How many contracts should you buy?
d. If the current exchange rate is \$1.67 = £1, the option strike price is \$1.65 = £1, and the option premium is \$0.0416 per £, what is the maximum potential loss for the firm after these contracts are purchased? (Ignore transactions costs.)

5. Consider the following exchange rates:

- The spot exchange rate for French francs is currently FFr6.06 = \$1.
- The swap contract that entitles its holder to purchase French francs today and to sell them in 3 months sets the exchange rate in 3 months at FFr6.08 = \$1.
- The swap contract that entitles its holder to sell French francs today and to purchase them in 3 months sets the exchange rate in 3 months at FFr6.139 = \$1.

What implications do these spot and swap rates have for the forward market?

SELECTED REFERENCES

Brown, Brendan. *The Forward Market in Foreign Exchange; A Study of Market-Making, Arbitrage, and Speculation,* St. Martin's Press, New York, 1983.

Fraser, Donald R., and Peter S. Rose, Editors. *Financial Institutions and Markets in a Changing World,* 3d edition, Business Publications, Inc., Plano, Texas, 1987.

Havrilesky, Thomas M., and Robert Schweitzer, Editors. *Contemporary Developments in Financial Institutions and Markets,* Harlan Davidson, Inc., Arlington Heights, Illinois, 1987.

Huat, Tan Chwee. *Financial Institutions in Singapore,* Singapore University Press, Singapore, 1981.

Jones, Eric T., and Donald L. Jones. *Hedging Foreign Exchange; Converting Risk to Profit,* John Wiley and Sons, Inc., New York, 1987.

Quirk, Peter J., Graham Hacche, Viktor Schoofs, and Lothar Weniger. *Policies for Developing Forward Foreign Exchange Markets,* International Monetary Fund, Washington, D.C., 1988.

CHAPTER 7

EUROMARKETS

CHAPTER OUTLINE

EUROMARKETS
- Eurodollars
  - Development of the Eurodollar market, Euromarket locations, Eurocurrencies
- Eurobonds and Foreign Bonds
- Eurocommercial Paper and Euronotes
- Euroequities

THE EUROPEAN COMMUNITY
- European Monetary System (EMS)
- Completing European Integration
- Monetary Union

INTERNATIONAL COMPARISONS:
- Canada
- France
- Germany
- Japan
- Netherlands
- Switzerland
- United Kingdom

CHAPTER OVERVIEW

This chapter:

- Discusses the development of Euromarkets
- Defines the instruments of Euromarkets, including deposits, bonds, commercial paper and notes, and equities
- Traces the growth of Euromarket instruments during the 1980s
- Provides background material on the European Community and outlines the objectives and goals of the Single European Market

Euromarkets, where home-currency instruments are traded outside national borders, continue to grow in importance, providing alternative financing vehicles and investment opportunities. Eurocurrencies, particularly Eurodollars, have proved effective in correcting international liquidity imbalances for banks, industrial firms, and sovereign governments. Eurocurrency markets that started in London are now found in other European cities and in Singapore, Hong Kong, Tokyo, the Cayman Islands, and the Bahamas, while London is still the site of most Eurobond issues and active secondary trading. Eurocommercial paper, Euronotes, and Euroequities have all grown rapidly.

The year 1992 marked the target date for full integration of the twelve-nation European Community markets for goods and services, including financial services. The Single European Market is a landmark event in the growth of cross-border financial investments.

EUROMARKETS

Euromarkets are financial markets that involve instruments either denominated in a currency that is not the local domestic currency or denominated in the domestic currency but sold in nondomestic markets or distributed by an international syndicate of investment bankers or merchant banks. This is a comprehensive definition that describes a multitude of financial instruments and arrangements. The instruments themselves can be placed in four general classifications:

(1) Eurodollars,
(2) Eurobonds,
(3) Eurocommercial paper and Euronotes, and
(4) Euroequities.

Eurodollars

Eurodollars form the core of international money markets transactions.

Eurodollars:
Deposits denominated in U.S. dollars issued by banks outside the United States. Even if the bank's home office is in the United States, the deposit is considered a Eurodollar deposit.

Development of the Eurodollar Market In the late 1950s and 1960s, banks in Western Europe, the Middle East, the Far East, and elsewhere began actively to trade U.S. dollars for reasons having to do with international trade and U.S. legislation.

In 1957, Great Britain severely restricted non-British borrowing and lending in British pounds. At about the same time, countries in Western Europe liberalized bank trading in U.S. dollars to facilitate formation of the European Common Market.

During the 1960s, U.S. exports of goods and services exceeded imports by $40 billion, which created a net international demand for dollars to pay for the American goods. The supply of dollars came primarily from capital outflows of $52 billion from the United States for large investments in foreign capital assets.

These large holdings abroad of U.S. dollars (still convertible into gold) and the accompanying conversions strained the nation's gold reserves and shook international faith in the soundness of dollar. The U.S. government reacted with several pieces of legislation to restrict capital outflows:

- Interest Equalization Tax
- Voluntary Foreign Credit Restraint Program
- Foreign Direct Investment Program

The *Interest Equalization Tax (IET)* of 1964 discouraged the issuance of foreign securities in the United States by effectively increasing by 1 percent the cost of financing for foreigners. When evidence showed that the IET merely encouraged more bank financing, bank loans were subsequently included in IET provisions.

The *Voluntary Foreign Credit Restraint Program (VFCRP)* of 1965 recommended limitation of the amount of foreign lending and investment by commercial banks, insurance companies, and pension funds. The program also asked industrial firms to improve their individual capital flows either by exporting more goods and services, by postponing marginal foreign direct investment, or by raising more funds abroad.

The 1968 *Foreign Direct Investment Program (FDIP)* placed mandatory restrictions on direct investment to advanced European economies, Australia, and South Africa. More liberal ceilings applied to developing countries.

The net effect of these regulations was to put pressure on the multinational customers of U.S. commercial banks to fund their foreign operations outside U.S. markets. Loan rates that banks could offer foreign borrowers were not as competitive as they would have been otherwise. Moreover, banks' corporate customers were encouraged to seek overseas financing, and foreign borrowers were discouraged. These factors combined to significantly reduce demand for bank loans.

At the same time, U.S. commercial banks were subject to Regulation Q (Reg Q) of the Federal Reserve, which placed ceilings on deposit interest rates. When, in 1966, Reg Q ceilings for negotiable certificates of deposit (NCDs) were below market rates, banks responded by offering more competitive NCD rates in their foreign offices, which were not subject to Reg Q. The overseas NCDs, known as *Eurodollar CDs,* became a significant source of funds for U.S. commercial banks, especially because they were not subject to costly reserve requirements and deposit insurance premiums.

Investment of the proceeds from Eurodollar CD sales was, likewise, not subject to the IET, VFCRP, or the FDIP. Thus, Eurodollars provided banks with liquidity to finance the foreign operations of U.S. multinational firms. Even after the Reg Q ceiling on domestic NCDs was removed in 1970 and the capital outflow legislation was abolished in 1974, the Eurodollar market continued to flourish, primarily because of the absence of reserve requirements and deposit insurance premiums.

Euromarket Locations London became the most important Eurodollar financial center because of its long tradition as an international financial center with well-developed money, interbank, and discount markets. Equally important is the absence of strict regulations with respect to foreign currency transactions by non-British financial institutions. As a result, banks from other countries have been able to establish a virtually unregulated presence in London.

Paris is the second-largest Eurodollar market, although its transactions volume is much less than that of London. Frankfurt, Amsterdam, Zurich, Basel, Geneva, Milan, and Vienna also maintain Eurodollar operations. The Cayman Islands and the Bahamas have become major Eurodollar markets primarily because of tax advantages.

Since 1968, when the withholding tax on interest payments made to nonresidents was removed, Singapore has been an important center for U.S. dollar deposits. Both Hong Kong and Tokyo are now also designated *Asiandollar* financial centers. Singapore has generally dominated Hong Kong and Tokyo, because its tax environment has been the most favorable and foreign exchange controls have been almost nonexistent. Dollar deposits even in Asia are frequently referred to as Eurodollar deposits. In fact, the *Euro-* prefix applies to any transaction made outside the home country of the currency involved.

Eurocurrencies While the U.S. dollar has dominated Euromarkets, deposits in other currencies are also traded. Notice in Exhibit 7-1 that the U.S. dollar represented almost 83 percent of 1983 Eurocurrency deposits, which totaled $1.6 trillion. Together, the other currencies shown accounted for 15 percent. The European Currency Unit (ECU), a basket of currencies created in 1979 as part of the European Monetary System which serves as a settlement currency among central banks of the European Community, in 1983 represented less than ½ percent of Eurocurrency deposits.

By 1987 Eurocurrency deposits had grown at an average annual rate of 19 percent to $3.2 trillion, while the U.S. dollar share had dropped to 69 percent. This decline in relative importance is attributable at least partially to the decline in the U.S. dollar value that began in 1985, but currency appreciation alone does not explain the increased market shares of other currencies. The most graphic example of this is Japan. From the fourth quarter of 1982 to the same period in 1986, the yen appreciated 62 percent. Yet the share of yen-denominated Eurocurrency deposits more than doubled from 1983 to 1987. As do-

EXHIBIT 7-1 EUROCURRENCY DEPOSIT BREAKDOWN, 1983 AND 1987

	1983		1987	
	Amount*	%	Amount*	%
U.S. dollar	1337.2	82.8	2210.6	68.9
Deutsche mark	113.5	7.0	338.8	10.6
Swiss franc	63.9	4.0	181.5	5.7
Japanese yen	21.7	1.3	137.2	4.3
British pound	14.6	0.9	67.0	2.1
French franc	11.3	0.7	35.0	1.1
Dutch guilder	11.4	0.7	22.6	0.7
ECU	7.0	0.4	69.4	2.2
Other	34.3	2.1	144.8	4.5
Total	1614.9		3206.9	

*In billions of U.S. dollars.
Source: Calculations based on data from *Comparative Economic and Financial Statistics; Japan and Other Major Countries 1988,* Bank of Japan.

mestic financial markets of other countries are deregulated, their currencies are likely to continue to have more prominence in international markets.

Eurobonds and Foreign Bonds

As robust as the Eurocurrency market is, growth has been even stronger in the longer-term market for Eurobonds. International bonds are either Eurobonds or foreign bonds. The major currency in the international bond market is the U.S. dollar, with growing participation in other currencies. Eurobonds developed after the Eurocurrency markets.

Eurobonds:
Bonds issued by parties outside their domestic capital markets, underwritten by an international investment banking syndicate, placed in at least two countries, and, perhaps, issued in more than one currency.

The firms that underwrite Eurobonds generally maintain offices in New York, London, Tokyo, and other Euromarket centers. An international underwriting syndicate and multinational placement distinguish Eurobonds from other international issues. Eurobond issuer and investor need not *necessarily* be in different countries. For example, a U.S. firm may issue a Eurobond and sell part of it to a U.S. insurance company.

In the case of foreign bonds, though, the country of origin of foreign bond issuers is *not* the same as that of the investor.

Foreign bonds:
Bonds issued by entities outside their own domestic capital markets in a foreign market, underwritten by a firm that is domestic to that foreign market, usually denominated in the currency of the market in which they are issued, but occasionally denominated in another currency.

Foreign bonds are sometimes referred to as *traditional* international bonds because they existed long before Eurobonds. *Yankee bonds* are foreign bonds issued in the United States. Foreign bonds issued in the United Kingdom are called *Bulldog bonds,* while those issued in Japan are known as *Samurai bonds.*

Immediately after World War II, the United States was the primary market for foreign bonds, but the interest rate disincentive of the Interest Equalization Tax caused much of the dollar-denominated borrowing to move to the Eurobond market. More recent trends in international bond issuance continue to favor Euromarkets.

Exhibits 7-2 and 7-3 show that, as recently as 1980, issuances in the Eurobond and foreign bond markets were roughly equivalent, at $20 billion and $18 billion, respectively. By 1986, however, Eurobond issuances had far outpaced new foreign bonds. Foreign bond issuances grew during the period at an annual rate of 14 percent to $39 billion, while Eurobond issuances expanded at an annual rate of 45 percent to $187 billion.

Switzerland, which has historically prohibited Eurobond issues, dominated the foreign bond market in 1980 with 42 percent of all issuances. Its dominance grew to 61 percent in 1986. The United States and Japan were a distant second and third.

Eurobonds denominated in dollars continue to represent the majority of issuances, even though the share has slipped somewhat. A gradual decline in the relative importance of the dollar is linked to several factors. Depreciation of the dollar and uncertainty about its future stability have contributed to the use of other currencies. Liberalization of regulations in the United Kingdom, Japan, Germany, and France have made international bond issuance easier. Lastly, the popularity of currency swaps has made it possible to issue Eurobonds in one currency and swap the proceeds for another currency.

Exhibit 7-4 graphs the relative growth of Eurobonds and foreign bonds during the 1980s. From 1980 to 1989 new issues of foreign bonds more than doubled from $18 billion to $42 billion. In 1989 the value of Eurobond issues at $212 billion was 10 times the 1980 value.

The currency composition of new international bonds (including both Eurobonds and foreign bonds) continues to become more diverse. Exhibit 7-5 shows that 50 percent of the value of new international bonds was denominated in U.S. dollars in 1989. The Japanese yen, Swiss franc, deutsche mark, ECU, British pound, and Canadian dollar made up 40 percent of the total in roughly equivalent proportions.

EXHIBIT 7-2 EUROBOND ISSUES BY CURRENCY OF ISSUE, 1980 AND 1986

	1980		1986	
	Amount*	%	Amount*	%
U.S. dollar	13.6	66.7	117.2	62.6
Deutsche mark	3.5	17.2	16.9	9.0
Japanese yen	0.3	1.5	18.7	10.0
British pound	1.0	4.9	10.5	5.6
ECU	—	—	7.0	3.7
Other	2.0	9.8	16.8	9.0
TOTAL	20.4		187.1	

*In billions of U.S. dollars.
Source: U.S. Securities and Exchange Commission, *Internationalization of the Securities Markets,* 1987.

EXHIBIT 7-3 FOREIGN BOND ISSUES BY COUNTRY OF ISSUE, 1980 AND 1986

	1980		1986	
	Amount*	%	Amount*	%
United States	2.7	15.0	6.1	15.8
Germany	5.0	27.8	—	—
Japan	1.5	8.3	4.8	12.4
United Kingdom	0.2	1.1	0.5	1.3
Switzerland	7.5	41.7	23.4	60.6
Netherlands	0.3	1.7	1.8	4.7
Other	0.8	4.4	2.0	5.2
TOTAL	18.0		38.6	

*In billions of U.S. dollars.
Source: U.S. Securities and Exchange Commission. *Internationalization of the Securities Markets,* 1987.

EXHIBIT 7-4 EUROBOND AND FOREIGN BOND ISSUES, 1980, 1983, 1986, AND 1989

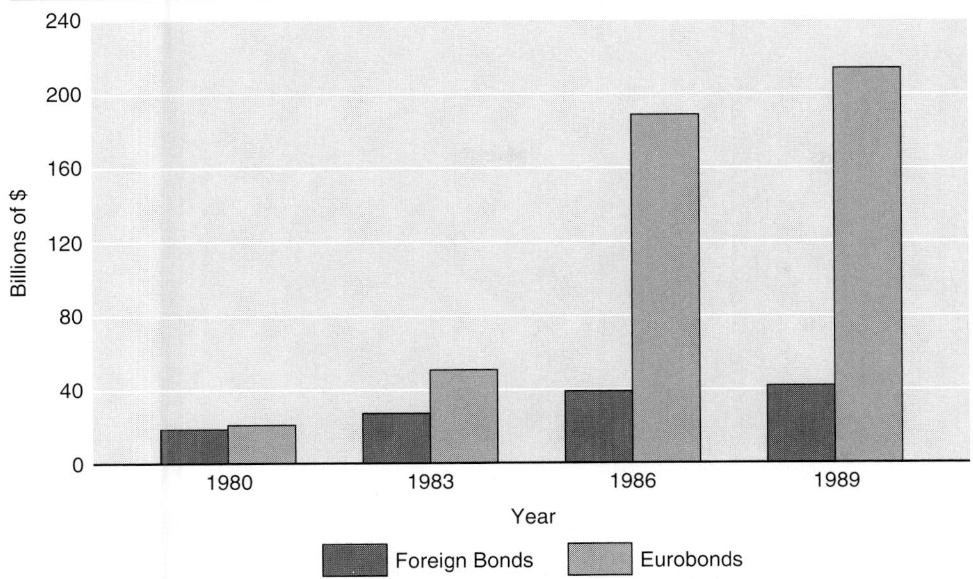

Source: Based on data from U.S.Securities and Exchange Commission, *Internationalization of the Securities Markets,* and International Monetary Fund, *International Capital Markets; Developments and Prospects,* April 1989 and April 1990.

Perhaps surprisingly, these countries were not so evenly represented among the ranks of bond issuers in 1989. Exhibit 7-6 shows that just under 39 percent of the new bonds were issued by Japanese concerns. The next largest share belonged to British issuers (8.4 percent). All other individual countries, including the United States, issued less than 6 percent of the total.

Japanese issuers are increasingly prominent in the international bond market. This may be partially explained by Japan's large international trade surpluses, much of which is tied to trade with the United States. The magnitude of this dollar-denominated trade gives Japan easy access to long- and short-term international financial markets.

Eurocommercial Paper and Euronotes

A relatively new short-term instrument in international arena is *Eurocommercial paper,* another offshoot of the Eurocurrency markets.

Eurocommercial paper:
Short-term unsecured notes issued by firms in markets outside their domestic markets.

This instrument is one of the more recent to develop in Euromarkets. Throughout the 1970s and early 1980s, both U.S. and foreign borrowers relied heavily on the U.S. commercial paper market. Even though the first issue of Eurocommercial paper was in 1970 by a U.S. firm, this form of financing did not gain widespread acceptance until 1985.

Arrangements that permit an issuer to request immediate sale of the paper or that allow a securities dealer to solicit an issue when the timing is most advantageous have made the market more appealing as an alternative to short-term bank loans. Advances in communications technology have made precise timing of the issues possible. In addition, commercial paper interest rates compare favorably with other sources of financing.

EXHIBIT 7-5 INTERNATIONAL BOND ISSUES BY CURRENCY, 1989

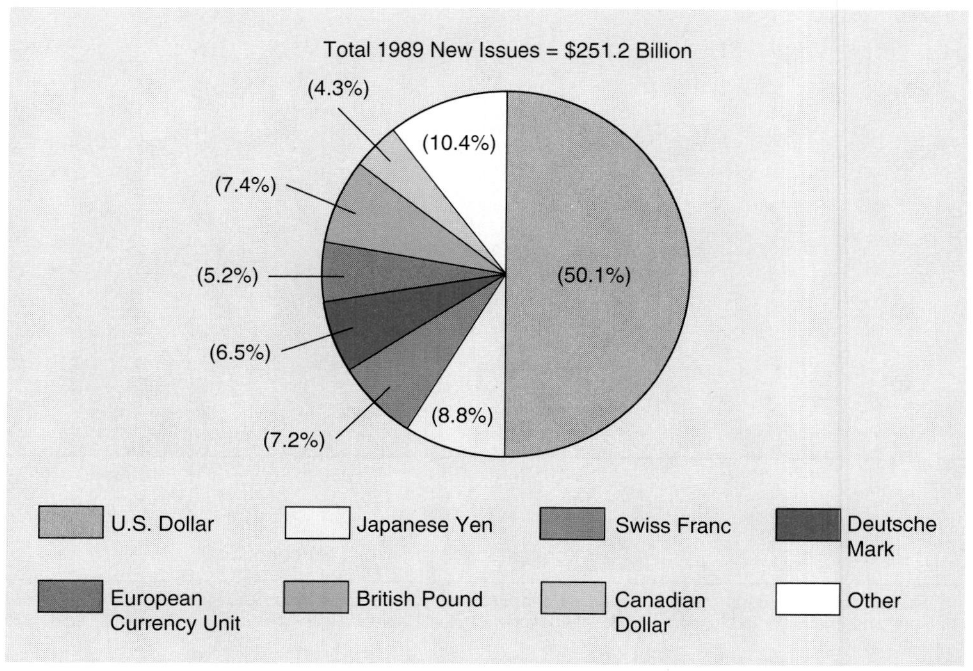

Source: Calculations and graphic based on data from International Monetary Fund, *International Capital Markets; Developments and Prospects,* April 1990.

EXHIBIT 7-6 INTERNATIONAL BOND ISSUES BY COUNTRY OF BORROWER, 1989

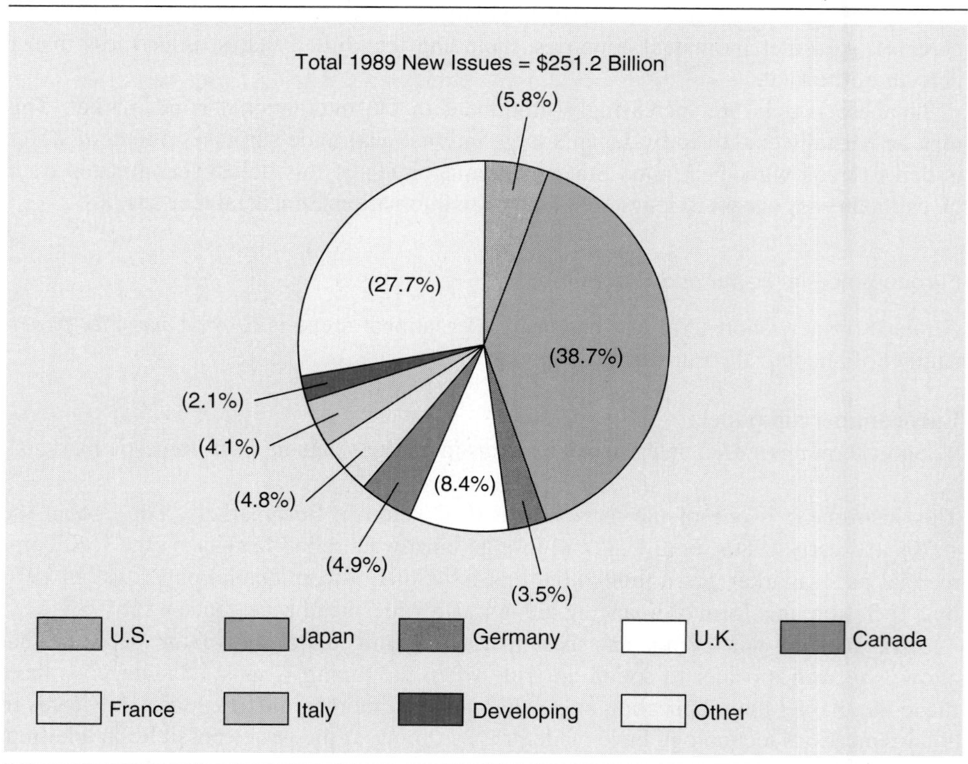

Source: Calculations and graphic based on data from International Monetary Fund, *International Capital Markets; Developments and Prospects,* April 1990.

The structure of Eurocommercial paper is not exactly the same as U.S. commercial paper.[1] While U.S. commercial paper ranges in maturity from 25 to 270 days, Eurocommercial paper usually has an original maturity of 6 months. U.S. commercial paper is a simple instrument that is backed by a bank line of credit. Eurocommercial paper is a more complex financial contract with no comparable guarantee. Lastly, U.S. commercial paper is typically a physical document. But Eurocommercial paper is increasingly issued in book-entry form, that is, with electronic record keeping only.

Euronotes are similar to Eurocommercial paper except that they include an additional agreement, a *Euronote facility* by an underwriter to place the issuer's notes, when issued, for a specified period of time. This makes a Euronote facility a medium-term credit arrangement.

Floating-rate notes (FRNs) are long-term obligations with a variable interest rate. The interest rate is usually tied to the London Interbank Offering Rate (LIBOR), but most FRNs guarantee a minimum rate of return.

During the 1980s, this market expanded rapidly. After its acceptance in 1985, Eurocommercial paper grew to an almost $60 billion industry 1 year later, more than double the size of Euronote issues. Exhibit 7-7 shows the composition of the market from 1983 through 1989. Note that the Eurocommercial paper market contracted during the second half of the 1980s. A factor contributing to this decline is the default of several Eurocommercial paper issuers. Another is adoption of international capital standards for commercial banks that penalize the off–balance-sheet commitments they make to back up Euronotes.

Euroequities

Another segment of international financial markets that experienced rapid growth followed by contraction during the 1980s is the *Euroequities* market.

[1]See Chapter 3 for a discussion of domestic commercial paper.

EXHIBIT 7-7 EUROCOMMERCIAL PAPER AND EURONOTE ISSUES, 1983–1989

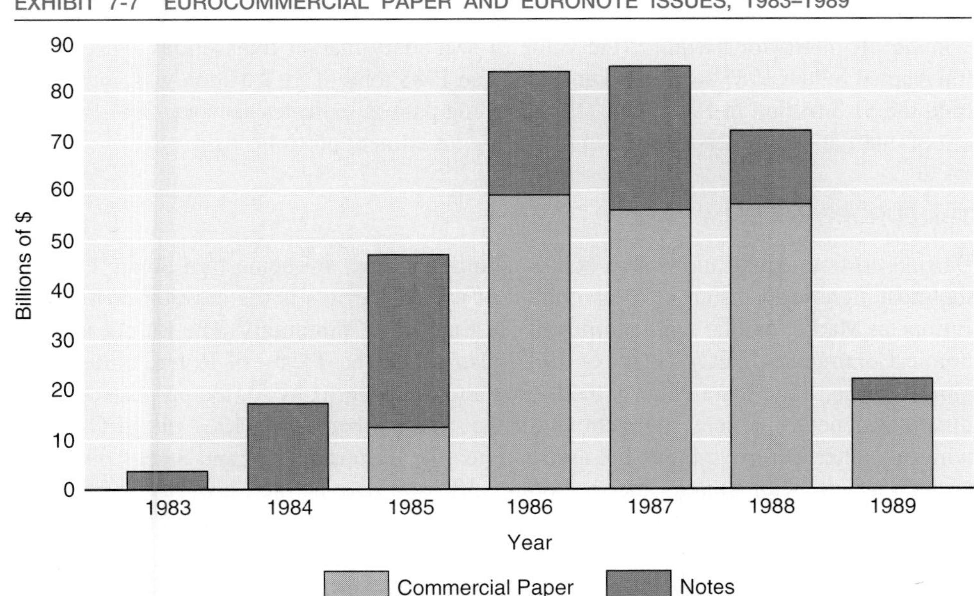

Source: Based on data from International Monetary Fund, *International Capital Markets; Developments and Prospects,* April 1990.

Euroequities:
Common and preferred stocks offered outside the issuer's domestic capital market in one or more foreign markets and underwritten by an international syndicate.

Issuing equities outside the home-country market is not a new practice; firms have often floated stock issues in other countries when their domestic market was too small to absorb a large issue. In many cases, firms have issued stock in London or other major capital markets.

Euroequities are differentiated from these more traditional international issues by the nature of the underwriting syndicate. The same network of investment firms and banks that has been active in the Eurobond market is now underwriting equity issues. To the extent that an issue or a portion of an issue is offered through such an international syndicate, it is a Euroequity issue. As is true with other Euromarkets, the home of the Euroequity market is London.

Frequently, large corporations issue two or more *tranches,* that is, groups of identical or similar securities, each offered under slightly different terms and conditions or being distributed in different ways. A multinational firm may offer domestic and international tranches, for example, with the international tranche distributed through a Euromarket syndicate, thereby qualifying as a Euroequity.

The best candidates for this form of distribution are firms that have an international product market, so that name recognition abroad will help ensure adequate investor interest. International placement helps issuing firms receive a price that is determined by worldwide market conditions and to diversify across a wider shareholder base. Firms from Germany, the United Kingdom, Italy, Switzerland, the United States, and France represent almost 90 percent of Euroequities issued.

Exhibit 7-8 shows international issues of $11.8 billion in common and preferred stock in 1986. In 1987, this amount increased to $18.2 billion, of which 44 percent was Euroequities. The stock market collapse in October 1987 put a damper on the market in 1988, with issues amounting to only $7.7 billion. Even so, the average annual growth rate of international equity issues from 1984 (when the total was $300 million) to 1988 was 125 percent.

Historically, the Euroequity market has been a primary market, with most secondary trading occurring in the domestic market of the issuer. The volume of secondary market trades outside the home market is increasing, however. Exhibit 7-8 shows that the trading volume of international equity (the value of secondary-market transactions) was barely interrupted by the 1987 stock market crash. The 1988 total of $1.2 trillion was not far behind the $1.3 trillion in 1987. This strong trading pattern indicates acceptance of the benefit of international diversification in managing investment portfolio risk.

THE EUROPEAN COMMUNITY

Barriers to free capital movement across national borders are being torn down. Perhaps the most significant instance of dissolution of capital barriers is the creation of a Single European Market among the countries of the European Community. The European Economic Community (EEC) Treaty of 1957, also called the Treaty of Rome, united Belgium, France, Italy, Luxembourg, the Netherlands, and Germany for the purpose of coordinating monetary policies and actions for their mutual benefit. In 1967 the EEC joined with two other European industrial associations (the European Coal and Steel Community and the European Atomic Energy Community) and became the European Community (EC). Starting in the late 1960s, the notion of even greater monetary integration began to gain support among its members.

A framework for the monetary union is described in the 1970 Werner Report, which recommended that:

EXHIBIT 7-8 INTERNATIONAL EQUITY ISSUES AND TRADING VOLUME, 1984–1988

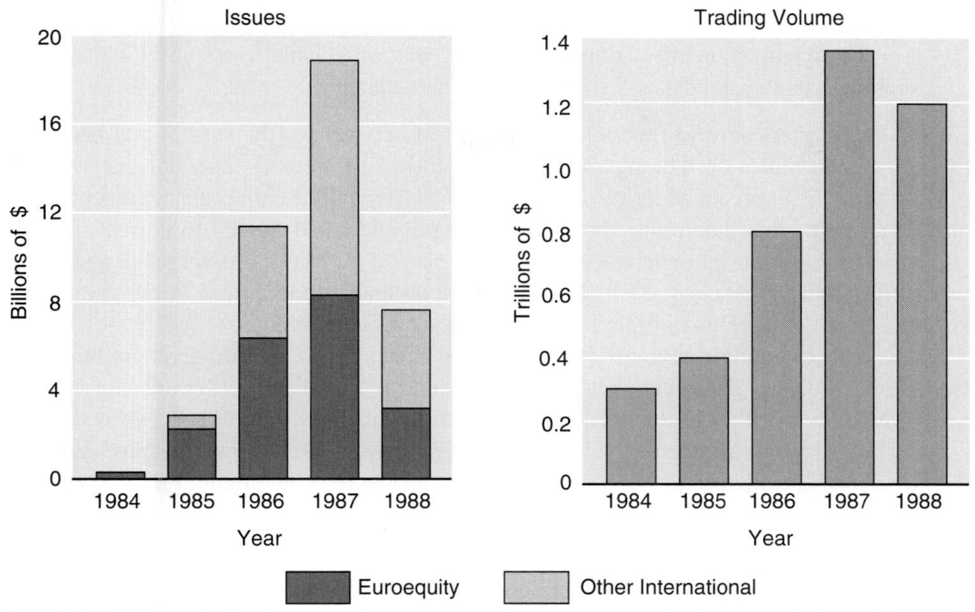

Source: Based on data from International Monetary Fund, *International Capital Markets; Developments and Prospects,* April 1990.

- European Community members should pool their reserves and settle any trade deficits or surpluses internally.
- Members should agree to maintain their relative currency exchange rates within predetermined limits, or parities.
- Adjustments to these parities should become less and less frequent, and the parities, eventually, should be fixed.
- The national currencies of the members should be replaced by one EC currency.

Implementation of these recommendations began during the 1970s and will continue through the 1990s.

European Monetary System

In 1979, the European Monetary System (EMS) was established. By this time, Denmark, Ireland, and the United Kingdom had joined the EC. It had four main results:

- The European Currency Unit (ECU) was created. The ECU is a GNP-weighted basket of member currencies, whose composition may change.[2] The ECU is used to denominate and settle central bank debts and claims of member countries.
- Short- and medium-term credit facilities were established for the members.
- Member countries agreed to maintain exchange rates within a band to be defined in terms of ECUs. The divergence indicator, a warning signal, would trigger action on

[2]In 1989, the ECU was composed of:

Belgian franc (7.6 percent)	Luxembourg franc (0.3 percent)
Danish krone (2.4 percent)	Netherlands guilder (9.4 percent)
French franc (19.0 percent)	British sterling (13.0 percent)
deutsche mark (30.1 percent)	Greek drachma (0.8 percent)
Irish pound (1.1 percent)	Spanish peseta (5.3 percent)
Italian lira (10.1 percent)	Portuguese escudo (0.8 percent)

the part of the EMS Council and the member country whose currency was involved. Presumably, members would intervene in the foreign exchange market to correct this divergence. This new arrangement is called the *Exchange Rate Mechanism (ERM).*

- The European Monetary Cooperation Fund was established to issue ECUs against member country deposits of gold and foreign exchange.

The ECU serves several functions—both unit of account for the system and basis for the divergence indicator. The maximum variation of a member country currency rate is plus or minus 2.5 percent of its value in terms of ECUs, with the divergence indicator set at 75 percent of this maximum spread. Members of the ERM agreed to correct the exchange rate variation of their respective currencies whenever the divergence indicator was activated. This means that ERM members are obligated to intervene in currency markets in unlimited amounts to bring their currency values back in line.

To help accommodate any needed intervention of this nature, a short-term credit facility was initiated. Any ERM member required to enter the market in order to bring its currency value back within limits has been given automatic and unlimited access to this facility. The European Monetary System and the Exchange Rate Mechanism have reduced the amount of speculation in European currencies and have brought about more cooperation in the management of money supply within the ERM.

Completing European Integration

In 1981, Greece joined the EC and in 1985 Portugal and Spain were the last of the current twelve countries to become part of the union. Also in 1985, a white paper (position paper) was developed by the EC Commission (the EC body that makes policy proposals) and approved by the EC heads of government. The paper includes 300 proposed directives to unify EC markets further. The proposed measures fall into three main categories:

- Liberalizing capital movements
- Abolishing cross-border restrictions in the provision of financial services
- Removing obstructions to the free movement of goods and services

To implement these recommendations, the Single European Act was adopted in 1986. According to this act, all barriers to the free movement of goods, persons, services, and capital are to be eliminated throughout the EC by December 31, 1992. The anticipated benefits of the unified market are given in Exhibit 7-9. The terms of the Single European Market have been and continue to be negotiated among the EC members in all areas of commerce.

Monetary Union

In 1988, the decision was made to ask an EC committee to study the process of creating a unified European currency as suggested in the 1970 Werner Report. The resulting Delors Committee Report, accepted in 1989, recommends that conversion to a unified currency take place in three stages:

1. A period of closer coordination and full participation of EC members in the Exchange Rate Mechanism
2. A transition phase during which (a) the central banks (monetary authorities) of EC countries would more closely coordinate monetary policy and (b) the framework for a European central bank, the Eurofed, would be established
3. The final point when the Eurofed assumes full control of European monetary policy and a single European currency circulates in lieu of existing national currencies

EXHIBIT 7-9 ANTICIPATED EFFICIENCIES FROM THE SINGLE EUROPEAN MARKET

The Single European Market of 1992 is intended to solve the problems within the European Community (EC) that arise because of the fragmentation of Europe into multiple markets with different laws and regulations. It is anticipated that efficiencies will be realized by reducing the following economic costs:

1 Administrative costs of maintaining different bureaucratic requirements
2 Transportation costs related to formalities at national borders
3 Cost of relatively short production runs because final output is subject to different national product standards
4 Duplication in research and development efforts
5 Costs associated with inefficient and noncompetitive state-run enterprises
6 Costs incurred by consumers because of a lack of competition among firms, including narrow product selection and relatively high prices
7 Opportunity costs that are sustained by firms that cannot easily expand across national borders to realize full market potential

Source: Task Force on the International Competitiveness of U.S. Financial Institutions, Committee on Banking, Finance and Urban Affairs, U.S. House of Representatives, *Report of the Subcommittee on Financial Institutions Supervision, Regulation, and Insurance,* October 1990.

The first stage was scheduled to end July 1990, but the United Kingdom joined the ERM only in October 1990 because of a philosophical struggle with the notion of relinquishing sovereign monetary control. Nevertheless, progress is being made in the Delors Report timetable. The second stage is due for completion by January 1, 1994.

In the meantime, the growing acceptance of the ECU can be seen in the increase in ECU-denominated bond issues. Exhibit 7-10 shows that, from very modest beginnings in 1981, the value of the new issues (national and international) grew to over 15 billion ECUs in 1988.

EXHIBIT 7-10 ECU BOND ISSUES, 1981–1988

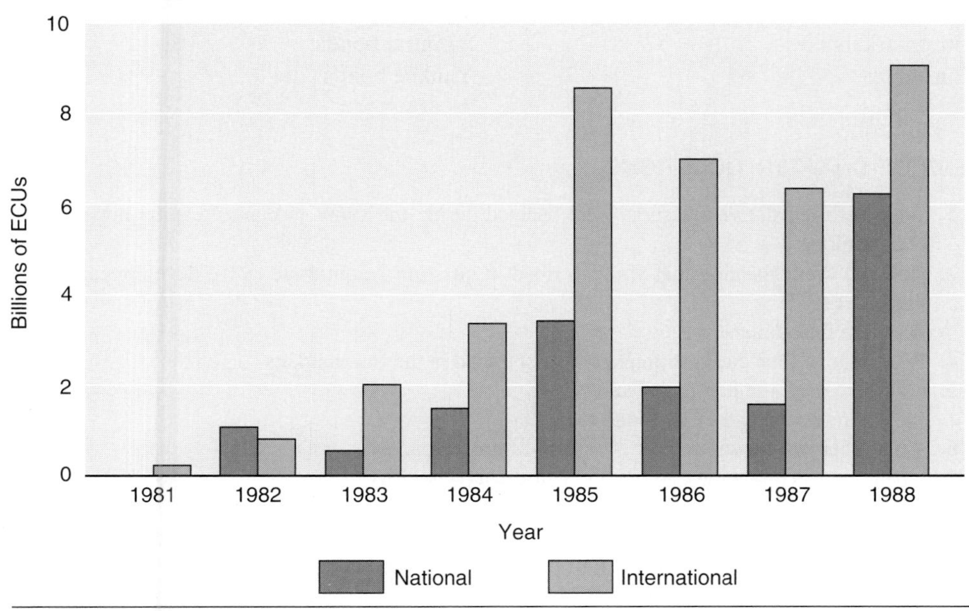

Source: Based on data from International Monetary Fund, *The European Monetary System in the Context of the Integration of European Financial Markets,* October 1989.

Economic integration of the European Community is moving forward. By January 1, 1993, there should be few impediments to trade throughout the EC. In the area of financial services, operations will be considerably simplified. A license in one country will entitle the holder to conduct its business throughout the EC. Banks, securities firms, and mutual funds are the financial firms that are expected to benefit most.

The Single European Community is perhaps the most dramatic example of financial market integration. However, cross-border exchanges are accelerating in all markets for currency, stocks, and bonds.

SUMMARY

The Euromarkets have grown from primarily wholesale money markets to a wide array of short- and long-term financial services and instruments. In general, growth in Eurobonds has far outpaced the growth in traditional international bonds. Eurocommercial paper and Euronote issues expanded rapidly during the early 1980s, only to contract somewhat during the late 1980s. Primary issues in the international equity market were slowed considerably by the stock market crash of 1987, but secondary market trading has continued at a strong pace.

A major initiative in financial market liberalization and integration is the Single European Market with planned implementation beginning January 1, 1993. Financial firms that have been constrained by varying rules and regulations in the EC will be able to operate throughout the twelve-nation region with a license from any one of them. Financial integration of Europe will be complete with an authoritative European central bank, Eurofed, and a single European currency, the ECU.

KEY TERMS

Bulldog bonds
Eurobonds
Eurocommercial paper
Eurodollars
Euroequities
Euromarkets
Euronotes
European Community (EC)
European Currency Unit (ECU)
European Monetary System (EMS)
Exchange Rate Mechanism (ERM)
Foreign bonds
Samurai bonds
Yankee bonds

END-OF-CHAPTER QUESTIONS

1. What U.S. legislative measures were enacted during the 1960s to control capital flows across U.S. borders?
2. How did the legislation that you described in question *1* contribute to the development of the Euromarkets?
3. What are Eurodollars?
4. What type of financial instrument was first traded in the Euromarkets?
5. **a.** Where were the first Euromarkets?
b. Where else may they be found today?
6. What other currencies are now considered Eurocurrencies?
7. Japanese banks now rank among the world's largest. Why do you think the U.S. dollar still remains the primary Eurocurrency rather than the yen?
8. What are the advantages of offering long-term financial securities in international markets?
9. What is the difference between a Eurobond and a foreign bond?
10. Who are the major participants in the Euroequity market?
11. What are ECUs? What was the motivation for their creation?

12. Refer to a recent edition of the *Wall Street Journal.* What is the current dollar value of the ECU?
13. How have foreign currency swaps facilitated Euromarket security issuance?
14. How does Eurocommercial paper differ from U.S. commercial paper?
15. Do you foresee any negative competitive implications of the Single European Market for U.S. financial services firms?

SELECTED REFERENCES

Abrams, Richard K., Peter K. Cornelius, Per L. Hedfors, and Gunnar Tersman. *The Impact of the European Community's Internal Market on the EFTA,* International Monetary Fund, Washington, D.C., December 1990.

Comparative Economic and Financial Statistics; Japan and Other Major Countries 1988, Bank of Japan, Tokyo, 1988.

Economic and Monetary Union, Commission of the European Communities, Luxembourg, 1990.

Einzig, Paul, and Brian Scott Quinn. *The Eurodollar System; Practice and Theory of International Interest Rates,* 6th edition, St. Martin's Press, New York, 1977.

Europe 1992; The Facts, Department of Trade and Industry and the Central Office of Information, London, 1989.

European Economy; One Market, One Money; An Evaluation of the Potential Benefits and Costs of Forming an Economic and Monetary Union, Commission of the European Communities, Directorate-General for Economic and Financial Affairs, Brussels, October 1990.

Folkerts-Landau, David, and Donald J. Mathieson. *The European Monetary System in the Context of the Integration of European Financial Markets,* International Monetary Fund, Washington, D.C., October 1989.

Fraser, Donald R., and Peter S. Rose, Editors. *Financial Institutions and Markets in a Changing World,* 3d edition, Business Publications, Inc., Plano, Texas, 1987.

Havrilesky, Thomas M., and Robert Schweitzer, Editors. *Contemporary Developments in Financial Institutions and Markets,* Harlan Davidson, Inc., Arlington Heights, Illinois, 1987.

Huat, Tan Chwee. *Financial Institutions in Singapore,* Singapore University Press, Singapore, 1981.

International Capital Markets; Developments and Prospects, International Monetary Fund, Washington, D.C., April 1989 and April 1990.

Scott, Robert Haney, K. A. Wong, and Yan Ki Ho, Editors. *Hong Kong's Financial Institutions and Markets,* Oxford University Press, Hong Kong, 1986.

Task Force on the International Competitiveness of U.S. Financial Institutions, Committee on Banking, Finance and Urban Affairs, U.S. House of Representatives. *Report of the Subcommittee on Financial Institutions Supervision, Regulation, and Insurance,* October 1990.

Tew, Brian. *The Evolution of the International Monetary System, 1945–81,* Hutchinson & Co., Ltd., London, 1982.

Ungerer, Horst, Juko J. Hauvonen, Augusto Lopez-Claros, and Thomas Mayer. *The European Monetary System: Developments and Prospectives,* International Monetary Fund, Washington, D.C., November 1990.

U.S. Securities and Exchange Commission. *Internationalization of Securities Markets; Report to the Senate Committee on Banking, Housing and Urban Affairs and the House Committee on Energy and Commerce,* Washington, D.C., 1987.

CHAPTER 8

INTEREST RATE FUNDAMENTALS

CHAPTER OUTLINE

CHAPTER OVERVIEW

This chapter:

- Describes the yield curve
- Explains the relationship between changes in interest rates and bond prices
- Develops explanations of the term structure of interest rates
- Examines the impact of inflation on real rates of return

The basic commodity that financial institutions trade among themselves and with others is money, and the price of money is the interest rate. Interest rates affect the value of money and capital market instruments, both domestically and internationally. Changes in interest rates have certain predictable effects on the price of fixed-income securities, or bonds.

Various theories of interest rate behavior suggest that current interest rate levels will depend on estimates of future market conditions, a basic preference to hold liquid assets, or particular preferences as to length of the investment period. Unbiased expectations theory represents the idea that interest rates are determined by an average of the market's estimate of future short-term rates. Liquidity preference theory adds the notion of a liquidity premium in longer-term rates. Market segmentation theory places more emphasis on the supply and demand for funds in particular maturities.

All interest rate theories include the notion of inflation, the decrease in purchasing power of money. Inflation is measured by changes in price indexes, such as consumer and wholesale price indexes and the GDP deflator.

INTEREST RATE THEORY

A number of factors influence interest rates and changes in interest rates, but an important fundamental relationship, the *term structure of interest rates,* is frequently analyzed.

Term structure of interest rates:
The relationship between time (term) and interest rates.

The *yield curve* is an analytical tool that helps describe this relationship.

Yield curve:
A graphic description of the relationship between time to maturity and yield to maturity for a given risk class of securities.

The Yield Curve

A yield curve plots the remaining time to maturity of a group of securities against yield to maturity.[1] The unique maturity date of each security in the group is represented by a point on the curve. As the objective of the analysis is to isolate the effect of time upon yield, all characteristics of the securities besides maturity are held constant.

Corporate bonds and U.S. Treasury bonds, for example, would not be included in the same yield curve. Treasury bonds are considered free of default (nonrepayment) risk; corporate bonds are not. A yield curve including both types of bonds would mix up differences related to risk with the effects of time. It would be misleading as well to group corporate bonds with municipal bonds, even if they are in the *same* default risk class, because the two classes of bonds are subject to different income tax treatment; that is, municipal bond

[1] The yield to maturity is the average annual rate earned by an investor who holds a security until it matures (Chapter 4).

EXHIBIT 8-1 EXAMPLES OF YIELD CURVES

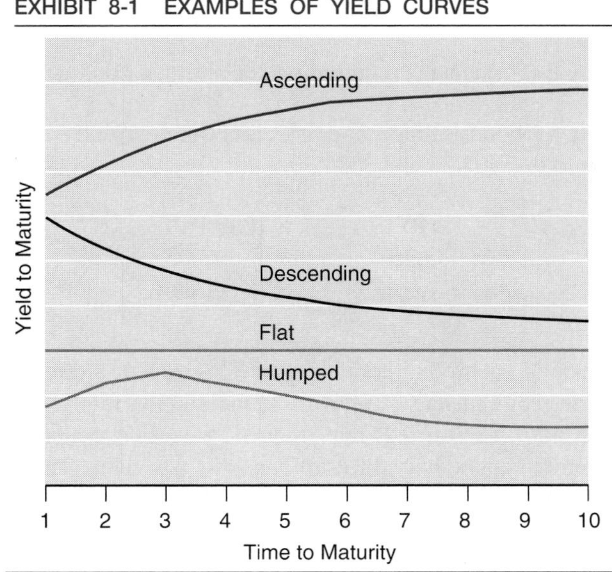

interest is not taxable. The differential tax treatment would be captured in such a combination, which also would distort the relationship between time to maturity and yield.

Exhibit 8-1 illustrates four possible yield curve shapes. All four types of yield curves have been observed in the United States at one time or another. The most common curve observed in the United States in fact has been the ascending yield curve, which describes lower short-term yields relative to long-term yields, in an environment of generally low rates. The descending curve was observed from 1906 to 1929, then again in the late 1960s and early 1970s, when the general level of U.S. interest rates was higher. Humped Treasury yield curves have been observed also during periods of high interest rates, specifically around 1960 and during 1966–1970. Flat yield curves prevailed from 1901 to 1905, when interest rates fluctuated between their historical highs and lows.

While the shape of these curves is objectively determined—maturity dates and yields are plotted on a graph—there are a number of differing theories that explain the *reasons* for the shapes. Before examining these theories, however, it is necessary to understand more fully the relationship between bond prices and interest rates.

Interest Rates and Bond Prices

The variability of bond prices depends on market conditions and specific bond characteristics. The factors that influence bond prices and changes in bond prices are:

- The relationship between required rate of return and coupon rate
- The remaining time to maturity
- Changing interest rate levels

Consider two bonds, A and B, each with a face value of $1000 and a coupon rate of 10 percent, paid semiannually. Bond A was issued 13 years ago with an original maturity of 15 years (so the remaining maturity is 2 years). Bond B also had an original maturity of 15 years, but it was issued 5 years ago (so it now has a remaining maturity of 10 years).

At time of issue, the going market rate for bonds in this risk class was 10 percent, leading issuers to set the coupon rates at 10 percent. According to the bond pricing formula, the price of each bond at issuance would be $1000.[2] This happens because the market rate (the rate of return required by investors) and the coupon rate are the same. This equality typically occurs at the time of bond issuance and is the basis for the first principle of bond pricing.

Bond Theorem 1:

When the coupon rate equals the required rate of return, a bond will sell at par.

If the market rate for bonds in the same risk class were currently 12 percent, prices for bonds A and B would be $965.36 and $885.30.[3]

$$P_0^A = 50(\text{PVIFA}_{.06,4}) + 1000(\text{PVIF}_{.06,4}) \qquad (1)$$
$$= 965.36$$

$$P_0^B = 50(\text{PVIFA}_{.06,20}) + 1000(\text{PVIF}_{.06,20}) \qquad (2)$$
$$= 885.30$$

In this case, the price of each bond is below par. This, too, is a direct result of the relationship between the required rate of return and the coupon rate. The coupon rate does not change, but the market (required) rate frequently does. A coupon rate that is *lower* than the required return causes a bond to sell *below* its par value. The same effect works in the opposite circumstance: When the coupon rate is *higher* than the required return, a

[2] The bond pricing formula is Equation 1 in Chapter 4.
[3] See Appendix A for time value of money tables.

bond sells *above* par value. These relationships (caused by changing required rates of return) are described by the second principle of bond pricing.

Bond Theorem 2:

When the coupon rate is less than (greater than) the required rate of return, a bond sells at a discount (premium).

In the example, bond B is selling farther below its par than bond A is. The reason for this is that bond A is closer to its maturity date. Bond A has 2 years to maturity; bond B has 10. The third principle of bond pricing addresses differences in the size of discount or premium that are attributable to differential time to maturity.

Bond Theorem 3:

All other things being equal, the price of a bond approaches its par value as its maturity date approaches.

Now assume that the general level of interest rates instantaneously increases, so that the required rate of return for these bonds is 14 percent. Again, applying the bond pricing formula yields prices for bonds A and B of $932.26 and $788.10. Both bond prices fell. If general interest rates had declined, the bond values would have risen. The fourth principle of bond pricing describes the relationship between changes in market rates and changes in bond prices.

Bond Theorem 4:

There is an inverse relationship between bond price movements and changes in required rate of return.

Again there is a differential effect in price that has to do with the remaining maturity of the bonds. The price of bond B fell by a larger percentage than that of bond A.[4] The fifth principle of bond pricing explains the relative price volatility of short-term and long-term bonds.

Bond Theorem 5:

Longer-term bonds are more price sensitive to a given change in required rate of return than are shorter-term bonds.

Bond B experiences a sharper price decline because it has 10 years left to maturity. This greater price sensitivity of longer-term bonds works in both directions. If interest rates decline, the prices of both bonds increase, but bond B's price increased by a larger percentage than bond A's. Basically, prices of long-term bonds are more volatile than those of short-term bonds for a given change in required rate of return.

Theories Explaining the Term Structure of Interest Rates

There are three basic theories explaining the term structure of interest rates:

(1) unbiased expectations theory
(2) liquidity preference theory
(3) market segmentation theory

While there is considerable academic research testing each of these theories, none of the evidence to date is conclusive enough to dismiss any of them. Each theory in fact appears to contribute some insight into the behavior of interest rates and is therefore useful in combination with the others.

[4] A: $(932.26 - 965.36)/965.36 = -.0343$
B: $(788.10 - 885.30)/885.30 = -.1098$

Unbiased Expectations Theory The *unbiased expectations theory* assumes that the shape of the yield curve is explained by the market's consensus about future interest rates. That is, the yield curve is the result of both current and anticipated interest rates.

If the market as a whole believes that rates will *rise,* people will prefer shorter-term securities so that they do not lock themselves into a lower rate when they can make more money at a higher rate in the future. If interest rates are expected to rise, more investors will want to invest only short-term, in order to take advantage of higher rates later. Also, when rates rise, prices of short-term securities will be less volatile and they will suffer smaller percentage decreases than longer-term securities. These factors will create strong demand for short-term securities that will bid up short-term security prices and push their yields down. Of course, selling pressure on long-term securities at the same time will create the opposite effect on their prices and yields. The net effect, according to the unbiased expectations theory, is that the yield curve will slope upward.

The converse would be an expectation that interest rates will *fall.* In this case, investors will want to invest in longer-term securities because longer-term investments will appreciate more in such an environment than their short-term counterparts. Also, investors will want to lock in the relatively high interest rates that are available today. This buying pressure will cause the price of long-term bonds to increase and long-term yields to decline vis-à-vis short-term yields. The yield curve will slope downward.

Unbiased expectations theory suggests that the short-term interest rates implied by the yield curve are *unbiased estimates* of the market consensus of future rates. Specifically, long-term rates are a geometric average of current and anticipated future short-term rates.

EXHIBIT 8-2 HYPOTHETICAL YIELD CURVE

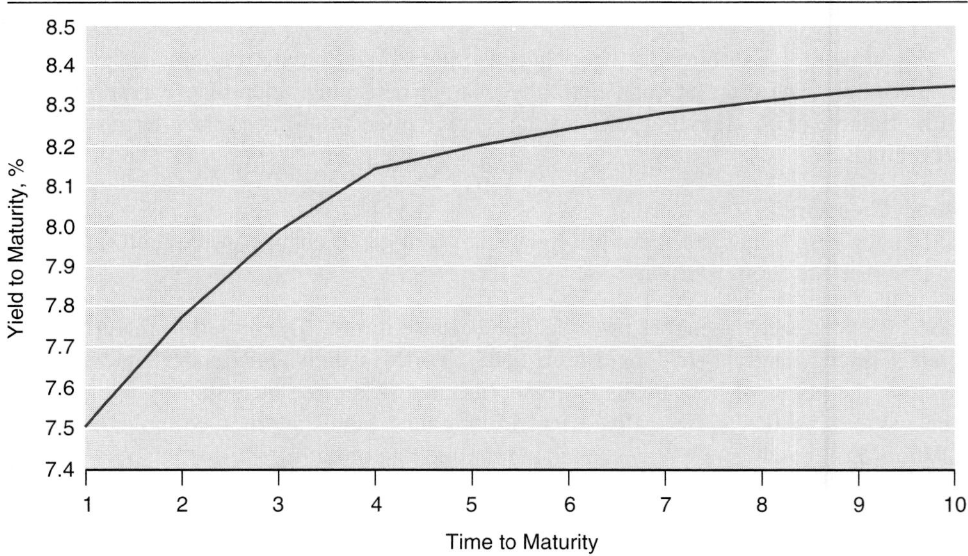

Years to maturity	Yield to maturity (%)
1	7.50
2	7.80
3	7.99
4	8.15
5	8.20
6	8.25
7	8.29
8	8.32
9	8.34
10	8.35

$$(1 + {}_0R_n)^n = (1 + {}_0R_1)(1 + f_2)(1 + f_3) \ . \ . \ . \ (1 + f_n) \quad (3)$$

where ${}_0R_n$ = the long-term rate applicable for the period from time 0 to time n
f_i = the implied future 1-year rate for year i ($i = 2, \ . \ . \ . \ n$)

Exhibit 8-2 is a hypothetical yield curve. The ascending curve begins at 7.50 percent for 1-year maturities and increases to 8.35 percent for 10-year maturities. All yields other than the 1-year rate, ${}_0R_1$, are averages of implied future short-term rates. The rate for a 2-year security, ${}_0R_2$, has a value of 7.80 percent and is a geometric average of ${}_0R_1$ and the 1-year rate during the second year, f_2.

$$(1 + {}_0R_2)^2 = (1 + {}_0R_1)(1 + f_2) \quad (4)$$
$$(1.0780)^2 = (1.0750)(1 + f_2)$$
$$f_2 = 0.0810$$

The implied future 1-year rate for year 2, f_2, is 8.10 percent. The same procedure is followed to determine the implied 1-year rate for year 3, f_3, and all the other short-term rates; that is, increase the value of n by 1 year, substitute the values of known variables, and solve for f.

To streamline the process, note that all the terms on the right-hand side of Equation 3 that precede $1 + f_n$ are equivalent to $(1 + {}_0R_{n-1})^{n-1}$. Thus

$$\frac{(1 + {}_0R_n)^n}{(1 + {}_0R_{n-1})^{n-1}} - 1 = f_n \quad (5)$$

To find the 1-year rate implied for year 10, substitute the yields to maturity for 10- and 9-year bonds, respectively, into Equation 5.

$$(1.0835)^{10}/(1.0834)^9 - 1 = f_{10} = 0.0844$$

Equation 3 may also be used to infer yields for future multiyear periods. Suppose that the specific period of interest begins at time m and ends at time n, representing $n - m$ periods. Adapting Equation 3 to these circumstances

$$(1 + {}_0R_n)^n = (1 + {}_0R_1)(1 + f_2) \ . \ . \ . \ (1 + f_m)(1 + f_{m+1}) \ . \ . \ . \ (1 + f_n) \quad (6)$$

where $(m + 1) < n$. Because time m is the *end* of year m, and

$$(1 + {}_0R_1)(1 + f_2) \ . \ . \ . \ (1 + f_m) = (1 + {}_0R_m)^m \quad (7)$$

then

$$(1 + {}_0R_n)^n = (1 + {}_0R_m)^m (1 + {}_mR_n)^{(n-m)}$$
$$\left[\frac{(1 + {}_0R_n)^n}{(1 + {}_0R_m)^m}\right]^{1/(n-m)} - 1 = {}_mR_n \quad (8)$$

To illustrate, suppose that an investor wants to determine the yield to maturity during the 4-year holding period beginning at time 6 (end of year 6) and that Exhibit 8-2 describes the yield curve. In this case $m = 6$ and $n - m = 4$. The 4-year yield implied by this curve is

$$\left[\frac{(1.0835)^{10}}{(1.0825)^{6}}\right]^{\frac{1}{4}} - 1 = 0.0850$$

This is the estimated yield to maturity (average annual rate of return) for the 4-year period beginning at the end of period 6. It is the geometric average of the short-term rates implied by the yield curve.

Under the assumptions of unbiased expectations theory, an investor should be indifferent between holding one long-term security and holding a series of 1-year securities because the terminal value is the same in either case. All long-term rates are simply averages of short-term rates. In the real world, there are transactions costs associated with frequent buying and selling that work against true indifference.

Liquidity Preference Theory Unbiased expectations theory assumes that everyone in the market correctly anticipates interest rate changes, so that each can make appropriate portfolio adjustments. *Liquidity preference theory* suggests that investors cannot be absolutely certain about future changes in the interest rate environment. To the extent that they hold long-term securities, investors' vulnerability to loss increases and they must be compensated for exposure to this additional risk.

As in an earlier example, bonds A and B both have 10 percent coupon rates paid semiannually, but bond A has only 2 years to maturity, while bond B has 10 years remaining before it matures. Suppose that two investors attempt to assess their risk exposure when the appropriate discount rate for the bonds was 12 percent. In a 12 percent interest rate environment, the prices of bonds A and B are $965.36 and $885.30. It is possible that one investor might expect interest rates to increase and therefore choose bond A with 2 years to maturity. The other may think, for some reason, that interest rates will drop; this investor would choose bond B with 10 years to maturity.

In the event that interest rates decline to 10 percent, the value of both bonds will increase to $1000 (because they both have 10 percent coupon rates). While for the holder of bond A, this represents a $34.64 increase (a 3.6 percent capital gain or increase in the market value of the bond), the holder of bond B realizes a much greater increase of $114.70 (a 13 percent capital gain). Current yields (from interest income) further enhance profitability—10.4 percent for bond A and 11.3 percent for bond B.

If interest rates increase to 14 percent, the prices of bonds A and B drop to $932.26 and $788.10. This results in a capital loss of 3.4 percent for bond A that is offset by the current yield of 10.4 percent, for a net return of 7 percent despite the price decline. In the case of bond B, the capital loss of 11 percent almost exactly offsets its 11.3 percent current yield. The longer-term bond B places investors in greater jeopardy of *loss of principal* or exposes them to greater *price risk* than the shorter-term bond A.

Compensation for this greater price risk is in the form of risk premiums that increase as time to maturity increases. This means that even if future 1-year rates are all *equal,* the yield curve will be upward sloping.

$$(1 + {}_0R_n)^n = (1 + {}_0R_1)(1 + f_2 + L_2) \ . \ . \ . \ (1 + f_n + L_n) \tag{9}$$

where L_i equals the liquidity premium applicable to period *i,*
and $L_n > L_{n-1} > \ . \ . \ . \ L_2 > 0$.

Liquidity preference theory rests on somewhat more subjective assumptions than unbiased expectations theory because liquidity premiums are not necessarily the same for everyone. The theory does, nevertheless, predict the shape of the yield curve that has been most common in the United States in the twentieth century.

Market Segmentation Theory Another approach to interest rate behavior is *market segmentation theory,* which suggests that investor time preferences involve more than price risk. That is, market participants operate essentially in one maturity band that is determined by their sources and uses of funds. Managers of insurance company and pension fund asset portfolios, for example, manage liabilities that typically are long-term in nature. If these managers invest in short-term asset portfolios, which are the least vulnerable to price risk, the company will face exposure to lower rates of return on investment that may be insufficient to service their liabilities. In other words, they face *reinvestment risk,* the potential loss of income.

Other types of financial intermediaries (commercial banks, for example) need to maintain shorter average maturities of asset portfolios. Increases in their short-term cost of funds could quickly erode their profitability spread if long-term asset portfolios are locked in at lower rates.

Market segmentation theory suggests that interest rates in a maturity band will depend on the supply of and demand for loanable funds with that maturity. Not everyone will prefer short-term securities or necessarily have a particular perception of future short-term vis-à-vis long-term rates.

The theory of *preferred habitat* is a compromise between market segmentation and unbiased expectations. This theory assumes that investors generally operate in the maturity class that is their preferred habitat, the maturity band in which they are most comfortable. Sufficiently high interest rates would lead them to switch to other maturities.

INTEREST RATES AND INFLATION

Anticipated rates of inflation also help determine interest rate levels. *Inflation* is the loss of purchasing power of a currency. The net effect of inflation is that prices of goods and services increase, with no corresponding increase in quality or quantity.

Inflation rate:
The percentage increase in prices of goods and services that results from the loss of purchasing power of a nation's currency.

Price Indexes

Inflation rates are most frequently measured in terms of general price increases expressed as changes in *price indexes.*

Price index:
The standardized value of a basket of goods and/or services.

Types of Price Indexes *Consumer* price indexes measure prices of goods and services commonly purchased by individuals—food, shelter, clothing, for example. *Wholesale* price indexes refer to goods normally bought by businesses—raw materials, component parts, and finished goods. These indexes are calculated by picking a *base year* when the price of a basket, or list, of goods is set at an arbitrary number, perhaps, 100.[5] If the aggregate price of the basket of goods the next year is 5 percent higher, the index value is 105.[6] The inflation rate for a given year is the percentage change in a specific price index

[5] Technically, the aggregate price at the base year is divided by itself to form a ratio of 1, and the ratio is multiplied by 100.

[6] The second-year aggregate price is divided by the first-year aggregate price, and this ratio is multiplied by 100.

EXHIBIT 8-3 CONSUMER PRICE INDEXES FROM SELECTED INDUSTRIALIZED COUNTRIES, 1980–1990

Year	U.S.	Japan	U.K.	Germany	France	Italy
1980	100.0	100.0	100.0	100.0	100.0	100.0
1981	110.3	105.0	111.9	106.3	113.4	117.9
1982	117.1	107.9	121.5	111.9	126.9	137.3
1983	120.9	109.9	127.0	115.6	139.0	157.5
1984	126.1	112.4	133.4	118.4	149.4	174.5
1985	130.5	114.7	141.4	120.9	158.0	190.5
1986	133.0	115.4	146.3	120.8	161.9	201.7
1987	138.0	115.5	152.3	121.0	167.3	211.2
1988	143.5	116.3	159.8	122.6	171.9	221.9
1989	150.4	118.9	172.3	126.0	177.9	235.8
1990	158.5	122.6	188.7	129.4	183.9	251.0

Source: Calculations based on data from International Monetary Fund, *International Financial Statistics,* Various Issues.

EXHIBIT 8-4 INFLATION RATES OF SELECTED INDUSTRIALIZED COUNTRIES, 1981–1990 (PERCENTAGES)

Year	U.S.	Japan	U.K.	Germany	France	Italy
1981	10.31	5.05	11.88	6.29	13.43	17.90
1982	6.15	2.73	8.60	5.23	11.84	16.48
1983	3.23	1.81	4.54	3.35	9.59	14.70
1984	4.32	2.30	5.01	2.41	7.50	10.76
1985	3.52	2.04	6.04	2.15	5.71	9.17
1986	1.90	0.60	3.40	−0.10	2.50	5.90
1987	3.73	0.10	4.16	0.20	3.32	4.72
1988	3.97	0.70	4.92	1.30	2.74	5.05
1989	4.82	2.27	7.79	2.76	3.49	6.27
1990	5.38	3.09	9.52	2.69	3.37	6.46

Source: Calculations based on data from International Monetary Fund, *International Financial Statistics,* Various Issues.

for that year. In the United States, the *gross domestic product (GDP) deflator* is the most comprehensive indicator, as it includes all goods and services produced. Consumer indexes, however, are the more frequently quoted.

International Comparisons Exhibit 8-3 shows consumer price indexes of six leading industrialized nations for the period 1980 through 1990, with 1980 as the base year.[7] Exhibit 8-4 provides the annual inflation rates implied by these index values. In 1981 the rate of inflation in the United States exceeded 10 percent. Purchasing power losses were even more pronounced in Italy, France, and the United Kingdom, with respective inflation rates of 18, 13, and 12 percent. A major contributing factor to the high levels of inflation during the early 1980s was significant increases in oil prices during the 1970s, reflected in both consumer and wholesale prices. Inflation rates have declined since that time, but while they persisted, market rates of interest also reached record levels.

The Fisher Effect

It is easiest to see the relationship between market rates of interest and inflation rates in terms of a simple example. Suppose a buyer wants to purchase an item 1 year from today because it will not be needed until that time and storage cost in the interim is prohibitive-

[7] Together, the countries shown in Exhibit 8-3 control a large share of the world's domestic financial markets. In 1989, their stock markets represented 87 percent of stock market capitalization of all industrialized countries.

ly high. The current price of the item is $110, so the buyer decides to invest $100 now so that it will grow sufficiently in 1 year to cover the cost of the item. Assuming no inflation, the market interest rate that must be earned is 10 percent; that is, 10 percent is the minimum-required rate of return.

Inflation will have an impact on minimum-required return. If the inflation rate is expected to be 5 percent, the price of the item will be $115.50 at the end of the year, (110)(1.05) = 115.50. The buyer now requires a higher rate of return to preserve the same amount of purchasing power. A 5 percent increase (the rate of inflation) is not sufficient because a 15 percent rate would produce only $115 at year-end, $0.50 less than the required amount. Both the original investment (principal) *and* the rate of return (interest) must increase by 5 percent to obtain the desired result.

$$100(1.10)(1.05) = 115.50 \tag{10}$$

This relationship is known as the *Fisher effect,* developed by Irving Fisher. Fisher describes market rates as *nominal* rates of return, made up of elements of *real return* and *inflation premium.*

$$(1 + r^*)(1 + I) = (1 + k) \tag{11}$$

where r^* = real rate of interest
I = expected rate of inflation
k = nominal (market) rate of interest

The inflation premium becomes $I + Ir^*$, or 0.055 in the example above.[8] The cross-term Ir^* is small (0.005 in the example) and, in practice, is usually disregarded.

[8] $(1 + r^*)(1 + I) = (1 + k)$
$1 + r^* + I + Ir^* = 1 + k$
$r^* + I + Ir^* = k$

EXHIBIT 8-5 GOVERNMENT BOND NOMINAL YIELDS: SELECTED INDUSTRIALIZED COUNTRIES, 1981–1990

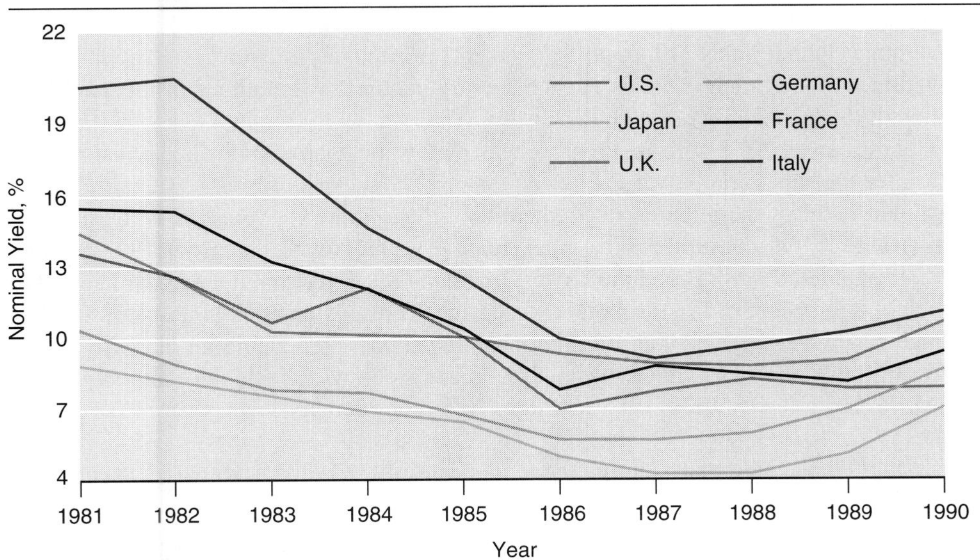

Source: Calculations and graphic based on data from International Monetary Fund, *International Financial Statistics.*

EXHIBIT 8-6 GOVERNMENT BOND REAL RETURNS: SELECTED INDUSTRIALIZED COUNTRIES, 1981–1990

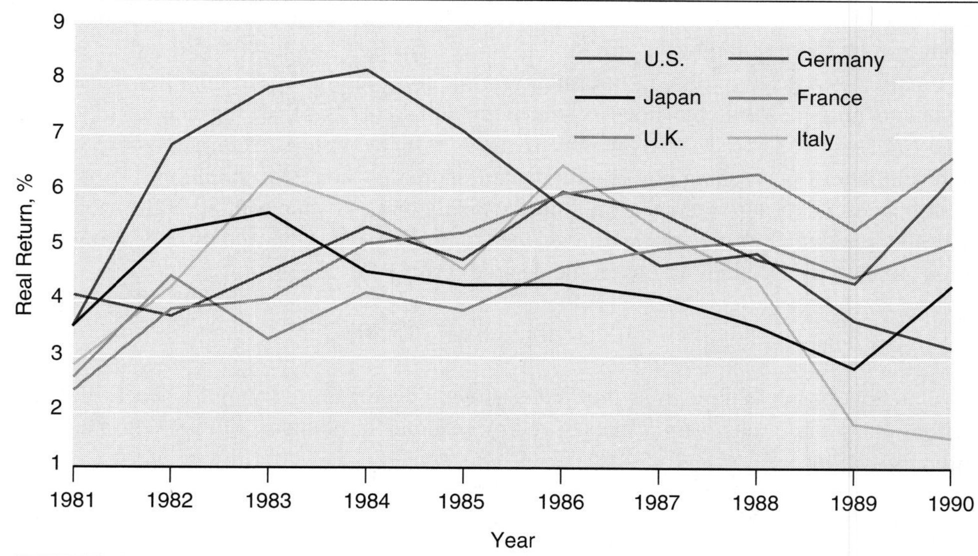

Source: Calculations and graphic based on data from International Monetary Fund, *International Financial Statistics.*

The real rate of return is what matters to an investor. Real rates indicate the increases in value of one's resources; the inflation premium merely restores lost purchasing power.

Nominal and Real Rates of Return in Selected Countries

Government securities entail minimal default risk. This makes them useful examples of historical real rates of return. Exhibit 8-5 shows 10 years' of nominal rates of return on government securities of the six industrialized nations in Exhibits 8-3 and 8-4. The highest bond yields in 1981 were offered by Italy (20.6 percent) and France (15.8 percent), the two countries with the highest inflation rates for that year (see Exhibit 8-4). The United Kingdom and the United States followed with nominal yields of 14.7 and 13.9 percent, respectively. Germany and Japan, with the lowest 1981 inflation rates, also had the lowest government bond yields (10.4 and 8.7 percent, respectively). Over the 10-year period, government bond nominal yields in each country declined as inflation subsided, an illustration of the Fisher effect.

Contrast Exhibit 8-5 with Exhibit 8-6, which plots the approximate annual real rates of return for the same group over the same period. The real rate of return, of course, is the nominal yield less the inflation rate, where the inflation rate is expressed as the percentage change in the consumer price index for the year.[9] Notice that from 1982 through 1985 the United States offered the highest real rate of return (from 6.8 percent in 1982 to a high of 8.2 percent in 1984). In other words, the decrease in nominal rates shown in Exhibit 8-5 was more than offset by inflation rate declines, producing an increase in real rates. In Italy and France, the two countries in the group with the highest *nominal* yields shown in Exhibit 8-5, 1982–1985 real rates were considerably lower than in the United States.

Then, in the United States during the second half of the 1980s, nominal yields dropped

[9] Technically, the inflation premium is the *average anticipated* inflation rate for the time period that is relevant for the observed interest rate.

and the inflation rate increased. The U.S. real rate of return had declined to 3.2 percent by 1990. In the United Kingdom nominal rates increased, as Exhibit 8-5 shows, but inflation increased even more, so that the real return dropped below 2 percent in 1989 and 1990. In France, where the inflation rate stayed under 3.5 percent, nominal yields (then roughly equivalent to those in the United States) delivered real rates of return that were consistently higher than those in the United States during the second half of the decade.

Controlling inflation is a critical concern for every country's government because only competitive *real* rates of return attract investment capital that is needed to sustain economic development. Moreover, high rates of inflation make it difficult for individual households to maintain a given standard of living and more costly for corporations to obtain operating funds.

SUMMARY

Evidence supports the ideas that interest rates are determined by supply and demand for money of a particular maturity (market segmentation theory), by expectations of future short-term rates (unbiased expectations theory), and by preferences to avoid the uncertainty of future investment opportunities (liquidity preference theory). These theories address the question of why interest rates have a certain pattern over time. The behavior of interest rates is important because the value of fixed-income securities, bonds, is closely related to this behavior. Bond prices will equal their par values only when the market rate equals a bond's coupon rate. When this is not the case, bonds sell at discounts or premiums, with bond prices moving in the opposite direction of market interest rate changes.

Expectations of changes in price levels (inflation) have a direct bearing on the magnitude of interest rate changes. Changes in price levels are measured by changes in consumer and wholesale indexes, or prices of specified baskets of goods and services. Inflation reduces the real rate of return, the difference between nominal yield and rate of inflation. When countries have difficulty controlling inflation, the lower real rates of return make their capital markets less appealing to domestic and international investors.

KEY TERMS

Fisher effect
implied interest rate
inflation
inflation premium
liquidity preference theory
liquidity premium
market segmentation theory
market value
par value
preferred habitat theory
price index
price risk
real rate of return
reinvestment risk
required rate of return
term structure of interest rates
unbiased expectations theory
yield curve

END-OF-CHAPTER QUESTIONS

1. What are the variables that define a yield curve? Explain their meaning.
2. What is the major difference between unbiased expectations theory and liquidity preference theory of interest rates?
3. What is the basic premise of market segmentation theory?
4. What process would you use to convert the price indexes in Exhibit 8-3 so that the 1985 value was 100?
5. Why do bond issuers attempt to estimate the rate of return required by the market for their new bonds and set this as the coupon rate?

6. Suppose that you are a bond portfolio manager. If you believe that interest rates are going to increase,
   a. What effect will this have on the value of the bond portfolio?
   b. What maturity preference do you have (short-term versus long-term)?
7. Consider the manner in which an investment grows over time and explain why you think that interest rate theory uses the geometric mean of short-term interest rates instead of the arithmetic mean (simple average).
8. In terms of the liquidity preference theory, why should liquidity premiums increase over time?
9. If nominal interest rates increase as inflation expectations increase, why should individuals' standard of living necessarily suffer in an environment of high inflation rates?
10. During the early 1980s, the United States attracted large amounts of overseas capital despite federal budget deficits (expenditures in excess of revenues) and large trade deficits (imports in excess of exports). Why do you think this was so?

END-OF-CHAPTER PROBLEMS

1. Construct a yield curve using U.S. Treasury securities quoted in the financial press.
2. Obtain the most recent edition of *International Financial Statistics* (published by the International Monetary Fund) in your school's library. Compute the real rates of return on government bonds for the six countries covered in this chapter, and compare them with the rates in Exhibit 8-6.
3. According to unbiased expectations theory and the yield curve shown in Exhibit 8-2, calculate the estimates of:
   a. The short-term rate anticipated for the year beginning at time 2 and ending at time 3 (f_3).
   b. The rate applicable to the 3-year holding period beginning at time 3 and ending at time 6 ($_3R_6$).
4. Considering the Fisher effect, what nominal rate of return would a government security have to yield in order to provide a 2 percent real rate of return when the rate of inflation is expected to be 5 percent.

SELECTED REFERENCES

Benoit, J. Pierre V. *United States Interest Rates and the Interest Rate Dilemma for the Developing World,* Quorum Books, Westport, Connecticut, 1986.

Brigham, Eugene F. *Fundamentals of Financial Management,* 5th edition, Dryden Press, Hinsdale, Illinois, 1989.

Cohen, Jerome B., Edward D. Zinbarg, and Arthur Zeikel. *Investment Analysis and Portfolio Management,* 5th edition, Richard D. Irwin, Inc., Homewood, Illinois, 1987.

Falkena, H. B., L. J. Fourie, and W. J. Kok, Editors. *The Mechanics of the South African Financial System; Financial Institutions, Instruments, and Markets,* Macmillan South Africa, Ltd., Johannesburg, 1984.

Havrilesky, Thomas M., and Robert Schweitzer, Editors. *Contemporary Developments in Financial Institutions and Markets,* Harlan Davidson, Inc., Arlington Heights, Illinois, 1987.

Homer, Sydney. *A History of Interest Rates,* 2d edition, Rutgers University Press, New Brunswick, New Jersey, 1977.

Nelson, Charles R. *The Term Structure of Interest Rates,* Basic Books, Inc., New York, 1972.

CHAPTER 9

INTEREST AND EXCHANGE RATE PATTERNS

CHAPTER OUTLINE

CHAPTER OVERVIEW

This chapter:

- Discusses the influence of default risk on interest rates
- Measures default risk premiums over time
- Highlights historical interest rate patterns
- Outlines factors that affect foreign exchange rates

Chapter 8 showed that interest rates during specific periods of time depend on anticipated inflation rates and investor preferences. Interest rates also depend on the characteristics of individual borrowers. When the likelihood that a borrower will default on a financial obligation is high, the interest rate that borrower must pay will also be relatively high. These default risk premiums increase when general economic conditions are more uncertain.

Interest rates, inflation, and foreign exchange rates are all linked in a world whose markets are becoming more integrated. The exchange rate of a country's currency will be influenced by a number of factors. Domestic inflation will tend to depreciate a currency. The balance of payments (difference between exports and imports) also causes exchange rates to adjust somewhat automatically when currency values are permitted to float, that is, are not fixed. All other things being equal, higher domestic interest rates attract foreign capital and increase the value of domestic currency. Capital flows can reverse quickly, however, so currency markets are volatile. Changing budget and trade circumstances will make a currency more or less attractive at a particular time.

DEFAULT RISK

Default risk affects interest rates just as inflation does. While inflation is an economywide factor, default risk has to do basically with characteristics of the borrower.

Default risk:
The risk that a borrower may not repay principal and/or interest as originally agreed.

Debt instruments issued by government bodies are virtually free of default risk, but the perceived default risk of other borrowers varies.

Bond Ratings

Corporate debt in the United States is evaluated by rating agencies, notably Standard and Poor's Corporation (S&P) and Moody's Investor Service. The S&P bond ratings range from AAA to D. Moody's ratings are similar.

AAA: Highest rating, suggesting extremely strong ability to pay principal and interest

AA: High-quality issuance with very strong repayment capacity, differing from AAA only by a small degree

A: Strong capacity to pay principal and interest but somewhat more susceptible to adverse economic conditions

BBB: Adequate capacity to pay principal and interest but more susceptible to adverse economic conditions than firms in the A category

BB, B, CCC, CC: Ability to pay principal and interest is to a greater or lesser degree speculative, with BB the least speculative and CC the most speculative

C: Inability to pay interest on an income bond[1]

D: In default; principal and/or interest in arrears

Ratings are based on a number of quantitative and qualitative criteria. Basic quantitative considerations include the firm's debt and its debt-servicing capacity. Structural aspects of the bond issue are also evaluated—mortgage, subordination, and guarantee provisions; sinking fund; and maturity—as applicable. Factors that are relevant to the firm's particular operating environment may include sales stability, labor relations, resource availability, political risk exposure in overseas operations, and unfunded pension liabilities. Government regulatory and environmental protection issues also come into play in the evaluation.

Bonds rated AAA through BBB are considered *investment grade* securities. In the United States, many financial institutions are not allowed to invest in securities other than investment grade. From an issuer's perspective, the higher the bond rating, the lower the interest rate required by investors. Understandably, firms are careful to protect their bond ratings.

[1] An income bond pays interest only if the issuing firm earns enough income.

The *default risk premium* associated with debt issues has consistently had an inverse relationship with bond ratings. The higher the bond rating, the less the borrower will need to offer to compensate the buyer of the bond.

Default risk premium:
The component of a required interest rate based on the borrower's perceived risk of default. All other things being equal, it is the difference between the required rate of return and the risk-free (government security) rate.

Higher-rated firms are subject to lower risk premiums, although the size of the premiums has varied over time.

Exhibit 9-1 graphs the yields (interest rates) for U.S. Treasury bonds, Aaa-rated corporate bonds, and Baa-rated corporate bonds for the period 1961 through 1990.[2] Notice that rates peak in the early 1980s. Notice also that the differences between the rates, the risk premiums, are not constant. During periods of difficult economic conditions, risk premiums increase.

Exhibit 9-2, which is based on the information in Exhibit 9-1, shows for each year the difference between the corporate bond rate and the rate for U.S. Treasury bonds. In 1961, both interest rates and risk premiums were low. The premium of Aaa bonds over Treasury bonds was 45 basis points; the Baa premium over Treasury bonds was 118 basis points.[3] Four years later in 1965, rates were at approximately the same levels, but risk premiums were even lower.

Both interest rates and risk premiums increased over time until, by 1975, the Aaa risk premium stood at 185 basis points and the Baa at 363 basis points. There were also rela-

[2] The corporate ratings are by Moody's. They correspond to the S&P AAA and BBB, respectively.

[3] A basis point is one-hundredth of a percent.

EXHIBIT 9-1 U.S. BOND YIELDS BY RATINGS, 1961–1990

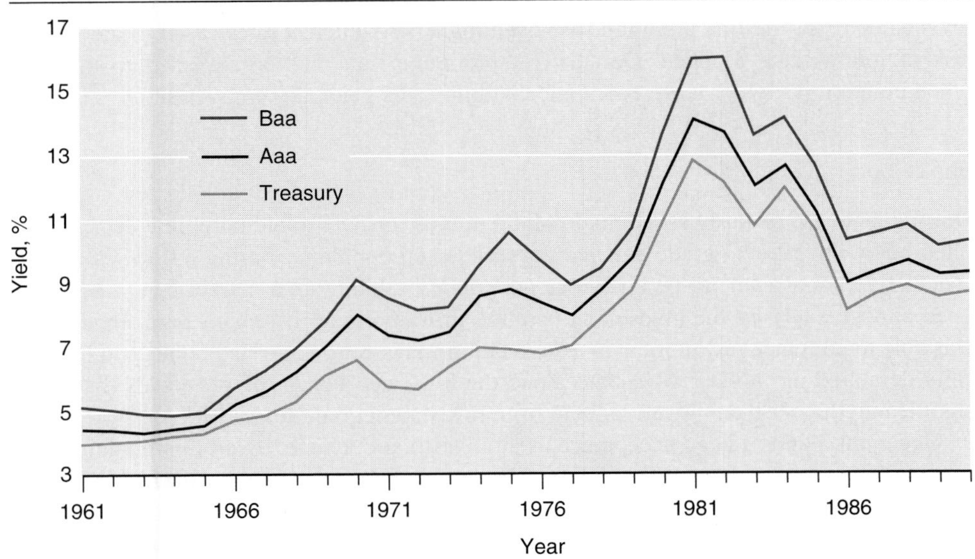

Source: Based on data from U.S. Department of Commerce, Bureau of Economic Analysis, *Business Statistics 1961–1988* and *Survey of Current Business.*

EXHIBIT 9-2 RISK PREMIUMS ON U.S. BONDS, 1961–1990

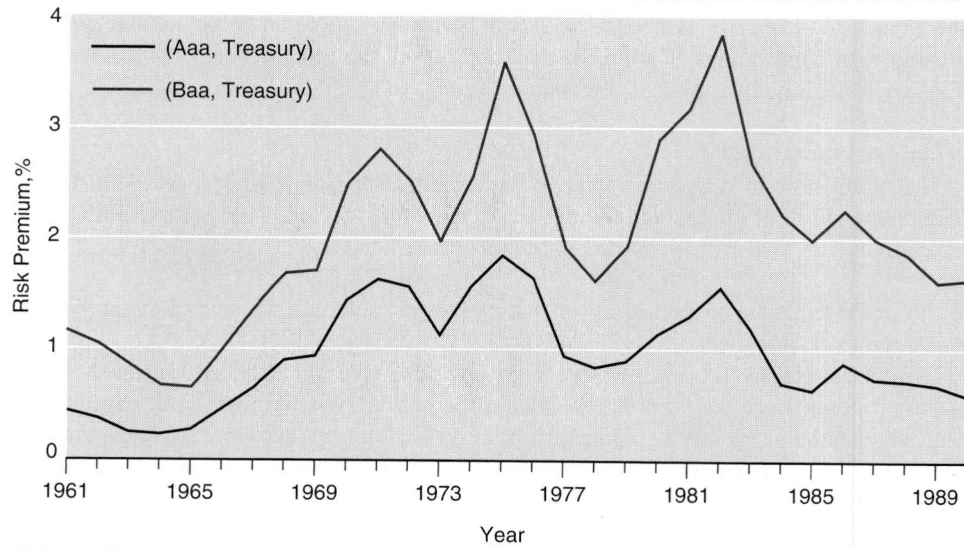

Source: Based on data from U.S. Department of Commerce, Bureau of Economic Analysis, *Business Statistics 1961–1988* and *Survey of Current Business.*

tively high premiums during the early 1980s. Notice, too, that the risk premium of Baa bonds increased by more than the risk premium for Aaa bonds.

Both the size of the premiums and the difference between Aaa and Baa are related to economic conditions. The first round of crude oil price increases in 1973 and 1974 caused general concern that all bond issuers would be adversely affected by the resulting higher cost of operations, and risk premiums increased. Presumably, the less creditworthy borrowers would be affected even more severely, necessitating an even higher risk premium.

Similar concerns were raised in the early 1980s. The 1979 oil price increases again affected the cost of operations, but this time the situation was complicated further by extremely high interest rates. While the risk premium for Aaa bonds rose to nearly the same level as in 1975, the Baa premium rose even higher. As interest rates eased in the 1980s, risk premiums also dropped. Default risk premiums can thus be expected to increase when inflation is high or when economic conditions are generally unfavorable.

Junk Bonds

Despite evidence of fairly substantial risk premiums for BBB-rated corporate debt, bonds rated below investment grade enjoyed unprecedented popularity during the 1980s. These speculative bonds came to be known as *junk bonds,* making up a market that was developed almost solely by the investment banking firm of Drexel Burnham Lambert. Drexel was able to convince institutional investors that firms issuing low-rated bonds had historically defaulted in only a few instances and the low-rated bonds offered yields that were significantly higher than those available from investment grade securities.

Once junk bonds gained acceptance as an investment vehicle, several particular applications began to develop for this form of financing. Firms that previously had been unable to tap public capital markets began to use junk bond financing instead of bank loans or direct placements with insurance companies. Investors who believed management of certain targeted firms was overly conservative, or otherwise inept, used junk bonds to finance corporate takeovers. Management teams issued junk bonds and undertook leveraged buyouts (LBOs) to convert their publicly owned companies to private ownership, hoping to use their increased control to improve operations.

The net result was that firms relying on junk bond financing became increasingly highly leveraged. Higher levels of debt and associated higher fixed interest payments make firms susceptible to failure during economic slowdowns and other periods of reduced sales. A number of highly publicized defaults in the late 1980s led many analysts to conclude that junk bond financing had been overused and that corporate America suffered from excessive exposure to downside risk.

The market value of junk bonds fell in response to these concerns, and Drexel saw the value of its large inventory of the speculative instruments decline significantly. When the firm had difficulty refinancing its short-term liabilities, it filed for protection under federal bankruptcy laws and was later liquidated.

INTEREST RATE PATTERNS IN SELECTED COUNTRIES

Interest rate levels are influenced by market conditions, supply-and-demand factors, inflation, and default risk. Government policy also plays an important role. While national approaches to interest rate management vary from one country to another and over time, no country permits its interest rates to be determined solely by market forces. Even when interest rates are not actually determined by the government, it is not uncommon for government agencies to act as market participants in attempts to achieve a desired interest rate environment. A proper balance of government expenditure and growth of private enterprise is necessary to promote domestic and international prosperity in any country.

Before World War II

In the United States, the Federal Reserve System was established in 1913 for the explicit purpose of maintaining a stable money supply. It implements monetary policy by setting the discount rate (the rate at which it lends to financial institutions). The U.S. system is not unique in this way. In fact, it was patterned after similar systems in Europe, and interest rates in Europe and the United States were maintained at nearly the same level before World War II (1939–1945).

Administration of interest rate policy in the United States has sometimes differed from that of European countries, however. An example can be seen in comparison of Fed actions with those of central banks in other countries in the thirties. In the face of the 1931 worldwide depression and banking crisis, Britain abandoned its gold standard after gold conversions threatened the country's reserves. At the same time, the British government *lowered* interest rates to encourage production and consumption domestically.

In the United States, interest rates had also declined dramatically after the 1929 stock market crash. The Federal Reserve lowered the discount rate from 3 percent in mid-1930 to 1.5 percent in mid-1931. When the dollar was then subjected to massive selling pressure, accompanied by drains on U.S. gold reserves similar to those in Britain, the Federal Reserve responded by *increasing* the discount rate to shore up the value of the dollar internationally. While higher U.S. interest rates would make investment from overseas more attractive, this U.S. response amounted to a policy that actually restrained the domestic economy during a depression.

Beginning in 1932, the business climate improved, commodity prices recovered, and interest rates started to decline. Between 1930 and 1932, bond yields were roughly equivalent in several countries. In the United States, the United Kingdom, and France, for example, high-quality corporate and government bond yields ranged from 3.5 to 4.5 percent. The rates in Germany were higher, with prime corporate and government bonds selling to yield 10 to 12 percent. As high as these rates were, relative to others at the time,

EXHIBIT 9-3 HYPERINFLATION IN GERMANY

After World War I, the Germany economy suffered crippling hyperinflation and currency devaluation. In early 1922, the *Reichsbank* (central bank) discount rate was 5 percent. To curb inflation (associated with war reparation payments) that had been mounting gradually for several years, the rate was raised to 7, then 8, then 10 percent, to no avail. In August 1923, the *Reichsbank* created a new form of discount: loans at "constant value." Such loans were repayable in not less than four-fifths of the British pound value of the amount lent. The discount rate for constant value loans was 10 percent, while the rates for loans that did not enjoy this constant value clause rose as high as 90 percent.

Inflation continued to worsen. In October 1923, the *Reichsbank* printed paper for its notes (money) in thirty different paper mills, but even this level of production was not sufficient. From January to June 1923, the value of the dollar rose from 3644 marks to 22,301 marks. On the Berlin money market, short-term loans in November 1923 were quoted at 30 percent per day, or 10,950 percent per year! In 1924, the mark stabilized, with mark loans down to 13 percent per year by October, while comparable loans in other currencies were priced at 7.2 percent. The German experience during the 1920s is a graphic example of the potentially devastating effect of uncontrolled inflation on interest rates and currency value.

they were *much* lower than the hyperinflationary rates in Germany in the early 1920s. (See Exhibit 9-3.) After 1932, German rates declined, as did rates in other countries.

Riskier bonds yielded substantially higher rates during the economically troubled years from 1930 through 1932. This is an example of the "flight to quality" during times of economic uncertainty. In the United States, for example, at the beginning of 1930 Baa bond rates were 125 percent of corresponding Aaa bond rates. By 1932 this ratio was 185 percent; that is, Baa bond yields were nearly twice those of Aaa bonds. As rates declined after 1932, so did the risk premiums for Baa bonds, bringing the Baa-Aaa yield ratio closer to 145 percent by 1936. After another period of economic depression in 1937 and 1938, the Baa-Aaa ratio peaked at over 180 percent again in 1939 but declined to just over 120 percent by 1945. Since then, the ratio has generally been less than 120 percent.

After World War II

After World War II, interest rates around the world rose. In the United States, wartime personal and corporate income had been high, while expenditures had been restricted. This combination created a pent-up demand that then exerted upward pressure on prices, reflected eventually in rising interest rates. Immediately after the war, in 1946, prime corporate and government yields averaged 2.5 and 2.2 percent, respectively. By 1959, they were 3.9 and 4.4 percent.

Interest rates in other countries also rose. During the immediate post–World War II period, government bond yields in France and the United Kingdom were higher than U.S. rates but lower than Japanese, German, and Italian rates. Increases in Germany were not as great as in other countries because German rates were already relatively high. The Japanese government placed interest rates under its control in 1947. Exhibit 9-4 shows that German and Japanese government bond yields were over 6 percent in the late 1950s, while U.S. government rates were approximately 3 percent. As U.S. rates rose through 1965, Japanese yields were held virtually constant through government control. German

EXHIBIT 9-4 GOVERNMENT BOND YIELDS: SELECTED INDUSTRIALIZED COUNTRIES, 1956–1980

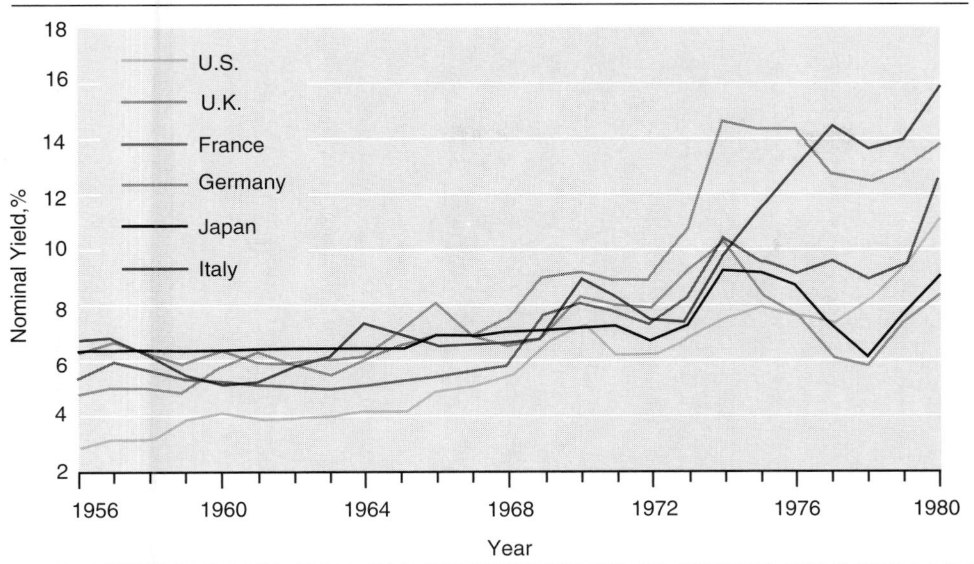

Source: Based on data from International Monetary Fund, *International Financial Statistics,* and Homer, Sydney, *A History of Interest Rates.*

yields showed little variability because, in the 1960s and 1970s, the German government instituted an aggressive program to control inflation.

In 1966, inflation heated up as a result of U.S. government social programs and the war in Vietnam. Payments for social programs rose from $29.4 billion in 1965 to $56.1 billion in 1970, or at an average rate of 13.8 percent per year.[4] Over the same period, national defense expenditures went from $50.6 billion to $81.7 billion, rising 10 percent a year. Federal budget deficits (excess of expenditures over receipts) from 1965 through 1970 totaled $54.2 billion, as compared with $19.6 billion for the 5 years before 1965. These deficits were financed by federal government borrowings and, because the federal government dramatically increased its demand for borrowed funds, interest rates (the price of those funds) also increased. From 1965 to 1970, U.S. government bond yields increased from 4.3 to 7.4 percent. Crude oil prices that quadrupled during 1973 and 1974 further fueled inflation and pushed U.S. yields to 8.0 percent in 1975.

These effects are illustrated in Exhibit 9-4. The interest rate levels in the six industrialized countries shown increased significantly, as did interest rate volatility. The increase in U.K. government yields is notable. While U.S. rates went from 4.3 percent in 1965 to 8.0 percent in 1975, U.K. government bond yields increased from 6.6 to 14.4 percent! This large increase in U.K. rates was the result of government policy that nationalized private industry after World War II, so that the government demand for funds extended to cover the investment needs of what had been private concerns. Also, large social welfare expenditures after 1960 were not accompanied by corresponding increases in industrial productivity. As investment capital left the United Kingdom, national debt increased, exports decreased, imports increased, and inflation and interest rates rose to unprecedented levels.

Exhibit 9-5 shows the interest rate differentials of the European countries included in Exhibit 5-11 vis-à-vis the United States from 1956 to 1980. Rate differentials are calculated as the applicable foreign rate minus the U.S. rate. These differentials dipped in 1959

[4] This represents federal payments for individuals or families for medical care, housing, and food and nutrition.

EXHIBIT 9-5 INTEREST RATE DIFFERENTIALS: SELECTED COUNTRIES VS. THE UNITED STATES, 1956–1980

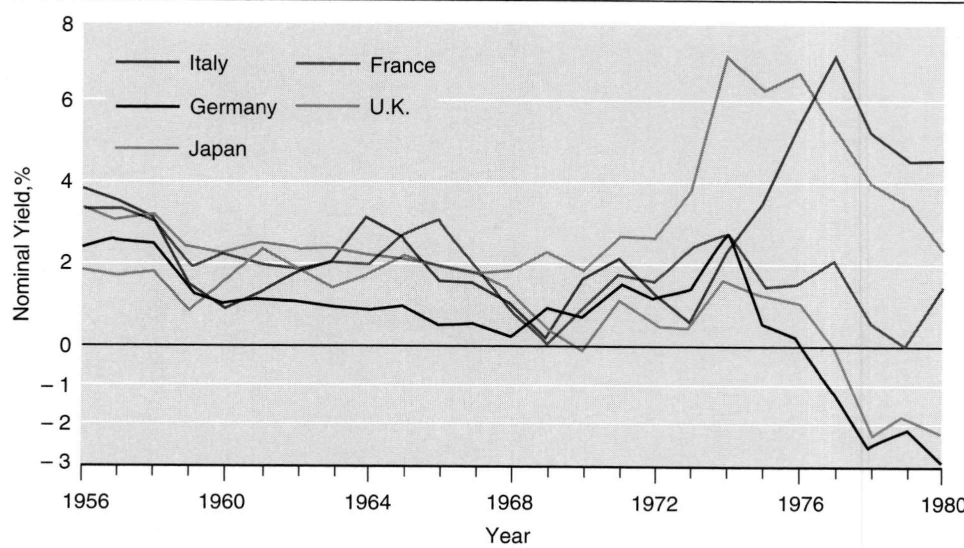

Note: Differential equals applicable foreign government bond rate minus U.S. government bond rate.
Source: Calculations and graphic based on data from International Monetary Fund, *International Financial Statistics,* and Homer, Sydney, *A History of Interest Rates.*

when U.S. rates peaked at 3.9 percent. From 1960 through 1964, the U.K. rates exhibited the most volatile differentials in the face of high social expenditures. After 1965 the differentials became increasingly volatile, as did the yields themselves. Again, the U.K. differential increased fastest, reaching 7.2 percent by 1974. During the 1980s, shifts in government policy to reduce consumption and to increase productivity have restored U.K. inflation rates of return to levels comparable to other major industrialized nations.

It is hard to overstate the role of governments and government agencies in the maintenance of appropriate interest rate levels and general business climate. All countries are interested in promoting domestic prosperity, although they implement different sorts of government policy to accomplish it.

FACTORS INFLUENCING CURRENCY EXCHANGE RATES

An important element of a nation's international economic well-being is how the value of its currency changes relative to others. Chapter 6 showed that interest rates influence forward currency exchange rates in a relationship referred to as *interest rate parity.* In this chapter it has been shown that inflation affects domestic interest rates, thereby affecting *forward exchange* rates.

Purchasing Power Parity

Spot exchange rates will also reflect inflation rate differentials *if* exchange rates are allowed to adjust freely. High rates of inflation generally will cause a currency to lose value, all other things being equal. This concept is called *purchasing power parity.*

Purchasing power parity:
The concept that homogeneous goods cannot have more than one price measured in any one currency. If the price increases domestically, the domestic currency will de-

preciate so that the price of the goods denominated in foreign currency remains the same. This is the *law of one price.*

Over the long term, purchasing power parity satisfactorily explains exchange rate changes. In the short term, however, it is less successful.

The connection between theory and practice breaks down for several reasons in the short term. Technically, only goods that are traded internationally should be subject to the law of one price. It is also not always clear how differences in service and quality of goods are accounted for. Price increases are not necessarily uniform over all products.

Other Factors

Other fundamental factors that influence spot currency exchange rates are:

- Trade imbalances
- Capital flows
- Domestic interest rates
- Political factors

Movements of goods and services across national borders are recorded in a country's *balance of payments,* a summary of international financial activity.

Balance of payments:
The description of financial transactions between a country and its trading partners. The categories include goods (merchandise), services, and investment capital.

Categories of merchandise and their Standard International Trade Classifications (SITC) are:

SITC	Description
1	Food and live animals
2	Beverages and tobacco
3	Crude material excluding fuels
4	Animal and vegetable oil
5	Chemicals
6	Basic manufactures
7	Machinery and transport equipment

Service categories include payments for:

- Professional and other business services
- Insurance and freight
- Interest payments
- Direct investment income

Transactions that are classified as investment capital include:

- Short-term loans
- Long-term loans and other securities
- Direct investment (equity capital)

If a country receives more funds than it disburses, the country has a *surplus* for the period. If the reverse is true, a *deficit* results.

Trade (goods and services) imbalances exert fundamental pressure on exchange rates that does not reverse itself. When a country imports more than it exports, downward pressure is exerted on the currency's value. This is true because paying for the *imports* creates a *demand* for foreign currency. *Exports* create a *supply* of foreign currency that must be converted into the domestic currency to pay for the exports. When a nation experiences a trade deficit (imports in excess of exports), the demand for foreign currency is only partially offset by the supply. The excess demand for foreign currency places upward pressure on foreign currency value and downward pressure on domestic currency value. A trade surplus has the opposite effect.

The effects of *capital flows* are generally reversible. When funds are borrowed abroad in a foreign currency, for example, demand for the foreign currency increases, exerting upward pressure on its value. When the loan is repaid, the relative supply of the foreign currency increases, with downward pressure on its value.

All other things being equal, increases in *domestic interest rates* tend to attract foreign capital and create stronger demand for domestic currency. When rates decline, foreign capital may tend to be reinvested in another country (and another currency), generating weaker demand for the domestic currency.

Although they may be less quantifiable than trade imbalances, capital flows, and interest rates, *political factors* also play a significant role in exchange rate fluctuations. Political stability has a favorable effect on the value of a country's currency. Loss of stability, or even *perceived* loss of stability, depresses its value.

The value of a country's currency can affect its different market sectors in different ways. High and increasing domestic currency values benefit importing sectors, because domestic currency then has relatively more purchasing power abroad. Exporting sectors may find in this case that their goods are not competitively priced in an international sense because the high value of the domestic currency makes their products more expensive overseas.

Domestic price levels and interest rates, trade balances, international capital flows, and political factors all influence currency values and can lead to frequent changes in exchange rates.

Exchange Rate Adjustments

If exchange rates are flexible—that is, if they are permitted to change in response to the factors that influence them—economic imbalances, theoretically, will *self-adjust.* As significant trade surpluses increase the value of the domestic currency, the effective prices for importing sectors are reduced and imports are stimulated.

The reverse is true for exporting sectors. As export prices become less competitive and exports decline, exporting sectors may try to maintain market share by decreasing domestic currency prices, accepting thinner profit margins.

These circumstances have a dampening effect on exports. Higher imports accompanied by lower exports will reduce the trade surplus and the value of the domestic currency along with it.

This self-adjusting process can take place only if exchange rates are allowed to *float* or to vary according to prevailing economic conditions instead of being restricted to a specified relationship with one or more currencies. To see how this works, consider a country with a relatively high rate of inflation and a strong economy. Its inflation rate is likely to be reflected in the country's domestic interest rate structure and currency value.

If the exchange rate with one of this country's trading partners is inflexible—that is, if the two rates are pegged—the domestic currency value will effectively export domestic inflation to its trading partner, but with none of the adjusting mechanisms. As prices rise domestically *and* the domestic currency value is not permitted to adjust, prices will tend to increase for the country's trading partner as well, according to the law of one price.

This line of reasoning suggests the rationale behind floating exchange rates. While floating rates may be desirable, if they become *extremely* volatile, countries that are dependent in a material way on either imports or exports will be exposed to harmful rate volatility. This was the situation in the 1930s—international financial chaos, widespread unemployment, protectionist sentiments, trade restrictions, and competitive currency devaluations that proved detrimental to other countries, all aggravated by abandonment of the gold standard.

RECENT PATTERNS OF FOREIGN EXCHANGE RATES

Exchange Rates during the 1980s—Selected Currencies

In the early 1980s high interest rates in the United States attracted capital from industrialized and developing nations alike. Federal budget deficits rose from $79 billion in 1981 to $128 billion in 1982 and $208 billion in 1983. The government's high demand for funds in the capital market helped push government bond yields from 8 percent in 1975 (Exhibit 9-4) to 13.9 percent in 1981 (Exhibit 8-5). Inflation rates subsided somewhat after 1981, as evidenced by real rates of return on U.S. government bonds of 6.8 percent in 1982 and 7.9 percent in 1983 (Exhibit 8-6).

The phenomenon of high nominal rates accompanied by low inflation is attributable in part to substantial inflows of foreign capital to the United States, a safe haven for investment dollars. The attraction became even stronger when the Tax Reform Act of 1984 eliminated the 30 percent withholding tax on new government and corporate bonds issued in the United States and sold to foreign investors. The value of the dollar reflected this inflow of capital. As can be seen in Exhibit 9-6, the dollar value of other major currencies dropped dramatically. The dollar appreciated on the order of 30 to 40 percent against most major currencies in the early 1980s.

This dramatic appreciation was possible because of the floating-rate system that had been adopted in the early 1970s. The high value of the dollar, of course, was detrimental to the U.S. manufacturing export sector, and trade deficits reached alarming levels. The Federal Reserve had the unenviable task of lowering the value of the dollar while not significantly discouraging providers of foreign capital.

In September 1985, the finance ministers and central bankers of the major industrial countries met at the Plaza Hotel in New York and agreed to facilitate the orderly appreciation of nondollar currencies. The Plaza Agreement marked the beginning of the decline in the value of the dollar. The U.S. government bond yields dropped from 12.5 percent in 1984 to 8.4 percent in 1987 (Exhibit 8-5); real returns went from 8.2 to 4.7 percent (Exhibit 8-6). The dollar value of foreign currencies increased accordingly.

But the other currencies appreciated more than originally anticipated. Despite massive dollar purchases by foreign central banks, the dollar continued to slide. At their meeting early in 1987, the financial ministers and central bankers agreed to help slow the dollar decline (the Louvre Accord). Since then, exchange rates have moderated.

The exchange rate volatility during the 1980s underscores the market's sensitivity to real economic factors. Lower interest rates and persistent trade deficits brought the value of the U.S. dollar down as quickly as high interest rates and tax incentives had pushed it up. It appears that such volatility is a trade-off that must be accepted to avoid the financial market chaos that characterized the last days of Bretton Woods, the system of pegged exchange rates that began in 1944 and ended in 1971 when the United States abandoned the gold standard.

The Case of Latin America

Floating exchange rates are not necessarily an antidote to financial chaos. Latin America is a case in point.

EXHIBIT 9-6 U.S. DOLLAR VALUE OF SELECTED CURRENCIES, 1980–1990

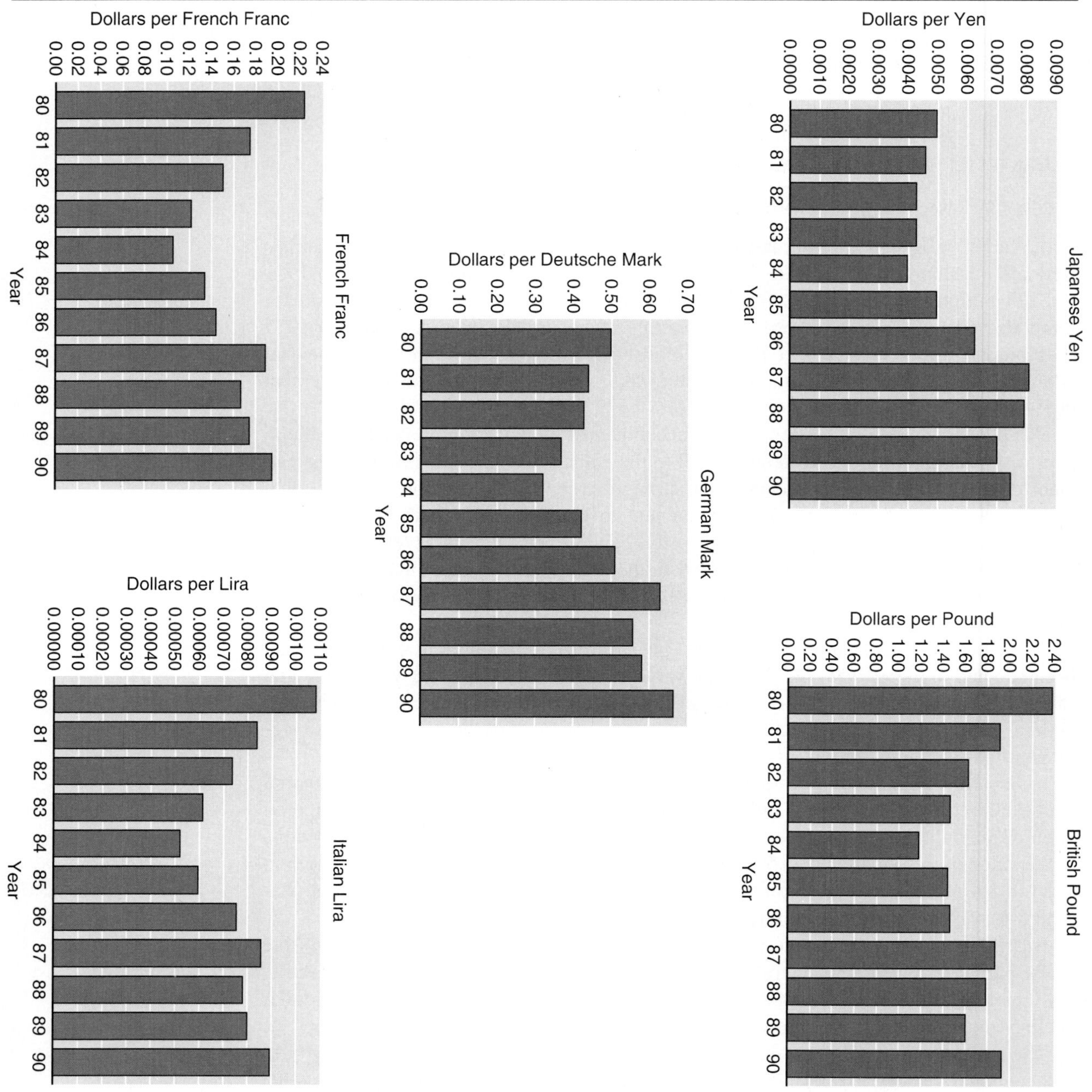

Source: Calculations and graphics based on data from International Monetary Fund, *International Financial Statistics.*

As crude oil prices increased in the 1970s, many developing countries found the value of their exports insufficient to cover the cost of the oil they needed, while oil-exporting countries found themselves with large trade surpluses to invest. In many cases, these surpluses were deposited in commercial banks and then loaned to oil-importing countries or *recycled* to help developing oil-importing countries cover their oil-import-driven trade deficits. Debt levels rose significantly.

From 1970 through 1980, the external debt (debt owed to foreign lenders) of all developing countries rose from $66.9 billion to $572.2 billion. Of the 1980 total, Latin American and the Caribbean countries owed $242.7 billion, or 42 percent. Just 2 years later, the external debt of all developing countries had grown by almost $200 billion to $752.9 billion, with Latin America and the Caribbean representing $333.5 billion, or 44 percent. In 1982 among the Latin American countries, Argentina ($43.6 billion), Brazil ($83.2 billion), and Mexico ($87.6 billion) accounted for $214.4 billion of external debt. (See Exhibit 9.7.)

Mexico was actually an oil exporter, but the country borrowed heavily against future oil revenues to finance infrastructure and industrial development projects. The effect of having so much external debt was that a large proportion of export earnings went to service the debt. When the price of oil dropped precipitously, Mexico's oil export earnings could no longer cover its interest and principal payments.

In 1982, Mexico announced that it could not make its payments, and the serious overburden of debt in many developing countries was recognized. Since that time, the governments and banks involved, along with international organizations such as the IMF and the World Bank, have worked to resolve the problem. Meanwhile, new debt was required to make the payments on old debt, and the mountain of debt only continued to grow. In 1989, Argentina ($61.9 billion), Brazil ($112.7 billion), and Mexico ($102.6 billion) owed a total of $277.2 billion to foreign lenders.

Debt payments have been rescheduled (delayed), and, in the case of Mexico some debt has been forgiven. All three countries have adopted austerity measures that include reducing imports that would have been used for capital investment. The almost continual debt renegotiation has discouraged new investment from outside the region, and some of the capital already invested was moved to safer havens.

These developments have caused the demand for the currencies of Argentina, Brazil, and Mexico to evaporate. Exhibit 9-8 provides a summary of the dollar values of their currencies from 1981 through 1990. The value of the Mexican peso went from $0.038 to

EXHIBIT 9-7 EXTERNAL DEBT: ARGENTINA, BRAZIL, AND MEXICO, 1970–1989

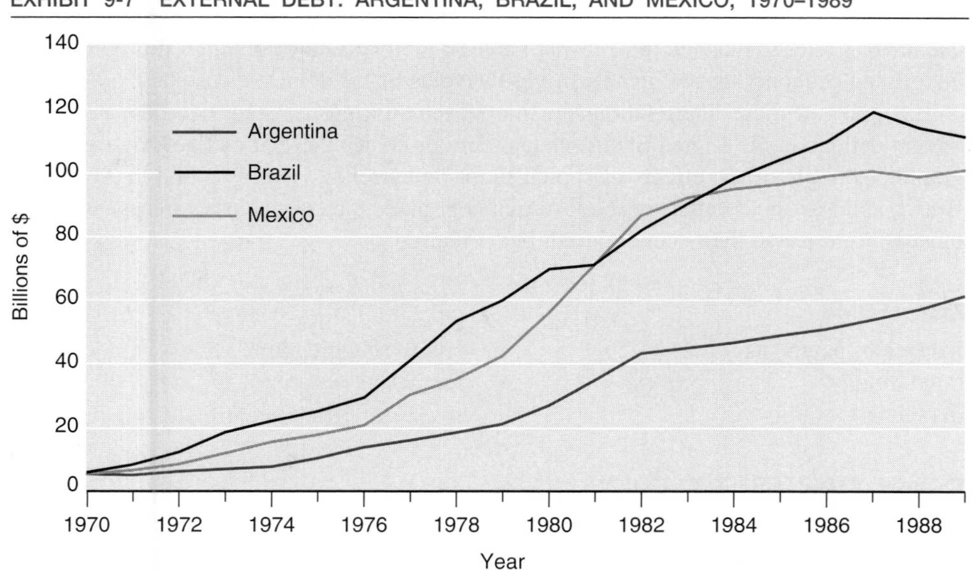

Source: Based on data from World Bank, *World Bank Debt Tables 1989–1990* and *Trends in Developing Economies 1989,* and United Nations, *Economic Survey of Latin American and the Caribbean 1988.*

EXHIBIT 9-8 EXCHANGE RATES FOR ARGENTINA, BRAZIL, AND MEXICO, 1981–1990*

Year	Argentina	Brazil	Mexico
1981	1163.960000	7682.307690	0.038168
1982	551.555000	4000.000000	0.010363
1983	43.622900	1020.408160	0.006949
1984	4.734080	314.465400	0.005192
1985	1.249624	95.328880	0.002690
1986	0.795312	67.114090	0.001083
1987	0.266670	13.840830	0.000453
1988	0.074794	1.306677	0.000438
1989	0.000557	0.088044	0.000379
1990	0.000179	0.005648	0.000239

*U.S. dollars per unit of local currency.

Source: Calculations based on data from International Monetary Fund, *International Financial Statistics.*

$0.0002. Argentina's currency value fell from over $1000 to less than a penny.[5] The Brazilian cruzeiro plummeted from over $7000 to less than a penny.

This breakdown in international financial viability all but brought these countries to their knees. Argentina, Brazil, and Mexico are tragic reminders of the interrelationship between domestic and international economics.

SUMMARY

Default risk has an effect on interest rates. The greater the perceived probability of borrower default, the greater the default risk premium that is included in interest rates. Even the highest-grade corporate bonds require a risk premium over the U.S. Treasury bond rate, and bonds with lower ratings require greater default risk premiums. Over time, default risk premiums have grown, especially during economic crises and especially for lower-rated bonds.

In a sound economy, high interest rates attract foreign investment. Demand for the currency increases, which increases its value. This linkage means that central banks can use interest rates to manage the external value of their currency, although it is a country's underlying economy that ultimately drives the value of the domestic currency.

Examples of these interrelationships have been striking in recent decades. Trade and budget deficits in the United States made other currencies more attractive. An even more graphic example of the effects of capital flight on currency value is found in Argentina, Brazil, and Mexico. Unmanageable external debt made the currencies of these nations almost worthless, and their economies all but collapsed.

KEY TERMS

balance of payments
bond rating
default risk
default risk premium
purchasing power parity
investment grade securities

END-OF-CHAPTER QUESTIONS

1. Both anticipated inflation rates and default risk influence interest rates.
  a. How do these factors differ?

[5] The peso was converted to the peso Argentino in 1983. The peso Argentino was converted to the austral in 1985.

b. How can you estimate the effect of the two factors?

2. Define default risk premiums.
3. What has been the pattern of default risk premiums for AAA corporate bonds? for BBB corporate bonds?
4. Obtain a recent edition of the *Wall Street Journal.* Calculate the approximate yield to maturity of an AT&T bond (New York Exchange Traded Bonds).
5. Using the same edition of the *Wall Street Journal,* compare your answer in *4* to the yield to maturity of a Treasury security of the same maturity (Treasury bonds, notes, and bills). To what do you attribute the difference?
6. Research one of the recent junk bond failures, and identify the factors that led to the firm's bankruptcy.
7. Historically, what has been the effect on domestic interest rates of budget deficits, inflation, and trade deficits? Give specific examples.
8. Describe purchasing power parity.
9. What is the balance of payments?
10. Under a floating foreign exchange system, how do exchange rates react to trade surpluses? to trade deficits?
11. Determine the current dollar value of Japanese yen, British pounds, German marks, French francs, and Italian lira. Compare these to the values shown in Exhibit 9-6.
12. What factors do you think have influenced your findings in *11?*
13. The U.S. Treasury Department initiated a plan to help resolve the Latin American debt crisis that was commonly referred to as the Brady Plan. Using library resources, determine the primary country that has been helped by this plan and the provisions of the plan.
14. Since the 1980s the U.S. budget deficit has not been reduced. Should foreign investors lose confidence in the ability of the U.S. government to repay its debt, what developments would you expect to occur in the United States?

SELECTED REFERENCES

Adams, T. F. M., and Iwao Hoshii. *A Financial History of the New Japan.* Kodansha International, Ltd., Tokyo, 1972.

Benoit, J. Pierre V. *United States Interest Rates and the Interest Rate Dilemma for the Developing World,* Quorum Books, Westport, Connecticut, 1986.

Comparative Economic and Financial Statistics; Japan and Other Major Countries, Bank of Japan, Tokyo, 1988.

Economic Survey of Latin America and the Caribbean 1988, United Nations, Santiago, Chile, 1989.

The European Monetary System: Developments and Perspectives, International Monetary Fund, Washington, D.C., November 1990.

Handbook of International Trade and Development Statistics 1988, United Nations, New York, 1989.

Historical Tables; Budget of the United States Government; Fiscal Year 1990, U.S. Office of Management and Budget, Washington, D.C., 1989.

Havrilesky, Thomas M., and Robert Schweitzer, Editors. *Contemporary Developments in Financial Institutions and Markets,* Harlan Davidson, Inc., Arlington Heights, Illinois, 1987.

Homer, Sydney. *A History of Interest Rates,* 2d edition, Rutgers University Press, New Brunswick, New Jersey, 1977.

Internationalization of the Securities Markets; Report to the Senate Committee on Banking, Housing, and Urban Affairs and the House Committee on Energy and Commerce, U.S. Securities and Exchange Commission, Washington, D.C., 1987.

Kaufman, Hugo M. *Germany's International Monetary Policy and the European Monetary System,* Brooklyn College Press, New York, 1985.

Onoh, J. K. *Money and Banking in Africa,* Longman Group, Ltd., London, 1982.

Trends in Developing Economies 1989, World Bank, Washington, D.C., 1989.

World Bank Debt Tables, Country Tables 1970–1979 and Analysis and Summary Tables 1989–1990, World Bank.

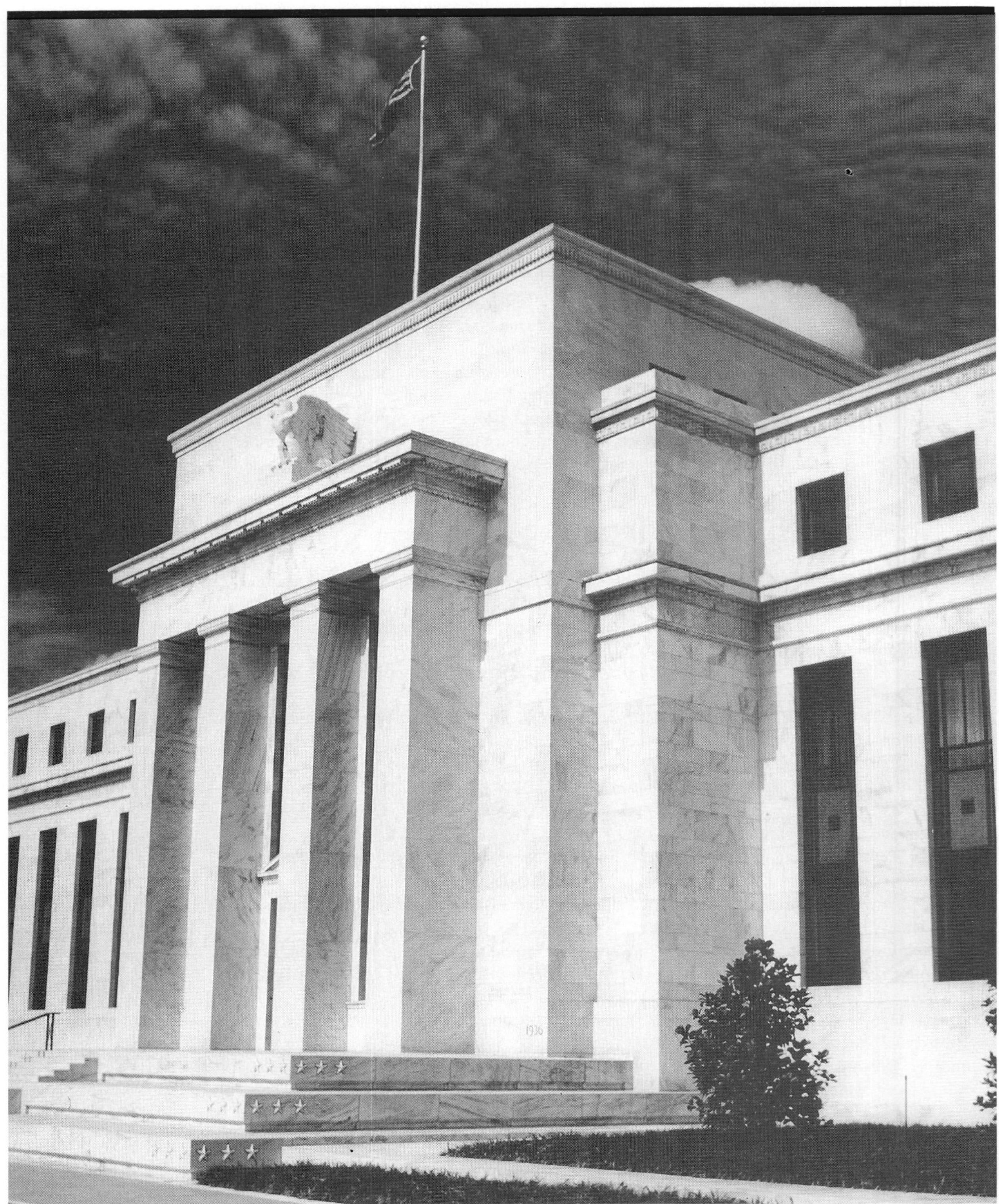
1936

PART TWO:

BANK REGULATION

CHAPTER 10

THE FORMATION OF U.S. BANK REGULATION AND THE FEDERAL RESERVE SYSTEM

CHAPTER OUTLINE

CHAPTER OVERVIEW

This chapter describes:

- The formation of the U.S. banking system
- Principles of central banking
- The origin, structure, and responsibilities of the Federal Reserve System
- The rationale for bank regulation
- Important regulatory legislation before 1980

The Federal Reserve System is one of several government organizations that play a significant role in the U.S. banking system. As the linchpin of the banking system, its responsibilities go far beyond maintenance of an orderly banking system. This chapter explains the Fed's regulatory functions and how they relate to regulatory activities of other government institutions.

Bank regulation has evolved for close to two centuries. Both state and federal authorities oversee bank operations. A historical difference between the degree of regulatory restriction at the two levels of government encouraged the development of a dual banking system in the United States. To some extent, bank regulation represents government reaction to adverse economic conditions at the time. Both the dual banking system and the regulatory environment are best understood after considering the development of commercial banking in the United States.

BANKING IN THE UNITED STATES: A HISTORICAL PERSPECTIVE

The first U.S. bank, the Bank of North America, was formed in 1781 by a group of patriotic merchants whose objective was to generate funds for the Continental Army. Even though it was a private financial institution, the American colonies and later the U.S. Congress (after the U.S. Constitution was ratified) pledged support and guaranteed depositors against loss. Operation of the bank ceased in 1791, when another institution assumed its functions. In the interim, other state-chartered banks began to operate.

The First Official U.S. Banks

In the early days of the United States, state-chartered banks issued liabilities, called bank notes, that circulated as money. These notes were backed by gold or silver (held as bank assets) and convertible into precious metal on demand. Because each bank issued its own "money," the country's currency was not uniform. Worse, some bankers were known to operate in unscrupulous ways—defrauding depositors or setting up their bank note conversion facilities in remote areas to discourage conversion. This history caused significant opposition to nationwide banking, despite the need for a uniform money creation function.

Alexander Hamilton, the first Secretary of the Treasury from 1789 to 1795, and the architect of the system, advocated a strong banking network. In 1790, during George Washington's first term as President, Hamilton conceived the idea of a national bank. It was not to be a central bank in the European sense; it would neither have a large number of branches nor be publicly owned.

A national bank with note-issuing powers could convert the national debt into a medium of exchange if government securities could be used to collateralize or back national bank notes.[1] The government could thereby standardize the nation's currency *and* finance its operations. A strong national bank would also promote business and industry. As one who believed that the industrial interests of a developing nation were of primary importance, Hamilton saw this as a powerful argument in favor of a national bank.

Hamilton's concept was not without opposition. Thomas Jefferson (drafter of the Declaration of Independence, Secretary of State from 1790 to 1793, and President from 1801 to 1809) opposed both strong central government and a national banking system. As an advocate for the agricultural sector and for the rights of the states and local authorities, he championed self-reliance, not government protection or planning, as the key to the success of America. In fact, he advised George Washington that a national bank was unconstitutional. But the President accepted Hamilton's argument, and in 1791 the 20-year charter of the First Bank of the United States was granted.

The First Bank of the United States The First Bank of the United States accepted deposits, made loans, and issued paper currency. It carried on both private business and the official business of the government. Soon it was the country's largest bank, with branches located in all major cities and notes circulating throughout the country. It began to be noted that requiring state banks to redeem their notes (convert them into specie—precious metal) constrained the money supply. This observation may have planted the

[1] See Chapter 2 for a description of the functions of money, including medium of exchange.

first seed of monetary policy whose implementation was later to become a major objective of the federal government.

The 20-year charter was apparently not long enough for the new bank to prove its worth. The power accruing to the First Bank because of its special relationship with the federal government was distasteful to some. Its relatively restrictive policy with respect to growth of the money supply was not well received, and those state banks that had been forced to redeem their own notes formed a strong lobby against the bank.[2] By 1811, when its charter expired, the Jeffersonians were in office. The charter was not renewed.

Between 1811 and 1816, the volume of circulating bank notes more than doubled to over $200 million, and the state banking system was found inadequate to accommodate the nation's needs. Complete convertibility became virtually impossible, given the limited supply of gold and silver coins. Indeed, the first bank failure in the United States is an example of the abuse of note-issuing powers: When a Rhode Island bank that had issued $800,000 in notes failed in 1809, it was discovered that the bank had only $45 in capital.

This kind of high-leverage potential encouraged bank creation. In 1781, there were only five commercial banks in operation, but by the time the charter of the First Bank of the United States expired, the number had grown to 250. The need for a national currency remained unmet, while practices like those of the Rhode Island bank fueled resistance to the banking industry.

The Second Bank of the United States During the War of 1812, a sizable national debt (in the form of government bonds) had been built up, and the money supply issued by state banks remained unstable. The Second Bank of the United States was chartered in 1816 to address the lack of a national currency. The Second Bank was entitled to repay the government bonds with bank notes backed by government securities, thus providing a uniform national currency.

It quickly became a powerful financial presence, holding the federal government's deposits and a large share of private wealth. Foreign currency exchange activity was almost exclusively coordinated by the Bank, and it had close relationships with large (money center) banks in New York, Chicago, and St. Louis. Smaller state banks looked to it as a lender of last resort, or the ultimate provider of liquidity in the event of crisis. The bank even acted to restrict the money supply when it was believed that speculative lending was accelerating at unacceptable rates.

Nevertheless, it enjoyed little popularity. Its branches crossed state lines, giving rise to territorial disputes with state banks. Andrew Jackson, President from 1829 to 1837, was also opposed to the Bank. He considered his constituency to be the farmers and laborers of the country—people who were opening up the frontier to agriculture and mining, developing roads and canals, and building new cities and towns. These people found their futures and fortunes tied to a concentration of power and wealth in the northeast, where the Second Bank of the United States was headquartered.

In 1832, Jackson vetoed legislation that would have kept the Bank alive. The following year, the Treasury withdrew its funds and redeposited them into a number of state banks. The Bank's charter was not renewed upon expiration in 1836, and no national bank following this model has been chartered since. So began the "free banking" era, a period of less regulation for the industry than at any other time in its history in the United States.

[2] Recall from Chapter 2 that removing liquidity (or reserves) from the banking system contracts the money supply by some multiple. In the early days of the United States, bank notes were the primary liabilities of banks and were convertible into specie (precious-metal reserves), and conversion had the effect of reducing the money supply.

The Free Banking Era

By 1836, the number of state banks had grown to 600. From that date until 1863, when the National Bank Act was passed, the federal government had no role in commercial banking. In the interim, 1600 state banks issued their own bank notes, or IOUs. Specie, generally gold or silver coins, continued to be legal tender, although the volume of notes that circulated often made guaranteed convertibility virtually impossible. Unscrupulous bankers generated large volumes of notes that could never be redeemed or issued notes and then avoided redemption requests. Not surprisingly, then, many of these banks failed.

To finance the Civil War (1861–1865), the administration of Abraham Lincoln (whose term as President coincided with the duration of the war) borrowed heavily, suspended gold convertibility of state bank notes, and issued *greenbacks.*

Greenbacks:
National paper currency printed by the federal government but not backed by gold.

The combination of these factors increased the money supply significantly, and prices rose by 74 percent from 1861 through 1864. Institutional changes were the natural response to the need to manage both the cost of the war and the growth in the money supply.

The National Bank Act of 1863

The National Bank Act of 1863 brought hope of lasting relief from the undependability associated with a nonuniform currency and an unregulated system. A new system of commercial banks was established—national banks. Specifically:

- National banks were to be chartered by a new Comptroller of the Currency (with reporting responsibility to the Secretary of the Treasury).
- Minimum capital requirements were set for national charters.
- National bank notes were backed by Treasury securities and printed by the Treasury to ensure uniformity.
- Minimum reserves against bank notes and deposits were held by the Comptroller.
- The Comptroller imposed restrictions on the lending activities of national banks in order to ensure liquidity and safety and could examine national banks regularly for compliance.

After the Civil War, with this new banking structure in place, the government gradually retired the greenbacks from circulation and reinstated gold convertibility. The hope had been that most state banks would convert to the new national charter, which would give the federal government more control over the money supply. By 1865, there were 1000 national banks, bringing the total number of banks to around 1600, a lower conversion rate than Congress had anticipated.

Conversions accelerated when Congress levied a 10 percent tax on state bank notes that proved to be a powerful incentive. In 1866, fewer than 400 of the 600 state banks remained; those that survived were the strongest of the group. State bank notes virtually disappeared, replaced by deposit funds, which became a critical part of state banking. Transactions accounts grew in popularity as state banks encouraged the use and acceptance of checks, which became a mainstay of commercial banking. (See Exhibit 10-1.)

The check was the key to state bank survival. Because state banking laws continued to be more lenient than federal ones, the number of state banks continued to grow, reaching 1500 by 1888. From 1900 to 1920, the total number of banks expanded from 12,427 to over 30,000, with new state bank charters accounting for 76 percent of the increase.

EXHIBIT 10-1 EARLY CHECKING ACCOUNTS IN THE UNITED STATES

A small group of Boston businessmen founded "The Fund at Boston in New England" in 1691, seeking to protect themselves against shortages of hard currency. The objective was to provide a ready source of coin, the only universally accepted medium of exchange at the time. To accomplish this goal, the group mortgaged their land and commodities and placed the proceeds in the fund. This enabled them to draw checks against the fund, which proved to be an idea before its time. Without a sound banking system in place, the checks were not readily accepted by other people, making the early checks an infeasible method of payment.

While there was now a uniform currency printed by the Treasury, national banks and state-chartered banks operated side by side in a *dual banking system.*

Dual banking system:

Banking system in which a bank may obtain either a federal charter (from the Office of the Comptroller of the Currency) or a state charter (from state banking authorities).

The Independent Treasury System

The government had been operating since 1836 without an official, or central, bank while the Treasury Department performed government finance functions. In 1846, the *Independent Treasury System* was introduced and operated outside the commercial banking system, as an alternative to a central bank. Subtreasuries in various cities held federal government reserves, primarily import duty receipts. The Treasury also paid interest on the national debt that accumulated during the Civil War.

The postwar economic expansion and high import duties resulted in large government surpluses, which were used to retire the national debt that had mounted during the Civil War. But Treasury redemptions were unpredictable and sometimes had destabilizing effects on the economy.

The banking system, moreover, was subject to serious fluctuations in reserves. Thousands of small national banks were required to keep their reserves on deposit at larger banks in forty-seven *reserve cities* designated by the Comptroller. These banks, in turn, had to keep their reserves on deposit at money center banks in the *central reserve cities* of New York, Chicago, and St. Louis. When demand for loans at the smaller banks peaked, the small national banks requested withdrawals from the reserve banks.

The money center banks generally maintained liquid assets that were more than sufficient to meet withdrawal demand. When necessary, they could organize groups, or *syndicates,* to satisfy the requests.

Bank syndicate:

Group of banks that together contribute the necessary financing for a transaction (deposit withdrawal or loan).

If withdrawal demand exceeded the available liquidity in money center banks, however, a *money panic* could ensue.

Money panic:

Rapid withdrawal of deposits from a commercial bank precipitated by fear that the bank will fail.

Whenever money center banks were unable to honor deposit withdrawal requests by local banks, the local banks were forced to deny customer loan requests. Depositors would then become uncertain of the soundness of the bank and withdraw funds at rates that banks could not sustain. If one bank failed, depositors of neighboring banks became fearful that their money was not safe and began the process again. These money panics could affect entire regions of the country. (See Exhibit 10-2.)

By 1900, it was apparent to Treasury officials that government expenditures had a significant impact on the economy. In 1902, when commercial bank reserves relative to deposits fell to a 20-year low, the Treasury stepped in. Prepayments of interest on government bonds, purchases of government bonds at premium prices, and deposits of government bonds in national banks pumped needed liquidity into the system, thereby averting one money panic.

At the same time, it appeared that purely economic considerations did not always motivate the Treasury's selection of banks that were to receive assistance. There was fear that politics might favor banks in some geographic regions over others. Recurrent money panics during the late 1800s encouraged acceptance of the need for a true central bank, as support for an independent central bank grew among the newly prosperous members of banking and manufacturing circles. A central bank would offer control over the money supply and improved credit availability.

The primary problems with the Independent Treasury System can be summarized as follows:

- The nation's economic growth was occurring primarily in the regions outside the

EXHIBIT 10-2 J. P. MORGAN: LENDER OF LAST RESORT

James Pierpont Morgan (1837–1913) amassed a vast fortune during the independent treasury era. He controlled banks, insurance companies, railroads, shipping lines, and communications systems. In many ways, J. P. Morgan acted as a central banker during this period. When there was need for reserves in the money center banks, it was often Morgan who organized the syndicates. In 1895, he even rescued the federal government. With the discovery of gold in Alaska and in South Africa in the 1890s, the money supply increased. The U.S. investors who became concerned that hyperinflation might make their portfolios worthless demanded gold for their currency to reinvest in Europe. In desperation, the Treasury turned to Morgan. He organized a syndicate and provided 3.5 million ounces of gold to bail out the U.S. government.

Ultimately, these arrangements could not be sustained. In 1907, Morgan turned to the government for help. Knickerbocker, New York's third-largest bank, was suddenly bankrupted as a result of usually high deposit withdrawal demand. Morgan organized $25 million in emergency loans, followed by another $10 million the next day, but panic would not be contained. Smaller banks feared being cut off by their money center banks and pressed for massive withdrawals. When Morgan appealed to President Theodore Roosevelt for help in October, the Treasury quickly deposited $25 million in the New York banks and controlled its own withdrawals across the country. The total infusion to New York banks eventually grew to $38 million. One month later, the Treasury issued $150 million in new government securities and allowed commercial banks to use them as collateral to create new money. A crisis of this dimension demonstrated how much the monetary system was in need of restructuring.

Source: Greider, William, *Secrets of the Temple: How the Federal Reserve Runs the Country,* Touchstone/Simon and Schuster, New York, 1987.

northeast, yet the money center banks in the northeast controlled a significant amount of the money supply. In other words, the money supply was not sensitive to needs for financing in the regions experiencing economic growth.

- The money supply was inelastic in that it was tied to the amount of gold and government securities, and the availability of gold constrained the extent to which the money supply could expand. In the 1890s, the discovery of gold in Alaska and South Africa increased the supply of gold (and the money supply) so dramatically that inflation became a threat to the economy. At the same time, the federal debt generally declined after passage of the National Bank Act, causing the money supply to contract. These responses were not necessarily appropriate to meet prevailing economic circumstances.
- The number of commercial banks had grown dramatically, despite the money panics, from 1600 in 1865 to 12,427 in 1900 to approximately 25,000 by 1912. Neither the Treasury Department nor the money center banks could adequately service the liquidity needs of such an extensive system.

The Federal Reserve Act

The bank created by the Federal Reserve Act in 1913 was not in the tradition of the first two experiments of 1791 and 1816 and attempted to avoid the problems of the Independent Treasury System. It was a decentralized and independent bank, with twelve regional banks as the basis of the system. Each had authority over a specific geographic region.[3] The regional banks were to be supervised by the Federal Reserve Board in Washington, D.C.

Federal Reserve System:
A system of twelve regional banks, coordinated by the Federal Reserve Board. It is the first system in the United States designed to perform all the traditional functions of a central bank.

Nationally chartered banks are required to be members of the Federal Reserve, and state banks can elect to be members. Member banks contribute the equity capital for their respective reserve bank, receiving in return a predetermined dividend (not a share of total Federal Reserve earnings). Member banks elect six of the nine directors of their reserve bank, of whom, no more than three can be bankers. Those directors not selected by member banks are appointed by the Federal Reserve Board.

The President of the United States originally appointed five of the seven members of the Federal Reserve Board; the Secretary of the Treasury and the Comptroller of the Currency occupied the remaining two seats. In the 1930s these two seats were relinquished to Presidential appointees so that currently all Board members are appointed.

The Federal Reserve System is not the first organization to have a national banking presence in the United States, nor is it the first to conduct monetary transactions on behalf of the government. It is the first, however, to assume the full range of central banking functions (performing banking activities for the government, regulating commercial banks, maintaining orderly financial markets, acting as lender of last resort, and managing the domestic currency value).

The initial objective of the Federal Reserve was to minimize the problems of instability of the money supply and credit availability. The reserve banks are charged with maintaining sound credit conditions and accommodating commerce, industry, and agriculture in their regions. Over time, the role of the Federal Reserve has grown beyond this initial responsibility.

[3] Regional Federal Reserve Banks are located in New York, Boston, Philadelphia, Richmond (Virginia), Atlanta, Cleveland, Chicago, St. Louis, Kansas City, Minneapolis, Dallas, and San Francisco.

The Federal Reserve was designed with responsibilities intended to prevent the money panics that had plagued the country prior to its creation. Specifically, regional reserve banks:

- Were given significant note issue authority
- Became fiscal agents of the federal government
- Were given the authority to rediscount commercial notes
- Were designated to hold the required reserves of members
- Became lenders of last resort in their respective regions

The Federal Reserve Board is clearly a more governmental body than the reserve banks. In supervising the reserve banks, the Board is to regulate the relationships between and among itself, the reserve banks, and the government. While it was unclear at the time of the legislation whether the regional banks or the Board had the authority (1) to intervene in the money market through securities transactions and (2) to adjust the interest rate at which commercial notes could be rediscounted, these functions became defined as U.S. bank regulation continued to take shape.

CHARACTERISTICS OF MODERN CENTRAL BANKING

Central banks serve a variety of functions. "Serve" is the key word. Unlike its eighteenth- and nineteenth-century predecessors, the First and Second Banks of the United States, the modern central bank is a financial institution that is not established to compete with commercial banks; profitability is not its primary objective. It serves government, banks, other financial institutions, and the public.

In any country, a compelling reason for a central bank is to inspire confidence in the nation's money. This motivation forms the basis for a central bank's relationships with government and the commercial banking system. The central bank helps manage a country's national debt. In some cases, it has enhanced the marketability of government securities by requiring that early commercial bank notes be collateralized by government securities.

As economies develop, the role of a central bank tends to expand. Stability of securities markets and other financial institutions is added to the list of objectives. Further, after the early 1930s, levels of national income and employment became issues for central banks, as well as federal governments. As increasing international trade caused interest rates and price levels of one country to affect those of its trading partners, central banks became international financial intermediaries. An outgrowth of this expanded scope has been a strong alliance between central bank and Treasury authorities.

Central bank:

A financial institution that carries out the financial transactions of the federal government, controls and regulates the money supply, maintains order in financial markets, promotes favorable economic conditions, and/or acts as a lender of last resort for other financial institutions.

In the United States, the Federal Reserve has acted in each of these capacities, meeting needs that the First and Second Banks of the United States were unable to satisfy.

Government Relations

The basic characteristic of central banks is, in one sense or another, a *close link to government.* Theoretically, there are two extreme types of relationship between the two entities. At one end of the continuum would be a central bank that is merely a subdivision of the Treasury. The motivation for such an arrangement is that if government is held accountable for every facet of the economy, monetary policy and the central bank must be under government control.

The other extreme, which the U.S. Federal Reserve System typifies, is a completely independent central bank. Independence from government influence preserves freedom from the conflict of interest involved when a single official entity both creates and spends money.

Central bank–government relationships throughout the world fall somewhere between the two extremes. A central bank generally acts in both *advisory* and *operational* capacities. Government policy decisions are made on the advice of central banks. The weight that this advice carries, of course, is a function of the institution's independence. If the bank is strongly independent, the "advice" constitutes a policy decision because the government has little power to reverse the central bank's decision. With respect to operations, central banks handle their governments' official transactions. Domestically, this encompasses Treasury security issuance, interest payments, and redemptions. Overseas responsibilities extend to foreign currency transactions. Given these responsibilities, it is not surprising that treasury departments and central banks tend to work in close harmony.

Commercial Banking Responsibilities

A second characteristic of central banks is their supportive role in *maintaining of a sound commercial banking system.* Historically, economic instability frequently arises out of *monetary* instability. Excessive bank lending can lead to inflationary pressures. Strict curtailment of loans and other forms of credit can have the opposite effect. When central banks exert some influence over the amount of available credit, it is possible to smooth the peaks and valleys of monetary and therefore economic growth. Stability is a common goal of national monetary policy, and the macroeconomic justification for the commercial bank–central bank relationship.

The microeconomic rationale for the relationship has to do with the nature of commercial banks. Banks are usually major participants in the payments mechanism of a country, and their demand and other deposits constitute a significant portion of the money supply. The aim of profit-seeking commercial banks, however, is to invest depositors' funds in assets that will earn bank shareholders a reasonable rate of return. As a result, bank asset portfolios are at least partially illiquid.

A sudden and unusually high level of deposit withdrawals can threaten a bank's solvency. If the demands are not met, the result has often been similar pressure on other institutions. Again, the net effect is undesirable monetary instability. When central banks act as *lender of last resort,* they mitigate this instability and help preserve confidence in the system.

Lender of last resort:
The financial institution from which other financial institutions may ultimately receive assistance during a liquidity crisis.

If such support were to be unqualified, it might lead to excessive risk taking by commercial bank management, so central banks often supervise and oversee commercial bank operations, including the degree of loan riskiness, the amount of bank capital, and compliance with bank laws and regulations.

Orderly Financial Markets

The lender-of-last-resort function goes beyond commercial banking. The third function of central banking is to *provide liquidity in any financial crisis.* As savings institutions, investment funds, and other institutions offer products that are essentially transactions (checking) accounts, a nation's vulnerability to monetary instability increases. Frequently, securities purchases are financed through credit arrangements. A sudden and dramatic decline in the value of marketable securities can create the need for additional liquidity to maintain adequate collateral for securities loans. Some economic circumstances could engender a systemwide liquidity crisis. Whatever the threat to monetary stability, a central bank must be prepared to remove it.

General Economic Conditions

Since the Great Depression in the 1930s, central banks have been held at least partially responsible for *preventing adverse economic fluctuations.* In order to achieve desired advances in employment and the general standard of living, governments have relied increasingly on central banks to ensure adequate credit availability for investment and consumption. This, in turn, has led central banks to adopt monetary growth targets, either growth in money supply or growth in outstanding credit. Income and employment goals are thus added to the goal of monetary stability.

Domestic Currency Value

Cross-border trade has increased significantly in recent decades, which means that price levels in foreign countries can have a significant impact on a domestic economy. Costs for importing raw materials and finished products will fluctuate with the value of the domestic currency vis-à-vis foreign currencies. Thus, the last defining characteristic of modern central banking is *management of the external value of the domestic currency.*

Actual management of the exchange value of the domestic currency can be quite complicated. If the value of the domestic currency is too low, imported goods can become prohibitively expensive. If its value is too high, imports are less expensive, but the country's exports may not be competitively priced.

Factors that influence the exchange value of the currency include domestic interest rates, international trade balance, and domestic fiscal policy. All other things being equal, high interest rates attract foreign capital and increase the value of domestic currency. International trade surpluses (exports in excess of imports) also increase demand for domestic currency, placing upward pressure on its value. Low interest rates and trade deficits depress currency value.[4]

Domestic budget deficits have a negative effect on currency value. When government expenditures exceed receipts of income tax and other revenues, either more money must be created or the national debt must increase. If more money is created, the value of each unit of currency declines; that is, inflation results. This causes domestic currency value to fall below its previous level vis-à-vis foreign currencies. Increased national debt has roughly the same effect, as more money must be created to pay the interest expense associated with the new debt. This is the case whenever debt is denominated in domestic currency.

If the new debt is denominated in foreign currency, national debt issuance places pressure on the export sector. Exports must increase by an amount sufficient to pay for imports *and* to accumulate foreign currency to service the debt. If this happens, private-sector productivity increases flow through to the government, with essentially a negative net effect for the private sector.

Central bank management of the external value of the domestic currency can have profound effects on the economy. The interrelationships are complex in that trade balances and fiscal policy influence the value of the currency as well.

[4]See also Chapter 9.

With the establishment of both the Office of the Comptroller of the Currency and the Federal Reserve System, U.S. commercial banking took on a decidedly different character. It was the funding requirements of the Civil War and persistent money crises that precipitated a shift toward more regulation, but there are even more fundamental reasons why commercial banks operate in a regulated environment.

The basic justification for bank regulation lies in the critical role of commercial banking in a domestic economy. Bank demand deposits are the primary component of the *money supply,* and the country's money transactions often take the form of exchanges of bank deposits. Disruption of this basic system can disrupt the entire economy.

The role of commercial banks in the economy goes beyond the payments system. Commercial banks establish a dependable payments system while investing a large percentage of deposits in illiquid assets. That is, what is not needed to maintain reserves can be invested in higher-yielding, less liquid assets. For this investment function to work well, depositors must have confidence that their money is safe; the failure of one bank should not precipitate massive deposit withdrawals, or *runs,* at other institutions. Bank regulation is intended to monitor the risk of failure in the system as a whole, to guard against a domino effect when one institution fails.

Regulation has two assumptions: (1) The *safety and soundness* of the banking system is too important to leave to chance, and (2) the relative illiquidity of bank portfolios makes *confidence* in the system essential.

Regulatory Problems in the Early 1900s

Establishment of regulation by the Comptroller and by the Federal Reserve has not always prevented serious problems in the banking industry. The requirement that reserves be held by Federal Reserve banks, for instance, was from the outset a significant disincentive to membership, because no interest is paid on these amounts. Reserve requirements of state and national banks continued to be different, and the less closely monitored state banking system continued to grow even after passage of the Federal Reserve Act. Of the over 17,000 banks chartered from 1900 through 1920, only 4000 were national banks. State banks had a very real presence—essentially outside the federal regulatory system.

Meanwhile, the Treasury once again borrowed heavily to finance World War I. The national debt mushroomed from \$1 billion to \$27 billion. After the war, inflation accelerated until it reached 15 percent in 1919. At that point, the Federal Reserve raised the discount rate (the rate charged to member banks that borrow from the Federal Reserve) from 4 to 7 percent to cool inflation. As other interest rates rose, the economy slipped into recession during 1920–1921. Then the economy rebounded, as labor productivity improved, the nation's output of goods rose dramatically, and the stock market posted impressive gains.

But the "roaring 20s" were also characterized by high unemployment, depressed commodity prices for the country's farmers, rising prices of industrial output, heavy consumer borrowing, and high interest rates. Bank failures during the 1920s reduced the number of commercial banks from 30,000 in 1920 to fewer than 25,000 by the end of the decade.

In 1927, the McFadden Act gave national banks more flexibility and power, although McFadden is frequently cited today as the legislation that denies national banks the ability to set up nationwide branch networks. Legislators in fact designed McFadden to give national banks more liberal branching rights prohibited prior to 1922. The Comptroller of the Currency's ruling in 1922 that branching was permitted if it was allowed by state law was confirmed by the national legislation. The law also increased the loan limit for a single borrower and broadened national bank investment powers to include corporate bonds and increased levels of real estate lending.

When, in 1929, the stock market crashed and the Great Depression began, the Federal Reserve did not respond to provide liquidity for the financial system, perhaps believing that a "correction" in the overpriced stock market was overdue. Billions of dollars of bank assets evaporated, as farmers and businesses defaulted and went bankrupt. As bank failures accelerated, the number of banks fell from under 25,000 in 1929 to just over 14,000 in 1933. The money supply shrank; bank deposits fell from $49 billion in 1929 to $32 billion by 1933, a decline of 35 percent. With the exception of a brief 4-month period in 1932 (when the Fed increased the money supply by $1.1 billion by buying Treasury securities), the Federal Reserve took no action to relieve the liquidity crisis. In fact, it actually increased the discount rate by 2 percentage points during a 2-week period in 1931.

When President Franklin Roosevelt (1933–1945) assumed office in 1933, the country's economy was devastated and the banking system had all but collapsed. Reform of the banking system was a top priority. The legislation that followed was an attempt to put more effective safeguards in place.

Key Legislation

Regulatory foundations, begun with the National Bank Act of 1863 and the Federal Reserve Act of 1913, were strengthened by legislation in the 1930s. The Banking Acts of 1933 and 1935 formed the basis of a system that was to remain virtually unchanged until 1980.

The Banking Act of 1933 Lenient state banking laws are frequently blamed for the bank failures during the Great Depression. Also of concern were certain commercial banking activities linking commercial banks with investment banking.[5] In some cases, commercial banks made questionable loans to clients of their investment banking affiliates. Underwriting by investment banking divisions was not always prudent, and new issues of firms in weak financial condition could be sold to the commercial bank's trust department. At other times, doubtful bank loans could be sold to investment banking affiliates to support the stock price of the parent bank.

Senator Carter Glass of Virginia, who served in the Senate between 1920 and 1946, had fruitlessly promoted separation of commercial and investment banking before the 1930s. By the time the 1933 act was drafted, economic conditions provided Senator Glass with ample support for the idea. The Banking Act of 1933 (frequently referred to as the Glass-Steagall Act) brought an end to an era. The act required commercial banks to divest themselves of investment banking affiliates, prohibited interest payments on demand deposits, and established government authority to regulate interest rates on time deposits. The provisions of Glass-Steagall have been debated vigorously almost since their enactment. Legislation in the early 1980s dismantled some of this law, and other changes are likely to follow.

The FDIC The 1933 Banking Act also created the first federal deposit insurance facility in the United States with the objective of preventing the massive failures that had occurred between 1929 and 1933. Regulators were particularly concerned with protection of small depositors who had suffered when banks failed during the depression. Prior to 1933, there had been only state insurance plans, all of which eventually failed. It was hoped that the Federal Deposit Insurance Corporation (FDIC) would be more successful.

[5] Investment banking is the process of bringing new issues of stocks and bonds to the market for sale (see Chapter 5).

Certain factors did improve the probability of success. First, the banks covered by the plan were a more diversified group than those that any single state might assemble. Second, the banks still operating in 1933 had been strong enough in the first place to weather the Great Depression. The most important advantage of the FDIC over comparable state plans, however, was its access to federal monetary authorities. No single state insurance scheme was capable of lending such credibility to its guarantees.

Insurance premiums from subscribing banks established the FDIC fund, and annual contributions added to its strength. Both national and state banks are eligible for coverage. Each account was originally insured up to $2500. Today, the limit is $100,000 per account.

Of course, to provide this safety net, it was felt that more supervision and regulation were necessary. The 1933 act added the FDIC to the ranks of federal bank regulators (Comptroller of the Currency and Federal Reserve) already charged with oversight responsibilities. The division of authority is such that the FDIC has primary responsibility for state banks that are not members of the Federal Reserve. The Federal Reserve and the comptroller examine state and national member banks, respectively. The FDIC is required to examine bank financial data periodically to enable the agency to assess a bank's operational and financial stability. When loan portfolios and/or management practices expose an institution to high potential loss, thereby threatening equity capital, the institution is designated as a "problem" bank, needing closer monitoring. Because the FDIC does not charter banks, it may not revoke a charter but can force a bank to cease operating. Only the Comptroller or a state banking authority has revocation rights, so the FDIC must work closely with other regulators.

The FDIC deposit insurance premiums were originally set at 1⁄12 percent of total deposits, or $0.083 for each $100 of deposits. Premiums cover FDIC operating expenses and maintain the insurance fund. Beginning in 1962, Congress required that two-thirds of these premiums be refunded to contributing banks. In 1981, Congress reduced the rebate to 60 percent of premiums paid, thereby increasing the effective premium. In 1989, the Financial Institutions Reform, Recovery, and Enforcement Act increased the premium to $0.12 per $100 of deposits for 1990 and $0.15 per $100 of deposits in 1991. Subsequent legislation increased premiums to $.23 per $100 of deposits.

The Banking Act of 1935 The Banking Act of 1935 significantly strengthened the Federal Reserve's powers with respect to monetary policy. This legislation gave the Fed greater authority over bank reserve requirements and made interest rates paid on bank time deposits subject to Federal Reserve limits. The Comptroller of the Currency and the Secretary of the Treasury came off the Federal Reserve Board in order to give the Board more autonomy, and the Board's name was changed to the Board of Governors of the Federal Reserve System (heads of the regional banks had been referred to as governors). This last change was symbolic of the greater authority conferred upon the Board, with the clear implication that policy decisions henceforth would be made in Washington.

Perhaps the most significant change accomplished by this legislation was formation of the *Federal Open Market Committee (FOMC).* No longer would there be any question as to which agency was responsible for open-market securities transactions. The twelve-member FOMC was composed of the seven members of the Board of Governors and five of the regional reserve bank presidents (the former governors) on a rotating basis, with the New York president always a member. The majority held by the Board of Governors ensures that, in the event of a conflict, national priorities would dominate in the setting of monetary policy. The New York Federal Reserve Bank acts as agent for the FOMC in executing open-market securities transactions. Exhibit 10-3 illustrates the organizational structure of the Federal Reserve System, including the FOMC.

The 1935 act also gave the Comptroller more authority to make decisions about national bank charter applications. Applicants are required to show both that the proposed bank is needed and would be successful (without hurting existing banks). Making it more difficult to charter a bank was intended to help prevent bank failure, and new bank charters dropped from an average of 360 per year to 50. Even during the post–World War II expansion from 1945 through 1960, annual new charters remained below 100.

Consumer Protection Legislation Several laws following this legislation in the 1930s were aimed primarily at protecting the rights of bank customers. Consumer protection law in commercial banking falls into one of three general categories:

- Adequate disclosure
- Access to credit
- Procedures in the event of dispute

Truth in lending laws prescribe the type and method of disclosure by banks (and other financial institutions) that make loans to consumers. The 1968 federal Consumer Protection Act (also known as the Truth in Lending Act) establishes specific consumer rights, with commercial bank disclosures monitored by the Federal Reserve. The Fed's Regulation Z stipulates that an annual percentage rate (APR) must be stated prominently, that a full accounting for all finance charges be made available to the consumer, and that other minimum disclosures be made. States have similar laws and regulations of their own.

The *Equal Credit Opportunity Act (ECOA)* of 1974 (and an amendment 2 years later) prohibits discrimination against borrowers because of gender, marital status, race, national origin, age, or income that is derived from public assistance.

The *Fair Credit Billing Act (FCBA)* of 1974 was enacted to protect consumers in use of credit cards. Credit card issuers must provide customers with notice of their rights and the exact procedures to follow in the event of a dispute. This law is also implemented by Federal Reserve Regulation Z.

These and other laws and regulations are applicable to consumer credit. They are intended to help ensure fair allocation of credit through complete information on rights and procedures. For lenders, the primary costs are increased administrative expense (disclosure forms and management time necessary to ensure compliance with truth in lending

EXHIBIT 10-3 THE FEDERAL RESERVE SYSTEM

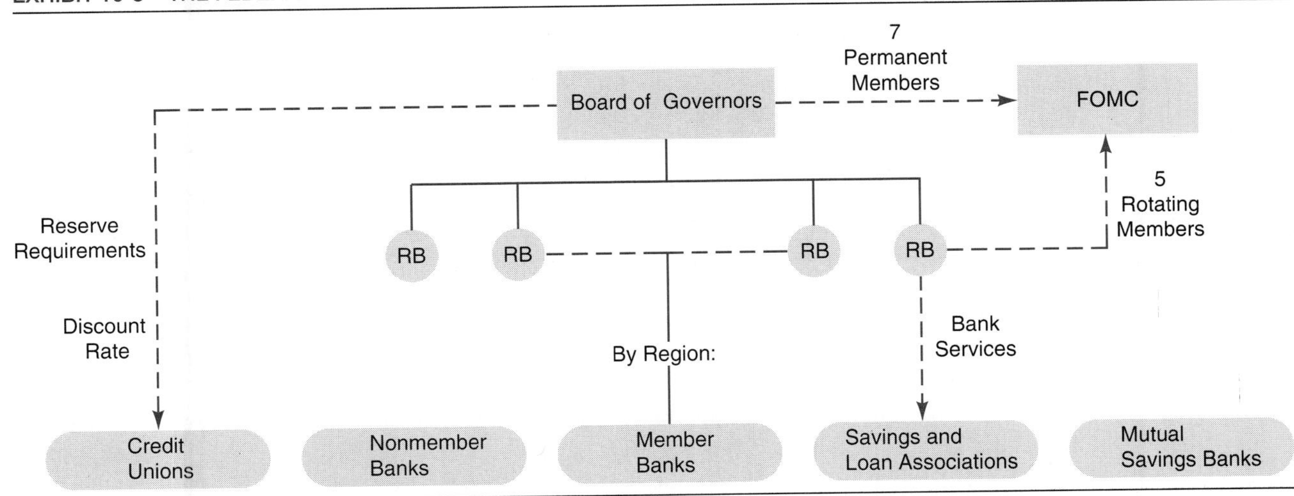

RB reserve bank

EXHIBIT 10-4 DISCRIMINATORY REGULATION

In the early 1980s, some suggested that U.S. bank regulations had gone too far.* What started as an effort to ensure safety and soundness in the nation's payments system became, in some cases, an exercise in protecting special interests at the expense of the small depositor.

From the late 1960s through the 1970s, the thrift industry (savings and loan associations and savings banks), the housing industry, and construction unions helped lobby for regulation that gave thrifts a higher deposit rate ceiling than commercial banks and raised the minimum denomination in which Treasury debt (especially the T-bill) was issued. These same interests also worked to prevent bank holding companies and nonfinancial corporations from issuing small-denomination debt (which would most likely carry interest rates close to market rates of return). At the same time, interest rate ceilings for large-denomination deposits were eliminated, allowing market rates of return to be paid on them. The result was a system that discriminated against small depositors to ensure banks and thrifts of a low-cost source of funds. The interest rate a small depositor could earn on savings thus depended upon a family's wealth and financial sophistication. These circumstances discriminated, in particular, against the young, the old, and the poor. The advent in the 1970s of money market mutual funds offering market rates of return to small investors caused large-scale withdrawals from depository institutions, particularly in the thrift industry, so the "discrimination" backfired in the end.

*Kane, Edward J. "Accelerating Inflation, Technological Innovation, and the Decreasing Effectiveness of Banking Regulation," *Journal of Finance,* Vol. 36, No. 2 (May 1981), pp. 355–367.

and FCBA) and having somewhat less information about their perspective loan customers (ECOA). (See also Exhibit 10-4.)

Community Reinvestment Act of 1977 Another significant consumer protection law that applies to commercial banks is the Community Reinvestment Act of 1977. It requires federal regulators (Comptroller, Federal Reserve, and FDIC) to encourage the banks they oversee to provide for the credit needs of the communities they serve.[6] The law mandates that regulators assess an institution's record of providing for the credit needs of the entire community, including low- and moderate-income neighborhoods. This record is to be considered when a bank seeks a new charter, acquires shares of another bank, or merges with another bank.

The objective of the Community Reinvestment Act was to discourage the practice of *redlining.*

Redlining:

The systematic withholding of bank loans from low- to moderate-income communities, while still accepting deposits in them, particularly communities with a significant minority population.

To the extent that economically deprived areas are systematically shut out from mortgage finance, loans to community organizations (churches, colleges, and professional organizations), and small businesses, their condition will continue to deteriorate. If banks wish to expand, this legislation requires that they demonstrate that they are not neglecting under-

[6] Similar provisions apply for savings and loan associations.

served, disadvantaged areas, although if a bank is not located to serve such an area, the law has virtually no effect on it.

The Financial Institutions Reform, Recovery, and Enforcement Act of 1989 (FIRREA) strengthened the 1977 law by requiring that regulators regularly prepare a written evaluation of each bank's community reinvestment. A portion of this evaluation that must now be made public includes the institution's rating:

- Outstanding
- Satisfactory
- Needs to improve
- Substantial noncompliance

The documentation for the rating must also be made public.

The confidential portion of the report includes (1) all references that identify employees or other individuals who provided information in confidence to a regulator and (2) sensitive or speculative statements obtained or made by regulators. The law allows disclosure of confidential portions of the report if the regulatory agency determines that such disclosure would promote the objectives of the act.

The FIRREA amendments to the Community Reinvestment Act have placed a significant burden on commercial banks to demonstrate compliance. Publication of a statement was intended to take advantage of public pressure to encourage banks to comply with objectives of the legislation. At the same time, small banks that already fully serve the entire community may find that the new law simply adds to the cost of regulatory documentation.

Regulation of Bank Holding Companies

After the financial system contraction brought on by the Great Depression, banking activities did not grow appreciably until World War II had ended, when the constraints imposed by the legislation of the 1930s appeared overly restrictive. In 1945, when the war ended, loans were only 16 percent of total bank assets, compared with 63 percent in 1925. As the economy expanded in the 1950s, banks became more aggressive and competitive, with the result

EXHIBIT 10-5 FEDERAL BANK REGULATORS, 1989

	Federal regulator			
	Office of the Comptroller of the Currency	Federal Reserve	FDIC	Total
Type of banks	National	State-chartered Fed member	Insured state-chartered non-Fed member	
Number of banks	4,179	1,034	7,500	12,713
Number of offices*	25,844	5,702	16,904	48,450
Assets†	$1,977,623	$540,934	$780,469	$3,299,026
Average size‡	$473.2	$523.1	$104.1	$259.5

*Main office plus branches.
†Millions of dollars.
‡Amount of assets in millions of dollars divided by number of banks.
Source: The Federal Reserve System; Purposes & Functions, Board of Governors of the Federal Reserve System, Washington, D.C., 1984, and, *Statistics on Banking 1989,* Federal Deposit Insurance Corporation, Washington, D.C.

that the ratio of loans began to rise once again. Certificates of deposit, Eurodollars, credit cards, repurchase agreements, and renewed interest in federal funds were all born in the 1960s, all permitting greater flexibility in a more vibrant banking environment.[7]

The most significant structural change in this period was the growth of *bank holding companies (BHCs):*

Bank holding company:
A corporation whose primary function is to own other corporations, specifically, one or more commercial banks.

This organizational form was not new or unique to the post–World War II era; the Banking Act of 1933 specifically addressed authority over BHCs that owned banks that were members of the Federal Reserve. The Fed could legally deny such a holding company the right to vote its stock in the member bank, although it also could examine the holding company and its affiliates in order to determine whether voting permission should be granted or denied. Other requirements for BHCs member banks included publication of periodic financial statements, maintenance of reserves, and divestiture of securities businesses. Holding companies that held nonmember banks were hardly regulated at all; they could invest in virtually any other type of firm, except a securities firm.

Despite hands-off treatment of nonbank activities, few BHCs survived after 1933 (in 1954 there were only forty-six). At least one of these was large enough to attract the attention of the Board of Governors. Transamerica Corporation controlled 41 percent of commercial bank office locations, 39 percent of commercial bank deposits, and 50 percent of commercial bank loans in Arizona, California, Nevada, Oregon, and Washington, leading the Board of Governors to bring an antitrust action in 1948. The decision came down in favor of Transamerica, requiring the firm to divest itself only of Bank of America stock. It was allowed to retain the remaining forty-six banks and to expand into other states if it wanted.

The Bank Holding Company Act of 1956 was the congressional response to the lenient court ruling. It was intended to avoid undue concentration by BHCs and to prevent the spread of BHCs (unaffected by Glass-Steagall) that owed investment banking firms. The objective was to stop interstate "branching." Already established holding companies, however, were permitted to retain those banks that they owned in 1956. That is, *grandfathering* gave BHCs permission to continue an activity already begun while prohibiting future expansion of that activity. The BHCs with less than a 25 percent ownership interest in a bank were exempt from the act, as were (initially) BHCs that owned only one bank.

Perhaps predictably, the one-bank holding company (OBHC) exclusion gave rise to large numbers of OBHCs, organized to take advantage of a structure allowing banks to engage in activities that otherwise were prohibited. In contrast to 1954, when there were only forty-six BHCs in total, by 1970 there were more than 1000 OBHCs alone. A 1970 amendment to the Bank Holding Company Act (effective 1971) closed the one-bank loophole, bringing all BHCs under the regulation of the Federal Reserve.

Bank holding companies are permitted a wide range of activities, which includes, but is not limited to, leasing, data processing, real estate appraisal, operation of a discount brokerage, and operation of a distressed savings and loan association. Moreover, holding companies control the vast majority of total commercial bank deposits. With such a large share of deposits, it makes sense that bank holding companies are regulated primarily by the Federal Reserve since the deposit base is a critical element in the nation's money supply. (See Exhibit 10-6.)

[7] See Chapter 3 for a discussion of certificates of deposit, federal funds, and repurchase agreements. Eurodollars and Eurodollar markets are covered in Chapter 7.

EXHIBIT 10-6 BANK HOLDING COMPANIES SUBJECT TO FEDERAL RESERVE REGULATION, 1960–1989

Year	Number of BHCs	Annual growth rate	% of U.S. bank deposits
1960	47*		7.9%
1970	121*	9.9%	16.2
1980	3,056	38.1	71.0
1989	5,871	7.5	90.0

*Includes only bank holding companies that control two or more banks.
Source: The Federal Reserve System; Purposes & Functions, Board of Governors of the Federal Reserve System, Washington, D.C., 1984 and Spong, Kenneth. *Banking Regulation; Its Purposes, Implementation, and Effects,* 3e, Federal Reserve Bank of Kansas City, Kansas City, 1990.

SUMMARY

The first U.S. banks were chartered and controlled by state authorities, and early attempts at a national banking system created no lasting structure. National banks did not become a permanent part of the financial landscape until 1863. The Office of Comptroller of the Currency was created to charter and supervise these new national banks. While the dual system of state and national banks has continued to exist, operational differences between the two types of banks diminished.

The Federal Reserve Act of 1913 created the nation's central bank to act as lender of last resort for commercial banks and to execute monetary policy. Through major bank legislation of the earlier 1930s, its role was strengthened and it became even more independent. At the same time, the federal deposit insurance system was initiated, after a series of failures had reduced the number of banks to one-half the 1920 total. Other legislation followed in the 1960s and 1970s that protected consumer rights and attempted to provide equity in bank services.

KEY TERMS

bank holding companies
central bank
dual banking system
Federal Deposit Insurance Corporation
Federal Reserve System
First and Second Banks of the United States
free banking era
grandfathering
greenbacks
lender of last resort
money panic
Office of Comptroller of the Currency
redlining
syndicate
truth in lending law

END-OF-CHAPTER QUESTIONS

1. How did the First and Second Banks of the United States differ from the Federal Reserve?
2. Describe the function of the Independent Treasury System from 1846 through 1913.
3. What were the deficiencies of the Independent Treasury System?
4. There are two possible extremes with respect to the type of relationship that a central bank may have with its government. Describe them and possible justifications for them.
5. Differentiate the macroeconomic and microeconomic relationship of a central bank to the commercial banking industry.
6. Give three reasons why commercial banks should be regulated.

7. Despite its charge to maintain stability in the money supply, the Federal Reserve did little to support the banking system after the stock market crash of 1929. Using library resources, determine the reaction of the Federal Reserve to the stock market crash of October 1987.
8. How was the Federal Reserve System reorganized in the Banking Acts of the 1930s?
9. How can a central bank influence the general economic climate of a country?
10. What is redlining?
11. If redlining is damaging to the development of individual communities, is it possible that a large presence of foreign banks in a market could present a similar problem?
12. Name the three types of consumer protection legislation, and describe the scope of these laws.
13. Why do you suppose that such a large percentage of the U.S. deposit base is controlled by bank holding companies?
14. Which banks are the primary supervisory responsibility of the Federal Reserve? the Comptroller of the Currency? the Federal Deposit Insurance Corporation?
15. Refer to Exhibit 10-5, and describe the differences you note with respect to banks regulated by the Office of the Comptroller, the Fed, and the FDIC.

SELECTED REFERENCES

Ciocca, Pierluigi, Editor. *Money and the Economy: The Central Bankers' Views,* Macmillan Press, London, 1987.

Cooper, S. Kerry, and Donald R. Fraser. *Banking Deregulation and the New Competition in Financial Services,* Ballinger Publishing Company, Cambridge, Massachusetts, 1984.

The Federal Reserve System; Purposes and Functions, Board of Governors of the Federal Reserve System, Washington, D.C., 1984.

Goodhart, Charles. *The Evolution of Central Banks,* The MIT Press, Cambridge, Massachusetts, 1988.

Greider, William. *Secrets of the Temple; How the Federal Reserve Runs the Country,* Touchstone/Simon & Schuster Inc., New York, 1989.

Spong, Kenneth. *Banking Regulation; Its Purposes, Implementation, and Effects,* Federal Reserve Bank of Kansas City, Kansas City, 1990.

Statistics on Banking 1989, Federal Deposit Insurance Corporation, Washington, D.C.

Toniolo, Gianni, Editor. *Central Banks' Independence in Historical Perspective,* Walter de Gruyter, Berlin, 1988.

CHAPTER 11

U.S. MONETARY POLICY, DEREGULATION, AND DEPOSIT INSURANCE

CHAPTER OUTLINE

CHAPTER OVERVIEW

This chapter describes:

- Federal Reserve monetary policy and implementation
- Bank deregulation legislation
- Crises in federal deposit insurance
- Proposed changes in bank regulation

The Federal Reserve uses tools to manage the money supply of the United States, including reserve requirements, the discount rate, and open-market operations. Of these, open-market operations are the most powerful and frequently used. The objectives of Fed monetary policy are to maintain price level stability and to create an economic environment that is conducive to economic growth, goals that can sometimes conflict. Moreover, although technically independent, the Federal Reserve has at times disagreed with the U.S. Treasury in terms of the correct monetary policy actions in a given situation.

In order to compete with other financial institutions, banks and savings and loan associations were given expanded powers in the early 1980s. The combination of government safeguards and deregulatory efforts, however, has left the system vulnerable in several important aspects. One of the most important of these is the threat to the country's deposit insurance system.

FISCAL POLICY

Bank regulation is not motivated solely by concern for the financial institutions themselves. It is part of the larger agenda of maintaining order in an economy. Generally, two broad categories of national financial policy affect an economy: *fiscal policy* and *monetary policy.*

Fiscal policy:
The policy of government with respect to government revenues and expenditures.

The legislative and executive branches of the federal government are primarily responsible for *fiscal policy.* They develop budgets of government expenditures. Tax revenues to meet these budgets may be less than, equal to, or greater than actual government expenditures. When revenues equal expenditures, the government has no impact on the aggregate level of economic activity. However, when revenues exceed expenditures, fiscal policy has the effect of dampening economic expansion. This is true because the government effectively removes purchasing power from the economy when it spends less than it collects.

Finally, when government revenues are less than government expenditures, the economy is stimulated by the incremental purchasing power that is introduced. In the United States, the federal government has run such deficits each year since 1970; indeed, between 1934 and 1969, the annual federal budget was in surplus on only eight occasions. Thus, U.S. government financial activity historically has provided economic stimulus. In some cases, the deficits have been deliberate attempts to apply Keynesian economics.[1] In other cases, particularly in more recent years, federal budget deficits have been simply a function of increased spending that has not been offset by increased tax revenues.

MONETARY POLICY

Monetary policy involves control of the nation's money supply, something early regulation of banks did little to accomplish.

Monetary policy:
The policy of government with respect to its money supply.

The National Bank Act of 1863 and its subsequent amendment did not effectively eliminate money created by state banks. While state bank notes became less prevalent, state bank checking account deposits grew more popular. As checks became readily accepted as money, state bank checking accounts became a portion of the money supply that was not subject to federal regulation. It was not until the creation of the Federal Reserve System in 1913 that the federal government gained more complete statutory power to manage the money supply.

The Tools of Monetary Policy

The tools of monetary policy have developed over time.

- The first was the imposition of *reserve requirements* against deposits.

[1]John Maynard Keynes (1883–1946), the English economist, advocated the use of government deficit spending in order to promote employment and to maintain (or increase) national income. His theories inspired national economic policies in the United States after the Great Depression. Keynes was also an advocate for the creation of the World Bank at the Bretton Woods Conference in 1944. See Chapter 2 for coverage of Bretton Woods.

- When the Federal Reserve was created, the *discount rate* was used.
- The most powerful tool was later to be refined; *open-market operations.*

Reserve Requirements The National Bank Act of 1863 attempted to control the portion of the money supply that could be affected at the federal level by specifying minimum reserve requirements for the new national banks. If a policy decision to reduce the money supply were to be made, the reserve requirements could be increased, causing loanable funds to decline.

Reserve requirement:
Minimum reserve assets that by law a depository financial institution must maintain. Reserve requirements are expressed in terms of a percentage of relevant bank deposits.

The imposition of reserve requirements on national banks was not completely effective, however, because state bank reserves were set at the discretion of state banking authorities. Perhaps for this reason, the use of the reserve requirement has had limited application as a tool of monetary policy. Furthermore, aggregate national bank notes outstanding were limited to the amount of the national debt, because all such notes were required to be collateralized by government securities. Thus, there was no way for federal regulators to increase the money supply within the provisions of the National Bank Act.

The Discount Rate With creation of the Federal Reserve System in 1913, reserve banks became the lender of last resort in their respective regions, thereby giving birth to an important tool of monetary policy, the *discount rate.*

Discount rate:
The rate of interest at which a depository institution borrows from the Federal Reserve bank in its district.

Lowering the discount rate tends to encourage bank borrowing at the Fed's "discount window," all other things being equal.[2] Greater borrowing from the Federal Reserve increases the money supply, which encourages business activity. Opposite effects should occur when the discount rate is raised.

Open-Market Operations Although the discount rate has played a more significant role than the reserve requirement in implementation of monetary policy, neither has been as frequently used nor as effective as *open-market operations.*

Open-market operations:
The purchase and sale of government securities by the Federal Reserve in the public securities market.

Open-market operations occurred to some extent in the early 1900s, but the practice was formalized and placed under the jurisdiction of the Federal Open Market Committee in 1935.

Intervention by the Independent Treasury System in 1902 is an early example of an open-market operation. The Treasury bought government securities (at premium prices) as part of a strategy to alleviate a tight money market. And it worked: The money panic was averted. Since then, open-market operations have become increasingly important.

[2] The discount window is a figurative expression, not a real location.

The Mechanics of Open-Market Operations

Open-market operations have a critical impact on the money supply. Buying and selling government securities is a way the Fed implements monetary policy.

The Federal Reserve Balance Sheet Exhibit 11-1 shows the balance sheet of the Federal Reserve as of March 31, 1991. The Fed's primary financial asset is government securities (75.6 percent of the total). Gold, foreign currency, and special drawing right (SDR) certificates are the next-largest component; they are items of international liquidity that have little impact on the domestic money supply.[3] Loans to domestic banks are generated when the Federal Reserve acts as lender of last resort for depository institutions, but the amount is minuscule compared with government securities.

The Fed's largest liability is currency in circulation (87.6 percent of the total). Currency in circulation and reserves of depository institutions form the country's *monetary base.*

Monetary base:

Claims against a central bank that serve as money (currency) and the reserves held by a central bank that form the basis for creation of money (reserves of depository institutions).

Reserves and the Money Supply Exhibit 11-2 summarizes the connection between reserves and transactions account balances, a major part of the money supply. When the Fed sells government securities, its balance in the government securities account declines.

[3] Special drawing rights (SDRs) are a form of money created by the International Monetary Fund (IMF) and used among the sovereign governments that are members of the IMF. (See Chapter 16.)

EXHIBIT 11-1 BALANCE SHEET OF THE FEDERAL RESERVE SYSTEM, MARCH 31, 1991

		Amount*	%
Financial assets			
Gold, foreign exchange, SDR certificates		51.1	15.6
Federal Reserve float†		2.5	0.8
Loans to domestic banks		0.2	0.1
Securities:			
Treasury issues	241.0		
Government agency issues	6.3	247.3	75.6
Other assets		26.0	7.9
Total assets		327.1	100.0
Financial liabilities			
Monetary base:			
Currency in circulation	286.6		
Reserves of depository institutions‡	24.1	310.7	95.0
Due to U.S. government‡		11.5	3.5
Due to foreign sector‡		0.3	0.1
Other liabilities		4.6	1.4
Total liabilities		327.1	100.0

* In billions of dollars.
† Cash items in the process of collection (CIPC).
‡ Deposit accounts.
Source: Board of Governors of the Federal Reserve System, *Financial Assets and Liabilities.*

EXHIBIT 11-2 THE RELATIONSHIP BETWEEN RESERVES AND TRANSACTIONS ACCOUNTS

The reserve base is a part of the money supply that can be held only by financial institutions. Because banks are required to keep a percentage of transactions accounts on deposit with the Federal Reserve (the reserve requirement), both the amount of reserves and the reserve requirement influence aggregate transactions account balances. The exact relationship is

$$T = mR$$

where T = aggregate transactions account balances
m = the transactions account multiplier (the inverse of the reserve requirement)
R = aggregate reserves of depository institutions

Changes in these parameters Δ will also be interrelated.

$$\begin{aligned} T + \Delta T &= (m + \Delta m)(R + \Delta R) \\ &= mR + R\Delta m + m\Delta R + \Delta m\Delta R \end{aligned}$$

Subtracting the two equations, the change in transactions account balances equals the amount of reserves multiplied by the change in the multiplier plus the multiplier times the change in reserves plus the change in multiplier times the change in reserves.

$$\Delta T = R\Delta m + m\Delta R + \Delta m\Delta R$$

When the multiplier does not change, a change in reserves will have the following potential effect on transactions account balances.

$$\Delta T = m\Delta R$$

Reference: Smith, Paul F., *Comparative Financial Systems,* Praeger Publishers, New York, 1982.

Because the transaction is settled through the banking system, reserves of depository institutions also decline. The reverse is true when the Federal Reserve purchases government securities. The balance of government securities increases, as do depository institution reserves. The effect on the money supply of either selling or buying is several times the amount of the original transaction because of the *transactions account multiplier.*

Transactions account multiplier:
The potential increase in transactions accounts for a $1 change in depository institution reserves—the inverse of the reserve requirement for transactions accounts.

If the reserve requirement for transactions accounts is 12 percent, a $1 change in reserves can change transactions account balances in depository institutions (part of the money supply) by $8.33, or $1(1/.12).

Exhibit 11-3 illustrates this principle. In this example, the Federal Reserve purchases $500 million in government securities from commercial banks. Payment is made through the banking system so that reserve accounts (Fed liabilities) increase by the same amount. On the books of commercial banks, securities balances decline and reserves at the Fed increase. This $500 million is now excess reserves for the banking system and, assuming a

EXHIBIT 11-3 EXPANDING THE MONEY SUPPLY THROUGH OPEN MARKET OPERATIONS (MILLIONS OF DOLLARS)

a

Federal Reserve	
Treasury Securities + 500	Due to commercial banks + 500

Commercial banks	
Due from Fed +500 Securities (500)	

b

Federal Reserve	
Treasury Securities + 500	Due to commercial banks + 500

Commercial banks	
Due from Fed + 500 Securities (500) Loans + 4165	Transactions accounts + 4165

(a) The Federal Reserve purchases government securities ($500 million).
(b) The initial government securities transaction and the eventual effect of the money supply (transactions accounts) and loans outstanding (a $4.2 billion increase).

12 percent reserve requirement, can support additional transactions account balances of $4.165 billion, or $500 million divided by .12. The new transactions accounts add to the money supply. This example assumes that the money supply increase is invested in loans, thereby boosting the amount of funds available for investment purposes and consumer purchases. Thus, open-market operations can be a powerful tool in managing the country's money supply.

Monetary Policy Implementation

Upon its creation, the Federal Reserve became responsible for holding member bank reserves previously controlled by the Treasury, for setting the discount rate, and for intervening in the nation's money market. Virtually all the tools of monetary policy belonged to the Federal Reserve. Its charge was to stabilize the money supply, act as lender of last resort for banks that found themselves in liquidity crises, supervise member banks, and generally promote price stability.

Federal Reserve Independence The Federal Reserve System was conceived as an independent, decentralized organization, and in the early years regional reserve banks had relative autonomy. Technically, the Federal Reserve System has political independence. Member banks capitalize each regional reserve bank and control two-thirds of the nine seats on the board of directors. The Board of Governors (appointed by the President of the United States) appoints the remaining three. Within the government, the Federal Reserve reports only to the U.S. Congress.

However, in a functional sense, that is, in terms of actually carrying out its responsibilities, the Federal Reserve is not altogether independent. Monetary policy is affected by fiscal policy as well as by national priorities as envisioned by Congress or the executive branch of government. The functional relationship between government and the Federal Reserve has at times been strained because of this interdependence.

The Early Years of U.S. Monetary Policy The Federal Reserve System began to operate at the time that World War I erupted. The United States attracted a substantial amount of capital from war-torn countries in Europe, and as gold flowed into the United States, the Federal Reserve could do little to minimize its effect. Only an increase in the reserve requirements and/or massive open-market operations could have absorbed the excess money. Yet the Federal Reserve did not then have the authority to modify reserve requirements, nor, because it was newly established, did it hold securities that could be sold. Predictably, from June 1914 to March 1917, the money supply rose by 46 percent and wholesale prices rose by 65 percent.

Once the United States became involved in the war, the Federal Reserve advocated financing U.S. involvement through a combination of taxation and bond selling. The Treasury did not agree to obtain part of the wartime cost from current revenues (taxes) and elected instead to finance the entire U.S. war effort with debt (government bond issues). To minimize the cost of debt service, the Treasury sold the bonds at low interest rates—so low that the Federal Reserve objected because of its concern about the inflationary effects of an easy money environment in the presence of the heavy inflow of capital from overseas. The Fed's role, despite its objections, was to facilitate government bond sales. It fulfilled this role through the commercial banking system. Individual investors borrowed from private banks to buy Treasury bonds. The banks, in turn, discounted the loan paper at their respective reserve banks, or in effect sold the loans that had been used to purchase Treasury bonds.

If the Federal Reserve had refused to assist the Treasury in the sale of bonds, the Treasury could have taken it over under wartime legislation in effect at the time but permitted to lapse after the war. The Federal Reserve's early attempt to assert its independence failed because the Treasury forced it to take actions that it considered unwise.

After World War I, the urgency of government financing eased, the close ties between the Treasury and the Federal Reserve moderated, and the Fed began to fine-tune its monetary policy instruments. Even so, within the Federal Reserve System, reserve banks and the Board did not agree on how to dampen the speculation of the 1920s. Reserve banks advocated raising the discount rate; the Board had more faith in "moral suasion." Following the stock market crash in 1929, the system more or less passively permitted two successive waves of bank failures—one in the fall of 1930, the other in the spring of 1931.

When the United Kingdom abandoned the gold standard in September 1931, the Federal Reserve reacted by raising the discount rate to support the value of the dollar and to discourage conversion of the dollar into gold. The higher rates made it more costly for banks to obtain funds, and more bank failures followed. The Federal Reserve engaged in a brief period of large-scale, open-market operations, purchasing government securities to increase the money supply, but only between April and August of 1932. Exactly why such purchases were not made earlier or why, once started, they were not continued is unclear.

From 1930 through 1933, over 9000 banks closed their doors. In March 1933 the new President, Franklin D. Roosevelt, closed all banks for an unprecedented bank holiday, as one of the first acts of his administration. The President and the Treasury were able to gain more authority over monetary policy through the Emergency Banking Act of 1933.

This emergency legislation (reminiscent of similar legislation during World War I) gave the Treasury explicit approval and veto power over all Federal Reserve banking business, subject to presidential approval. Decision making was shifted from district reserve banks almost entirely to the Federal Reserve Board in Washington (a shift of power that would be made permanent by federal legislation in 1935). This is perhaps one of the best examples of the functional *interdependence* of the Federal Reserve with other branches and agencies of government.

During World War II, the U.S. central bank, the Federal Reserve, again helped finance wartime activities by buying government securities. In fact, the Federal Reserve intervened in the market to maintain interest rates on the securities between .375 (Treasury bills) and 2.5 percent (long-term Treasury bonds). The considerable purchases that were necessary to sustain rates at these low levels inflated bank reserves and the money supply. Price controls held wages and prices in check.

After the war, controls were lifted and price levels rose, but the Federal Reserve took no action to check inflation, partially because of its commitment to keep the Treasury's interest costs low; raising interest rates to slow inflation would have been counterproductive. Maintenance of low Treasury expense was not the only reason for the Fed's lack of action. All available government resources, including the Federal Reserve, were being used to achieve the top priority goal of "maximum employment" in accordance with the Employment Act of 1946. Consumers, manufacturers, and investors in securities sought bank loans to finance consumer purchases and investments that had not been possible during the war, and the banking system was obliged to satisfy this demand. With memories of the Great Depression still fresh, the Federal Reserve took no severe action to reduce the money supply. Economic growth was not sacrificed to achieve price stability.

By 1951, however, the Federal Reserve was extremely concerned about the expanding money supply and openly challenged the U.S. Treasury on several occasions. To end these disputes, a negotiated settlement, the Treasury-Federal Reserve Accord, was reached. The Treasury accepted the principle of higher interest rates and more flexibility for the Fed in managing the country's money supply. The 1951 accord became the basis of increased Federal Reserve independence in its fight to maintain price stability.

Monetary Policy in the 1960s and 1970s The financial climate of the country then remained fairly steady until the 1960s, with only occasional peaks in inflation. From 1958 through 1964, wholesale and consumer price indexes rose an average of 1 percent or less per year. Inflation heated up to about 2 percent a year from 1964 through 1972. Between 1972 and 1978, however, inflation averaged 10 percent per year.

Major contributing factors to these inflationary trends were the need to finance both the war in Vietnam and the Great Society domestic reforms initiated during the 1960s. The perceived need for government expenditures to reduce unemployment, eliminate poverty, and improve the quality of life for Americans may have been motivated by the growing tensions associated with the war. Whatever the connection between the two, the outcome was that both the money supply *and* interest rates climbed sharply, suggesting that the increasing supply of money still was not sufficient to keep pace with the increasing demand since interest rates continued to increase. The Federal Reserve raised the discount rate from 4.0 to 4.5 percent, a change that met with strong and immediate criticism from the executive branch. The Fed subsequently found itself in the delicate position of attempting to discourage inflation and simultaneously promote full employment.

Several actions of the Federal Reserve in this period helped avert a disruption of the financial markets. In the case of Penn Central Transportation Company in 1970, the Federal Reserve set aside its monetary targets to maintain money market order. When Penn Central had difficulty refinancing its commercial paper, only recently accepted as a short-term financing vehicle for nonfinancial firms, the entire market reacted with uncertainty. The Federal Reserve stepped in and permitted member banks to borrow at the discount window on favorable terms in order to refinance commercial paper that could not be rolled over. Deposit interest rate ceilings also were relaxed to make it easier for banks to raise funds in the open market.

Such examples notwithstanding, by 1975 inflation was not under control, and the country was in deep recession. What came to be called *stagflation* brought calls from Congress for the Federal Reserve to report to Congress periodically with respect to targets for money supply growth and other monetary policies.

Stagflation:
Inflation that occurs simultaneously with stagnant economic growth (recession).

The shift from regulation of interest rates to regulation of monetary aggregates had begun.

Monetary Policy since 1979 While Congress emphasized periodic reports on money supply statistics, the Federal Reserve continued to target, or concentrate on, interest rates. In attempting to control and lower interest rate levels, money was added to the system, but these liquidity infusions only served to fuel inflation. In October 1979, the Federal Reserve announced that it would no longer target interest rates; instead its monetary policy would focus on the growth rates of the money supply. Interest rates would be permitted to find their own level.

The Fed then pursued a classic tight money policy, and interest rates soared. The discount rate (which had been 5.5 percent in 1976) rose from its 12 percent level in 1979 to a high of 14 percent in 1981. The federal funds rate increased from 5 percent in 1976 to almost 14 percent in 1979 and to 19 percent in 1981.

The United States suffered a recession in 1981 and 1982, as the unemployment rate rose to 11 percent (from less than 6 percent in 1979). After the inflation rate dropped by more than 10 percentage points, the Federal Reserve relaxed its tight money policy in 1982 and once again targeted interest rate levels as well as monetary aggregates.

The economy began to recover, but the interest rates remained relatively high, with a federal funds rate of just under 10 percent in 1983 and 1984, while the inflation rate ran only about 4 percent. Persistently high real interest rates (nominal rate less the inflation rate) hurt business expansion efforts. The strong value of the dollar, attributable at least in part to attractive U.S. interest rates, kept U.S. exports from being price-competitive. Private and government debt swelled, but the borrowed money was not used for investment in industrial equipment and infrastructure. Instead, it went largely for corporate takeovers, personal consumption, and government deficits. While the stock market soared in the mid-1980s, the economic recovery stalled. Oil and gas, agriculture, and real estate prices fell dramatically, and manufacturing plants closed.

The Federal Reserve responded by lowering the discount rate modestly. The Fed was again at odds with the government. Rates would not be reduced further until the federal government reduced its budget deficit. To reduce rates in the presence of such high deficits, the Fed reasoned, would give an "easy money" signal to the market that might lead to high rates of inflation again and would surely cause the value of the U.S. dollar to fall drastically.

Bringing down the value of the dollar was precisely what the Treasury wanted, however, to help U.S. business be more price-competitive at home and overseas. In cooperation with the governments of Germany, Japan, France, and the United Kingdom, the U.S. Treasury began to intervene in the foreign exchange markets, selling large amounts of dollars to reduce the value of the currency. After the five governments pursued this strategy, the Federal Reserve recognized that both the dollar value and interest rates had been too high for too long, and both declined.

The damage to the economy from high interest rates since 1979 and a strong dollar was not easily reversed, however. Demand for domestically manufactured products remained sluggish so that significant increases in production capacity were not necessary. Agriculture, oil, and real estate prices showed few signs of rebounding. Only the financial markets seemed to benefit as stock and bond prices increased between 1985 and 1987.

The reality of the situation caught up with the financial markets in October 1987 when the stock market crashed, losing about 20 percent of its value in only 2 trading days. The Federal Reserve acted to prevent the same sequence of events that had occurred after the crash in 1929 by providing needed liquidity to the financial markets.

The Fed has been generally more accommodating to the economy in the late 1980s and early 1990s than it had been during the early 1980s. Nevertheless, the structural problems of the economy have not been corrected by more lenient monetary policy. Low interest rates in the early 1990s have done little to stimulate the U.S. economy. It appears that the cost of fighting the early 1980s inflation continues to be paid in terms of sluggish growth.

DEREGULATION

In the wake of the high and volatile interest rates of the 1970s, commercial banks and other depository institutions found themselves at a competitive disadvantage in financial services markets. As market interest rates rose and mutual funds and securities firms began to compete with commercial banks and savings and loan associations, the flow of funds to depository institutions declined.

Disintermediation

Money market mutual funds offered small savers market rates of interest for a substantially smaller investment than once required. The funds then pooled these small investments to purchase Treasury securities, large bank certificates of deposit (not subject to interest rate ceilings after 1970), commercial paper, and banker's acceptances. Individual investors not only earned high rates of return but also received limited check-writing privileges. In 1974, money market funds controlled roughly $2 billion in assets; by 1980, the total was $200 billion.[4] The growth of these funds was one of the major motivations behind elimination of deposit interest rate regulation.

Securities firms, too, offered transactions accounts in direct competition with bank checking accounts. Besides earning interest on their accounts, clients received a full range of brokerage services. Competition from these two sources resulted in *disintermediation.*

Disintermediation:
The withdrawal of funds from depository institutions for the purpose of investing in other vehicles.

Two government studies analyzed the problems of depository institutions and made specific recommendations to address them:

- The Hunt Commission report
- The FINE study

In 1971, the *President's Commission on Financial Structure and Regulation (the Hunt Commission)* suggested that savings and loan associations, credit unions, and mutual savings banks be permitted to offer transactions accounts. The Hunt Commission also recommended that deposit interest rate ceilings (Regulation Q) be eliminated after a phase-out period and reinstated only if necessary.

Of course, eliminating ceilings was feasible only if investment powers were also expanded. Institutions had to have the power to make investments that would earn high enough rates of return to provide a reasonable margin over deregulated deposit interest rates. In order to put all depository institutions on an equal footing, the commission suggested instituting uniform reserve requirements and giving the Federal Reserve regulatory authority over all such institutions.

[4]Currently, money market funds hold over $500 billion in assets. See Chapter 21 for a description of money market funds.

In 1975, the House Banking Committee conducted the *Financial Institutions and the Nation's Economy (FINE) Study.* Several of its recommendations coincided with those of the Hunt Commission:

- Thrift institutions (savings and loan associations and mutual savings banks) should receive broader investment powers.
- Reserve requirements should be uniform.
- Deposit interest rate ceilings should be eliminated.

The study suggested furthermore that regulatory and insurance functions be consolidated. Even with this unanimity of opinion, federal legislation was not enacted until several years after these studies.

The Reform Movement

The 1979 shift in the Federal Reserve's emphasis from interest rate control toward control of monetary aggregates forced depository institutions to operate in a regulatory environment that was out of step with the rest of the market. Maintaining deposit interest rate ceilings, as other market interest rates found their natural level, was inconsistent policy. Competitive pressures mounted until depository institutions were essentially in crisis.

Commercial banks withdrew from Federal Reserve membership at an unprecedented rate. Nonmember state banks had the advantages of often lower reserve requirements and the freedom to invest reserves in interest-bearing investments (unlike those held at Federal Reserve banks). The Federal Reserve became concerned that such wholesale defection would impair its ability to implement monetary policy.

The Federal Home Loan Bank Board, then the chief regulator of savings and loan associations, also pressed for reform. The deposit instruments S&Ls could offer were hardly competitive under the circumstances. Individual S&L managers also sought expanded deposit and investment powers.

Even consumer groups lobbied for deregulation. They argued that Regulation Q discriminated against small investors. Since 1970, the deposit rate ceilings for certificates of deposit in excess of $100,000 had been eliminated. Only rates paid to small depositors were still maintained at artificially low levels.

At the state level, mutual savings banks had won the right to offer NOW (negotiable order of withdrawal) accounts that were in fact interest-bearing checking accounts. However, such permission had been won primarily in the northeast, the region in which mutual savings banks are concentrated; NOW accounts were not available nationwide. The U.S. Congress had little alternative. In 1980, the first major legislative overhaul of depository institutions since the 1930s was carried out.

The Depository Institutions Deregulation and Monetary Control Act of 1980

The Depository Institutions Deregulation and Monetary Control Act (DIDMCA) provided for expanded asset and liability powers and, simultaneously, increased the authority of the Federal Reserve.[5] Its main features are listed below.

1 New reserve requirements for both member and nonmember commercial banks were set. This provision virtually eliminates the motivation to withdraw from the Federal Reserve. (See Exhibit 11-4.)
2 The Federal Reserve was instructed to provide services to *all* depository institutions, including access to the discount window.
3 The reserve requirements applicable to commercial banks were applied to other

[5]The DIDMCA is also known as the Monetary Control Act of 1980 and as the Omnibus Banking Act.

EXHIBIT 11-4 UNIFORM RESERVE REQUIREMENTS SPECIFIED IN THE DIDMCA OF 1980

Type of deposit	Percentage
Transactions Accounts	
$0 = $26.3 million*	3
Over $26.3 million	12
Nonpersonal time deposits†	
Less than 2.5 years	3
2.5 years or more	0
Eurocurrency liabilities	3

*This amount is adjusted each year by 80% of the change in total transactions accounts for all depository institutions; e.g., the 1988 base amount was $41.5 million.

†By original maturity.

Source: Cooper, S. Kerry, and Donald R. Fraser, *Banking Deregulation and the New Competition in Financial Services,* 1984, p. 117.

depository institutions. Savings and loan associations, mutual savings banks, and credit unions are now subject to uniform reserve requirements.

4 The Federal Reserve was instructed to establish a schedule of fees for services. Prior to DIDMCA, there were generally no fees.

5 The Depository Institutions Deregulation Committee (DIDC) was created to oversee the phaseout of Regulation Q deposit interest rate ceilings over a 6-year period. Voting members of the DIDC were Secretary of the Treasury, and the chairs of the Federal Reserve, the Federal Deposit Insurance Corporation, the Federal Home Loan Bank Board, and the National Credit Union Administration. The Comptroller of the Currency was a nonvoting member.

6 Interest-bearing transactions accounts became legal products for all depository institutions. All banks and thrifts could offer negotiable order of withdrawal (NOW) accounts. Credit unions were permitted to offer share drafts. Only individuals and nonprofit organizations, however, could take advantage of NOW accounts, and the interest rate was set at slightly over 5 percent.

7 The limit of insurance for accounts in depository institutions was raised from $40,000 to $100,000.

8 The S&Ls could now offer credit cards and were permitted to make commercial real estate loans and consumer loans, each up to 20 percent of total assets.

9 Mutual savings banks could make business loans and offer demand accounts to business clients.

10 State usury laws were effectively eliminated for mortgage, business, and agricultural loans.

With the DIDMCA, the scope of Federal Reserve authority has been expanded from state bank members to *all* depository institutions. Depository institutions are more competitive in that they may now offer interest-bearing checking accounts. The legislation mandated the phased-out elimination of all deposit interest rate ceilings and allowed S&Ls and mutual savings banks to move into more diversified and profitable, albeit more risky, lines of business. At the same time, the deposit insurance ceiling increased by 150 percent. In other words, as more potential risk was introduced into depository institutions, the government safety net expanded—a dangerous combination.

Problems in the thrift industry did not completely disappear, of course. Moreover, both commercial banks and thrifts continued to operate at a competitive disadvantage vis-à-vis money market mutual funds, whose rates of return to investors were not constrained in any way. Legislation in 1982 attempted to correct these deficiencies.

The Garn–St Germain Act of 1982 sought to expand financial institutions' powers still more and to facilitate the rescue of failing institutions. Its major provisions are:

1 The money market deposit account (MMDA) was legalized for depository institutions. The MMDAs could compete directly with money market mutual funds. If the accounts were owned by individuals, there were no reserve requirements. A 3 percent reserve requirement was stipulated for business accounts.
2 Federal, state, and local governments were permitted to own NOW accounts.
3 Federally chartered S&Ls were empowered to offer demand accounts to persons or organizations with whom they had business relationships.
4 The DIDC was instructed to eliminate (Regulation A) deposit rate differentials between commercial banks and thrifts.
5 Savings and loan associations were permitted to diversify asset portfolios further, up to certain percentages of total assets:

Commercial real estate loans	40%
Secured and unsecured commercial loans	5%
Commercial leasing	10%
Consumer loans	30%

6. Savings and loan associations could add state and local government revenue bonds to their asset portfolios. Before 1982, only investments in general obligation bonds were allowed.
7. Federal regulators received more financial and geographic flexibility for rescuing thrifts, making it possible for financial and nonfinancial firms to purchase thrifts on more favorable terms for the buyers.
8. The percentage of capital that a national bank could lend to a single borrower was increased from 10 to 15 percent, plus an additional 10 percent for loans collateralized by readily marketable assets.
9. National banks were permitted to form bank service companies and to invest in export trading firms. These provisions gave national banks more operational flexibility.
10. The transfer of assets (excluding low-quality assets) between bank holding companies and affiliated banks was substantially liberalized.
11. The Federal Deposit Insurance Corporation (FDIC), the Federal Savings and Loan Insurance Corporation (FSLIC), and the National Credit Union Administration (NCUA) were instructed to study the federal deposit insurance system and to identify and evaluate possible alternatives.

The Garn–St Germain Act made it easier for regulators to close failing thrift institutions. Under the act, depository institutions can now compete directly with money market funds, by offering a similar instrument *with* deposit insurance coverage. For commercial banks, lending limits to individual customers were increased and the scope of activities expanded. The S&Ls' powers were so transformed that, at least in terms of statutory powers, it became difficult to distinguish S&Ls from commercial banks.

Even these expanded powers did not bring an end to the problems in the S&L and commercial banking industries. In fact, the 1980s would witness bank and S&L failure rates that had not been seen since the 1930s.

DEPOSIT INSURANCE

In 1989, Congress was compelled to restructure the deposit insurance system and make major changes in regulatory oversight. (See Exhibit 11-5.) The federal deposit insurance agencies that were created in the early 1930s have only recently been seriously chal-

EXHIBIT 11-5 THE THEORY OF DEPOSIT INSURANCE

The introduction of federal deposit insurance in 1933 added stability to the banking system. While its benefits to depositors are clear-cut, its implications for bank management and FDIC financial exposure may be less straightforward, as some academic researchers show.

John J. Mingo found that the rate at which commercial banks increased their capital investment was negatively related to the percentage of total deposits covered by FDIC insurance.* In other words, commercial banks substitute the government guarantee of deposits for shareholder equity. Some part of the risk taking that is normally associated with equity ownership is thereby shifted to the FDIC.

Robert C. Merton suggests that deposit insurance is similar to a common stock put option, which entitles the buyer of the option to sell stock at a specified (exercise) price to the seller of the option.† Stock option buyers do not exercise the option unless the value of the stock falls below the exercise price. In the case of deposit insurance, depositors do not receive payment from the FDIC unless the value of the bank's assets is less than the amount necessary to repay depositors, that is, unless the bank becomes insolvent. The value of this option is the cost that is imposed on the FDIC as a result of this arrangement. According to option-pricing theory, the value of the option is positively related to the bank's deposit-to-asset ratio, volatility of underlying asset returns, and time. In other words, the true cost to the FDIC increases when the bank uses more debt financing, the rate of return on assets is more variable, and the term of insurance coverage increases.

The work of these researchers and others indicates that appropriate deposit insurance premiums can be set only after assessing bank capital levels, the composition of bank asset portfolios, and their trends over time.

* Mingo, John J., "Regulatory Influence on Bank Capital Investment," *Journal of Finance,* Vol. 30, No. 4 (September 1975), pp. 1110–1121.

† Merton, Robert C. "An Analytic Derivation of the Cost of Deposit Insurance and Loan Guarantees," *Journal of Banking and Finance,* Vol. 1 (1977), pp. 3–11.

lenged. During the 37 years from 1943 through 1979, only 210 banks failed. But in the 6-year period ended 1985, 300 failed. Another 769 failed between 1986 and 1989. Thus, in the 1980s, over 1000 banks failed, five times the number of failures in the previous 4 decades. Contraction of the savings and loan industry has been even more severe. The S&Ls numbered over 5000 in 1979. By 1989, only 3000 remained, and the number continues to decline each year.

Too Big to Fail

Not all the bank failures have been handled in the same way. When the troubled bank is large, it is more likely that all depositors and creditors will be paid by the FDIC. The controversial arrangement for large banks is attributed to the "too big to fail" theory of deposit insurance. In essence, it means that depositors in large institutions have implicit insurance on all deposits, including those with balances in excess of $100,000, and that general creditors (without the status of deposits) will also face no loss. The concept is controversial because it:

- Involves differential treatment of bank depositors by a government agency
- Discourages depositors in large banks from forcing market discipline on those

banks, as the depositors can remain confident that their investments are safe regardless of bank behavior
- Causes depositors to have less confidence in small banks, thereby making them less competitive
- Greatly increases the exposure of FDIC to loss, thereby indirectly exposing the U.S. taxpayers to greater loss

The FDIC's reason for handling large, troubled banks in this way is the potential effect to the banking system as a whole should a large bank fail. A large bank failure could bring systemwide instability and bank runs. The cost of this instability is thought to be greater than the cost of an unconditional bank bailout.

The first instance of this special treatment was Continental Illinois National Bank in 1984, with liabilities of $33 billion, of which only $3 billion were insured. All claims of depositors and creditors were completely guaranteed by the government. To rescue the bank, the coordinated efforts of the FDIC, the Federal Reserve, and a private bank syndicate were necessary.

The Crisis and FIRREA

In the savings and loan industry, there are no institutions that are too big too fail. In fact, most operate with relatively little regulatory oversight. The new powers of the 1980 and 1982 legislation, combined with higher deposit insurance, were tailor-made for abuse in a lax regulatory climate. Many S&Ls attracted *brokered deposits,* large CDs sold through securities brokers. Since the CDs were completely insured as long as the deposit did not exceed $100,000, investors were confident that their money was safe and asked few questions about the soundness of the S&L. The S&L had a ready source of cash then to invest in new activities permitted to it, including junk bonds, commercial loans, commercial real estate loans, and direct real estate investments. The originally conservative residential mortgage finance industry was transformed into a freewheeling, high-risk money machine, completely insured by the federal government.[6]

The failure rate became so high that the Financial Institutions Reform, Recovery, and Enforcement Act (FIRREA) was passed in August 1989. Under the strain of widespread failures, the Federal Savings and Loan Insurance Corporation (FSLIC) was declared insolvent and absorbed by the FDIC.[7] The FDIC resources had also been strained. Bank failures have accelerated because of third-world bank loans and domestic loans in the oil and gas and commercial real estate sectors. The Bank Insurance Fund (the renamed FDIC fund), which stood at $18 billion at the beginning of 1988, fell to $11.4 billion as of June 1990.[8]

FIRREA mandated that the FDIC adjust insurance premiums so that the fund balance be maintained at an amount between 1.25 and 1.40 percent of estimated insured deposits. At the end of 1989, the ratio of insurance fund balance to insured deposits was only .70 percent. By June 1990, the ratio stood even lower at 0.57 percent.

To reverse this trend, deposit insurance premiums have gone from .083 percent of deposits before FIRREA to .195 percent of deposits in 1991 and, according to provisions in FIRREA, could go as high as .325 percent. It is apparent, however, that increased insur-

[6]See also Chapter 19.

[7]The fund that insures savings and loan associations is still maintained separately from the bank insurance fund. Under the FDIC, the S&L fund is designated the Savings Association Insurance Fund (SAIF).

[8]By 1991, the fund balance was down to $8.4 billion and in danger of being depleted if not for injection of new capital.

ance premiums will not be sufficient to restore the fund and that federal government assistance will be necessary.[9]

At the same time that FSLIC was absorbed by FDIC, the Federal Home Loan Bank Board, once essentially an independent agency, was converted into the Office of Thrift Supervision (OTS) and brought under the authority of the Treasury Department.

Those S&Ls that had been closed by federal regulators and others, still open because FSLIC lacked the funds to close them but in unstable financial condition, became the responsibility of the Resolution Trust Corporation (RTC), created by FIRREA to liquidate failed savings institutions. As of August 1989, RTC held over 250 institutions with assets of over $100 billion in conservatorship. The chairperson and the director of FDIC each serves the same function in RTC. The RTC Oversight Board, the policy-making body, includes the Secretary of the Treasury (as chairperson), the Chair of the Federal Reserve, and the Secretary of Housing and Urban Development. With such a far-flung policy-making board, the RTC is a cumbersome structure in terms of making timing decisions about asset liquidation and has been criticized because of this. FIRREA mandates that the RTC will operate only until December 31, 1996.

FIRREA attempts to correct some of the excesses of the early 1980s legislation by requiring higher capital levels and more prudent investment policies for thrifts, shoring up the federal insurance fund, and limiting the use of brokered deposits. Exhibit 11-6 outlines the major provisions of this legislation.

While there are no definite amounts identified as the total cost of cleaning up the S&L industry, estimates range from $150 billion to $500 billion. How the bailout is to be financed is the subject of much debate. The federal budget deficit is a stubborn financial problem, even before considering the savings and loan issue. Current commercial bank failures, moreover, although not as widespread as S&L failures, do not bode well for the long-term solvency of the FDIC.

The liabilities of institutions that have already been closed and the even worse *potential* exposure of the U.S. government have brought the concept of federal deposit insurance under scrutiny.

Reform Proposals

FIRREA also instructed the Treasury Department to conduct major studies on the issue of federal deposit insurance, and in fact the current deposit insurance system has sometimes been cited as a significant cause of the instability in the banking industry. The rationale for this argument is that the government guarantee encourages excessive risk taking by managers of financial institutions. The incentive is said to be strong because any failure of risky investments to pay off as originally anticipated will not hurt depositors; the federal government will assume the deposit liabilities. The converse is that if these risky investments *do* pay off, the bank and its managers will prosper. This situation is often referred to as a *moral hazard:* investing with all the attendant benefits but passing the costs along to another party. Possible reforms to the deposit insurance system involve:

- Abolition of federal deposit insurance
- Modifying insurance coverage
- Charging risk-adjusted premiums

[9]The FDIC Assessment Rate Act of 1990 gave the FDIC board broad authority to set premiums in order to maintain desired reserves to deposit ratios for the boy interest franc (BIF) and interest franc (SAIF). Assessment feelings and rate increases were eliminated. The FDIC Improvement Act of 1991 gave the FDIC the power to borrow $70 billion from the Treasury Department and from member banks. In addition, the FDIC Improvement Act stipulated that the weighted average bank assessment may not fall below .23 percent of deposits until the (ratio of fund) balance to insured deposits reached 1.25 percent.

EXHIBIT 11-6 THE FINANCIAL INSTITUTIONS REFORM, RECOVERY, AND ENFORCEMENT ACT (FIRREA) OF 1989

FIRREA includes provisions affecting commercial banking and savings and loan associations. Major provisions are:

1. The Federal Home Loan Bank Board (previously the primary regulator of savings and loan associations) and the Federal Savings and Loan Insurance Corporation were abolished. The Office of Thrift Supervision (within the Treasury Department) became the chief regulator, and the FDIC took over the insurance function. The FDIC now maintains two funds: the Bank Insurance Fund (BIF) and the Savings Association Insurance Fund (SAIF).
2. The Resolution Funding Corporation was created to sell bonds to raise the funds necessary to complete the liquidation of failed S&Ls. The Resolution Trust Corporation (RTC) oversees the liquidations.
3. Insurance premiums increased for both S&Ls and commercial banks. The S&L premiums per $100 of deposits were to increase from $0.208 to $0.23 in 1991, then decrease to $0.18 in 1994 and to $0.15 in 1998. Bank insurance premiums per $100 of deposits were to increase from $0.083 to $0.12 in 1990 and to $0.15 in 1991. FIRREA also gave FDIC the right to increase the rates in either fund, if necessary, to ensure solvency of SAIF and BIF. Premiums may not exceed $0.325 per $100 of deposits or be raised by more than $0.075 per year.
4. The Community Reinvestment Act of 1977 was amended to require public disclosure of a depository institution's regulatory rating with respect to community reinvestment. In addition, member institutions of Federal Home Loan Banks were to establish special funds to help finance home purchases, housing rehabilitation, and economic development for low- and moderate-income families.
5. For S&Ls, minimum tangible capital was set at 1.5 percent of total assets.* Minimum core capital was set at 3 percent of total assets. By the end of December 1992, thrifts are required to meet the same capital requirements as commercial banks (prescribed by the Office of the Comptroller of the Currency).
6. Any insured depository institution that does not meet minimum capital requirements may not accept brokered deposits.†
7. Savings institutions may no longer invest in bonds that are not rated investment grade. All holdings of such "junk" bonds must be sold as soon as possible but no later than 1994.
8. The penalties for bank fraud were stiffened. The maximum fine increased from $5000 to $1 million, and the maximum prison term increased from 10 to 20 years.

* Tangible capital includes common stock equity, noncumulative preferred stock, nonwithdrawable deposit accounts, pledged deposits, and minority interest in consolidated subsidiaries. Core capital is tangible capital plus qualifying intangibles, including goodwill (the premium paid by an investor when purchasing a troubled thrift institution).

† Brokered deposits are placed with a depository institution through a third party, typically a securities broker. The broker tries to find the highest rate of return available in an institution that is federally insured. Previously, troubled institutions could attract large amounts of brokered deposits by offering high interest rates, putting even more pressure on profits.

Source: Meyer, Dianne, and Sandra A. Ballard, "Issues in Lending: A Guide to FIRREA," *Journal of Commercial Bank Lending,* Vol. 72 (January 1990), pp. 11–23.

Proponents of the proposal to *abolish* federal deposit insurance suggest that closer market scrutiny, not government oversight, will restore discipline to the market. Those opposed to the abolition of federal deposit insurance argue that its absence would destroy confidence in the system and lead to domino-effect bank runs. Proponents of abolition assert that the Federal Reserve *can* and *would* provide needed liquidity to shore up the system; it would not passively allow large-scale bank failures as it did in the 1930s.

EXHIBIT 11-7 THE BUSH ADMINISTRATION'S PROPOSAL FOR BANK REFORM

In 1991, Nicholas Brady, Treasury secretary in the Bush administration, proposed a plan for bank reform. In essence, the proposal seeks to allow well-capitalized banks more freedom of operation, to limit federal deposit insurance coverage, and to bring more market discipline to banking. The features of the plan include the following:

1. Permit those banks that meet minimum capital requirements to branch nationwide and to engage in securities underwriting. (Those banks not meeting the capital requirements would be liquidated or absorbed by other institutions.)
2. Limit insurance coverage to $100,000 per person per bank for regular banking purposes. Provide an additional $100,000 per person per bank for retirement accounts.
3. Base deposit insurance premiums on the adequacy of bank capital, with strongly capitalized banks paying lower premiums.
4. Eliminate insurance coverage of brokered deposits and nondeposit liabilities, frequently covered in large bank liquidations.
5. Give bank regulators more authority to correct bank deficiencies sooner.
6. Force banks to disclose the true market value of assets and liabilities.
7. Permit nonbank financial firms and nonfinancial firms to own commercial banks through the holding company structure.
8. Limit the ability of state-chartered banks to engage in activities not permitted for national banks to prevent the FDIC from being exposed to the risk of covering losses associated with these activities.

The proposals address important issues in U.S. banking and would help make banks more competitive and financially viable. Congress, however, generally has failed to enact necessary legislation to adopt the proposals.

Source: Modernizing the Financial System: Recommendations for Safer, More Competitive Banks, U.S. Department of the Treasury, 1991.

Other alternatives involve *modification of insurance coverage,* rather than abolition of insurance. Sharing risk with the insured party is referred to as *coinsurance.* In one type of coinsurance plan, each depositor would be required to pay the first dollars of loss. A variation, *fixed-proportional sharing,* requires the insured to pay a fixed percentage of every dollar of loss. Opponents of this type of modification argue that the current system is already coinsurance, because the government pays the first $100,000, and the depositor pays the remainder.

Another modification is to *lower the maximum coverage.* The relatively high $100,000 limit is forty times the original limit of $2500, yet from 1934 to 1980 (when the higher limit was established), general price levels increased only seven times. A lower limit might reduce the moral hazard, as it would be more difficult for institutions to raise funds quickly by raising deposit rates; that is, several smaller insured deposits would be necessary to equal one $100,000 insured deposit. At the same time, small depositors would be completely protected as the original 1933 legislation intended.

Risk-adjusted premiums are probably the most widely proposed alternative to the deposit insurance system. Such premiums are likely to impose a certain amount of discipline on the insured institution because more risky operations would cause its insurance premiums to rise. In fact, this is the practice in virtually all insurance arrangements other than those for depository institutions. The FDIC Improvement Act of 1991 requires the FDIC to develop risk-based insurance assessments by January 1, 1994.

Proper evaluation of portfolio risk has always been a challenge for federal regulators. This difficulty is compounded further by a traditional reluctance to disclose negative information about the regulated institutions. The usual justification for this stance has been that such disclosure could cause a lack of confidence in the institution and would result in bank runs. There are signs today that this protective attitude is giving way to more pressing concerns of restoring discipline to the industry.

Whatever the ultimate disposition of federal deposit insurance, it is safe to say that it has turned into one of the most urgent issues in bank regulation in decades. Not since the bank failures of the Great Depression has the regulatory structure of the U.S. banking system faced so much uncertainty. (See also Exhibit 11-7.)

SUMMARY

The basic tools of monetary policy are reserve requirements, the discount rate, and open market operations. The Federal Reserve has the responsibility to conduct monetary policy so as to maintain price stability and to encourage economic growth, but the two goals sometimes conflict. Which should take priority has often been the basis for debate between the Federal Reserve and the U.S. Treasury Department. Over time, the Federal Reserve has gained the independence to implement monetary policy essentially as it sees fit.

During the early 1980s, attempts to constrain growth of the money supply led to extremely high interest rates. Concentrating on money supply targets did not have the desired effect, however, as private and public debt increased significantly. The effects of high interest rates and mounting debt continue to be felt in the early 1990s. Most troubling is the lack of response of the economy to traditional means of stimulation. A low interest rate policy by the Fed has not renewed the economy's vigor.

After the major bank legislation of the 1930s, the structure of the commercial bank system remained virtually unchanged until 1980, when depository institutions were deregulated in order to overcome competitive disadvantages vis-à-vis nondepository financial institutions. Thereafter, institutions failed at rates not seen since before the 1930s legislation. The federal agency responsible for savings and loan insurance (FSLIC) folded. Commercial bank failures accelerated, causing assets in the commercial bank insurance fund (FDIC) to decline for the first time since its inception. Without government assistance, the future of the FDIC is also questionable.

The 1980s brought significant change to the regulatory environment of depository institutions. Further, with the amount of uncertainty that still surrounds the system, the 1990s will almost certainly witness additional changes.

KEY TERMS

Depository Institutions Deregulation and Monetary Control Act of 1980
deposit insurance
discount rate
disintermediation
Financial Institutions Reform, Recovery, and Enforcement Act of 1989
fiscal policy
Garn–St Germain Depository Institutions Act of 1982
monetary base
monetary policy
open-market operations
reserve requirements
stagflation
transactions account multiplier

END-OF-CHAPTER QUESTIONS

1. Why has the Federal Reserve has been criticized for its actions after the stock market crash in 1929?
2. The Federal Reserve System is often characterized as being independent and autonomous. In what way is this not a completely accurate description?

3. How were the powers of the Federal Reserve increased by the legislation of 1980?
4. Define the primary tools of monetary policy, and indicate their relative importance.
5. Refer to the *Federal Reserve Bulletin* in your university library.
   a. How many times in the last 2 years has the discount rate been changed?
   b. Why do you suppose the Fed made these changes?
6. Why do the goals of the Federal Reserve to maintain price stability and economic growth sometimes conflict?
7. What factors led to the "deregulation" of banks?
8. a. What type of monetary target has the Federal Reserve historically used in the implementation of monetary policy?
   b. Why did this change in 1979?
   c. What was the effect of the change?
9. What were the major provisions of the Depository Institutions Deregulation and Monetary Control Act of 1980?
10. What were the major provisions of the Garn–St Germain Depository Institutions Act of 1982?
11. In what ways did the Financial Institutions Reform, Recovery, and Enforcement Act of 1989 attempt to correct the excesses of the 1980s?
12. Why is federal deposit insurance a topic of current debate?
13. Why does deposit insurance present a moral hazard?
14. a. Define the coinsurance approach to deposit insurance.
    b. Why is the U.S. deposit insurance system a form of coinsurance?
    c. In some cases, the U.S. deposit insurance system is not a coinsurance system. Can you present a convincing argument to support this statement?
15. Some analysts suggest that lowering the maximum coverage of deposit insurance will discourage brokered deposits. Do you agree?
16. Why do you suppose that the concept of risk-adjusted deposit insurance premiums receives a good deal of support?

SELECTED REFERENCES

Benston, George J., and George G. Kaufman. *Risk and Solvency Regulation of Depository Institutions: Past Policies and Current Options,* Salomon Brothers Center for the Study of Financial Institutions at the Graduate School of Business Administration of New York University, New York, 1988.

Ciocca, Pierluigi, Editor. *Money and the Economy: The Central Bankers' Views,* Macmillan Press, London, 1987.

Cooper, S. Kerry, and Donald R. Fraser. *Banking Deregulation and the New Competition in Financial Services,* Ballinger Publishing Company, Cambridge, Massachusetts, 1984.

The Federal Reserve System; Purposes and Functions, Board of Governors of the Federal Reserve System, Washington, D.C., 1984.

Goodfriend, Marvin. *Monetary Policy in Practice,* Federal Reserve Bank of Richmond, Richmond, Virginia, 1987.

Goodhart, Charles. *The Evolution of Central Banks,* The MIT Press, Cambridge, Massachusetts, 1988.

Greider, William. *Secrets of the Temple; How the Federal Reserve Runs the Country,* Touchstone/Simon and Schuster, New York, 1989.

Modernizing the Financial System; Recommendations for Safer, More Competitive Banks, U.S. Department of the Treasury, Washington, D.C., 1991.

Spong, Kenneth. *Banking Regulation; Its Purposes, Implementation, and Effects,* Federal Bank of Kansas City, Kansas City, Missouri, 1990.

Toniolo, Gianni, Editor. *Central Banks' Independence in Historical Perspective,* Walter de Gruyter, Berlin, 1988.

CHAPTER 12

CENTRAL BANKS AND REGULATORY SYSTEMS OUTSIDE THE UNITED STATES

CHAPTER OUTLINE

CENTRAL BANKING BEFORE 1900
- Swedish Riksbank
- Bank of England
- Bank of France
- National Bank of Belgium
- Banca d'Italia
- German Reichbank
- Swiss National Bank
- Bank of Japan

FOUNDATIONS OF MODERN CENTRAL BANKING
- Lessons Learned from Early Central Banks
- Specific Central Bank Development

REGULATORY ENVIRONMENTS
- Government Finance
  - The Bank of England, The Reichbank (Bundesbank predecessor), The Federal Reserve, The Bank of China
- Industrial Finance
  - Japan, Germany
- Regulatory Trends
  - Regulatory systems
  - International cooperation

MONETARY POLICY
- Interest Rate Regulation
- Reserve Requirements
- Open-Market Operations

DEREGULATION
- United Kingdom
- Canada
- Japan

DEPOSIT INSURANCE

INTERNATIONAL COMPARISONS:
- Belgium
- Canada
- China
- Commonwealth of Independent States (former republics of the Soviet Union)
- France
- Germany
- Hong Kong
- Italy
- Japan
- Sweden
- Switzerland
- United Kingdom

CHAPTER OVERVIEW

This chapter:

- Traces the origins of central banks outside the United States
- Describes the regulatory environment in various countries as it relates to government and industrial finance
- Pinpoints certain trends in the evolution of financial system regulation
- Provides a cross-country comparison of the use of the tools of monetary policy
- Highlights the pace of deregulation in other countries
- Compares deposit insurance schemes of selected countries

The U.S. Federal Reserve System is a product of the twentieth century. In other countries, central banks date back to the seventeenth century. By the time the Federal Reserve was created, many lessons of central banking had been learned. In some cases, these institutions traveled a rocky road to stability and solvency. In other cases, central banks made a smooth transition from a competing commercial bank to a nonprofit, quasi-government organization. In still other cases, the central bank is simply an arm of the government with little of the independence of the Federal Reserve. In this chapter, there are comparisons of these systems with the U.S. system with respect to central bank origin, commercial bank regulation, monetary policy, and deregulation.

With sometimes significant differences in origin and orientation, one of the biggest challenges to today's central banks in industrialized countries is to manage their role in a global environment and to coordinate their activities with the rest of their counterparts. The following section describes the starts and stops in the evolution of central banking among the world's oldest institutions.

CENTRAL BANKING BEFORE 1900

Swedish Riksbank

Sweden is credited with having the world's first central bank. In 1668, parliament took over ownership and supervision of the *Rikets Standers Bank* (the Bank of the Estate of the Realm). The bank had originally been established in 1656 as a private institution. After running into financial trouble, it was reorganized in 1668. Still, it operated independently of the crown and, for almost 200 years, was the only bank in Sweden. As the country's sole bank, it was also the primary note (paper money) issuer.

In 1726, when the Rikets Standers Bank once again ran into financial difficulty, this time because of the overissuance of notes in connection with unsecured government loans, the government resolved the crisis by making the bank's notes legal tender. These bank notes remained legal tender until 1873 when Sweden adopted the gold standard. In the interim, the government authorized private note-issuing banks in 1824 (with explicitly no state support promised or implied), and in 1867 the name of the central bank was changed to the *Swedish Riksbank.* In 1897, the Riksbank received the sole right of note issue.

However, there is little evidence that the world's first central bank performed many of the now traditional functions. In fact, during the banking crisis of 1907–1908 (which would lead to creation of the Federal Reserve System in the United States), the Riksbank was able to maintain currency convertibility only by virtue of a deposit of state funds that were, in turn, proceeds of an overseas loan.

Bank of England

Nearby, the *Bank of England* was chartered by parliament in 1694 for the purpose of facilitating government fund-raising. In contrast to the Swedish Riksbank, the Bank of England continued to operate as a private bank until 1946, when it was nationalized. In exchange for raising money for the government, the Bank received preferential note-issuing privileges, and, in 1833, Bank of England notes became legal tender. In 1844, the Bank was effectively granted the sole right to issue notes. However, this action did not give the Bank of England complete control over the money supply because checks were becoming a readily accepted form of payment.

Nevertheless, the Bank enjoyed a close relationship, with the government and a competitive advantage vis-à-vis other commercial banks. Because of its privileged position and its size, the central bank had a great deal of influence over the banking industry as a whole.

Bank of France

Napoleon Bonaparte helped establish the *Bank of France* in 1800. He believed that other banks had failed to maintain stable discount rates for commercial bills of exchange. The Bank of France was essentially a privately owned bank with strong government support. By 1806, the administrators of the Bank, the governor and two deputy governors, had become government appointees. Thus, private citizens owned the state-run central bank.

In keeping with Napoleon's desire for stable discount rates, the Bank of France received exclusive note-issuing power in Paris in 1803. By 1848, after banking crises brought the collapse of many smaller banks, this exclusive right extended throughout France. After 1848, the Bank of France issued notes and, following the English example, the four largest commercial banks that had survived issued deposits up to 1.5 times capital. A check clearinghouse was established in Paris in 1872, after the passage of the 1865 law that prescribed checking account regulation.

In addition to fulfilling its macroeconomic responsibilities for maintaining orderly markets, the Bank of France recognized its microeconomic role of lender of last resort in 1882. Interestingly, it was not a commercial bank that first received this assistance. The Bank rescued the Stock Exchange after particularly speculative behavior led to a liquidity crisis. Shortly thereafter, several smaller banks required similar help. Again, in 1889, the Bank of France supported one of the four major commercial banks, Comptoir d'Escompte, after its speculation in the copper market led to massive losses. These and other episodes underscored the need for bank supervision in connection with the facility of lender of last resort.

National Bank of Belgium

The *Bank of Belgium* was established in 1835 to compete with the existing bank that had performed most government financial functions before Belgium separated from Holland in 1830. But the Dutch management of the existing bank, Societe Generale, felt no obligation to take supervisory directives from the new Belgian government. The newly created Bank of Belgium did accept government oversight. The new bank was also just as committed to financing industrial enterprises as the original bank and was, therefore, just as illiquid. Because the Bank of Belgium was newer and smaller, it required government rescue in 1839 and ceased currency conversions in 1842.

Although Societe Generale had also been adversely affected by illiquidity in its asset portfolio, it was able to maintain currency conversion and took over once again as the government's cashier. However, a banking crisis in 1848 was more than even Societe Generale could withstand, and it, too, suspended note conversion.

These events led to the development of a new concept of central banking. In 1850, the *National Bank of Belgium* received the right of unlimited note issue in exchange for the strict requirement to maintain cash reserves. While the new Bank had note-issuing freedom, it also had strict operational restrictions. The actual amount of cash reserves was to be determined through negotiation by the Minister of Finance and the Bank, whose governor was appointed by the King. The initial reserve requirement was set at 25 percent of notes and demand deposits and later raised to 33.33 percent in 1872.

These requirements may appear high, but they did not represent a binding constraint. Since the National Bank refused to pay interest on demand deposits, it attracted few such accounts. Consequently, the combination of notes and demand deposits made up only 10 percent of the Bank's total liabilities at the time.

Although the National Bank of Belgium was subject to reserve requirements, other commercial banks appeared to have no such requirement. Nevertheless, operational restrictions on the National Bank of Belgium were an important refinement of bank regulation.

Banca d'Italia

The central bank in Italy has more contentious origins than any of its counterparts. A note-issuing bank, which had originated in Genoa in 1844, merged with another institution to become *Banca Nazionale* in 1849. By 1874, it was the largest Italian bank, but by no means was it the exclusive note issuer. Even individuals and nonfinancial firms issued notes. A law was passed in 1874 to attempt to bring some measure of uniformity to the nation's currency. Since regional influences were strong, no *single* bank received exclusive note-issuing privileges. Instead, six banks were designated: Banca Nazionale, Banca Nazionale Toscana, Banca Toscanadi Credito, Banca Romana, Banca di Napoli, and Banca di Sicilia. (See Exhibit 12-1.)

The system worked reasonably well until competition among the banks accelerated (1883–1885). The Banca Nazionale began to compete with Banca di Napoli in the south (Naples). Initially, the territorial competition enhanced the earnings of Banca Nazionale. However, after 1885, two problems emerged. The Italian agricultural sector suffered from competition with North America. Second, a bank-led building boom in Naples and Rome collapsed, leaving banks holding uncollectible loans.

The generally poor condition of banks and the imprudent banking practices of the period led to a new banking law in 1893. Banca Nazionale and the two Tuscan banks were merged into *Banca d'Italia.* Banca Romana was liquidated. The two remaining banks became affiliates of Banca d'Italia. While Banca d'Italia remained a private bank, an inspector general (within the Ministry of Finance) held veto power over every note-issuing institution. All notes and demand deposits were subject to a 40 percent metallic reserve requirement.

EXHIBIT 12-1 THE INFAMOUS BANCA ROMANA

In 1850, the same year that the conservative restructuring of the National Bank of Belgium was legislated, Banca dello Stato Pontifico began operations, and here the similarity ends. The bank was located within the Papal States, Italian territory over which the Pope (head of the Roman Catholic Church) had civil authority from A.D. 754 until 1870. In 1870, Italy reclaimed sovereignty over most of this land, leaving only Vatican City under the control of the Pope. To say that Banca dello Stato Pontifico, chartered by the Pope, was plagued by imprudent banking practices is an understatement. By 1870, Banca dello Stato Pontifico had accumulated capital of 3 million lira and losses of 9 million lira.

Because it was the only bank in the Papal States that Italian troops had seized, the bank was not liquidated but, instead, was reorganized and became Banca Romana. Unfortunately, bank management did not mend its ways. A government audit of all note-issuing banks was conducted in 1888. During the audit of Banca Romana, a cash shortage of 8 million lira was detected. The audit was suspended while the governor of Banca Romana borrowed the funds from the Banca Nazionale, the largest note-issuing bank in Italy at the time. The audit continued and the accounts were declared in order.

The imprudent practices finally caught up with the bank, forcing it to cease note redemption in 1891. Again, for political reasons, the government did not order liquidation. Instead, Banca Romana was permitted to receive more loans from Banca Nazionale and was relieved of any legal obligation to redeem its notes.

An economist unearthed the report of the 1888 audit and disclosed it to the public in 1893. Banca Romana collapsed, an uproar arose in Parliament, and a new, more restrictive, banking act was passed.

Conditions improved, metallic reserves increased, and the Italian system sustained relatively little damage during the banking crisis of 1907. Meanwhile, Banca d'Italia (or its predecessor Banca Nazionale) performed the lender-of-last-resort function on a number of occasions: 1888 (Banca Romana), 1889 (banks in Turin), 1893 (a secondary bond and stock market decline), and 1905–1906 (bank portfolios adversely affected by a stock market decline).

German Reichbank

The German *Reichbank* was established in 1875 for the expressed purpose of unifying the currency and coin system. In addition, a more effective payments system was needed. From the outset, the Reichbank was structured as a government institution, with no stated goal for profit maximization. However, private shareholders received a limited dividend and elected a central committee that met each month with the officially appointed directorate.

In connection with the second objective of a more effective payments system, the Reichbank initiated a Berlin-based clearinghouse for checks in 1883. Reichbank branches in key cities served as note issuers and sites for clearinghouse settlement. Understandably, the use of checks became increasingly popular.

As was eventually the case in Belgium, Germany's central bank portfolio was restricted. The Reichbank could hold only high-grade bills. Further, the central bank paid no interest on its deposits, although it possessed the statutory right to issue interest-bearing deposits up to the amount of its capital and reserves. Thus, the Reichbank represented little or no competition for German commercial banks but stood ready to support the commercial banks by discounting commercial bills for those banks that experienced liquidity problems.

The Reichbank served to strengthen the German system from a macroeconomic perspective by performing as a noncompetitive, non-profit-maximizing, collateralized liquidity facility. In the early years, however, the Reichbank was *not* a lender of last resort, as were its counterparts in France, the United Kingdom, and Italy. Neither did the Reichbank perform any supervisory functions. Part of the explanation for the difference may rest with the fact that German banks conducted much more portfolio management business than demand deposit business prior to 1900.

Swiss National Bank

In Switzerland, individual cantonal (state) banks each issued notes. However, they relied primarily on the French system to clear checks and transfer balances. In 1862, the larger Swiss banks organized a clearing mechanism in which each would accept the others' notes as payment. This only led to a multitude of notes circulating throughout the country. Meanwhile, the Franco-Prussian War interrupted French clearing services.

In 1881, as thirty-six different bank notes circulated, a new federal law constrained note issue by requiring that notes be backed by 40 percent legal tender and 60 percent other liquid assets. The 1881 law successfully regulated notes, but stipulated no reserve for deposits. Further, rumors of war in 1886 caused cantonal banks to restrict credit for fear that the Bank of France would again deny them access to discounting and other services. Clearly, this profit-motivated restriction of credit was not necessarily in the best interest of the country as a whole. In addition, if Switzerland were to adopt a gold standard, note issue would have to be centralized.

After lengthy negotiation over the matters of ownership and location, the *Swiss National Bank* became a reality in 1905. The Bank was modeled after the Reichbank with a combination of private and public ownership. Dividends paid to private shareholders were limited by law. Interest payments on deposits were prohibited to any party other than the government in order to prevent central bank competition with other banks.

The Swiss National Bank was, thus, a noncompetitive, non-profit-maximizing institution whose primary responsibility was the macroeconomic management of the monetary system. Regulation and oversight of commercial banks were responsibilities of other federal agencies.

Bank of Japan

A central bank in Japan was organized for the same reason as in a number of other countries—currency reform. After the Meiji Restoration of 1868, the first step in reform, a national system of bank chartering, was intended to provide a better framework for government finance and the monetary system in general. The U.S. national bank system (U.S. National Bank Act 1863) became its model. Sixty percent of initial bank capital was to be invested in inconvertible government securities. The government securities were then to be surrendered to the government and exchanged for 6 percent government bonds. The new securities formed the basis for bank note issuance. The remaining 40 percent of initial capital was to be invested in specie (silver) and held as reserve assets.

At the time, market interest rates were closer to 10 percent. The issuance of government debt drove up the price of specie that was required to purchase the bonds, thus encouraging note conversion. Because of the relatively high 40 percent specie reserve requirement, in combination with these factors, only four national bank charters were requested and granted. To encourage more national charters, the government changed the requirements in 1876. Eighty percent (instead of 60 percent) of capital could be invested in existing government bonds to back bank notes. The remaining 20 percent reserve requirement became government notes instead of specie. National banks were no longer required to convert their notes into specie. Instead, only conversion into government securities was necessary. Not surprisingly, the number of national banks grew. In the next few years, the government granted 153 national bank charters.

While the national bank system produced the desired market for government securities, it did not provide control over the money supply, a uniform currency, or finance for international trade. Accordingly, the government created the *Bank of Japan* in 1882. Organizationally, the Japanese central bank resembled the Bank of Belgium. Its operational guidelines resembled those of the German Reichbank. Yet the Bank of Japan developed into an institution that was functionally unlike its Belgian and German counterparts.

As was true with respect to the National Bank of Belgium, top officials (governor and vice-governor) were government appointees. The government was initially a large shareholder of the Bank of Japan. Theoretically, private shareholders of the National Bank brought financial market discipline to the bank's management. However, any private party who wished to become a shareholder was required to first receive permission from the Minister of Finance. From its inception, the Bank of Japan has been subject to strong government influence.

The German Reichbank did not act as lender of last resort in its early years. The Bank of Japan did so almost immediately. Its contact with commercial banks was close, albeit selective. The Bank of Japan primarily supported the larger banks, approximately forty institutions in Tokyo, Osaka, Kyoto, and Yokohama. Since there were over 2300 banks in Japan at the turn of the century, these larger institutions represented less than 2 percent of the total. Assistance for the small group of banks that *did* have relationships with the bank took the form of loans at below-market interest rates with relatively illiquid stocks as collateral.

So that the Bank could gain control over the money supply, bank charters of national banks were not renewed. As charters expired, the national banks were permitted to become ordinary banks with no note-issuing privileges. Only the Bank of Japan retained the right of note issue, thus creating a uniform currency.

To facilitate international trade, the Bank of Japan worked closely with the government-controlled Yokohama Specie Bank. The Specie Bank had been established in 1880 to encourage foreign trade and to import foreign specie. The Bank of Japan assisted these efforts by advancing funds at an interest rate of 2 percent and discounting commercial bills.

It should be noted that all overseas sales of government securities and all other transactions by the Treasury were handled by the Yokohama Specie Bank, instead of the Bank of Japan. Coordinated efforts of the central bank and the Specie Bank helped place Japan on much sounder footing with respect to external finance.

During the early days, the Bank of Japan focused primarily on microeconomic concerns. The management of interest rates and changes in money supply do not appear to have been top priorities.

FOUNDATIONS OF MODERN CENTRAL BANKING

Lessons Learned from Early Central Banks

These early experiments in central banking laid the foundation for central banking as we know it today. The Swedish Riksbank, the Bank of England, and the Bank of France initially followed the competitive, commercial bank model. The restructured National Bank of Belgium was the first to be organized as a *nonprofit institution,* paying *no interest on deposits* and holding a *restricted asset portfolio.* The troubled evolution of Banca d'Italia illustrates the potential problems that can arise when *note-issuance privileges* are given to more than one institution, in a competitive environment. The Reichbank and the Bank of Japan, from the outset, were subject to *strong government influence.* In its design, the U.S. Federal Reserve System reflects these features.

Together with the United States and Canada, the countries of Japan, Germany, the United Kingdom, France, and Italy have some of the most developed banking systems. The Swiss franc is the third-most important currency in Eurocurrency markets, after the U.S. dollar and the German deutsche mark. Sweden and Belgium have contributed significant historical precedents in central banking. Exhibit 12-2 shows the percentage breakdown of money supply (M_2) in these countries in 1989. The aggregate of their currency and deposits (demand, time, and savings) constituted 90 percent of the total for all industrialized nations. The rest of the chapter will concentrate on these countries.

As noted in Chapter 11, the modern central bank has several characteristics or functions:

1 A close link to government
2 Support for maintenance of a sound commercial banking system
3 Provision of liquidity in any financial crisis
4 Responsibility for avoidance of adverse economic fluctuations
5 Management of the external value of the domestic currency

The extent to which central banks perform the above-mentioned functions depends on their historical background.

Specific Central Bank Development

The *Bank of England* has performed its functions since 1844, essentially gaining powers of regulation and oversight through its special relationship with the government, rather than legislative mandate. The Bank was not nationalized until 1946 through the Bank of

EXHIBIT 12-2 MONEY SUPPLY (M_2) FOR INDUSTRIALIZED COUNTRIES, 1989

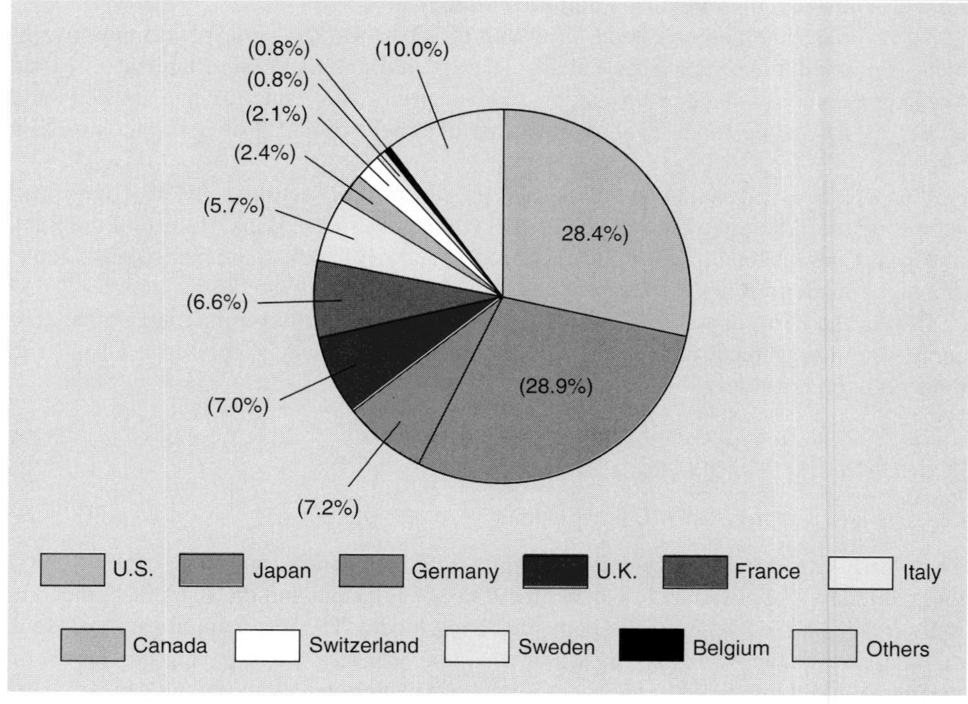

Source: Data from International Monetary Fund, *International Financial Statistics Yearbook 1990*, Washington,

England Act. At that time, the Bank became particularly involved with postwar monetary policy, currency conversion issues, and management of the large money supply that had accumulated during the war. Still, its role as central bank continued to evolve without legislative action. The 1979 Banking Act was intended to codify the Bank's responsibilities, to establish regulatory authority over other financial institutions, and to conform with bank statutes of other European Community countries.

The *Bank of France* was also nationalized, at approximately the same time (1945). Unlike the Bank of England, the Bank of France has operated in a much more strictly legislated environment. *The Swiss National Bank* (SNB), in contrast, continues to be both publicly and privately owned. However, the National Bank Law of 1953 dictated SNB's relationship to the government.

The *German Bundesbank* and the *Bank of Japan* have modern structures that have not evolved entirely domestically. Both West Germany and Japan were occupied by Allied forces after World War II. As a result, both have strongly centralized systems, similar to the U.S. model. Yet, as noted in the following section, the evolution of the Bundesbank and the Bank of Japan have followed distinctly different paths.

With respect to strong, centralized systems, the systems of the former *Soviet Union* and *Eastern Europe* serve as good examples. In 1917, the Soviet banking system was nationalized after the October revolution. Vladimir Lenin, Soviet leader at the time, believed that the state should have a monopoly on investment capital in a socialist economy. The Gosbank (State Bank) was established in 1921. Monetary objectives were (1) to introduce currency reform and (2) to encourage trade.

Excessive competition between the Gosbank and other banks led to legislation in 1927 to distribute capital more effectively. The doctrine of "one client–one bank" meant that

EXHIBIT 12-3 20TH-CENTURY DATES OF IMPORTANCE FOR CENTRAL BANKS IN SELECTED COUNTRIES

Bank	Date	Event
Bank of England (United Kingdom, owned by treasury)	1928	Given exclusive right of note issue
	1946	Nationalized
	1979	Given legal status to (1) continue previous central bank practices and (2) conform with statutory requirements of the European Community
Deutsche Bundesbank (West Germany, owned by government)	1922	Reichbank made autonomous by law as a condition for moratorium on reparations payments associated with World War I
	1923	Rentebank organized under law to issue notes Reichbank to continue to conduct banking functions
	1930	Foreign supervision ended
	1933	Private ownership abolished. Directors appointed by government
	1937	Reichbank placed under complete control of government
	1945	Reichbank ceased to exist (after World War II); banking system decentralized
	1949	West German constitution provided for central bank (Bundesbank) creation
	1951	Allied supervision of banking system ended
	1957	Bundesbank created
Bank of Japan (owned by public and private entities)	1942	Converted from a joint-stock company to a special corporation, in which shareholders were entitled to only a fixed investment return
	1949	Policy board (with public and private membership) established to formulate monetary policy, as stipulated by U.S. occupation authorities
Bank of France (owned by government)	1936	Taken over by the government
	1945	Nationalized by law
Bank of Italy (publicly owned)	1926	Granted exclusive right to issue bank notes
	1936	Prohibited from discounting bills of exchange for nonbank firms, i.e., became bankers' bank; became an institution owned by public entities
	1947	Received responsibility for supervising other banks
Swiss National Bank (publicly and privately owned)	1953	Bank's structure and relationship to government established (law amended in 1978)
Gosbank (Soviet Union, owned by government)	1917	Soviet banking system nationalized
	1921	Gosbank established
	1927	Implementation of "one client–one bank" doctrine

only one institution would provide credit for a given enterprise. This provision formed the foundation for credit allocation under the system of planned economies in the Soviet Union and its satellite countries (until the late 1980s when many of these satellites broke economic ties with the Soviet Union). Investment capital allocation was decided by government planning, instead of competitive supply and demand forces. Currently, the nations of Eastern Europe and, indeed, former Soviet republics are working to dismantle this system of investment capital distribution in favor of more efficient financial institutions and markets.

If the Soviet Union was at one end of the spectrum of state control, *Hong Kong* is at the other, with no formal central bank at all. Instead, a private commercial bank (the Hong Kong and Shanghai Banking Corporation) acts as lender of last resort and one of the two note-issuing banks of this dynamic, Asian city-state.

Certain aspects of regulatory systems are tied to the relationships between central banks and their governments. The Bank of England, the Reichbank (Bundesbank predecessor), the Federal Reserve, and the Bank of China are useful examples of these relationships. Other aspects are related to the relationships between banks and industrial firms. In this regard, the systems in Japan and Germany provide interesting contrasts with the United States.

Government Finance

Independence of central banks from government fiscal authorities is considered desirable because it helps to avoid potential overissue of notes or money. However, this independence is not always perfect.

The Bank of England Until 1914, the Bank of England operated independently of the Treasury. Rarely did the policy position of one conflict significantly with the policy position of the other. However, World War I (1914–1918) and the banking crisis of 1914 (during which the Treasury increased its deposits at the Bank to help resolve the crisis) necessitated a much closer coordination of the two operations. Afterward, the close working relationship continued. While the availability of credit and the level of interest rates were sometimes points of contention between the Bank and the Treasury, the Bank was not really subservient to the Treasury at any point. Even after nationalization in 1946, when the government began to manage the economy, the Bank of England has appeared to operate as an autonomous, full partner in the relationship.

The Reichbank (Bundesbank Predecessor) This was *not* the case in Germany, however, where in the past the government exercised a great deal of influence over the German central bank. At the beginning of World War I, Germany ceased gold conversion of its currency in order to conserve reserves. The government also lifted a previously imposed tax on excessive bank note issue. The objective was, of course, to *encourage* increased bank note issuance.

The government instituted other measures to increase its access to Reichbank credit. Before the war, by law, two-thirds of note issue was backed by commercial bills of exchange. The remaining one-third required gold reserves. These requirements were changed to enable the Reichbank to use Treasury bills to meet the two-thirds' requirement. This created a ready market for government securities and a source of bank notes for the government.

In addition, the one-third gold requirement was changed to allow banks to back this portion of notes with "loan bureau" notes. However, loan bureaus were simply subsidiaries of the Reichbank that issued notes backed by commodities or bonds, and loan bureau notes also circulated as money. Thus, government war bonds backed loan bureau notes, which, in turn, satisfied the one-third requirement. This arrangement created another market for government securities and added to money supply.

Loan bureau notes could even be exchanged for Reichbank notes. Once exchanged, loan bureau notes became the basis for issuing more bank notes (one-third of which were backed by the newly acquired bureau notes) and prompted the purchase of more Treasury bills (to back the remaining two-thirds of newly issued bank notes). This arrangement constituted a virtual "credit machine" for the government. In 1921, the one-third reserve requirement was completely eliminated.

The resulting inflation in the German economy is now legendary.[1] Understandably, in 1922 one of the conditions for granting Germany a moratorium on war reparations payments (through international treaty) was the enforcement of autonomy of the Reichbank. The following year, the Reichbank refused a government request to discount Treasury bills. This was the first real assertion of independence by the Reichbank since its formation in 1875. The relative autonomy continued until 1933 (after the worldwide banking collapse associated with the Great Depression) when *all* private ownership, and thus all private influence, ceased. After 1933, the Reichbank progressively became more an instrument of the government and a captive source of government finance.

From 1933 to 1937, the objectives of the Reichbank and the German government tended to converge. The Reichbank wanted employment expansion; the government wanted military armaments buildup. However, since international treaties prohibited the Reichbank from discounting Treasury bills, a new instrument was devised. Firms that manufactured armaments for the government drew commercial bills of exchange. The Reichbank discounted *these* bills instead of Treasury bills. In this way, both the military buildup and employment expansion were facilitated. This arrangement was an indirect form of government finance without the use of government securities.

By 1937, the Reichbank became concerned about the inflationary effects of continuing this practice. The government ceased issuance of the disputed instruments, and the central bank tightened credit. Unfortunately, commercial banks already held enough government bills of exchange to frustrate the central bank's money-tightening measures. Commercial banks simply discounted those bills held in their portfolios to increase liquidity. In 1937, a change in the law placed the Reichbank under the complete authority of the government. Shortly thereafter, the government selected and appointed a new Reichbank president, ensuring more accommodation of government financial needs.

The Allies disbanded the Reichbank at the end of World War II. Its successor, the Deutsche Bundesbank, has *never* operated as a vehicle for government finance in the manner of the Reichbank. The Bundesbank Act of 1957 stipulates that central bank's primary responsibility is to manage the money supply. It is, of course, obligated to support the general economic policy of the government, but, in the event of a conflict, its primary responsibility must have a higher priority. (See Exhibit 12-4.)

The Federal Reserve Although not as dramatically as the Reichbank case, the Federal Reserve has struggled with the U.S. Treasury over matters of money supply control versus economic growth. The (post–World War II) Employment Act of 1946 made "maximum employment" a top priority for every arm of the federal government, including the Federal Reserve. Demand for credit came from the government, from consumers who had pent-up demand from the war years and from businesses that wanted to invest in equipment and inventory to satisfy the consumer demand. The rate of inflation went from 8.5 percent in 1946 to 14.4 percent the next year. Even so, the Federal Reserve was obligated to keep interest rates low, despite its objections. It was not until 1951 that the Treasury–Federal Reserve Accord between the two agencies gave the Federal Reserve more flexibility and obligated the Treasury to accept somewhat higher interest rates.

The Federal Reserve used this independence to manage the rate of inflation during the early 1980s. The discount rate went from 6 percent in 1975 to 13 percent in 1980 to 14 percent in 1981. Inflation cooled but an economic recession also followed.

As the economy recovered, fiscal deficits also grew and the Federal Reserve objected. The Federal Reserve was determined not to allow inflation to get out of hand again. As

[1]See Chapter 2.

EXHIBIT 12-4 ECONOMIC GROWTH VS. CURRENCY STABILITY

Upon assuming office Helmut Schlesinger, the Bundesbank president who succeeded Karl Otto Pöhl on August 1, 1991, faced what seemed to be a terrible dilemma, the choice between economic growth and a strong currency. The reunification of East and West Germany (October 1990) had placed a heavy burden on the German economy. New taxes amounting to $10 billion were necessary for reconstruction of the former East Germany and for social services for its former citizens, many of whom became unemployed after reunification. For the first time in many years, the German current account trade surplus (exports of goods and services *less* imports) disappeared. The rate of growth in the German economy had stalled, threatening to fall from an annual 4 percent in 1990 to less than 3 percent in 1992.

Lower interest rates may have helped this situation, lowering the cost of borrowing and, thereby, encouraging investment and production in Germany. Other industrialized nations (including the United States) stressed that, indeed, the health of the global economy could be threatened by high interest rates in Germany.

However, Schlesinger made no pretense about his primary objective. Maintaining the value of the deutsche mark was most important. The value of the currency could only be protected if the German inflation rate was contained, a priority that he had emphasized throughout his career as Bundesbank chief economist. The rate of inflation had gone from well under 3 percent per year in the middle and late 1980s to closer to 4 percent in the early 1990s. The deutsche mark had lost 17 percent of its value within the last year. For Schlesinger, these were the most worrisome developments, and higher interest rates could help on both accounts. Schlesinger's goal was clearly to avoid any situation that even remotely resembled the hyperinflation of past decades.

Source: Riemer, Blanca, and John Templeman, "Inflation? Don't Even Say That Word around Helmut Schlesinger," *Businessweek,* July 29, 1991.

the government and business sectors pushed for lower interest rates to keep the recovery going, the Federal Reserve asserted its independence by keeping interest rates relatively high and even increased the discount rate from 8.5 percent (at which level it had been maintained since January 1983) to 9.0 percent in May 1984.

One of the by-products of the high interest rates was a high foreign currency value of the dollar as foreign investment was attracted by the interest rate environment in the United States. This high dollar value hurt the export manufacturing sector. The dispute between the government and the Federal Reserve intensified. In September 1985, the U.S. government and the heads of the governments of Germany, Japan, France, and the United Kingdom agreed to intervene to lower the value of the dollar (the Plaza Agreement). At this point the Federal Reserve agreed to cooperate. This was at least tacit acknowledgment that the Federal Reserve had used its independence inappropriately and had gone too far in its fight against inflation.

The Bank of China Government financing activities of the German central bank during the first half of the twentieth century is a useful example of the potential conflict of interest when there is strong government control over a central bank. However, the experience in China presents quite a different picture.

The People's Bank of China is essentially modeled after the Gosbank of the former Soviet Union. Resources flow through the banks based on government allocation. With the exception of consumer purchases, transactions take the form of book transfers at the

People's Bank. Unlike the Gosbank, the People's Bank has established a bridge between its socialist system and the capitalist West.

The Bank of China was for many years a state-owned corporation that was a subsidiary of the central bank, the People's Bank of China. However, in 1979, the People's Republic of China (PRC) undertook, among other things, a reorganization of the Bank of China. Instead of reporting directly to the People's Bank, the Bank of China now reports directly to the government and enjoys greater status. While it has certain domestic responsibilities with respect to negotiating the financing for central government projects and record keeping, its international functions are of particular interest.

The Bank of China maintains branches in Hong Kong, London, Singapore, Luxembourg, New York, and Tokyo, with the Hong Kong branch being the largest. In a sense, this branch has acted as China's point of observation in the West, where, since 1949, international trade and finance have been discussed and negotiated. The Bank oversees thirteen affiliated banks, called "sister banks" and even state-controlled nonbank enterprises that are located in Hong Kong. Apart from its official capacity, it operates as a competitive commercial bank, providing short-term financing, especially for local merchants that purchase goods from mainland China. In addition, the Bank of China provides a full range of conventional banking services.

The London branch of the Bank of China plays an even greater role in government affairs overseas. The branch has served both the Nationalist government (until 1949) and the Communist government. Historically, the branch accepted sterling deposits from Hong Kong, Australia, and other countries that used sterling as a means of payment. In order for the government to pay its own import bills, the London branch sold sterling in exchange for hard currency.

After 1970, the London branch introduced a new form of accommodation in the form of "supplier credits." The Bank traditionally maintained numerous correspondent accounts with other Western banks. Generally, the accounts balanced; that is, the Bank of China deposit in the correspondent bank equaled the correspondent bank deposit in the Bank. However, when the government required more foreign currency than this arrangement provided, the London branch started arranging special supplier credits. A supplier of goods to China arranged credit with its own bank. The supplier's bank set up a deposit at the London branch of the Bank of China, which deposit was used to pay the import bill. Once there was sufficient government-owned foreign currency on deposit at the London branch, the transaction was reversed. Supplier credits are fundamentally interbank transactions that facilitate the government's international transactions.

The London branch is now the site of *most* of China's world money market transactions. Credit for the state and for state-owned enterprises is routinely arranged and negotiated at the London branch. In addition, Euromarket transactions of the Bank of China are conducted there.

These examples suggest that the role of central banking in government finance is only partially a function of organizational structure. The Bank of England facilitated government finance without official status until 1946, and its powers were not codified until 1979. On the other hand, the Reichbank circumvented the technical separation of government and central banking to place both the economy and the central bank at peril. The Bank of China is a wholly owned and supervised subsidiary of the government that operates competitively and efficiently as a bridge between a socialist domestic system and a capitalist Western world.

Industrial Finance

The extent to which industrial firms are financed by bank credit is a partial function of the regulatory environment. In the United States, where capital markets are highly developed, industrial firms have less reliance on bank financing. The alternatives of stock and bond issuance have caused long-term bank loans to be less important to U.S. firms than to their counterparts in Japan and in Germany. The 1933 Glass-Steagall Act separated the functions of commercial and investment banking in the United States. Bank portfolio holdings of corporate stock are prohibited, and holdings of corporate bonds are restricted. If developed capital markets had been absent, such restrictions could have severely constrained U.S. industrial growth by forcing an overreliance on bank loan financing.

Japan The bank regulatory system of Japan has several features in common with that of the United States. Article 65, like the Glass-Steagall Act in the United States, prohibits commercial banks in Japan from underwriting corporate stock. Historically, interest rates have been closely regulated and are, only now, being liberalized. As noted earlier, policies of the Bank of Japan are essentially extensions of *government* policy.

Before the war, the *zaibatsus* dominated Japan.

Zaibatsu:

A Japanese holding company with a wide variety of subsidiary firms, a form of business organization that existed after the Meiji Restoration of 1868 until the end of World War II.

These huge industrial groups represented joint ownership of financial institutions and diverse nonfinancial firms. The banks channeled funds to the industrial firms. After the war, Allied powers dismantled the legal ties to reduce the concentration of economic power.

After World War II, the close link between the banking and industrial sectors was still undeniable. The legal structure disappeared, but economic ties remained. The more loosely constructed groups, *keiretsus,* continued to function.

Keiretsu:

A system of joint corporate ownership without a formal holding company. Each member of the group owns a small portion of stock in all the other members so that as much as 80 percent of the stock of each is held by affiliated companies.

This heritage has had a profound effect on the regulatory environment in Japan, where banks are permitted to hold large portfolios of corporate stocks. Short- and medium-term loans have historically been rolled over with the effect that they essentially became long-term loans. Using these close ties between financial and nonfinancial sectors, the Bank of Japan has given preferential loan rates to banks to fund loans specifically targeted for industries that the government has considered high priorities. Through *window guidance,* the Bank of Japan controls all aspects of commercial credit and money supply.

Window guidance:

Persuasion used by the Bank of Japan to convince commercial banks to support those industries deemed important for the country's growth and development.

In this way, the government indirectly influenced the post–World War II reconstruction of Japan through its central bank.

One outgrowth has been high debt ratios in Japanese firms as compared with U.S. companies. However, as Japanese capital markets have developed, corporations have begun to rely much less on their *keiretsu* banks. Today, stocks and bonds are much more common sources of corporate finance than previously has been the case.

Germany German corporations also have close relationships with their banks. As was true in Japan, these ties were instrumental in Germany's post–World War II industrial buildup. There is an important difference, however. The strong influence of the government over the banking system during the 1920s and 1930s and the disastrous results, as outlined above, led to a much less regulated banking system.

An important manifestation of this relative freedom from regulation is the ability of West German banks to underwrite and hold corporate stocks and bonds. In fact, German banks offer such a wide range of services that they are called *universal banks,* offering these services to their customers in a competitive environment.

Universal bank:
A bank that has the legal authority to offer all financial services and may, thus, be engaged in securities and insurance underwriting as well as the full range of more traditional banking services.

While interest rate deregulation in the United States and Japan *began* in the late 1970s, West German rate deregulation *was completed* in 1976. Thus, in a legal structure emphasizing minimal government interference, German banks have been free to compete vigorously in the provision of corporate finance and other services.

Regulatory Trends

Regulatory Systems There are essentially two distinctly different forms of bank regulation. The first is a *formal regulatory system,* complete with specific requirements and guidelines for balance sheet ratios. The objective of such legal stipulation is to ensure stability of bank activity and monetary conditions. Examples of formal regulatory systems are those of the United States, Japan, and continental Europe.

The second type of system has involved much more informal control. This is not to suggest that orderliness is a lower priority under less formal systems. Instead, the difference appears to be more related to financial system infrastructure. Where a small number of banks has existed or where banks and other financial institutions have been concentrated within a limited geographical area, a *system of nonstatutory supervision* has evolved.

The geographically concentrated financial markets of the United Kingdom, Belgium, and Luxembourg are examples. Frequent interaction between senior bank management and supervisory authorities has made it possible for authorities to adequately assess bank operations and attendant risks. To the extent that such close contact has been effective, there exists little incentive to formalize the relationships.

Nevertheless, deregulation of financial services and the blurring of past lines of distinction between financial institutions has led to a trend toward *increased statutory guidelines* and even more effective oversight. The U.K. Banking Act of 1979 created a legislative framework for authorization of deposit-taking activity and supervision by the Bank of England. Before 1979, supervision was largely informal.

In Canada, there is a combination of informal and formal controls. The banking system there developed after its U.S. counterpart, with the first commercial bank being chartered in 1817 and the Bank of Canada (central bank) not being created until 1934. This time difference allowed Canadians to observe some of the problems in the United States associated with having a large number of unit banks. Nationwide branching was accepted in Canada from the outset. As a result, five Canadian banks now control about 90 percent of all bank assets. This structure makes it easy to coordinate policies with fewer laws and regulations. Formal controls consist mainly of laws that mandate public disclosure and regulate permissible bank activities. Laws have also been passed to allow supervisory authorities to issue formal regulations with respect to cash and secondary reserves, capital adequacy, and liquidity levels. Thus far, however, banks are subject only to guidelines for cash and secondary reserves.

International Cooperation Another significant worldwide trend is toward greater *international cooperation* among supervisory authorities. Until the 1970s, there was no formalized international coordination. Then the Herstatt Bank, one of Germany's largest privately held banks, failed. This $900 million bank ran up foreign currency exchange losses in June 1974 that sent it to the Bundesbank for emergency funds. The Bundesbank found that the record keeping was so poor that it could not determine the extent of loss within a short period of time. The bank was closed at 4 P.M., German time. New York banks were still open but unable to complete their currency transactions with the closed Herstatt. This, of course, also exposed the U.S. banks to loss. In the final accounting, Herstatt's losses amounted to $500 million. The growing interdependence of systems and the ease with which risk is sometimes spread across borders have led to more structured international communications.

The European Community (EC) has an ultimate goal of uniform bank regulation throughout the region.[2] The 1977 directive was the first step in this direction. Guidelines for bank licensing and supervision were to be formulated in as consistent a fashion as possible across EC members. The Banking Act of 1979 in the United Kingdom was drafted to comply with this first banking directive. To encourage the flow of information across borders, the second banking directive in 1989 is based on the concept of a single banking license. With one license a bank has the right to operate throughout the EC. (Similar provisions have been made for securities firms and insurance companies.) With this license, banks will be able to engage essentially in universal banking throughout the EC as long as there is "mutual recognition" in the home country of the bank.

The list of permissible activities includes:

1. Deposit taking and other forms of borrowing
2. Financial leasing
3. Money transmission services
4. Guarantees and commitments
5. Trading for the bank's own account in CDs, bonds, government securities, futures and options, foreign currency and securities
6. Issuance of securities
7. Money brokering
8. Portfolio management
9. Securities safekeeping services
10. Credit reference services

Mutual recognition essentially means that the banks from the host country must be permitted the same scope of activities in the home country of the bank being licensed.

The final stage of monetary union for EC countries includes a functional European central bank, or *Eurofed.* The central bankers within the EC differ with respect to the degree of autonomy that the members should have to determine national monetary policy. There is also debate as to the autonomy of the Eurofed itself. On one hand, monetary policy can be considered only one part of an agenda aimed toward economic policy coordination. In this sense, it is possible that the objectives of the Eurofed could change over time, given changing needs for employment and economic growth. On the other hand, monetary policy can be considered a cornerstone not to be disturbed; that is, price stability is an objective that would not change under differing economic conditions. Of course, the second interpretation implies a more independent Eurofed, such as the Federal Reserve or the Bundesbank. The exact status of the Eurofed must be developed by EC members over a number of years. But whatever its form, the European central bank will significantly increase international cooperation among central banks.

[2]This objective is part of the larger goal of creating *one* economic market that is composed of the twelve member nations. See Chapter 7 for a full description of the EC initiative.

International cooperation extends beyond the EC. The Organization for Economic Cooperation and Development (OECD) organized the Basel Committee on Banking Regulations and Supervisory Practices to address the relevant issues of international banking. The committee's report, known as the Basel Concordat, was completed in 1975 and subsequently revised.[3] It was endorsed by the regulators of the Group of Ten and Luxembourg in 1983 and subsequently endorsed by the regulators of several other countries.[4] The concordant is the basis for international coordination among banking authorities.

The two broad, primary principles of the concordat are that (1) no foreign banking institution in a given host country should be without supervision and (2) supervision should be adequate. The concordat also outlines basic areas of responsibility for oversight, assigning some functions to host country authorities and others to parent country authorities.

Functional assignments are in the areas of *solvency, liquidity,* and *foreign exchange operations.* Supervision to ensure solvency of foreign *branches* is the primary responsibility of the parent country. The solvency of foreign *subsidiaries* is assigned to the host country, while that of *joint ventures* falls to the country of incorporation.

The level of liquidity of both branches and subsidiaries falls within the purview of host country supervisory bodies. Again, for joint ventures, the country of incorporation is held accountable. However, the liquidity of foreign offices can affect the liquidity of the group to which it belongs. So parent countries are held responsible for adequacy of control systems and procedures.

Last, foreign exchange operations are the shared responsibility of host and parent countries. The host country monitors the foreign exchange position of those institutions operating within its territory. The parent monitors the position of the entire institution.

In general, regulators seek to coordinate their financial systems across national borders with the same objectives that operate within—safety and soundness, efficiency, and competitiveness. As these systems evolve, the changing environment will require flexibility for the oversight function to keep pace with, but not constrain, the evolution. (See Exhibit 12-5.)

MONETARY POLICY

As is true in the United States, monetary policy of other countries is formed primarily by the same authorities responsible for oversight of financial institutions. The tools of policy implementation include, but are not limited to, interest rate regulation, reserve requirements, and open-market operations.

Interest Rate Regulation

Interest rate regulation is one of the most widely used forms of monetary control. Unlike open-market operations, the successful implementation of interest rate policy does not require a developed money market. Over time, however, interest rate regulation has become less important as a monetary control vehicle.

Immediately after World War II, "easy money" policies were not uncommon. In the United Kingdom, the discount rate was set at 2 percent, where it was to remain until after 1950.[5] The only monetary policy tools used at the time were credit allocation and admin-

[3]The Basel Accord addresses the coordination of bank capital requirements. See Chapter 15.

[4]The Group of Ten consists of Belgium, Canada, France, Germany, Italy, Japan, the Netherlands, Sweden, the United States, and the United Kingdom. Switzerland is an associate member.

[5]Clearing (commercial) bank liquidity adjustments are made through lending to and borrowing from discount houses. In turn, the Bank of England enters into money market transactions with discount houses. See Chapter 3.

EXHIBIT 12-5 BCCI: THE BANK OF CROOKS AND CRIMINALS?

The Bank of Credit and Commerce International (BCCI) presents an unfortunate case of the failure of international regulatory cooperation. The bank had operations in sixty-nine countries and assets of $20 billion when authorities stepped in to seize it in 1991. It seems the bank had long been involved in illicit activities, had used political influence to avoid detection and prosecution, and had accumulated losses of up to $10 billion that had not been disclosed.

The shutdown played havoc with banking operations in a number of countries. In London, $400 million in deposits, representing 120,000 accounts of individuals and small businesses, were frozen. In China, the BCCI branch in Shenzhen Special Economic Zone, center of the private enterprise initiative in that country, was closed. In Hong Kong, twenty-five BCCI branches with 40,000 accounts stopped operating as thousands of other depositors withdrew funds from Standard Charter Bank, a BCCI affiliate. In the United States, the scandal touched First American Bankshares, headquartered in Washington, D.C., and chaired by Clark Clifford, a former U.S. defense secretary. After allegations that he knew that BCCI had secretly and illegally purchased First American, Clifford resigned and was later indicted for crimes in connection with BCCI. The controversy soiled his otherwise spotless reputation in government and banking.

The first illicit activities were detected as early as 1986, but it was not until the results of a 1990 audit report were subsequently made public that regulators stepped in. While BCCI is clearly an isolated case of deception and fraud, the case does underscore the importance of timely international cooperation among bank regulators.

Source: Greenwald, John, "Taken for a Royal Ride," *Time,* July 22, 1991.

istrative control. While the Bank of England maintained the position that fiscal policy should keep the money supply in check, the Treasury became alarmed about the magnitude of bank loans to the private sector.

In France, where the discount rate was set at less than 2 percent, the money supply increased at an annual average rate of 30 percent in the 3 years ended 1948. The Bank of France found itself in the position of financing large government deficits, often against its best judgment. Steps were taken in late 1947 to slow the increase in money supply. The discount rate was raised to 2.5 percent, and certain large loans were restricted to "preapproval" by the Bank of France. In 1948, the discount rate was raised again to 3.5 percent.

The Bundesbank, the new central bank of Germany, reacted in a much more vigorous way that was to become characteristic of its vigilance against the threat of inflation. In 1950, as the economy began to expand, the discount rate rose to 6 percent, an unusually high rate at the time. The government did not agree with this measure but had little power to reverse it. This occurred again in the mid-1950s. From August 1955 to May 1956, the German central bank raised the discount rate from 3 to 5.5 percent, again against the government's wishes. By this time, the central bank's autonomy could not be denied.

Meanwhile, in France, the discount rate of 3 percent was raised to 4 percent in 1957 to ward off inflation. More selective credit restrictions were also imposed to fight inflationary trends.

In the United Kingdom, a severe drop in reserves was brought on as a result of the Korean war. The Bank of England abruptly changed its rate policy of the preceding 20 years. The discount rate increased from 2 to 2.5 percent in November 1951 to 4 percent in March 1952. The rate was subsequently lowered, only to be raised again when balance-of-payment problems developed. By 1957, the Bank rate stood at 7 percent.

Greatly increased social expenditures in Germany led to another conflict between fiscal and monetary policy in the mid-1960s. The Bundesbank tightened credit to offset the effect of the large public expenditures. The Bank maintained this tight money policy even though the first major recession in West Germany had set in. It was not until 1976 that the government began to take steps to balance the budget and the Bundesbank lowered its discount rate.

Clearly, the discount rate had been a powerful monetary policy tool in Germany, as it was in other countries. Its usefulness diminished, however, when regulation of German interest rates ended in 1976. In its place, minimum reserve requirements became much more critical in adjusting the economy's liquidity levels.

Japanese monetary policy has also had a long history of reliance on the discount rate. The high leverage of both commercial banks and nonfinancial corporations made its application particularly effective. In 1962, however, the Bank of Japan began to develop the country's money market, at least in part, in order to facilitate the use of open-market operations. By the 1970s, the money supply became less sensitive to changes in interest rates. In the mid-1970s the Bank of Japan switched its emphasis from interest rate levels to control of the growth rate of the money supply.

In the United Kingdom, a 1971 announcement by the Bank of England dismantled the interest rate cartel of the country's clearing banks. Even though the Bank of England does not loan money directly to commercial banks in the United Kingdom, this caused interest rates to became sensitive to market forces. The net result was that the money supply expanded even faster than it had before the announcement. A real estate and financial sector "boom" and "bust" followed in 1973. The Bank of England stepped in to shore up the banking system after massive bank deposit withdrawals. By 1976, the Bank rate was 15 percent, and a new monetary target was adopted.

High interest rates worldwide were to follow in the late 1970s and early 1980s.[6] During the latter 1980s the discount rate in the United States showed relatively less volatility than rates in other countries. Exhibit 12-6 shows discount rates in 1987 and 1991 in selected countries. Notably, 1991 discount rates in Japan, Germany, Canada, Switzerland, Sweden, and Belgium were higher than in 1987. In the United States the discount rate increased somewhat after 1987 but was lowered again so that the 1987 and 1991 rates are both 6 percent. Thus, Exhibit 12-6 shows that the discount rate had an upward trend in several industrialized countries during this period. It also shows that there is some convergence of discount rates among the major Euromarket currencies of the U.S. dollar, Japanese yen, deutsche mark, and Swiss franc.

Nevertheless, the earlier experiences of Japan and the United Kingdom illustrate the difficulty of effective application of rate changes.[7] The increasing complexity of financial markets has made it necessary for monetary authorities to adopt additional measures of control, monetary aggregates being one of the most common targets.

Reserve Requirements

As discussed in Chapter 11, reserve requirements are minimum percentages of bank liabilities that must be held as liquid assets. Changes in reserve requirements will affect the nation's money supply. If reserve requirements are increased, banks have less money to lend, the money supply decreases, and economic expansion slows. If the requirements are lowered, banks have more money to lend and the economy expands.

Reserve requirements, however, can only be effective if a central bank has authority over the major credit-issuing institutions. In the United States, the 1980 Depository Insti-

[6]See Chapter 9.

[7]There was a similar experience in the United States. See Chapter 11.

EXHIBIT 12-6 DISCOUNT RATES

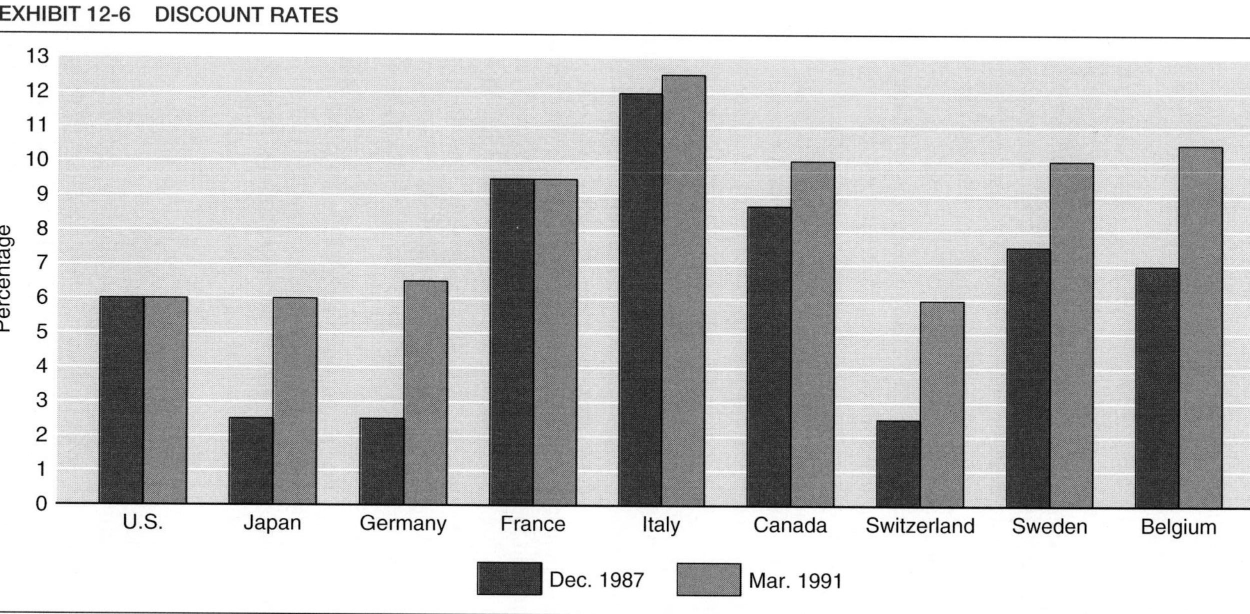

Source: Data from International Monetary Fund, *International Financial Statistics*, May 1991, p. 63.

tutions Deregulation and Monetary Control Act brought *all* depository institutions under the authority of the Federal Reserve. Through this act, the Federal Reserve gained control over the reserve requirements of not only commercial banks but also savings and loan associations, mutual savings banks, and credit unions.

In order for reserve requirements to be an effective monetary tool, it is also necessary for banking authorities to enforce these requirements on the primary forms of money. The United Kingdom presents an interesting case. In 1960, clearing banks maintained a minimum of 30 percent of deposits in the form of liquid assets—a liquidity rate *suggested* by the Bank of England but not *held* by the Bank.

At the time, the Bank of England believed that there was excess liquidity in the economy. To absorb the excess, the Special Deposits Scheme was introduced. In addition to normal liquidity requirements, *clearing* (commercial) banks were required to deposit a percentage of liabilities with the Bank of England. The deposits earned interest but were not classified as liquid assets. While the percentage varied, the basic scheme continued until 1980.

The United Kingdom's *nonclearing* banks also created a significant amount of liquidity. The Bank of England threatened to extend the special deposits scheme to these institutions if they refused to constrain their lending voluntarily. This example illustrates the importance of control over all segments of the money supply if reserve requirements are to be an effective tool. Since such control is *not* typical in most industrialized nations, interest rates and open-market operations are generally more powerful monetary policy tools.

In 1981, the only remaining liquidity or reserve requirements in the United Kingdom was a non-interest-bearing account with the Bank of England equal to .5 percent of all sterling-denominated liabilities. In addition, banks availing themselves of the discount facility are required to maintain an average of 5 percent of assets on deposit at discount houses. (See Exhibit 12-7.)

Open-Market Operations

After the change of policy in 1981, the implementation of U.K. monetary policy shifted more to open-market operations. In addition to purchases and sales of short-term Treasury and commercial bills, monetary authorities started "overselling" long-term Treasury securities. Selling more bonds than necessary to finance government absorbed excess liquidity more efficiently than the special deposits scheme.

However, the resulting upward pressure on interest rates led to cessation of the technique in 1985. The Bank's holdings of government securities was to be gradually liquidated.

Monetary policy has been complicated in Germany by the need to stabilize the value of the deutsche mark. In the late 1970s, when the value of the deutsche mark increased relative to that of other currencies, the cost of imports declined and kept inflation quite low (3.7 percent). However, by 1980, oil price increases caused German import prices to soar and inflation to reach almost 7 percent. As German interest rates rose, money flowed into the country. The Bundesbank attempted to counteract the effect of these speculative capital flows by selling deutsche marks. The resulting increase in money supply overshot the target for monetary growth.

Switzerland faced the same dilemma in 1978, and monetary targets were exceeded. However, despite massive interventions by the central banks of West Germany and Switzerland, the devaluation of the U.S. dollar (and, hence, the appreciation of German and Swiss currencies) did not slow until U.S. policy changed to fight inflation more aggressively in the United States.

This is the heart of the dilemma. Countries with few capital movement restrictions can be affected by speculative investments. Large and rapid investments in the domes-

EXHIBIT 12-7 MINIMUM RESERVES REQUIREMENTS FOR SELECTED COUNTRIES

Country	%	Liabilities
Belgium*	none	
Canada	10.00	Sight (demand) deposits
	1.00	First $500 million of time deposits
	3.00	Time deposits in excess of $500 million
France	5.50	Demand deposits
	3.00	Time deposits
Germany	12.10	Maximum rate for demand deposits of residents in excess of DM100 million
	12.10	Demand deposits of nonresidents
	4.95	Time deposits
	4.15	Savings deposits
Italy	22.50	Maximum rate on total customer deposits, net of capital
Japan	2.50	Maximum rate for demand deposits in excess of ¥2.5 trillion
	1.75	Maximum rate for time deposits in excess of ¥2.5 trillion
Sweden	10.00	Deposits†
Switzerland‡	35.0 to 70.0	
United Kingdom	0.45	Eligible liabilities of banks with more than £10 million in sterling liabilities (excluding interbank deposits) maturing in less than 2 years

*The Banking Commission has the power to issue regulations with respect to liquidity if necessary. However, the Banking Commission does regularly monitor banks' liquidity position.

†This is a liquidity requirement, rather than a reserve requirement; that is, liquid assets (not just central bank deposits) satisfy this requirement.

‡This is also a liquidity requirement. Depending on the mix of short-term versus long-term liabilities, the ratio of liquid assets (cash holdings and other very liquid assets) to short-term liabilities (those repayable within 1 month plus 15% of savings deposits) must fall between .35 and .70.

Source: Organization for Economic Cooperation and Development, *Regulations Affecting International Banking Operations of Banks and Non-banks,* 1981; International Monetary Fund, *The European Monetary System in the Context of the Integration of European Financial Markets,* 1989; and Subcommittee on Financial Institutions Supervision, Regulation and Insurance, *Report of the Task Force on the International Competitiveness of U.S. Financial Institutions,* 1990.

tic currency cause equally rapid currency appreciation. As a result, export sectors are placed at a competitive disadvantage. As was true in 1978 in Germany and Switzerland, the fiscal policies of one country can materially disrupt the economies of other countries. For this reason, increased international coordination of monetary authorities is observed.

DEREGULATION

Deregulation is even more easily observed than increased international coordination. While Swiss and German universal banks have long been permitted a full range of activities, the United Kingdom, Canada, and Japan have made significant strides in liberalizing their financial markets.

United Kingdom

In the United Kingdom, the 1971 Competition and Credit Regulations of the Bank of England dismantled the interest rate cartel of clearing banks, with the primary objective of placing financial institutions on more equal footing. In a sense, these regulations were precursors of the 1980 U.S. Monetary Control Act. The Bank of England regulations have resulted in more vigorous competition among clearing banks and, in general, among *all* financial institutions. Banks are now permitted to operate as primary dealers in the market for Treasury securities. Building societies (savings and loan associations) may sell mutual fund shares, offer credit cards, and compete in banking services. The shares of new and small companies may now trade on the London Stock Exchange's Third Market, created in 1987.

Canada

Competition among Canadian financial institutions has increased since 1967, as a result of the Canadian Bank Act. The act removed deposit rate ceilings and granted expanded lending powers to depository institutions. Chartered (commercial) banks began to offer deposits at market rates of interest and to cultivate mortgage and consumer loan business.

Foreign bank entry into the Canadian market had been difficult because of the high concentration of assets in the five largest banks and because of the close relationship of these five with the government. However, the 1980 Bank Act introduced a new type of bank, a Schedule B bank. Banks already existing were designated Schedule A banks. New Canadian-owned banks may be incorporated as Schedule A or Schedule B banks, but no more than 25 percent of ownership shares may be held by non-Canadians. In addition, no more than 10 percent of the shares of a Schedule A bank may be held by one party. On the other hand, as long as the capital of a Schedule B bank does not exceed $750 million, the 10 percent ownership restriction does not apply. This means that foreign banks may now enter the Canadian market under this Schedule B framework and establish a subsidiary that may remain closely held as long as capital does not exceed $750 million.

Like their U.S. counterparts, Canadian banks have also sought permission to engage in securities underwriting. In 1986 a plan for further deregulation included a provision that banks be permitted to engage in these activities. While all the provisions have not been enacted, banks may now own securities firms in Canada. Eventually, this permission will be extended to all other types of financial service firms. Many Canadian banks have exercised this right by investing in existing securities firms. In this respect, Canadian deregulation is ahead of U.S. efforts.

Japan

The heavily regulated system of Japan has been liberalized but not to the same extent. Previously denied access to money markets, commercial banks have enjoyed expanded powers since the late 1970s, notably the right to issue negotiable certificates of deposit (NCD). Banking reform in 1982 was the most comprehensive in over 50 years. Since 1982, Japanese banks have been permitted to purchase, sell, and underwrite government securities. Subsequent regulatory changes have allowed even more flexibility in banks' money market operations. From 1984 to 1985, the minimum denomination of NCDs was reduced from ¥500 million to ¥300 million to ¥100 million. The maximum maturity was extended from 1 month to 3 months. The Euro-yen NCD was authorized in 1984 and the yen banker's acceptance market permitted a year later. In 1985, banks were permitted to offer money market certificates with interest tied to money market rates. In the same year, interest rate ceilings were liberalized for deposits of ¥1 billion or more and then liberalized for deposits of ¥500 million in 1986. This deregulatory trend will most certainly continue.

Deregulation is a common theme in many financial markets today. As noted earlier, the increased interaction among markets makes these changes necessary to maintain and enhance competitive position. At the same time, there is also a recognized need for adequate supervision and investor protection. As a result, deposit insurance schemes increased in number.

DEPOSIT INSURANCE

Many industrialized nations have some form of deposit insurance. However, there are some exceptions. The Australian central bank, the Reserve Bank, has the authority to take over a troubled institution if it appears unlikely that it will be able to meet its obligations. There is no formal deposit insurance scheme. The government of New Zealand has expressly prohibited deposit insurance on the grounds that it would interfere with the existing high standards of performance and safety. Luxembourg hosts significant international and wholesale banking activity. Accordingly, small-depositor insurance does not appear to be warranted.

Although *participation* in deposit insurance arrangements is generally voluntary, competitive forces make it difficult *not* to participate. This is particularly true for smaller banks. In Canada, Switzerland, and the United Kingdom, insurance is provided by the banking authorities. In Japan and Belgium, banks and the authorities jointly operate insurance facilities. The deposit insurance systems in France, Germany, Italy, and Sweden are administered by the banking industry.

The *coverage* of deposit insurance is far less uniform than the rates of participation. Interbank deposits are usually not covered. There may also be limitations with respect to the type of deposit that is covered for nonbank depositors. However, these restrictions do not apply in Canada and the United States. Deposits of foreign branches and subsidiaries are usually eligible for coverage, although Japan does not cover Japanese branches of foreign banks. Germany, Italy, and Japan extend coverage of domestic banks to their foreign branches.

EXHIBIT 12-8 DEPOSIT INSURANCE FOR SELECTED COUNTRIES

		Coverage Limit	
Country	Name of Insurer (year originated)	Local Currency	U.S.S.*
Belgium	Rediscount and Guarantee Institute (1985)	BFr500,000	13,750
Canada	Canada Deposit Insurance Corp. (1967)	C$60,000	52,422
France	Deposit Guarantee Fund (1980)	FFr400,000	66,812
Germany	Deposit Security Fund (1966)	30% of liable capital per depositor	N/A
	Savings Bank Security Fund (1969)	100% of deposits and credits	N/A
	Credit Cooperatives Security Scheme (1976)	100% of deposits and credits	N/A
Italy	Interbank Deposit Protection Fund (1987)	100% of first L200 million, 75% of next L800 million	610,000
Japan	Deposit Insurance Corporation (1971)	¥10,000,000	70,600
Sweden	Deposit Insurance Fund for Savings Bks (N/A)	N/A	N/A
Switz.	Deposit Guarantee Scheme (1984)	SFr30,000	19,869
U.K.	Deposit Protection Fund (1982)	75% of deposit up to £20,000	25,050

*As of June 1991.

Source: U.S. Department of the Treasury, *Modernizing the Financial System; Recommendations for Safer, More Competitive Banks,* Chapter XXI, February 1991.

Like the United States, countries often set *maximum deposit coverage.* Exhibit 12-8 provides examples of these coverage limits. German limits are tied not to deposit amount but to bank capitalization. The limit is 30 percent of capital per depositor. The system of the United Kingdom incorporates a true coinsurance feature.[8] Seventy-five percent of sterling deposits up to a specified amount are guaranteed. The objective is to encourage depositor assessment of risk in placing funds with specific institutions. Other systems generally have a flat, ceiling amount as does the U.S. system. With the exception of Italy (with a limit that is equivalent to over $600,000), most of these coverage limits are lower than in the United States.

For the most part, deposit insurance arrangements are at least partially funded. Premiums based on insured deposits (total deposits in the United States) are the norm. However, the guarantees in France, Italy, and Switzerland (all administered by the banking industry) are unfunded. Any funds disbursed by French authorities to cover insured deposits are to be reimbursed by contributions by other insured institutions.

Within the EC, the 1986 Banking Directive recommended deposit insurance schemes to cover all credit institutions in the Community. This at least partially explains the rather recent formation of many of these deposit schemes. Here, too, there is a trend toward more statutory guidelines for oversight, even as deregulation expands the flexibility of financial services firms.

SUMMARY

Central banking began as early as 1668 when the predecessor of the Swedish Riksbank was taken over by parliament. The early central banks were usually private commercial banks that also facilitated government finance. The need for a uniform currency motivated the creation of the majority of these institutions. Accordingly, it was typical for central banks to be granted the exclusive right of note issue not long after designation as official banks.

The responsibilities of central banks now involve a wider scope of activities. Central banks are charged with maintaining a stable money supply, implementing monetary policy that will accommodate the government objectives of national income and employment, and stabilizing the domestic currency in international markets. At times, these objectives may conflict.

Increased interaction of financial markets has driven much of the change in regulatory environments. Since world trade transmits many of the characteristics of one market to those of its trading partners, increased coordination among monetary authorities has become necessary. Even within national borders, competition among different financial institutions has led to deregulation of interest rates and investment powers. Nevertheless, wider scope of activity places even heavier responsibilities on the shoulders of regulators to maintain the systems' safety and soundness.

KEY TERMS

Basel Committee on Banking Regulations
Basel Concordat
cantonal bank
discount rate
Eurofed
keiretsu
open market operations
reserve requirements
universal banking
window guidance
zaibatsu

[8]See Chapter 11 for a discussion of coinsurance.

END-OF-CHAPTER QUESTIONS

1. Why were the early central banks given the right of note issue?
2. What was the consequence in Italy when the issue privilege was given to six different banks?
3. Describe the Japanese experiment with U.S.-style national banking in the late nineteenth century. What steps were taken to encourage more national bank charters? When did the system end?
4. Why is it important that a central bank be noncompetitive and non-profit-maximizing?
5. Why should the U.S. Federal Reserve be concerned about the level of interest rates in Germany?
6. Explain the potential conflict of interest when a central bank is overly influenced by government. Use the case of Germany during the interwar period (World War I and World War II) to illustrate your answer.
7. How did the interwar experience in Germany affect West Germany's post–World War II regulatory environment?
8. What has been the role of the Bank of China in government finance? Does the potential conflict of interest appear to have compromised the Bank?
9. Explain current trends with respect to bank regulation.
10. Why is interest rate regulation a less effective tool for monetary control than it was in the past?
11. Discuss the U.S. and Canadian banking systems. In your answer, address the issues of market concentration, branching, deregulation, and deposit insurance.
12. With regard to the single bank license in the EC, is it possible that U.S. banks may not be able to take advantage of the universal banking privileges provided for in the Second Banking Directive? Explain.
13. In several countries, there is a recent trend toward more statutory regulation of the banking system.
    a. Why do you think this is so?
    b. What took the place of statutory regulation previously?
    c. Generally, contrast these systems with the U.S. banking system.

SELECTED REFERENCES

Adams, T. F. M., and Iwao Hoshii. *A Financial History of the New Japan,* Kodansha International Ltd., Tokyo, 1972.

Binhammer, H. H. *Money, Banking, and the Canadian Financial System,* Nelson Canada, Scarborough, Ontario, 1988.

Bronte, Stephen. *Japanese Finance: Markets and Institution,* Publications, London, 1982.

Bureau of Economic Analysis, U.S. Department of Commerce. *Business Statistics 1961–1988,* Washington, 1989.

Ciocca, Pierluigi. *Money and the Economy: Central Bankers' Views,* Macmillan Press, London 1987.

Cooper, S. Kerry, and Donald R. Fraser. *Banking Regulation and the New Competition in Financial Services,* Ballinger Publishing Company, Cambridge, Massachusetts, 1984.

Department of Trade and Industry. *Europe 1992: The Facts,* London, February 1989.

Economic Council of Canada. *Globalization and Canada's Financial Markets,* Canadian Government Publishing Centre, Ottawa, Canada, 1989.

Folkerts-landau, David, and Donald J. Mathieson. *The European Monetary System in the Context of the Integration of European Financial Markets,* International Monetary Fund, 1989.

Francke, Hans-Hermann and, Michael Hudson. *Banking and Finance in West Germany,* Croom Helm, London, 1984.

Friesen, Connie M. *International Bank Supervision,* Euromoney Publications, London, 1986.

Goodhart, Charles. *The Evolution of Central Banks,* MIT Press, Cambridge, Massachusetts, 1988.

Grady, John, and Martin Weale. *British Banking, 1960–85,* Macmillan Press, London, 1986.

Greenwald, John. "Taken for a Royal Ride; In the Wake of the B.C.C.I. Debacle, a Trustful Sheik and More Than a Million Depositors Are Left Holding the Bag." *Time,* vol. 138, no. 3 (July 22, 1991).

Greider, William. *Secrets of the Temple,* Simon & Schuster, Inc., New York, 1987.

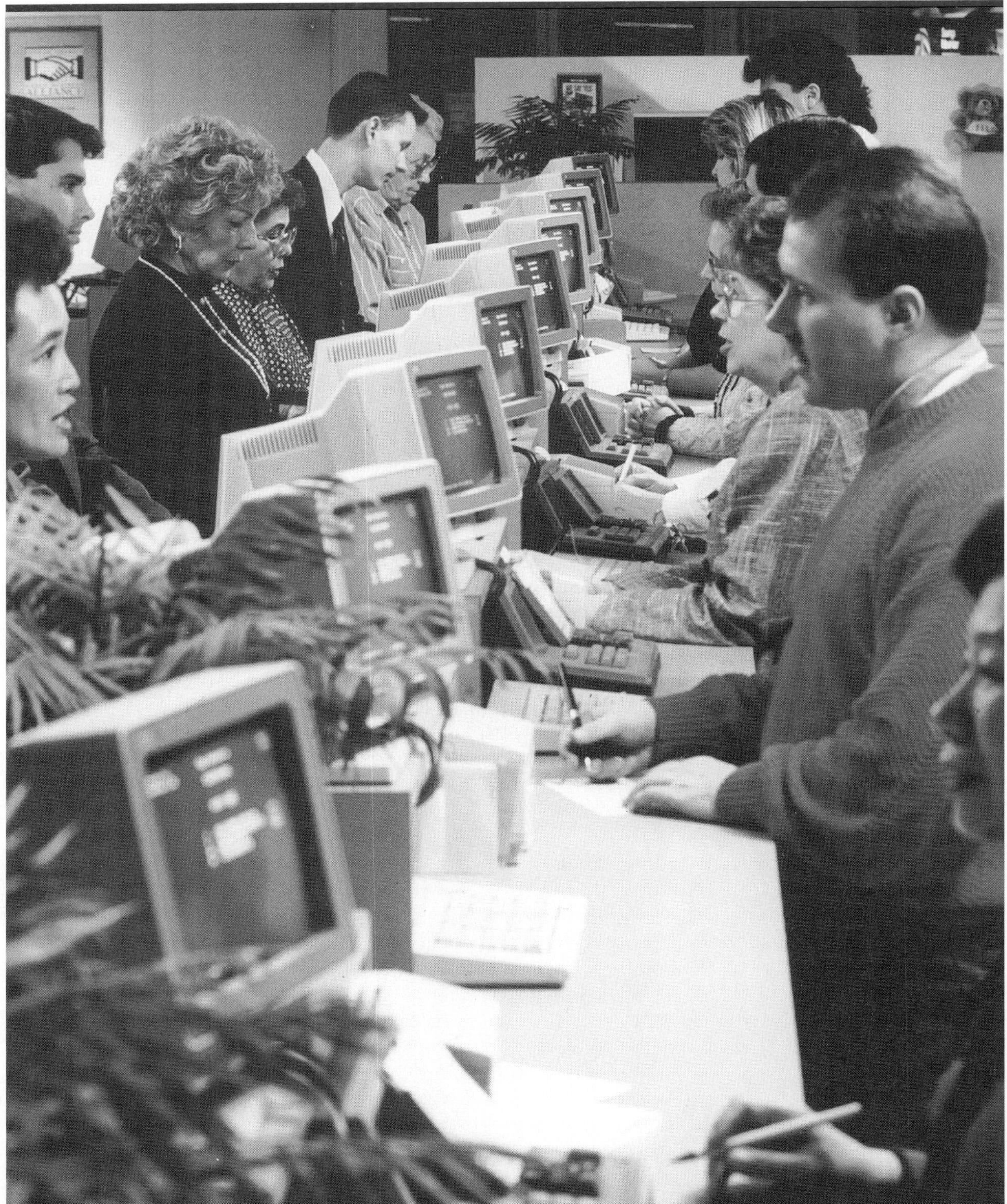
ALLIANCE

PART THREE

BANK MANAGEMENT

CHAPTER 13

BANK PROFITABILITY, LIQUIDITY, AND LIABILITY MANAGEMENT

CHAPTER OUTLINE

BANK PROFITABILITY
- Assets
  - Liquid assets, investment securities, assets, banking industry assets
- Liabilities
  - Deposits, other liabilities and capital, banking industry liabilities
- Income and Expense
  - First National, banking industry
- Rates Earned and Paid
  - First National, banking industry rates

LIQUIDITY MANAGEMENT
- The Need for Liquidity
  - Loan demand, deposit withdrawal
- Estimating Liquidity Needs
  - Structure of deposits approach, statement of cash flows approach
- Meeting Liquidity Needs
- Regulating Liquidity
  - Regulatory issues, regulatory approaches in selected countries in the OECD
- Observed Liquidity Levels in Selected Countries

LIABILITY MANAGEMENT
- Liability Mix and Cost of Funds
- Observed Liability Mix in Selected Countries

INTERNATIONAL COMPARISONS:
- Austria
- Belgium
- Canada
- Finland
- France
- Germany
- Greece
- Italy
- Japan
- Luxembourg
- Netherlands
- Norway
- Portugal
- Spain
- Sweden
- Switzerland
- United Kingdom

CHAPTER OVERVIEW

This chapter:

- Describes a commercial bank balance sheet
- Explains a bank's income statement and measures of profitability
- Discusses the need for bank liquidity
- Outlines methods for estimating liquidity needs
- Traces the development of liability management in the United States and the attendant changes in bank financing
- Compares liquidity and liability mix in selected countries

The banking system is vital to every country's economic well-being and financial stability. One of the important challenges to the U.S. banking system is the volatility of interest rates. To a great extent, the cost of bank funds can change virtually overnight. If a bank is to maintain adequate profitability, asset portfolios must reflect these changes. The analysis of bank profitability necessarily begins by examining the balance sheet, the income statement, and related ratios.

In recent years, perhaps the most dramatic changes in bank balance sheets have occurred in the liabilities section. The *mix* of liabilities has changed to offer depositors interest rates that are more competitive with other financial institutions, such as money market mutual funds. The *use* of liabilities has changed to afford commercial bank managers more flexibility in managing liquidity needs and in raising funds for investment. At the same time, the increased flexibility of liability management can also add to instability of profits or sources of funds. This paradox is an important issue in bank management today.

BANK PROFITABILITY

Banks realize profits as long as interest earned on assets exceeds interest paid on interest-bearing liabilities.[1] Other noninterest income and expense items also affect bank profits.

$$P = II - IE + NIIE - T \tag{1}$$

where P = bank profits
II = interest income and fees
IE = interest expense
NIIE = net noninterest income and expense
T = income taxes

By far, the most important categories are interest income on assets and interest expense on liabilities. Over time, asset and liability combinations have changed significantly. The asset portfolio that was once dominated by short-term commercial loans now includes more real estate and consumer loans. These and other asset categories have enhanced interest income but, at the same time, have contributed to reduced *bank liquidity.*

Bank liquidity:
The ability of a bank to meet its current obligations for cash outflow and to respond to changes in customer demand for loans and cash withdrawals *without* selling assets at a substantial loss. Bank assets are liquid to the extent that they may be easily converted into cash without loss.

On the other hand, a significant portion of low-cost demand and time deposits has been replaced by certificates of deposit, subordinated debentures, Eurocurrency deposits, and commercial paper. These instruments have helped banks have more control over access to funds, that is, increased liquidity. However, they have also increased interest expense because interest paid on them is higher.

Assets

Liquid Assets Exhibit 8-1 is the balance sheet of First National Bank, a hypothetical bank, as of December 31, 1992. Like balance sheets of nonfinancial corporations, bank

[1]In addition, fee income is an important feature of bank operations. However, this section concentrates on the more traditional determinants of bank profitability.

EXHIBIT 13-1 FIRST NATIONAL BANK BALANCE SHEET DECEMBER 31, 1992 (IN MILLIONS)

Assets		
Cash and due from banks	$ 2,491	7.6%
Interest-bearing time deposits in other banks	1,103	3.4
Federal funds sold and securities purchased under agreement to resell	1,063	3.2
Investment securities:		
U.S. Treasury and government agencies	$ 2,192	6.7
Obligations of states and political subdivisions	696	2.1
Other securities	1,261	3.8
Total investment securities	4,149	12.6
Loans:		
Commercial, financial, and agricultural	$ 9,168	27.9
Real estate–construction	4,762	14.5
Real estate–mortgage	1,838	5.6
Credit card	2,793	8.5
Installment	2,407	7.3
Lease financing	975	2.9
Foreign	479	1.4
Unearned income	(245)	(0.7)
Total loans, net of unearned income	22,177	67.4
Reserve for possible credit losses	(460)	(1.4)
Net loans	21,717	66.0
Customers' liability on acceptances outstanding	105	0.3
Investments in subsidiaries	632	1.9
Premises and equipment	420	1.3
Other assets	1,212	3.7
Total Assets	$32,892	100.0
Liabilities and Stockholders' Equity		
Domestic deposits:		
Non-interest-bearing demand	$ 4,544	13.8
Interest-bearing transactions accounts	1,539	4.7
Money market deposit accounts	4,889	14.9
Time, $100,000 or more	6,847	20.8
Other time	3,189	9.7
Savings	1,622	4.9
Total domestic deposits	$22,630	68.8
Foreign deposits	1,737	5.3
Total deposits	24,367	74.1
Short-term borrowings:		
Federal funds purchased and securities under agreements to repurchase	$ 3,411	10.3
Commercial paper	388	1.2
Other	954	2.9
Total short-term borrowings	4,753	14.4
Long-term borrowings	395	1.2
Bank acceptances outstanding	104	0.3
Other liabilities	724	2.2
Total liabilities	30,343	92.2
Common stock	$ 150	0.5
Capital surplus	359	1.1
Retained earnings	2,040	6.2
Total equity	2,549	7.8
Total Liabilities and Stockholders' Equity	$32,892	100.0

balance sheets begin with cash and other liquid assets. The balance in *cash and due from banks* is the amount of vault cash and demand accounts held at other banks. Demand deposits at other banks are used for check-clearing purposes. Larger banks that clear checks with many other banks maintain relatively high cash balances as a result. Other bank balances that are liabilities for First National appear in a transactions deposit account in the liability section. *Cash* accounts also include balances held at the regional Federal Reserve bank so that the bank's minimum required reserves are reflected here. These are the bank's *primary reserves.*

Interest-bearing time deposits in other banks hold large-denomination certificates of deposit, both negotiable and nonnegotiable. Such deposits are liquid assets but not quite as readily liquidated as demand accounts. The rates earned are comparable to those earned on *federal funds sold and securities purchased under agreements to resell (repos).* Federal funds and repos are money market investments with typical maturities that do not exceed a few days. Since U.S. money markets are so well developed and these assets so readily marketable, interest-bearing time deposits, federal funds, and repos are commonly considered *secondary reserves.*

Investment Securities The investment securities portfolio of a commercial bank contains fixed-income securities, a large percentage of which are *U.S. Treasury and government agency securities.* In addition, banks hold substantial quantities of municipal and corporate bonds. Interest earned on municipal bonds is exempt from federal income tax. The implications of this tax-exempt feature are discussed later in this section.

While these securities are less liquid than deposits, federal funds, and repurchase agreements, they should not be considered *illiquid.* Within this category, Treasury securities are most easily convertible into cash, and government agency securities are the next most liquid. The liquidity of municipal and corporate bonds depends on the issuer and prevailing market conditions. The bank's objective in managing its investment securities portfolio is profitability rather than liquidity.

Loans While liquid assets and investment securities constitute 14.2 and 12.6 percent, respectively, of First National's total assets, *loans* represent 66 percent. This is true for most commercial banks. The largest and *most profitable* asset category is loans. *Commercial, financial, and agricultural* loans are the single largest category of First National's loans, but *real estate, credit card, consumer installment,* and *lease financing* loans are also important sources of revenue.

Note that as the largest and most profitable asset classification, loans are the *least liquid.* This is the conflict and the trade-off in bank asset management. Maximizing the loan portfolio, all other things being equal, will maximize bank profits but minimize bank liquidity. Both liquidity and profitability are important for safety and soundness in the banking system.

Other Assets The remaining assets are a small portion (7.2 percent) of First National's total assets. *Customers' liabilities on acceptances, investments in subsidiaries,* and *premises and equipment* are typically a minor part of commercial bank investments. This is in sharp contrast to a nonfinancial firm in which fixed assets of land, plant, and equipment often dominate the balance sheet.

Banking Industry Assets Exhibit 13-2 shows the composition of bank industry assets from 1964 through 1991. In 1964, commercial banks held 7.2 percent of financial assets as cash and much of that with Federal Reserve banks. These percentages have consistently grown smaller so that by 1991, only 1.4 percent of financial assets was cash. Securities have declined even more—from 33.3 percent of assets in 1964 to 20.8 percent by 1991. On the other hand, loans and investments in subsidiaries (by bank holding companies) have become more important categories over time. These changes help to underscore the reduced liquidity in the system as a whole. Nevertheless, the most dramatic balance sheet changes have occurred in the composition of bank liabilities.

Liabilities

Deposits The largest classification of liabilities for a bank is its *deposits.* Again referring to Exhibit 13-1, deposits are 74.1 percent of First National's liabilities and shareholders' equity. Before the introduction of negotiable certificates of deposits in 1961, banks obtained the bulk of deposit funds from *non-interest-bearing demand deposits* and *savings deposits.* Savings paid low rates of interest, and demand deposits paid no interest at all. For First National, these combined categories provide only 18.7 percent of total funds.

In contrast, *time deposits of $100,000 and more* alone contribute 20.8 percent to the total. *Interest-bearing transactions (N.O.W.) accounts,* introduced by the Monetary Control Act of 1980, have to some extent replaced non-interest-bearing demand accounts, representing 4.7 percent of First National's total liabilities and capital. The 1982 innovation of *money market deposit accounts* has had a profound effect on bank financing. In this example, 14.9 percent of the bank's assets have been financed with these deposits. Since large time deposits and money market deposit accounts pay market interest rates, *at least* 35.7 percent of First National's deposit funding is associated with relatively high interest rates.

Other Liabilities and Capital Another 11.5 percent from short-term borrowings also carries market interest rates. *Federal funds purchased* and *commercial paper* (sold by the holding company) provide 10.3 and 1.2 percent, respectively.

Other liabilities and equity make up 11.5 percent of the balance sheet. Note that the *equity ratio* is only 7.8 percent of total assets.

EXHIBIT 13-2 FINANCIAL ASSETS OF DOMESTIC AND FOREIGN COMMERCIAL BANKS IN THE UNITED STATES, 1964–1991 (PERCENTAGES)

	1964	1969	1974	1979	1984	1989	1991
Financial assets (billions)	$312	$472	$836	$1356	$2106	$2954	$3345
Cash:							
Vault cash and due from banks	1.5%	1.6%	1.5%	1.5%	1.3%	0.9%	0.8%
Reserves at FRBS*	5.7	4.7	3.1	2.2	1.0	1.3	0.6
Total cash	7.2	6.3	4.6	3.7	2.3	2.2	1.4
Commercial paper and BAs†	2.1	2.6	3.3	3.5	4.0	2.3	1.6
Securities	33.3	26.9	23.6	21.6	21.6	20.6	20.8
Loans	56.3	61.6	63.0	63.6	61.1	63.3	61.8
Investments in subs.:‡	—	0.8	4.4	6.3	7.5	8.2	7.9
Misc. assets	1.1	1.8	1.1	1.3	3.5	3.4	6.5
Total	100.0	100.0	100.0	100.0	100.0	100.0	100.0

*Federal Reserve banks.
†Banker's acceptances.
‡Investments in bank and finance company subsidiaries by bank holding companies.
Source: Board of Governors of the Federal Reserve System, *Flow of Funds; Financial Assets and Liabilities.*

$$ER = \frac{TE}{TA} \qquad (2)$$

where ER = equity ratio
TE = total equity (common stock, capital surplus, and retained earnings)
TA = total assets

This is typical for commercial banks. Compared with nonfinancial corporations, with closer to 50 percent equity financing, commercial banks are thinly capitalized. All other things being equal, a relatively small equity base improves the rate of return on equity. Of course, the combination of low capital ratios and illiquid loan portfolios can threaten bank safety and liquidity. If a significant number of loans is not repaid, the resulting losses can amount to more than the sum of all capital accounts. When this happens, liabilities exceed assets and the bank becomes insolvent; that is, the bank fails.

Banking Industry Liabilities Exhibit 13-3 shows the changes that occurred in U.S. commercial bank liability structure from 1964 through 1991. In 1964, deposits were 96.2 percent of financial liabilities, with checkable (or transactions) accounts constituting over half the total. Together, federal funds purchased, repos, commercial paper, and bonds were less than 1 percent. Notice, however, that large time deposits, most of which are negotiable certificates of deposit, had already become an important part of bank financing. Almost 9 percent of financial liabilities was derived from these relatively new instruments.

After the credit crunch of 1966, however, the 1969 level of large time deposits had dropped significantly to less than 7 percent and transactions accounts declined to 45.7 percent. The small increase from 35.4 to 37.1 percent in savings and small time deposits was not sufficient to sustain the higher level of deposit funding observed only 5 years

EXHIBIT 13-3 LIABILITIES OF DOMESTIC AND FOREIGN COMMERCIAL BANKS IN THE UNITED STATES, 1964–1991 (PERCENTAGES)

	1964	1969	1974	1979	1984	1989	1991
Liabilities (billions)	$290	$447	$822	$1344	$2092	$2924	$3248
Checkable deposits (*)	52.1%	45.7%	28.8%	25.1%	15.5%	16.5%	17.1%
Small time and savings deposits	35.4	37.1	32.1	31.9	39.0	37.2	40.6
Large time deposits	8.7	6.8	19.7	16.8	15.3	15.0	13.5
Total U.S. deposits	96.2	89.6	80.6	73.8	69.8	68.7	71.2
Deposits of banks in U.S. possessions	0.4	0.7	0.6	0.7	0.4	0.4	0.8
Federal funds and security repos	0.2	2.0	3.4	7.0	7.4	8.6	7.4
Commercial paper	—	1.0	1.0	1.5	2.1	1.6	0.7
Total short-term borrowings	0.2	3.0	4.4	8.5	9.5	10.2	8.1
Bankers' acceptances	1.2	1.2	2.3	2.5	3.6	2.1	1.5
Taxes payable	0.2	0.1	0.1	0.1	—†	—†	—†
Bonds	0.3	0.4	1.3	1.6	2.5	2.7	3.4
Equity in subsidiaries	—	1.8	7.9	8.9	10.6	9.6	6.4
Miscellaneous liabilities	1.5	3.2	2.8	3.9	3.6	6.3	8.6
Total financial liabilities	100.0	100.0	100.0	100.0	100.0	100.0	100.0

*Includes net interbank claims.
†Less than .1 percent.
Source: Board of Governors of the Federal Reserve System, *Flow of Funds; Financial Assets and Liabilities.*

earlier. By 1969, deposits represented less than 90 percent of financial liabilities, but federal funds, repos, and commercial paper had grown to 3 percent.

In 1970, the Federal Reserve removed the Regulation Q deposit interest rate ceiling on large time deposits. Commercial banks were free to offer rates that were competitive with other money market instruments, notably Treasury securities. This caused a significant change in the amount of large time deposits outstanding. From 1969, these deposits increased from less than 7 percent of bank liabilities to almost 20 percent by 1974. At the same time, the rates banks could offer to small savers were still limited by Regulation Q. These deposits declined by 5 to 32 percent during the 5 years ended 1974. Transactions accounts declined even more, to less than 30 percent, as money market mutual funds offered higher interest rates than bank checking and savings accounts. By 1974, deposit liabilities had declined to just over 80 percent of bank financial liabilities.

Still higher interest rates in the late 1970s and the accompanying disintermediation brought deposit liabilities below 74 percent by 1979. All three deposit categories declined in importance in the 5-year period after 1974. A dramatic change in bank financing accompanied this shift. Federal funds, repos, and commercial paper generally carry lower interest rates than large time deposits. Because of this, borrowed funds and commercial paper were less expensive sources of funds from the bank's perspective. In 1964, these short-term borrowings were less than .5 percent of the total. By 1979, they were a full 8.5 percent. Since then, they have consistently represented over 8 percent of total financial liabilities of the banking system.

Legislation of 1980 and 1982 allowed U.S. commercial banks to offer more competitive rates for transactions and small savings accounts. Small time and savings account balances recovered from their low level of 32 percent of liabilities in 1979 to over 40 percent in 1991. However, the share of low-yielding transactions accounts has declined significantly, from over 50 percent in 1964 to roughly 17 percent in 1991. These changes have had a significant impact on commercial bank profits.

Income and Expense

A commercial bank income statement does not follow the same format as that of a nonfinancial firm. Instead, interest income and expense are the first two classifications, reflecting their importance to the bank. The difference between interest income and interest expense is *net interest income.*

Net interest income:

The difference between interest earned on time deposits, investment securities, loans, and other earning assets and interest paid on deposits and other interest-bearing liabilities.

All other income and expense items follow net interest income.

First National Exhibit 13-4 is First National's income statement for the year ended December 31, 1992. Since loans are the most important assets, *interest and fees on loans* is listed first. *Interest on investment securities* is next, with interest from taxable investments shown separately from tax-exempt interest. *Interest on time deposits and interest on federal funds sold* follow.

Interest expense includes the major categories of *interest on deposits* and on *short-term* and *long-term borrowings.* With total interest income and expense of $3.010 billion and $1.874 billion, respectively, First National's net interest income is $1.136 billion. The bank's provision for credit losses is an amount set aside in the current year to cover future uncollectible loans. The cumulative provision is a contra-asset account (see balance sheet). Deducting the 1992 provision of $280 million brings the after-provision net interest income to $856 million.

EXHIBIT 13-4 FIRST NATIONAL BANK INCOME STATEMENT 1992 (IN MILLIONS)

Interest Income	
Interest fees on loans	$2417
Interest on investment securities	
Taxable	331
Exempt from federal income taxes	66
Total	397
Interest on time deposits in other banks	128
Interest on funds sold and repurchase agreements	68
Total interest income	3,010
Interest Expense	
Interest on deposits	1374
Interest on short-term borrowings	462
Interest on long-term borrowings	38
Total interest expense	(1874)
Net Interest Income	1,136
Provision for possible credit losses	(280)
Net interest income after provision for possible credit losses	856
Other Operating Income	
Trust department income	53
Service charges on deposit accounts	97
Credit card fees	222
Other service charges and fees	63
Servicing fees from asset sales	151
Investment securities gains (losses)	(3)
Other income	179
Total other operating income	762
Other Operating Expenses	
Salaries and employee benefits	506
Occupancy expense of premises	74
Equipment expense	61
Other expense	477
Total other operating expenses	(1118)
Income before income taxes	500
Applicable income taxes	(116)
Net Income	$384

Noninterest expense for the year ($1.118 billion) exceeds noninterest income ($762 million) by $356 million. This reduces taxable income to $500 million. After deducting taxes, net income is $384 million. Thus, First National earned $384 million on a year-end asset base of $32.892 billion in 1992.

Banking Industry Exhibit 13-5 illustrates industry revenues and profits for the years 1983 through 1989. Revenues (gross interest and fees) grew from $217 billion in 1983 to $317 billion 6 years later. This is an average increase of $16.6 billion per year. Of course, interest expense also grew. Over the same period, net interest income went from $73 billion for the industry to $112 billion, or an average annual increase of $6.5 billion per year.

The distance between the gross interest income and net interest income lines represents interest expense. From 1983 to 1986 net interest income improved despite drops in revenue. That is, even though revenues declined, interest expense declined even further so that net interest income grew. However, from 1986 to 1989, there is definite acceleration in the revenue curve that is not noted in the net interest income curve. This suggests that while interest income showed robust improvements, interest expense increased almost as much.

EXHIBIT 13-5 INCOME OF INSURED COMMERCIAL BANKS, 1983–1989

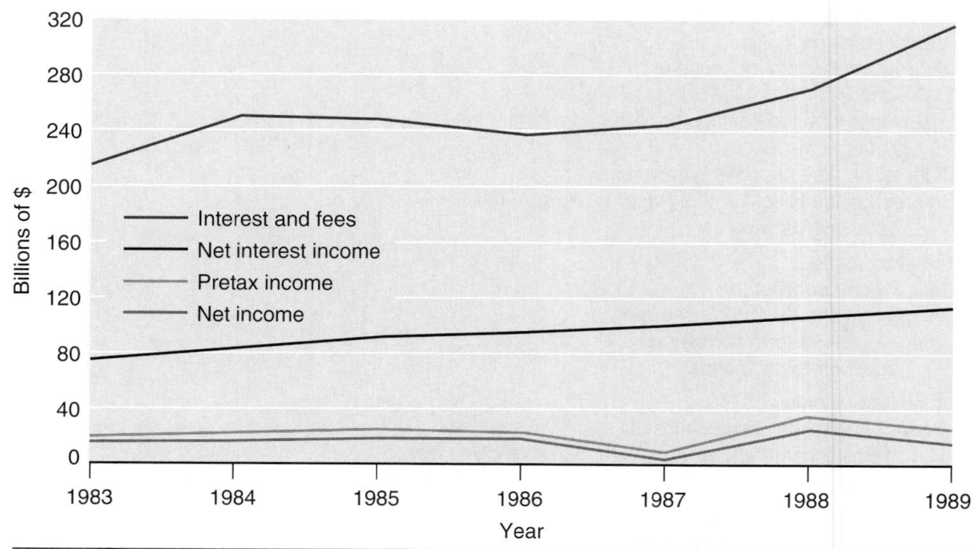

Source: Data from Federal Deposit Insurance Corporation, *Statistics on Banking,* 1988 and 1989.

The third line of the graph is pretax income. The difference between net interest income and pretax income is net noninterest income and expense, the distance between the second and third lines. The net is consistently negative and was a larger negative in 1983 than in 1989.

The fourth line is net income. Income tax is represented by the distance between the third and fourth lines. Essentially, even though bank revenues virtually mushroomed by \$100 billion from 1983 through 1989, interest expense, net noninterest expense, and taxes almost exactly kept pace. Industry net income in 1983 was \$14.9 billion. The same figure in 1989 was only marginally higher, \$15.6 billion.

This illustrates the profit pressure under which banks operate. However, it is not a complete analysis. Analyzing *rates* of return gives an even clearer picture of the bank profitability.

Rates Earned and Paid

First National When computing rates of return and interest rates paid, both income statement and balance sheet items are used. However, year-end balance sheet totals can give misleading results, particularly if account balances have changed significantly during the year. Average balances are preferable because they capture these changes and are a better match for the income and expense stream for the year. Since most bank accounting systems are now automated, average balances are relatively easy to generate. Figure 13-6 shows average balances of the accounts of First National Bank for 1992. They are computed as follows.

$$\bar{A}_i = \frac{\left(\sum_{t51}^{n} A_{it}\right)}{n}$$

where $\bar{A}_i$ = average balance of asset or liability account i

n = total number of dates used to calculate the average balance

A_{it} = balance of account i at time t

EXHIBIT 13-6 FIRST NATIONAL BANK DETAIL OF INTEREST INCOME AND EXPENSE AND RELATED RATES EARNED AND PAID, 1992

	Income or Expense (in millions of $)	Average Balance* (in millions of $)	Rate† (percentage)
Assets			
Time deposits in other banks	128	1,391	9.20
Federal funds sold and repurchase agreements	68	895	7.60
Investment securities			
Taxable	331	3,917	8.45
Tax-exempt	100‡	962	10.40
	431	4,879	8.83
Loans			
Commercial, financial, agricultural	896	8,699	10.30
Real estate–construction	386	3,509	11.00
Real estate–mortgage	184	1,688	10.90
Credit card	430	3,071	14.00
Installment	353	2,942	12.00
Lease financing	109	1,147	9.50
Foreign	59	567	10.41
Total loans	2,417	21,623	11.18
Total interest-earning assets	3,044	28,788	10.57
Cash and due from banks		2,252	
Other assets		2,107	
Reserve for possible credit losses		(408)	
Total assets		32,739	
Liabilities			
Deposits:			
Interest-bearing transaction accounts	78	1,500	5.20
Money market deposit accounts	319	4,984	6.40
Time, $100,000 or more	517	6,544	7.90
Other time	240	3,004	7.99
Savings	92	1,720	5.35
Foreign–time	128	1,753	7.30
Total interest-bearing deposits	1,374	19,505	7.04
Short-term borrowings:			
Federal funds purchased	276	3,603	7.66
Commercial paper	112	1,503	7.45
Other short-term	74	931	7.95
Long-term borrowings	38	386	9.84
Total funds borrowed	500	6,423	7.78
Total interest-bearing liabilities	1,874	25,928	7.23
Demand deposits		3,695	
Other liabilities		759	
Total liabilities		30,382	
Stockholders' Equity		2,357	
Total liabilities and stockholders' equity		32,739	
Net interest income and interest rate spread	1,170		3.34
Net interest income as % of earnings assets			4.06

*Average balances are computed using Equation 3.
†Rate is computed using Equation 4.
‡Interest income has been adjusted to its taxable equivalent amount. See Equation 5.

Banks commonly generate monthly financial statements. However, this section discusses the rates for First National Bank for the entire year of 1992. The amounts shown on the balance sheet in Exhibit 13-6 should be thought of as the average of either 12 month-end balances or 360 daily balances.[2]

In addition to average balances, Exhibit 13-6 contains details of interest income and expense. Rates earned or paid are simply the relevant interest amounts divided by the average balances.

$$r_i = \left(\frac{I_i}{A_i}\right)\left(\frac{360}{N}\right) \tag{4}$$

where r_i = interest rate earned or paid on account i (annual basis)
I_i = interest income or expense associated with asset or liability account i during the period
N = number of days in the period

Equation 4 explains the computation of all rates in Exhibit 13-6, with one exception. The rate earned on tax-exempt investment securities is based on interest income of $100 million (Exhibit 13-6), instead of the $66 million recorded in the income statement (Exhibit 13-4). All other sources of income are taxable and have been recorded on a before-tax basis. Since municipal bond interest is not taxable, the income of $66 million is also the after-tax amount. In order to compare municipal interest income (after tax) with other taxable income (before tax), municipal bond interest has been increased to a *taxable-equivalent amount.*

Taxable-equivalent amount:
The amount of before-tax income from a taxable source that is equivalent to a corresponding amount of tax-exempt income, once applicable taxes have been considered.

To determine a taxable-equivalent amount, the relationship between before- and after-tax amounts must be identified. Beginning with the definition that an after-tax amount equals the corresponding before-tax amount *less* taxes, the following relationship develops.

$$\begin{aligned} \text{AT} &= \text{BT} - \text{tax} \\ \text{AT} &= \text{BT} - \text{BT}\,(t) \\ \text{AT} &= \text{BT}\,(1 - t) \\ \frac{\text{AT}}{(1 - t)} &= \text{BT} \end{aligned} \tag{5}$$

where AT = after-tax amount
BT = before-tax amount
t = tax rate

In the case of First National, the marginal tax rate is assumed to be 34 percent. Thus, the amount of taxable income that is equivalent to $66 million, after tax, is $100 million [($66 million)/(1 − .34)]. The resulting rate of return is the *equivalent* of 10.40 percent from a taxable source. Note that this compares favorably with the bank's rate of return on taxable securities (U.S. Treasury securities, government agency securities, and corporate bonds) of 8.45 percent. All other things being equal, the municipal bond taxable-equivalent yield varies positively with the tax rate; that is, higher tax rates result in higher taxable-equivalent yields.

[2]Twelve 30-day months produces a 360-day year.

The rates of return associated with loan categories range from a low of 9.50 percent for lease financing to a high of 14.0 percent for credit card loans. Generally speaking, loans are higher-yielding assets than time deposits in other banks and investment securities. The average rate of return on First National's investment securities was 8.83 percent [($431 million/$4,879 million) (360/360)], while the average return on the loan portfolio was 11.18 percent [($2,417 million/$21,623 million) (360/360)]. More specifically, consumer and real estate loans are two of the highest-yielding categories.[3]

Total interest income for the year is $3.044 billion, and the average balance of all earning assets was $28.788 billion. The *yield on earning assets* was, therefore, 10.57 percent.

$$k_{\text{EA}} = \frac{\text{II}}{\text{EA}} \tag{6}$$

where k_{EA} = yield on earning assets
II = total interest income and fees
EA = average balance of earning assets

Interest rates paid on interest-bearing deposits range from 5.20 percent for interest-bearing transactions accounts to 7.99 percent for time deposits. Note that transactions and regular savings accounts carry lower rates of interest than time deposits. Note also that the relatively high level of time deposits as a percentage of total deposits causes the average rate paid on interest-bearing deposits to be slightly over 7.0 percent.

The cost of other borrowings is, in every case, well over 7 percent. Long-term borrowings (bonds) cost First National almost 10 percent. Total interest expense for the year totaled $1.874 billion. On an average liability base of $25.928 billion, the *average rate paid on interest-bearing liabilities* was 7.23 percent.

$$k_{\text{IBL}} = \frac{\text{IE}}{\text{IBL}} \tag{7}$$

where k_{IBL} = average rate paid on interest-bearing liabilities
IE = total interest expense
IBL = average balance of interest-bearing liabilities

The *interest rate spread,* or *net interest margin,* is the difference between the yield on earning assets and the average rate paid on interest-bearing liabilities.

$$\text{IS} = k_{\text{EA}} - k_{\text{IBL}} \tag{8}$$

where IS equals the interest rate spread. Spread measures the rate of return per dollar invested in earning assets *less* the rate paid per dollar of borrowed funds. First National's spread for 1991 was 3.34 percent (10.57 − 7.23).

Another measure of the cost of funds for a commercial bank is the *cost of funding earning assets.* This is essentially the interest expense per dollar of earning assets.

$$k_{\text{FEA}} = \frac{\text{IE}}{\text{EA}} \tag{9}$$

where k_{FEA} equals the cost of funding earning assets. For 1991, this cost was 6.51 percent ($1.874 billion/$28.788 billion) for First National.

Net interest income measures bank profits that are linked to interest-sensitive assets

[3]It should also be noted that real estate loans are risky in that they are exposed to the cyclical nature of the real estate industry.

and liabilities. First National's net interest income is $1.17 billion, that is, $3.044 billion of interest income *less* $1.874 billion of interest expense.

Net interest yield is net interest income as a percentage of earning assets, that is, a measure of return on those assets that are devoted to a bank's primary activities of borrowing and reinvesting funds. Alternatively, net interest yield can be calculated as the difference between yield on earning assets and the cost of funding earning assets.

$$\text{NIY} = \frac{\text{NII}}{\text{EA}} \tag{10}$$

$$\text{NIY} = k_{\text{EA}} - k_{\text{FEA}} \tag{11}$$

First National's net interest income and average earning assets of $1.17 billion and $28.788 billion, respectively, provide a 4.06 percent net interest yield on earning assets. Alternatively applying Equation 11 gives the same result (10.57 − 6.51 = 4.06 percent).

Recently, competition for deposits from money market funds and transactions accounts offered through brokerage firms has led to deregulation of interest rates, as explained in Chapter 11. Deposit interest rate deregulation, in turn, has meant that banks rely more on interest-sensitive deposits and other borrowings, placing significant pressure on interest rate spreads. As a result, emphasis on higher-yielding assets has increased.

Another trend in commercial banking is increasing lines of business that generate fee income. Included here are longer-term commercial loans with origination fees that are paid at the beginning of the term of the loan. Mortgage loans also generate "up-front" fees in the form of points, or percentages of the loan amount (usually between 1 and 5 percent) that are paid at the time the loan is disbursed.

Still another major activity that brings fee income to the bank is credit card issuance to both consumer and business clients. As shown in Exhibit 13-4, First National realized $222 million in 1991 from these annual charges to credit card holders. This amount was almost 30 percent of the bank's noninterest income for the year. These fees are in addition to the $430 million earned as interest on credit card loans, reflected in Exhibit 13-6.

When *all* categories of income and expense are considered, the bank's net income is $384 million (Exhibit 13-4). A bank's profit margin is called the *net margin after tax* and is net income as a percentage of total revenues.

$$\text{NMAT} = \frac{\text{NI}}{(\text{II} + \text{GNI})} \tag{12}$$

where NMAT = net margin after tax
NI = net income
II = interest income and fees
GNI = gross noninterest income

First National's profit margin after tax was 10.09 percent [$384 million/($3.044 billion + $762 million)].

Return on assets (ROA) and *return on equity* (ROE) are also based on net income.

$$\text{ROA} = \frac{\text{NI}}{\text{TA}} \tag{13}$$

$$\text{ROE} = \frac{\text{NI}}{\text{TE}} \tag{14}$$

First National's return on assets and return on equity were 1.17 percent ($384 million/$32,739 million) and 16.29 percent ($384 million/$2,357 million), respectively. Each of these ratios measures the amount of net income per dollar invested.

The ROA and ROE are related to each other through the *equity multiplier* (EM), the inverse of the equity ratio.

$$EM = \frac{TA}{TE} \tag{15}$$

The equity multiplier is the number of asset dollars supported by each dollar of equity. As the equity multiplier increases, the amount of equity supporting each asset dollar declines. In addition, ROE is the product of ROA and the multiplier.

$$\begin{aligned} ROE &= \left(\frac{NI}{TA}\right)\left(\frac{TA}{TE}\right) \\ &= (ROA)(EM) \end{aligned} \tag{16}$$

Applying Equations 15 and 16 to First National, the equity multiplier is 13.8901 ($32.739 billion/$2.357 billion) and ROE is 16.29 percent [(.011729) (13.8901)], as before.

Bank regulators are placing considerable emphasis on increasing capital ratios (equity capital as a percentage of total assets) in order to enhance the safety of the banking system. obviously, increasing profits improves ROA, ROE, and capital ratios. However, decreasing total assets, all other things being equal, has the same effect.

Securitization of loans allows a bank to sell some of the loans on its balance sheet. While proceeds of asset sales can be used to fund new loans, a bank may also reduce the size of its balance sheet by retiring debt with the proceeds.[4] For a given level of income, securitization increases both ROA and capital ratios because the denominator of each ratio is reduced while its numerator is unchanged.

Even after the sale of securitized assets, a bank may continue to service the loans, that is, maintain records, send account statements, and collect payments. Compensation for these services takes the form of additional fee income. These incremental fees on loans that no longer appear on the balance sheet improve earnings and boost ROE. First National has adopted the practice of securitizing its credit card loans. Servicing fees appear as "servicing fees from asset sales" in the other operating income section of the bank's income statement (Exhibit 13-4). In 1991, these fees amounted to $151 million, just under 20 percent of other operating income, and helped offset the cost of the interest-sensitive deposits.

Banking Industry Rates Generally, industry profitability ratios in recent years reflect a considerable profit squeeze due to high interest costs and noninterest expense. The pressure has been only partially relieved by asset securitization and other fee-generating activities.

Exhibit 13-7 provides ratios for the U.S. banking industry as a whole for 1988 through 1990. The yield on earning assets did not decline over the period, but the cost of funding those earning assets was high enough to prevent a significant change in net interest yield. Other nonoperating expense levels were sufficiently high to push down the industry's return on assets and return on equity.

[4]See also "Securitization" in Chapter 4.

EXHIBIT 13-7 SELECTED INDUSTRY RATES IN THE UNITED STATES, 1989–1990

	1988	1989	1990
Yield on earning assets	9.84%	11.44%	11.06%
Cost of funding earning assets	5.96	7.40	7.07
Net interest yield	3.88	4.05	3.99
Return on assets	0.86	.50	.50
Return on equity	10.03	7.82	7.73

Source: Federal Deposit Insurance Corporation, *Quarterly Banking Profile,* various issues.

These industry ratios clearly show the profit squeeze. However, these averages are not representative of every type of bank. There are significant differences for different bank size groups.

Exhibit 13-8 shows a breakdown by four size groups. Larger banks can earn more on asset portfolios but must also rely more on borrowed funds and large CDs, both of which are quite sensitive to market conditions. The net effect is that net interest yield is lower for larger banks. Their returns on assets and equity are also often lower than the smaller

EXHIBIT 13-8 SELECTED INDUSTRY RATES IN THE UNITED STATES BY SIZE OF BANK, 1988–1989

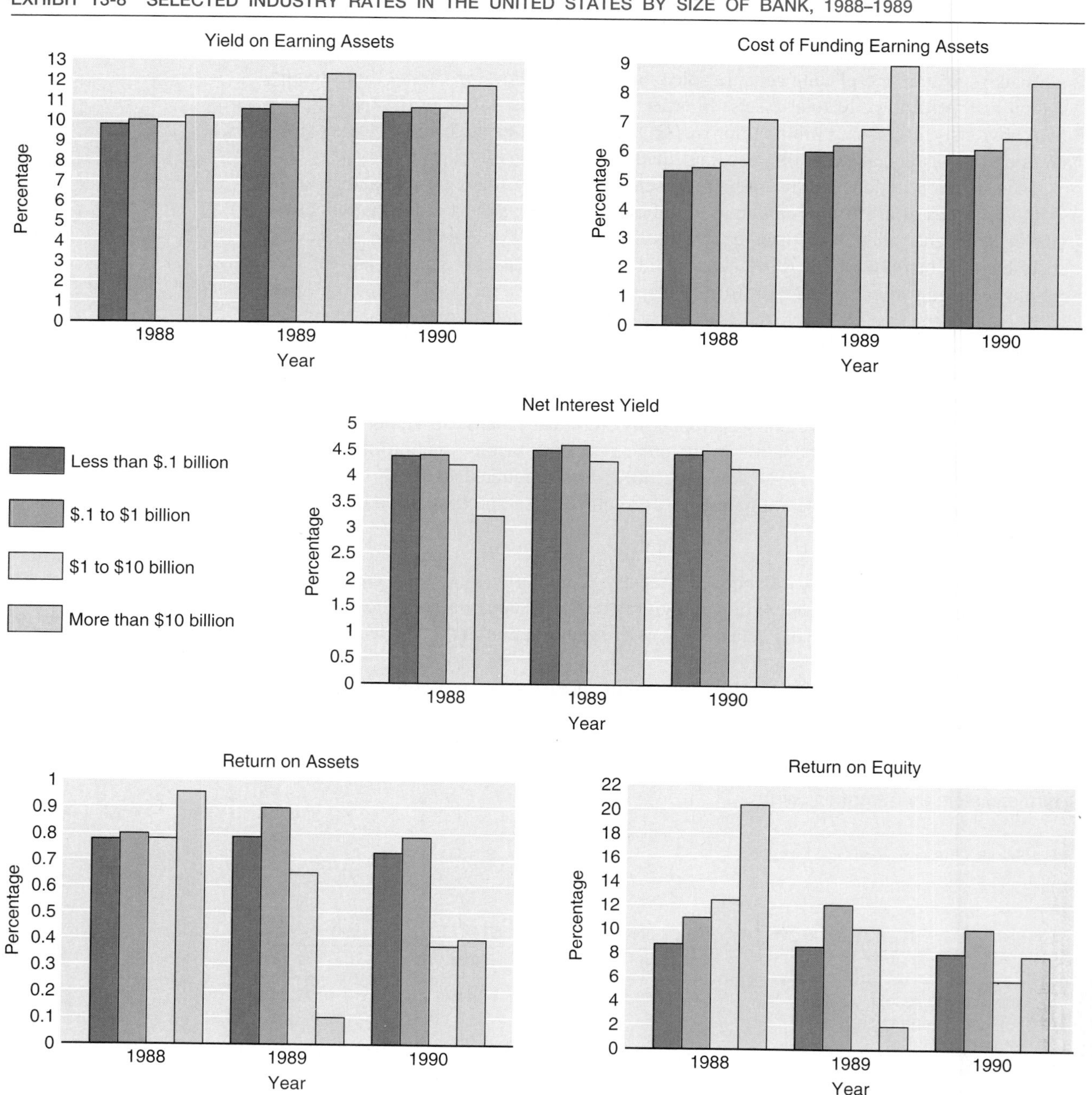

Source: Data from Federal Deposit Insurance Corporation, *Quarterly Banking Profile,* various issues.

banks' returns. Basically, larger banks operate on much thinner margins so that the profit pressures noted earlier are even greater for them.

LIQUIDITY MANAGEMENT

The recent pressure on bank profits has, of course, not removed the need for adequate liquidity within individual banks or the system as a whole. Interestingly, the interest-sensitive deposits and other borrowings that have challenged profitability have also significantly altered practices of liquidity management.

Since a bank can realize higher profits from assets that are relatively illiquid, there is a natural trade-off between profitability and liquidity. Commercial banks must invest as profitably as possible within reasonable limits of liquidity. Because of this potential conflict, regulators in a number of countries have established certain minimum liquidity requirements.

The Need for Liquidity

Loan demand and *deposit withdrawal* are primary reasons that banks need liquidity. Loan demand fluctuates with several factors—interest rate levels, business opportunities, consumer demand for high-ticket items, and income levels, for example. If a bank is unable to respond to higher loan demand, it may find itself at a competitive disadvantage when compared with other financial institutions. Likewise, a bank that cannot easily meet deposit withdrawal requests will lose the confidence of depositors.

Loan Demand Because banks are subject to *partial* reserve requirements, it is not always necessary for a bank to have a liquidity injection equal to 100 percent of the anticipated increase in loan demand. To a large extent, a bank can "create" the money to fund a loan. This is particularly true since most loans are extended in the form of a deposit.

For example, consider ABC Corporation, a customer of Bank A who desires a $100 loan. Bank A may not "create" the deposit for its customer (liability) and the offsetting loan (asset) without considering the minimum required reserve for the deposit. For this example, assume that the deposit will be a transactions account and that the minimum reserve requirement is 12 percent.[5] Thus, no more than 88 percent of the deposit increase may be loaned. In other words, the bank needs a liquidity injection sufficient to support a $100 loan.

If the $100 loan is to represent 88 percent of the deposit increase, the remaining 12 percent must be placed on deposit with a Federal Reserve bank to satisfy the reserve requirement. The total deposit increase must equal $113.64 [100/(1 − .12)]. The bank may "create" $100, but $13.64 must be in the form of a liquid asset, either a currency deposit or the transfer of a deposit from another bank.

Assume, for purposes of illustration, that Bank A attracts a customer deposit from another bank for $13.64. John Smith writes a check for $13.64 on Bank B to open an account at Bank A. Bank A now has a deposit liability to John Smith for $13.64 *and* a claim on Bank B (due from Bank B), the latter of which may be converted into a claim on a Federal Reserve bank (due from Federal Reserve). With this liquidity injection, Bank A may now "create" the loan for ABC Corporation by increasing its loan account by $100 and its transactions deposits account by the same amount. Total new deposits equal $113.64. Twelve percent, the reserve requirement, equals $13.64 and is on deposit at the Federal Reserve.

In general, the liquidity necessary to fund a loan under these assumptions is (17)

[5]See Chapters 11 and 12.

$$
\begin{aligned}
LR &= \left[\frac{LD}{(1 - r)}\right] - LD \\
&= LD\left\{\left[\frac{1}{(1 - r)}\right] - 1\right\} \\
&= LD\left\{\frac{[1 - (1 - r)]}{(1 - r)}\right\} \\
&= LD\left[\frac{r}{(1 - r)}\right]
\end{aligned}
$$

where LR = liquidity required to satisfy loan demand
LD = amount of loan demand
r = minimum required reserve percentage

Of course, this result depends on the assumption that the ABC Corporation will write checks to its own vendors and suppliers, merely transferring deposit balances among banks. If, in fact, ABC Corporation or any of its payees withdraws cash from Bank A, the \$13.64 in minimum reserves will not be sufficient. Equation 17 is the *minimum* liquidity required to meet a given level of loan demand.

Deposit Withdrawal The second source of liquidity need is *deposit withdrawal.* In general, the degree to which the public leaves money on deposit at banks depends on the public's confidence in a particular bank or in the banking system. As described in Chapters 10 through 12, when there is a crisis of confidence, central bank and other government assistance is often required to maintain order in the system. However, there is frequently demand for cash that is not related to public confidence. It is this type of deposit withdrawal that is considered here.

Of course, it is possible that the two types of deposit withdrawal are related. Indeed, if the more routine demand for cash is not met quickly and efficiently, depositor confidence will erode as a result. Thus, while meeting loan demand is important from a competitive standpoint, satisfying deposit withdrawal demand is *critical* with respect to bank viability.

Estimating Liquidity Needs

There are several approaches for estimating liquidity needs. Two are discussed in this section.

Structure of Deposits Approach The first approach concentrates on vulnerability to deposit withdrawal and the *structure of deposits.* Following this approach, deposits are classified in one of several classifications. For example,

1 *"Hot money."* Deposits that are the least stable require maintenance of high levels of liquidity because they may be withdrawn quickly and completely.
2 *Stable deposits.* Stable deposits are subject to sizable withdrawals but are rarely ever completely withdrawn.
3 *Core deposits.* These deposits are the most predictable of all. Fluctuations are small.

Deposits in the first category may include time deposits in excess of \$100,000, liabilities that are very sensitive to small differences in interest rates. These deposits commonly have relatively short maturities which contribute further to faster turnover. It is advisable to set aside a large percentage of these deposits in liquid assets, up to 100 percent of these "hot money" deposits.

Stable deposits may also be characterized by large denominations. However, in this second category, depositors often have an ongoing relationship with the bank. Corporate clients holding interest-bearing transactions accounts or large, short-term deposits use these accounts to manage their own liquidity and transactions needs. They may also have loans from the bank. The corporations' deposit balances vary but are unlikely to be withdrawn altogether. It is reasonable to maintain no more than 30 to 40 percent of these deposit balances in liquid assets.

Examples of *core deposits* include regular savings accounts and 2.5-year small saver certificates of deposit. Because of low variability of these deposit balances, it is often necessary to maintain no more than 5 to 10 percent in liquid assets.

These percentages are applied to the appropriate deposit categories. The sum of these computed dollar amounts is a bank's estimated liquidity need according to the structure of deposits approach.

Statement of Cash Flows Approach Note that the structure of deposits method does not consider loan demand. A more comprehensive approach is the *statement of cash flows* approach, for which both loan demand and deposit withdrawal must be anticipated. Changes in both can often be estimated with reasonable accuracy. This approach recognizes that projected deposit increases can help fund increased loan demand.

For example, if management anticipates that loan demand could result in an increase in loans of $100 million *and* that the bank will be able to attract an additional $40 million in deposits in the normal course of business, the statement of cash flows approach reflects these projections as follows.

	DR	CR
Change in loans	$100	
Change in deposits		$40

Forty percent of anticipated loan demand will be satisfied with normal deposit base growth. The remaining $60 million is, therefore, the bank's liquidity need for the future time period.

Assuming the same loan demand as noted above, consider the effect of normal deposit base increases totaling $150 million.

	DR	CR
Change in loans	$100	
Change in deposits		$150

In this case, the bank will actually have $50 million more liquidity than needed to satisfy anticipated future loan demand. In this environment of relatively weak loan demand, management must work to identify investment vehicles that will earn an acceptable rate of return and satisfy profitability goals. This sort of situation can occur when interest rates are high—attracting deposits but discouraging loan demand.

Even more of a challenge is the combination of higher loan demand and weak deposit growth.

	DR	CR
Change in loans	$100	
Change in deposits	$50	

Here, $100 million more in loans will be demanded, but the deposit base will actually shrink by $50 million. The bank's projected liquidity needs total $150 million. This situation is more likely to happen when interest rates are relatively low, motivating depositors to seek higher-yielding alternatives but stimulating loan demand.

The examples above stressed identification of future liquidity needs. Once identified, these projected needs must be met. Before banks began to invest in relatively illiquid assets, meeting the need was a relatively simple process.

The *commercial bank,* or *real bills,* theory of banking suggests that investments are self-liquidating, for the most part. According to the theory, banks invest in commercial bills of exchange. The bills are backed by a transaction in real goods. In fact, the bill is a kind of short-term inventory financing. Since inventory cycles are fairly short, the bills self-liquidate, providing the bank with regular liquidity infusions.

Of course, this model of banking has not accurately described the U.S. banking industry for more than 100 years. Today, commercial banks are diversified into a wide range of loans and securities. So it is necessary to make specific arrangements to meet liquidity needs.

Most approaches fall into one of three categories:

- Asset management
- Liability management
- Funds management

Asset management involves setting aside sufficient funds now to satisfy the future need. For example, in the last illustration above, \$150 million was the estimated future liquidity need. If this amount is required in 6 months, bank management should invest in short-term securities that, upon maturity, have a value of \$150 million. If the bank chose U.S. Treasury bills, the required purchase would depend on the yield. Since Treasury bills are discount securities, the purchase price is less than face value.[6] Assuming an 8 percent annual yield, the required purchase would amount to \$144 million.

$$P = 150\left[1 - \left(\frac{180}{360}\right)\right]$$
$$= 144 \qquad (18)$$

where P = the purchase requirement.

It is clear from this exercise that the asset management approach can place constraints on bank operations. If assets must be set aside for anticipated future liquidity needs, these investments can reduce management's flexibility. Worse yet, investment in low-yielding assets can have an adverse effect on bank profits in the meantime.

Liability management frees the asset portfolio from these constraints. Managing liquidity through liabilities effectively means raising funds in deposit and other markets at the time they are needed. In the example above, at the point that the bank identifies a \$150 million need in 6 months, no action is taken. Instead, the bank plans to attract deposits or borrow short-term funds in 6 months. In the interim, assets may be invested without consideration of the future need. The net effect is more flexibility and, therefore, more profit potential.

The use of liability management began in 1961 when banks began to issue negotiable certificates of deposit. The 1966 credit crunch threatened the renewal of maturing certificates of deposit because regulated domestic deposit rates were not competitive with Treasury security rates. To circumvent the problem of low, noncompetitive rates, U.S. banks issued dollar-denominated negotiable CDs overseas. Since rate ceilings did not apply to overseas deposits, competitive rates could be offered. Foreign branches raised funds that

[6] See Chapter 3 for a complete description of Treasury bill auctions and pricing.

could not be raised domestically. These events gave birth to a much more active liability management and to the Eurodollar market.[7]

While liability management does enhance flexibility, it also increases the risk of bank operations. Should interest rates rise unexpectedly, management may face increases in the cost of funds that are not immediately offset by higher rates of return on longer-term assets with fixed interest rates. Variable-rate loans (whose rates change when market rates change) have helped reduce this problem.

Generally, neither asset management nor liability management is used exclusively. Instead, a combination, or *funds management,* is more typical. Liquidity considerations are an integral part of asset management, but management will also change its interest rate to attract funds or borrow in money markets to meet short-term liquidity needs.

Regulating Liquidity

Regulatory Issues The adequacy of bank liquidity is tied to solvency of the banking system. From a regulatory perspective, liquidity means a bank's ability to meet its obligations when they are due. Before the widespread use of liability management, liquidity was more easily measurable. Maintaining high-quality, liquid assets assured both the public and the regulators.

The ability to convert these assets into cash meant that even heavy deposit withdrawal could be met. In turn, this situation led to confidence in the bank's solvency, so that "runs" were unlikely. However, it is not always possible to assess exactly the liquidity of certain assets. Municipal bonds are a good example. Large sales of municipals can depress their market value since secondary markets for municipals are not as well developed as markets for Treasury securities. Nevertheless, municipal bond yields frequently compare favorably with government bond yields. From the bank's perspective, then, the less liquid municipal bonds may be preferable.

Another shortcoming of attempting to measure liquidity based on asset holdings is that this approach does not consider the dynamic aspect of banking. Using the 1966 credit crunch mentioned above as an example, measuring liquid asset levels as a percentage of deposits would probably not have revealed the impending problem. That is, the balance sheet alone does not reflect the ease or difficulty that a bank may have in refinancing maturing deposits or other liabilities.

Regulatory Approaches in Selected Countries in the OECD[8] Because of these considerations, many regulators have moved more to a *cash flow* approach in assessing bank liquidity. In general, cash flow techniques attempt to measure any mismatch in the maturity structure of asset and liability portfolios.

The specific regulatory approach varies by country. Continental European countries still apply variations of specific liquidity measures. Denmark has maintained a ratio of liquid assets to liabilities. The Netherlands and Switzerland vary required liquidity coefficients (coverage percentages) for specific balance sheet accounts (liabilities) based upon type and maturity.

In Germany, guidelines are established by law for maintenance of liquidity. However, regulators reserve the right to impose stricter or more lenient ratios or guidelines as conditions warrant.

Some countries have fewer formal requirements. Instead, liquidity review is a part of the regular oversight process. In Canada, this is accomplished through informal monitoring of maturity mismatching. In the United Kingdom, cash flow over the next 12 months is routinely reviewed.

[7]See also Chapter 7.

[8]The acronym OECD represents the Organisation for Economic Co-operation and Development.

The approach in the United States is a combination of fixed-ratio maintenance and cash flow analysis. Smaller banks are evaluated primarily on the basis of liquid asset levels. Larger banks, considered to have greater access to money and capital markets, are assessed on the basis of projected cash flow or maturity mismatches.

The CAMEL rating system is used in the United States. The specific qualities considered are:

C Capital adequacy
A Asset quality
M Management and administrative ability
E Earnings level and quality
L Liquidity level

Each bank is scored between 1 (best) and 5 (worst). Banks with poor results are examined more frequently by federal regulators.

Observed Liquidity Levels in Selected Countries

Actual liquid asset holdings vary significantly. Exhibit 13-9 highlights the range of variation from one country to another. In 1989, among members of the OECD, U.S. banks held less than 10 percent of total assets as cash, deposits at the central bank, and interbank deposits. Canadian banks were somewhat less liquid with just under 9 percent invested in liquid assets. Banks in the United Kingdom were considerably more liquid with a liquidity-to-assets ratio of almost 19 percent.

EXHIBIT 13-9 LIQUID ASSETS AS A PERCENTAGE OF TOTAL ASSETS FOR SELECTED COUNTRIES, 1989

Country (institutions)	Cash*	Interbank Deposits	Total Liquid Assets
Austria (large banks)	2.39%	32.86%	35.25%
Belgium (banks)	.18	43.40	43.58
Canada (domestic banks)	1.41	7.30	8.71
Denmark (banks and savings banks)	1.60	16.20	17.80
Finland (commercial banks)	3.52	1.74	5.26
France (large banks)	1.52	42.78	44.30
Germany (commercial banks)	2.82	24.86	27.68
Greece (large commercial banks)	13.48	5.07	18.55
Italy (all commercial banks)	.38	8.19	8.57
Japan (all ordinary banks)	—†	16.14	16.14
Luxembourg (banks)	.20	60.23	60.43
Netherlands (banks)	2.58	25.13	27.71
Norway (commercial banks)	1.32	3.76	5.08
Portugal (banks)	12.81	12.06	24.87
Spain (commercial banks)	7.69	10.16	17.85
Sweden (commercial banks)	2.71	22.96	25.67
Switzerland (large banks)‡	3.21	29.45	32.66
United Kingdom (commercial banks)	1.58	17.02	18.60
United States (insured commercial banks)	5.05	4.63	9.68

*Includes deposits at central bank.
†Included in interbank deposits.
‡Data is from 1987.
Source: Organisation for Economic Cooperation and Development, *Bank Profitablity Statistical Supplement, Financial Statements,* 1981–1989.

Banks in Luxembourg are the most liquid of the group, with over 60 percent of asset holdings in interbank deposits. This underscores Luxembourg's importance as an international banking center, where 88 percent of bank assets are claims on nonresidents and the population per bank is 3000 people. In comparison, in the United States, population per bank is closer to 20,000. In Germany and Japan, the corresponding statistics are even higher at approximately 230,000 and 850,000, respectively. The relatively high concentration of banks in Luxembourg makes it an important center for interbank and wholesale transactions. The degree of liquidity is influenced by this mix of banking activities.

Larger banks, which have numerous correspondent relationships with other banks, tend to maintain higher cash balances to accommodate the clearing function. For example, the roughly 370 largest banks in the United States invested almost 12 percent in cash and interbank deposits in 1989, and the 13 city banks of Japan, 20 percent, both higher percentages than the respective banking industries as a whole. Advances in interbank and wholesale money markets have made it possible for banks to manage both liquidity positions and liabilities.

LIABILITY MANAGEMENT

As noted earlier, the advent of negotiable certificates of deposits in 1961 dramatically changed the nature of bank liquidity management. Commercial banks became much more active participants in money market transactions and far less dependent on traditional deposit-taking activity.

Liability Mix and Cost of Funds

From the perspective of bank management, the mix of liabilities will materially affect profitability. Recall that First National Bank's average cost of funds on interest-bearing liabilities was 7.23 percent (see Exhibit 13-6). In general, the average cost of funds is

$$k_{\text{IBL}} = \sum_{i=1}^{n} w_i r_i \tag{19}$$

where k_{IBL} = cost of interest-bearing liabilities or the weighted average cost of funds
w_i = weight of liability i as a percentage of total interest-bearing liabilities
r_i = average interest rate associated liability i
n = total number of interest-bearing liabilities

Equation 19 makes it possible to change the assumptions of liability mix and/or the cost of specific interest-bearing liabilities. Of particular importance is the effect of changes for liabilities that carry market rates of interest. Assume that money market participants considered First National's asset mix to be somewhat riskier than originally assessed.

This might stem from the bank's investments in real estate and consumer loans. Note from Exhibit 13-6 that, on average, almost 40 percent of First National's earning assets were invested in these categories. The average balances in the categories of real estate–construction, real estate–mortgage, credit card, and installment total $11.21 billion, or 38.9 percent of the average balance of total interest-earning assets of $28.788 billion.

Referring again to Exhibit 13-6, assume further that the perceived higher risk affects the cost of time deposits and short-term borrowings. If the rates paid on time deposits and short-term borrowings each increased by 60 and 50 basis points, respectively, the average rate paid on interest-bearing liabilities would also increase from its present level of 7.230 percent.[9]

Exhibit 13-10 includes the new higher rates for the three time deposit accounts and the three short-term borrowing accounts. The exhibit also includes the weight of each average balance for interest-bearing liabilities given in Exhibit 13-6. Applying Equation 19, the revised average rate paid is 7.6062 percent, approximately 38 basis points higher, or less than .5 percentage point greater than the original average cost.

As small as this change may seem (a 5 percent increase in the average cost), it translates into a larger effect on bank profitability. A revised interest expense amount is implied by the new rate on interest-bearing liabilities. Note that it is also possible to apply Equation 7 to arrive at total interest expense. Substituting the revised cost of funds of 7.6062 percent and the average interest-bearing liability balance of $25.928 billion (Exhibit 13-6), implied interest expense for the year becomes $1.972 billion.

As a result, taxable-equivalent net interest income drops from $1.170 billion to $1.072 billion, an 8.4 percent decline.

Interest income	$3.044 billion
Interest expense	−1.972 billion
Net interest income	1.072 billion

Net interest income as a percentage of earning assets declines at the same rate to 3.72 percent ($1.072 billion/$28.788 billion). The increase in the rate paid on liabilities reduces the interest rate spread by the same 38 basis points to 2.96 percent. Note, however, that the 5 percent increase in cost of funds (from 7.23 to 7.61 percent) produces an 11.4 percent drop in interest rate spread (from 3.34 to 2.96 percent). Thus, changes in the cost of funds can produce more than proportional changes in net interest income and interest rate spread.

Of course, First National's net income will also be adversely affected. The $98 million increase in interest expense ($1.972 billion − $1.874 billion) reduces reported income

[9]A basis point is .01 percentage point.

EXHIBIT 13-10 FIRST NATIONAL BANK COST OF FUNDS

	Weight* (1)	Cost† (2)	Weighted cost‡ (3)
Deposits			
Interest-bearing transaction accounts:	.058	5.20%	.3016%
Money market deposit accounts	.192	6.40	1.2288
Time deposits ≥ $100,000	.252	8.50	2.1420
Other time	.116	8.59	.9964
Savings	.066	5.35	.3531
Foreign–time	.068	7.90	.5372
Short-term borrowings			
Federal funds purchased	.139	8.16	1.1342
Commercial paper	.058	7.95	0.4611
Other	.036	8.45	0.3042
Long-term borrowings	.015	9.84	.1476
Total	1.000		7.6062

(1) *Percentage of total interest-bearing liabilities.
(2) †Interest rate after change.
(3) ‡Column 1 *times* column 2.

before taxes to $402 million (see Exhibit 13-4). Applying the bank's average tax rate *t,* net income for the year is revised downward to $309 million.

$$
\begin{aligned}
t &= \frac{\text{income taxes}}{\text{income before taxes}} \\
&= \frac{\$116{,}000{,}000}{\$500{,}000{,}000} \\
&= .232 \qquad (20)
\end{aligned}
$$

$$
\begin{aligned}
\text{NI} &= \$402{,}000{,}000(1 - .232) \\
&= \$308{,}736{,}000 \qquad (21)
\end{aligned}
$$

This represents an almost *20 percent reduction* in net income (from $384 million to $309 million), return on assets (from 1.17 to .94 percent), and return on equity (from 16.29 to 13.10 percent).

$$
\begin{aligned}
\text{ROA} &= \frac{\$308{,}736{,}000}{\$32{,}739{,}000.000} \\
&= .0094 \qquad (22)
\end{aligned}
$$

$$
\begin{aligned}
\text{ROE} &= \frac{\$308{,}736{,}000}{\$2{,}356{,}000{,}000} \\
&= .1310 \qquad (23)
\end{aligned}
$$

As this example shows, seemingly small changes in interest rates paid on liabilities can have *significant* impact on bank profitability. To prevent this, it is critical that adjustments in asset portfolios be made in an attempt to compensate for increases in the cost of funds. Thus, active liability management should be accompanied by equally rigorous asset management.

Under these circumstances, it is not surprising that bank regulators have begun to emphasize the cash flow approach of liquidity review, particularly with respect to banks that are active participants in money markets. Of particular importance are maturity mismatches of assets and liabilities. Chapter 15 discusses the application of asset-liability management techniques.

Observed Liability Mix in Selected Countries

For the most part, U.S. banks rely on individual and nonbank corporate customers for deposit funds. And despite the fact that it is more common now than in the past, bond financing is less frequently used by banks in the United States than in other countries. Exhibit 13-11 shows that 73 percent of total U.S. bank assets in 1989 were financed with nonbank deposits. For the largest 370 U.S. banks the percentage was somewhat lower at 67 percent.

In contrast, banks in Austria, Belgium, and Luxembourg rely much more on *interbank* deposits and *bonds,* with 50 to 60 percent in these categories. At the same time, these sources contributed only 5 percent to U.S. bank funds. Notice, too, that within these European banking systems, 45 percent or more of total liabilities and capital are in the form of interbank deposits alone. As noted earlier, banks in these countries concentrate more on wholesale banking activities, involving large transactions at market interest rates.

Small changes in market interest rates can have a major impact on profits, particularly if a significant proportion of liabilities is sensitive to market rates. To reduce this exposure, a large percentage of assets should also be rate-sensitive. Referring to Exhibit 13-9, we find that this is the case in Austria, Belgium, and Luxembourg. In each of the three in-

EXHIBIT 13-11 LIABILITIES AS A PERCENTAGE OF TOTAL ASSETS FOR SELECTED COUNTRIES, 1989

Country (institutions)	Interbank Deposits	Nonbank Deposits	Bonds	Total
Austria (large banks)	44.60%	33.28%	14.69%	92.57%
Belgium (large banks)	57.94	28.77	4.50	91.21
Canada (domestic banks)	11.87	74.35	1.81	88.03
Denmark (banks and savings banks)	25.64	46.79	—	72.43
Finland (commercial banks)	3.73	46.10	8.18	58.01
France (large banks)	44.70	35.28	6.57	86.55
Germany (commercial banks)	27.66	48.40	8.91	84.97
Greece (large banks)	1.01	92.33	—	93.34
Italy (all commercial banks)	9.04	45.03	—	54.07
Japan (all ordinary banks)	—*	76.09	0.76	76.85
Luxembourg (banks)	49.97	38.48	3.19	91.64
Netherlands (banks)	22.26	47.63	15.55	85.44
Norway (commercial banks)	16.84	51.60	11.93	80.37
Portugal (banks)	4.90	73.20	0.89	78.99
Spain (commercial banks)	14.11	60.43	1.53	76.07
Sweden (commercial banks)	35.03	33.65	4.56	73.24
Switzerland (large banks)†	24.70	50.27	11.51	86.48
United Kingdom (commercial banks)	—*	86.99	3.63	90.62
United States (insured commercial banks)	4.39	72.82	0.67	77.88

*Included in nonbank deposits.
†Data is from 1987.
Source: Organisation for Economic Cooperation and Development, *Bank Profitability, Statistical Supplement, Financial Statements of Banks,* 1981–1989.

stances, no less than 33 percent of total assets has been invested in interbank deposits, whereas U.S. banks invested less than 5 percent in this way.

In general, Canadian, Greek, and Portuguese banks follow the U.S. pattern of nonbank deposit funding. Canadian banks, however, maintain a somewhat higher proportion of interbank deposits, 12 percent of total assets in 1986.

The universal banks of Germany and Switzerland fall somewhere in between these two extremes. Approximately half the assets are financed with nonbank deposits, versus 73 percent in the United States and less than 40 percent in Luxembourg. Swiss (25 percent) and German (28 percent) banks rely on interbank deposits more than U.S. banks (4 percent), but less than their counterparts in Luxembourg (50 percent). In addition, these universal banks use more bond financing than U.S. banks, as also shown in Exhibit 13-11. The liability mix of Swiss and German banks is indicative of their active participation in both interbank money markets and industrial finance.

The typical banking activities in a country will be reflected in the industry's balance sheet composition. However, the fundamental principles of rate sensitivity and maturity matching are applicable in every instance.

SUMMARY

Bank profitability, liquidity, and liability management are interrelated. There is a tradeoff between bank profitability and liquidity. This is especially true in the United States and other countries in which deposit interest rates vary with market interest rates. Profitability, in terms of net interest margin, interest rate spread, and returns on assets and equity, is quite sensitive to changes in rates paid on interest-bearing liabilities.

There is, then, an incentive to invest in more profitable asset categories, notably loans. However, loans are usually illiquid and provide little or no protection against unanticipated deposit withdrawals. As a result, access to money markets has become important in accommodating liquidity needs. Especially for larger banks, liquidity is now *less* a function of the existing balance sheet and *more* a function of the ability to issue large-denomination time deposits, to purchase federal funds and repos, and to issue commercial paper.

Nevertheless, the actual mix of liquidity and liabilities depends on primary banking activities. In countries where international banking dominates, a relatively large percentage of assets and liabilities will be composed of interbank balances. In countries where banks are more involved in consumer and industrial finance, balance sheets reflect less reliance on interbank transactions. Regardless of the composition of banking business, however, the principles of maturity matching and interest sensitivity apply.

KEY TERMS

asset management
asset utilization
core deposits
cost of funding earning assets
cost of funds
equity multiplier
equity ratio
hot money
interest rate spread (net interest margin)
liability management
liquidity
net interest income
net interest yield
net margin after tax
return on assets
return on equity
statement of cash flows
structure of deposits
taxable-equivalent rate
yield on earning assets

END-OF-CHAPTER QUESTIONS

1. In the United States, what are the major assets and liabilities of commercial banks?
2. Under what circumstances can a bank be considered illiquid even when liquid asset holdings appear adequate?
3. Define net interest income and interest rate spread.
4. What two primary factors influence the liquidity needs of a commercial bank?
5. Describe three alternative approaches that a bank can take to bolster capital. What are the advantages and disadvantages?
6. Given the current regulatory climate throughout the industrialized world, do you believe that bank profits in the United States will improve in the near term? Explain.
7. Which type of banks, regionals or money center banks, would you expect to have a higher proportion of core deposits? Why?
8. What circumstances led to increased reliance on liability management in the United States?
9. How has the liability mix of U.S. commercial banks changed over the past 25 years? What were some of the primary contributing factors in this change?
10. Contrast the levels of interbank balances in Austria, Belgium, and Luxembourg to those of the United States. Explain any observed difference.

END-OF-CHAPTER PROBLEMS

1. **a.** Calculate the annual interest rate earned from an investment security with an average balance of $1,250,000 for which $5312.50 of income is received each month.
   b. Now, calculate the taxable-equivalent annual interest rate, assuming that this investment is a municipal bond and that the marginal tax rate is 34 percent.
2. Refer to Exhibits 13-6 and 13-10. Recall that certain rates paid on liabilities were assumed to

increase in Exhibit 13-10. Now assume that rates earned on certain assets also increase by 50 basis points. The assets categories that are affected are:

Time deposits in other banks
Federal funds sold and repurchase agreements
Commercial, financial, and agricultural loans
Construction (real estate) loans

a. Recompute annual interest earned for each asset category and in total.
b. Recompute the ratios in Equations 6 through 14.

3. With respect to loan demand, why is it not always necessary for a bank to generate 100 percent of a given loan request in the form of additional liquid assets? Suppose that a loan request for $1.75 million is submitted to a bank whose minimum reserve requirement is 10 percent. What is the minimum liquidity that is required to fund this loan?

4. Obtain an annual report from a local bank in your area. Compare the local bank's profitability and with First National Bank's in this chapter.

5. Using the guidelines suggested in connection with the structure of deposits approach for estimating liquidity needs, calculate the need for liquidity, assuming the following deposit account balances (in millions of dollars).

"Hot money"	$ 50
Stable deposits	130
Highly stable deposits	85
Total	$265

6. Applying the statement of cash flow approach, estimate future liquidity needs if the following changes are projected in specific accounts.

Account	Projected Change (millions)
Commercial loans	$−1.0
Mortgage loans	+5.0
Credit card loans	+2.5
Transactions deposit accounts	−6.0
Small time deposits	+10.0
Large time deposits	−7.5

SELECTED REFERENCES

Board of Governors of the Federal Reserve System. *Flow of Funds Accounts, Financial Assets and Liabilities,* Washington, D.C., various issues.

Calomiris, Charles W., and Charles M. Kahn. "The Role of Demandable Debt in Structuring Optimal Banking Arrangements," *American Economic Review,* vol. 81, no. 3 (June 1991), pp. 497–513.

Federal Deposit Insurance Corporation. *Statistics on Banking,* Washington, D.C., 1988 and 1989.

Federal Deposit Insurance Corporation. *Quarterly Banking Profile,* various issues.

International Bank for Reconstruction and Development/ The World Bank. *The World Bank Atlas 1988,* Washington, D.C., 1988.

Jacklin, Charles J., and Sudipto Bhattacharya. "Distinguishing Panics and Information-Based Bank Runs: Welfare and Policy Implications," *Journal of Political Economy,* vol. 96, no. 3 (June 1988), pp. 568–592.

Organisation for Economic Cooperation and Development. *Bank Profitability, Statistical Supplement, Financial Statements of Banks, 1982–1986,* Paris, 1988.

Pecchioli, R. M. *Prudential Supervision in Banking,* Organization for Economic Co-operation and Development, Paris, 1987.

Spong, Kenneth. *Banking Regulation; Its Purposes, Implementation, and Effects,* 3d Edition, Federal Reserve Bank of Kansas, 1990.

United States Department of Commerce, Bureau of the Census. *Statistical Abstract of the United States, 1989, 109th Edition,* Washington, D.C., 1989.

Wallace, Neil. "Another Attempt to Explain an Illiquid Banking System: The Diamond and Dybvig Model with Sequential Service Taken Seriously," *Federal Reserve Bank of Minneapolis Quarterly Review,* Fall 1988, pp. 13–16.

Whalen, Gary. "Concentration and Profitability in Non-MSA Banking Markets," *Economic Review,* Federal Reserve Bank of Cleveland, First Quarter 1987, pp. 2–9.

Williamson, Stephen D. "Liquidity, Banking, and Bank Failures," *International Economic Review,* 29, February 1988, pp. 25–43.

Wilson, J. S. *Banking Policy and Structure; A Comparative Analysis,* Croom Helm Ltd., London, 1986.

CHAPTER 14

BANK INVESTMENT AND LOAN PORTFOLIO MANAGEMENT

CHAPTER OUTLINE

INVESTMENT SECURITIES

LIQUIDITY CONSIDERATIONS
- Yield Considerations
- Interest Rate Expectations
  - Bondholder return, interest rate changes

INVESTMENT SECURITIES MANAGEMENT
- Interest Rate Risk
- Managing Interest Rate Risk
  - Passive management, laddered maturity approach, barbell maturity approach
- Default Risk
- Tax Rate and Municipal Securities
  - Indifference tax rate, impact of legislative changes, optimal mix of taxable and tax-exempt securities
- Trends in Bank Holdings of Investment Securities

LOAN PORTFOLIO MANAGEMENT
- Loan Portfolio Diversification
- Regulation of Loan Concentration
  - The United States, selected countries in the OECD
- Trends in Loan Portfolio Composition
- Commercial Bank Market Shares
- Characteristics of Bank Loans
  - Commercial loans, real estate loans, consumer loans
- Credit Analysis
- Loan Pricing

OBSERVED COMBINATIONS OF SECURITIES AND LOANS IN THE OECD

INTERNATIONAL COMPARISONS:
- Austria
- Belgium
- Canada
- Denmark
- Finland
- France
- Germany
- Greece
- Italy
- Japan
- Luxembourg
- Netherlands
- Norway
- Portugal
- Spain
- Switzerland
- United Kingdom
- United States

CHAPTER OVERVIEW

This chapter:

- Outlines the objectives of investment securities management
- Discusses interest rate risk and default risk
- Describes management techniques to ensure both liquidity and profitability in the investment portfolio

- Analyzes the optimal mix of taxable and tax-exempt securities
- Examines trends in the composition of bank portfolios of investment securities and loans
- Describes categories of commercial, real estate, and consumer loans
- Discusses credit analysis and loan pricing

The primary earning assets for commercial banks are investment securities and loans. In the United States, these two categories account for over 80 percent of banking industry assets. But the dramatic change in bank liabilities that was discussed in Chapter 13 has forced adjustments in bank asset portfolios as well. The increasing cost of funds has led to a smaller proportion of assets in the form of safe and liquid Treasury securities. The trend in blue-chip corporate America toward direct financing through instruments such as commercial paper has meant that commercial banks have had to look to other areas for high-yielding loans. But these changes have not come without risk. Corporate bonds and real estate loans are subject to default and credit risk that must be properly managed in order to maintain profitability and solvency.

INVESTMENT SECURITIES

United States commercial banks hold many of the debt securities described in Chapter 4, including Treasury issues, government agency bonds, municipal bonds, and corporate bonds. However, U.S. banks may not invest in equity securities with the exception of Federal Reserve Bank stock, stock in subsidiaries, and stock held temporarily as collateral on defaulted loans. While the debt securities that are permitted are quite liquid, they do not merely satisfy the bank's liquidity needs. The *composition* of the investment portfolio will also depend on yield considerations and expectations of future interest rates. Profitability is a much more important decision variable in the management of securities than in the management of bank liquidity.

Loan demand will determine the *amount* of securities held. When loan demand is weak, securities are the next best investment alternative for a bank. Conversely, when loan demand is strong, security balances can be reduced in order to provide the liquidity that is necessary to meet loan demand. In this sense, the securities portfolio is the *residual* of loan demand.

LIQUIDITY CONSIDERATIONS

Treasury issues are the most liquid securities a bank can hold.

Asset liquidity:
The extent to which an asset may quickly be converted to cash without realizing a loss on the transaction.

An extensive secondary market in Treasury securities helps to ensure the quick sale of Treasury bills and bonds at the going market price. Even large sales will not tend to depress the price. Commercial banks held 7 percent of outstanding Treasury securities in 1991, down from 20 percent in 1971.

Government agency securities are almost as liquid as Treasury issues. Government securities firms (described in Chapter 3) regularly trade both Treasury and government agency obligations. Agency securities include those issued by the Federal National Mortgage Association (Fannie Mae) and the Federal Home Loan Mortgage Corporation (Freddie Mac).[1] In 1991, commercial banks held 20 percent of all government agency securities. As was true with Treasury issues, banks held a much higher percentage in 1971, 36 percent of the total outstanding.

Municipal bonds are significantly less liquid than Treasury and government agency securities. State and local governments have issued approximately 75 percent of municipals. Another 15 percent have been issued by nonfinancial corporations to fund local projects that qualify for tax-exempt treatment (industrial revenue bonds). Because of this, municipal bond trading tends to be concentrated in more narrow geographical regions than Treasury and government agency securities trading. Nevertheless, banks have been major participants in the market, holding 13 percent of all outstanding issues in 1991. Twenty years earlier, the proportion was 51 percent.

Corporate bonds are also not as liquid as government securities. But, when issued by major firms, they may be actively traded on organized exchanges and, thus, reasonably liquid. At the same time, significant, unexpected developments may have an adverse effect on their market value. For example, an announcement that the issuing firm plans to initiate a highly leveraged takeover of another firm can produce uncertainty about the quality of already existing bonds and drive down their market price.

Nonetheless, commercial banks have become much more active participants in the corporate bond market because of the relatively high yields on corporates. In 1971, banks held 1.7 percent of outstanding corporate bonds. By 1991, the proportion had grown to 5.5 percent.

With the exception of corporate bonds, commercial banks hold a smaller share of these securities presently than they have in the past. This change is in response to the higher cost of funds that resulted, first, from rising and volatile interest rates of the 1970s and, second, from deposit interest rate deregulation in the 1980s.

Yield Considerations

As bank deposits have become increasingly interest rate–sensitive, the yield earned on investment securities has become even more critical. The greater emphasis on corporate bonds is due to their higher rates of return.

Government agency issues share many of the attributes of Treasury securities. They are readily marketable and are backed by at least an implicit guarantee by the federal government. However, since they are not direct liabilities of the Treasury, they yield a slightly higher return to compensate for the higher risk. Also, many agency securities are pass-through certificates backed by mortgage loan pools. Since mortgage loan rates are substantially higher than Treasury rates, these pass-through certificates enjoy a competitive advantage with respect to rate.

The competitiveness of municipal bonds will depend not only on the bond's coupon rate but also on the bank's marginal tax rate. Recall that the taxable-equivalent yield of a municipal bond may be calculated as follows.[2]

$$k_{\mathrm{TE}} = \frac{k_M}{(1 - t)} \tag{1}$$

where k_{TE} = taxable-equivalent yield
k_M = municipal bond yield
t = marginal tax rate

[1]See Chapter 4 for a description of Treasury and government agency bonds and other capital market instruments (including municipal and corporate bonds).

[2]See Chapter 13.

If a municipal bond has a yield of 7 percent and the bank's marginal tax rate is 46 percent, the bond's taxable-equivalent yield is 12.96 percent:

$$k_{TE} = \frac{7\%}{(1 - .46)} = 12.96\%$$

At this tax rate, this relatively low-yielding municipal bond is equivalent to a much higher-yielding corporate bond.

However, if the marginal tax rate is lowered, the same municipal security is less attractive. For example, a marginal tax rate of 34 percent reduces the taxable-equivalent yield to 10.61 percent. Thus, tax rate structure is a fundamental determinant in investment portfolio composition.

Interest Rate Expectations

The anticipated direction of interest rate changes will also affect portfolio composition. If interest rates are expected to decline, portfolio managers will seek to "lock in" the high rates of return currently available. Conversely, expectations of higher interest rates in the future would motivate managers to invest on a short-term basis in order to take advantage of the higher yields, when available.

Bondholder Return While this analysis is intuitively appealing, it is necessary to examine more closely the rate of return to an investor in fixed-income securities. As noted in Chapter 4, rate of return is composed of the current yield and the capital gains yield.

$$k_B = \text{CY} + \text{CGY} \tag{2}$$

where k_B = rate of return to a bond investor
CY = current yield (interest payment as a percentage of bond value at the beginning of the period)
CGY = capital gains yield

For a particular security, the current yield will depend on the bond's coupon rate and the value of the bond at the beginning of the holding period. Thus, the current yield for the year is a unique value that can be identified at the beginning of the year.

However, the capital gains yield, or percentage price change, will depend on the value of the bond at the end of the period. In turn, the end-of-period value will depend on interest rate changes. For example, on January 1, a 10 percent coupon bond (bond A) that pays interest annually, has a remaining maturity of 2 years, and has a required return of 12 percent will sell at \$966.21.

$$\begin{aligned} P_0 &= 100\,(\text{PVIFA}_{.12,2}) + 1000\,(\text{PVIF}_{.12,2}) \\ &= 100(1.6901) + 1000(.7972) \\ &= 966.21 \end{aligned} \tag{3}$$

A 10-year bond (bond B) with the same features but a 12.5 percent required return will sell for \$861.59 on January 1.[3]

[3] The .5 percent difference in required return is a liquidity premium as discussed in Chapter 8.

The *current* yields of bond A and bond B are 10.35 percent ($100/$966.21) and 11.6 percent ($100/$861.59), respectively. The *capital gains* yields are functions of both beginning and ending prices P_0 and P_1.

$$\text{CGY} = \frac{(P_1 - P_0)}{P_0} \tag{4}$$

$$\text{CGY}_\text{A} = \frac{(982.14 - 966.21)}{966.21}$$

$$= .01649 \tag{5}$$

$$\text{CGY}_\text{B} = \frac{(869.29 - 861.59)}{861.59}$$

$$= .00894 \tag{6}$$

Thus, total return to an investor in bond A during the year is 12 percent (10.35 + 1.65). The corresponding return on bond B is 12.5 percent (11.61 + 0.89). Each bond yields exactly the required return, even though the mix of current and capital gains yields is different.

Interest Rate Changes Now suppose that interest rates decline during the year such that required returns fall by 1 percent for all securities. In this case, end-of-year prices for bonds A and B will be $990.99 and $918.53, respectively. The capital gains yields increase to 2.56 percent and 6.61 percent, respectively.

$$\text{CGY}_\text{A} = \frac{(990.99 - 966.21)}{966.21}$$

$$= .02556 \tag{7}$$

$$\text{CGY}_\text{B} = \frac{(918.53 - 861.59)}{861.59}$$

$$= .06609 \tag{8}$$

Total return from bond A becomes 12.91 percent(10.35 + 2.56), .91 percent higher than before. However, total return for bond B is 18.22 percent (11.61 + 6.61), 5.72 percent higher.

Before the change in interest rates, the rate of return differential between the two bonds was .5 percent. After the decline, the differential is 5.31 percent. This example illustrates the actual price behavior of short-versus long-term bonds in a declining interest rate environment; that is, long-term investments result in higher total rates of return.

Of course, should rates increase, the greater volatility of long-term bonds works to the disadvantage of the investor. Assuming an *increase* of 1 percent, end-of-year prices of bonds A and B are $973.45 and $823.68, respectively. Resulting capital gains yield and total return for bond A are .75 and 11.10 percent, respectively. Corresponding figures for bond B are −4.40 and 7.21 percent.

While bond A's total return declined by .9 percent from that in the stable-rate environment, bond B's total return is 5.29 percent lower. When interest rates increase, smaller declines in total rate of return will result when shorter-term bonds are held.[4]

The direction of interest rate change can have significant impact on the market value of a bond portfolio. At the same time, short-term securities can sacrifice earnings potential for the bank.

[4]This and other aspects of bond price behavior are discussed in Chapter 8.

Interest Rate Risk

Since it is difficult to predict the direction and magnitude of interest rate changes, bank investment portfolios can be exposed to significant *interest rate risk.*

Interest rate risk:
Risk associated with fixed-income securities because of changing interest rates.

Any investment in a fixed-income instrument creates interest rate risk. At this point, the discussion of interest rate risk will be focused on investment securities. However, in Chapter 15 it is shown that the principles also apply generally to bank portfolios of assets and liabilities.

Two types of interest rate risk are relevant for portfolio managers: *price risk* and *reinvestment risk.*

Price risk:
The risk that the market value of a fixed-income security will decline when interest rates increase.

Reinvestment risk:
The risk that it may not be possible to reinvest the proceeds of maturing fixed-income securities at rates equivalent to those of the maturing securities because of generally declining interest rates.

The examples in the last section show that longer-term bonds will be subject to greater price risk. Similarly, short-term securities present more reinvestment risk.

Managing Interest Rate Risk

Passive Management Actual management of interest rate risk may take several forms. *Passive management* involves purchasing long-term securities with the intention of holding them until they mature. As long as the bank does not need the funds to meet loan or other liquidity demands, this strategy may work reasonably well. Since the yield curve is usually upward sloping, longer maturities will produce higher yields, all other things being equal.

However, should interest rates increase significantly, holding the long-term bonds at the previous, lower rates can result in a substantial opportunity cost for the bank: The bank cannot earn the higher rates that are available. Selling the bonds in order to reinvest at the now higher market rate presents another problem. The higher-rate environment has reduced the market value of the current portfolio. Selling will produce "losses on securities transactions" that must be reported in the financial statements, reducing the bank's net income for the period. Thus, the passive management approach has a built-in incentive to avoid recognizing losses in market value by simply holding the securities until maturity. A hidden cost is that opportunities for enhanced cash flow from higher market yields may be forgone.

More active liability management has led to more aggressive asset management, as well. Flexibility in the securities portfolio can provide both liquidity and higher yields.

Laddered Maturity Approach The *laddered maturity approach* for investments provides such flexibility. This approach spreads investment dollars evenly over several maturities. For example, if bank management decided that a 10-year investment horizon was appropriate, one-tenth of the portfolio would be invested in securities maturing in 1 year. Another one-tenth would be invested in bonds maturing in 2 years. This process continues until the final one-tenth is invested in bonds with 10 years to maturity.

If the bank needs additional liquidity at any point, it may sell securities with the shortest time to maturity. These can be sold at prices close to par, producing little or no loss upon sale. Medium- to long-term securities continue to earn, presumably, higher returns for the bank. To maintain the "ladder," proceeds of maturing issues are reinvested into the longest term of the investment horizon. Using the example above, funds from maturing issues would be reinvested in 10-year bonds. This approach ensures the bank of regular liquidity infusions from short-term maturities while also allowing it to earn relatively higher rates of return from longer-term investments.

Barbell Maturity Approach Another approach that is geared for even greater liquidity and high-yield potential is the *barbell maturity approach.* Here, a large portion of the portfolio is invested short-term, perhaps 5 years or less. The remaining is invested in long-term securities, perhaps 15 years or more. For example, 40 percent may be invested in securities with 1 to 4 years until maturity, perhaps with 10 percent in each of the four maturity classes. These investments provide a continual supply of liquidity and a reserve in the event of additional liquidity needs.

The remaining 60 percent can be spread over maturities from 15 to 25 years, enabling the bank also to realize maximum available yields in a normal (upward sloping) yield curve environment. As long as the yield curve slopes upward, it could even be possible to sell the longer-term bonds at a capital gain when 12 to 13 years remain until maturity. As before, proceeds are reinvested in the longest term on the bank's investment horizon.

Both the laddered maturity approach and the barbell maturity approach provide liquidity and income-earning capability and are superior to the passive approach (which does not consider price or reinvestment risk). With its greater concentration in the longer maturities, the barbell maturity approach provides even more income than the laddered maturity approach. However, these are both ways to manage interest rate risk and do not address the issue of default risk.

Default Risk

The elements of risk that are discussed above involve changes in market conditions. Managers of bank investment portfolios also face *default risk.*

Default risk:
The risk that the issuer of a fixed-income security may fail to pay interest and/or principal.

Bank managers usually do not evaluate default risk of bond issuers. In the case of Treasury and government agency issues, there is little or no risk. In the case of municipal and corporate bonds, bank regulators strongly urge institutions to invest only the highest-rated bonds.[5] National banks may not invest in bonds that have a rating lower than the top four ratings of AAA, AA, A, and B. Individual states have similar restrictions for state-chartered banks.

Other regulatory provisions are also applied. Type I securities are considered least risky and include Treasury, government agency, and (highest-quality) general obligation bonds of states and local political subdivisions. The Federal Reserve permits its members to hold an unlimited amount of these securities and to underwrite their issuance.

[5]Chapter 9 describes bond ratings by Moody's Investor Service and Standard & Poor's Corporation.

Type II securities are issued by certain public agencies (federal and state) that are not backed by the full faith and credit of the United States or by the full taxing authority of municipalities. Banks may invest up to 15 percent of the sum of capital and surplus in the securities of any single issuer. Underwriting is also permitted. Classification as a Type II security is an issue-specific designation.

Type III securities include all other investment-grade securities. Bank investments are limited to 10 percent of capital and surplus. Underwriting and dealing in these securities are prohibited.

These regulations define the population of securities in which commercial banks may invest. The actual combination of securities, however, is essentially left to bank management.

Tax Rate and Municipal Securities

In addition to considerations of interest rate and credit risk, the mix of *taxable* and *tax-exempt securities* can have significant impact on bank profitability. As noted in Equation 1, the taxable-equivalent yield of a municipal security depends on the bank's marginal tax rate. Thus, the desirability of tax-exempt bonds will also depend on *tax rates.*

Indifference Tax Rate Recall the example of First National Bank in Chapter 13. Exhibits 13-4 and 13-6 show the bank's income and yield on both categories of securities. The rate of return on taxable securities is 8.45 percent.

$$k_T = \frac{\$331{,}000{,}000}{\$3{,}917{,}000{,}000}$$

$$= .0845$$

Actual tax-exempt income is \$66 million. Since the average balance is \$962 million, the nontaxable-equivalent yield is 6.86 percent. With these two yields, it is possible to derive the *indifference tax rate.*

Indifference tax rate:

That rate which produces an after-tax yield on taxable securities that is equal to the municipal yield, causing an investor to be indifferent between the two types of securities.

$$k_T(1 - t^*) = k_M \tag{9}$$

where k_T = yield on taxable securities

k_M = yield on tax-exempt (municipal) securities

t^* = indifference tax rate

Substituting the yields above, t^* is 18.8 percent.

$$.0845(1 - t) = .0686$$

$$-t^* = \left(\frac{.0686}{.0845}\right) - 1$$

$$t^* = 1 - \left(\frac{.0686}{.0845}\right)$$

$$= .1882 \tag{10}$$

Any tax rate greater than 18.8 percent causes the tax-exempt securities to provide a higher yield than their taxable counterparts. Since the marginal tax rate for First National (and most banks) is 34 percent, tax-exempt securities with this yield are attractive investments under these circumstances.[6]

Impact of Legislative Change Prior to 1983, commercial banks were able both to earn tax-exempt income and to deduct interest paid on deposits (and other funds) that were used to finance municipal securities. Only depository institutions were permitted to engage in this practice. Because of this, before the 1980s, commercial banks invested in a large percentage of municipal bonds. For example, 51 percent of all tax-exempt securities in 1971 were held in commercial bank portfolios. In 1983, Congress passed legislation to partially restrict interest expense deductibility. After 1983, only 80 percent of interest paid on funds used to finance tax-exempt securities was deductible.

The net effect of the change is that it levied a kind of tax on tax-exempt securities. The amount of implicit tax is the amount of tax shelter that was lost. The amount of funds used to finance tax-exempt investments M multiplied by the interest rate paid on this liability k_L is the dollar cost of funds. This quantity multiplied by the marginal tax rate t is the unadjusted amount of tax shelter. Finally, multiplying this quantity by 20 percent measures the amount of lost tax shelter. This result as a percentage of municipal income is the implied tax rate on municipal bond income.

$$\begin{aligned} t' &= \frac{.20(k_L)(M)(t)}{(k_M)(M)} \\ &= \frac{.20(k_L)(t)}{k_M} \end{aligned} \tag{11}$$

where t' equals the implied tax rate on municipal, tax-exempt securities with a 20 percent exclusion of interest expense. Assuming a cost of funds of 8 percent and a marginal tax rate of 34 percent, the implied tax rate in the example above is 7.93 percent.

$$\begin{aligned} t' &= \frac{.20(.08)(.34)}{.0686} \\ &= 0.0793 \end{aligned}$$

Equation 9 may now be restated to incorporate this implied tax rate on municipal bonds.

$$\begin{aligned} k_T(1 - t^*) &= k_M(1 - t') \\ -t^* &= \left[\frac{k_M(1-t')}{k_T}\right] - 1 \\ t^* &= 1 - \left\{\frac{[k_M(1-t')]}{k_T}\right\} \end{aligned} \tag{9a}$$

Recalculating the indifference tax rate using Equation 9a, the result is 25.25 percent.

[6]The Tax Reform Act of 1986 established the following corporate tax rates:

Taxable Income, $	Tax Rate
0–50,000	.15
50,001–75,000	.25
75,001–100,000	.34
100,001–335,000	.39
>335,000	.34

$$
\begin{aligned}
t* &= 1 - \left\{\frac{[k_M(1-t')]}{k_T}\right\} \\
&= 1 - \left[\frac{.0686(1-.0793)}{.0845}\right] \\
&= .2525
\end{aligned}
\qquad (9b)
$$

The indifference tax rate increase from under 19 to over 25 percent after the 1983 legislative change is reflected in this example. Nevertheless, tax-exempt securities continued to be attractive for bank portfolios if used in appropriate proportions.

The Tax Reform Act of 1986 placed more restrictions on income exemptions and interest expense deductions. After August 1986, only municipal securities issued for public purposes retained complete tax exemption on interest income. Those issued for private purposes (industrial revenue bonds) became subject either to alternative minimum tax or to full taxation of interest income.

Also, commercial banks could no longer deduct interest expense on funds used to finance municipal securities purchased after 1986. The only exception to this general rule was public purpose bonds issued by municipalities with $10 million or less in total issues per year.

Assume that First National's municipals were issued prior to August 1986 for a private purpose (retaining tax exemption for interest income) but were purchased by the bank *after* August 1986 (losing the interest expense deduction). The change in treatment of interest expense materially affects both the implied and indifference tax rates.

Since 100 percent of interest expense is disallowed as a deduction, the forgone tax shelter increases significantly. Substituting 100 percent for 20 percent in Equation 11, the implied tax rate is restated as follows.

$$
t'' = \frac{1(k_L)(t)}{k_M} \qquad (11a)
$$

where t″ equals the implied tax rate on municipal tax-exempt securities with a 100 percent exclusion of interest expense. In our example, t'' is equal to 39.65 percent.

$$
\begin{aligned}
t'' &= \frac{1(.08)(.34)}{.0686} \\
&= .3965
\end{aligned}
$$

The indifference tax rate becomes 51.01 percent.

$$
\begin{aligned}
t* &= 1 - \left[\frac{.0686(1-.3965)}{.0845}\right] \\
&= .5101
\end{aligned}
$$

Using this example, taxable securities would be preferable for any tax rate lower than 51 percent. To verify this, note that, when the marginal tax rate is 34 percent, the after-tax return on taxable securities is 5.58 percent [.0845 (1 − .34)]. Using the implied tax computed above, tax-exempt securities yield 4.14 percent [.0686(1 − .3965)].

In order to be attractive for First National, *these* municipals must qualify as public purpose bonds of small municipal issuers, retaining interest expense deductibility. Others, which do not qualify in this way, must offer higher interest rates to be competitive. Because of these changes in tax law, qualifying municipal issues are in great demand and the commercial bank share of municipal bond holdings declined to 13 percent by 1991.

If income can be excluded from taxable income and 80 percent of associated interest expense deducted, municipal bonds are attractive investments for the bank. This is true, however, only if the bank has income from other sources to shelter from taxation.

Optimal Mix of Taxable and Tax-Exempt Securities All other things being equal, a bank's investment portfolio should provide it with the highest after-tax yield possible within established parameters of interest rate risk and default risk. However, exactly what this means in terms of the mix of taxable and tax-exempt securities depends on the bank's projected income and expense composition.

Notice that First National's after-tax yield on taxable bonds is 5.58 percent [.0845(1 − .34)]. With an implied tax rate of 7.93 percent, the corresponding rate for tax-exempt bonds is 6.32 percent [.0686 (1 − .0793)]. Therefore, tax-exempt bonds are generally preferable for this bank given these interest rates. However, this rule of thumb is valid only if income from other sources exceeds the bank's anticipated expenses. If there is no income to shelter, tax-exempt bonds become less attractive.

Referring to Exhibit 13-4, notice that the total income from loans, time deposits, and federal funds sold is $2.613 billion. The net of interest expense, provision for credit losses, and other operating income and expense is $2.51 billion. The resulting $103 million excess of income over expense can be at least partially sheltered from taxation.

If this were not the case, the decision to invest excessive amounts in tax-exempt securities would be ill-advised. Considering an alternative situation, assume that income from sources other than securities is again expected to be $2.613 billion but that expense will be closer to $2.900 billion and that the cost of funds is 8 percent. Assume also that the same rates are expected to be available on investments and that an average securities balance of $4.879 billion will be maintained, as indicated in Exhibit 13-6.

Under these new assumptions, projected expenses exceed income by $287 million. The importance of the tax shelter is diminished since non-securities-related operations are expected to produce a net loss, that is, no tax liability. In this case, the bank should invest in taxable securities sufficient to offset exactly the $287 million loss. At a rate of return of 8.45 percent, this implies an average investment of $3.396 billion ($287 million/.0845 = $3.396 billion). Taxable earnings on this amount are $287 million. The remaining $1.483 billion can then be invested in tax-exempt securities to earn $102 million.

As shown in Exhibit 14-1, this optimal mix results in income before tax of $102 million. However, since this amount is earned from tax-exempt securities, only the disallowed portion of interest expense is taxable. Net income is $93.84 million.

Notice that neither 100 percent tax-exempt nor 100 percent taxable investments yield as high a net income as does the optimal mix. A reduced amount of taxable securities forgoes higher yields in exchange for no corresponding tax benefits. A greater amount of taxables encroaches on the income range in which the effective tax-exempt yields exceed taxable yields.

Essentially, the optimal mix of securities will depend on the bank's marginal tax rate and its investment opportunities. Any tax benefits associated with municipal securities may be realized only if there is sufficient other income to shelter from taxation. As long as there is taxable income from other operations of the bank, bank management should focus on rates of return net of both explicit and implied tax rates.

Trends in Bank Holdings of Investment Securities

The reduced attractiveness of municipal bonds and the pressure to cover the higher cost of funds has led to a reduction in the importance of investment securities in bank portfolios. In 1964, fully one-third of bank financial assets was held as securities. Referring to Exhibit 14-2, notice that Treasury securities dominated at over 20 percent. Next in impor-

EXHIBIT 14-1 THE MIX OF TAXABLE AND TAX-EXEMPT SECURITIES ($ MILLIONS)

	Optimal	100% Tax Exempt	100% Taxable
Income from non-securities-related operations	(287)	(287)	(287)
Income from securities:			
Taxable	287[a]	0	412[h]
Tax-exempt	102[b]	335[f]	0
Income before tax	102	48	125
Taxable income:			
Less tax-exempt earnings	(102)	(335)	0
Plus loss of interest expense deduction	24[c]	78[g]	0
Taxable income	24	(209)	125
Tax[d]:			
First $335 million	(.1139)	0	(.1139)
Remaining taxable income	(8.0461)	0	(42.3861)
Total tax	(8.1600)	0	(42.5000)
Net income[e]	93.84	48	82.5

[a]($3396) (.0845) = $286.96.
[b](1483) (.0686) = $101.73.
[c](.20) ($1483) (.08) = $23.73.
[d]See footnote 2 in main text for corporate tax brackets.
[e]Income before tax less tax.
[f]($4879) (.0686) = $334.70.
[g](.20) ($4879) (.08) = $78.06.
[h]($4879) (.0845) = $412.28.

tance were tax-exempt securities, 11 percent of financial assets. Government agency and corporate bonds together represented approximately 2 percent.

Over time, the relatively low returns available on Treasury securities have caused bank managers to shift away from them in favor of other higher-yielding investment alternatives. Government agency bonds, with the next lowest default risk, grew from less than 2 percent of assets to almost 9 percent in 1991. At the same time, Treasury issues had fallen to less than 6 percent. The 1991 share of corporate bonds (2.7 percent) was over six times the corresponding number in 1964. Not surprisingly, in view of the changes in tax treatment, the share of tax-exempt securities declined from 10.8 percent of financial assets in 1964 to 3.4 percent in 1991.

Overall, these changes reflect the trend toward more interest-sensitive liabilities. In response, a greater percentage of funds is invested in the highest-yielding assets that a bank holds—loans.

EXHIBIT 14-2 INVESTMENT SECURITIES, U.S. BANKS, 1964–1991

	1964	1969	1974	1979	1984	1989	1991
Financial assets (billions)	$311.5	$471.6	$836.4	$1335.9	$2105.8	$2954.4	$3344.7
Securities as a % of financial assets:							
Treasury	20.4%	11.8%	6.7%	7.3%	8.8%	6.9%	5.8%
Government agency	1.7	2.1	4.0	3.8	3.7	5.9	8.9
Tax-exempt	10.8	12.6	12.1	10.0	8.3	5.1	3.4
Corporate & foreign	0.4	0.4	0.8	0.5	0.8	2.7	2.7
	33.3%	26.9%	23.6%	21.6%	21.6%	20.6%	20.8%

Source: Board of Governors of the Federal Reserve System, *Flow of Funds Accounts, Financial Assets and Liabilities,* various issues.

Loan Portfolio Diversification

Loans represent the core of commercial banking. Originally, banks catered to the needs of business borrowers. These loans were often unsecured and short-term. After World War II (1939–1945), banks began to make more loans backed by real estate. Many real estate borrowers were mortgage companies that carried their own customers' loans until mortgages could be set up. Also, banks began to make mortgage loans directly, that is, to make "conventional" mortgage loans for which the banks assumed the ultimate risk. Growth in these loans (with original maturities of 25 to 30 years) and construction loans (with typical original maturities from 18 months to 3 years) coincide with major construction in the United States during the post–World War II years.

Also after 1946, commercial banks sought to further diversify their loan portfolios with consumer installment loans. Expanding branch networks helped reach ultimate consumers. Establishing relationships with appliance and automobile dealers also helped. In dealer relationships, banks purchased loans or "paper" from the dealers after consumers had made their purchases of these durable, high-ticket items. Generally, the bank withheld a small percentage of the price paid for the paper as a reserve against future default. Once the consumer paid the loan in full, the reserve was released to the dealer.

Banks also began to provide inventory financing directly to durable-good dealers. Through "floor planning," manufacturer's invoices for durable goods were paid by the bank, with the loans being repaid when consumers purchased the items. Credit cards are another avenue through which banks have expanded loans to consumers and businesses.

These and other loan products have helped commercial banks diversify and, at the same time, improve the rate of return on their asset portfolios. Regulators also recognize the benefits of diversification and have established guidelines to prevent undue concentration in the loan portfolio.

Regulation of Loan Concentration

The United States Regulators examine bank loan portfolios to spot excessive concentration of *long-term loans.* While commercial banks are not precluded from making loans for 15 to 30 years, if a substantial share of the portfolio is devoted to long-term loans, the bank may be effectively taking equity positions with client firms. Such positions are, of course, to be avoided since banks *are prohibited* from holding nonfinancial corporate stock. This is particularly true if the client is not well capitalized.

An excessive amount of long-term loans that have a *fixed rate of interest* can also expose the bank to risk if interest rates increase. Deposits are short-term liabilities that can quickly reflect a higher level of interest rates. If the bank holds large quantities of long-term, fixed-rate loans, interest expense on deposits can increase much faster than interest income on loans and put considerable strain on bank profitability.

While there is no established maximum percentage of long-term, fixed-rate loans that a bank may hold, concentration in terms of a *single borrower* is more explicitly regulated. If a bank devotes too much of its resources to one borrower, the solvency of the bank itself can depend on the financial circumstances of that client. The concept of single borrower is extended to direct and indirect obligations of the borrower. Indirect obligations include those of a partnership in which the client has ownership interest and those for which the client is an endorser or guarantor for another party. In the case of corporate clients, obligations include those of both parent and subsidiaries.

National banks in the United States may not lend more than 15 percent of capital to any single borrower that is not completely collateralized. If the loan is completely collateralized by readily marketable assets, the limit is 25 percent of capital (an additional 10 percent). State banks are also subject to single-borrower limits, but these limits vary from one state to another. There are also legal guidelines on loan concentrations to single borrowers outside the United States.

Selected Countries in the OECD Exhibit 14-3 shows restrictions on loan concentration in several member countries of the OECD. Most of the guidelines are set in terms of capital, as is true in the United States. However, the percentages vary. In Austria, France, Germany, and Italy, there are specific limits on "large loans." In Austria, France,

EXHIBIT 14-3 REGULATORY GUIDELINES CONCERNING LOAN CONCENTRATION FOR SELECTED COUNTRIES

Country	Description	Regulatory Guideline
Austria	Large-scale loans (>15% of capital)	800% of capital
	Single borrower	50% of capital
Belgium	Single borrower	50% of capital
Canada	Single borrower	25% of capital
Denmark	Single borrower	35% of capital
Finland	Single borrower	—*
France	Large loans (>25% of capital)	800% of capital
	Single borrower	50% of capital
Germany	Each large loan (>15% of capital)	50% of capital
	All large loans	800% of capital
Greece	Single borrower	20% of capital
Italy	Large loans (>20% of capital)	40% of deposits
Japan	Single borrower	20% of capital
Luxembourg	Single customer	30% of capital
Netherlands	Single customer	25% of capital
Norway	Single borrower	50% of capital
Portugal	Single borrower	10% of capital plus 1% of local currency deposits
Spain	Single borrower	—†
Sweden	Single borrower	—‡
Switzerland	Single borrower—secured loan	40% of capital
	Single borrower—unsecured loan	20% of capital
United Kingdom	Single borrower	25% of capital
United States	Single borrower—not fully secured	15% of capital
	Single borrower—fully secured by readily marketable collateral	25% of capital

* Bank may not lend such amount that may endanger the solvency of the bank.

† Exposure to a single borrower is controlled through the coverage ratio of capital to loan balances (one of several such ratios prescribed by regulators). As the exposure increases, the required coverage ratio also increases. Exposure is measured by the ratio of single-borrower exposure to total assets.

Exposure to Total Assets, %	Required Coverage Ratio, %
<1.25	6
1.25–2.5	12
2.5–5.0	18
over 5.0	24

‡ Bank may not lend to the extent of endangering the financial situation of the bank.

Note: Single borrower includes affiliated groups or borrowers linked through equity holdings.

Source: Pecchioli, R. M., *Prudential Supervision in Banking,* Organisation for Economic Co-operation and Development, 1987.

and Germany, all large loans may not exceed 800 percent of capital. In Italy, these loans may not exceed 40 percent of deposits. Austria and France also limit any loans to a single borrower (including affiliates) to 50 percent of capital.

No explicit guidelines exist in Finland and Sweden, but concentration levels are monitored by regulators. In Spain undue concentration is discouraged by requiring higher and higher amounts of capital to offset the risk that such concentration adds to the bank.

These regulations underscore a universally recognized principle borrowed from financial theory. Diversification is an essential element for sound loan portfolio management.

Trends in Loan Portfolio Composition

The diversification noted above and generalized profit pressures have had significant impact on U.S. loan portfolios. Exhibit 14-4 shows some of these changes. Notice that loans have grown from 56 percent of bank financial assets in 1964 to about 62 percent in 1991. *Business loans* have increased somewhat with the most significant growth in noncorporate business loans from about 2 to 4 percent. For the industry as a whole, business loans were 21 percent of 1991 financial assets.

The largest increase, however, is due to *mortgage loans.* Home, multifamily, and commercial loans have all shown significant increases in their proportions of bank assets. The farm mortgage percentage has essentially been stable over the 27-year period. In 1964, mortgage loans were only 14 percent of financial assets, 6 percent less than business loans. By 1991, mortgages encompassed almost 5 percent more of financial assets than business loans. This increased exposure has led to loan losses (particularly in the northeast section of the country) because of an oversupply of housing and commercial real estate. The oversupply hampers the efforts of bank customers to sell or lease the projects involved and makes repayment less likely.

Household and *consumer* loans are the third-largest category of bank loans and have consistently represented about 14 percent of financial assets over the period shown. *For-*

EXHIBIT 14-4 U.S. BANK LOANS, 1964–1991

	1964	1969	1974	1979	1984	1989	1991
Financial assets (billions)	$311.5	$471.6	$836.4	$1355.9	$2105.8	$2954.4	$3344.7
Loans as a % of financial assets:							
Business							
Corporate	16.1%	20.9%	19.1%	15.1%	16.7%	16.0%	16.1%
Noncorporate, nonfarm	1.9	2.6	4.3	5.4	5.9	5.8	3.9
Farm	2.3	2.2	2.2	2.3	1.9	1.0	1.0
	20.3	25.7	25.6	22.8	24.5	22.8	21.0
Foreign	2.1	1.3	2.1	3.9	1.5	.7	.6
Financial institutions	3.2	2.4	3.8	2.0	1.4	1.1	1.0
Mortgages							
Home	8.7	8.8	8.9	11.0	9.3	10.7	13.9
Multifamily	.5	.7	.9	.8	1.0	1.2	1.2
Commercial	4.0	4.7	5.2	5.6	7.3	10.8	10.1
Farm	.8	.8	.7	.6	.5	.6	.5
	14.0	15.0	15.7	18.0	18.1	23.3	25.7
Household and consumer	13.7	14.8	14.2	15.4	13.9	14.0	12.4
Security credit	3.0	2.4	1.6	1.5	1.7	1.4	1.1
	56.3	61.6	63.0	63.6	61.1	63.3	61.8

Source: Board of Governors of the Federal Reserve System, *Flow of Funds Accounts, Financial Assets and Liabilities,* various issues.

eign loans, loans to financial institutions, and *loans to finance securities* complete bank loan portfolios, usually making up 10 percent or less.

In terms of the share of credit made available through commercial banks, there has been a decided change over this period. Less business finance but more mortgage finance now originates in commercial banks.

Commercial Bank Market Shares

Exhibit 14-5 helps illustrate the trend of more direct financing by U.S. businesses. While bank loans to nonfarm business more than doubled from $277 billion in 1979 to $669 billion in 1991, the share of total business financial liabilities dropped from 17 to 14 percent. Commercial paper and long-term debt instruments have become much more important sources of finance for corporations.

But what has been lost in the business sector has been gained in the mortgage market. In 1979 bank mortgage loans amounted to $244 billion, or 18.5 percent of all mortgages as shown in Exhibit 14-6. By 1991, commercial bank mortgages loans were $859 billion, or 22.1 percent of all mortgages outstanding. Within the general category, multifamily and commercial mortgages have grown even faster. In 1979 banks held 23.5 percent of this subset, by 1991 35.5 percent.

In the consumer sector, as Exhibit 14-7 shows, the share has been more consistent. Commercial banks provided 52.8 percent of all consumer credit in 1979 and 47.4 percent by 1991.

Banks are important providers of finance in all three markets. A substantial amount of consumer credit is through commercial banks. Mortgage lending continues to be a growth sector. Business loans show much less promise for growth in future commercial lending.

Characteristics of Bank Loans

Loans may be classified in a number of ways, one of which is *maturity*. Business loans are often short-term loans, that is, 1 year or less in original maturity. However, long-term,

EXHIBIT 14-5 COMMERCIAL BANK LOANS AS A PERCENTAGE OF BUSINESS LIABILITIES, 1964–1991

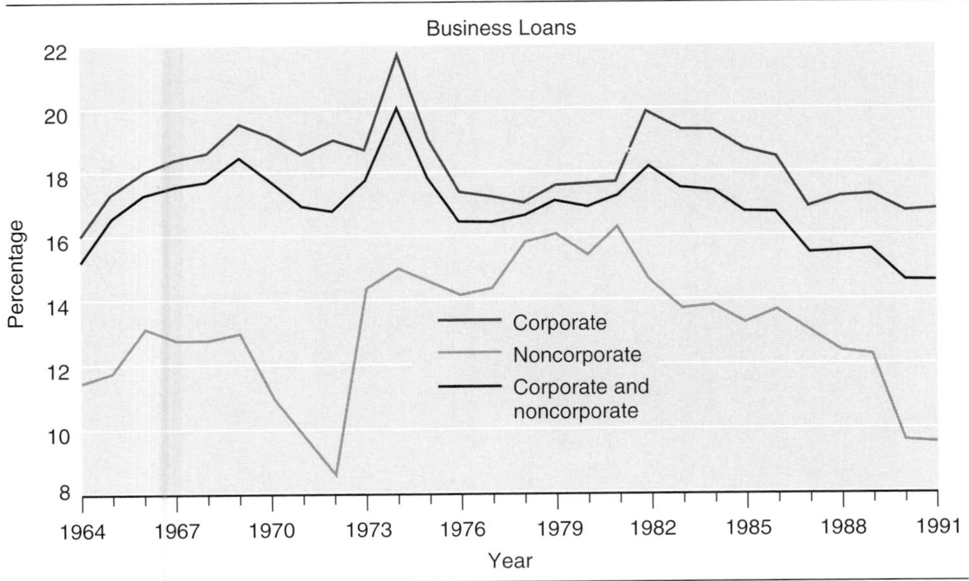

Source: Data from Board of Governors of the Federal Reserve System, *Flow of Funds Accounts, Financial Assets and Liabilities,* various issues.

EXHIBIT 14-6 COMMERCIAL BANK SHARE OF MORTGAGE LOANS, 1964–1991

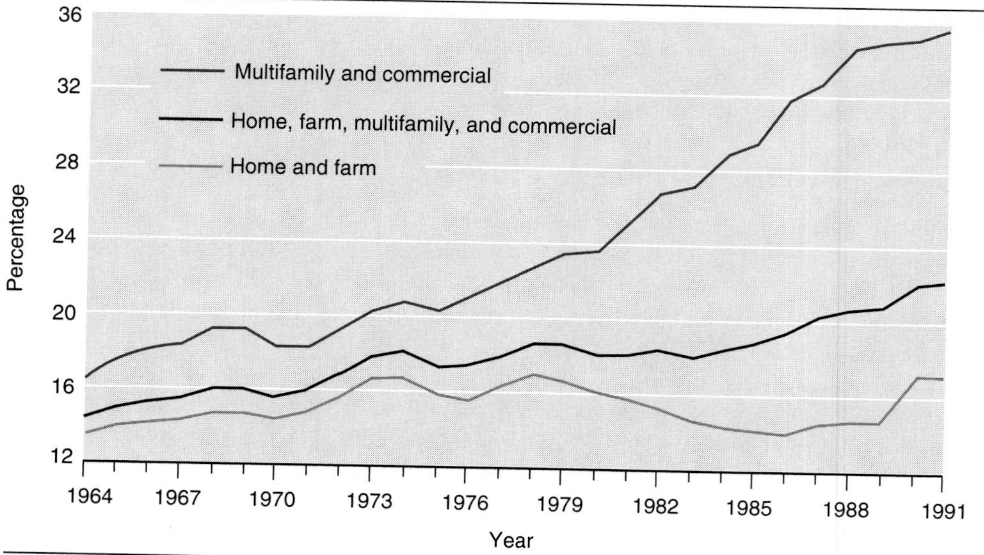

Source: Data from Board of Governors of the Federal Reserve System, *Flow of Funds Accounts, Financial Assets and Liabilities,* various issues.

or "term," loans are now a significant portion of commercial bank portfolios. The collateral, if any, that secures the loan determines whether the loan is a *secured* or an *unsecured loan.* In the event that a borrower fails to repay a secured loan, the lending institution may seize the collateral as partial (or complete) satisfaction of the unpaid balance. If there is no collateral, the loan is unsecured.

Commercial Loans Businesses require *working capital loans* in order to sustain themselves through their *operating cycles.*

EXHIBIT 14-7 COMMERCIAL BANK LOANS AS A PERCENTAGE OF CONSUMER CREDIT, 1964–1991

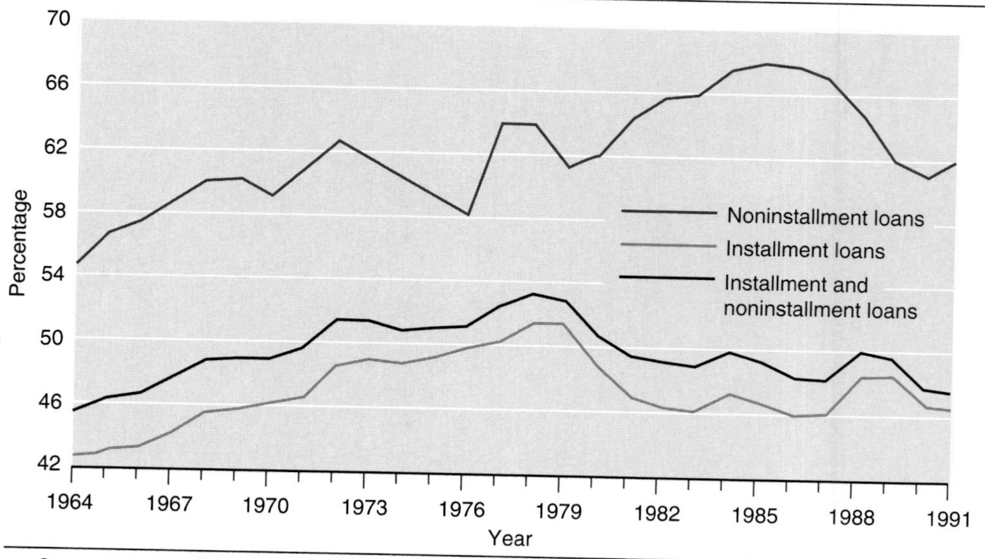

Source: Data from Board of Governors of the Federal Reserve System, *Flow of Funds Accounts, Financial Assets and Liabilities,* various issues.

Operating cycle:
The length of time that it takes for a firm to produce its final product, sell to its customers, and collect proceeds of the sale in cash.

Inventory is necessary either to manufacture a final product or to stock wholesale goods for subsequent retail sales. To the extent that the business enterprise extends credit to its own customers, more time will elapse between the sale and actual cash collection. The enterprise may obtain trade credit from its vendors, but trade credit may not be available for any more than 30 days. The difference between the level of current assets (cash, accounts receivable, and inventory) and current liabilities (accounts payable and other accruals) is *net working capital.*

If net working capital is fairly consistent over the course of a year, there is a permanent working capital need. This may be financed with long-term funds. However, if there are major seasonal fluctuations, there is also a fluctuating portion of working capital that is more appropriately financed with short-term loans.

These seasonal working capital loans are repaid from the proceeds of sales and/or accounts receivable collections. While banks may require that their commercial customers secure the seasonal loans with inventory or accounts receivable, collateral is often not required because risk is relatively low.

A working capital loan may be offered as a *line of credit.* Typically, the bank and its customer agree on the terms of the line of credit once each year. They mutually agree upon the maximum amount of credit that will be available, the interest rate, and the *commitment fee.*

Line of credit:
A preapproved credit facility (usually for 1 year), enabling a bank customer to borrow up to the specified maximum amount at any time during the relevant period of time.

Commitment fee:
The rate charged to a bank customer for the unused portion of a line of credit.

Interest is charged only on actual borrowings. The commitment fee (usually less than 1 percent per annum) is charged on the part of the credit line that the client does not use. In addition, the bank will commonly require its customer to reduce borrowings to zero at least once a year in order to verify seasonality of the financing need.

A *standby letter of credit* is not intended for seasonal working capital. A standby letter of credit is used only as a form of guarantee to back up another obligation of the client. It may be used by a customer who issues commercial paper. The line of credit is an added assurance that the bank customer can redeem its commercial paper when it matures.

An *asset-based loan* is any loan that is secured by assets of the client that are directly related to loan repayment. For example, a short-term loan based on accounts receivable will be repaid from collections of receivables. The actual amount of such a loan will vary from 50 to 80 percent of the face value of the receivables. Loans for leveraged buyouts are asset-based loans to investors who intend to purchase a firm that may hold undervalued assets. Once the firm has been purchased, some of the undervalued assets are sold at prices closer to true value and the proceeds are used to repay the loan.

Term loans extend beyond 1 year. *Revolving lines of credit* may extend beyond 1 year and are, as such, a combination of working capital and term loans. The more strict interpretation of a term loan involves repayment over a period of years. The purpose of the loan may be acquisition of plant or equipment, in which case funds are advanced in full, right away. If the need is related to a higher anticipated requirement for permanent working capital, funds may be advanced as needed. In either case, however, the bank looks to its customer's future profitability for loan repayment, not specific assets or liquidity levels.

Real Estate Loans Many *commercial real estate loans* are construction loans, used to complete development of commercial real estate. Upon completion, the project is funded by permanent financing. If the project is an office building or a retail facility, an adequate number of tenants is critical to its success. If the project is a development of residential units, ultimate sales are the key. The bank faces maximum exposure to loan loss when the real estate developer has not preleased or presold the project and there is no commitment for permanent financing.

Residential mortgages are loans made to individuals and families for primary or secondary residences. The viability of these loans is based on a different set of criteria from commercial real estate loans. The key factors are property appraisals, down payment, and income and other indebtedness of the borrowers. Residential mortgages commonly have original maturities of 25 to 30 years. However, because of resale, the effective maturity is closer to 7 years on average.

Home equity loans are in addition to the first mortgage on a residence. A home equity loan maybe a second mortgage or a revolving line of credit. During the 1980s, these loans became popular because of rapidly appreciating residential property values. In this environment home equity, the difference between market value and mortgage balance, grew rather quickly. In addition, the Tax Reform Act of 1986 marked the beginning of a phase-out of tax deductibility of interest on consumer debt. By 1991, only interest on first mortgages and home equity loans could be deducted from taxable income. Banks have successfully promoted home equity lines of credit as a result. To protect itself from downturns in the real estate market, a bank will lend only 50 to 70 percent of equity. Other factors such as general indebtedness and income are also considered.

Consumer Loans Consumer loans are of particular importance to smaller banks, some of which have consumer portfolios that are larger than their commercial portfolios. Individuals obtain these loans for a number of reasons, including durable-good purchases, vacations, medical expenses, and education. The three major classifications are installment loans, credit cards, and noninstallment loans.

Installment loans are the largest overall category of consumer credit. Typically, the borrower makes monthly payments of interest and principal until the balance is repaid. *Unsecured installment loans* are usually in smaller denominations than secured installment loans. Because of the relatively small size of these loans, the interest earned is often not sufficient to offset the administrative cost and still provide the bank a reasonable profit. Credit cards and revolving lines of credit have become more cost-effective alternatives from the bank's point of view.

Consumers obtain *direct secured installment loans* from their banks, primarily to purchase automobiles. Other types of collateral include mobile homes, recreational vehicles, boats, large appliances, and financial assets. These loans mature in 4 to 7 years.

Indirect secured installment loans are generated through dealers (retailers). The consumer completes a credit application, which the dealer sends to the bank for processing. Upon approval, the bank notifies the dealer who, in turn, prepares the relevant loan documents, completes the transaction with the purchaser, and forwards the completed package to the bank. When the bank receives the loan package, the dealer's deposit account is credited and a loan account is established for the purchaser. In addition, if the bank has provided the dealer with floor planning (inventory financing), wholesale cost of the durable good and accrued interest are deducted from the dealer's account.

Credit cards offer consumers predetermined maximum amounts of credit. MasterCard and Visa are the most widely held versions. Service and payment processing are centralized to afford operational efficiency. Participating banks pay annual fees to the credit card network based upon the number of their active accounts. Banks earn revenues both from their cardholders and from the establishments that accept the cards. Cardholders pay an annual fee and interest on unpaid balances. Vendors that accept the cards receive from 2 to 5 percent less than the face value of the transaction. This percentage off face value represents a discount on the draft, or signed transaction document. The greatest source of credit card income to banks is interest on unpaid balances.

Overdraft lines of credit are facilities that enable bank customers to write checks for amounts in excess of their transactions account balance. The amount of the overdraft is, of course, a loan. This facility may be connected with the consumer's credit card account.

Single-payment loans are the smallest category of consumer loans. Customers request these loans for short periods of time, often until another financial transaction occurs. For example, a customer may need a loan until a certificate of deposit matures or may need the down payment for a new home until the current home is sold. From the bank's perspective, the most important consideration is verification of the source of future cash flow for loan repayment.

Credit Analysis

The evaluation of a prospective borrower's loan request for credit risk is crucial to maintain the soundness of the loan portfolio. The criteria for this analysis are frequently referred to as the "three C's" of credit: character, capacity, and collateral.

Assessing the borrower's *character* includes an evaluation of past performance. If the request is for a commercial loan, managerial experience and proficiency are important. If it is a consumer loan request, payment history and other accounts should be examined. In a sense, evaluation of character is an evaluation of *willingness* to repay the loan.

Capacity is a measure of *ability* to repay. For business loans, capacity will depend upon the type of loan. As noted above, short-term loans are repaid from liquidity, long-term loans from profits. Ratio analysis of a firm's financial statements is often helpful to arrive at succinct descriptive variables of the firm's financial position. Comparisons of these data to industry statistics can help highlight any major deviations from industry norms for further investigation. In addition, any present or anticipated conditions that may have a significant impact on future cash flows should also be a part of the analysis.

Consumer credit decisions can usually be made in a more objective way. A consumer's income relative to existing debt is, perhaps, the best measure of capacity. If the bank analyzes the profile of its individual customers over time, the characteristics that have been associated with timely loan repayment will help the bank identify the best potential customers in the future. This process is called *credit scoring.*

Collateral is of particular importance for asset-based loans, since loan repayment is directly tied to the asset's cash flow potential. The bank should obtain every reasonable assurance that the collateral is adequate. For other types of loans, the bank should attempt to anticipate fluctuations in market value of the securing property so that the loan does not become seriously undercollateralized. For example, an automobile loan whose unpaid balance declines at a slower rate than the value of the auto can leave the loan undersecured. In addition, the borrower then owes a loan balance that exceeds the value of the property, providing him or her with a disincentive to repay the obligation.

Of course, general economic conditions will have an impact on credit analysis. In strong economies, corporations are better able to service debt because sales volume is more predictable. Individuals are less likely to have their employment interrupted and, therefore, better able to repay loans. In expanding economies, relatively strong demand for real estate will support the value of property that is used as loan collateral.

Loan Pricing

Banks may offer loans at either *fixed* or *variable* rates of interest. A fixed-rate loan removes uncertainty for the borrower, particularly with respect to commercial term loans and residential mortgage loans. Should interest rates increase, the borrower's debt-servicing cash flow is unaffected. However, the lending institution sustains an opportunity cost because it is unable to reinvest at the higher rates. At the same time, for competitive reasons, banks permit more timely adjustments of deposit interest rates. These conditions can have significant adverse implications for bank profitability.

Variable-rate loans relieve this pressure for lending institutions. Still, the pressure is not eliminated; it is simply shifted to the borrower. As a result, borrowers are willing to pay a higher interest rate for fixed-rate loans than for their variable-rate counterparts, particularly if interest rates are expected to increase.

In terms of consumer loans, only residential mortgages have been issued in significant numbers with variable rates attached. The differential between variable and fixed rates may be as much as 3 percent. Interest rate caps for variable-rate loans are commonly established to limit both the amount of rate increase for a given *year* and over the *term* of the mortgage. The rate itself is tied to either a quoted interest rate or the bank's average cost of funds.

Floating-rate commercial loans are more common than consumer variable-rate loans. Further, many that are technically fixed are of a short enough term so as to expose the bank to minimal interest rate risk. The bank's CD rate or average cost of funds serves as a base rate. Alternatively, the London Interbank Offer Rate (LIBOR) can be the base. The contractual (loan) rate equals the base rate plus 2 percent or less.

Pricing a specific loan requires consideration of the cost of debt funds, default risk and term premiums (for fixed-rate, long-term loans), and expected administrative expense. The cost of funds is the marginal or incremental cost of borrowing rather than the historical cost. To illustrate, consider First National Bank once again. According to Exhibit 13-6, 60 percent of average assets were financed with interest-bearing deposits, 20 percent borrowed funds, 11 percent demand deposits, 2 percent other liabilities, and 7 percent equity.

Assume that these *proportions* will be constant in the future but that the *cost* of interest-bearing deposits will increase to 7.25 percent (from the current 7.04 percent) and that the *cost* of borrowed funds will increase to 7.85 percent (from 7.78 percent). Note that demand deposits and other liabilities have no explicit cost associated with them.[7] If the target return on equity at 17.5 percent (up from 16.3 percent), the weighted cost of debt funds is expected to be 7.15 percent [(.60)(.0725) + (.20)(.0785) + (.07)(.175)]. If default risk and term premiums are 1 percent each and administrative expense is expected to be .5 percent of the loan amount, the loan is appropriately priced at 9.65 percent.

In general,

$$k_L = \left(\sum_{i=1}^{n} w_i r_i \right) + \text{DRP} + \text{TP} + A \qquad (12)$$

where k_L = loan rate

$\sum_{i=1}^{n} w_i r_i$ = cost of interest-sensitive liabilities (debt-funds)

DRP = default risk premium

TP = term premium

A = administrative expense

[7] Technically, required reserves impose an implicit cost on transactions accounts and short-term nonpersonal time deposits. The opportunity cost is the reserve requirement percentage multiplied by the earning rate that is forgone.

Alternatively, compensating balances may be required in connection with a lower stated rate. For example, suppose that First National wishes to earn an effective rate of 9.65 percent while quoting an 8.65 percent loan rate. The compensating balance that is required causes 8.65 percent of the gross loan to equal 9.65 percent of the net funds.

$$k_L = k_E (1 - x) \tag{13}$$

where k_E = loan rate
x = compensating balance of gross loan

where k_E is the effective rate of the loan and x is the compensating balance as a percentage of the gross loan. Substituting the specifics of our example, $x = .1036$, that is, a 10.36 percent compensating balance will bring the effective rate to 9.65 percent. Intuitively, if a bank client pays 8.65 percent of the loan amount as interest but can actually use only 89.64 percent of the loan $(1 - .1036)$, the effective interest rate is 9.65 percent.

Whatever approach is taken, it is important to consider all relevant factors. Not only are cost considerations crucial, but competitive factors play a role in the loan-pricing decision. A bank must offer its client a package that meets his or her needs for efficient service and, at the same time, provides bank depositors and investors a reasonable rate of return. Otherwise, bank customers may elect the alternatives to commercial bank services, such as commercial paper, that are increasingly available.

OBSERVED COMBINATIONS OF SECURITIES AND LOANS IN THE OECD

As can be observed from Exhibit 14-8, the banks of a number of other countries hold loan portfolios in proportions roughly comparable to those of the United States. Canadian banks hold an even higher concentration of loans than U.S. banks while maintaining a smaller aggregate investment portfolio.

Banks of Japan, Germany, and the United Kingdom hold smaller investment portfo-

EXHIBIT 14-8 SECURITIES AND LOANS AS A PERCENTAGE OF TOTAL ASSETS FOR SELECTED COUNTRIES, 1989

Country	Institutions	Securities, %	Loans, %
Austria	Large banks	12.19	48.04
Belgium	Banks	23.34	28.54
Canada	Domestic banks	10.15	77.00
Denmark	Banks & savings banks	21.71	43.09
Finland	Commercial banks	14.79	62.81
France	Large banks	3.98	39.77
Germany	Commercial banks	11.66	58.33
Greece	Large commercial banks	43.26	33.33
Italy	All banks	13.15	32.11
Japan	All ordinary banks	13.29	53.70
Luxembourg	Banks	7.28	23.86
Netherlands	Banks	8.75	56.49
Norway	Commercial banks	12.89	75.40
Portugal	Banks	15.00	37.39
Spain	Commercial banks	19.57	46.02
Sweden	Commercial banks	11.72	50.80
Switzerland*	Large banks	12.14	47.74
United Kingdom	Commercial banks	6.44	60.81
United States	Insured commercial banks	18.22	65.23

*Data from 1987.
Source: Organisation for Economic Co-operation and Development, *Bank Profitability, Statistical Supplement, Financial Statements of Banks,* 1981–1989.

lios. Recall from Exhibit 13-9, however, that the banks in these countries held larger proportions of liquid assets, particularly interbank deposits. Also, banks of Austria, Belgium, and Luxembourg invest much smaller percentages of assets in securities and loans. This is again indicative of the wholesale nature of banking in these countries.

Exhibit 14-9 shows gross interest income for these countries in 1989. Notice that the returns in Japan and Germany are lower than in the United States. This is due primarily to lower interest rate levels in these countries during the year analyzed. On the other hand, higher interest rate environments in other countries are reflected in the gross earnings of their commercial banks. These rates are also measures of the cost of obtaining loans in the respective countries. It should be remembered that as nonfinancial U.S. firms compete with Japanese and German firms in world export markets, the cost of bank loans historically has been lower, perhaps giving these firms a competitive advantage. At a minimum, this rate differential encourages U.S. firms to look for alternatives to traditional bank financing.

SUMMARY

Securities and loan portfolios represent as much as 80 percent of bank assets in the United States. Management of these portfolios is interrelated. Strong loan demand may necessitate partial liquidation of securities portfolios in order to generate required liquidity. Generally, the share of bank assets represented by investment securities has declined, as commercial banks have focused more on higher-yielding loans. More competitive, interest-sensitive liabilities have escalated banks' costs of funds. Larger loan portfolios are a natural consequence.

Management of investment securities should incorporate considerations of both liquidity and profitability. When the yield curve slopes upward, long-term, fixed-income securities provide the highest yields but also expose a portfolio to maximum price volatility. Laddered and barbell approaches to securities management afford both liquidity and high-yield potential.

The optimal mix of taxable and tax-exempt bonds will depend on available rates, tax

EXHIBIT 14-9 GROSS INTEREST INCOME AS A PERCENTAGE OF TOTAL ASSETS FOR SELECTED COUNTRIES, 1989

Country	Institutions	%
Austria	Large banks	8.03
Belgium	Banks	9.90
Canada	Domestic banks	11.29
Denmark	Banks & savings banks	8.59
Finland	Commercial banks	9.60
France	Large banks	8.49
Germany	Commercial banks	7.08
Greece	Large commercial banks	13.22
Italy	All banks	8.49
Japan	All ordinary banks	5.53
Luxembourg	Banks	9.00
Norway	Commercial banks	12.10
Portugal	Banks	12.31
Spain	Commercial banks	11.01
Sweden	Commercial banks	9.85
Switzerland*	Large banks	5.00
United Kingdom	Commercial banks	12.36
United States	Insured commercial banks	9.87

*Data from 1987.

Source: Organisation for Economic Co-operation and Development, *Bank Profitability, Statistical Supplement, Financial Statements of Banks,* 1981–1989.

structure, and the financial position of the bank. Legislation in the 1980s placed restrictions on both interest income exclusions and interest expense deductions associated with municipal bond investments, reducing the opportunities for tax sheltering. As long as a bank realizes net *income* from non-securities-related operations, the form of security that offers the highest after-tax yield is preferable. When a bank has a net *loss* from non-securities-related operations, management should invest in higher-yielding taxable bonds in sufficient quantity to realize full deductibility of the net expenses.

Loan portfolio management continues to evolve as the portfolio itself becomes more diversified. Short-term commercial loans, once the mainstay of banking, are now offered along with more long-term facilities. The latter loans finance both increases in permanent working capital and fixed-asset acquisitions. In consumer lending, credit cards and revolving lines of credit are commonly offered in addition to installment loans. Real estate loans have today become as important to the bank portfolio as traditional commercial loans.

Each of these areas requires different forms of analysis for successful management. However, considerations of character, capacity, and collateral of respective borrowers continue to be basic principles of effective loan portfolio management.

KEY TERMS

asset-based loan
barbell maturity approach
capital gains yield
collateral
commercial loans
commitment fee
credit cards
current yield
home equity loans
implied tax rate
indifference tax rate
installment loan
interest rate risk
laddered maturity approach
line of credit
operating cycle
passive management
price risk
real estate loans
reinvestment risk
taxable-equivalent yield

END-OF-CHAPTER QUESTIONS

1. What are the major categories in bank investment securities portfolios? Are these securities held primarily to provide the bank with liquidity?
2. What are the two components of return attributable to security investments?
3. a. Describe interest rate risk.
b. Differentiate price risk from reinvestment risk.
4. Management of the securities portfolio is somewhat simplified by easily determined market values of the instruments. Why do you think that the market value of loans is more difficult to determine?
5. Differentiate the laddered approach of securities management from the barbell approach.
6. Describe a line of credit. How does it differ from a standby line of credit?
7. What are the primary components of credit analysis?
8. Name five factors that have contributed to the changing composition of U.S. bank asset portfolios.

END-OF-CHAPTER PROBLEMS

1. At the beginning of the year, assume that bond A has a 10 percent coupon rate, paid annually, matures in 4 years, and has a required return of 10 percent. Assume also that bond B has the same coupon rate, paid annually, but matures in 20 years, and has a required return of 11 percent. If, during the year, all interest rates increase by 1 percent, what will be the total returns realized by holders of bonds A and B?

2. Suppose that a bank may invest in either qualified municipal bonds that pay 7.5 percent interest or taxable bonds that pay 11 percent interest. Suppose further that the marginal tax rate and cost of funds are 34 and 8 percent, respectively. Which bonds provide the higher after-tax yield?
3. Recompute the appropriate loan rate for the example presented in the section "Loan Pricing," assuming a funding mix of 40 percent interest-bearing deposits and borrowed funds each.
4. Referring to problem 4, what general guidelines for the mix of taxable and tax-exempt securities would you recommend?
5. Suppose that bank management priced a loan at 11.5 percent but also required a 15 percent compensating balance. What would be the effective interest rate?
6. One of the investment alternatives available to your bank is a 6.5 percent municipal bond that qualifies for the 80 percent interest expense deduction. Another option is a 7.8 percent municipal bond that does not qualify. If the cost of funds is 8.2 percent and the marginal tax rate is 34 percent, which would you recommend?
7. Referring to problem 6, what statutory tax rate would make you indifferent between these two municipal bonds?

SELECTED REFERENCES

Board of Governors of the Federal Reserve System. *Flow of Funds Accounts, Financial Assets and Liabilities,* various issues.

Cherin, Antony C., and Ronald W. Melicher. "Branch Banking and Loan Portfolio Risk Relationships," *Review of Business and Economic Research,* vol. 22, no. 2 (Spring 1987), pp. 1–13.

Ford, John K., and Thomas O. Stanley. "An Objective Technique for Loan Officer Evaluation," *International Journal of Bank Marketing,* vol. 6, no. 1 (1988), pp. 49–54.

Johnson, Frank P., and Richard D. Johnson. *Commercial Bank Management,* Dryden Press, Hinsdale, Illinois, 1985.

Koch, Timothy W. *Bank Management,* Dryden Press, Hinsdale, Illinois, 1988.

Laderman, Elizabeth A., Ronald H. Schmidt, and Gary C. Zimmerman. "Location, Branching, and Bank Portfolio Diversification: The Case of Agricultural Lending," *Federal Reserve Bank of San Francisco Economic Review,* issue 1 (Winter 1991), pp. 24–38.

Wilson, J. S. G. *Banking Policy and Structure; A Comparative Analysis,* Croom Helm Ltd., London, 1986.

CHAPTER 15

BANK CAPITAL AND ASSET-LIABILITY MANAGEMENT

CHAPTER OUTLINE

BANK CAPITAL
- Equity Capital
- Nonequity Capital
  - Allowance for loan loss, subordinated notes and debentures
- The Need for Bank Capital
- Regulation of Bank Capital
  - United States, international coordination
- Capital Ratios in the United States
- Capital Management outside the United States
  - Capital ratios in the OECD, income effects

ASSET-LIABILITY MIX AND GAP
- Interest Rate Sensitivity
- Gap
  - Gap and Gap ratio, Security Bank, First National Bank
- Gap Applications
- Gap Strategies

INTEREST RATE RISK AND BANK CAPITAL
- Interest Rate Changes and Net Worth
- Duration
- Duration and Net Worth

HEDGING BANK PORTFOLIOS
- Interest Rate Futures
- Options on Futures Contracts
- Interest Rate Swaps

MARKET VALUE ACCOUNTING

INTERNATIONAL COMPARISONS:
- Austria
- Belgium
- Canada
- Denmark
- Finland
- France
- Germany
- Greece
- Italy
- Japan
- Luxembourg
- Netherlands
- Norway
- Portugal
- Spain
- Sweden
- Switzerland
- United Kingdom

CHAPTER OVERVIEW

This chapter:

- Describes bank capital
- Examines the need for bank capital
- Highlights international coordination of capital standards
- Explores the impact of interest rate risk on bank assets, liabilities, and capital

- Illustrates gap and duration analysis
- Describes the use of interest rate futures, options on futures, and swaps to reduce interest rate risk
- Discusses market value accounting

The challenge to bank management is to maximize shareholder wealth while maintaining solvency and adequate liquidity. As illustrated in Chapters 14 and 15, bank profitability is closely linked to the composition of the balance sheet. A major challenge to bank regulators is to encourage both profitability and soundness. The proper management of bank capital is central to all these objectives, but a philosophical tug-of-war often results when bank managers and regulators address the issue of the "right" level of capital. If the level is too high, the resulting cost of funds can put the bank at a competitive disadvantage. If the level is too low, the bank will be in danger of insolvency.

The right level of bank capital is a difficult issue at the domestic level. It is even more complicated at the international level. Nevertheless, the central bankers of the industrialized West have designed a uniform set of capital standards to help place banks in international circles to compete on a more level playing field.

Volatile interest rates can threaten a bank's capital base. Equity is the difference between assets and liabilities, that is, net assets. Whenever the market value of assets and/or liabilities changes, the market value of equity also changes. The proper combination of rate-sensitive assets and rate-sensitive liabilities can help shield the bank from this risk. Yet it is not necessarily easy to achieve this balance by merely accepting deposits and making loans. Derivative securities, such as interest rate futures, options, and swaps, can be useful in protecting bank equity from the adverse effects of interest rate volatility.[1]

BANK CAPITAL

Capital includes preferred and common stock, paid-in surplus, and undivided profits. This is the definition according to generally accepted accounting principles (GAAP). Bank regulators include in the definition of capital other items that are not normally regarded as capital in nonfinancial corporations. This is a major difference between GAAP and regulatory accounting principles (RAP).

Equity Capital

Common stock represents an ownership claim on a commercial bank in proportion to the number of shares held. Common shareholders have residual claims on the bank in that interest and preferred stock dividends are paid before common shareholders receive dividends. The common shareholders are also the last to receive a distribution if the bank is liquidated. Often common stock has a legally specified par value that is established when the stock is authorized. The market value of the stock is determined in secondary stock market trading and is almost always higher than the par value.

Paid-in surplus (or additional paid-in capital) is associated with common stock that has a legal par value. Whenever the bank issues new shares, the surplus account is subject to change. If the stock's market value exceeds its par value, the excess over par is recorded in paid-in surplus.

Undivided profits (or retained earnings) represent accumulated earnings of the bank. Cash and stock dividend payments reduce the balance. *Reserves for contingencies and*

[1]Interest rate changes can have a significant impact on any firm with large portfolios of interest-sensitive financial assets and liabilities. While the discussions in this chapter focus on commercial banks, the principles can be applied to a wide range of financial institutions.

other reserves are amounts of past earnings that have been specifically set aside to meet anticipated future obligations.

The categories noted above are considered *common equity capital. Preferred stock* is another source of equity capital. Preferred stock is a hybrid of common stock and bonds. It is an ownership claim on the bank that entitles its owner to a periodic dividend payment that is fixed or, at least, limited in some way. When the dividend is *not* fixed, it is generally tied to an index, much like a variable-rate liability. Unlike bond interest payments, however, preferred stock dividends are not tax-deductible. The stock itself may be perpetual or have a limited life. It may also be callable or convertible into common stock.

Nonequity Capital

Allowance for Loan Loss According to RAP, the *allowance for loan loss* (or allowance for credit loss) is also considered capital. The allowance is an asset valuation account associated with loans, that is, a contra-asset account. A contra-asset account is one that has a credit balance but is recorded in the asset section with accounts that have a debit balance. The net effect of this arrangement is that the asset balance is lower than it would be otherwise.[2]

Each year (or, in some cases, each month), bank management estimates the amount of loss that should be recorded for the period. This amount is not usually *actual* loss. Instead, it is an amount considered necessary to cover anticipated *future* loss and to maintain an adequate allowance. The amount is recorded as *provision for loan loss* (or provision for credit loss), an expense for the period. The offsetting entry is to allowance for loan loss. For example, suppose that the management of a $500 million bank (total assets) estimates that $10 million is an appropriate provision given current economic conditions and the specific loans in its portfolio. The accounting entry is as follows (in millions of dollars).

	DR	CR
Provision for loan loss	$10	
Allowance for loan loss		$10

The provision reduces income before taxes by $10 million and ultimately reduces capital. The allowance entry reduces the carrying value of loans by the same amount. Ignoring taxes, the size of the bank is reduced to $490 million. An important advantage of the allowance method is that provisions can be structured to smooth the impact on earnings over time. The alternative *direct charge-off* method requires recognition of loss in the amount and the period of actual loan write-off. Application of the direct charge-off method can cause undesirable volatility of reported earnings since actual loan write-offs may not be evenly distributed over time. (Of course, since the provision under the allowance method is subjectively determined, it is possible to conceal actual loan portfolio weakness by understating the provision.)

Under the *allowance method,* when loans are actually written off, the allowance (not operating income) is reduced. For example, if bank management determines that an $8 million loan is uncollectible, the following entry is made (in millions of dollars).

	DR	CR
Allowance for loan loss	$8	
Loans		$8

[2]A common example of a contra-asset account is accumulated depreciation, recorded in the fixed-assets section of the balance sheet. Gross fixed assets *less* accumulated depreciation *equals* net fixed assets.

While the appropriate amount of provision for loan loss is a subjective determination by individual bank management, the aggregate provision for all U.S. commercial banks in recent years has ranged from 1 to 2 percent of total loans. For tax purposes, however, the amount of provision that may be used as a deduction is limited.

Before the Tax Reform Act of 1986, bank management could elect either the reserve (allowance) method or the direct charge-off method. If the reserve method was selected, the Internal Revenue Service permitted a maximum allowance that was directly related to the size of the loan portfolio or to the bank's actual loan loss experience.[3] Commonly, bank managers elected the reserve method based on a maximum percentage of the loan portfolio because this method minimized tax liability. Since provision was deductible, a large provision reduced taxable income and tax liability.

The Tax Reform Act of 1986 restricted the reserve method to those banks with no more than $400 million in assets or those that hold problem loans equal to 75 percent of the loan portfolio. All other banks are required to use the direct charge-off method for tax purposes. This change in the tax law does not prevent a bank from using the reserve method for the shareholders' GAAP-prepared financial statements.

Subordinated Notes and Debentures In addition to the allowance for loan loss, *subordinated notes and debentures* are also considered bank capital for regulatory purposes. Before 1962, regulators did not permit a bank to classify these debt instruments as capital unless the institution was in financial distress. The Comptroller of the Currency allowed the classification for all national banks in 1962. Thereafter, state banking authorities modified state regulations to conform with the change. As noted in Exhibit 13-3, these long-term debt instruments grew from .3 percent of systemwide financial liabilities in 1964 to 3.4 percent in 1991.

The features of subordinated debt make it an attractive source of long-term financing. Unlike stock dividends, interest payments are tax-deductible. To the extent that the rate of return on earning assets exceeds the after-tax interest cost, the difference accrues to equity investors. In other words, subordinated debt provides important leverage effects.

However, the fixed nature of interest payments can present cash flow problems. When interest income slumps, fixed interest payments can adversely affect net income. Any sinking fund requirements (money that must be set aside before the obligations mature) magnify this effect. Any failure to repay interest and/or principal constitutes default and can lead to the bank's liquidation.

In order to *qualify* as bank capital, debt instruments must meet certain criteria. The claim of debt holders must be subordinated to *all* depositors, insured and uninsured. In addition, only debt issues with a weighted average original maturity of 7 years or more qualify, according to regulations of the FDIC and the Comptroller's office.

The Need for Bank Capital

Bank capital serves much the same functions as capital in a nonfinancial firm. It provides a *buffer for temporary operating losses.* Capital absorbs these losses until profitability is restored so that the firm remains *solvent.*

Solvency:
: The financial condition of a bank in which the book value of its assets exceeds the book value of liabilities.

[3]The allowance could not exceed 1.82 percent of eligible loans in 1969. By 1982, the percentage had been reduced to .6 percent. Eligible loans *excluded* federal funds sold, commercial paper, government-guaranteed loans, and loans secured by government securities or deposit balances.

Theoretically, the solvency of a bank should be determined by *market value* of assets and liabilities rather than *book value.* However, the market value of some bank assets, especially loans, is difficult to specify. Bank regulators are studying ways in which more market value accounting can be used, but, in the meantime, it is the book value of equity that determines solvency and that absorbs any operating losses.

The ability of bank capital to absorb operating losses is not, of course, unlimited. Sustained losses will eventually erode the capital base and leave creditors' claims exposed. This will occur when cash inflows from operations (income statement activity) are insufficient to cover cash outflows. Conceptually, under these circumstances, the bank must liquidate assets in order to satisfy the shortfall (excess of expenses over revenues). As assets decline while liabilities do not, the capital base shrinks. If the process continues, asset values decline until liabilities are greater than assets. This function of capital as a cushion is common to all business organizations.

Bank capital also serves other functions. Perceived capital adequacy increases *public confidence* in an institution. If public confidence is maintained, management can avoid unexpectedly high deposit withdrawals (bank runs). On the surface, bank runs may not appear to present a risk of insolvency since, presumably, the value of liquidated assets equals the value of deposits and other liabilities to be satisfied. However, when large quantities of assets must be sold quickly, the bank may realize less than asset-carrying values, that is, sustain losses upon sale. These losses deplete capital just as operating losses do. Since usually no more than 5 to 10 percent of bank assets is financed with capital, liquidating as little as 5 percent of assets below carrying value can bring the bank close to insolvency.

Even if asset liquidation is not necessary, a loss of public confidence can increase the bank's cost of funds. If the increase is significant enough, profitability will be hurt, once again putting pressure on an already thinly capitalized institution. Thus, capital adequacy can help preserve public confidence and avoid either bank runs or high costs of doing business.

From a regulatory perspective, bank capital places *constraints on bank growth.* In this sense, minimum capital requirements prevent unlimited deposit taking and lending (or other investment activities). With a given capital ratio, dividend payout ratio, and rate of return on equity, a bank can expect to grow in the normal course of operating profitably.

$$\Delta\text{TA} = (\text{ROE})(E)(b)(\text{EM}) \tag{1}$$

where ΔTA = change in the asset base for 1 year
ROE = return on equity (net income as a percentage of equity)
E = equity (dollar amount)
b = retention ratio (percentage of net income not paid as dividends)
EM = equity multiplier (total assets to equity)

The expression (ROE) (E)(b) is the change in retained earnings that can be projected. This addition to retained earnings forms a new equity layer that will support asset growth. When the equity multiplier is high (or the capital ratio is low), the bank's asset base can grow relatively faster. All other things being equal, regulators usually prefer to see a lower equity multiplier (higher capital ratio) because of the greater buffer against loss that it implies. Of course, regulators must seriously consider the impact of minimum capital requirements on bank profitability and competitiveness.

Regulation of Bank Capital

United States Until recently, bank regulators established capital guidelines by reference to peer groups. Banks were classified by size, and banks within a given size category were expected to maintain minimum *capital ratios.*

Capital ratio:
Capital as a percentage of bank assets.

In addition to these minimum ratios, regulators established target, or desirable, capital ratios within each size category.

Generally, larger banks maintained lower capital ratios. This disparity was justified by the shorter-term, more commercially oriented loan portfolios of large banks. In addition, larger banks held more diversified (therefore, less risky) loan portfolios. Nevertheless, this system did not prevent significant erosion of bank capital ratios over time. The aggregate ratio of total capital to assets of all insured U.S. banks fell from 12 percent in 1935 to 6.5 percent by 1990.

In 1981, regulators standardized suggested capital ratios for national banks, state-chartered Federal Reserve member banks, and bank holding companies. Three size categories were preserved: multinational banks (assets greater than $15 billion), regional banks (assets between $1 billion and $15 billion), and community banks (assets less than $1 billion). Acceptable capital ratios for community and regional banks were 7 and 6.5 percent, respectively, according to Federal Reserve and Comptroller standards. Ratios below these acceptable levels resulted in closer and more frequent monitoring. The FDIC established similar standards for banks within its jurisdiction (state-chartered, nonmember banks). Multinational banks (seventeen in total) were to be monitored on an individual basis.

In addition, regulators refined capital definitions in 1981, differentiating between primary and secondary capital.

Primary capital is the sum of:

1 Equity capital (common stock, perpetual preferred stock, paid-in surplus, undivided profits, and contingency and other capital reserves)
2 Mandatory convertible instruments (up to 20 percent of other primary capital)
3 Allowance for loan loss
4 Minority interest in subsidiaries

Secondary capital is the sum of:

1 Limited-life preferred stock
2 Mandatory convertible instruments not eligible for primary capital
3 Subordinated notes and debentures (original maturity of at least 7 years, with the maximum amount less than 50 percent of primary capital)

Total capital is the sum of primary and secondary capital.

Through the International Lending Supervision Act of 1983, Congress gave regulatory agencies statutory authority to establish minimum capital levels. The regulators' guidelines were that primary capital could be no less than 5.5 percent of adjusted total assets.[4] Also, total capital could be no less than 6 percent of adjusted total assets. Banks were expected to operate above these minimum levels. At the same time, banks from other countries, notably Japan and Germany, operated with much thinner capital bases, giving them a lower cost of funds and greater growth potential. Shortly after the 1983 legislation, U.S. regulators helped formulate a policy for capital adequacy that would be accepted by all major industrialized countries.

International Coordination The Federal Reserve worked within the OECD to encourage a harmonization of capital policy among the member countries. The objectives of these coordination efforts were:

[4]Adjusted assets are total assets minus the sum of intangible assets, loans with a high probability of nonrepayment, and a small percentage of loans for which payment is at least questionable.

1 To reduce international differences in capital levels that gave some countries competitive advantages
2 To make capital requirements sensitive to the differences in risk profiles of bank balance sheets
3 To take into account the level of off–balance sheet risk exposure
4 To remove any disincentives for holding safe, liquid assets

As a first step, in January 1987, the Federal Reserve and the Bank of England announced an agreement on common standards of capital. Capital would be defined as:

- Equity
- Retained earnings
- Minority interest in subsidiaries
- Perpetual debt

Also, each class of assets would be weighted depending upon riskiness of the category, and contingent liabilities would be included in the calculations.

The Federal Reserve and the Bank of England then attempted to get support for this scheme from other OECD members, especially France, Japan, and Germany. However, Japan and Germany resisted the plan for similar reasons. Japanese banks have significant amounts of land and equity stock recorded on their balance sheets at historical book values that are considerably below market value. Under the U.S.-U.K. plan, these "hidden" reserves could not be used to satisfy capital requirements. Likewise, German banks have large holdings of equity stock that would be considered capital. The Japanese, Germans, and French argued that defining an appropriate capital standard for all banks would be impossible.

In December of the same year, the Cooke Committee (Committee on Banking Regulation and Supervisory Practices of the Bank for International Settlements, also known as the Basel Committee) announced agreement on international convergence of capital standards. This agreement, the *Basel Accord,* addressed concerns of Japan and Germany in two ways. *Capital definitions* included asset revaluation reserves. Within prescribed limits, *risk weights* were left to the discretion of individual countries.

The definition of capital under the Basel Accord is as follows:

Tier I (core) capital:

- Shareholders' equity
- Perpetual preferred stock, net of goodwill

Tier II (supplemental) capital:

- Perpetual and term subordinated debt
- Mandatory convertible debt
- Asset revaluation reserves
- Other supplementary items at the discretion of individual countries

Tier II capital is limited to 100 percent of Tier I capital. According to the accord, beginning January 1993, international banks must maintain both Tier I and Tier II capital equal to 4 percent of risk-weighted assets for a total capital ratio of 8 percent. Germany and Japan are permitted to use 45 percent of unrealized gains on equities held as investments toward the Tier II capital requirement.[5]

Exhibit 15-1 shows the risk weights and capital definitions that have been adopted in the United States. Essentially, cash and cash equivalents have no capital requirements.

[5]In late 1991 and early 1992, the value of Japanese equities fell dramatically because of a collapse in real estate prices and a general recession. As much as half of the unrealized gains that had been available were eliminated in the sharp market decline, threatening the ability of Japanese banks to comply with the Basel Accord.

EXHIBIT 15-1 RISK-BASED CAPITAL GUIDELINES

Risk Weighting

Category	Weight, %
Cash	
Balances due from Federal Reserve banks	
Transactions balances due from U.S. depository institutions	
Balances due from OECD central and commercial banks in immediately available funds	
U.S. Treasury and government	
Loans to OECD governments	0
Long-term claims on U.S. and OECD-based banks	
Short-term claims on banks in non-OECD countries	20
Residential mortgage assets	50
Long-term claims on banks in non-OECD countries	
Claims on the domestic and foreign private sector	
Foreign currency loans to non-OECD countries	
Loans to non-OECD governments	
100% of general guarantees	
50% of note issuance facilities	
20% of trade commitments	100

Capital Guidelines

Capital	Required Ratio to Risk-Weighted Assets, %
Tier I	
Shareholders' equity	
Minority interest in subsidiaries	4
Tier II	
Allowance for loan loss (up to 1.25% of risk-weighted assets)	
Subordinated debt (up to 50% of Tier I capital)	4

Source: Subcommittee on Financial Institutions Supervision, Regulation, and Insurance, *Report of the Task Force on the International Competitiveness of U.S. Financial Institutions,* 1990, and Economic Council of Canada, *Globalization and Canada's Financial Markets,* 1990.

Less liquid assets have weights that range from 20 to 100 percent. Risk-weighted asset totals are computed by multiplying balances in accounts and contingent liabilities by the appropriate weight. When these are aggregated, the result is the asset base used for the 4 percent guidelines. In the United States, most banks are in compliance with the Basel Accord. However, the accord guidelines are more of a challenge for larger banks.

Capital Ratios in the United States

For the industry as a whole, the equity capital to total assets has recently ranged between 6 and 6.5 percent. Since equity capital is part of the Tier I category, these rates suggest that U.S. banks should have little difficulty complying with the Basel Accord. However, Exhibit 15-2 shows the extent to which capital ratios vary by bank size.

Banks with assets under $100 million are well capitalized with an average equity of 9 percent of assets. For banks with assets between $100 million and $1 billion, the ratio drops to under 8 percent. Those with assets between $1 billion and $10 billion, it is between 6 and 6.5 percent. Ratios for the largest banks (with assets over $10 billion) are barely over 5 percent.

There are over 9000 banks in the first size group but less than 3000 in the second. The

EXHIBIT 15-2 U.S. BANK CAPITAL RATIOS BY SIZE, 1988–1990

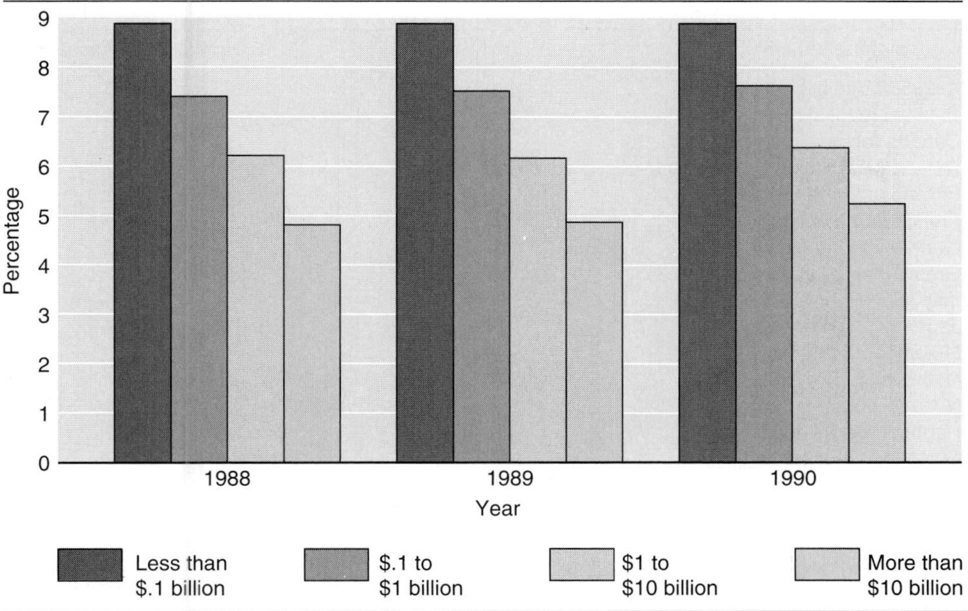

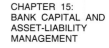

Source: Data from Federal Deposit Insurance Corporation, *Quarterly Banking Profile,* various issues

third group has just over 300 banks, and the largest group in terms of assets is composed of less than 50 banks. So, the vast majority of U.S. banks meet the requirements. It is the larger money center banks that have had to restructure their operations in order to be in compliance with the Basel Accord.

Capital Management Outside the United States

Capital Ratios in the OECD On average, the capital levels in the United States are similar to those in several other countries. Exhibit 15-3 compares the average capital ratios of selected OECD members. The ratios for Canada, Finland, Italy, and Switzerland are within 100 basis points of the 1989 U.S. ratio. For Denmark, Portugal, and Spain, the ratios are noticeably higher. All the other countries shown, including Japan and Germany, have much lower capital ratios. The average German capital ratio is less than 80 percent of that of the average U.S. bank. In the United States, each dollar of assets is supported by capital of $0.0621. In Japan, each dollar of assets is backed by less than $0.03 of capital. The lowest ratio belongs to Sweden, with $0.0153 of capital per dollar of assets in 1989.

The variation of these ratios has important implications for the competitiveness of these banking systems. The leverage effects translate directly into income effects for bank shareholders.

Income Effects All other things being equal, low capital ratios improve rate of return on equity (ROE). Recall from Chapter 13, Equation 16, that ROE is the product of the return on assets (ROA) and the equity multiplier (EM).

$$\text{ROE} = (\text{ROA})(\text{EM}) \tag{2}$$

Starting from any level of ROE, notice that a higher ROE can be achieved by increasing ROA *or* the EM.

EXHIBIT 15-3 CAPITAL AS A PERCENTAGE OF TOTAL ASSETS FOR SELECTED COUNTRIES, 1989

Country (institutions)	Capital/Total Assets, %*
Austria (large banks)	4.25
Belgium (banks)	3.39
Canada (domestic banks)	5.46
Denmark (banks and savings banks)	8.72
Finland (commercial banks)	7.00
France (large banks)	2.19
Germany (commercial banks)	4.87
Greece (large commercial banks)	2.87
Italy (all commercial banks)	6.34
Japan (all ordinary banks)	2.97
Luxembourg (banks)	3.20
Netherlands (banks)	4.37
Norway (commercial banks)	4.21
Portugal (banks)	10.32
Spain (commercial banks)	9.62
Sweden (commercial banks)	1.53
Switzerland (large banks)†	6.09
United Kingdom (commercial banks)	4.89
United States (insured commercial banks)	6.21

*Capital includes reserves but excludes bonds.
†Data is for 1987.
Source: Organisation for Economic Co-operation and Development, *Bank Profitability, Statistical Supplement, Financial Statements,* 1981–1989.

Exhibit 15-4 shows this relationship for the same group of OECD nations. Among these countries, the highest ROE in 1989 was in Sweden at 24.84 percent. Sweden's ROA is actually lower than the U.S. ratio, but the Swedish EM is four times the U.S. equity multiplier.

On the other hand, the results for Canada and Switzerland are quite comparable. The EM, ROA, and ROE are roughly the same as the U.S. case. In Canada, gross income is a slightly higher percentage of assets than in the United States, but the mix of assets and liabilities is very similar.[6] The Swiss banking system is much more liquid than the U.S. system, and gross income on assets is only 50 percent as high as the U.S. average. The relatively high returns on assets and equity are due to a much lower cost of funds for Swiss banks than for U.S. banks.

The ROEs of Germany, Japan, and France are all higher than in the United States. Germany's ROA is about the same even though the German banking system is much more liquid. The higher average German ROE is a direct result of the leverage effects in that country. The equity multiplier is 20.5 versus 16.1 in the United States. Japan's ROA is only half the U.S. average, but the EM of 33.7 causes the Japanese ROE to be just about the same as the U.S. ROE. The French case is similar except that the French EM is an even higher 45.7, and the resulting French ROE (11.87 percent) is much higher than in the United States (7.73 percent).[7]

[6]Chapters 13 and 14 discuss the asset and liability mix of these countries. Specific information is found in the following exhibits:

Item	Exhibit
Liquid assets	13-9
Liabilities	13-11
Securities and loans	14-8
Gross income	14-9

[7]It should be noted that Norwegian and U.K. banks recorded an unusually high provision for loan loss in 1989, causing ROA to be unusually low.

Country (institutions)	Equity Multiplier*	R0A, %	ROE,%†
Austria (large banks)	23.53	.34	8:00
Belgium (banks)	29.50	.10	2.95
Canada (domestic banks)	18.32	.47	8.61
Denmark (banks and savings banks)	11.47	.22	2.52
Finland (commercial banks)	14.29	.14	2.00
France (large banks)	45.66	.26	11.87
Germany (commercial banks)	20.53	.42	8.62
Greece (large commercial banks)	34.84	.32	11.15
Italy (all commercial banks)	15.77	.75	11.83
Japan (all ordinary banks)	33.67	.24	8.08
Luxembourg (banks)	31.25	.21	6.56
Netherlands (banks)	22.88	.48	10.98
Norway (commercial banks)	23.75	.09	2.14
Portugal (banks)	9.69	.78	7.56
Spain (commercial banks)	10.40	1.09	11.33
Sweden (commercial banks)	65.36	.38	24.84
Switzerland (large banks)‡	16.42	.48	7.88
United Kingdom (commercial banks)	20.45	.01	20
United States (insured commercial banks)	16.10	.48	7.73

*Inverse of the capital ratio.
†Equity multiplier multiplied by ROA.
‡Data is for 1987.
Source: ROA from Organisation for Economic Co-operation and Development, *Bank Profitability, Statistical Supplement, Financial Statements of Banks, 1981–1989,* and equity multiplier and ROE from calculations based on data from Organisation for Economic Co-operation and Development, *Bank Profitability, Statistical Supplement, Financial Statements of Banks, 1981–1989.*

These examples illustrate the importance of the capital ratio in international banking. If a bank can operate with less capital than the competition, it can afford to realize a lower ROA and still produce a strong ROE. This latitude with respect to ROA means that the bank can also offer its services with thinner profit margins and, thus, be more competitive in the international marketplace.

However, operating with low capital ratios has definite drawbacks. The bank's capital base will be even more susceptible to the adverse effects of volatile interest rates.

ASSET-LIABILITY MIX AND GAP

In Chapter 13, both financial position and profitability were analyzed from a static perspective. However, one of the greatest risks to bank solvency and profitability is linked to the *dynamic* nature of interest rates.

Interest Rate Sensitivity

Bank assets and liabilities are always affected by changes in interest rates because of respective fixed cash flows. Short-term instruments may be associated with different interest rates as they mature and asset proceeds are reinvested or liabilities are reissued. In some cases, instruments are *rate-sensitive.* Their interest rates will change at predetermined intervals, that is, *float* with a specific publicly quoted rate or index.

Rate-sensitive assets and liabilities:
Assets and liabilities whose rates earned and paid change with market interest rates. They have floating interest rates instead of fixed rates.

If rate-sensitive assets and liabilities are significantly different proportions of the bank balance sheet, earnings will be volatile in an environment of changing interest rates.

Security Bank is a case in point. Referring to Exhibit 15-5, notice that Security is well capitalized with 7 percent of average assets financed with equity. The exhibit also includes the average rates earned and paid on assets and liabilities. Loan rates range from 10.42 to 12.56 percent, while deposit rates are 8 percent or less. Even long-term borrowing costs are less than 10 percent. In the base case (before assuming any interest rate changes), interest income exceeds interest expense by $1.106 billion.

Note, too, that the 1992 bank's assets include interest-bearing time deposits and federal funds that either have floating interest rates or are extremely short term so as to almost immediately reflect rate changes. Also, a small portion of loans is rate-sensitive. Total rate-sensitive assets equal $10.69 billion. The remaining assets ($22 billion) are considered fixed-rate assets; that is, a change in rates will not affect associated cash flows right away. On the other hand, *most* of Security's liabilities are highly rate-sensitive ($25.078 billion).

If it is assumed that the bank's net noninterest expense is $636 million, 1992 income before taxes is $470 million ($1.106 billion − $636 million) in a stable interest rate environment. Should interest rates change, however, bank earnings could be subject to considerable volatility.

EXHIBIT 15-5 SECURITY BANK RATE, SENSITIVITY, 1992

	Average Balance (millions)	Base Rates (%)	Income or Expense (millions)
Rate-sensitive assets:			
Interest-bearing time deposits	$1,391	9.20	$128
Federal funds sold and repos	600	7.60	46
Variable-rate loans	8,699	10.42	906
	10,690		1,080
Fixed-rate assets:			
Investment securities	5,174	8.14	421
Fixed-rate loans	12,924	12.56	1,623
Cash and due from banks	2,252	—	—
Premises and other assets	1,699	—	—
	22,049		2,044
Total assets	$32,739		3,124
Rate-sensitive liabilities:			
Money market deposit accounts	$5,984	6.40	$383
Time deposits, $100,000 or more	8,548	7.90	675
Foreign time deposits	2,753	7.30	201
Short-term borrowings	7,532	7.65	576
Variable-rate, long-term borrowings	261	9.84	26
	25,078		1,861
Fixed-rate liabilities and equity:			
Interest-bearing transactions accounts	500	5.20	26
Other time deposits	1,000	7.99	80
Savings deposits	720	5.35	39
Fixed-rate, long-term borrowings	125	9.84	12
Demand deposits	2,200	—	—
Other liabilities	759	—	—
Equity	2,357		—
	7,661		157
Total liabilities and equity	$32,739		$2,018

Exhibit 15-6 illustrates the potential effect on bank earnings of 1 percent changes in short-term rates. For this example, assume instantaneous changes in the rates earned and paid on floating-rate assets and liabilities. Thus, only rate-sensitive instruments are affected. Profit is measured for the full year.

When short-term rates increase by 1 percent, rate-sensitive assets earn more interest income than would have otherwise been the case. Since the average balance of these assets is $10.69 billion, projected interest income grows by $106.9 million. Similarly, rate-sensitive liabilities of $25.078 billion necessitate an additional $250.78 million in interest payments. Incremental interest income ($106.9 million) net of incremental interest expense ($250.78 million) produces a decrease in net interest income and earnings before taxes of $143.88 million. Under this assumption, the change in earnings is 30.6 percent.

When short-term rates are assumed to decrease by 1 percent, the reverse is true. Projected interest expense declines more than interest income. Security Bank profits climb by $143.88 million, or 30.6 percent.

Gap

Gap and Gap Ratio The projected volatility of Security's earnings is directly related to the difference between its rate-sensitive assets and liabilities. This difference is the bank's *gap*.[8]

Gap:
The difference between rate-sensitive assets and liabilities.

Gap may be measured in absolute dollar terms.

$$\text{Gap} = A_s - L_s \tag{3}$$

where A_s = rate-sensitive assets
L_s = rate-sensitive liabilities
gap = the bank's gap

Gap may also be measured in relative terms.

$$\text{Gap ratio} = A_s/L_s \tag{4}$$

[8] Gap should not be confused with GAAP, or generally accepted accounting principles.

EXHIBIT 15-6 SECURITY BANK, PROFITABILITY ANALYSIS, 1992 (MILLIONS)

	Base Rates	1% Increase	1% Decrease
Interest income:			
Rate-sensitive assets	$1,080	$1,186.90*	$ 973.10†
Fixed-rate assets	2,044	2,044.00	2,044.00
Interest expense:			
Rate-sensitive liabilities	(1,861)	(2,111.78)‡	(1,610.22)§
Fixed-rate liabilities	(157)	(157.00)	(157.00)
Net interest income	1,106	962.12	1,249.88
Net noninterest expense	(636)	(636.00)	(636.00)
Earnings before taxes	$ 470	326.12	$613.88
Percentage change in earnings		−30.6	+30.6

*$1080 plus .01($10,690) = $1186.90.
†$1080 minus .01($10,690) = $973.10.
‡$1861 plus .01($25,078) = $2111.78
§$1861 minus .01($25,078) = $1610.22.

Security Bank Applying Equation 3, Security Bank's gap is a negative \$14.388 billion; that is, rate-sensitive liabilities exceed rate-sensitive assets by \$14.388 billion. An assumed 1 percent increase interest rates produced earning declines of 1 percent of gap.

$$\Delta \text{NII} = \Delta k(\text{Gap}) \tag{5}$$

where ΔNII = change in net interest income
Δk = change interest rates

Generally, increasing interest rates will have a negative effect on earnings when rate-sensitive liabilities exceed rate-sensitive assets. Conversely, lower rates will relieve the interest expense burden more than they will reduce interest income, and earnings will improve.

A positive gap (more rate-sensitive assets than liabilities) will create opposite reactions to short-term rate changes. Increasing rates will boost interest income more than interest expense, and profits will improve. However, when rates drop, deteriorating interest income more than offsets lower interest expense, and profits slump.

The gap ratio in Equation 4 measures the amount of rate-sensitive assets for every dollar of rate-sensitive liabilities, that is, measures rate-sensitive assets as a percentage of liabilities. In the case of Security Bank, the gap ratio is .426 (\$10.690 billion/\$25.078 billion). The bank's rate-sensitive assets represent less than half the corresponding liabilities.

Whenever the gap (in absolute terms) is negative, the gap ratio will be less than 1. Similarly, a gap ratio that is greater than 1 implies a positive dollar value gap. Theoretically, when the gap and gap ratio are 0 and 1, respectively, earnings volatility (attributable to interest rate changes) is minimized.

First National Bank In practice, a zero gap is difficult to maintain. However, it *is* possible to achieve a smaller gap than Security's. Another hypothetical bank, First National, was analyzed in Chapter 13. Security and First National are comparable in a number of ways. Total asset levels and rates earned and paid on specific categories are identical. We can even assume that net noninterest expense is the same for both. The primary difference between the two banks is the mix of assets and liabilities. Specifically, First National holds more rate-sensitive assets and fewer rate-sensitive liabilities.

As can be seen in Exhibit 15-7, First National's rate-sensitive assets are also less than liabilities. However, the difference is smaller than that noted with Security. First National's gap is a negative \$3.24 billion (\$16.208 billion − \$19.448 billion), and its gap ratio is .833. In the base case, projected interest income and expense are \$3.01 billion and \$1.874 billion, respectively.[9] After deducting net noninterest expense, earnings before tax equal \$500 million.

Again assuming 1 percent interest rate changes, the nonzero gap produces earnings volatility (Exhibit 15-8). A 1 percent increase in short-term rates reduces profits by the same percentage (1 percent) of gap, or \$32.4 million. However, because the gap (on the same asset base) is smaller, both the aggregate change and the percentage change (negative 6.48 percent) are smaller than was true for Security Bank. Similarly, if short-term rates decline, the improvement in earnings is smaller.

Gap Applications

These two examples illustrate the manner in which bank portfolios can be constructed to minimize earnings variability when assets and liabilities are classified as either rate-sensi-

[9]Average balances, rates, interest income, and interest expense are consistent with Exhibit 13-6. Specific categories have been reclassified by rate sensitivity.

EXHIBIT 15-7 FIRST NATIONAL BANK, RATE SENSITIVITY, 1992

	Average Balance (millions)	Base Rates %	Income or Expense (millions)
Rate-sensitive assets:			
Interest-bearing time deposits	$1,391	9.20	$128
Federal funds sold and repos	895	7.60	68
Variable-rate loans	13,922	10.42	1,450
	16,208		1,646
Fixed-rate assets:			
Investment securities	4,879	8.14*	397
Fixed-rate loans	7,701	12.56	967
Cash and due from banks	2,252	—	—
Premises and other assets	1,699	—	
	16,531		1,364
Total assets	$32,739		3,010
Rate-sensitive liabilities:			
Money market deposit accounts	$ 4,984	6.40	$1319
Time deposits, $100,000 or more	6,544	7.90	517
Foreign time deposits	1,753	7.30	128
Short-term borrowings	6,037	7.65	462
Variable-rate, long-term borrowings	130	9.84	13
	19,448		1,439
Fixed-rate liabilities and equity:			
Interest-bearing transactions accounts	1,500	5.20	78
Other time deposits	3,004	7.99	240
Savings deposits	1,720	5.35	92
Fixed-rate, long-term borrowings	256	9.84	25
Demand deposits	3,695	—	—
Other liabilities	759	—	—
Equity	2,357	—	
	13,291		435
Total liabilities and equity	$32,739		1,874

*This rate is not taxable-equivalent.

EXHIBIT 15-8 FIRST NATIONAL BANK, (PROFITABILITY ANALYSIS, 1992 (MILLIONS)

	Base Rates	1% Increase	1% Decrease
Interest income:			
Rate-sensitive assets	$1,646	$1,808.08*	1,483.92†
Fixed-rate assets	1,364	1,364.00	1,364.00
Interest expense:			
Rate-sensitive liabilities	(1,439)	(1,633.48)‡	(1,244.52)§
Fixed-rate liabilities	(435)	(435.00)	(435.00)
Net interest income	1,136	1,103.60	1,168.40
Net noninterest expense	(636)	(636.00)	(636.00)
Earnings before taxes	$500	$467.60	$532.40
Percentage change in earnings		−6.48	+6.48

*$1,646 plus .01($16,208) = $1,808.08.
†$1646 minus .01($16,208) = $1,483.92.
‡$1439 plus .01($19,448) = $1,633.48.
§$1439 minus .01($19,448) = $1,244.52.

tive or fixed rate. Practically, however, this classification scheme is often more involved than it may first appear.

Strictly speaking, maturing assets and liabilities expose banks to as much earnings volatility as do rate-sensitive instruments. So, items subject to *repricing* include both variable-rate instruments and those fixed-rate instruments that mature in the near term. Exhibit 15-9 shows the time periods within which First National's assets and liabilities are either due to be repriced (rate-sensitive instruments) or mature (fixed-rate).

Measurements of gap occur in each time period analyzed. In the first 90 days, liabilities exceed assets. Thus, there is a negative gap of $2.776 billion with a corresponding gap ratio of .845. In the 91- to 180-day period, the gap is a positive $88 million and the gap ratio is 1.096. However, this positive gap is not large enough to offset the negative gap in the 0- to 90-day period. Cumulatively, that is, for the first 180 days, First National has a negative gap of $2.688 billion and a gap ratio of .857.

The 181- to 365-day period (second 6 months of the year) also has a positive gap that, again, is not large enough to offset the negative gap of the first 90 days. The greatest gap exposure is in the 0- to 90-day period. Whether the bank attempts to modify this position depends on its customer base, interest rate expectations, and its inclination to use other financial instruments to hedge the balance sheet.

Gap Strategies

Bank management's reaction to a negative gap will vary. If First National's management believes that interest rates are likely to decline, it may not attempt to eliminate the gap. To do so would eliminate potentially higher earnings, as interest expense declines more

EXHIBIT 15-9 FIRST NATIONAL BANK, GAP ANALYSIS 1992 (MILLIONS)

	Interest Sensitivity Period				
	0–90 Days	91–180 Days	181–365 Days	Over 1 Year	Total
Assets:					
Money market instruments*	$1,990	$ 195	$ 101	—	$ 2,286
Investment securities	496	375	534	3,474	4,879
Loans	12,696	433	874	7,690	21,623
Other assets[†]	—	—	—	3,951	3,951
Total	15,112	$1003	$1,509	15,115	$32,739
Liabilities and equity:					
Non-interest-bearing deposits[‡]	—	—	—	$3,695	$ 3,695
Interest-bearing deposits[§]	$11,799	$897	$1,211	5,598	19,505
Short-term borrowings	5,980	10	47	—	6,037
Long-term borrowings	109	8	13	256	386
Other liabilities	—	—	—	759	759
Equity	—	—	—	2,357	2,357
Total	$17,888	$915	$1,271	$12,665	$32,739
gap	(2,776)	88	238	2,450	
gap ratio	.845	1.096	1.187	1.193	
Cumulative gap	(2,776)	2,688)	(2,450)	0	
Cumulative gap ratio	.845	0.857	.878	1.000	

*Interest-bearing time deposits, federal funds sold, and repurchase agreements.
[†]Cash and due from banks, premises, allowance for possible credit loss, and other assets.
[‡]Demand deposits.
[§]Money market deposit accounts, time deposits ≥ $100,000, foreign time deposits, interest-bearing transactions accounts, other time deposits, and savings accounts.

than interest income. If short-term rates decline by 1 percent in the first 90 days, earnings will be \$27.8 million higher than would otherwise be the case.[10] To the extent possible, the bank *may* decide to make the gap even more negative. Emphasizing fixed-rate loans and/or issuing more floating-rate or short-term deposits would accomplish this. New longer-term loans with fixed rates would fall outside shorter-term gapping periods. Effectively, First National could attempt to lock in the now-available higher rates on assets. Interest paid on new variable-rate or short-term deposits would decrease when short-term rates fall.

Thus, it is clear from this example that a negative gap may be *desirable* if bank management anticipates falling interest rates. At the end of an expansionary economic cycle, during which short-term interest rates have reached relatively high levels, a negative gap will enhance profitability as rates decline to more normal levels.

On the other hand, if the economy is poised at the beginning of a period of anticipated economic expansion, during which interest rates are expected to increase, a positive gap may be advisable. In the case of First National, reversing its near-term negative gap might involve offering more variable-rate loans or stressing short-term loans and investments in order to position the bank to take advantage of subsequent repricing at higher rates. At the same time, locking in longer-term deposits would result in less exposure on the liability side.

Creating or increasing a negative gap when management expects interest rates to decline and taking the opposite approach when management expects interest rates to increase are theoretically sound but highly speculative strategies. If management is to succeed in these attempts, projections of future interest rates must be accurate. If actual rate movements are in the opposite direction, earnings could deteriorate seriously. Accurate interest forecasting is an imprecise science, at best. Making deliberate, substantial changes in the bank's gap to widen it in one direction or the other can be a risky proposition. It amounts to gambling the bank's capital, and perhaps its solvency, on management's interest rate projections. This is clearly not sound management.

Even if management *could* predict interest rates with certainty, bank customers may not be anxious to accommodate the necessary changes in interest rate exposure. When the market consensus is that rates will decline, the appropriate bank strategy is to increase rate-sensitive liabilities relative to rate-sensitive assets. This may mean asking bank clients to accept fixed-rate loans. Yet if clients have the same rate expectations, fixed-rate loans will appear unattractive to them. Likewise, variable-rate or extremely short term deposits will not be particularly appealing.

These gap strategies are feasible only to a certain extent. They are, at best, difficult to achieve and, at worst, speculative and may threaten the bank's soundness. The difficulty of predicting interest rates complicates administration of the schemes. The financial sophistication of bank clients can preclude necessary portfolio adjustment.

INTEREST RATE RISK AND BANK CAPITAL

In addition to the practical limitations of gap management, there are more fundamental problems associated with gap analysis.

Interest Rate Changes and Net Worth

Adjusting the timing of asset and liability repricing to achieve a zero gap will not necessarily protect an institution from adverse changes in net worth.

[10]This amount is 1 percent of Gap.

Net worth:
The difference between the *market values* of assets and liabilities. In this context, net worth is to be distinguished from GAAP-defined shareholders' equity and from RAP-defined capital.

The simple example in Exhibit 15-10 will help to illustrate. Suppose that two banks, A and B, each have total assets of $100 million, liabilities of $95 million, and net worth of $5 million.

Each bank holds fixed-rate loans that mature in 5 years on the same date. Liabilities consist of 5-year certificates of deposit that mature on the same date as the loans. In all gapping periods up to year 5, there are no potential repricings. Since all repricings occur on the same date in year 5, each bank has a positive $5 million gap in that period and a gap ratio of 1.05.

$$\text{Gap} = \$100 \text{ million} - \$95 \text{ million}$$

$$= \$5 \text{ million} \tag{6}$$

$$\text{Gap ratio} = \frac{100}{95}$$

$$= 1.0526 \tag{7}$$

The only difference in the portfolios of Banks A and B is the type of loans held. Bank A's loans pay 12 percent interest each year on the face amounts, with principal due at maturity. Bank A plans to receive $12 million per year until the maturity date, at which time the last interest payment and principal repayment will be received.

Bank B's 12 percent loans, however, will be completely repaid in year 5. The bank will receive no cash flows until maturity, at which time its customers will repay all accrued interest and principal.[11] Given these terms, loan repayments for Bank B will total $176.234 million ($100 million × 1.12^5).

The 10 percent CDs are identical. At the end of 5 years, each bank will pay a total of $152.998 million to depositors ($95 million × 1.10^5). Notice that at required loan and

[11]We assume that both banks assessed loan origination fees sufficient to cover all operating expenses during the 5-year period.

EXHIBIT 15-10 ANTICIPATED CASH FLOWS FOR BANKS A AND B

	Year*				
	1	2	3	4	5
Bank A					
Loans	12	12	12	12	112
CDs	0	0	0	0	(152.998)
Bank B					
Loans	0	0	0	0	176.234
CDs	0	0	0	0	(152.998)

Bank	Instrument	Rate, %	Value at Year 0*
A and B	Loans	12	$100
A and B	CDs	10	95
A	Loans	11.5	101.82
B	Loans	11.5	102.26
A and B	CDs	9.5	97.19

*Millions of dollars.

CD rates of 12 and 10 percent, respectively, the present values are also identical. Loans are valued at $100 million, CDs $95 million. Net worth, of course, is $5 million.

Now, assume that interest rates decline by 50 basis points across the board. Loan and CD rates fall to 11.5 and 9.5 percent, respectively. Anticipated cash flows will not change, but their present values will. Since there is an inverse relationship between interest rate changes and changes in market value, present values increase.[12]

The present value of CDs increases to $97.19 million for both banks. However, changes in loan market values are not equal. Bank B loans increase more in value than those held by Bank A. After the rate change, loan portfolios of Banks A and B are worth $101.82 million and $102.26 million, respectively. Bank B's loan portfolio value increases more because of the time pattern of its cash flows. All cash flows occur in year 5. As noted in Chapter 8, longer-term instruments are more price-sensitive to changes in yield. Bank B's loan portfolio will be more rate-sensitive since Bank A receives a portion of its cash flows in the interim years 1 through 4.

Note, too, that these different changes in asset values cause net worth of the two banks also to differ after interest rates decline.[13] The market value of equity drops from $5 million to $4.63 million for Bank A ($101.82 million − 97.19 million) and increases to $5.07 million for Bank B ($102.26 million − 97.19 million). Gap analysis does not satisfactorily explain this phenomenon because the technique does not consider the time value of money.

Duration

Gap analysis considers only dates of maturity or repricing. The objective of gap analysis is to measure the impact on earnings of mismatched combinations of rate-sensitive assets and liabilities. It does not address the issue of changes in the market value of assets and liabilities. So gap analysis necessarily does not address the change in net worth noted in the example above. The market value of assets and liabilities will depend not only on maturity or repricing dates, but also on the timing of future cash flows.

Duration is a concept that measures a financial instrument's *average life,* or the *weighted average time of cash receipt.* The time of each cash receipt is weighted by the proportion of total present value which that cash flow represents.

$$D = \frac{\left\{\sum_{t=1}^{n}\left[\frac{\mathrm{CF}_t t}{(1+k)^t}\right]\right\}}{\sum_{t=1}^{n}\left[\frac{\mathrm{CF}_t}{(1+k)^t}\right]} \tag{8}$$

where D = duration
CF_t = cash flow in time t
t = number of periods before CF_t occurs
k = appropriate discount rate for the instrument
n = number of periods before instrument matures

To the extent that the durations of two financial instruments differ, their price sensitivity to interest rate changes will differ. Exhibit 15-11 illustrates duration calculations for

[12]See Chapter 8 for a discussion of bond price behavior. These principles apply to any fixed-income instrument, including loans and CDs.

[13]In the discussion of duration, net worth and capital ratio refer to the market value concept of these terms. Neither GAAP-reported capital nor RAP-defined capital changes.

EXHIBIT 15-11 DURATION ANALYSIS FOR BANKS A AND B

Instrument (1)	Bank (2)	Year (3)	CF* (4)	PVCF* (5)	(3)×(5)* (6)	Duration (years)† (7)
Loan (12%)	A	1	$12	$10.71	10.71	
		2	12	9.57	19.14	
		3	12	8.54	25.62	
		4	12	7.63	30.52	
		5	112	63.55	317.75	
				100.00	403.74	4.0374
Loan (12%)	B	1	0	0	0	
		2	0	0	0	
		3	0	0	0	
		4	0	0	0	
		5	176.234	100	500	
				100	500	5.0
CD (10%)	A & B	1	0	0	0	
		2	0	0	0	
		3	0	0	0	
		4	0	0	0	
		5	152.998	95	475	
				95	475	5.0

*Millions of dollars.
†Duration equals the total of column 6 divided by the total of column 5.

Banks A and B. Bank A will receive interest payments prior to year 5. So the weighted average time of cash receipt, or duration, is less than 5 years. On the other hand, Bank B loans generate no interim cash flows, and as a direct result, these loans have a duration of exactly 5 years. The same is true for both banks' CDs.

Just as the stated maturity of a financial instrument suggests its degree of price sensitivity to yield changes, duration also helps describe price sensitivity. The following formula uses duration to estimate the percentage price change that will be associated with a particular change in rates.

$$\frac{\Delta P}{P} = -D\left[\frac{\Delta k}{(1+k)}\right] \tag{9}$$

where P = market value of financial instrument
ΔP = change in market value of financial instrument
D = duration
k = appropriate discount rate
Δk = change in discount rate

The algebraic sign of the percentage change in market value is inversely related to the algebraic sign of the change in rates; that is, the relationship between price and rate changes is inverse. Note, too, that the greater an instrument's duration, the greater the *absolute value* of its change in market value for a given change in rate. This is consistent with the concept of greater price volatility for longer-term instruments. Equation 9 works well for relatively small changes in rates.[14]

[14]Equation 9 is an approximation formula specifying that percentage price changes are a linear function of rate changes. The actual relationship is nonlinear. This means that for small changes in rate the approximation will give a fairly accurate result. However, the larger the change in rate, the less accurate the approximation.

Referring again to Banks A and B, the durations of their loan portfolios are 4.0374 and 5 years, respectively. For Bank A, Equation 9 predicts a positive 1.802 percent change in price:

$$\frac{\Delta P}{P} = -4.0374\left(\frac{-.005}{1.12}\right)$$
$$= .018024$$

The actual change was 1.820 percent. Similarly, the predicted change for Bank B's loan portfolio is 2.232 percent

$$\frac{\Delta P}{P} = -5\left(\frac{-.005}{1.12}\right)$$
$$= 0.022321$$

while the actual change was 2.260 percent. In general, when rates decline, the predicted price increase is less than the actual increase. When rates increase, Equation 9 will predict a greater percentage price decline than will actually occur. However, for very small rate changes, the error will also be small.

Duration and Net Worth

The most significant implication of duration analysis is that bank asset and liability portfolios with the same duration will have similar market value sensitivity to interest rate changes. The process of matching durations of asset and liability portfolios can significantly *reduce* interest rate risk. However, this matching will not necessarily *eliminate* the risk.

Notice that, when interest rates declined, the net worth of Bank A declined from $5 million to $4.63 million and that the capital ratio fell from 5 to 4.55 percent (4.63/101.82). However, the corresponding results for Bank B were less severe. After the rate change, net worth was $5.07 million and the capital ratio fell to only 4.96 percent (5.07/102.26). That is, the interest rate risk to net worth was reduced, but not eliminated, by matching the duration of assets and liabilities.

When the durations of two instruments are equal *and* the instruments are discounted by the same rate, Equation 9 suggests that a given change in interest rate would produce equivalent percentage changes in their respective values. Further, the difference between the values of the two instruments should change by the same percentage. If *both* conditions had existed, the net worth of Bank B would have increased by this same percentage.

However, we note that for Bank B this was not the case. This result is due to the differential rates at which loans and CDs were discounted. The .5 percent decline in rates represented a larger percentage change in deposit rates than in loan rates. In essence, the present value of the liabilities changed by a greater percentage than the present value of loans.

Notice from Equation 9 that the percentage change in market value has an inverse relationship with rate level prior to any change in rates. Thus, a 50-basis-point decline will produce a greater proportional change for a 10 percent financial instrument than a 12 percent instrument. Bank B's CDs increased by 2.30 percent, loans by only 2.26 percent. Thus, the capital ratio declined by .4 percent.

The case of Bank A is further complicated by the unmatched durations of loans and CDs. Bank A's aggregate CD value also increased by 2.30 percent, but loan values increased by only 1.82 percent because the duration of the loan portfolio was just over 4 years. The combination of shorter asset duration and differential discount rates resulted in a larger decline in net worth than would have been true if durations were matched and both assets and liabilities discounted at more similar rates.

Certain points should be remembered when applying duration analysis. Unless the instrument involved is a zero-coupon instrument (no cash flows until maturity), duration will not equal time to maturity. Duration changes as time passes and as market interest rates change. If the instruments have any embedded options that may alter the future cash flows, the objective of duration analysis can be frustrated. An example of such an embedded option is a mortgage prepayment option which can severely shorten the future cash flow stream of a mortgage loan. Last, if interest rate changes for assets do not equal interest rate changes for liabilities, matched durations will not help at all.

HEDGING BANK PORTFOLIOS

As explained above, bank management will not always be able to adjust asset and liability portfolios to completely protect the institution from interest rate risk. However, it is possible to use other external means to *hedge* portfolios.

Hedging:
Using one or more financial innovations to protect the market value of specific assets and liabilities (microhedge) or of equity (macrohedge) from adverse effects of interest rate changes.

In particular, *interest rate futures, futures options,* and *swaps* can be used effectively. The mechanics of futures, options, and swap markets are discussed in Chapters 5 and 6 in the context of domestic securities and foreign currency transactions. This section extends these principles to the other segments of bank balance sheets.

Interest Rate Futures

Interest rate futures are contracts to buy or sell fixed-income financial securities at some future specified date. Exhibit 15-12 provides a description of the most common contracts for interest rate futures. Treasury bond and Treasury bill futures have historically been the most actively traded.

EXHIBIT 15-12 INTEREST RATE INSTRUMENTS

	Instruments	Denominations	Exchange*
Futures	Treasury bonds	$100,000	CBT, LIFFE
	Treasury bonds	$50,000	MCE
	5-yr. Treasury notes	$100,000	CBT, FINEX
	2-yr. Treasury notes	$200,000	FINEX
	Treasury bills	$1 million	IMM
	Municipal bond index	$1000 times Bond buyer MBI	CBT
Options on futures	Treasury bonds	$100,000	CBT
	Treasury notes	$100,000	CBT
	Municipal bond index	$100,000	CBT

*CBT Chicago Board of Trade
FINEX Financial Instrument Exchange, a division of the New York Cotton Exchange
IMM International Monetary Market at Chicago Mercantile Exchange
LIFFE London International Financial Futures Exchange
MCE MidAmerica Commodity Exchange

A futures contract entitles the buyer to purchase the underlying asset at a future date at a specific price. If in the interim, the value of the underlying asset increases, the value of the futures contract also increases. If the purchaser chose to sell the contract instead of taking delivery of the underlying asset, he or she would realize a profit. This is the basic principle that makes the use of futures a viable method of hedging against portfolio loss.

A bank securities portfolio manager holding Treasury bonds may be concerned that the value of the portfolio will decline if rates increase. The appropriate hedge would be to take the opposite position in the futures markets. Since the bank holds Treasury bonds, it is said to have a "long position" in bonds in the cash market (asset). Accordingly, the bank portfolio manager would take a "short position" in the futures market by selling Treasury bond futures contracts for subsequent delivery (liability).

If rates do, indeed, increase, the long portfolio will decline in value. However, the futures position can be closed by buying an offsetting contract (settling the liability) at a now lower price. The profit in the futures market will work to offset the loss in the cash market.

To the extent that the cash market asset is similar to the underlying asset in the futures market, profits in one market will be close to the amount of losses in the other market. Bank assets do not always match futures contract underlying assets. As a result, hedges can be subject to *basis risk,* the risk that changes in the price of cash market assets will not exactly coincide with price changes in the futures market.

Nevertheless, futures hedging can reduce potential loss. When cash market and futures market instruments are not the same, the transaction is considered a *cross-hedge.* Exhibit 15-13 illustrates a cross-hedge using Treasury note futures contracts. On January 1, bank management makes a 5-year loan to a valued customer at a fixed rate of 10 percent. If interest rates increase, the bank could incur a significant opportunity cost in interest income.

Management decides to construct a cross-hedge with intermediate-term Treasury note contracts. Ten of the $100,000 contracts cost $953,125 on January 1. A short position (liability) in the futures market hedges a long position (asset) in the cash market. When the futures contract expires in 6 months, rates have increased. The bank has sustained an opportunity cost of $5000 in interest income, but the $6875 in futures market profits more than offset the loss.

EXHIBIT 15-13 HEDGING A FIXED-RATE LOAN IN THE FUTURES MARKET

	Cash Market	Futures Market
Jan. 1	Bank makes $1,000,000, 5-yr, fixed-rate loan at 10%.	Bank sells 10 Treasury note futures contracts for delivery in 6 months at 95-10.*
June 30	Loan rates have increased such that the average rate for the 6-month period was 11%.	Treasury notes are now selling at 94-20. Bank buys 10 Treasury note futures contracts to close its position.
	Opportunity cost = 0.01(1,000,000)(.5) = 5000	Price = $946,250
Gain (loss)	$(5000)	$6875

*Note that 95-10 means Treasury bonds are selling at $95\frac{10}{32}$ percent of face value, i.e., $95.3125 for every $100 of face value. One $100,000 futures contract would, therefore, cost $95,312.50.

†$1,000,000/$95,312.50 = 10.49. The bank buys 10 contracts.

It should be noted that if interest rates had declined, the loss in the futures market would have more than offset the bank's interest income "windfall." Thus, hedging activities will prevent the realization of gains that might otherwise be possible.

To purchase or sell a futures contract, an initial deposit, or *margin,* is required. Margin ranges from 3 to 10 percent of the initial price. At the end of each trading day, however, contracts are marked to market by the futures exchange (that is effectively the "other side" of the transaction). The change in value of the contract is recorded in the bank's account. If losses deplete the margin below minimum maintenance levels, the bank must add additional funds to the account.

Commercial banks may use futures contracts only to hedge interest rate exposure. Because of regulatory restrictions, banks may not speculate in the futures market; that is, banks may not trade futures contracts only for the purpose of generating trading profits in a manner unrelated to interest rate exposure.

In addition, if the futures contract is not related specifically to a given balance sheet item or category, gains or losses must be reported in the bank's financial statements each accounting period. Thus, a general balance sheet hedge (macrohedge) can result in reported losses due to an open futures position that has been marked to market, while the corresponding gains in the cash market may *not* be reported until the asset is sold or otherwise liquidated. Hedges put in place for specific categories (microhedges) are eligible for deferring the reporting of gains and losses until the contract is closed out.

Options on Futures Contracts

Options on futures contracts can be used in much the same way as futures contracts themselves in terms of constructing the hedge. The primary differences are cost and related obligations.

A futures contract purchaser (seller) must accept delivery of (deliver) the underlying asset or sell (purchase) an offsetting contract to close the position. The purchaser of a call or put option may allow the option to expire without taking any action at all. After an option is purchased, the buyer has *no obligation* to do anything further. This is in contrast to a futures contract in which some later action must be taken to close the contract. A call option for a futures contract entitles the purchaser to buy the underlying futures contract at the specified price. A put option entitles the purchaser to sell the contract.

The prices of options are paid in full at the time of purchase. Prices are quoted in full points (percentage of face value) plus fractional points (sixty-fourths). For example, a quotation of 2-42 on a Treasury note contract ($100,000 face value) means $2\frac{42}{64}$ percent of face value, or $2656.25. Often, option prices are lower than the required initial margin for a futures contract. Thus, a bank may put in place an options hedge for considerably less expense than a futures hedge. In addition, maximum loss is limited to the price of the option. Basis risk can be avoided by purchasing options on futures contracts instead of futures contracts themselves.

The maximum loss is limited to the price of the option as long as the bank purchases the option. Selling, or writing, an option exposes the writer, in some cases, to unlimited risk. Bank portfolio options hedges are best constructed through options purchases.

Interest Rate Swaps

Interest rate swaps do not involve purchasing financial market instruments. Instead, the rights to future cash flows are exchanged. Alternatively, the obligations to pay future cash may be exchanged. The fundamental concept is to exchange a fixed-rate cash flow stream with a floating-rate stream.

While parties design swaps in any number of combinations, the most basic interest rate swap is a *coupon swap* in which a floating rate is exchanged for a fixed rate. For example, a financial institution may hold a large portfolio of fixed-rate loans, while most of its deposit liabilities are floating-rate CDs. Another bank may hold considerable variable-rate investments with fixed-rate obligations. To minimize interest rate risk, the two institutions agreed to swap interest payments on liabilities.

They agree upon a *notational principal,* or the amount of liabilities for which interest rates will be swapped. The maturity of the swap and the frequency of payments are also established. For example, Bank C may enter into an agreement that stipulates a $10 million notional amount for 4 years with payments made semiannually.

If the fixed rate is 9 percent for Bank C, it may agree to swap a fixed 9 percent for a floating rate of the "Treasury bill rate plus 1," meaning 1 percentage point above the Treasury bill rate. When paid to the other party in the swap, recorded interest expense on the notational amount is the same as would otherwise be the case every 6 months:

	DR	CR
Interest expense	$450,000	
Cash		$450,000

In addition, the bank records the interest rate swap when the floating-rate payment is received. If Treasury bill plus 1 is 8.5 percent, the bank has saved .5 percent on an annual basis for this 6-month period. When the payment is received, the following entry is made:

	DR	CR
Cash	$25,000	
Interest expense		$25,000

The .5 percent difference for 6 months on $10 million is $25,000. Bank C receives this payment from its counterpart in the swap and its own interest expense is reduced.

Because the success of this arrangement depends on the creditworthiness of the two parties involved, the role of intermediator has become increasingly important. In the early days of the interest rate swap market, large U.S. money center banks and investment banks acted primarily as brokers. Currently, these institutions frequently act as principals in offsetting swaps, providing more credit assurance for all involved.

In addition, interest rate swaps enable commercial banks to offer loans and deposits with competitive features. Even if these products expose the bank's balance sheet to undesirable interest rate risk, an interest rate swap may be constructed to reduce the risk to a more acceptable level while still offering its clients a full range of banking services.

MARKET VALUE ACCOUNTING

This chapter has illustrated the sensitivity of bank performance to interest rate changes. Historically, this interest rate sensitivity is perhaps best illustrated by the distress of the savings and loan industry during the 1970s and early 1980s (with many of its problems still unresolved). During this time, the market value of long-term, low-interest, fixed-rate mortgage loans held by these thrifts declined dramatically as interest rates soared. At the same time, the value of short-term, high-interest deposits did not decline. The economic reality was that, in all too many cases, the value of assets was lower than the value of liabilities; that is, many thrifts were insolvent. This economic reality was not recognized in the financial statements of these institutions, however, because of the GAAP (generally accepted accounting principles) practice of recording assets at historical cost, not current market value, until the assets were actually sold or otherwise disposed of.

Before the 1970s this GAAP practice was not a real issue because interest rates were stable and most deposit interest rates were regulated. The volatile interest rates of the late

1970s and early 1980s and the attendant problems in the financial services industry led to a reevaluation of reporting practices. The Financial Institutions Reform, Recovery, and Enforcement Act (FIRREA) of 1989 directed the U.S Treasury Department to examine the question of *market value accounting* for depository institutions. In 1991 the Treasury concluded that increased market value disclosure was desirable, but not comprehensive market value accounting (marking all assets and liabilities to market).

Even before congressional action in 1989, the Financial Accounting Standards Board (FASB), the body that is responsible for defining generally accepted accounting principles, began to examine the question. For some time, GAAP has required banks to report (1) securities held for short-term trading purposes and (2) interest and foreign exchange contracts at market values. In addition, estimates of the market value of other investment securities have been required for supplemental (footnote) disclosure.

The FASB and the Securities and Exchange Commission (SEC) are strong advocates for increased market value accounting (MVA). There are several benefits of increasing MVA:

- The capital of each depository institution can be better estimated.
- Regulators will be better able to identify those institutions that are capital-impaired.
- The accountability of management for its decisions will be facilitated by the more transparent measurement of economic performance.
- Transactions motivated strictly by accounting considerations will be discouraged. An example is "gains trading," in which securities that have appreciated in value are sold to reflect the gain in current operations, and securities that have depreciated are not sold to avoid recognizing the loss. Under MVA both gains and losses would be recognized, eliminating the incentive to gains trade.

As a step in the direction of full MVA, in 1991 the FASB framed the Statement of Financial Accounting Standards 107 (SFAS 107) that requires footnote disclosure of the market value of all financial instruments, including loans for all financial statements issued after December 15, 1992. Also being considered is complete MVA for all marketable securities and related liabilities (not just trading account securities). This means that even bonds held as assets for long-term investment purposes and the bank's own bonds payable would be reflected in the financial statements at market value on each reporting date. Any gains or losses would be absorbed in the income statement or directly in the equity accounts of the balance sheet.

The benefits of MVA are clear. The challenge in realizing these benefits is to be able to generate the necessary information in a cost-effective way, especially in smaller institutions. However, computerized systems and mass-marketed software applications should help contain the cost of producing the necessary market value information.

SUMMARY

Bank capital protects depositors by absorbing temporary losses, inspiring public confidence, and placing reasonable constraints on asset growth. Capital consists primarily of equity (common and preferred stock) and subordinated debt. Over time, capital ratios have declined worldwide. In some cases, this has placed U.S. banks at a competitive disadvantage. Competing banks, especially from Japan, have benefited from lower capital ratios by being able to offer bank services at discount prices. At the same time, Japanese returns on equity have remained relatively strong because of the effect of high equity multipliers. The Basel Accord (fully operational beginning in 1993) attempts to level the playing field among international banks by prescribing uniform capital standards among OECD countries. In recognition of the difference among banking systems, central banks are given some discretion in terms of how these standards are administered.

Even with harmonized capital standards, however, interest rate risk can still pose a threat to bank profitability and solvency. This risk is especially worrisome when the amount of rate-sensitive assets is significantly different from the amount of rate-sensitive liabilities. Gap analysis attempts to identify the time periods in which the greatest maturity mismatching of assets and liabilities exists. The primary objective of gap analysis is to help protect the income stream from adverse changes in interest rates.

But gap analysis does not consider the time value of money. Changes in the market value of equity can occur when cash flow streams from assets are substantially different from the cash flow streams for liabilities. Duration captures the difference in cash flow timing. It is a more theoretically sound approach, but it is also more difficult to apply practically.

External hedging approaches can help compensate for these theoretical and practical difficulties. Futures contracts, options on futures contracts, and interest swaps can be used to reduce interest rate risk significantly.

The exposure of banks to interest rate risk has motivated a reassessment of the way that assets and liabilities are reported. The FASB and the SEC are moving banks and other financial institutions in the direction of recognizing the impact of market dynamics by requiring more disclosure of market value in periodic financial statements.

KEY TERMS

allowance for loan loss
bank capital
Basel Accord
capital ratio
common stock
direct charge-off
duration
gap
hedging
interest rate futures
interest rate options
interest rate swaps
market value accounting
net worth
preferred stock
primary capital
provision for loan loss
rate-sensitive asset
rate-sensitive liability
risk-based capital
secondary capital
solvency
subordinated debt

END-OF-CHAPTER QUESTIONS

1. List the elements in bank capital. Differentiate GAAP-defined capital from RAP-defined capital.
2. In your opinion, do you think that the Basel Accord will reverse the international trends in returns on equity noted in Exhibit 15-4? Why or why not?
3. What are the three functions of bank capital?
4. What is the difference between a futures contract and an options contract?
5. **a.** What is the objective of gap analysis?
   b. In order to minimize interest rate risk, what should be an institution's objective with respect to gap?
   c. How easy or difficult is it to achieve the objective that you indicated in *b?*
6. Why does gap analysis not always fully explain interest rate risk?
7. **a.** What is duration?
   b. Why is duration analysis theoretically superior to gap analysis?
8. Explain the rationale of using futures or options contracts to protect a bank balance sheet from interest rate risk.
9. Name the advantages and disadvantages of using futures and options hedges.
10. **a.** What is an interest rate swap?
    b. How can an interest rate swap be used to protect against interest rate risk?

END-OF-CHAPTER PROBLEMS

1. Refer to Exhibits 15-5 and 15-6, and assume an average tax rate of 25 percent.
   a. What is Security Bank's ROA and ROE in the base case?
   b. If Security's equity ratio declined by 1 percent, by how much could ROA decline and still maintain the same ROE? What amount of net income does this difference in ROA imply?
2. Refer to Exhibits 15-7 and 15-8 for First National Bank. If interest rates increase by 400 basis points, what would be the bank's earnings before tax for the year?
3. Refer to Exhibits 15-5 and 15-6 for Security Bank. If interest rates increase by 400 basis points, what would be the bank's earnings before tax for the year? Compare this result to your answer for problem 2.
4. Your bank has accepted a $1 million deposit in the form of a CD at 8 percent. Interest rates are high and expected to decline soon. Your customer bought this CD in order to lock in this rate. But this also means that your bank will be paying higher than market rates on the CD when rates decline. Construct an appropriate hedge using 6-month futures contracts on 2-year Treasury notes assuming that the price is 98-14.
5. Referring to problem 4, assume that interest rates fell during the 6-month period that the hedge was in place. Shortly after the CD was issued, the rate on these instruments fell to 6.5 percent. Upon expiration of the futures contract, the price of 2-year Treasury notes is 99-7. Compute the profit and loss in cash and futures markets when the bank closes out its position.
6. Refer to Exhibit 15-11. Calculate the duration for Bank A's loan portfolio if the appropriate market rate is 10 percent. (Note that future cash flows do not change.)

SELECTED REFERENCES

Bank for International Settlements. *Recent Innovations in International Banking,* April 1986.

Bierwag, Gerald O. *Duration Analysis; Managing Interest Rate Risk,* Ballinger Publishing Company, Cambridge, Massachusetts, 1987.

Brodt, Abraham I. "Optimal Bank Asset and Liability Management with Financial Futures," *Journal of Futures Markets,* vol. 8, no. 4 (August 1988), pp. 457–481.

Chicago Board of Trade. *CBOT Financial Instruments Guide,* Chicago, 1987.

Economic Council of Canada. *Globalization and Canada's Financial Markets,* Ottawa, 1990.

Fraser, Donald R., and Peter S. Rose. *Financial Institutions and Markets in a Changing World,* 3d ed., Business Publications, Inc., Plano, Texas, 1987.

Giokas, D., and Vassiloqlou, M. "A Goal Programming Model for Bank Assets and Liabilities Management," *European Journal of Operational Research,* vol. 50, no. 1 (January 7, 1991), pp. 48–60.

Grumball, Clive. *Managing Interest Rate Risk,* Quorum Books, Westport, Connecticut, 1987.

International Monetary Fund. *International Capital Markets; Developments and Prospects,* Washington, D.C., April 1989.

Koch, Timothy W. *Bank Management,* Dryden Press, Hinsdale, Illinois, 1988.

Mitchell, Karlyn. "Interest Rate Risk at Commercial Banks: An Empirical Investigation," *Financial Review,* vol. 24, no. 3 (August 1989), pp. 431–455.

Pecchioli, R. M. *Prudential Supervision in Banking,* Organization for Economic Co-operation and Development, Paris, 1987.

Sprenkle, Case M. "Liability and Asset Uncertainty for Banks," *Journal of Banking and Finance* (Netherlands), vol. 11, no. 1 (March 1987), pp. 147–159.

Subcommittee on Financial Institutions Supervision, Regulation, and Insurance. *Report of the Task Force on the International Competitiveness of U.S. Financial Institutions,* Committee on Banking, Finance, and Urban Affairs, Washington, D.C., October 1990.

Thistle, Paul D., Robert W. McLeod, and B. Lynne Conrad. "Interest Rates and Bank Portfolio Adjustments," *Journal of Banking and Finance* (Netherlands), vol. 13, no. 1 (March 1989), pp. 151–161.

U.S. Department of the Treasury. *Modernizing the Financial System; Recommendations for Safer, More Competitive Banks,* Washington, D.C., February 1991.

Wetmore, Jill L., and John R. Brick. "Interest Rate Risk and the Optimal Gap for Commercial Banks: An Empirical Study," *Financial Review,* vol. 25, no. 4 (November 1990), pp. 539–557.

BANK OF TOKYO TRUST
NYCE

PART FOUR

BANKS AROUND THE WORLD

CHAPTER 16

COMMERCIAL AND NONCOMMERCIAL BANKS

CHAPTER OUTLINE

COMMERCIAL BANKS
- United States
- United Kingdom
- Canada
- Germany
- France
- Switzerland
- Japan
- A Cross-Country Comparison
  - Total assets, average size, population per bank, growth rate of assets

NONCOMMERCIAL BANKS
- Bank for International Settlements
  - Origin and objectives, structure and membership, operations
- International Monetary Fund
  - Objectives, structure and quotas, special drawing rights, balance sheet
- The World Bank Group
  - International Bank for Reconstruction and Development, International Development Association, International Finance Corporation, Multilateral Investment Guarantee Agency

INTERNATIONAL COMPARISONS
- Canada
- France
- Germany
- Japan
- Switzerland
- United Kingdom

CHAPTER OVERVIEW

This chapter

- Provides a historical overview and structural description of the commercial banks of the United States, the United Kingdom, Canada, Germany, France, Switzerland, and Japan
- Describes the background and functions of the Bank for International Settlements, the International Monetary Fund, and the World Bank Group

Commercial banks are common in all industrialized countries. Yet the scope of activities of banks in other countries differs considerably from that in the United States. In general, U.S. banks are prohibited from several important activities that are permitted for banks in major trading partners of the United States. This difference and the basic structure of the U.S. banking system put U.S. banks at a competitive disadvantage that will not be corrected until the system is restructured.

Outside the commercial banking realm there are several international institutions that affect financial operations in a global sense. Central bankers coordinate their activities through the Bank for International Settlements. The International Monetary Fund and the World Bank Group help smooth out the international liquidity imbalances and promote economic expansion in less developed countries.

COMMERCIAL BANKS

The regional distribution of the world's top 1000 banks in 1988 appears in Exhibit 16-1. In terms of number of banks, the largest concentration is in Europe, followed by North America and Asia. In terms of total capital and assets, however, the banks of Europe and Asia manage a much larger share of the total. European banks represent 44 percent of capital and 41 percent of assets of the largest 1000. Asian banks represent 29 percent of capital and 39 percent of assets. The North American shares are 20 and 15 percent. Because the most significant banking activity occurs in these regions, the commercial banks of the United States, the United Kingdom, Canada, Germany, France, Switzerland, and Japan are discussed in this chapter. In each case, bank development and structure is analyzed.

United States

The United States has a large number of both state-chartered and national commercial banks. The number peaked at 30,000 in 1920 but because of failures and mergers is now approximately 12,000. One-third of U.S. banks are nationally chartered, hold 60 percent of U.S. bank assets, and control 53 percent of U.S. bank offices. In terms of number of banks, the largest group is non–Federal Reserve member state institutions representing about 60 percent of all commercial bank charters. These smaller institutions, however, represent only 24 percent of bank assets and 35 percent of bank offices. The smallest group in terms of number of charters, Federal Reserve member state banks, hold roughly 8 percent of bank charters, but 16 percent of assets and 12 percent of offices.[1]

As a result, national banks have average total assets of about $470 million, state-chartered Federal Reserve member banks $520 million, and non-Fed member state-chartered banks $100 million. Across all banks, the average size is $260 million. While New York is often described as the U.S. money center because the country's largest banks are headquartered there, the structure of the U.S. banking system is essentially a diverse collection of institutions with limited geographic service areas. Among industrialized countries, the United States is unusual in this regard. Even when regional banks operate in other countries, a strong system of banks that branch nationwide is the rule rather than the exception.

[1]See Chapter 10 for coverage of U.S. bank regulation.

EXHIBIT 16-1 THE WORLD'S TOP 1000 BANKS BY REGION, 1988

Region	No. of banks	Capital* ($ mil.)	Assets ($ bil.)	Pretax return %
North America	214	151,160	2,627	20.2
South America	41	19,286	267	24.1
Europe	477	323,053	7,458	17.4
Middle East and Africa	66	32,057	604	15.2
Asia and Pacific	202	215,802	7,075	19.2
Total	1,000	741,358	18,031	18.6†

*Capital represents the sum of shareholders' equity and disclosed reserves.
†Of the top 1000 banks, 168 did not report profits.
Source: The Banker, July 1989, p. 41.

Exhibit 16-2 shows the growth of U.S. bank assets during the 1980s. In 1981 U.S. bank assets totaled $2 trillion. By the end of the decade, the total stood at $3.3 trillion, representing an annual increase of 6.2 percent. The assets of commercial banks expanded rapidly during the 1980s because of a general expansion in the U.S. money supply.[2] Capital levels, however, did not keep pace, and, by the early 1990s, expansion of bank assets slowed as bank regulators placed more emphasis on building capital levels, a policy position observed in many industrialized countries.[3] Exhibit 16-3 shows the top twenty U.S. banks ranked by capital ratio in 1988.

United Kingdom

The center of the U.K. financial system is London. In fact, prior to 1914, London was recognized as the world's center for international finance. The pound sterling was the major currency of the world because London has historically provided significant amounts of long-term investment capital and short-term trade finance. Furthermore, the government of the United Kingdom has a long tradition of facilitating domestic and international trade.

The foundations of the system are the 1844 legislative acts—the Bank Charter Act and the Joint Stock Bank Act—which required that any bank with more than six partners to incorporate. In order to incorporate, a bank disclosed names and addresses of all shareholders and the bank's capital, including number of shares to be issued. These acts ended the practice of bank note issuance by a multitude of banks because sole note-issuing powers were given to the Bank of England, although it was not formally designated as central bank at that time.

For centuries, the Bank of England oversaw all banking operations and monetary policy. After being nationalized in 1946, the Bank received the power to give directives to other banks, a power that it did not exercise. Instead, its quasi-official status and its

[2]See Chapter 11 for a discussion of U.S. monetary policy.
[3]See Chapter 15 for a discussion of the Basel Accord on international capital standards.

EXHIBIT 16-2 U.S. BANK ASSETS, 1981–1989

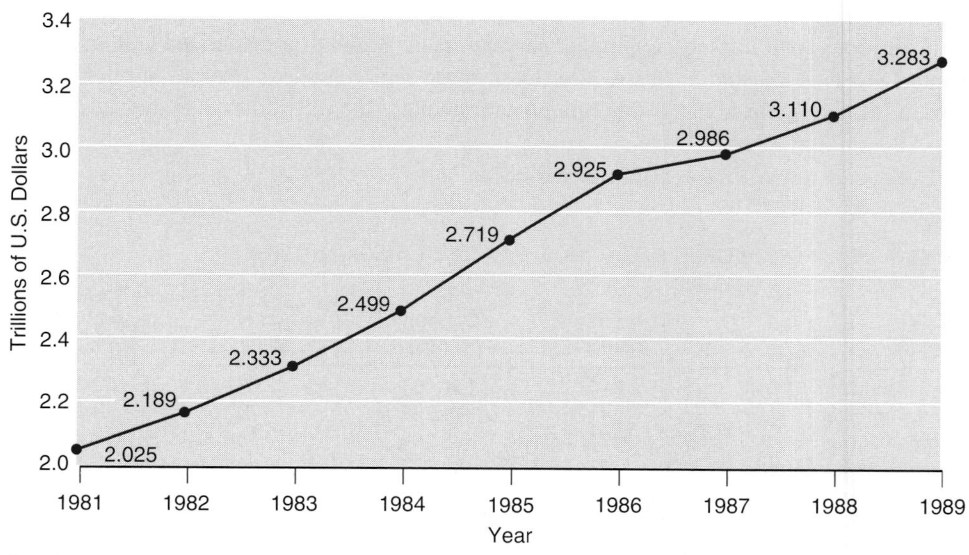

Source: Calculations and graphic based on data from *Bank Profitability, Statistical Supplement; Financial Statements of Banks 1981–1989,* Organisation for Economic Cooperation and Development, 1991.

EXHIBIT 16-3 TOP 20 U.S. BANKS RANKED BY CAPITAL TO ASSETS RATIO,* 1988

Rank	Bank	Percentage
1	BancOne	8.09
2	Meridian	7.81
3	First American	7.65
4	First of America	7.40
5	United Jersey	7.35
6	First Wachovia	7.18
7	J.P. Morgan	7.06
8	Fleet/Norstar	7.05
9	CoreStates	7.04
10	Society	6.91
11	Boatmen's	6.75
12	U.S. Bancorp	6.74
13	Midlantic	6.73
14	Ameritrust	6.69
15	NCNB†	6.58
16	Signet Banking	6.57
17	Suntrust Banks	6.49
18	Republic NY	6.44
19	Citizens and Southern†	6.42
20	Sovran Financial†	6.39

*Capital is defined as equity capital plus disclosed reserves.
†NCNB, Citizens and Southern and Sovran Financial have merged to become NationsBank.
Source: The Banker, July 1989, p. 42.

ability to affect the liquidity of other commercial banks, just as the Federal Reserve does in the United States, made it possible for the Bank of England to achieve its desired results through requests. In general, the banking system of the United Kingdom is based on convention and mutual understanding between government, the Bank of England, and other institutions.

Clearing banks in the United Kingdom perform the same functions as commercial banks in the United States. In particular, clearing banks provide the nation's primary payments mechanism (checks and other forms of payment) and short-term liquidity to industrial firms through extensive overdrafts.

Overdraft:
A check written for which there are insufficient bank funds but which the bank honors, effectively granting the check writer a short-term loan.

Unlike U.S. banks, British clearing banks branch nationwide. This system has resulted in a relatively small number of clearing banks that process 80 percent of all check and credit card transactions. Among these, the largest are Barclay's, Lloyd's, Midland, and National Westminster.

Secondary banks, also known as merchant banks, offer primarily time, rather than demand, deposits.[4] Competition among secondary banks is aggressive, and the banks use interest rates to attract large, wholesale deposits. To match the average maturity of deposits and loans, secondary banks generally make longer-term loans, frequently to non-British enterprises.

[4]See Chapter 5 for a discussion of merchant banks.

Both clearing and merchant banks use discount houses to adjust their liquidity levels.[5] The Bank of England does not make direct loans to or conduct open market operations with banks, as the Federal Reserve does in the United States. Instead, the Bank of England conducts these transactions with discount houses; in turn, the discount houses deal directly with the banks.

Exhibit 16-4 shows the growth in assets of the forty-seven clearing and secondary banks in the United Kingdom. From slightly over $300 billion in 1981, the total assets of U.K. banks increased at an average rate of 11 percent per year to reach $731 billion by 1989. In terms of total assets, the size of the U.K. banking system is thus less than one-quarter the size of the U.S. system, but the average size (total system assets divided by number of banks) of a U.K. bank is $15 billion, much larger than the average U.S. bank.

Canada

The Canadian banking system is a blend of the U.S. and U.K. systems. Structurally, it resembles the U.K. system in that banks branch nationwide, but its monetary policy implementation is similar to that of the United States with the Canadian central bank having direct relations with the commercial banks.

The earliest banks in Canada prior to the 1800s were not really banks but merchants who performed banking functions. Once banks developed, bank note exchange facilitated the flow of goods and services.

The Bank of Montreal, the first true bank, began operations in 1817 and received a charter in 1822. The bank's charter contained provisions that illustrate the strong governmental influence over Canadian banks. The original charter was granted for only 10 years, prohibited the bank from owning real estate other than bank premises and from making loans collateralized by real estate, required annual reports to shareholders with specified information, and placed a ceiling of 6 percent on loan interest rates. In the

[5] See Chapter 3 for coverage of discount houses.

EXHIBIT 16-4 U.K. BANK ASSETS, 1981–1989

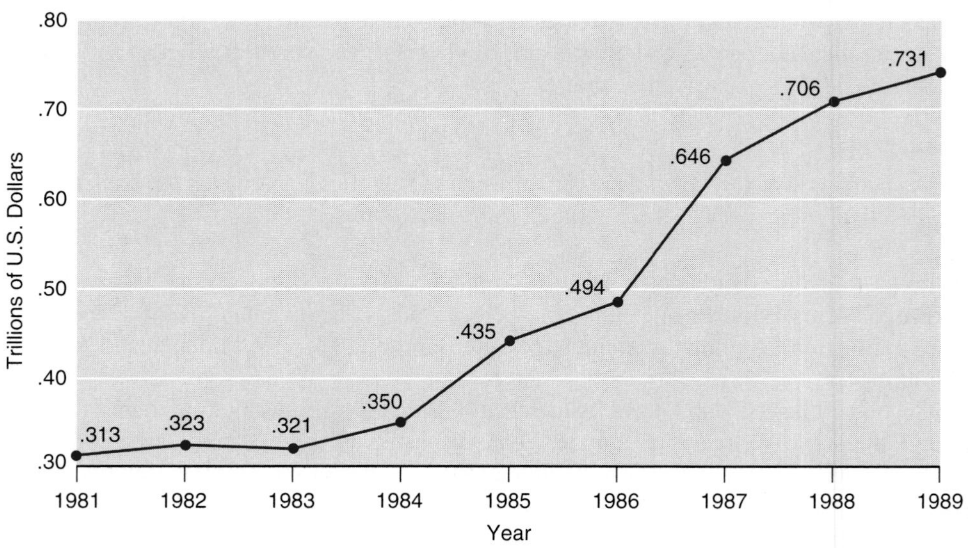

Source: Calculations and graphic based on data from *Bank Profitability, Statistical Supplement; Financial Statements of Banks 1981–1989,* Organisation for Economic Cooperation and Development, 1991, and *International Financial Statistics,* International Monetary Fund, Yearbook 1990.

United States, in contrast, strict government supervision of commercial banks did not begin until enactment of the National Bank Act of 1863.

The Finance Ministry of Canada implements both fiscal and monetary policy. The original Bank Act was passed in 1871, and subsequent amendments to the act have shaped the financial system over time. The Bank Act amendment of 1924 established the Office of the Inspector General of Banks, Canada's primary bank examiner. The Canadian central bank, the Bank of Canada, was created by a 1934 amendment to the Bank Act.

Restrictions of bank operations have eased over time. Residential mortgage loans with a 15 percent government guarantee have been permitted since 1936. In the mid-1940s, the government began to guarantee short- and intermediate-term bank loans to farmers and veterans. Also, the government lifted loan interest rate ceilings in 1967 (13 years before the major deregulatory thrust in the United States), allowed banks to offer discount brokerage services in the early 1980s, and permitted banks to own securities firms in the late 1980s (a practice only a few commercial banks in the United States were allowed).

Generally, there has been a good relationship between government and the banking industry. Canadian banks have been permitted to expand lending powers as desired and have enjoyed virtually complete freedom to offer a variety of deposits. This contrasts with the U.S. experience in which expansion of banking powers has been permitted primarily by bank regulators rather than by legislators because of the reluctance of legislators to pass further bank liberalization laws.

The Canadian equivalent of commercial banks is *chartered banks.* Between 1820 and 1970, 157 charters were granted. Sixty of these, however, were never used, forty-five banks either failed or ceased operation for some other reason, and there were a number of bank mergers. These factors have caused the number of Canadian banks to be much smaller than the number of U.S. banks. Five chartered banks control roughly 90 percent of Canadian bank assets: the Royal Bank of Canada, the Bank of Montreal, the Bank of Nova Scotia, the Toronto-Dominion Bank, and the Canadian Imperial Bank of Commerce. Unlike U.S. money center banks, these five operate branching networks throughout Canada, a practice prohibited for U.S. banks.

Exhibit 16-5 shows total Canadian bank assets in U.S. dollars from 1981 through 1989. On average the assets of Canadian banks increased at the rate of 4 percent per year over this period. The slump in growth in the early 1980s is attributable primarily to the strength of the U.S. dollar versus the Canadian dollar at that time. In general the size of the Canadian banking system is 12 percent the size of the U.S. banking system. Because there are only ten banks, however, the average size of a Canadian bank is $39.5 billion.

Germany

Commercial banks in Germany have even greater operational freedom than Canadian banks. Past abuses of power by the government have resulted in a general disdain for government intervention in the banking system.[6]

Moreover, individual states in Germany have a long history of regional strength and independence from the central government, resulting in several cities with significant economic influence. Bonn has historically been the political center; Hamburg is the country's largest city and busiest port; Dusseldorf is a major manufacturing site; and Frankfort is the financial center. In this respect, German banking is comparable to U.S. banking, with a large number of state and regional banks.

In contrast to the U.S. system, however, the Deutsche Bundesbank, the German central bank, does not restrict the scope of bank activities. German banks offer corporate under-

[6]The evolution of the relationship between the German government and central bank is described in Chapter 12.

EXHIBIT 16-5 CANADIAN BANK ASSETS, 1981–1989

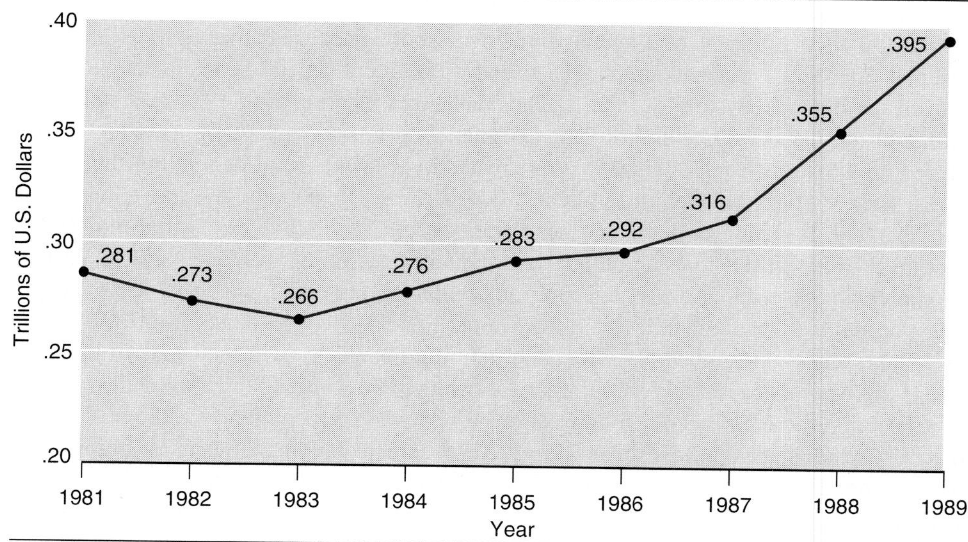

Source: Calculations and graphic based on data from *Bank Profitability, Statistical Supplement; Financial Statements of Banks 1981–1989,* Organisation for Economic Cooperation and Development, 1991, and *International Financial Statistics,* International Monetary Fund, Yearbook 1990.

writing services and hold the common stock of their clients as investments. Because of this wide range of bank services, German banks are called *universal* banks. The central bank does, however, perform customary roles of lender of last resort and facilitator of monetary policy. The German banking system has operated in this way since shortly after the end of World War II.

In addition to the state and regional banks, there are six big banks in Germany—Deutsche Bank, Dresdner Bank, and Commerzbank and their subsidiaries in Berlin. With average assets of $51 billion each, these banks control almost half of all German bank assets and branches and, like Canadian banks, operate nationwide.

Exhibit 16-6 shows the strong growth in total German banking assets in the 1980s. From $271 billion in 1981, total assets increased at an annual rate of 12 percent to reach $670 billion in 1989. Part of this is attributable to the depreciation of the U.S. dollar in the second half of the decade, but even in German deutsche marks, bank assets increased at an average rate of 8 percent a year. Total assets in the German banking system are 11 percent of the U.S. total, but because there are only 264 banks in that system, the average size of a German bank is $2.5 billion, ten times the U.S. average.

France

Prior to World War I, Paris was second only to London as an international financial center. Although France was ravaged by both World Wars, Paris has since regained much of its former status in world finance. In 1945, the four largest deposit banks were nationalized, and all banks were required to assume one of three forms: *deposit bank, banque d'affaires* (or business bank), or *medium- to long-term credit bank.* Deposit banks receive demand deposits or any deposits repayable within 2 years. Business banks underwrite new securities issues. Medium- to long-term credit banks offer loans and accept time deposits that have longer terms than the deposit bank instruments.

In 1966, however, the distinction between deposit banks and business banks was effectively eliminated in a move toward bank deregulation. Currently, French deposit banks

EXHIBIT 16-6 GERMAN BANK ASSETS, 1981–1989

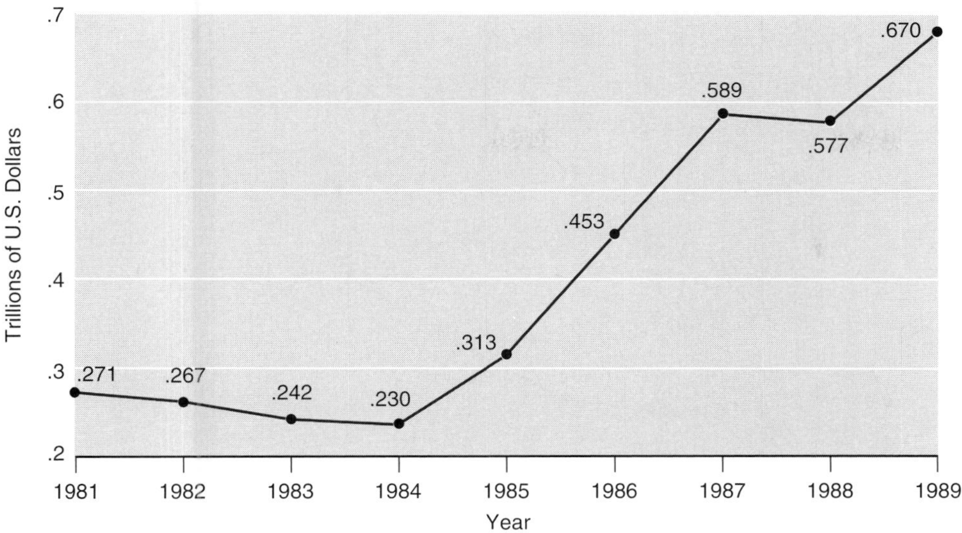

Source: Calculations and graphic based on data from *Bank Profitability, Statistical Supplement; Financial Statements of Banks 1981–1989,* Organisation for Economic Cooperation and Development, 1991, and *International Financial Statistics,* International Monetary Fund, Yearbook 1990.

offer a full line of financial services, including short- and medium-term loans, demand and time deposits, and securities dealing and underwriting.

Like Germany, France has a number of large banks that dominate the industry. The top three French banks control 80 percent of all bank deposits versus 20 percent for the top three banks in the United States. The largest French banks are Banque Nationale de Paris, Credit Lyonnais, Societé Générale, Banque Paribus, Banque Indosuez, and Credit Commercial de France.

Exhibit 16-7 shows that the eight big banks of France are larger than the 47 British, 10 Canadian, or 264 German banks described thus far. Assets of these French banks increased at an average rate of 12 percent from $410 billion in 1981 to over $1 trillion in 1989.[7] With average assets of $129 billion, these large now-universal banks play a major role in European finance.

Switzerland

Swiss commercial banks operate in an environment of privacy that is unmatched in the rest of the world. The 1934 Banking Law, the first federal banking law in that country, contained provisions that protected depositors in Swiss banks. Banks are prohibited from revealing details of financial transactions to outsiders unless an illegal act, according to Swiss law, is involved. This secrecy provision was partially motivated by attempts of agents of Nazi Germany to determine the nature and amount of Swiss deposits owned by German citizens. The bank secrecy law protected private citizens from the misguided whims of government by allowing depositors to use accounts identified with numbers only, the so-called numbered accounts, and by preventing transactions disclosure.

The provisions of the 1934 act have, nevertheless, created some tensions between the governments of Switzerland and other countries. Tax evasion and insider stock trading, for example, are considered criminal acts in the United States but are prosecuted adminis-

[7]Fluctuations in the value of the French franc played no role in the increase, as there was a 12 percent increase in bank assets in French franc terms as well.

EXHIBIT 16-7 FRENCH BANK ASSETS, 1981–1989

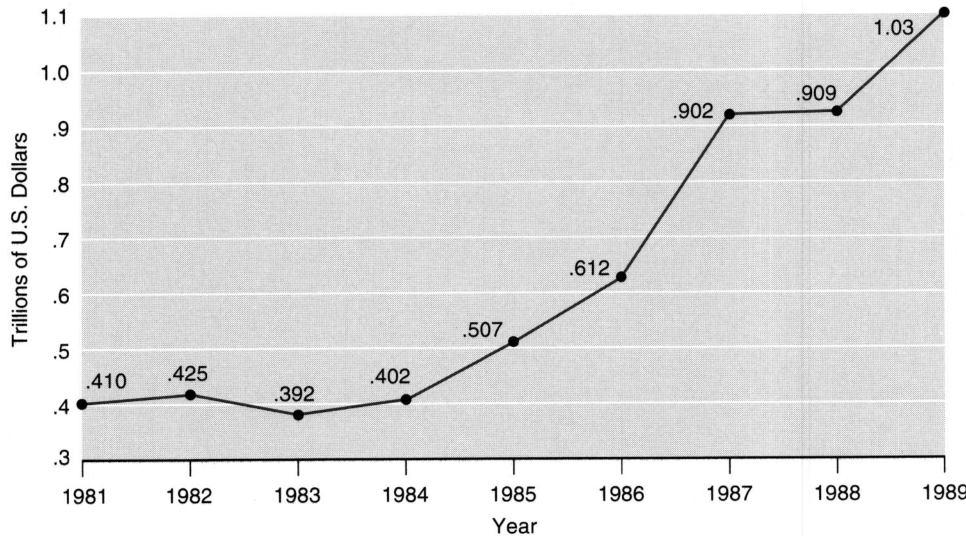

Source: Calculations and graphic based on data from *Bank Profitability, Statistical Supplement; Financial Statements of Banks 1981–1989,* Organisation for Economic Cooperation and Development, 1991, and *International Financial Statistics,* International Monetary Fund, Yearbook 1990.

tratively (in civil proceedings) in Switzerland. Because they are civil offenses in Switzerland, these acts do not override the bank secrecy law. In the interest of good international relations, however, the Swiss government has cooperated with the United States in some cases involving insider-trading violations. Along these same lines, beginning in 1991, the actual owner of all Swiss bank accounts, not a lawyer or other agent for the depositor, must be known by at least two bank officials.

Switzerland has had a favorable financial climate for other reasons. The Swiss people themselves have long been ardent savers, with the result that the country has consistently been a net exporter of capital. Consistent with its respect for privacy, Switzerland has remained politically neutral, avoiding burdensome expenses of war. Stability of the Swiss franc and the Swiss banking system after World War I contributed to its reputation as a safe haven for funds. As a result, during the 1920s and 1930s, the country's commercial banks received large deposits, primarily from Germany.

Over time, Switzerland's economic stability, political neutrality, and bank secrecy law have attracted capital worldwide. Foreign banks have likewise been attracted to Switzerland's stable financial markets.

Liechtenstein is a sovereign state approximately 1 hour's drive from Zurich and shares its currency, legal structure, and customs with Switzerland. Because of these shared characteristics, Liechtenstein has also become involved in the world of international banking.

Like German banks, the major banks in Switzerland are also universal banks. The five largest institutions control almost 50 percent of all Swiss bank assets and $72 billion each on average. The "big three" are Union Bank of Switzerland, the Swiss Bank Corporation, and Credit Suisse Bank. As compared to even German and French banks, Swiss banks are more involved in capital markets and equity investments in industrial firms.

Cantonal banks are publicly owned and restricted to the geographic areas in which they are located. While these twenty-nine institutions are considered banks, they tend to specialize in savings deposits and mortgage loans. Controlling roughly one-quarter of bank assets, cantonal banks are the second most important group of banks.

Foreign banks represent the third-largest presence in Switzerland, greater than domes-

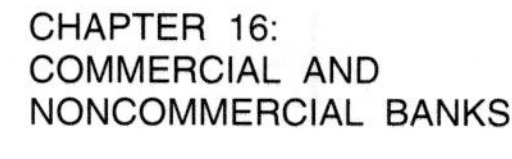

EXHIBIT 16-8 SWISS BANK ASSETS, 1981–1989

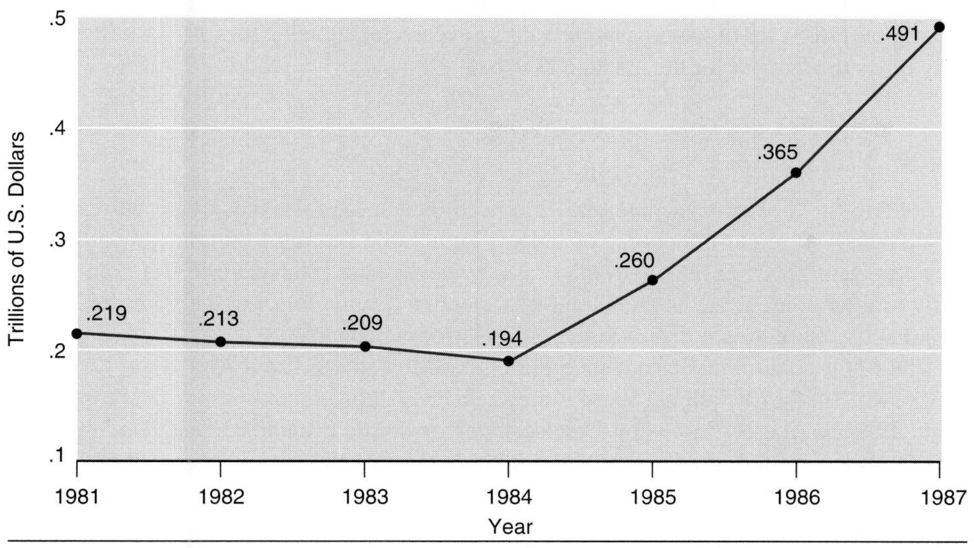

Source: Calculations and graphic based on data from *Bank Profitability, Statistical Supplement; Financial Statements of Banks 1981–1989,* Organisation for Economic Cooperation and Development, 1991, and *International Financial Statistics,* International Monetary Fund, Yearbook 1990.

tic savings banks and credit cooperatives. With over 100 foreign institutions, Switzerland is one of the world's largest international financial centers.

Exhibit 16-8 shows the assets of big banks and cantonal banks from 1981 through 1987. Growing at 14 percent a year, Swiss bank assets totaled $491 billion by 1987. The

EXHIBIT 16-9 EUROPE'S TOP 10 BANKS RANKED BY CAPITAL AND ASSET SIZE, 1988 ($ BILLIONS)

Rank	Bank	Capital*
1	National Westminster, London	$10.9
2	Barclay's London	10.5
3	Credit Agricole, Paris	8.7
4	Union Bank of Switzerland, Zurich	6.7
5	Deutsche, Frankfurt	6.5
6	Swiss Bank Corp., Basel	6.1
7	Lloyd's, London	5.9
8	Banque Nationale, Paris	5.6
9	Midland, London	5.6
10	Credit Lyonnais, Paris	5.4
		Assets
1	Credit Agricole, Paris	$214.4
2	Bank Nationale, Paris	197.0
3	Barclay's, London	189.4
4	Credit Lyonnais, Paris	178.9
5	National Westminster, London	178.5
6	Deutsche, Frankfurt	170.8
7	Group Eucreuil, Paris	150.3
8	Societe Generale, Paris	145.7
9	Dresdner, Frankfurt	129.7
10	Paribas, Paris	121.6

*Capital is defined as the sum of shareholders' equity and disclosed reserves.

Source: The Banker, July 1989, p. 46.

appreciation of the Swiss franc accounted for a portion of the high rate of growth, but even so, banking system assets in Swiss francs grew at an average rate of 8 percent per year. The thirty-four big and cantonal banks have average total assets of $14 billion, over fifty times the amount for the average U.S. bank.

Japan

Exceeding the size of Canadian and European banks, Japanese banks are currently the world's largest primarily because of Japan's large trade surpluses and the strength of the Japanese yen. This was not always the case, however. The 1868 Meiji Restoration was an early turning point in the economic development of Japan, replacing the prior feudal system that had generated little economic progress for the country.

The Meiji government established the Osaka Mint in 1871 and passed the New Currency Act. The 1872 National Bank Act established national banks, similar to those in the United States. The objectives of these acts were to create a stable currency and to mobilize funds for needed development. Although there were 153 national banks by 1879, the individual savings rate was quite low, most loans were agricultural, and there was limited availability of small business loans.

Rapid expansion of the money supply through the new national banks led to widespread inflation in 1877 through 1880. In turn, the inflation necessitated an amendment of the National Bank Act that created Japan's central bank to facilitate industrial finance, lower interest rates, and increase the resources available to financial institutions. The Bank of Japan began operations in 1882 and was given sole note-issuing power after 1899. All other banks were reorganized as ordinary banks.

The ordinary bank classification is composed of *city banks* and *regional banks.* City banks are large, nationwide organizations that target major industrial firms, while regional banks cater to the needs of smaller businesses and individuals. The activities of regional banks are typically limited to one prefecture or state.

Prior to World War II (1939–1945), Japanese banks were often members of large industrial combinations called *zaibatsus.* Through this mechanism, strong ties between banks and industrial firms were formed with the largest *zaibatsu* banks, Sumitomo, Mitsui, and Mitsubishi being particularly instrumental in Japan's economic development.

After World War II, *zaibatsus* were dismantled and *keiretsus,* or industrial groups with interlocking ownership, formed.[8] Former *zaibatsu* banks still provided the majority of debt financing to their *keiretsu* affiliates. Although the regional banks channeled their savings deposits to the *keiretsu* city banks through interbank loans, until the 1970s city banks were consistently overloaned.

Overlending:
The situation in which a bank's loan demand consistently exceeds available deposits and capital.

The Bank of Japan relieved the overlending by making loans to the city banks. The Bank of Japan encouraged loans to high-priority industries by offering its loans to city banks at favorable interest rates, which were then reflected in favorable interest rates to industrial firms. Overlending ended after the 1970s when Japan became a net capital exporter because of large trade surpluses. While industrial firms are now less dependent on their *keiretsu* banks, they still maintain close relationships.

In the late 1920s, there were approximately 1000 ordinary banks in Japan. During

[8]See also Chapter 12 for a discussion of *zaibatsus* and *keiretsus.*

World War II, many were liquidated or consolidated so that by 1945, only sixty-one ordinary banks remained. Today, the thirteen city banks hold almost 70 percent of total bank assets. With nationwide branch networks, these thirteen institutions control over 20 percent of all bank offices. The largest include Dai-Ichi Kangyo, Fuji, Sumitomo, Sanwa, Mitsubishi, Tokai, Mitsui, Daiwa, Taiyo Kobe, Saitama, Hokkaido, Kyoma, and the Bank of Tokyo. The average asset base of a city bank is $273 billion, more than twice as large as the average French big bank.

Exhibit 16-10 illustrates the rapid growth of Japanese bank assets for all ordinary banks. From a total of $1.2 trillion in 1981 Japanese bank assets increased at the rate of 20 percent a year to reach $5.3 trillion in 1989, more than 1.5 times as large as the total assets of all U.S. banks. Part of this increase is attributable to the appreciation of the Japanese yen, but even in yen terms, Japanese bank assets grew at almost 14 percent per year during the 1980s. The average assets for these 145 banks is $37 billion. There is no question that Japanese trade surpluses have moved these banks to the forefront of international finance as indicated in Exhibit 16-11.

A Cross-Country Comparison

When the banking system of the United States is compared with the systems in other industrialized countries, the contrasts are striking. Several points are clear:

- The amount of total assets in the U.S. banking system is smaller than the Japanese but larger than the others.
- The average bank size in the United States is smaller than in any other country analyzed.
- The growth rate of U.S. bank assets is slower than that of other countries.

Total Assets Exhibit 16-12 shows the relative proportions of bank assets in the seven countries discussed above. Japanese bank assets alone are almost half of the total, and the United States represents over 25 percent. The other shares range from 3.3 to 8.7

EXHIBIT 16-10 JAPANESE BANK ASSETS, 1981–1989

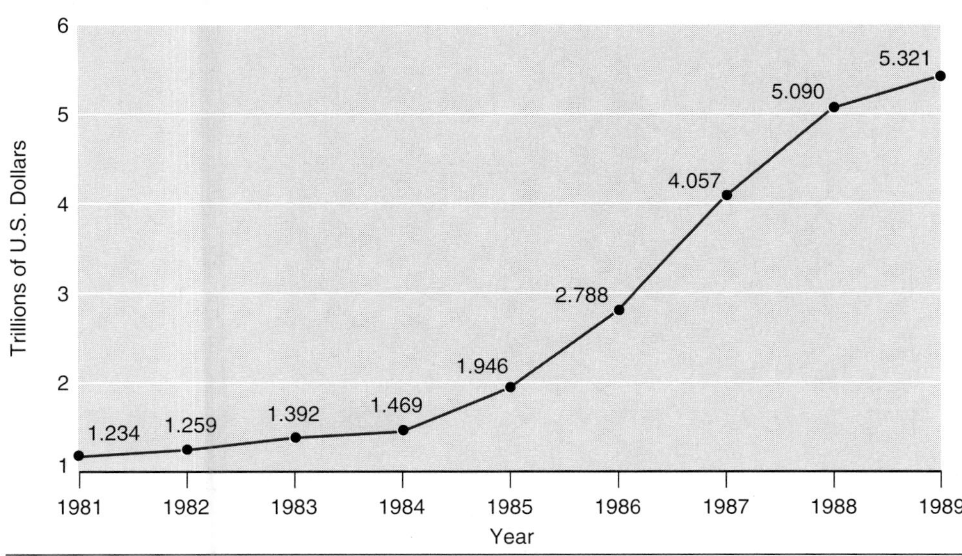

Source: Calculations and graphic based on data from *Bank Profitability, Statistical Supplement; Financial Statements of Banks 1981–1989,* Organisation for Economic Cooperation and Development, 1991, and *International Financial Statistics,* International Monetary Fund, Yearbook 1990.

EXHIBIT 16-11 THE WORLD'S TOP 10 BANKS RANKED BY CAPITAL AND BY ASSET SIZE, 1988 ($ BILLIONS)

Rank	Bank	Capital*
1	National Westminster, London	$10.9
2	Barclay's, London	10.5
3	Citicorp, New York	9.9
4	Fuji, Tokyo	9.0
5	Credit Agricole, Paris	8.7
6	Sumitomo, Osaka	8.6
7	Dai-Ichi Kangyo, Tokyo	8.5
8	Mitsubishi Bank, Tokyo	8.2
9	Industrial Bank of Japan, Tokyo	8.2
10	Sanwa, Tokyo	7.6
		Assets
1	Dai-Ichi Kangyo, Tokyo	$352.5
2	Sumitomo, Osaka	334.7
3	Fuji, Tokyo	327.8
4	Mitsubishi Bank, Tokyo	317.8
5	Sanwa, Tokyo	307.4
6	Industrial Bank of Japan, Tokyo	261.5
7	Norinchukin, Tokyo	231.7
8	Credit Agricole, Paris	214.4
9	Tokai, Nagoya, Japan	213.5
10	Mitsubishi Trust, Tokyo	206.0

*Capital is defined as shareholders' equity plus disclosed reserves.
Source: The Banker, July 1989, p. 41.

EXHIBIT 16-12 BANK ASSETS OF SELECTED INDUSTRIALIZED COUNTRIES, 1989

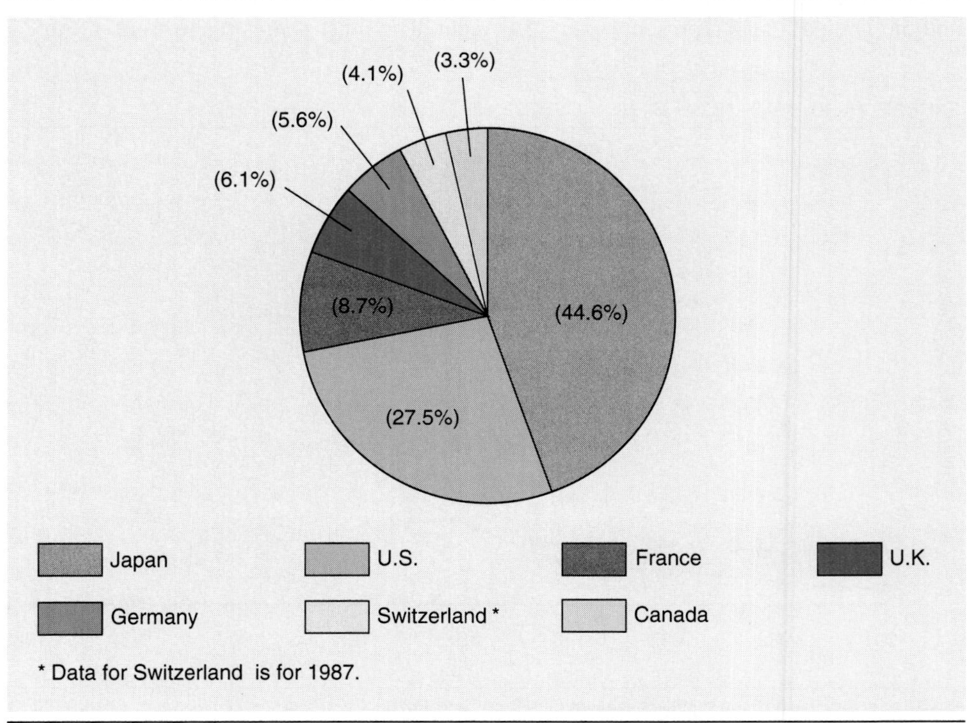

Source: Calculations and graphic based on data from *Bank Profitability, Statistical Supplement; Financial Statements of Banks 1981–1989,* Organisation for Economic Cooperation and Development, 1991, and *International Financial Statistics,* International Monetary Fund, Yearbook 1990.

percent. Taken in the aggregate, the U.S. banking system is the second-largest banking system in the world.

Average Size Even with a large share of total banking assets, U.S. banks operate at a competitive disadvantage because their average size is so much smaller. Consider the following breakdown of average bank size for these countries in 1989.

	Number of banks	Assets ($ billions)
United States	12,689	.26
United Kingdom	47	15.55
Canada	10	39.50
Germany	264	2.54
France	8	129.13
Switzerland	34	14.44
Japan	145	36.69

The average size of U.S. banks is 10 percent the size of the average German bank, .2 percent the size of the average French bank, and somewhere in between these percentages for the banks in the other countries. This significant size difference is important because a growing share of banks operating in the United States are foreign banks that compete directly with U.S. domestic banks. To the extent that U.S. banks are smaller and less able to offer a full range of services, domestic banks will continue to lose market share on their own turf.[9]

The size difference is also important because industrial firms operate increasingly in a global environment. The future international competitiveness of the United States will depend in large measure on the ability of small- and medium-size firms to sell their goods and services abroad. Just as the large *zaibatsu* banks helped Japanese industrial firms compete and expand internationally, so, too, can U.S. banks assist U.S. firms. The assistance can be limited by the size of the bank, however, because a smaller bank's loan portfolio can more easily become overly concentrated in one industry. Furthermore, it is not certain that foreign banks will have the same kind of commitment to U.S. firms that U.S. banks have.

Population per Bank The relative small size of U.S. banks is not tied to the lack of banking assets in this country but to the large number of banks. The number of banks in the United States is almost fifty times the number in Germany and almost ninety times the number in Japan. The populations of these countries are also smaller than the U.S. population but not so much as to reconcile the difference in number of banks. Exhibit 16-13 shows that the population per bank in the United States is 20,000 people. Switzerland has the next smallest population per bank at 192,000 people, ten times the U.S. figure, and France has the highest at over 7 million people per bank, 350 times the U.S. ratio. Exhibit 16-13 also shows that availability of banking services has not necessarily been compromised by the smaller number of banks because the population per bank branch among the six countries shown is remarkably similar. In the United States, France, the United Kingdom, and Switzerland, the population per bank branch is between 4000 and 5000 people. In Japan and Germany, the number is no more than twice this level. Thus, the convenience and availability of banking services need not be compromised in a banking system of larger institutions.

Growth Rate of Assets The competitive pressures on U.S. banks domestically and internationally are partially reflected in the growth rate of U.S. bank assets. The annual

[9]See Chapter 1 for a description of the increasing trend of foreign bank loans as a percentage of total bank loans in the United States.

EXHIBIT 16-13 POPULATION PER BANK AND PER BRANCH, 1989

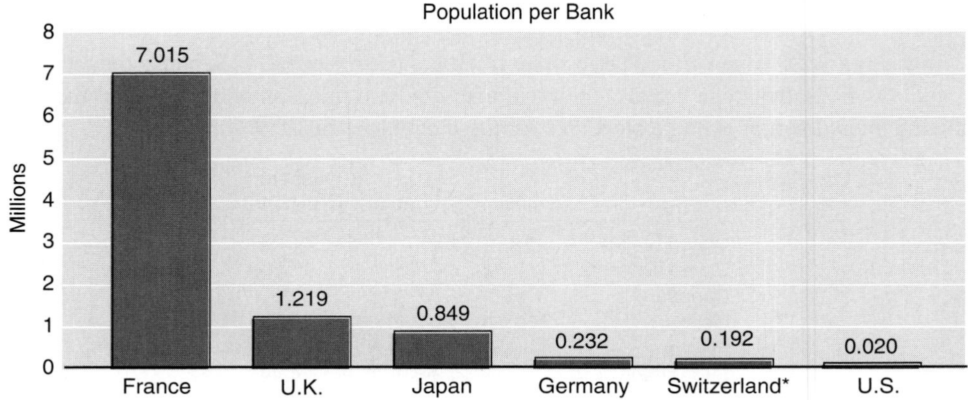

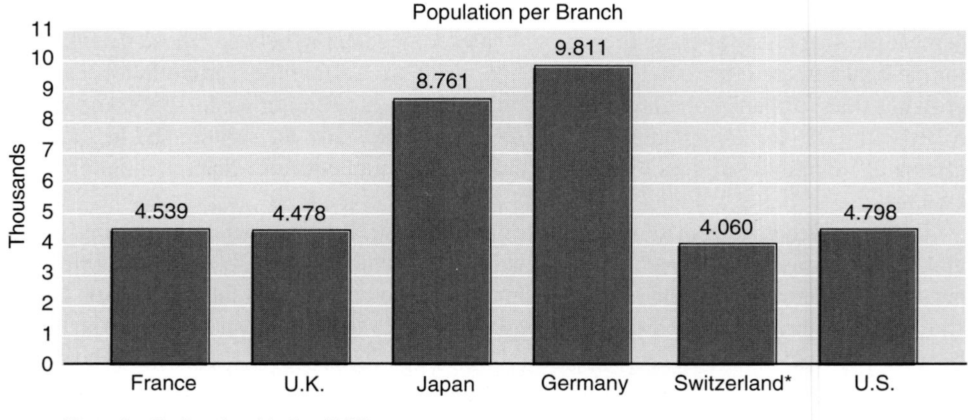

*Data for Switzerland is for 1987.

Source: Calculations and graphics based on data from *Bank Profitability, Statistical Supplement; Financial Statements of Banks 1981–1989,* Organisation for Economic Cooperation and Development, 1991, and *The World Bank Atlas 1990,* The World Bank, 1990.

growth rates of bank assets during the 1980s in the seven industrialized countries included here are:

	% in local currency	% in U.S. dollars
United States	6.2	6.2
United Kingdom	13.6	11.2
Canada	4.0	4.4
Germany	8.1	12.0
France	12.4	12.2
Switzerland	8.1	14.4
Japan	13.8	20.0

The U.S. growth rate was second lowest. U.S. bank regulators are now emphasizing higher capital ratios, leading some banks to reduce their overall size in order to boost the capital ratio. But the Basel Accord on capital standards applies to international banks in all these countries.[10] Thus, regulators are emphasizing capital standards in all the industrialized countries.

[10]See Chapter 15 for a description of the Basel Accord.

The fact remains that U.S. bank assets are not growing at the same pace as those in other major trading partners. All other things being equal, this means that the competitive disadvantage of smaller U.S. banks will be compounded only in the future. It will be difficult for the large number of banks to all increase in size and market share, particularly given a slow rate of growth within the U.S. domestic economy. The problem can be alleviated, however, if banks are allowed to branch nationwide and to merge and consolidate freely across state lines. Permitting U.S. banks to compete in other forms of financial services, such as securities underwriting, can also add to bank profitability and growth potential.

NONCOMMERCIAL BANKS

Commercial banks perform intermediation functions that are vital to an individual country's economic growth and development. In an international context, there are banks that focus on the development and economic coordination of a number of countries. Three examples of such banks are:

- The Bank for International Settlements
- The International Monetary Fund
- The World Bank

Bank for International Settlements

The Bank for International Settlements (BIS) in Basel, Switzerland, is a central bank for central banks. It is technically a commercial bank with a Swiss license but has immunity from government interference in its operations through an international treaty. Its depositors are central bankers, who meet privately ten times a year to discuss monetary issues and policies in the major industrialized countries of the world. The Committee on Banking Regulations and Supervisory Practices of the BIS issued the recommendation for international coordination of capital standards that has been adopted and will be implemented by 1993. Despite its confidential nature, the BIS has far-reaching effects on monetary systems.

Origin and Objectives There had been little coordination among central banks prior to 1914. After World War I (1914–1918), however, central banks began to work together ad hoc to stabilize the value of major currencies and to make settlements of payments used for postwar reconstruction. Also, the war reparations of Germany were transformed into less political payments through the Young Plan of 1929, which specified that Germany would make loans abroad to satisfy its remaining obligation. The loans would be repaid over a period of time on a normal commercial loan basis. An official bank was needed to channel these loans and to accept the repayments.

To accommodate these needs, the Bank for International Settlements was organized in 1930 with several objectives:

- To promote the cooperation of central banks
- To provide additional facilities for international financial operations
- To act as trustee or agent in regard to the international financial settlement entrusted to it under agreements with the parties concerned

The first role of the BIS was as agent for the Young Plan to handle the German war reparations.

Structure and Membership The BIS was established as a commercial bank with special international recognition. This form prevented the bank from being subjected to political forces and allowed it to maintain its independence. The original shareholders of the bank were the central banks of Belgium, France, Germany, Great Britain, Italy, and Japan—and a financial group from the United States that was composed of J.P. Morgan and Company, First National Bank of New York, and First National Bank of Chicago. Belgium, France, Germany, Italy, and the United Kingdom hold over 50 percent of the outstanding shares. The U.S. allocation of shares was sold to the public, but Citibank of New York is designated to exercise the voting rights of these shares. The Federal Reserve System did not purchase shares because it wanted to avoid any conflict of interest that may result from owning a private bank, but the Fed does participate actively as a member of BIS committees. Currently the central banks of twenty-eight countries are shareholders.[11]

To enable it to carry out its objectives, the bank has specific powers to:

- Buy, sell, and hold gold, currency, and securities for its own account and for the accounts of central banks
- Make loans to and to borrow from central banks against gold and high-quality, short-term securities
- Accept and maintain deposit accounts for central banks
- Accept deposit accounts for governments only in connection with international settlements
- Act as agent for any central bank that requests this service

Thus, the BIS can perform almost any financial service for central banks. The deposits of gold, currency, and securities are held at the central banks that are its correspondent banks. The Federal Reserve Bank of New York is the correspondent for the BIS in the U.S. market.

Certain practices are prohibited. The Bank for International Settlements may *not:*

- Issue notes payable at sight of bearer
- "Accept" bills of exchange
- Make loans to or open demand deposit accounts for governments
- Acquire a predominant interest in any business concern
- Remain any longer than necessary the owner of real property that comes into its possession as satisfaction for claims due to it
- Operate in such a way as to impair its short-term liquidity

The BIS must not create money in the way that a conventional bank might or act in the capacity of an industrial financier. It is also not permitted to directly finance government operations or to facilitate government payments except in special cases of international settlements.

Operations Although the BIS followed the guidelines of its original mission, some question arose as to the role of the Bank in its dealings with the German central bank during World War II. Prior to the war, the customary practice was for European countries to pay interest on the Young Plan loans by making deposits in the BIS to be transferred to Germany's account. The allegations of wrongdoing involved a suspected pro-German sentiment on the part of the BIS and knowing acceptance of looted gold from countries that Germany occupied, gold that had been stolen rather than received in the normal course of business.

After the war, the origins of all such gold transfers were investigated. The amount of

[11]The shareholders of the BIS include the central banks of Australia, Austria, Belgium, Bulgaria, Canada, the former Czechoslovakia, Denmark, Finland, France, Germany, Greece, Hungary, Iceland, Ireland, Italy, Japan, the Netherlands, Norway, Poland, Portugal, Romania, South Africa, Spain, Sweden, Switzerland, Turkey, the United Kingdom, and the former Yugoslavia.

gold illegally transferred was identified as 3740 kilograms, or 120,244 troy ounces, valued at $4.2 million at that time, or $48 million at today's price.[12] Because of this controversy, the United States advocated disbanding the BIS, but the Western European governments did not agree. The BIS made the gold available to the countries from which it had been illegally seized and then resumed operations as before the war. The stigma of this episode, however, stayed with the BIS and prevented it from being accepted as a dominant international financial institution.

Despite reservations about the operations of the BIS on the part of the treasuries of western governments, the central banks of the same countries have consistently used the BIS as a forum to resolve issues concerning the world's money supply, currency values, and interest rates. At their meetings in Basel, held once a month for 10 months of the year, the central bankers exchange information on their countries' problems and the international monetary situation. A central bank governor who is contemplating a policy change can discuss it confidentially with the others and get their reaction to it. The meetings are essentially free from formal documentation, either public or private. Instead, "gentlemen's agreements" are reached, and each is bound by his word to the others.

On a daily basis, the foreign exchange officers of central banks and BIS officers communicate in multilateral conversations via telephone to discuss the currency markets. The BIS provides the central banks with a cloak of anonymity in that their deposits are pooled and then invested in currencies and loans on behalf of the BIS without any particular national identity being associated with the investment.

An example of this anonymity at work is the case of Mexico's financial distress in 1982. Mexico had been borrowing overnight funds for months in the U.S. federal funds market, with each day's borrowing increasing in order to pay the interest on the borrowing from the day before. By August, Mexican borrowing represented almost 25 percent of the entire U.S. federal funds market. Mexico had a commitment of $4.5 billion from the International Monetary Fund, but several months would pass before the money could actually be disbursed. By that time, Mexico would have absorbed even more of the Fed funds market. Furthermore, if the Federal Reserve blocked Mexico's access to the federal funds market, a quarter of the highly liquid market would have been completely frozen, precipitating a financial crisis.

Mexico needed $1.85 billion to pay off its federal funds purchases; the BIS came to its aid. Publicly, the BIS provided Mexico the needed $1.85 billion. Privately, however, the loan was made by central banks through the BIS: $925 million from the U.S. Federal Reserve and the rest from the central banks of Germany, Switzerland, the United Kingdom, Italy, and Japan. This example illustrates the spirit of the central bankers who belong to the Bank for International Settlements: a crisis for the central banker in one country is a crisis for all of them.

International Monetary Fund

The International Monetary Fund (IMF) is an organization conceived by the Treasuries of the United States and the United Kingdom during World War II. The objectives were to ensure free convertibility of currencies in trade and to avoid currency devaluations (to make exports more price competitive) that brought chaos to currency markets. While the Bank for International Settlements was formed by central banks, the International Monetary Fund was formed through the cooperation of national treasuries.

Objectives The fund was to involve a finite pool of funds that could be drawn upon by countries experiencing balance-of-payment deficits, that is, imports in excess of ex-

[12]At the time, gold was valued at $35 per ounce; today the price is closer to $400 per ounce.

ports. The assets of the fund would be composed of gold and currencies. Each member country would contribute a specified amount of its own currency and gold, to be determined from that country's general economic strength. Forty-four countries reached agreement in 1944 at Bretton Woods, New Hampshire, to create the International Monetary Fund. There are now over 150 members.

The objectives of the IMF are to:

- Promote international monetary cooperation through a permanent institution which provides consultation and collaboration
- Facilitate the expansion and balanced growth of international trade and contribute to promotion and maintenance of employment and income
- Promote currency exchange stability
- Assist in the establishment of a multilateral system of payments and in the elimination of foreign exchange restrictions
- Make it possible for members to cover their temporary trade imbalances
- Shorten the duration of trade imbalances

The IMF thus seeks to help member countries manage their external trade situation. With resources available to cover balance-of-payments deficits and give assistance to correct these imbalances, members could avoid international monetary crises.

Structure and Quotas The IMF is composed of two main departments: the General Department and the Special Drawing Rights Department. The special drawing right (SDR) is the first reserve asset (that is, money) to be created by international decision. Membership in the IMF confers the right to participate in the Special Drawing Rights Department.

Within the General Department, each member has a general resource account (GRA). Each member deposits in its GRA the *quota* that it is assessed.

Quota:

The minimum subscription (contribution) that a country must pay in order to become a member of the International Monetary Fund.

The sum of these quotas forms the pool of funds available to members as needed. A country's quota is based on several economic factors, including gross domestic product, international reserves (gold and foreign exchange), international payments and receipts, and the variability of international payments.

A member satisfies its quota subscription by depositing (1) freely usable (convertible) currencies and/or SDRs and (2) its own currency. At least 25 percent of the subscription must be in freely usable currencies and/or SDRs, on which the IMF pays remuneration or interest. Quotas are reviewed at least once every 5 years.

The aggregate of quota subscriptions is available to other members as needed. When a member experiences a balance-of-payments deficit, it essentially faces a shortage of currencies other than its own. It may then tap the resources of the IMF, with the first resource being its *reserve tranche.*

Reserve tranche:

The excess of a country's quota over the holdings by the International Monetary Fund of its own currency.

When a country first joins the IMF, its reserve tranche is 25 percent of the quota, that is, the portion contributed in SDRs and other freely usable currencies. A member can use its reserve tranche to satisfy a balance-of-payments deficit by exchanging its own currency for the freely usable currencies. There is no obligation to reverse this transaction, that is, to repurchase its own currency because the reserve tranche is considered the member's own international liquidity.

If the reserve tranche is insufficient to satisfy the need, *credit tranches* may be obtained. These tranches are denominated in four increments, each equal to one-quarter of the member's quota. As long as the member is making efforts to correct its balance-of-payments deficit, the first tranche is liberally available and subject to few terms and conditions other than repurchase, that is, repayment of the loan. Subsequent tranches, called *upper-credit tranches,* are subject to increased scrutiny and conditionality. The IMF has also instituted a number of special programs to assist members that find themselves in chronic balance-of-payments difficulties.

Special Drawing Rights The SDRs are a form of money created by the IMF that may be used only by monetary authorities and other official agencies. A member obtains SDRs by participating in the Special Drawing Rights Department, and SDRs allocated to the member entitle it to obtain freely usable currencies from other IMF members. A participant in the Special Drawing Rights Department agrees to accept SDRs from any other participant designated by the IMF and to provide the designated participant with an equivalent amount of freely usable currency. The allocation of SDRs is in proportion to a member's quota. The IMF may periodically add to or subtract from the SDRs outstanding depending upon economic conditions. There are currently SDR21 billion outstanding.

The value of the SDR is tied to the value of specified units of five major currencies. Currently the currencies and units are:

Currency	Number of units
U.S. dollar	.4520
Deutsche mark	.5270
French franc	1.0200
Japanese yen	33.4000
British pound	.0893

These five countries have the largest amount of exports among IMF members, and the number of units reflects the relative size of their exports and holdings of currencies in the IMF. Early in 1991, the dollar value of the SDR was $1.3463.

Balance Sheet Exhibit 16-14 shows the balance sheet of the General Department of the IMF for fiscal 1989. Assets totaled SDR 100 billion, with 92 percent invested in currencies and securities. The other major categories are SDR holdings, gold, and receivables. The liabilities of the IMF are primarily member quotas which constitute almost 90 percent of the total.

The World Bank Group

The World Bank Group is composed of four affiliates:

- The International Bank for Reconstruction and Development (IBRD, also frequently called the World Bank)
- The International Development Association (IDA)
- The International Finance Corporation (IFC)
- The Multilateral Investment Guarantee Agency (MIGA)

The common objective of all these organizations is to help raise the standard of living in developing countries by channeling financial resources from developed countries to developing regions.

EXHIBIT 16-14 INTERNATIONAL MONETARY FUND BALANCE SHEET, 1989*

	Millions of SDRs	Percentage
Assets		
Currencies and securities	92,017	91.8
SDR holdings	976	1.0
Gold holdings	3,620	3.6
Receivables†	1,228	1.2
Other	2,449	2.4
Total	100,290	100.0
Liabilities		
Quotas	89,988	89.7
Reserves	2,178	2.2
Borrowings	5,607	5.6
Payables‡	387	0.4
Other	2,130	2.1
Total	100,290	100.0

*Balance sheet date is April 30, 1989, on which date the dollar value of an SDR was SDR1 = $1.29566.
†Interest income.
‡Interest expense.
Source: Calculations based on data from *International Monetary Fund 1990 Annual Report.*

International Bank for Reconstruction and Development The IBRD, or World Bank, was created at the same time as the IMF during the Bretton Woods conference in 1944. While the IMF concentrates primarily on short-term financial difficulties, the World Bank is concerned with long-term development. The two organizations generally hold their annual meetings jointly, and a prerequisite for membership in the World Bank is membership in the IMF. Currently there are over 150 World Bank members.

According to its charter, the World Bank must lend for productive purposes and must stimulate economic growth in the developing countries in which it lends. Specifically, the purposes of the Bank are to:

- Assist in the reconstruction and development of territories of members by facilitating investment for productive purposes
- Promote private foreign investment by means of guarantees or participations in loans and other investments made by private investors
- Promote long-term, balanced growth of international trade by assisting in raising productivity, the standard of living, and improving conditions of labor in member countries
- Arrange loans so that the more useful and urgent projects are dealt with first
- Assist in bringing about a smooth transition from a wartime to a peacetime economy

World Bank loans must be made to governments with all due consideration to ensure repayment and be guaranteed by that government. In this way, IBRD loans are not considered concessional loans, that is, containing some form of grant assistance. The loans are generally repayable in 15 to 20 years, and the purposes for the loans include:

- Agriculture and rural development
- Education
- Energy
- Education
- Transportation
- Urban development

Obtaining a World Bank loan is a lengthy process that involves six steps—identification, preparation, appraisal, negotiation, implementation and supervision, and evaluation. In the *identification* phase the borrowing country decides which project should be proposed with the help of the World Bank. This may take 1 to 2 years. *Preparation* for the project will also take between 1 and 3 years and requires detailed analysis of all aspects of the project—technical, economic, financial, and social. Identification and preparation are the responsibilities of the borrowing country even though it may receive assistance from the IBRD. *Appraisal* of the project is done by the World Bank over a 3- to 6-month period. Rarely is the project rejected at this stage, but some modifications may be required. Once the project appraisal is completed, the Bank and the borrowing country enter into *negotiations* on the terms of project implementation. The negotiated conditions are documented in the loan agreement. This stage usually takes between 1 and 2 months. Project *implementation* is the responsibility of the borrowing country, but the IBRD does supervise both procurement of needed materials and project implementation. The implementation may require 6 years or more. Once the project is completed and the loan has been fully disbursed, the World Bank performs an *evaluation* of the project, comparing the actual results with the anticipated results. The results of these evaluations are then published in the Bank's annual review of projects.

Exhibit 16-15 shows the balance sheet of the World Bank in 1989. Of the total $108 billion in assets, $78 billion, or 72 percent, was devoted to loans to member countries. Government securities and time deposits were roughly 10 percent each of the total.

Bank capital was 16 percent of total liabilities and capital. Medium- and long-term borrowings totaled approximately 70 percent. Unlike the IMF, which is funded primarily

EXHIBIT 16-15 WORLD BANK BALANCE SHEET, 1989

	Millions of dollars	Percentage
Assets		
Cash:		
Due from banks	791	0.7
Time deposits	10,404	9.6
Government securities	11,735	10.9
Receivables*	3,457	3.2
Loans	77,942	72.1
Other	3,830	3.5
Total assets	108,159	100.0
Liabilities and capital		
Liabilities		
Payables†	4,980	4.6
Short-term borrowings	7,918	7.3
Medium- and long-term borrowings	75,085	69.4
Reserve for loan loss	800	0.8
Other liabilities	1,762	1.6
Total liabilities	90,545	83.7
Capital		
Capital stock	8,652	8.0
Reserves	7,868	7.3
Unallocated retained earnings	1,094	1.0
Total capital	17,614	16.3
Total liabilities and capital	108,159	100.0

*Currency swaps, securities sold, interest income on loans and securities.
†Currency swaps, securities purchased, interest expense on borrowings.
Source: Calculations based on *The World Bank Annual Report 1989.*

through member quotas, or contributions, the IBRD issues debt instruments in money and capital markets to fund the largest share of its loans to member countries.

International Development Association The International Development Association (IDA) is the concessional affiliate of the World Bank Group. Its loans, for similar purposes as IBRD loans, are made to the poorest member countries, countries that are not able to qualify for IBRD loans. The wealthier members contribute to IDA, which then makes interest-free loans, called credits, repayable in 35 to 40 years. The IDA assets totaled $59 billion in 1989, and 60 percent was invested in development credits. In the liability section, subscriptions and contributions represented 91.5 percent of total sources of funds.

Exhibit 16-16 shows the breakdown of external debt of developing countries by region in 1988. While the amount of external debt varies, the contribution of the IBRD and IDA has been significant in each case. Between 8 and 9 percent of total financing for developing countries in Europe, Latin America, and North Africa has been derived from these organizations. East Asia (14 percent), sub-Saharan Africa (17 percent), and south Asia (30 percent) have depended on the World Bank and IDA for even more of their external financing. Both organizations perform an extremely important function in terms of development assistance in the countries that are recipients of their services.

International Finance Corporation The International Finance Corporation (IFC) makes private-sector investments, rather than loans to governments. It was established in 1956, and its capital is provided by 135 member countries. The IFC:

- Provides long-term loans and risk capital, without government guarantees, to private enterprises that have difficulty raising funds from other sources on reasonable terms
- Mobilizes additional project finance from other investors and lenders

EXHIBIT 16-16 DEVELOPING COUNTRY EXTERNAL DEBT BY REGION, 1988

	Sub-Saharan Africa	East Asia and Pacific	Europe and Mediterranean	Latin America	North Africa and Middle East	South Asia
Total (millions)	$118,498	$168,648	$136,054	$366,576	$106,081	$84,221
Official creditors						
Concessional credit*						
IDA	9.7%	1.9%	.1%	.2%	1.5%	22.3%
Other	25.9	20.1	9.0	5.5	32.3	41.0
Nonconcessional credit						
IBRD	7.1	12.4	8.5	8.1	6.6	8.1
Other	24.5	8.6	25.0	13.3	26.9	2.0
	67.2	43.0	42.6	27.1	67.3	73.4
Private creditors						
Bonds	.4	9.3	4.5	4.8	4.8	2.1
Commercial banks	18.7	34.3	44.2	62.0	10.2	20.8
Other	13.7	13.4	8.7	6.1	17.7	3.7
	32.8	57.0	57.4	72.9	32.7	26.6
	100.0	100.0	100.0	100.0	100.0	100.0

*Loans that have a grant element of 25 percent or more of the loan.
†International Development Association.
‡International Bank for Reconstruction and Development.
Source: World Debt Tables 1989–90; External Debt of Developing Countries, The World Bank, 1989.

- Encourages the flow of foreign and domestic private capital to developing countries through the establishment or expansion of capital markets and financial institutions

The operations of the IFC are unique within the World Bank Group with respect to its assistance in development of financial markets. The organization advises governments on the fiscal, legal, and regulatory frameworks that are required for healthy, market-oriented financial sectors. When it gives financial and technical assistance to local financial institutions, it is often the first such assistance in the host country. The IFC attracts international investors to host country securities markets by sponsoring, underwriting, and distributing the shares of both individual host country companies and funds that invest in host country securities.

In 1990 the IFC had total assets of $5.6 billion, with 58 percent in loans and equity investments and 39 percent in cash, deposits, and securities. Equity was 33 percent of liabilities and capital. Forty-eight percent of liabilities and capital was derived from market sources with maturities in excess of 2 years. Another 16 percent came from borrowings from the IBRD, with both short- and long-term maturities. Like IBRD, the IFC relies heavily on capital markets for its funding.

Multilateral Investment Guarantee Agency The Multilateral Investment Guarantee Agency (MIGA) is the newest member of the World Bank Group, beginning operations in 1988. The MIGA guarantees foreign investors against the danger associated with noncommercial risk and, in conjunction with the International Finance Corporation, provides policy and advisory services to promote the flow of foreign investments to developing countries and to assist developing countries in creating an attractive and hospitable investment climate.

The Guarantee Program provides insurance protection for foreign investors that might otherwise avoid long-term commitments in developing countries because of perceived political risks. The MIGA guarantees projects against specific risks for typically a 15-year period. Guarantees are provided against *currency transfer risk,* that is, the risk that conditions for converting and repatriating currency (transferring it to the home country of the foreign investor) will deteriorate. Investors are also protected against *expropriation risk,* or the risk of being unwillingly deprived of the investment or the benefits from the investment. *Risk of war, revolution,* and *civil disturbance* are covered in that the investor will be compensated for loss of physical assets and business interruption from a military action or civil disturbance in the host country. If the host country denies the investor justice in contractual matters, the investor will be compensated under the *breach of contract* coverage.

The MIGA may insure up to 90 percent of an investment, with a limit of $50 million. There is no minimum amount of coverage. By mid-1989, 1 year after its formation, MIGA had received sixty-nine applications for project insurance coverage in twenty-four member countries. The MIGA promises to be an important addition to the World Bank Group in terms of promoting more foreign investment from the private sector.

SUMMARY

Commercial banks are an integral part of the economy in all industrialized countries. In the United States, commercial banks serve a relatively small geographic area because nationwide branching is not permitted. In other major trading partners of the United States, there is no such prohibition. One of the consequences of this is that U.S. banks are on average much smaller than banks in other industrialized countries. Furthermore, the large trade surpluses of Japan have led to that country's banks dominating the ranks of the world's largest. The competitive position of U.S. banks could be improved, however, if the number of banks was reduced through consolidation and nationwide branching were permitted.

Several international, noncommercial banks have special roles in international finance. The Bank for International Settlements serves the central bankers of the world. Through it, coordinated monetary policy is implemented and monetary crises averted. The International Monetary Fund helps countries alleviate balance-of-payments problems by making pooled resources available to its members and by issuing a unique form of money, called Special Drawing Rights. The World Bank Group concerns itself with the long-term development issues of its members by providing long-term loans, equity investments, advice concerning capital market formation, and insurance to protect against political risk. The members of the World Bank Group are the International Bank for Reconstruction and Development, the International Development Association, the International Finance Corporation, and the Multilateral Investment Guarantee Agency.

KEY TERMS

Bank for International Settlements
banque d'affaires
cantonal bank
chartered bank
city bank
clearing bank
deposit bank
International Monetary Fund
overdrafts
overlending
quota
special drawing right (SDR)
universal bank
World Bank

END-OF-CHAPTER QUESTIONS

1. Does it appear that commercial banking systems must follow a particular format with respect to structure and branching in order for an industrial economy to thrive? Why or why not?
2. Discuss the contributory factors in the emergence of Japanese banks as the world's largest.
3. In what ways has the Canadian banking system been more deregulated than the U.S. system?
4. Name a factor that is common to both German and Japanese banks with respect to industrial firms.
5. Among the commercial bank systems discussed in this chapter, in which system(s) is nationwide branching not permitted?
6. In what ways is the Canadian banking system a blend of both the U.K. and the U.S. systems?
7. Explain the bank secrecy law in Switzerland.
8. Compare the commercial banks of Germany with those of the United States.
9. Compare the total banking assets of the United States with those of the other countries included in this chapter.
10. **a.** Which country in this chapter has the largest average bank asset base?
    b. How does this compare with the United States average?
11. In what ways are the founders of the Bank for International Settlements different from those of the International Monetary Fund?
12. What is a special drawing right?
13. Why does the BIS not have an equivalent to the IMF's special drawing right?
14. What kinds of financial assistance does the IMF offer its members?
15. How is the financial assistance offered by the IMF different from that offered by the International Bank for Reconstruction and Development?
16. Why would a country that can obtain loans from the International Development Association not qualify for loans from the IBRD?

17. How do the sources of funds of the IMF differ from those of the World Bank (IBRD)?
18. Why did the BIS not take over the major international monetary functions in 1944?
19. How do the operations of the International Finance Corporation differ from those of the IBRD?
20. How does the Multilateral Investment Guarantee Agency encourage foreign investment in developing countries?

SELECTED REFERENCES

Adams, T. F. M., and Iwao Hoshii. *A Financial History of the New Japan,* Kodansha International, Ltd., Palo Alto, California, 1972.
Auboin, Roger. *Bank for International Settlements 1930–1955,* International Finance Section, Department of Economics and Sociology, Princeton University, Princeton, New Jersey, 1955.
Bank Profitability, Statistical Supplement, Financial Statements of Banks 1981–1989, Organisation for Economic Co-operation and Development, Paris, 1991.
Edwards, Richard W., Jr. *International Monetary Collaboration,* Transnational Publishers, Inc., Dobbs Ferry, New York, 1985.
Emery, Robert F. *The Financial Institutions of Southeast Asia. A Country-by-Country Study,* Praeger Publishers, New York, 1970.
Financial Organization and Operations of the IMF, International Monetary Fund, Washington, D.C., 1990.
Grady, John, and Martin Weale. *British Banking: 1960–85,* St. Martin's Press, New York, 1986.
Horne, James. *Japan's Financial Markets,* George Allen and Unwin, North Sydney, Australia, 1985.
How the World Bank Works with Nongovernmental Organizations, The World Bank, Washington, D.C., 1990.
International Finance Corporation Annual Report 1990, International Finance Corporation, Washington, D.C. 1991.
International Financial Statistics, International Monetary Fund, Washington, D.C., Yearbook 1990.
International Monetary Fund 1990 Annual Report, International Monetary Fund, Washington, D.C.
King, Mary L. *The Great American Snafu,* Lexington Books, Lexington, Massachusetts, 1985.
Lees, Francis A., and Maximo Eng. *International Financial Markets: Development of the Present System and Future Prospects,* Praeger Publishers, New York, 1975.
M.I.G.A. Annual Report 1989, Multilateral Investment Guarantee Agency, Washington, D.C. 1990.
Mullineux, Andrew. *International Banking and Financial Systems: A Comparison,* Graham and Trotman, London, 1987.
Neufeld, E. P. *The Financial System of Canada,* Macmillan Company of Canada, Toronto, Canada, 1972.
Pressnell, L. S. *Money and Banking in Japan,* St. Martin's Press, New York, 1973.
Revell, Jack. *The British Financial System,* Macmillan Press, Ltd., London, 1973.
Schloss, Henry. *The Bank for International Settlements,* New York University, Graduate School of Business Administration, New York, 1970.
Skully, Michael T. *Financial Institutions and Markets in the Far East; A Study of China, Hong Kong, Japan, South Korea, and Taiwan,* St. Martin's Press, New York, 1982.
Suzuki, Yoshio. *Money and Banking in Contemporary Japan,* Yale University Press, London, 1980.
Viner, Aron. *Inside Japanese Financial Markets,* Dow Jones–Irwin, Homewood, Illinois, 1988.
World Bank Annual Report 1989, The World Bank, Washington, D.C. 1990.
World Bank Atlas 1990, World Bank, Washington, D.C., 1990.
World Debt Tables 1989–90; External Debt of Developing Countries, vol. 1, The World Bank, Washington, D.C., 1989.

CHAPTER 17

THE DOMESTIC OPERATIONS OF COMMERCIAL BANKS

CHAPTER OUTLINE

CHAPTER OVERVIEW

This chapter:

- Describes recent trends in the provision of payment services by commercial banks
- Highlights changes in corporate services in the U.S. banking system
- Includes a description of German bank and industry relations
- Discusses the emergence of bank discount brokerages
- Outlines basic tenets of socialist and Islamic banking
- Examines the issue of U.S. bank branching in theory and in practice

Banking services in the United States have evolved from an early emphasis on deposit taking (primarily demand deposits and savings accounts) and short-term loans into a much wider range of deposits and loans. As banking clientele has become more financially sophisticated, so have bank operations. Commercial banks have always played a vital role in the country's payments system. Now that role is more highly automated in order to expand capacity and to provide more convenient, round-the-clock service to customers. Large corporate clients are now more financially independent and have substituted direct financing (via commercial paper, for example) for previous bank loans. This has led banks to look more to fee-generating services for large corporations (letters of credit to back commercial paper, for example) and increasingly to small- and medium-size firms.

At the same time, bank entry into many fee-generating activities (securities underwriting, for example) has been frustrated by federal law that prohibits these activities. State law has permitted state-chartered banks more latitude, and federal regulators have begun to grant specific powers on a case-by-case basis. Nevertheless, domestic banks remain unable to offer a full range of services within the United States.

There are numerous issues. How can the banks remain profitable when large corporate business continues to offer thinning margins? How can income be augmented when fee-generating activities are restricted? How can risk in the banking industry be contained when banks must turn increasingly to smaller, *more risky* clients to boast profit margin? How can banks maintain their market share if competitors may provide banklike services while banks may not expand their product offerings?

As the legislative battle over bank powers is waged, some points are clear. One of these is that to remain profitable, banks must reduce costs. This premise has far-reaching implications. One of these is that merger with another bank may be one of the most cost-effective ways for a bank to grow. Another is that the cost of accepting a deposit or providing a deposit withdrawal can be greatly reduced through automation. Because of this, the nature of the payments mechanisms in the United States is changing.

PAYMENT MECHANISMS

Checks

United States Historically, *checks* have been the second most preferred method of payment in the Unites States, with *cash* representing the greatest number of transactions. Yet in terms of volume, checks have represented a larger dollar amount of payments. The dollar amount of checks written is more than ten times the dollar amount of cash transactions, but checks are written in only about 25 percent of all transactions. On the other hand, cash payments constitute roughly 70 percent of all transactions. Smaller transactions are almost always settled in cash.

Individuals write the greatest number of checks (over 50 percent) in the United States. The payees of these checks are primarily businesses, with government and other individuals receiving less than 10 percent of them. The next most frequent check writers are businesses, making payments to other businesses (23 percent), to individuals (16 percent), and to government (1 percent). Governmental bodies write about 5 percent of checks.

Upon receiving the check, the payee will frequently deposit it in his or her own transactions account. If the payor and the payee are in the same city, their banks will often clear these transactions directly. Exhibit 17-1 illustrates this process. The payor mails the check on day 1, and the payee receives it on day 2. The check may not be deposited into payee's Bank B until day 3. That evening, the payee's account is increased (credited) by the amount of the check, and the check is prepared to be sent to payor's Bank A. After

EXHIBIT 17-1 CHECK CLEARING IN THE SAME CITY

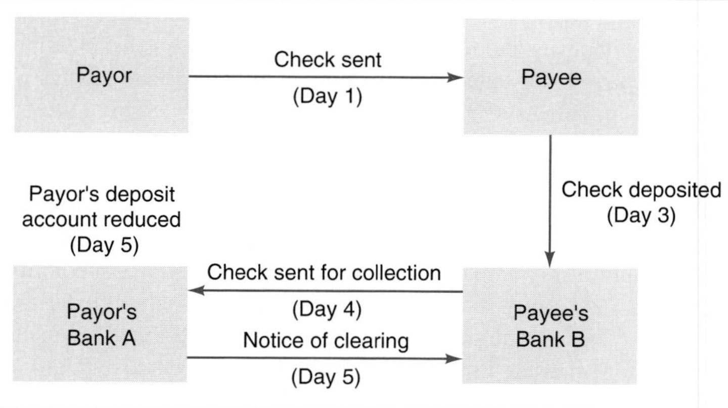

the payor's Bank A receives the check on day 4, the payor's account is reduced (debited) that evening. The opening balance in the payor's account on day 5 reflects the reduction. In terms of the interbank accounts, the cash balances change accordingly.

The accounting entries are as follows:

Day	Bank		DR	CR
3	B	Cash items in collection	X	
		Deposits (payee)		X
4	A	Deposits (payor)	X	
		Due from Bank B		X

Frequently, checks cross state lines. In these cases, the Federal Reserve System facilitates the check-clearing process. Since no commercial bank is permitted to branch nationwide, the Federal Reserve has established forty-eight check-clearing facilities around the country. Exhibit 17-2 shows an example. In the case of an out-of-state check, the payee may not receive the check until day 3 and deposit it on day 4. As before, the check is sent for collection the next day, day 5. However, instead of being sent to Bank A, it goes to the Federal Reserve Bank in that district. The Federal Reserve Bank, which maintains deposit accounts for both banks, reduces (debits) Bank A's account and increases (credits) Bank B's account. Both banks are notified on day 6. Bank A reduces the payor's account that evening, and the payor's opening balance on day 7 reflects the change. In this case, the accounting entries are:

Day	Bank		DR	CR
4	B	Cash items in collection	X	
		Deposits (payee)		X
5	Fed	Due to Bank A	X	
		Due to Bank B		X
6	A	Deposits (payor)	X	
		Due from Federal Reserve		X

In some cases, large correspondent banks perform the same function as the Federal Reserve for smaller, respondent banks.

One of the consequences of this system is that payors benefit from *check float.*

EXHIBIT 17-2 CHECK CLEARING ACROSS STATE LINES

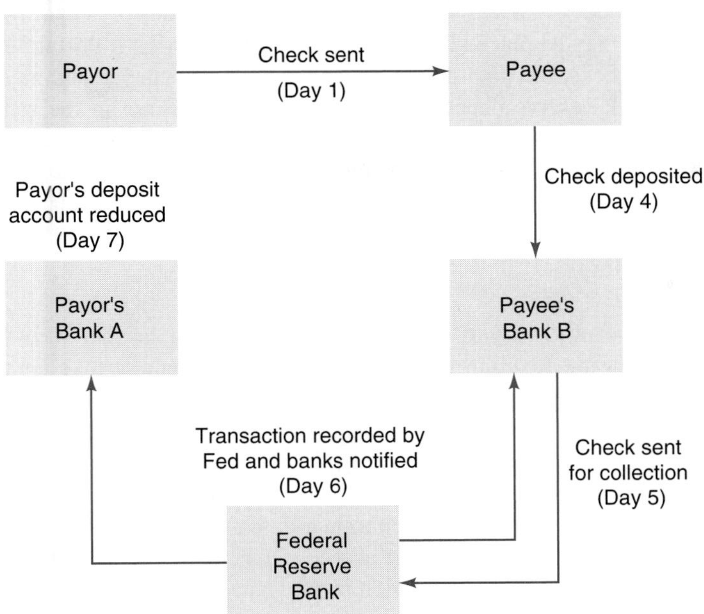

Check float:
The time that elapses between the payee's receipt of a check and the corresponding reduction in the payor's account.

Float exists because a check is technically not paid until the payor's bank receives it and verifies sufficiency of available funds. The greater the distance between payee and payor, the greater the float. In the interim, the payor's balance is not reduced and any applicable interest continues to accrue. This situation favors payors (who receive credit for the payments as soon as the payees receive the checks) at the expense of payees (who must wait until checks clear before funds are available to them). Further, the payee's bank may not prevent him or her from having access to the funds beyond a reasonable period of time that is stipulated by law.

Regulation of Funds Availability in the United States In the past, some payee banks placed holds on checks until they cleared payor banks. If the payees were not advised of these "holds," they could write checks that exceeded their *available balance.*

Available balance:
That portion of the account balance that may be withdrawn immediately.

In some cases, banks would not pay interest on the deposit until the end of the predetermined "hold period," even if the deposited check cleared before that time.

To correct these problems, Congress passed the Expedited Funds Availability Act of 1987. The act did not prohibit holds because banks have a legitimate need to protect themselves against check fraud or forgery. Instead, the law set a maximum hold period on specific accounts. The law states when interest on the deposit must begin accruing and requires that the bank tell its customers when funds will be available.

Not all accounts are covered by the legislation. Only transaction accounts are subject to the law. This includes demand deposits and negotiable order of withdrawal (N.O.W.) accounts. No holds may be placed on U.S. Treasury checks or U.S. Postal Service money orders. For other checks, the hold period depends on whether payee and payor banks are in the same Federal Reserve check-processing zone. If they are in the same zone, the maximum hold is 1 business day. If they are not, the maximum is 4 business days.

The Federal Reserve is responsible for implementing this law. Federal Reserve regulation CC is the enforcement regulation. This provision in the law is a relatively recent development. In other countries, the issue of fast and efficient funds availability has been resolved in different ways.

Canada, Europe, and Japan The check-writing habit is also well-developed in Canada, but the clearing function is much different. Five major banks control approximately 90 percent of total bank assets: the Royal Bank of Canada, the Bank of Montreal, the Bank of Nova Scotia, the Toronto-Dominion Bank, and the Canadian Imperial Bank of Commerce. Reciprocal agreements among them have all but eliminated payor float. Consumer checks are paid on a same-day basis, despite the fact that actual settlement occurs the next day. Writers of checks in denominations of $50,000 or more (business transactions) are assessed any float costs that accrue. Of course, this system is possible because there is a high degree of concentration in the Canadian banking system. In addition, nationwide branching of the five major banks has resulted in distributed locations and comparable market share.

In Europe, most countries have a *giro system* that performs the function of checking accounts in the United States.

Giro system:
A nonbank payments system (frequently at the post office) that transfers funds from one account to another on a same-day basis.

Because payments are effected at a centralized location, there is no payor float. The bank transaction in the United States that is most similar to a giro transfer is an "on-us" check, that is, a check deposited in the same bank on which it is drawn.

Interestingly, the giro system of the United Kingdom is not used as frequently as its continental European counterparts. This is partially because the U.K. Post Office Giro system was not introduced until 1968. More fundamentally, however, British clearing banks have long emphasized personal banking services, introduced branching nationwide, and encouraged the use of checks. The four major U.K. banks dominate the retail banking market, controlling 80 percent of all personal bank accounts. They are Barclay's, Lloyd's, Midland, and National Westminster.

In contrast, in Japan, checks and giro transactions originate almost exclusively in the business sector. Japanese payments are much more frequently in the form of cash or electronic transfer. The Japanese postal savings system has no parallel in the United States. The system accumulates savings from individuals and small businesses. It is a popular outlet for savings because the interest income was tax-exempt for deposits up to ¥3 million until 1988 and because there are over 20,000 locations, compared to approximately 10,000 bank branches. Currently, accounts may be maintained with balances up to ¥5 million. While interest income on these accounts is no longer tax-exempt, the interest rate is attractive as opposed to other alternatives. Also, the postal system is extremely convenient. Through the postal savings system, wire transfers are easily done.[1] Transfers are

[1]This and other forms of electronic payment are discussed in the section "Electronic Payments" that follows.

possible not only to all domestic locations but also to eighty-two other countries that have agreements between their postal authorities and Japan's.

Automation has clearly affected the payment mechanisms in Japan. The impact of automation on payments exceeds beyond cash transfers, however.

Credit Cards

United States Although a relatively new means of payment, credit cards have become extremely popular. The first cards were introduced in the 1950s, at which time, card payees had to telephone each transaction for authorization. The current technology involves plastic cards with magnetic stripes on the back. The magnetic stripe enables payees to verify cards electronically before accepting them as payment. This verification is via a communications network set up over telephone lines. Credit cards are convenient and reduce the need to carry cash. Because card verification is now so streamlined, many retail establishments frequently accept credit cards more readily than checks.

For banks, credit cards are a profitable product line. Income is realized in several ways. In every case, the payee accepting the credit card for payment does not receive the full amount shown on the *credit card draft.*

Credit card draft:
The sales slip created in a credit card transaction, showing amount, payee, payor, credit card issuer, and payor signature.

The draft is an instruction by the payor to the credit card issuer to pay the amount shown to the payee. However, when the draft is presented to the credit card issuer, it is discounted by 3 to 5 percent. The *discount* is a source of income for commercial banks that issue credit cards.

If the bank charges an *annual fee* to cardholders (usually \$25 to \$50), these fees are also income for the bank. The payor receives a monthly statement from the bank that lists the transactions for that month. If the cardholder pays the bank for these transactions before the specified due date, no interest is charged. If not, the bank earns *interest income* on unpaid balances. The interest rate on credit cards loans is higher than other forms of consumer lending, often in excess of 18 percent. Because of this high rate, the discounts, and annual fees, credit card operations can be quite profitable. Of course, there is also a relatively higher probability of uncollectible loans since the majority of credit cards are unsecured.

In the United States, Citicorp is the largest bank credit card issuer, with over 25 million accounts nationwide. Its MasterCard and Visa accounts are only a portion of its credit card businesses. The corporation also owns Diner's Club and Carte Blanche travel and expense cards. In addition, Citicorp has designed private-label credit cards for retail merchandisers such as Goodyear and Tandy Radio Shack.

Originally, Citicorp began card operations in New York State, subject to a 12 percent usury law loan rate ceiling. Subsequently, the state of South Dakota relaxed entry requirements for bank holding companies and eliminated interest rate ceilings. Citicorp transferred all its credit card operations to a bank in Sioux Falls where loans and receivables are subject to no interest rate ceilings. This strategic move is but one of many innovative techniques that Citicorp, the largest bank holding company in the United States, has employed to maintain a competitive advantage with respect to retail banking.

United Kingdom and Japan Of course, Citicorp is now only one of many issuers of bank credit cards in the United States. Cards have also gained prominence outside the United States. In the United Kingdom, the Barclaycard was the first. In some ways, the innovative spirit of Barclay's is similar to that of Citicorp. Barclay's is also the largest of Britain's clearing banks, with 5000 branches worldwide, more than any other bank.

In general, consumer banking services have been slower to evolve in Japan than in the United States or the United Kingdom. This is primarily because the thirteen larger city banks have historically focused on large corporate clients. The sixty-four regional banks that did cater to individuals had neither comparable nationwide networks nor management. However, at the urging of the Ministry of Finance and certain political factions, city banks began to issue credit cards in the 1960s. The Japan Credit Bureau (JCB) is the most widely distributed. Initiated in 1961, the JCB is offered by Sanwa, Mitsui, Kyowa, Daiwa, Hokkaido Takushoku, and Taiyo Kobe.

The Union Credit card, the second most popular, is also jointly operated by Fuji, Dai-Ichi Kangyo, Saitama, and Taiyo Kobe. Sumitomo, Mitsubishi, and Tokai have each independently marketed their own credit cards.

It should be noted that there may still be considerable payor float involved with credit card transactions. In this case, the float is the time necessary to process, invoice, and collect the sales drafts. In essence, card-issuing banks are compensated for this sometimes considerable float through the discount.

Telecommunications technology has enhanced the use of bank credits as a part of the payments system in the United States and abroad. In a similar way, the use of direct electronic payments has increased.

Electronic Payments

Electronic payments may take several forms, as illustrated in Exhibit 17-3. The *automated clearing house (ACH)* is similar to the European giro system in that both account balances change on the same day, with no payor float. The Federal Reserve processes most ACH transactions in the United States.

These transfers were the first electronic link between banks, an indirect connection. Large volume, regular payments are recorded by the bank's customer on a magnetic tape. The clearing house computer simply sorts the transactions on the tape, creating a new separate tape for each bank on the other side of the transfers. Output tapes are then used to adjust interbank balances.

Exhibit 17-4 illustrates this process. Bank A has a utility company account. Individuals make their utility payments at Bank A. On this particular day, four customers, whose

EXHIBIT 17-3 METHODS OF ELECTRONIC PAYMENT

Method	Description
Automated clearing house (ACH)	After documentation with a written agreement, one party is entitled to initiate a transaction with another party. With 1 or 2 days' notice to the bank, a given transaction is effected with hard-copy detail of the transaction following. Most common examples are payroll direct deposit, U.S. government payments, and recurring payments such as insurance premiums.
Wire transfers	Same-day transmission of funds on a transaction-specific basis.
Point-of-sale (POS) debit card	A transaction-specific transfer of funds that immediately reduces the payor's bank account balance and increases the payee's. Transfer takes place before payor leaves the retail establishment.
Automated teller machine (ATM) or cash dispenser (CD)	CDs are unmanned facilities that may be accessed with plastic cards with magnetic stripes. Cash withdrawals reduce the balance of the relevant account (checking, savings, etc.). ATMs dispense cash and provide other services, such as transfers among the individual's accounts, routine bill payments, balance verification, and deposits.

EXHIBIT 17-4 EXAMPLE OF AUTOMATED CLEARING HOUSE TRANSACTION

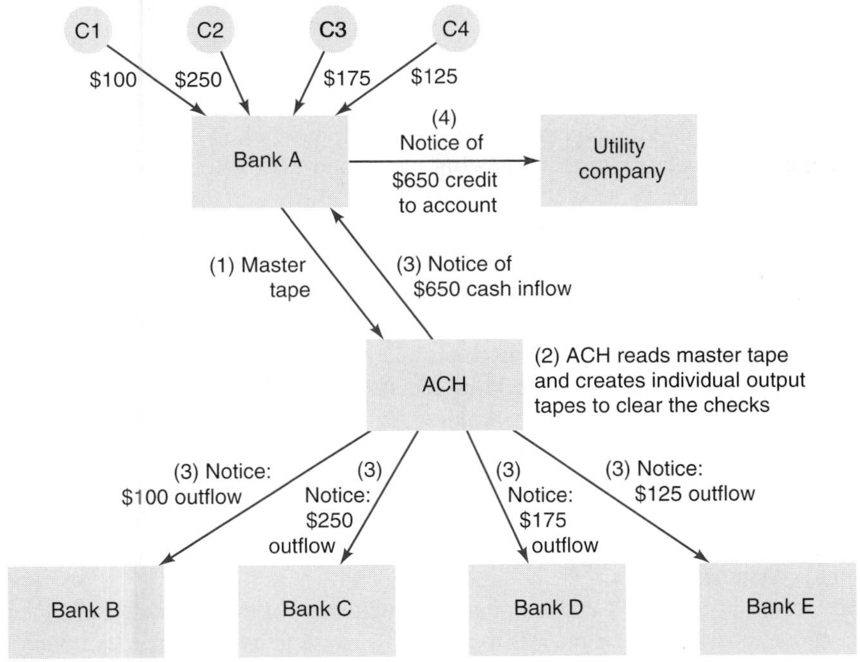

checking accounts are not with Bank A, make a total of $650 in utility invoice payments. The payments are first recorded on a master tape, and the tape is sent to the ACH.

At the ACH, the master tape is read, and for each bank on which a check has been written, an output tape with the details of that bank's check is created. Each output tape is run to actually change the interbank deposit balances. Each bank is then notified, and Bank A notifies its utility company customer.

This example has been simplified for purposes of illustration. Actual transactions involve a much larger number of checks.

Wire transfers eliminate the need for magnetic tapes and are more direct electronic links. Through Fedwire (Federal Reserve), CHIPS (Clearing House Interbank Payment, New York), SWIFT (Society for Worldwide Interbank Financial Telecommunications), or Cashwire (international, regional, and national private-sector firms), large interbank transactions are settled on a same-day basis. Wire transfers are an extension of the special handling for important transactions such as money market purchases or sales. Currently, immediately available funds can be transferred to any other party almost instantaneously.

Point-of-sale (POS) electronic links theoretically accomplish the same objective as wire transfers. However, while wire transfers typically involve large denominations, POS is geared to the smaller, high-volume retail market, for example, grocery stores and service stations. In this context, *convenience* and *cost* are important considerations.

In order to be convenient, a standardized system with adequate distribution is necessary. Standardization may be achieved with plastic *debit cards* with magnetic strips that contain information about the payor's account.

Debit card:

A card whose use results in reduction of the payor's bank account balance, that is, a "debit" to the deposit account of that payor. The offsetting "credit" is to the payee's deposit account or, alternatively, to the deposit account of the payee's bank.

Telecommunications equipment that connects the records of participating banks makes it possible to simultaneously reduce the account balance of the payor by the amount of the retail transaction and increase the balance of the retailer.

However, unless the number of banks and retailers in the areas is relatively small, coordination of all systems involved can become complicated and make it difficult to distribute the service. For example, an early POS experiment in Los Angeles was discontinued because there were multiple competing banks and no single grocery store enjoyed even a 10 percent market share.

Cost considerations are in terms of both out-of-pocket expense and security. Required hardware and software development can entail substantial initial investment. These fixed expenditures require a high volume of transactions to bring per-unit cost within a reasonable range. However, high volume will at least partially depend on public acceptance of this means of payment. From the consumers' perspective, the greatest benefit is the reduced need to carry cash. Yet checking accounts serve virtually the same function. Switching from checks to debit cards requires that consumers relinquish payor float. So, unless participating banks can price POS services in such a way that they are competitive with checks, the immediate advantages for consumers are not clear.

In the long run, POS can significantly reduce the cost of check processing on the part of participating banks. In the interim, startup costs may be too high to pass completely through to consumers.

Aside from out-of-pocket expense, banks participating in the on-line arrangement described above must open their records to access by a system over which they do not exercise complete control. The more secure alternative of off-line transactions (perhaps through ACH) increases the probability of loss through use of invalid cards. The considerations of cost and security can be significant deterrents in the implementation of POS technology.

Cash dispensers (CDs) were the first applications of automation in retail banking. These early machines usually dispensed a fixed amount of currency in a single denomination, and most were off-line. Fairly rapid advances have made it possible to receive larger amounts of currency and to perform other functions, such as loan payments, deposits, transfers between accounts owned by the customer, and payments to third parties. The later generations are referred to as *automated teller machines (ATMs).*

Some ATMs are positioned in an outside wall of the bank building to provide 24-hour access to bank services. Others are located in the lobby of the bank or in separate, adjoining lobbies. The enclosed ATMs provide greater customer security while using an ATM. Increasingly, ATMs are on-line operations, particularly in the United States.

Shared ATMs away from bank branches enable several banks to establish a "branch" in high-density areas such as factories, hospitals, universities, and airports. Generally, banks have been reluctant to share ATMs on their own premises. Banks in various geographic regions have agreed to such arrangements in order to provide convenient service for traveling customers.

Generally, ATMs have been well received both in the United States and abroad. Full-service machines tend to be more common in the United States. However, universally, customers use ATMs primarily as cash dispensers.

CORPORATE SERVICES

In the past, U.S. commercial banks fostered relationships with corporate clients such that one bank provided a number of services for a given firm. Loan pricing was a function of all the other services and their respective profitability. Recently, however, surplus corporate cash is more frequently invested in money market instruments, instead of bank deposits. Corporate loan pricing must now be competitive with commercial paper rates for

EXHIBIT 17-5 THE SLOW PACE OF MODERNIZATION IN NIGERIA

As banks in the United States and other developed countries modernize facilities to provide even faster and more convenient payment mechanisms, other countries, with less developed communications and banking systems, face considerable difficulty instituting features that are taken for granted in the West.

As recently as 1980, the Nigerian banking system had not been successful in promoting the wide acceptance of checks. There was little public confidence in this means of payment. A primary reason for this situation was the excessive time required for check clearing. The central bank's clearing houses were few in number and not automated. Consequently, 2 months might elapse before an intercity check cleared the system. Transferring funds from one bank office to another could also require several months. Even telephone calls between banks were not easily accomplished because intercity telephone lines were inadequate to handle all calls dependably.

This picture of the Nigerian banking system underscores the importance of computerized facilities and telecommunications capabilities in a modern banking system.

large, creditworthy clients. Thus, while relationship banking is still an important concept, performance and profitability measurement of individual services are critical.

Because of the diversity of clients, corporate services are often custom-tailored. In fact, banks engage in corporate banking to varying degrees. While Citicorp management places heavy emphasis on retail banking, other money center banks have tended to specialize in corporate accounts. J.P. Morgan, the holding company of Morgan Guaranty, is an example of this. Morgan Guaranty's management has shaped the organization into a wholesale operation, with only 2 percent of the New York metropolitan area branches of Citibank. The holding company also owns, partially or completely, subsidiaries engaged in trust, real estate, investment, international, and merchant banking activities.

Whatever the degree of emphasis on corporate services, certain trends are undeniable. Historically, commercial banks have earned substantial spreads by assuming credit risk of their corporate clients and financing these loans with relatively inexpensive deposit funds (demand or savings deposits). Deposit funds are now much more expensive. Further, larger corporations more frequently use commercial paper financing at lower interest rates. Thus, traditional spreads are no longer available on loans to major corporations.

One consequence of this situation is that medium-size firms represent a market segment with significant future growth potential. Because these corporations have relatively less access to money and capital markets, they must necessarily depend more heavily upon commercial banks and other financial intermediaries.

Another consequence of the thinner spread availability on traditional corporate loans is that fee income has become a much more important part of bank profitability. Thus, conventional services such as checking accounts and associated activities (for example, stop payment orders and items returned for insufficient funds) are now important fee income generators.

Expansion of Services

In addition to traditional lines of business, commercial banks have begun to offer other services, many of which produce fee income. Larger banks provide some services to smaller banks:

- Check clearing
- Investment advisory service

Banks now emphasize other services for nonbank clients:

- Foreign exchange and treasury services
- Data processing
- Highly leveraged loans
- A greater volume of commercial real estate loans
- Off–balance sheet commitments

Bank Clients The relationship between large banks and their smaller correspondent banks is not new. Correspondents have long relied on respondents for investment advice and securities safekeeping. Because lending limits are sometimes binding constraints for smaller banks, larger banks often purchase the excess amounts of particular loans, the "overlines."

Enhanced technology has also made it possible for larger institutions to clear checks for correspondents on a scale that was previously not possible. Even when correspondents are members of the Federal Reserve, these arrangements are often faster than the federal clearing service. For example, many larger banks have established clearing facilities at airports to eliminate the time required to transport the items into the city and back again. Some of these operations run two or three work shifts per day to provide the fastest possible turnaround. Foreign items are also handled, and immediate credit is given for cash items.

During certain periods of the year, more rural banks may find themselves with excess liquidity. For example, some banks in Maine and the Cape Cod banks in Massachusetts experience peak loan demand during the summer vacation season. In Minneapolis, agricultural loans also have a definite seasonality. Kentucky banks find themselves with excess funds after tobacco crops have been harvested.

While government securities, sale of federal funds, and repurchase agreements, are suitable outlets for temporary liquidity, commercial paper typically yields higher rates of return. City banks advise rural banks on the selection of particular firms' paper and even carry inventories of commercial paper after analyzing the financial statements of issuing firms and verifying backup lines of credit. In many cases, respondent banks hold correspondents' commercial paper in safekeeping and collect the funds upon maturity. Growth in the commercial paper market during the last 2 decades has encouraged these interbank arrangements.

Nonbank Corporations New services for nonbank corporate clients include foreign exchange and treasury operations. Multinational clients with domestic and international telecommunications networks can contract with the bank for worldwide cash flow information. With the assistance of the bank, receipts and disbursements can be more readily offset, often reducing the required number of foreign currency transactions. The bank performs all the required transactions, sometimes including risk management techniques that compensate for the multinationals' total exposure in specific currencies. To the extent that bank cash management techniques and technology are more advanced than those of its client, the client is more likely to contract with its bank.

Smaller corporate clients will not usually require such assistance. Instead, payroll or general ledger maintenance may be an appealing and appropriate service. This arrangement generally involves little or no incremental cost for the bank but enables it to sell unused time on its computer system. Since the bank already has cash flow details in connection with its clients' deposit and loan accounts, it has a comparative advantage over other data processing services.

In other cases, banks have become involved in *leveraged buyouts (LBOs),* particularly in the 1980s.

Leveraged buyout (LBO):
The purchase of the common stock of a firm with borrowed funds.

The objective for an LBO is to gain control of the company. Presumably, the group that gains control will be able to manage the firm more effectively. The assets of the firm form the basis for the transaction and are sometimes at least partially sold to repay the borrowing. When bonds are used to raise the money to buy the stock, they are often referred to as junk bonds because the credit rating is not investment grade. When bank loans are used to raise the money, these loans are referred to as highly leveraged transactions (HLTs).

These HLTs carry an attractive interest rate, but they are also risky. In an economic downturn, companies have difficulty paying the high rates of interest on relatively large amounts of debt. This, of course, puts the lender at risk of default. In 1991, HLTs amounted to $150 billion, roughly 20 percent of all commercial and industrial loans by U.S. banks.

Commercial real estate loans have also offered attractive returns to help replace the blue-chip commercial borrowers that have turned to the commercial paper market. But this market is also risky. In 1991, commercial real estate loans totaled $380 billion, or 20 percent of *total* bank loans.

Both HLTs and commercial real estate loans have reduced the safety of the banking system as a whole. In 1990 and 1991, these high levels of risky loans caused regulators considerable concern, and they required banks to set aside large loan loss provisions. This, together with the need to meet the 8 percent capital ratio target of the Basel Accord by 1992, created a tense regulatory climate. Commercial banks responded by severely reducing their lending activity. The "credit crunch" that resulted was at least partially blamed for the slow recovery from the 1991 economic recession in the United States.

It may be true that the banks were overly aggressive in the 1980s. But the profit pressures are no less real. The high cost of deposits and borrowed funds motivates banks to search for high-yielding loans and sources of fee income. Many *off–balance sheet* activities are good sources of fee income.

Off–balance sheet activity:
An activity or service that does not appear on the bank's financial statements, that is, a contingent obligation or an obligation to provide service in the future.

Examples of off–balance sheet activities include:

- Commitments to make or purchase loans
- Futures and forward contracts
- Letters of credit
- Standby letters of credit
- Commitments to purchase foreign currencies
- Interest rate swaps

In 1984, the dollar value of these contingencies and commitments was just under 60 percent of those liabilities recorded on the balance sheet. By 1989, this percentage had grown to almost 120 percent. The growth in these activities is clear evidence of the emphasis on fee income.

At the same time, unchecked growth in contingent liabilities is not necessarily the best way to boost earnings. Besides which, the 1992 Basel Accord capital requirements stipulate that banks must provide capital to cover these contingencies and commitments.

It may be preferable to allow commercial banks to engage in other financial services to earn additional fee income. One of these is securities underwriting.

Securities Underwriting

The Glass-Steagall Act Since 1933, when the Banking Act (Glass-Steagall) was passed by Congress, U.S. banks have been restricted with respect to investment banking activities.[2] The act required that commercial banks divest themselves of investment banking affiliates. No national bank or state bank that was a member of the Federal Reserve could *directly* deal in, underwrite, or purchase securities. Further, no entity engaged in the business of issuing, underwriting, selling, or distributing securities could accept deposits. While Glass-Steagall *did* permit national banks to buy and sell securities, without recourse as agents for their customers, subsequent rulings by the Comptroller of the Currency prohibited commercial banks from engaging in brokerage activities.

Until recently, most securities activities continued to be off-limits. Exceptions to this general rule were transactions involving fixed-income, investment-grade securities, such as federal government securities and general obligations of state and local governments. Glass-Steagall allowed national banks to own, deal in, and underwrite these instruments in U.S. markets and to engage in private placements.

Overseas and Foreign Exceptions Full-scale underwriting activities by U.S. banks are permitted in overseas markets. The net result of this regulatory difference is that only those banks that are large enough to maintain substantial overseas operations have been able to enter the securities business to any meaningful extent. At least in this respect, small- to medium-size banks have found themselves at a competitive disadvantage as compared with larger institutions.

While U.S. commercial banks are not permitted to engage in securities underwriting in the United States, foreign banks have long been permitted to do so. This is because, before 1978, foreign banks operating in the United States were not subject to Glass-Steagall. The *International Banking Act of 1978* had the effect of prohibiting foreign banks from engaging in securities underwriting. However, seventeen foreign banks were grandfathered, that is, permitted to continue to operate existing securities affiliates in the United States. Among these, there are eight German firms, three French, three Swiss, and one Japanese. Of course, the ability of these firms to do securities underwriting places domestic firms at a competitive disadvantage.

Federal legislators have thus far not been responsive to these apparent competitive inequities. While recent banking laws have served to remove interest rate ceilings and to provide for more attractive deposit instruments (for example, N.O.W. accounts, small-saver certificates, and money market deposit accounts), they have *not* relaxed prohibitions against securities operations. In 1991, the secretary of the treasury proposed, among other things, that commercial banks in sound financial condition be permitted to engage in securities transactions through a separate affiliate. To date, there has been no congressional action on this recommendation.

Regulatory Expansion of Securities Activities In the absence of legislative measures, U.S. bank regulators have granted expanded powers with respect to securities activities. During the 1980s, the Federal Reserve Board and the Comptroller of the Currency permitted bank holding companies and national banks to:

1. Underwrite commercial paper, mortgage-backed securities, municipal revenue bonds, and consumer-related receivables through subsidiaries that underwrite U.S. government securities
2. Place commercial paper without recourse for the account of customers
3. Transfer the commercial paper to a holding company subsidiary

[2]See Chapter 5 for a description of investment banking.

4 Issue, underwrite, and deal in collateralized mortgage obligations through finance subsidiaries
5 Offer securities brokerage and investment advisory services to institutions
6 Offer and sell units in a unit investment trust solely on the order and for the account of the bank's customer through a bank or bank holding company subsidiary
7 Make limited investments in an investment bank
8 Create and sell interests in a publicly offered common trust fund for individual retirement account assets

Beginning in 1987, the Federal Reserve interpreted the Glass-Steagall Act in such a way as to permit banks to engage *indirectly* in securities activities. Section 20 of the Glass-Steagall Act prohibits Federal Reserve member banks from affiliating with any organization "engaged principally" in the issue, flotation, underwriting, public sale, or distribution of securities. (Other provisions of the act prohibit a bank from participating in these activities *directly.*) The Federal Reserve interpreted Section 20 as permitting a bank to affiliate with a firm engaged in securities transactions as long as securities transactions are not the principal business of the firm.

The Federal Reserve gave bank holding companies the right to establish nonbank subsidiaries that earn up to 10 percent of revenue from otherwise prohibited securities transactions. These transactions include underwriting of and dealing in:

- Commercial paper
- Mortgage-backed securities
- Municipal revenue bonds
- Securitized assets
- Corporate bonds
- Corporate equities

To ensure that the affiliation with banks is truly indirect, "firewalls" must be constructed and maintained. These firewalls limit transactions between the Section 20 subsidiary and the bank so as to limit risk to the bank, limit bank subsidies to the Section 20 subsidiary, and prevent conflicts of interest between the two.

It should be noted that state, nonmember banks are not subject to Section 20 of the Glass-Steagall Act. That is, while state nonmembers may not engage *directly* in securities transactions, the law is silent with regard to their affiliation with securities firms.

Exhibit 17-6 provides a list of Section 20 subsidiaries that were authorized as of June 1990. Of the total twenty-nine securities subsidiaries, sixteen are in the New York district. Of these sixteen, nine are foreign banks. When the Bank of Montreal (Chicago district) is included, the total number of foreign Section 20 subsidiaries is ten and the number of domestic subsidiaries nineteen. When the seventeen foreign banks that were grandfathered under the International Banking Act of 1978 are considered, foreign bank securities operations in the United States outnumber those of domestic, Federal Reserve member banks.

Even so, the U.S. securities industry has challenged these developments, but these attempts have generally been unsuccessful. Perhaps Congress will validate these powers and further expand the scope of banking activities. While it is not likely that U.S. bank powers will expand to such an extent, the German banking system presents an interesting case of commercial bank involvement in industrial finance.

Bank and Corporate Relations in Germany

While U.S. banks attempt to provide a wider range of fee-generating services to corporate clients in order to bolster profitability, German banks have long enjoyed a much broader

EXHIBIT 17-6 COMMERCIAL BANK SECURITIES (SECTION 20) SUBSIDIARIES, JUNE 1990

Banking organization	Date authorized
Boston District:	
Bank of Boston Corp.	August 1988
Fleet/Norstar Financial Corp.	October 1988
New York District:	
Amsterdam–Rotterdam Bank	June 1990
The Bank of Nova-Scotia	April 1990
Bankers Trust N.Y. Corp.	April 1987
Barclays Bank PLC	January 1990
Canadian Imperial Bank of Commerce	January 1990
Chase Manhattan Corp.	May 1987
Chemical N.Y. Corp.	May 1987
Citicorp	April 1987
The Long-Term Credit Bank of Japan, Ltd.	May 1990
Manufacturers Hanover Corp.	May 1987
Marine Midland Banks	July 1987
J.P. Morgan and Co.	April 1987
The Royal Bank of Canada	January 1990
The Sanwa Bank, Ltd.	May 1990
The Toronto–Dominion Bank	May 1990
Westpac Banking Corp.	March 1989
Cleveland District:	
Huntington Bancshares, Inc.	November 1988
PNC Financial Corp.	July 1987
Richmond District:	
First Union Corp.	August 1989
NCNB Corp.	May 1989
Sovran Financial Corp.	Feb. 1990
Atlanta District:	
Barnett Banks	January 1989
South Trust Corp.	July 1989
Chicago District:	
The Bank of Montreal	May 1988
First Chicago Corp.	August 1988
St. Louis District	
Liberty National Bancorp	April 1990
Minneapolis District:	
Norwest Corp.	December 1989

Source: U.S. Department of the Treasury, *Modernizing the Financial System; Recommendations for Safer, More Competitive Banks,* 1991.

scope of corporate activity. German banks underwrite corporate securities and hold large portfolios of stock. As long as a German bank is adequately capitalized, there is virtually no regulatory limit on equity investments or other involvement in nonbank corporations.

In addition to their own equity positions, German banks are major depositories for individual shareholders. These individuals may authorize their depository bank to vote their shares during annual shareholder meetings. Because most agree with their bank's policy position with respect to a given industrial firm, bank influence over the corporate sector is even further enhanced.

Thus, it is common for bank representatives to hold seats on corporate boards of directors. Since German banks (1) hold significant shares in their own accounts, (2) represent most of the votes of shares deposited with them, and (3) provide the bulk of debt finance to industry, corporations also seek bank financial advisory service. Firms generally have a "house bank" that exercises significant influence over managerial decision making.

The house bank has close day-to-day contact with its corporate client, not simply as a cash manager or arm's-length third party but as an industry specialist, a readily accessible research facility, and a confidant. While French and Japanese banks also have close working relationships with their corporate clients, the German model is, perhaps, the *best* example of the extent to which bank and industry relations can be developed to facilitate industrial development. In contrast, in the United States relationships have not been permitted to evolve to this extent.

EXPANSION OF OTHER BANK POWERS

Discount Brokerage

In 1983, the Federal Reserve Board permitted BankAmerica Corporation to purchase Charles Schwab Corporation. Since then more than 2000 banks and bank holding companies in the United States have begun to offer discount brokerage services.

During the early 1980s, stock market participation by individual investors increased significantly, largely because of strong, broadly based stock price increases. The Dow Jones Industrial Average (an index of thirty blue-chip stocks in the United States) rose from 836 at the end of 1979 to 2225 in October 1987, or at an average rate of 13 percent per year. During the same period, the annual inflation rate (as measured by changes in the consumer price index) averaged 5 percent. The 8 percent average real rate of return (13 − 5) available in the early and mid-1980s lured many individual investors into the stock market. The subsequent stock market crash in October 1987 discouraged many individuals and caused this segment of the market to contract. But in the meantime, discount brokerage firms grew faster than more traditional, full-service brokers. This phenomenon is also due to demographic factors. As the "baby boom" generation (born shortly after World War II) ages, its members have more time to analyze their investments, that is, will be less dependent on the *advice* of brokers. For these investors, convenient, low-cost transactions are an appealing alternative.

Beyond demographic considerations, individual investors are becoming more sophisticated with respect to investment opportunities. A consequence of this heightened awareness is interest rate and price sensitivity. This sensitivity helps to account for the growth in interest-sensitive bank deposits and the discount brokerage business.

Within the discount industry, bank brokerages appear to have enjoyed particularly strong growth. Commercial banks do possess some comparative advantages. The name recognition of the bank is a strong marketing tool in that *confidence* in the brokerage firm is easier to establish. Also, bank clients are already familiar with the institution, making it possible to incur less *advertising* expense. Last, existing bank customers are ideal *prospects* for brokerage services. Thus, while nonbank discounters have had to rely on television and newspaper advertising, bank brokerages have been able to use successfully less costly advertising such as direct mail and bank statement enclosures.

The securities industries, both corporate services and retail brokerage, have substantial growth potential for commercial banks. As the conventional intermediation functions of accepting deposits and making loans continue to be challenged by nonbank competition and shrinking spreads, banks will seek these and other avenues to diversify their product mix. The insurance industry also holds promise.

Insurance

When the office of the U.S. Treasury Secretary recommended in 1991 that well-capitalized banks be permitted to engage in securities activities, it was also proposed that full-service insurance activities be permitted. The National Bank Act (1863) permits national banks to engage only in underwriting and brokerage of insurance that is incidental to banking. This includes credit life, accident, and health insurance. The Bank Holding Company Act (1956) and the Garn–St Germain Act (1982) prohibit bank holding companies from engaging in *any* insurance activity. However, existing insurance operations were grandfathered when the legislation was passed.

The banking industry has long taken the position that banks should be allowed a more active role in the insurance industry. Arguably, insurance is quite similar to banking in that:

- Banks accept deposits; insurance companies accept premiums.
- Both types of institutions invest the money in order to generate a profit.
- Eventually both depositors and policyholders are repaid.

If permitted to perform these functions in the insurance industry, the bank would be an *insurance underwriter.*

Insurance underwriter:
The company that assumes full responsibility for paying the benefits promised in an insurance policy.

Because insurance underwriting can give rise to large liabilities associated with benefit payments, the U.S. Treasury recommended that any bank-run insurance operations be confined to a separate insurance affiliate and that "firewalls" be constructed around the bank. This is similar to the Treasury recommendation for a separate securities affiliate for those banks on sound financial footing. A separate affiliate with bank firewalls limits risk to the bank.

Even if a bank does not engage in full underwriting activities, a bank-run *insurance agency* can increase noninterest income significantly.

Insurance agency:
A company that sells insurance policies for an insurance underwriter.

Since the insurance underwriter bears the ultimate burden of paying insurance claims, the commissions earned by an insurance agent are riskless income. Also, banks could provide cost-effective "packages" of:

- Mortgage loans and mortgage insurance to repay the mortgage in the event of death or disability of borrower
- Auto loans and auto insurance
- Small business loans and "key individual" insurance to cover those people essential to business operation
- Corporate loans and corporate life or property/casualty insurance to cover all employees and property of the corporation

As is true in the case of securities operations, federal regulators have attempted to liberalize national bank powers. The Office of the Comptroller of the Currency (which charters national banks) has given permission to national banks to underwrite and sell title insurance (protecting the buyer of real estate property from ownership claims of previous owners) and property insurance related to loan collateral. National banks have also been granted the right to broker fixed-rate annuities (insurance policies that pay a stream of fixed payments rather than a lump sum).

Federal regulators work within the framework of existing federal law that relates to national banks, state banks that are members of the Federal Reserve, and banking holding companies. Only U.S. congressional action can change the federal law. Meanwhile, state-chartered banks that are not members of the federal reserve are not subject to many of these existing laws. More than half of all bank charters belong to state-chartered nonmembers. The expansion of bank powers is much more pronounced within this group.

The Expanded Powers of State-Chartered Banks

Exhibit 17-7 is a summary, by state, of the activities in which state-chartered banks may participate. National banks and bank holding companies are precluded from operating in these areas. The general categories are insurance, real estate, and securities. Twenty-one states allow banks to underwrite securities and five permit insurance underwriting. Brokerages in securities and insurance are allowed in twenty-three and sixteen states, respectively. In twenty-five states, state-chartered banks may engage in real estate development and project ownership. Real estate brokerage is allowed in nine states.

Real estate activity is the most frequently noted expanded power among these. Real estate involvement has also been the source of many of the recent loan losses in the banking industry. This has essentially placed federal regulators in the position of insuring operations over which they have relatively little authority. The 1991 U.S. Treasury recommendations also included a provision to limit these state-granted powers. Specifically, the recommendations with respect to state banks were:

1 Prohibit *direct equity investment* in *real estate* and other commercial ventures.
2 *Limit* state bank activities to those permitted to *national banks* unless:
  a The bank is fully capitalized.
  b The FDIC verifies that the activities do not create a substantial risk of loss to the insurance fund.

The restrictions do not apply to agency activities, that is, those for which the bank does not assume the ultimate risk of loss, for example, an insurance agency. The FDIC Improvement Act of 1991 reflects these recommendations. No state bank may engage in insurance underwriting and equities investments that are prohibited for national banks. All state banks proposing to act as principle in any other activity not permitted for a national bank must comply with all capital standards and have the FDIC's written determination that the activity poses no significant threat to the Bank Insurance Fund.

These measures are aimed at protecting the Bank Insurance Fund (BIF) under supervision of the FDIC. The rationale is that if state banks are not allowed to participate in activities prohibited to national banks, there will be less risk of state bank failure, failure that necessarily results in losses that must be covered by the BIF and the U.S. taxpayer if BIF resources prove inadequate. Of course, the irony is that state banks have also been the most innovative and the closest approximation of banks in other countries with which the United States competes internationally.

Bank Powers in Canada, Germany, Japan, and the United Kingdom

Exhibit 17-8 is a comparison of the bank powers in the United States and four of its major trading partners: Canada, Germany, Japan, and the United Kingdom. The powers indicated for the United States are for national banks as permitted by federal law.

Among these, the Japanese system is most similar to the U.S. system. One major difference is that Japanese banks are permitted to invest in equities, or stocks. It is through these equity investments that Japanese banks maintain their close relationships with industry, many as part of *keiretsu* arrangements, that is, cross-holdings of stock among companies in the same group.[3]

[3]See Chapter 12 for a discussion of Japanese *keiretsus*.

EXHIBIT 17-7 EXPANDED ACTIVITIES FOR STATE-CHARTERED BANKS MAY, 1990

	Insurance		Real estate			Securities	
State	Underwriting	Brokerage	Equity participation	Development	Brokerage	Underwriting	Brokerage, no underwriting
Alabama		X					
Alaska							
Arizona			X	X		X	X
Arkansas			X	X			
California		X	X	X		X[a]	
Colorado			X	X			
Connecticut			X	X			X
Delaware	X	X				X	X
District of Columbia							
Florida			X	X		X	X
Georgia			X	X	X		X
Hawaii							
Idaho	X	X				X	X
Illinois							
Indiana		X[b]				X[c]	X[d]
Iowa		X[e]			X	X	X
Kansas						X[f]	X
Kentucky			X	X			
Louisiana							
Maine			X	X	X[g]	X	X
Maryland							
Massachusetts			X	X	X	X	
Michigan				X		X	X
Minnesota							X
Mississippi							
Missouri			X	X		X[h]	

[a] May underwrite mutual funds.
[b] Cannot broker life insurance; all other types permitted.
[c] May underwrite municipal revenue bonds, money market mutual funds, and mortgage-backed securities.
[d] May conduct discount brokerage.
[e] Property and casualty only.
[f] May underwrite municipal bonds.
[g] May own or operate brokerage firm to dispose of bank-owned property.
[h] May underwrite mutual funds and may underwrite securities up to state legal loan limit.

EXHIBIT 17-7 EXPANDED ACTIVITIES FOR STATE-CHARTERED BANKS MAY, 1990 *(Continued)*

State	Insurance		Real estate			Securities	
	Underwriting	Brokerage	Equity participation	Development	Brokerage	Underwriting	Brokerage, no underwriting
Montana						X^{i}	
Nebraska		X				X^{j}	X
Nevada			X	X			
New Hampshire			X	X			
New Jersey		X	X	X	X	X	X
New Mexico							
New York							X
North Carolina	X	X	X	X	X	X^{k}	X
North Dakota							
Ohio			X	X			
Oklahoma							
Oregon		X		X	X		
Pennsylvania			X			X^{l}	X^{g}
Rhode Island			X	X			
South Carolina		X					
South Dakota	X	X	X	X			
Tennessee			X^{n}			X	X
Texas							X
Utah	X^{m}	X	X	X	X	X	X
Vermont							X
Virginia			X	X			
Washington		X^{o}	X	X		X	
West Virginia			X	X		X	X
Wisconsin		X	X^{p}	X^{p}	X		
Wyoming		X					

[i] May underwrite bonds only.
[j] May underwrite U.S. government securities.
[k] May underwrite U.S. government, federal farm loan act, and general obligation municipal bonds.
[l] May underwrite municipal and mortgage-related securities.
[m] Grandfathered institutions.
[n] Banks may not be active partners in real estate development.
[o] Banks in small towns may engage in insurance activity without geographic limitation.
[p] As of May 1986, commissioner of banking may establish rules under which state banks may engage in activities authorized for other financial institutions in the state.
Source: U.S. Department of the Treasury, *Modernizing the Financial System; Recommendations for Safer, More Competitive Banks,* 1991.

EXHIBIT 17-8 INTERNATIONAL COMPARISON OF BANK POWERS

	Canada	Germany	Japan	United Kingdom	United States
Insurance:					
Brokerage	No	Yes	No	Yes	No†
Underwriting	No	Yes*	No	Yes*	No
Equities:					
Brokerage	Yes*	Yes	No	Yes	Yes
Underwriting	Yes*	Yes	No	Yes*	No
Investment	Yes	Yes	Yes	Yes*	No
Other underwriting:					
Government debt	Yes	Yes	No	Yes*	Yes
Private debt	Yes*	Yes	No	Yes*	No
Mutual funds:					
Brokerage	Yes	Yes	No	Yes	No
Management	Yes*	Yes	No	Yes	No
Real estate:					
Brokerage	No	Yes	No	Yes	No†
Investment	Yes	Yes	No	Yes	No
Other brokerage:					
Government debt	Yes	Yes	Yes	Yes	Yes
Private debt	Yes	Yes	Yes	Yes	Yes

* Not directly by the bank.
†With exceptions.
Source: U.S. Department of the Treasury, *Modernizing the Financial System; Recommendations for Safer, More Competitive Banks,* 1991.

The banks in Canada, Germany, and the United Kingdom all have a much broader range of powers than those in the United States. It is also true that these systems are much more concentrated with a few banks controlling from 50 percent (Germany) to 90 percent (Canada) of bank assets. This high degree of concentration makes it relatively easy for regulators to oversee the operations of banks. In contrast, in the United States there are over 12,000 banks, and bank supervision is complicated by this large number.

Yet this does not change the reality that, according to federal law, U.S. national banks cannot offer the same range of services as banks in other developed countries. Removing the expanded powers of state-chartered banks will only make these inequities worse.

The comparison of the U.S. banking system with others in the developed West is useful as a frame of reference as world economies become more interrelated through trade and finance. However, not all banking systems follow the western model. Particularly noteworthy in this regard are socialist and Islamic systems.

OTHER BANKING SYSTEMS

Socialist Banking

Even though the United States seems overly regulated when compared to other western systems, it appears relatively free of regulation when compared with socialist banking systems. In the early 1930s, the Soviet Union restructured its system in accordance with doctrines that were later to be followed by most socialist countries. Initially, all parties (state, collective, and private enterprises) were required to deposit all funds with the state bank. This step accomplished three objectives.

1 The government wished to gain control of private-sector activities in order to limit future development, monitor funds use, and exercise monetary control over such enterprises.

2 State banks sought to orchestrate economic and industrial development in public-sector enterprises.
3 Control of any private-sector surpluses would facilitate their reallocation to the public sector.

As socialist systems developed, the need for specialized attention in several areas arose. As a result, foreign-trade, agricultural, industrial, and savings banks appeared.

The state bank has always acted as a buffer between the domestic and foreign sectors through its *foreign-trade* bank branch. A typical arrangement involves both a foreign-trade enterprise and a domestic enterprise. Using metal ore as an example, a domestic enterprise wishing to sell ore overseas first sells it to a state-owned, foreign-trade enterprise, receiving a predetermined price in local currency. The foreign-trade enterprise, in turn, sells the iron ore to a foreign buyer in exchange for foreign currency. The foreign-trade enterprise exchanges the foreign currency for local currency at the foreign-trade bank. The original domestic enterprise is thus insulated from world commodity price fluctuations. Further, the difference between the local currency purchase and sale prices indicates the efficiency of the transaction and the industry's contribution to centralized plans for the national economy.

While foreign-trade banks are somewhat uniform from one socialist country to another, *agricultural banks* tend to vary more. In all socialist societies, considerable time was required to bring about land reform, that is, to dismantle large estates, distribute land to peasants, and help the newly endowed peasants increase agricultural output.

In the German Democratic Republic (before reunification with the Federal Republic of Germany), capitalist farmers were permitted to retain 20 to 100 hectares of land and to employ workers.[4] However, the government required these farmers to deposit their funds in the agricultural cooperative bank. Further, capitalist farmers were not eligible for long-term financing. Instead, peasants holding 6 to 10 hectares of land received interest-free loans that they did not, in some cases, have to repay. Subsequently, the government encouraged small landowners to form cooperatives in order to better afford more farm equipment, which could then be financed through the state.

In the People's Republic of China, a less centralized approach to agricultural finance was adopted. While a state-level agricultural bank was formed in 1951 (2 years after the Communist government gained control), the state encouraged a certain amount of self-help on the part of peasant farmers. In addition to state financing, the government encouraged formation of rural credit cooperatives, largely funded by short-term deposits made by the peasants themselves. By 1955, there were 130,000 such cooperatives. In 1958, they became credit departments of the communes being formed, acting as local offices of the People's Bank, the state bank.

Initially, in the areas of *industry* and *commerce,* state bank branches usually made only short-term loans. Separate, specialized banks financed long-term, capital projects. Over time, the separation of state and investment bank functions has been reduced in order to provide more financing flexibility. Nevertheless, industrial and commercial enterprises generally must still maintain their accounts in a specific state bank branch so that the state can monitor productivity.

Savings banks hold the deposits of individuals. To encourage saving, a low interest rate (approximately 3 percent) is offered. With almost no other investment opportunities, a 3 percent rate is apparently felt to be sufficient to attract savings. Housing loans are generally also available.

At this time, the monetary and banking systems of the Commonwealth of Independent States and Eastern Europe are undergoing changes to make them more compatible with

[4]A hectare is an area equal to 10,000 square meters, or 2.471 acres. The capitalist farmers could, therefore, retain approximately 50 to 250 acres.

their western counterparts. The Soviet Union had allowed the formation of approximately 100 private commercial banks. But the greatest advancements in this region have been made by Hungary. Since 1987, the Hungarian central bank has been structured as only a note-issuing (currency-issuing) institution with control over the country's money supply. This paves the way for development of other financial institutions to provide western-style banking services in Hungary. Nevertheless, the transition from highly regulated, centrally planned economies will not be simple. It is hoped that, in the long run, improved productivity and output will more than offset the problems encountered during transition.

Islamic Banking

As some socialist banking systems attempt to become more similar to western institutions, other nonwestern systems attempt to distinguish themselves from western banks. Islamic banks are good examples.

The Koran is the Islamic equivalent of the Bible. Unlike the Bible, however, the Koran addresses specific economic issues including inheritance, hoarding, usury, and the use of financial resources. *Interest* and *profit* are considered fundamentally different forms of compensation. The objective of trade-related activities should be profit. In fact, Islam encourages its followers to invest productively. The investment function should, of course, include a determination of the proper distribution of any resulting profit (or loss). Since ultimate proceeds cannot be known with certainty at the time of the investment, final distributions also cannot be known with certainty.

Interest, or *riba,* is considered exploitative since its fixed nature ignores the possibility that ultimate proceeds of the investment may be inadequate to repay both interest and principal. Thus, Islamic banks accept deposits but do not guarantee the amount to be repaid. Similarly, bank loans are granted with the same understanding.

However, most of the *first* commercial banks established in the Muslim world were European branches or subsidiaries. At least initially, most governments were content to overlook the violations of Islamic principles in exchange for economic and technical advancements. However, as religious fundamentalists gained more influence, these religious issues began to be raised.

The first Islamic bank was formed in rural Pakistan in the 1950s. Deposited funds were loaned after deducting only a small, permissible administrative fee to cover the bank's operating expense. However, new deposit funds did not materialize, and trained personnel was scarce. The bank effectively self-liquidated during the early 1960s.

The Nasser Social Bank, the oldest existing Islamic bank, was formed in 1972, with over $2 million of capital invested by the Egyptian government. Currently, over sixty Islamic institutions operate worldwide, most having been established by private Muslim citizens. Pakistan and Iran are the only countries that have implemented nationwide Islamic banking. (See Exhibit 17-9.)

In addition to a prohibition against interest, among other things, Muslim law prescribes segregation of the genders in matters of finance. This implies no joint bank accounts for spouses. Inheritance law dictates that a wife inherits one-quarter of her husband's estate. If the wife is deceased before the husband, he inherits half the wife's estate. In either case, children receive the remainder of the estate with distributions to sons being twice as large as distributions to daughters. Through this system, many women accumulate substantial fortunes.

Conservative Islamic women may hesitate to frequent male-dominated banks or to commingle funds in their spouses' accounts. In response to these dynamics, Saudi Arabia has initiated banks operated by women for women, the first in 1979. As more Saudi women enter the work force, it is expected that these institutions will increase in economic significance.

EXHIBIT 17-9 SELECTED ISLAMIC BANKS

Name	Date founded
Nassar Social Bank (Egypt)	1972
Islamic Development Bank (Saudi Arabia)	1974
Dubai Islamic Bank	1975
Faisal Islamic Bank of Egypt	1977
Faisal Islamic Bank of Sudan	1977
Kuwait Finance House	1977
Jordan Islamic Bank for Finance and Investment	1978
Bahrain Islamic Bank	1979
Iran Islamic Bank	1979
Islamic Investment Company (Nassan)	1979
Islamic Investment Trust (Geneva)	1980
Dar Al-Maal Al-Islami (Bahamas, Geneva)	1980
Bank Islam Berhad (Malaysia)	1983
Muslim Commercial Bank	—*
National Investment Trust	—*
Investment Corporation of Pakistan	—*
House Building Finance Corporation	—*

* These Pakistani banks were nationalized in 1974 and converted to Islamic institutions in 1984.

As Muslim economies have grown, greater observance of Islamic principles has been called for. As Islamic women gained more financial resources, the demand for banking services for women has grown. Likewise, in the United States, as population demographics have changed, so have banking services.

BANK BRANCHING

In the United States during the 1950s and 1960s, population and industrial production expanded rapidly. With this growth came increased demand for bank services. Bank size or "bigness" became a focal point of management. There were also significant population shifts from cities to suburbs. The service industries that catered to these residents, including banks, were obliged to follow them. Further, the demographic changes were not uniformly distributed, the west coast, the southwest, and, later, the southeast experiencing strongest growth.

The ability to branch is an important way for banks both to grow in an aggregate sense and to shift geographic concentration. In fact, successful retailing operations almost always required a branch network to gather deposits from small savers and to launch an effective consumer lending program. The requisite branch network could be established by building branches from the ground up, so-called *de novo* branches, or by merging with another bank that already operated several branches.

Branching Laws

However, existing laws in the United States prohibit unrestricted bank branching. The McFadden Act of 1927 gives national banks the right to branch within the state to the same extent that state banks are permitted to branch. A state permitting no branching whatsoever is termed a *unit-banking* state. Branching permitted throughout a state is called *statewide branching*. In other cases, branching is permitted but not on a statewide basis; this is called *limited branching*. Exhibit 17-10 shows the classification of all states and the District of Columbia.

Where branching is limited, *group banking* has evolved. Combinations of separate banking corporations have effectively circumvented unit-banking laws. The bank holding

EXHIBIT 17-10 BANK BRANCHING LAWS BY STATES

Unit (2)			
	Colorado	Wyoming	
Limited (9)			
	Arkansas	Minnesota	
	Illinois	Missouri	
	Iowa	New Mexico	
	Kentucky	Tennessee	
	Louisiana		
Statewide (40)			
Alabama*	Idaho	Nevada	Rhode Island
Alaska	Indiana*	New Hampshire	South Carolina
Arizona	Kansas*	New Jersey	South Dakota
California	Maine	New York	Texas
Connecticut	Maryland	North Carolina	Utah
Delaware	Massachusetts	North Dakota*	Vermont
District of Columbia	Michigan	Ohio	Virginia
Florida*	Mississippi	Oklahoma*	Washington
Georgia*	Montana*	Oregon	West Virginia
Hawaii	Nebraska*	Pennsylvania	Wisconsin

*Statewide branching by merger.

Source: U.S. Department of the Treasury, *Modernizing the Financial System; Recommendations for Safer, More Competitive Banks,* 1991, pp. XVII–7.

company is the organizational structure that binds related banks. In some respects, the holding company structure is *more* desirable because the Federal Reserve permits the parent firms to engage in activities "closely related" to banking, including leasing, mortgage servicing, factoring, and data processing. (See Exhibit 17-11).

Actually, many of these activities are more the result of a legislature oversight than conscious decisions on the part of the Federal Reserve. The 1933 Glass-Steagall Act brought bank holding companies under the purview of federal regulations. However, this law exempted from federal restrictions on interstate banking those holding companies whose bank ownership *already* crossed state lines. First Interstate Bancorp is an example of one such exempted firm with over twenty banks in twelve western states.

Subsequently, holding companies entered lines of business that were not expressly prohibited by law but that federal regulators believed to be outside the business of banking. The Bank Holding Company Act of 1956 was passed presumably to discontinue this practice. Congress gave the Federal Reserve the right to register and regulate the formation and activities of bank holding companies, including requiring the parent firms to divest themselves of nonbank affiliates.

However, the 1956 act defined bank holding companies as those owning two or more banks. As described in Chapter 10, one-bank holding companies proliferated until this loophole was closed in 1970. Currently, the holding company is the dominant organizational form of banks in the United States.

Interstate Banking

As mentioned above, federal law permits national banks and bank holding companies to branch to the extent allowed by state law. As a result of this and the bank holding company structure, banks now operate across state lines. In 1981, Keys Bank of Albany, New York, purchased Depositors Corporations of Maine, capitalizing on reciprocal banking

EXHIBIT 17-11 NONBANKING ACTIVITIES AUTHORIZED FOR BANK HOLDING COMPANIES

1 Making and servicing loans
  a Consumer finance
  b Credit card
  c Mortgage
  d Commercial
  e Factoring
2 Industrial banking
3 Trust company functions
4 Investment or financial advice
5 Leasing personal or real property (restricted)
6 Community development
7 Data processing (restricted)
8 Insurance agency and underwriting credit insurance (restricted)
9 Operating savings associations
10 Courier services (restricted)
11 Management consulting to depository institutions
12 Issuing money orders, savings bonds, and traveler's checks
13 Real estate and personal property appraising
14 Arranging commercial real estate equity financing (restricted)
15 Securities brokerage (restricted)
16 Underwriting and dealing in government obligations and money market instruments
17 Foreign exchange advisory and transactional services (restricted)
18 Futures commission merchant (restricted)
19 Investment advice on financial futures and options on futures
20 Consumer financial counseling
21 Tax planning and preparation
22 Check guaranty services
23 Operating a collection agency
24 Operating a credit bureau

Source: Subcommittee on Financial Institutions Supervision, Regulation, and Insurance, *Task Force Report on the International Competitiveness of U.S. Financial Institutions,* 1990, p. 307.

laws in the state of Maine. Since that time, a number of regional agreements have been effected.

Exhibit 17-12 gives a summary of the state laws regarding interstate banking. Generally, states fall into one of four categories:

1 *No law.* The state does not have a law that permits the purchase of banks by out-of-state bank holding companies (BHCs).
2 *Regional reciprocal entry only.* Within a selected group of states, each state permits the acquisition of its banks by BHCs headquartered in the other states of the group as long as each state has the same right.
3 *Currently regional reciprocal/becomes nationwide.* The law is now regional reciprocal but becomes nationwide at some point in the future.
4 *Nationwide entry.* The state allows BHCs from any other state to acquire its banks. In some cases, reciprocity (the right for BHCs in the state of the acquired bank to do the same in the state of the acquiring BHC) is required.

Conspicuous in its absence from regional agreements is the state of New York. These interstate pacts appear to be attempts to gather regional strength in preparation for the an-

EXHIBIT 17-12 INTERSTATE BANKING LAWS

No law (4)			
Hawaii	Kansas	Montana	North Dakota
Regional reciprocal entry only (14)			
Alabama Arkansas District of Columbia Florida	Georgia Iowa Maryland Minnesota	Mississippi Missouri North Carolina South Carolina	Virginia Wisconsin
Currently regional reciprocal/becomes nationwide entry (6)			
California Colorado	Illinois Indiana	Nebraska	Tennessee
Nationwide entry (27)			
Alaska Arizona Connecticut* Delaware* Idaho Kentucky* Louisiana*	Maine Massachusetts* Michigan* Nevada New Hampshire New Jersey* New Mexico	New York* Ohio* Oklahoma Oregon Pennsylvania* Rhode Island* South Dakota*	Texas Utah Vermont* Washington* West Virginia* Wyoming

* Reciprocity required.

Source: Subcommittee on Financial Institutions Supervision, Regulation, and Insurance, *Task Force on the International Competitiveness of U.S. Financial Institutions,* 1990, p. 313.

ticipated, eventual introduction of full-scale nationwide branching, in line with the 1991 recommendation of the U.S. Department of the Treasury. The entry of money center banks is *not* a welcome prospect for smaller institutions.

The Interstate Presence of Money Center Banks

In the meantime, a number of larger banks have already begun to make their presence felt outside New York State. Citicorp is, perhaps, the best example. The Garn–St Germain legislation of 1982 allowed interstate acquisitions of failed thrift institutions. In September of the same year, Citicorp purchased Fidelity Savings and Loan of Oakland, California. Two years later, the restructured Citicorp Savings controlled ninety-two offices in sixty-six cities of the state. In 1984, Citicorp was also permitted to purchase failed thrifts in Chicago and Miami. The following year, the holding company entered Las Vegas in the same manner.

Failed thrifts are not the firm's only interstate operations. Its bank card facility is located in South Dakota. Offices for Diners Club card are in Chicago. Citicorp also owns a mortgage banking concern in St. Louis and roughly 200 consumer finance offices in over 25 states. It is not inconceivable that at such time as legislative power to branch nationwide is granted, Citicorp could easily convert its consumer finance offices into full-scale commercial banks.

Before merging with Chemical Banking Corporation in 1991, Manufacturers Hanover Corporation—holding company for another large money center bank, Manufacturers Hanover Trust Company—positioned itself for the advent of full-scale, nationwide branching. Manufacturers, or "Manny Hanny," has purchased C.I.T. Financial Corporation, a major source of financing for medium-size business concerns complementing Manufacturers client base of larger firms. In addition, C.I.T. has factoring, leasing, and consumer-lending divisions. Notably, C.I.T. offices operate in forty-four states.

Strictly speaking, nationwide branching remains prohibited. However, the existence of grandfathered interstate banks, parties to regional banking agreements, and far-flung bank holding company subsidiaries renders this prohibition more a legislature technicality than a practical reality.

SUMMARY

Universal functions of commercial banks include accepting deposits and making loans. In most cases, these deposits represent a significant part of a country's money supply. However, technological advances have led to changes in both the delivery and form of payment services. Credit cards and the use of ATMs now frequently substitute for check writing. Point-of-sale facilities are also operational, although currently to a lesser extent.

Greater access to money and capital markets by large corporate bank clients has meant thinner margins in corporate lending activities. As a result, banks have turned increasingly to fee-generating services and to the middle segment of the corporate market. Cash management, data processing, commercial paper underwriting, and provision of discount brokerage facilities are some of the services being emphasized.

Regulatory barriers to other services are being challenged. Section 20 subsidiaries have been authorized by the Federal Reserve to permit bank affiliates to engage in securities transactions to a limited extent. State banking authorities allow state-chartered banks a much wider range of functions, including securities, insurance, and real estate participation. Even so, the United States has a more restrictive regulatory structure than other countries in the developed West.

Political and cultural differences can alter the nature of the domestic operations of commercial banks, however. Socialist economies have much more centralized and regulated banking systems than those observed in the West. In the Muslim world, Islamic banks have emerged in an attempt to reconcile modern finance and fundamentalist principle.

While Japanese, German, and British banks enjoy relative freedom with respect to geographic distribution within national borders, U.S. banks continue to grapple with the issue of interstate and nationwide branching. Nevertheless, over time, many U.S. banking offices have spilled over state lines so that their current structure *resembles* a nationwide branch network, even though it may not, technically, be so defined.

The U.S. banking industry is involved in radical change. Many of these changes are necessary to first maintain and then improve bank profitability. A conflict between bankers and legislators (and, at times, regulators) arises because the need of bankers to compete effectively must be balanced with the need to maintain a safe, stable banking system in the United States.

KEY TERMS

automated clearing house
automated teller machine
available balance
check float
credit card draft
credit cards
debit card
discount brokerage
German "house bank"
giro system
group banking
insurance underwriting
insurance agency
International Banking Act of 1978
Islamic banking
leveraged buyout
off–balance sheet activity
payment mechanisms
point-of-sale transaction
securities underwriting
socialist banking
unit banking
wire transfer

1. What is payor float? How is payor float reduced in Canada?
2. **a.** Describe a European giro system.
   b. How does a giro system differ from the Japanese postal system?
3. What are some of the contributing factors to the widespread acceptance and use of credit cards in the United States?
4. Contrast an automated clearing house transaction with a wire transfer.
5. Why is the middle-market corporate sector considered to have high-growth potential for commercial banks?
6. The main provisions of the Glass-Steagall Act have not been repealed. Yet commercial banks have received permission to engage in certain securities operations. Explain this apparent inconsistency and the activities that have been permitted.
7. **a.** Discuss the reasons why all parties were required to deposit funds with the state bank in the early years of socialist banking.
   b. Instead of the state bank providing loans based on the central planning budget, how should bank funds be allocated as the systems are reformed?
8. Why is interest prohibited in Islamic banking? What is the alternative?
9. **a.** Describe the general nature of regional banking agreements. Which states have entered such pacts?
   b. Does the trend at the state level appear to be in the direction of regional pacts? Explain.
10. Money center banks are generally not parties to the regional banking agreements mentioned in question 9. How have these banking organizations managed to expand their operations beyond the state of New York?
11. The issue of nationwide banking has been hotly debated. Name several advantages and disadvantages of interstate banking from the perspective of both consumers and bank managers.
12. What potential problems might arise if U.S. banks are allowed to establish relationships with corporate clients as German banks have?
13. Suppose that you live in Michigan and you receive a check drawn on a bank in California. If you deposit this check in your account on Monday, by what day must the funds be available to you according to Federal Reserve regulations?
14. Does your answer to 13 change if the check is drawn on a bank in your city? How?
15. Banks often sell "overlines," the portion of loans that is in excess of their legal lending limit, to other banks.
   a. To what activity in the securities industry is this similar?
   b. What competitive strengths can banks bring to the securities industry?
   c. What are the potential dangers of banks being involved in the securities industry?
16. Obtain the latest annual report of a bank in your area.
   a. Is this bank a state or national bank?
   b. Does this bank engage in any of the expanded powers discussed in this chapter?

SELECTED REFERENCES

Abdeen, Adnan M., and Dale N. Shook. *The Saudi Financial System; in the Context of Western and Islamic Finance,* John Wiley and Sons, New York, 1984.

Bayliss, B. T., and A. A. S. Butt Philip. *Capital Markets and Industrial Investment in Germany and France; Lessons for the U.K.,* Saxon House, Westmead, England, 1980.

Boreham, Gordon F. "Canadian and U.S. Banking Systems: Some Comparisons," *Canadian Banker,* vol. 94, no. 3 (1987), pp. 6–14.

Bronte, Stephen. *Japanese Financial: Markets and Institutions,* Germany Publications, London, 1982.

Coler, Mark, and Ellis Ratner. *Financial Services; Insiders' Views of the Future,* New York Institute of Finance, New York, 1988.

Compton, Eric N. *The New World of Commercial Banking,* Lexington Books, Lexington, Massachusetts, 1987.

Gart, Alan. *Banks, Thrifts, and Insurance Companies; Surviving the 1980s,* Lexington Books, Lexington, Massachusetts, 1985.

Hultmann, Charles W. "Foreign Banks and Interstate Banking in the U.S.," *International Journal of Bank Marketing,* vol. 4, no. 4 (1986), pp. 14–22.

Johnson, Hazel J. *Dispelling the Myth of Globalization; The Case for Regionalization,* Praeger Publishers, New York, 1991.

Kawashima, Mutsuho. "Citicorp Branches Out in Japan," *Tokyo Business Today,* January 1989, pp. 32–35.

Lawrence, Colin, and Robert P. Shay. *Technological Innovation, Regulations, and the Monetary Economy,* Ballinger Publishing Company, Cambridge, Massachusetts, 1986.

McRae, Hamish, and Frances Cairncross. *Capital City; London as a Financial Centre,* Methuen, London, 1984.

Mullineux, Andrew. *International Banking and Financial Systems: a Comparison,* Graham and Trotman, London, 1987.

Mullineux, A. W. *U.K. Banking after Deregulation,* Croom Helm, London, 1987.

Onoh, J. K., Editor. *The Foundations of Nigeria's Financial Infrastructure,* Croom Helm, London, 1980.

Pecchioli, R. M. *Prudential Supervision in Banking,* Organisation for Economic Co-operation and Development, Paris, 1987.

Revell, J. R. S. *Banking and Electronic Fund Transfers,* Organization for Economic Co-operation and Development, Paris, 1983.

Rosenbluth, Frances McCall. *Financial Politics in Contemporary Japan,* Cornell University, Ithaca, New York, 1989.

Seidman, Ann. *Money, Banking and Public Finance in Africa,* Zed Books, Ltd., London, 1986.

Seznec, Jean-Francois. *The Financial Markets of the Arabian Gulf,* Croom Helm, London, 1987.

Spong, Kenneth. *Banking Regulation; Its Purposes, Implementation, and Effects,* 3d ed., Federal Reserve Bank of Kansas City, 1990.

Subcommittee on Financial Institutions Supervision, Regulation, and Insurance. *Report of the Task Force on the International Competitiveness of U.S. Financial Institutions,* Committee on Banking, Finance, and Urban Affairs, U.S. House of Representatives, Washington, D.C., 1991.

Suzuki, Yoshio. *The Japanese Financial System,* Oxford University Press, New York, 1987.

U.S. Department of the Treasury. *Modernizing the Financial System; Recommendations for Safer, More Competitive Banks,* Washington, D.C., 1991.

Wilson, J. S. G. *Banking Policy and Structure; a Comparative Analysis,* Croom Helm, London, 1986.

Wilson, Rodney. *Banking and Finance in the Arab Middle East,* St. Martin's Press, New York, 1983.

Wohlers-Scharf, Traute. *Arab and Islamic Banks; New Business Partners for Developing Countries,* Development Centre of the Organisation for Economic Co-operation and Development, Paris, 1983.

CHAPTER 18

THE INTERNATIONAL OPERATIONS OF COMMERCIAL BANKS

CHAPTER OUTLINE

CHAPTER OVERVIEW

This chapter:

- Explains the motivations for entering international banking markets
- Describes the organizational forms of international banking
- Highlights foreign bank operations in the United States
- Examines the role of government in international banking
- Outlines international banking services
- Discusses risk in international banking
- Traces the origins third-world debt crisis

International financial transactions date back to ancient times when Egyptians and Sumerians wrote letters of credit on papyrus and "checks" on clay tablets to finance cross-border trade. Merchants in Babylonia and Assyria used bills of exchange to achieve the same objective.

In more recent times, the Medicis of Florence operated branches in Rome, Venice, Milan, Paris, Avignon, Bruges, London, and Geneva. The Baring Brothers of London established extensive correspondent relationships with other banks, including a representative office in the United States. Other London-based merchant banks maintained substantial Latin American and South African branch networks. By the 1860s, British bank branches in California and the Far East were not uncommon.

In this century, international banking has become even more widespread. As industrial firms find growth markets overseas, their banks follow them abroad. In many respects, U.S. banks have been modern international market pioneers, having engineered such innovations as the Eurodollar certificate of deposit. However, ironically, U.S. institutions are no longer the major players in international banking. Just as Japanese industrial firms have overtaken many U.S. counterparts, Japanese banks now dominate the ranks of the world's largest banks.

Whether this trend will continue at least partially depends on the ability of large U.S. banks to strengthen their balance sheets. Aggressive lending to third-world countries during the 1970s and early 1980s has created large portfolios of questionable loans that have required massive loan loss provisions and numerous debt reschedulings.

Problems in domestic loan portfolios (such as commercial real estate) have only compounded this problem. Yet the fact remains that the most dynamic growth in commercial banking has been and will be in the international sector.

REASONS FOR INTERNATIONAL EXPANSION

There are three main reasons that banks begin to operate internationally. Banks seek to:

- penetrate local markets,
- serve domestic clients, or
- participate in the Euromarkets.

Penetrating Local Markets

A primary motivating factor for international expansion is to gain direct access to the *host country's markets.* Perhaps, indigenous (host country) banks are not competitive in *lending* activities, either in terms of loan pricing or servicing. Alternatively, host country banks may not realize their full potential in *deposit taking.*

If a bank can offer lower loan rates, higher deposit rates, and/or better service, expansion into a foreign market can be profitable. When indigenous banks react to the foreign presence by improving their own product offerings, host country residents clearly benefit from this heightened competition.

The targeted market may be nonfinancial corporations, other banks, government, or individuals. The government and banking sectors are generally most easily penetrated. Corporate and individual clients may be more difficult to lure away from local institutions. Also, availability of sufficient information needed to evaluate corporate and individual creditworthiness may initially be limited.

However, just as many U.S. banks have sought to expand their retail markets domestically, a number have also found that some overseas consumer markets have not been fully exploited. This appears to be particularly true in countries with a highly concentrated banking structure. It may be that a relatively small number of indigenous banks will not feel significant competitive pressure to innovate products and services.

U.S. Banks For example, Citibank conducts consumer banking in over thirty countries, providing transactions and savings accounts as well as consumer loans (some through finance company subsidiaries). Bank of America caters to upscale clients abroad through its Global Consumer Division. Chase Manhattan operates automated teller machines in Singapore and Hong Kong. A Chase subsidiary in the Netherlands serves approximately 300,000 customers by opening accounts and selling products through direct mail. (See Exhibit 18-1.)

Bank of China China presents a particularly interesting case of local-market penetration through international bank operations. Chinese who live outside mainland China, called overseas Chinese, and residents of Hong Kong and Macao, called compatriots, regularly remit funds to family members in mainland China. This remittance of funds has taken place since the People's Republic of China was established in 1949. The government encourages these payments because they improve the country's balance of payments.

Bank of China overseas branches and branches in mainland regions from which large numbers of Chinese citizens have immigrated facilitate this process. Funds sent through the banking system are denominated in foreign currency. Once the foreign currency is received, the recipient must deposit it in exchange for *renminbi* (Chinese local currency).

This type of government involvement in overseas retail markets is rare. However, a later section describes generalized government intervention in international bank operations. (See also Exhibit 18-2.)

Serving Domestic Customers

Banks also begin operating abroad in order to serve corporate clients that expand internationally. In the 1960s and 1970s, U.S. multinational corporations greatly increased worldwide operations. As these firms established facilities in Canada and Western Europe, their banks followed them into these regions. Foreign direct-investment trends shifted toward the United States in the 1970s and 1980s. Likewise, European, Canadian, and Japanese banks followed their clients to the United States.

However, serving corporate clients in this way can be complicated. In some cases, host country governments impose restrictions on foreign bank entry or operations. Also,

EXHIBIT 18-1 CREDIT CARDS IN GERMANY

Travel and entertainment cards have been available in Europe for some time. However, bank credit cards are a recent innovation. With widespread acceptance and issuance of bank cards in the United States, American banks have turned to Europe for possible market expansion. In Germany, where bankers rely heavily upon their clients' presence in bank offices to cross-sell a number of products, the bank credit card received a cool reception.

To the displeasure of German banks, American Express purchased a Frankfurt bank through which insurance and other services were sold via credit card. Attempts to block this activity with regulatory intervention and with agreements among German banks for nonparticipation in the card venture proved unsuccessful. Unable to stop the introduction of the bank card, German banks joined with their own version, the Eurocard. In 1987, retailers announced plans to issue their own cards.

The introduction of credit cards by U.S. firms has facilitated market expansion. As a result, German residents now enjoy a broader range of financial services.

EXHIBIT 18-2 ORIENTAL CULTURE IN THE SUBURBS OF NEW YORK

A few years ago, the Flushing area of Queens, New York, had few Asian residents. Currently, more than 140,000 Chinese and Korean immigrants reside there. Oriental banks are, likewise, an important element of the economy. The oldest Chinese-American bank in Flushing is Asia Bank. Others include Amerasia Bank and Hong Kong–Shanghai Banking Corporation.

One of the newest entrants is China Trust, the largest private bank in Taiwan. In its first 2 weeks of operation, China Trust took in $6 million from 400 depositors. American banks compete aggressively for Oriental deposits. For example, ATMs in Flushing offer transactions in three languages, and the employees in Citibank's Asian Banking Center speak Korean, Mandarin, and Cantonese. Nevertheless, the Oriental banks have certain competitive advantages:

- Deposit interest rates are higher than at American banks.
- Weekend banking hours are maintained.
- In some cases, free parking (a rare commodity) is provided.
- The reputations and past records of customers from the home country are considered in credit evaluations.
- Gifts are often distributed during Chinese New Year.

The success of Oriental banks in Flushing is not an accident. Competitive pricing, a high level of service, and cultural links all contribute.

Source: Lorch, Donatella, "Banks Follow Immigrants to Flushing," *New York Times,* August 7, 1991.

as noted earlier, indigenous banks will generally compete to maintain or expand their own market share.

Once a bank has expanded internationally, it is even possible for conflicts between bank and customer to arise. The U.S. multinational is most likely a very creditworthy firm that can command the most competitive loan rates and fees for bank services. On the other hand, local industrial firms may be associated with more credit risk and, therefore, larger spreads and increased bank profitability. If the overseas bank operation neglects its U.S. multinational client to develop local client relationships, relations between the parent firm and the parent bank can become strained.

Notwithstanding these potential complications, attempts by banks to continue to provide services to their domestic clients account for a significant portion of international expansion.

Participating in Euromarkets

Recent developments in money and capital markets have also provided impetus for overseas operations. As discussed in Chapter 7, Euromarkets began to develop in the 1960s. Initially, interest rate ceilings in the United States threatened to severely constrict new negotiable certificates of deposit (CDs) as market interest rates climbed above the Federal Reserve Regulation Q limits on deposit interest rates. However, these ceilings did not apply to deposits offered in overseas offices of U.S. banks. Large money center institutions were the primary issuers of the new instruments, and they responded by offering CDs with competitive rates in offices located in Europe, especially London.

Thus, an important funding source, the negotiable CD, was protected from noncompetitive interest rate ceilings. As a further consequence of the relative freedom from regulatory oversight, overseas operations avoided reserve requirements and federal deposit insurance premiums. Without these added costs of doing business, Eurocurrency loan rates were set below the rates that were feasible domestically.

At the same time, growing deficits in the U.S. balance of payments (trade and capital flow deficits) prompted the Federal Reserve to restrict further overseas investment. This effectively prevented multinational banks from repatriating profits earned abroad and subsequently redeploying them overseas. As a result, these offshore profits became new bank capital investment outside the United States. This higher capital base supported even more deposit gathering.

In the 1970s unprecedented crude oil price increases generated correspondingly high international trade surpluses for oil-exporting countries. The Eurocurrency market provided an efficient mechanism for the absorption of resulting liquidity. Investment of the Organization of Petroleum Exporting Countries (OPEC) surpluses within the domestic financial markets of the United States and other industrialized countries sometimes met with governmental resistance, because such large infusions of liquidity complicated the efforts of monetary authorities to control money supply and inflation. But investing OPEC funds in the unregulated Eurocurrency markets posed no such problem.

Historically the primary participants in the Eurodollar market have been larger banking institutions. For example, in the 1970s only twenty institutions held over 90 percent of all foreign branch assets of U.S. banks. By the early 1980s, Citicorp attributed 80 percent of earnings to overseas operations, in which 50 percent of its total assets were invested.

As other countries relaxed banking regulations and tax laws, they, too, became prime locations for Euromarket activity. The prestige and the potential for job creation associated with the Euromarkets appear to have had some bearing on bank regulatory changes in Belgium, Luxembourg, and the Netherlands. Outside of Europe, Singapore, Hong Kong, and the Caribbean have attracted considerable "Euromarket" activity.

ORGANIZATIONAL FORMS FOR INTERNATIONAL BANKING

Various forms of international banking have existed in the United States before Euromarkets, some as early as the nineteenth century. However, a specific institutional framework for international operations for national banks was created through amendments to the Federal Reserve Act, the *Edge Act corporation.* The state bank equivalent is the *Agreement corporation.* Both types of corporations operate in the United States. In terms of overseas locations, banks may establish *representative offices, agencies, branches,* or *subsidiaries.* When an overseas location is chosen because of tax advantages or greater freedom from regulation, the location is called an *offshore center.* Banks also may participate in international activities by investing in *export trading companies.*

It is now possible to derive some of the same benefits available in offshore centers by establishing an *international banking facility* in the United States.

Edge Act and Agreement Corporations

The 1913 Federal Reserve Act gave national banks permission to establish foreign branches, a privilege they did not enjoy previously. Before the act, only state banks and private, unincorporated banks were allowed to have foreign offices. Beginning in 1913, national banks electing to open overseas branches were to obtain permission from the Comptroller of the Currency. The requirements included $1 million in domestic bank capital and full disclosure with respect to foreign branch operations.

This provision of the act was intended to facilitate foreign trade. However, during the next 3 years, only one national bank started an overseas branch. A 1916 amendment of the Federal Reserve Act empowered national banks (with $1 million of capital) to invest up to 10 percent of capital in state-chartered banks or corporations that were to be engaged primarily in international banking. A condition of such an arrangement was that the state-chartered corporation enter into an agreement to conduct its business subject to limitations and restrictions imposed by the Federal Reserve Board. These institutions have come to be referred to as *Agreement corporations.*

However, even this increased flexibility to operate an Agreement corporation under more lenient state laws did not stimulate much interest. In the next 3 years, only three Agreement corporations received charters. In 1919, the Edge Act created a *federally* chartered institution for foreign transactions through another amendment of the Federal Reserve Act.

In some ways, an *Edge Act corporation* was subject to more restrictions than an Agreement corporation. For example:

- All Edge Act corporation directors must be U.S. citizens.
- Ten percent of all domestic deposits must be held in reserve.
- Total liabilities must never exceed ten times the sum of capital plus surplus.

However, Edge Act corporations were permitted to invest in nonbank financial institutions, an activity in which agreement corporations were *not* explicitly allowed to engage.

Early Edge Act corporations were established primarily to engage in nonbanking enterprises. Later, banks used this framework in order to open facilities outside the home state. These corporations now compete with the foreign banks in the United States.

Currently, approximately 200 Edge Act facilities operate throughout the United States. Most Edge Act corporations are located in New York, Miami, Chicago, San Francisco, Los Angeles, and Houston. This geographic concentration may be partially explained by the capital requirement of $2 million. Given this requirement, a substantial volume of international transactions is necessary in order to ensure profitability. Many engage primarily in export and import financing, usually on a short-term basis, for clients that are either individuals or corporations. (See Exhibit 18-3.)

EXHIBIT 18-3 COMPARISON OF EDGE ACT AND AGREEMENT CORPORATIONS

	Agreement	Edge Act
Date of authorization	1916	1919
Charter	State	Federal
Minimum capital	No federally mandated minimum	$2 million
Nationality restrictions for ownership	None	Directors: U.S. citizens
Authority to invest conferred by	Federal Reserve Board	Statute
Powers	International banking	International banking and investment in nonbank financial institutions engaged in international operations
Reserve requirements	None	10% on all deposits accepted in the U.S.
Restrictions on debt issuance	None	Total liabilities not to exceed 10 times the sum of capital and surplus

There are four general forms of business organizations through which a bank may conduct overseas operations. The *representative office* is the most restricted of the four. Representative offices may *not* accept deposits, make loans, or conduct any banking services. They are simply points of contact between parent banks and their clients.

Agencies have somewhat more authority. They may accept predetermined payments in connection with international trade or deliver undisbursed portions of loans made by the parent bank. However, deposit-taking or fiduciary activities (such as portfolio management) are strictly prohibited. Essentially, no credit decisions are made by agencies. Agencies may only execute credit decisions made by the parent.

Branches and *subsidiaries* perform all normal banking functions. In the United States, a foreign *branch* must be licensed by either the state in which it is located or by the federal government. Technically, the results of operations are not distinguished from those of the parent bank. As a result, its lending limits are tied to the capital and surplus of the parent. Laws and regulations of the home country govern branch activities.

Subsidiaries are separate legal entities, incorporated by the government of the country in which they operate. Each has its own capital base. However, it is not uncommon for the parent bank to own 100 percent of the subsidiary's stock. Generally, laws of the host country govern the operation of overseas subsidiaries.

The choice of organizational form will depend upon a number of circumstances. If the bank has a large number of clients in the overseas location or a small number of major clients, a full-service bank (branch or subsidiary) may be preferable. On the other hand, a representative office is a cost-effective way to explore a new geographic market before setting up more extensive operations. In fact, in some cases, tax and other advantages associated with a foreign market may be exploited without a substantial investment in physical facilities or personnel.

Offshore Centers

An *offshore center* is a site (country or city) that has made special provisions to attract international banking business. International banking can be broadly defined in one of three ways from the perspective of a commercial bank.

International banking:

Transactions with (1) domestic clients denominated in foreign currency, (2) foreign clients denominated in foreign or domestic currency, or (3) domestic clients denominated in domestic currency but *recorded* or *"booked"* in another country.

Notice that the first two definitions describe situations that are easily classified as "international," whether the transactions are recorded in the home country or abroad. However, the third definition requires that the transactions be recorded in a location other than the home country in order for them to be considered international transactions.

The third type of transaction will be cost-effective only when the foreign location offers an incentive. An offshore banking center has a tax or regulatory advantage that makes the third type of transaction an attractive arrangement. Of course, once the center has attracted a sufficient number of institutions, it may encourage a wider range of services and evolve into a full-scale international banking center.

As explained earlier, London was the site of early offshore activity by U.S. banks. These dollar-denominated transactions were between U.S. banks and other U.S. residents but carried out in London. Nonresident transactions have been free from reserve requirements and deposit insurance premiums while being afforded favorable tax treatment. Indeed, London continues to be the largest offshore market. Nevertheless, because of its already considerable stature as an international financial center, London is not usually *classified* as an offshore center.

The term is usually reserved for cost-effective locations whose money and capital markets are relatively new and whose laws and regulations have been intentionally designed to attract financial firms. Examples are the Bahamas, the Cayman Islands, Bahrain, Hong Kong, Luxembourg, Panama, and Singapore.

Offshore centers may be either *paper* or *functional* centers. Paper centers are merely locations of record with little actual banking activity in the country. The Bahamas is an example of a paper center. Over 250 financial institutions are licensed to do business in the Bahamas, but only fifty-five of them actually have employees in the Bahamas. The rest transact business through a post office address. No clients are seen and no decisions are made in the Bahamas. Functional centers develop other related financial markets. Singapore and Hong Kong are good examples of functional centers. Eurobonds are issued and traded in these locations. The stock markets of both countries are considered important emerging markets. Singapore has been an important financial intermediary in the region. In the early 1980s, over $13 billion in crude oil–related surpluses of oil-exporting countries was deposited in Singapore banks and rechanneled to other Asian countries.

Because of its limited offering of financial services, a paper center will be more vulnerable to increases in its own tax structure. Banks make minimal capital investments in paper centers because their primary advantage is a favorable tax environment. In functional centers, banks derive additional benefit from related services and other advantages associated with the location. Many functional centers have increased taxes without seriously damaging their market share of world financial transactions.

It should be noted, however, that London, Tokyo, and New York now all offer "offshore" facilities. These and other areas will become increasingly attractive sites as deregulation continues to evolve. This trend could threaten the long-term viability of even the functional offshore centers. (See Exhibit 18-4.)

International Banking Facilities

As a reaction to the diversion of dollar-dominated bank business away from U.S. locations, in 1978 the state of New York introduced legislation that authorized International Banking Facilities (IBFs), exempt from New York State and city taxes. The legislation made implementation contingent on exemption of IBF deposits from reserve require-

EXHIBIT 18-4 FEATURES OF CARIBBEAN OFFSHORE CENTERS

Tax haven provisions*	Bermuda	Bahamas	Cayman Islands	Netherlands Antilles
No tax	X	X	X	
Low tax				X
Best for				
1. Trusts	X	X	X	
2. Holding Companies				X
No tax treaties	X	X	X	
U.S. tax treaty				X
Bank secrecy		X	X	
Numbered bank accounts		X		
Bearer shares		X	X	X

*These provisions are applicable to nonresident companies and trusts.
Source: Johns, Richard Anthony, *Tax Havens and Offshore Finance; A Study of Transactional Economic Development,* 1983, p. 193.

ments and interest rate ceilings that were in force at the time. The objective was to provide the same advantages associated with offshore centers.

By late 1980, the Federal Reserve agreed in principle with the concept. Effective December 1981, the Federal Reserve authorized a new category of "IBF time deposits" that were not subject to reserve requirements or interest rate ceilings. The IBFs were neither branches nor subsidiaries. Instead, they were merely separate records within a U.S.-chartered depository institution, a U.S. branch or agency of a foreign bank, or a U.S. office of an Edge Act corporation. (See Exhibit 18-5.)

Only nonresident deposits and loans qualified as IBF transactions. The objective was to separate this activity from domestic banking. To maintain this separation, no deposit instrument could be issued in negotiable form. Thus, negotiable CDs did not qualify for IBF treatment. In order to prevent the deposits from being used as transactions accounts, the minimum denomination for nonbank IBF deposits was set at $100,000.

Like Edge Act offices, IBF locations are concentrated in major cities. Of the approximately 500 IBFs, over 200 are in New York. Most of the others are in California, Florida, and Illinois. In terms of dollar value, however, New York dominates with approximately 80 percent of IBF deposits.

Export Trading Companies

In 1982, Congress enacted the Export Trading Company (ETC) Act to encourage exports. Any businesses engaged in international trade are known as ETCs if over 50 percent of revenues are derived from the export of goods or services.

The act gave bank holding companies the power to lend to ETCs or to acquire, partially or wholly, ETCs through equity investment. Edge Act corporations were also given this power. Just 2 years later, twenty-four bank holding companies had received approval from the Federal Reserve to establish ETC subsidiaries. Through such subsidies, commercial banks can enhance their image in international business with little increase in risk while earning fee income from letters of credit and banker's acceptances (discussed later in the chapter).

EXPANSION OF INTERNATIONAL BANKING

The number of U.S. banks with foreign offices has increased significantly since 1950. In 1950, only seven banks had overseas locations. By 1989, this number had grown to 247. These foreign offices controlled assets of $402 billion in 1989, or 12 percent of the total assets of all FDIC-insured commercial banks.

The expansion of international banking by U.S. institutions has occurred in three distinct phases:

EXHIBIT 18-5 RESTRICTIONS IMPOSED ON U.S. INTERNATIONAL BANKING FACILITIES

	Restriction
1. Clients	Nonresidents only (or other IBFs)
2. Transaction type	Written notice to nonbank clients that deposits and loans must be used in connection with offshore activities
3. Transaction form	May not be bearer or negotiable instrument
4. Maturity	At least 2 working days
5. Denomination	At least $100,000 for nonbank customers (unless to withdraw interest or close account)

1 The *first phase* started in the early 1960s and continued into the 1970s. Large multinational industrial corporations expanded their international operations. United States banks accommodated this expansion by increased international lending to their corporate customers.
2 The *second phase* began in the early 1970s and ended in the early 1980s. During this phase, the trade surpluses of oil-exporting countries were deposited in U.S. banks (and banks in other industrialized countries). These surpluses were recycled as loans to countries experiencing trade deficits and to governments of less developed countries (LDCs) that wished to undertake economic development projects. International lending grew very rapidly during this period. At the end of this phase, it was apparent that many of these loans would not be repaid as originally agreed. (The issue of third-world debt is discussed in the last section of this chapter.)
3 The *third phase* is the current phase, having begun in the early 1980s. United States banks are concentrating on managing their troubled international loan portfolios. There is no longer an emphasis on international asset growth. Instead, U.S. banks are retrenching from the international loan market.

Not all banks have been involved in these phases to the same extent. Large money center banks have been the primary participants. Regional banks in the United States have been involved to a lesser extent.

U.S. Money Center Banks

The international activity of U.S. banks has been highly concentrated in a small number of money center banks. Four banks hold 50 percent of international assets; ten banks hold 80 percent. Even so, the rapid expansion in international lending by these banks in the 1970s is now being followed by a mass exodus from the international sector. The following examples help illustrate this trend.

- Chase Manhattan (New York) sold its affiliate in the Netherlands with assets of over $5 billion to Credit Lyonnais of France. In total, Chase has reduced its foreign presence from fifty-five countries to thirty-three.
- Bank of America (California) sold its profitable Italian affiliate to Deutsche Bank of Germany.
- Wells Fargo and Company (California) divested of all its foreign offices before its merger with Security Pacific.
- Chemical Bank (New York) once had operations in thirty foreign countries (before its merger with Manufacturers Hanover of New York). The number is now nine. Many of the eliminated offices had been in Europe.

This emphasis on international downsizing has affected the worldwide standing of U.S. banks. Of the world's largest banks, fourteen are Japanese, five are European, and only one is from the United States. Citicorp, with assets of over $200 billion, is only half as large as Dai-Ichi Kangyo, the Japanese bank that is currently the world's largest. Also, Citicorp is the only U.S. money center bank aggressively developing its international operations. (See Exhibit 18-6.)

There are three primary reasons for the current retreat from international markets:

1 Third-world loan losses have stimulated a withdrawal from developing country loans.
2 United States banks have divested of foreign affiliates in order to purchase domestic banks and failed depository institutions (savings and loan association and commercial banks).
3 The capital standards of the Basel Accord have made it necessary for money center banks to raise their capital ratios. Because bank stock prices have been depressed, issu-

EXHIBIT 18-6 CITIBANK IN ASIA

While reducing its work force in the United States, Citibank has continued to increase its Asian personnel, for it has targeted affluent Asians. The strategies and services of its Asian program include the following:

- In Asia, the name *Citibank* is readily recognized as a high-quality provider of financial service. The bank capitalizes on this image.
- Each customer with a minimum $100,000 deposit has a personal banker.
- These clients are seen in a luxurious private office and served tea or coffee in fine China.
- Financial transactions can be conducted in eight different currencies.
- The same type of service is available to these clients when they travel to other countries.

This Asian program should be profitable. The Singapore affiliate of Citibank estimates 1992 revenues of $1 billion and net profit of $200 million.

Source: Kraar, Louis, "How Americans Win in Asia," *Fortune,* October 7, 1991, p. 140.

ing equity would only depress prices further. Selling overseas affiliates serves the same purpose by reducing the amount of risk-weighted assets.[1]

These are legitimate reasons for withdrawing from international activities. However, the unfortunate consequence is that relationships in lucrative and potentially lucrative markets have been relinquished. It may be difficult to reestablish them at a later date.

Foreign Banks in the United States

While the U.S. banks that followed their corporate clients abroad have withdrawn in many cases, the banks in other countries that followed their clients to the United States have not retreated. The size of the U.S. market has also been an attraction for foreign banks. The importance of the dollar in U.S. trade has also played a role.

Exhibit 18-7 is a list of the twenty-five largest foreign banks in the United States and their U.S. assets. Fifteen of the twenty-five are Japanese banks. Three are Italian, and two are based in the United Kingdom and France each. Hong Kong, Canada, and Switzerland are the home countries for the remaining three. Together, these banks controlled $440 billion in assets in 1989, or 13.3 percent of the total assets of all FDIC-insured banks.

This is a significant share of U.S. bank assets. However, in terms of location, these banks are concentrated in larger cities. Exhibit 18-8 shows the geographic breakdown as of 1989. Almost half are located in New York, with other large concentrations in Los Angeles, Chicago, Houston, and San Francisco. Representative offices and branches are the most common organizational form, followed by agencies.

In terms of the markets that these banks serve, most are involved in corporate banking. This is also true of Japanese banks that serve more than 1000 subsidiaries of Japanese industrial firms in California. In addition, these banks cater to the large Japanese population in that state. They have also gained significant market share by offering banking services with thin profit margins. The current trend of Japanese banking is to seek more profitable transactions in the middle market, that is, medium-size corporations. Of course, this is the same corporate market that U.S. banks have targeted for future growth. This means that the competition between U.S. and Japanese banks in the United States will probably increase in the future.

[1]See Chapter 15 for a discussion of the Basel Accord.

EXHIBIT 18-7 LARGEST FOREIGN BANKS IN THE UNITED STATES, 1989

Bank	Total assets*
1. Bank of Tokyo (Japan)	45.2
2. Dai-Ichi Kangyo (Japan)	34.0
3. Mitsubishi Bank (Japan)	31.5
4. Fuji Bank Limited (Japan)	29.7
5. Industrial Bank (Japan)	28.1
6. Sanwa Bank (Japan)	28.0
7. Hong Kong and Shanghai Bank (Hong Kong)	24.8
8. Sumitomo Bank (Japan)	24.5
9. National Westminster Bank (United Kingdom)	22.3
10. Bank of Montreal (Canada)	17.8
11. Tokai Bank (Japan)	17.7
12. Mitsui Trust and Banking Corp. (Japan)	12.1
13. Daiwa Bank (Japan)	11.5
14. Swiss Bank Corp. (Switzerland)	11.4
15. Mitsui Bank (Japan)	11.2
16. Long-Term Credit Bank of Japan (Japan)	10.5
17. Mitsubishi Trust and Banking Corp. (Japan)	10.2
18. Sumitomo Trust and Banking Corp. (Japan)	9.8
19. Banque National de Paris (France)	9.4
20. Banca Nazional del Lavoro (Italy)	9.1
21. Banco di Roma (Italy)	8.7
22. Barclays Group (United Kingdom)	8.6
23. Taiyo Kobe Bank (Japan)	8.4
24. Credit Lyonnais (France)	8.2
25. Banco di Napoli (Italy)	7.7
	440.4
Total assets of FDIC-insured banks, 1989	3299

*Billions of dollars.

Source: Subcommittee on Financial Institutions Supervision, Regulation, and Insurance, *Task Force Report on the International Competitiveness of U.S. Financial Institutions,* 1991, p. 53.

EXHIBIT 18-8 LOCATION OF FOREIGN BANKS IN THE UNITED STATES, 1989

	Number of locations						
City	Representative offices	Agencies	Branches	Subsidiaries	Edge Act banks	Investment companies	Total
New York	161	35	233	33	6	11	479
Los Angeles	24	60	30	13	—	—	127
Chicago	29	—	53	5	2	—	89
Houston	55	14	—	—	6	—	75
San Francisco	19	28	7	7	2	—	63
Miami	7	35	—	3	9	—	54
Atlanta	12	15	—	—	—	—	27
Washington, D.C.	10	—	3	—	1	—	14
Dallas	13	1	—	—	—	—	14
Seattle	5	—	9	—	—	—	14
All other	41	13	29	40	1	—	124
Total	376	201	364	101	27	11	1080

Source: Subcommittee on Financial Institutions Supervision, Regulation, and Insurance, *Task Force Report on the International Competitiveness of U.S. Financial Institutions,* 1991, p. 42.

The general focus on international banking is not limited to Japanese banks. Exhibit 18-9 shows the extent of international activity among the banking systems with the largest international portfolios. International investments are the smallest percentage of total assets for U.S. banks at 8.6 percent in 1990. The highest percentages are Luxembourg and Belgium, at 96.1 and 54.2 percent, respectively. The data help to illustrate the outward focus of other banking systems relative to the United States. In some cases, this outward focus is encouraged and facilitated by government agencies.

U.S. Regional Banks

United States regional banks also sought to increase their overseas activities. Their objectives were to share in the profitable Eurocurrency markets and to better compete with larger institutions that internationalized earlier.

However, regionals have had to face a number of challenges abroad. *First,* since U.S. regional banks began overseas operations after money center banks, the market available to them is sometimes limited. The U.S. multinational firms will not necessarily break off relations with banks that served them up to the point of a regional's entry into a foreign market.

Second, a regional's international branch network may be insufficient to offer the level of service demanded by U.S. firms. For services such as cash management and foreign exchange risk management, the regional must have a physical presence where the U.S. firm operates. It is not enough for the regional to simply have a branch on the same continent.

Third, the quality and diversity of service must also be competitive. High-quality service entails specialized personnel in adequate numbers. However, if the foreign branch of a regional bank has a low volume of activity, such an investment of talent may be prohibitively expensive. Further, without a full complement of personnel, the range of services may also be limited.

These factors help explain the dominance of money center banks over regional institutions in international activities. However, given the problems with third-world debt during the 1980s, the limited involvement of regional banks in lending to developing countries may actually be a fortunate turn of events.

EXHIBIT 18-9 INTERNATIONAL INVESTMENTS AS A PERCENTAGE OF TOTAL ASSETS FOR SELECTED COUNTRIES, 1990

Country	Percentage*
Belgium	54.2
Canada	13.4
France	40.4
Germany	16.3
Japan	13.9
Luxembourg	96.1
Netherlands	36.2
Switzerland	26.2
United Kingdom	45.0
United States	8.6

*Foreign assets of depository institutions (excluding monetary authorities) as a percentage of total assets.

Source: Calculations based on data from International Monetary Fund, *International Financial Statistics,* May 1991.

For historical reasons, in the United States, the relationship between government and business has been a somewhat arm's-length arrangement. This appears to be due to two primary factors. Large concentrations of financial power have never been readily accepted, as evidenced by an extensive body of antitrust law and court cases. Second, strong emphasis on public disclosure of government activity has produced "sunshine" and freedom-of-information laws.

These factors have made it difficult for commercial banks and government officials in the United States to develop extremely close working relationships. From the banks' perspective, the loss of confidentiality that would accompany a closer relationship with government could be a disadvantage, particularly if the bank sought greater market share or contemplated a politically unfavorable (albeit completely legal) strategy.

The result is that any dialogue between bankers and foreign policy officials in the United States is not routine. Talks between the two groups are often on an ad hoc basis after a difficult, or even crisis, situation has developed. This contrasts sharply with the situation in Germany or Japan, where bankers and government officials have a functional working relationship and meet regularly.

Germany

The banks of Germany have generally conducted international business in a way that was consistent with the government's foreign policy interests. Recall from Chapter 12 that historical abuses of government power over the financial system ultimately led to less formal regulation of German banks. In addition, the export sector has consistently been the key to German economic viability.

The result is that a few powerful banks have emerged that cooperate with the German government to achieve mutually desirable outcomes. For the reasons noted above, government officials hesitate to influence bank activity *directly.* An effective way to elicit commercial bank support of overseas trade has been the *government guarantee* of loans for international trade. These guarantees signal official desires, without resorting to directives. *Moral suasion* and implied *future government assistance* (as needed) have also been used.

Standard guarantees, for exports and raw materials, available on a fee basis, help both to stimulate the export sector and to ensure sufficient quantities of necessary raw materials for a properly functioning industrial sector. Most individual transactions have little or no impact on foreign policy. Thus, the *Hermes guarantee,* as such a guarantee is called, is important to a German bank only if the financial risk of the underlying international loan exceeds the bank's comfort level.

In some cases, however, specific transactions have considerable significance for foreign policy. In those situations, *exceptional guarantees* may be issued. The standard Hermes guarantees cover from 85 percent of the loan (in the case of a German export) to 95 percent (in the case of a German import). In exceptional circumstances, insurance coverage may be reduced or increased.

For example, in 1976, the potential sale of nuclear reactors to Brazil had significant consequences for the German nuclear energy sector. At the time, the domestic market was saturated, with only 70 percent utilization of the manufacturing facilities for nuclear power plants. The government had invested $5 billion in research and development. Up to 13,000 domestic jobs were at stake. Further, if this transaction were completed, the government might be in a much better position to obtain long-term supplies of uranium from deposits in Brazil.

The Hermes guarantee associated with the sale of these reactors covered 95 percent of the loan, rather than the customary 85 percent. The term of the guarantee was 20 years, an unusually long period of time for an export–import transaction. Thus, the government worked with the banking industry to effect a desirable outcome for the German economy.

Not all exceptional cases involve more *favorable* terms. If the government wishes to discourage a particular international transaction, the Hermes guarantee may be less generous than normal.

Other countries also have export credit agencies like Hermes. Exhibit 18-10 provides a list of the agencies in major industrialized countries. While all of them support international trade, they do not all operate with the close governmental relationship noted in Germany. This is particularly true in the United States.

Japan

As is true in Germany, the Japanese government also tends to coordinate its own foreign policy objectives with international banking. However, there is a fundamental difference between the two systems. The German government is a more or less equal partner with only slightly more influence in the government–bank balance of power. On the other hand, the balance of power in Japan is decidedly in favor of the Japanese government.

Coordination between the two sectors is not necessarily driven by the government's more powerful position. Instead, the major Japanese banks view matters from a long-term perspective in which their own success is tied to the nation's economic viability. As a result, the government and the banks often respond in a similar way in the face of long-term trends and economic needs.

Japanese banks frequently concentrate on lending and deposit taking in countries that are major trading partners. Since Japan is quite dependent on imported raw materials and other goods, there are numerous overseas bank locations in resource-rich nations.

Yet coordination with the government goes beyond industry-specific support. Frequently, the government has used international lending to offset deficits and surpluses in the country's balance of payments.

In the early 1970s, Japan enjoyed trade surpluses and a buildup of official international reserves (foreign currency). From 1970 to 1973, foreign currency–denominated loans were permitted for the first time, and restrictions on capital export (overseas loans and other investments) were relaxed. The government itself deposited substantial amounts of foreign currency in the banking system which enabled commercial banks to develop a Euroloan portfolio.

EXHIBIT 18-10 EXPORT CREDIT AGENCIES

Country	Agency
Belgium	Office National du Ducroire (OND)
Canada	Export Development Corporation (EDC)
France	Compagnie Française d'Assurance pour le Commerce Extéreuer (COFACE)
Germany	Hermes Kreditversicherungs–A.G. (Hermes)
Italy	Sezione Speciale per l'Assicurazione del Credito all 'Esportazione (SACE)
Japan	Export-Import Insurance Division, International Trade Policy Bureau, Ministry of International Trade and Industry (EID/MITI)
Netherlands	Nederlandsche Creditverzekering Maatschappij, N.V. (NCM)
Spain	Compañia Española de Segurosde Crédito a la Exportación S.A. (CESCE)
Sweden	Exportkreditnamnden (EKN)
United Kingdom	Export Credits Guarantee Department (ECGD)
United States	Export-Import Bank (Eximbank)

Source: Johnson, G. G., Matthew Fisher, and Elliott Harris, *Officially Supported Export Credits; Developments and Prospects,* 1990, p. v.

From 1973 to 1975, Japanese surpluses turned into deficits as crude oil price increases took their toll. The government reacted by restricting nonresidents to medium- and long-term loans denominated in foreign currency and, at the same time, incentives to encourage capital inflow (borrowing from overseas sources).

As the balance of payments has changed from surplus to deficit and then back again, the Japanese government has adjusted the restrictions on international banking accordingly. At times, action has gone beyond even these measures.

In 1980, special incentives were put in place to attract OPEC trade surpluses to Japan. The 5.5 percent interest rate ceiling on yen deposits was lifted, and normal withholding taxes on interest earned on bank deposits was waived for deposits by foreign governments and by international institutions. The Japanese government supplemented these measures with direct diplomatic consultations with Middle Eastern governments. Predictably, foreign deposits rose dramatically. Although implemented in a different way, Japanese government policy with respect to international banking has been just as effective as the German.

INTERNATIONAL LENDING

Cross-Country Comparisons

The true effectiveness of Japanese government and banking coordination is better understood by examining Exhibit 18-11. This exhibit shows the foreign assets of commercial bank systems as a percentage of all such assets for all industrialized countries in 1975 and 1990. Foreign assets includes claims on banks and nonbank clients. In 1975, Japan's holdings were less than 5 percent of the total. The United Kingdom (home of the Euromarkets) held 28 percent and the United States 12 percent. By 1990, the U.S. share was roughly the same, as were most of the others. However, the U.K share was under 21 percent, and the Japanese share was almost 19 percent.

The large increase for Japan came largely from an erosion in the U.K. banking system. Essentially, Japan now surpasses both the United States and the United Kingdom as leader in international banking.

Exhibit 18-12 is similar to Exhibit 18-11, except that only international loans to nonbanks have been included; that is, interbank transactions have been excluded. This information relates to loans to corporate businesses and to governments. In this sector, Japanese banks had not yet surpassed U.K. banks in 1990. However, the U.S. share declined from 16 percent in 1975 to 7.5 percent in 1990. The reverse was true for Japan. A roughly 6 percent share grew to over 15 percent.

It is interesting to note that in Exhibits 18-11 and 18-12 that the German banking system has maintained its share of the total and the nonbank markets. This is also true of those countries that have given their banks more liberal powers to provide a wider range of financial services. These include Belgium-Luxembourg, France, the Netherlands, and Switzerland. All these banking systems are strong competition for the United States.

In terms of the services offered by banks to their international clients, many of these products have been discussed in previous chapters. Examples include:

Services	Chapter
Banker's acceptances	3
Letters of credit to back commercial paper	3
Negotiable certificates of deposit	3
Interest rate swap contracts	5
Currency forward, option, and swap contracts	6

EXHIBIT 18-11 FOREIGN ASSETS OF BANKS

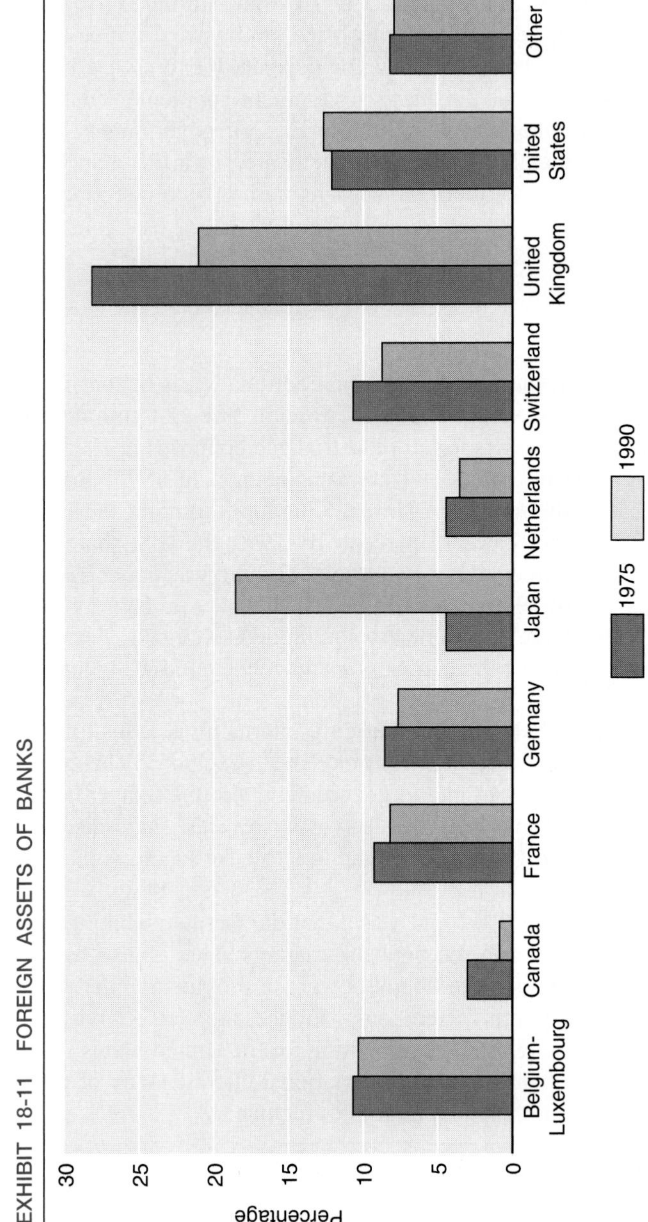

Source: Data from International Monetary Fund, *International Financial Statistics,* May 1991, p. 49, and Yearbook 1990, p. 73.

EXHIBIT 18-12 INTERNATIONAL LOANS TO NONBANK CLIENTS

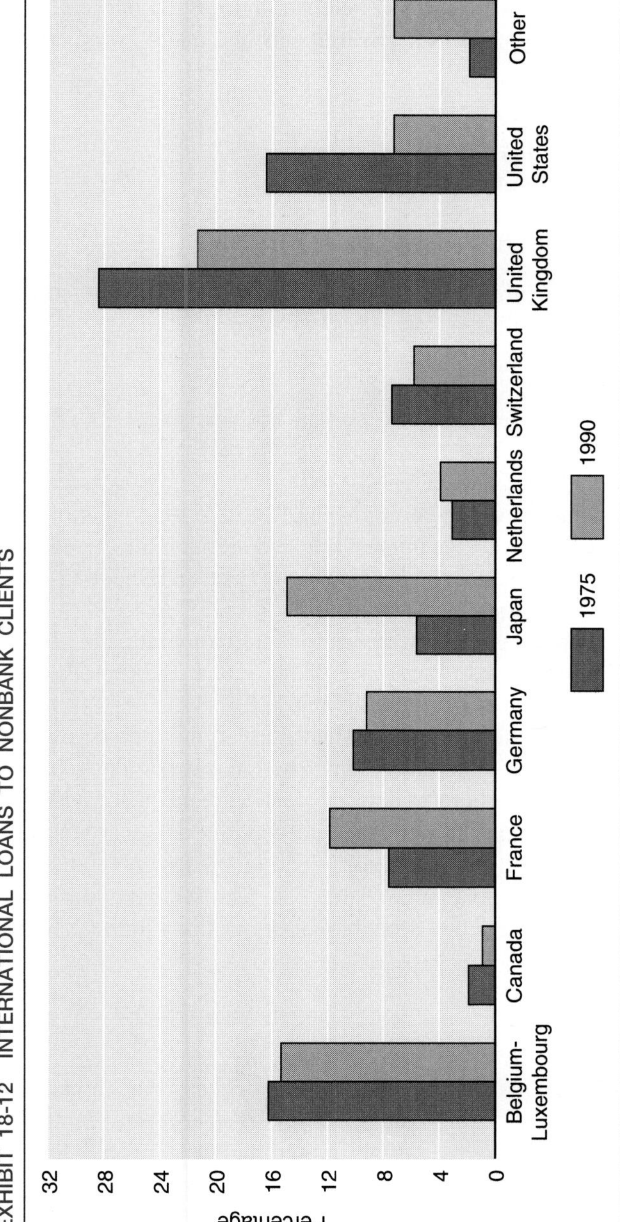

Source: Data from International Monetary Fund, *International Financial Statistics*, May 1991, p. 55, and *Yearbook 1990*, p.79.

In addition to these, there are two other important services in international banking: syndicated loans and note-issuance facilities.

Syndicated Loans

A *syndicated loan* differs from a conventional commercial loan in that a number of banks provide credit instead of one institution. The model for the syndicated loan in Euromarkets was the multibank, floating-rate loan that was developed and refined in the United States. The vehicle has been particularly useful for governments and major corporations. The reasons for its development were:

1 Increasingly larger individual loans
2 A desire by international bankers to diversify risk
3 Fee income potential for management of the loan
4 Favorable public visibility for participating banks
5 Enhanced working relationships with other banks

The interest rate associated with a Euromarket syndicated loan is usually quoted as a spread over LIBOR, London Interbank Offered Rate.

LIBOR:
The rate of interest at which short-term funds are exchanged between banks in London.

For example, "LIBOR plus 1" is one percentage point over LIBOR. A lead bank or syndicate manager negotiates with the borrower this interest rate and all other terms and conditions of the loan, documenting them in the loan agreement. Each participating bank then purchases some portion of the total loan.

London has historically served as the primary location for international loan syndications. Other sites that have developed include Singapore, Hong Kong, Bahrain, Luxembourg, and the Caribbean.

The participating banks will expect that the normal, necessary conditions of prudent lending be satisfied. The borrower should be creditworthy, the interest rate competitive, and appropriate restrictive covenants incorporated into the loan agreement. In addition, participating banks expect the lead manager to perform in a way that is consistent with their own financial interests. Ultimately, however, participating banks accept the full credit risk of the borrower for their respective parts of the loan. The syndication process enables regional banks to take part in large international transactions that might otherwise be unavailable to them.

Note-Issuance Facilities

In recent years, the heightened regulatory emphasis on capital adequacy has, in part, led to greater securitization in capital markets.[2] *Note-issuance facilities (NIFs)* provide financing for highly creditworthy borrowers through securities, rather than through bank loans.

The NIFs are structured to permit the borrower to issue a series of short-term notes ("Euronotes") over a medium term. Like the syndicated loan, an NIF is a legal commitment between the borrower and the banks. *Unlike* a syndicated loan, however, an NIF commitment does not appear on bank balance sheets. The NIF arranger establishes a mechanism whereby *other investors* will provide funds as needed by purchasing for its clients short-term notes, as issued.

[2]See Chapter 4 for a discussion of securitization.

The NIF arranger acts as an underwriter, by either purchasing only those notes that the issuer is unable to sell or providing standby credit to back the notes. The standby credit is similar to letters of credit that are issued to support commercial paper domestically. The underwriting commitment does not appear on the balance sheet of the NIF arranger *unless* the bank actually purchases notes (or pays them in the event of borrower default). However, the 1992 international capital standards (Basel Accord) require that one-half of the dollar amount of the standby credit be included in the computation of risk-weighted assets.

In the cases of both syndicated loans and NIFs, credit evaluation is extremely important. However, this process is decidedly more complex because of the nature of the underlying transactions.

Risk in International Lending

To the extent that international lending is denominated in a foreign currency, commercial banks will be exposed to *foreign exchange risk.* Forward contracts, currency swaps, foreign exchange futures, and options on futures are useful in the management of this form of risk.[3]

Commercial banks also face *country risk* when they expand into overseas markets.

Country risk:
Risk associated with the creditworthiness of a borrower with residence outside the home country of the lending institution.

In the evaluation of country risk, historical data with respect to the economic and financial profile of the country is vital. Commonly, a weighted system is used. Specific variables are weighted according to their historical behavior. Variables typically include inflation rate, balance-of-payments deficits, international reserve positions, GNP growth rates, and international debt service payments. Qualitative factors such as political and social stability are also considered. Exhibit 18-13 is an example of some of these factors.

Unfortunately, *political risk* is difficult, if not impossible, to assess in an objective sense. However, when the quantitative variables suggest a favorable lending environment, the bank must next consider the probability that these conditions will persist. In a developing country, this is equivalent to the probability that the fundamental political system will *not* change.

The less developed the country, in general, the higher the probability of disruptive political change. Important variables to consider are the extent to which the government is a collective process (reflecting the wishes of a broad spectrum of citizens), the likelihood that actions of a strong leader may anger another powerful group in the country (such as

[3]See Chapter 6 for a description of these management techniques.

EXHIBIT 18-13 DYNAMIC AND DEVELOPMENTAL COUNTRY RISK FACTORS

Dynamic	Developmental
Growth in real GNP per capita	GNP per capita
Export growth	GNP
Share of manufactured goods in total exports	Ratio of agriculture, investment, savings to GNP
Debt-service ratio	
Ratio of reserves to imports	
Rate of inflation	

Source: Mathis, F. John, Editor, *Offshore Lending by U.S. Commercial Banks,* 2d ed., 1981, pp. 50–55.

the military), the depth of leadership talent (should the government change), and the existing mechanism for a smooth transition in government. (See Exhibit 18-14.)

Third-World Debt

The Buildup of Debt At the time of world oil price increases in the 1970s, commercial banks became a primary source of international finance to offset widespread balance-of-payment deficits. In 1973, the price of oil climbed from $3 to $11.70 per barrel. In 1974, oil-importing countries paid oil exporters $90 billion. Subsequently, a worldwide recession occurred and oil consumption dropped. Nevertheless, in 1976, oil-producing countries earned $113 billion in oil export revenues, of which $42 billion represented trade surpluses. Of course, oil-importing countries sustained offsetting trade deficits.

Developing countries were hit especially hard because they tended to run trade deficits even before the oil price increases as part of their long-term economic strategies. Economic development often requires imported goods and capital in the early stages. However, the dramatic price increase for such a basic commodity was clearly disruptive.

Meanwhile, oil-exporting countries exhibited a strong preference for low-risk, high-yield assets such as government securities in high-income, industrialized countries, stock and bonds of western corporations, and the deposits of large multinational banks. The United States and the United Kingdom were initially the primary beneficiaries of OPEC trade surpluses.

EXHIBIT 18-14 CHASE MANHATTAN AND THE SHAH OF IRAN

During the last years of the Pahlavi dynasty in Iran, Chase Manhattan acted as syndicate manager, or comanager, in eleven syndicated loans to Iran. While other U.S., German, British, Canadian, and Japanese banks were also active in Iran, Chase Manhattan was, by far, the most involved bank in the region. The shah had agreed to have all payments for Iranian oil flow through the National Iranian Oil Company (NIOC) account at Chase. Before the government transition, Chase Manhattan had been able to depend on a deposit flow from Iran of up to $15 billion per year.

After the shah was forced to leave the country, the new Iranian government no longer permitted oil revenues to flow through the NIOC account because it was suspected that the shah had used the account to misappropriate funds. Up to this time, Chase had maintained Iranian loans in amounts roughly equivalent to Iranian deposits. However, most of the deposits were quite short term, while loans were longer-term with maturities up to several years.

To make matters worse, several of the syndicated loans had not been approved by the National Consultative Assembly, that is, the parliament. With the shah deposed, enforceability of the loans became questionable. Further, since Chase Manhattan had acted as syndicate manager, the bank might also be liable for losses by participating banks. Chase had been aware of the nonapproval but had *not* advised participating banks of this omission.

When Iranian deposits (and other holdings) in the United States were frozen by the U.S. government, Chase declared the Iranian loans in default. Thus, the bank maintained both the loans and deposits until Iranian assets were released. The Iranians agreed to allow the right of offset. The $4.7 billion in syndicated loans was satisfied when Iranian deposits of $5.5 billion were released, netting Iran $800 million.

Source: Hulbert, Mark, *Interlock; The Untold Story of American Banks, Oil Interests, the Shah's Money, Debts and the Astounding Connections between Them,* 1982.

Both countries had close political ties to the three large oil producers: Saudi Arabia, Kuwait, and United Arab Emirates. In addition, the United States and United Kingdom were the home countries of the seven major oil companies. Further, most payments for oil were denominated in U.S. dollars, followed next by British pounds. Last, at that time, London and New York were the only two international financial centers large enough to absorb the surpluses.

Given these circumstances, commercial banks found themselves in a much better position to finance developing country trade deficits than the international organizations that normally did so. At the end of 1976, Citicorp assets of $64 billion were three and a half times the assets of the International Monetary Fund. In addition, governments of industrialized countries were not in a position to increase foreign aid in sufficient amounts to finance these deficits.

Oil price increases in 1979 brought another round of OPEC surpluses and trade deficits in oil-importing countries. Within 6 years, U.S. foreign loan portfolios increased from $105 billion (1975) to $400 billion (1981). The OPEC trade surpluses, or petrodollars, as they were called, were thus recycled. However, at least in retrospect, the magnitude of the third-world loans was excessive.

A significant amount of U.S. loans to Latin American countries appears to have found its way into the hands of individuals who then invested the proceeds outside their national borders. For example, 1980 increases in Argentinean debt totaled $9 billion. In the same year, foreign assets held by Argentinean citizens rose by $6.7 billion. Mexican debt increases of $16.4 billion were accompanied by increases in foreign assets held by Mexican citizens of $7.1 billion.

The third-world debt *situation* became a debt *crisis* in 1982 when the scope of the problem was publicized for the first time following a joint annual meeting of the World Bank and the International Monetary Fund. Mexico announced that it would not be able to repay its loans as scheduled. Subsequently, numerous debt reschedulings have been undertaken to resolve the difficult matter of third-world debt repayment. These restructurings typically involve deferring payments, lowering interest rates, and, in some cases, debt forgiveness.

In exchange, the debtor nation is often required to undertake domestic austerity measures in order to be better able to meet its newly structured debt service requirements. However, it is usually a painful economic process that, to date, has not resulted in debt repayment or sustained economic development. (See Exhibit 18-15.)

The Brady Plan The U.S. Treasury Department has implemented a plan to resolve the third-world debt crisis. It is called the "Brady Plan," as it was designed by Treasury

EXHIBIT 18-15 THE UNITED STATES WAS ONCE A DEVELOPING COUNTRY TOO

In 1854, the Secretary of the Treasury analyzed U.S. government and corporate securities and found that 50 percent of all U.S. debt was held by foreigners. A bond issue to help build Washington, D.C., had been floated by the Dutch. A Welsh nobleman owned the Manhattan Banking Company. The Boston Copper and Gold Mining Company was incorporated in London. The Arizona Copper Company was Scottish. The British owned 100 percent of the Alabama, New Orleans, Texas, and Pacific Junction Railroad.

As has been true of other developing countries, the United States was built on borrowed money. Exports did not exceed imports until 1873. The country remained a net borrower until well into the twentieth century.

Source: Wriston, Walter B., *Risk and Other Four-Letter Words,* 1986, p. 164.

Secretary Nicolas Brady. The plan follows a menu approach in that it gives creditors (primarily commercial banks) several options from which to choose. One of the most successful applications has been the plan for Mexico in 1989. Options under this plan included:

1 Old loans exchanged for new bonds with a 30-year maturity. These zero coupon bonds carried a market rate of "LIBOR plus 13⁄16." However, in exchange for the market rate, creditor must forgive 35 percent of the old loans.
2 Old loans exchanged for new bonds with a 30-year maturity. These interest-paying bonds carried a below-market rate of 6.25 percent but required no debt forgiveness.
3 New money loans, including medium-term loans and medium-term trade credit. New loans could be made up to the amount of 25 percent of the creditor's holdings of Mexican bonds.

The new Mexican bonds were collateralized by U.S. Treasury securities purchased partially with funds from the International Monetary Fund and the World Bank. It was hoped that commercial banks would provide new money for Mexican investment under the third option, as well as exchange loans for bonds under the first two options. This was not the case.

At the time of the debt rescheduling, Mexico's commercial bank debt was $84 billion. Only $19.6 billion was rescheduled under the first option and $22.5 billion under the second. Most disappointing was the amount of new money raised—only $1.6 billion.

The plans for third-world debt rescheduling to date have all been less than completely successful. Banks are reluctant to provide new money for investment or to forgive significant amounts of the debt for fear of the precedent this may set for other debtors. And since this rescheduling is on a more or less piecemeal basis, there is some incentive for banks to "free-ride." A bank free-rides when it does not participate in debt rescheduling in anticipation of being one of the last banks with which the country negotiates. The rationale is that, at that point, the debtor nation may be willing and able to repay the remaining commercial bank debt.

U.S. Commercial Bank Exposure Nevertheless, the desire of the U.S. Treasury Department to resolve the debt crisis is well-motivated. Because U.S. banks led the way in OPEC oil surplus recycling, they are most exposed to the questionable loans. The loans are concentrated in the nation's largest banks.

Exhibit 18-16 is an analysis of the most troublesome loans for U.S. banks: Latin American debt. Of the total $36.4 billion owed to commercial banks as of March 1991, $28.5 billion (78 percent) was owed to the country's nine money center banks. By far, the largest amounts outstanding are loans to Mexico and Brazil.

These loans are part of the reason that U.S. money center banks are retreating from the international sector. However, this retreat does not necessarily bode well for the future competitiveness of these banks. It is unfortunate that the "misdeeds" of the past may continue to have a negative impact on the future of U.S. banking.

SUMMARY

Commercial banks enter international markets for a variety of reasons. Penetrating local markets, following domestic clients, and participating in Euromarkets have been the dominant reasons for doing so.

EXHIBIT 18-16 U.S. COMMERCIAL BANK LOANS TO ARGENTINA, BRAZIL, CHILE, COLUMBIA, AND MEXICO, MARCH 1991

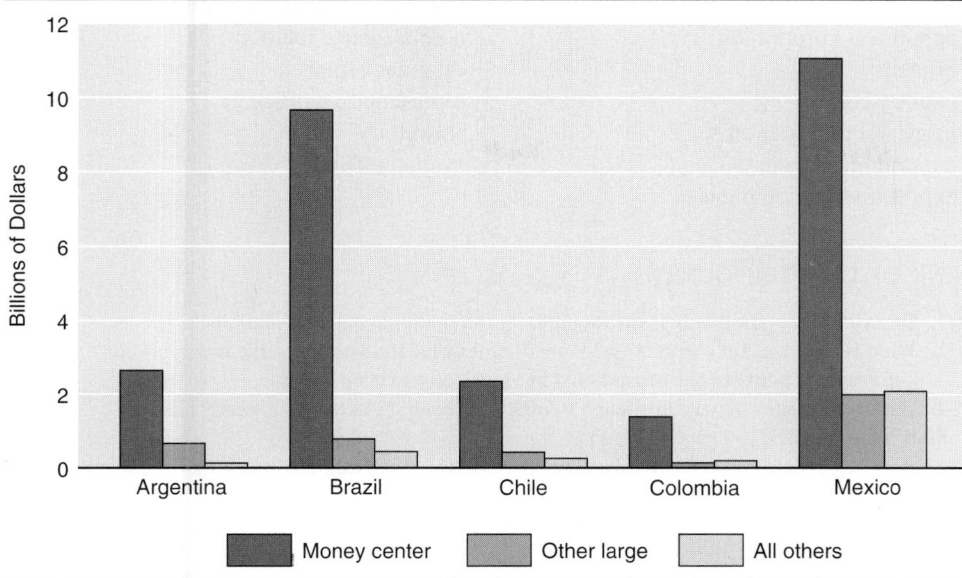

Nine money center banks: Bank of America, Citibank, Chase Manhattan Bank, Manufacturers Hanover (before merger), Morgan Guaranty, Chemical Bank (before merger), Continental Illinois, Bankers Trust, and the First National Bank of Chicago.

Twelve other large banks: Security Pacific (before merger), Wells Fargo (before merger), Marine Midland, Mellon Bank, First Interstate Bank of California, First National Bank of Boston, National Bank of Detroit, Texas Commerce Bank, Bank of New York, NCNB Texas National Bank, Republic National Bank of New York, and First City National Bank of Houston.

All U.S. banks, excluding the nine money centers and twelve other large banks.
Source: Data from Board of Governors of the Federal Reserve System, *Country Exposure Lending Survey,* March 1991.

The organizational structure of overseas operations will usually take the form of a representative office, an agency, a branch, or a subsidiary. In the United States, Edge Act and Agreement Corporations, International Banking Facilities, and Export Trading Companies have been designed and authorized by Congress in order to promote international trade and/or banking.

Primarily, the country's money center banks have engaged in international banking. Recently, however, these banks, with the exception of Citicorp, have retreated from the international sector. Excessive lending to Latin American countries in the 1970s and early 1980s has weakened their balance sheets and caused them to downsize in an effort to meet the international capital standards of 1992.

Meanwhile, foreign banks in the United States continue to secure stronger footholds. This is particularly true of Japanese banks, which promise to compete vigorously for corporate clients.

At the same time, U.S. government involvement in international banking has, in some ways, been minimal. German government loan guarantees for international transactions have been an effective inducement for export trade and essential imports. Japanese government officials have even more influence over the banking industry, tailoring administrative central measures to the country's prevailing economic needs and helping that country's banks rise to a position of dominance in international banking.

KEY TERMS

agency
agreement corporation
branch
country risk
Edge Act corporation
export credit agency
export trading companies
international banking facilities
note-issuance facility
offshore center
representative office
subsidiary
syndicated loan

END-OF-CHAPTER QUESTIONS

1. Describe three possible reasons for entering international banking markets.
2. What is an Edge Act corporation? How does it differ from an Agreement corporation?
3. Differentiate between an international bank branch and a subsidiary.
4. What advantages may be attributed to offshore centers? Are they generally all alike?
5. What is an IBF?
6. Why have regional banks not developed as extensive international networks as money center banks?
7. Are the bank-government relationships of the United States, West Germany, and Japan roughly equivalent? Explain.
8. For what reasons did syndicated loans become widely used on Euromarkets?
9. In what ways are note-issuance facilities preferable to syndicated loans.
10. What economic factors led to the massive buildup of third-world debt in the 1970s?
11. What consequences do you foresee (positive and negative) if foreign banks continue to gain market share in the United States?
12. Do you believe there is a connection between the competitive strength of multinational industrial firms and international banks? Why or why not?
13. What additional measures do you think could be taken to resolve the Latin American debt crisis?
14. Beginning in 1993, a single European banking license will enable a commercial bank to operate throughout the European Community. Do you believe that U.S. money center banks are positioning themselves for this? What impact do you think this will have on U.S. banks' worldwide competitiveness?
15. If oil prices should increase significantly again, do you believe that another buildup of third-world debt will occur?
16. How can regional banks take advantage of the Single European Market and its single banking license?

SELECTED REFERENCES

Bank for International Settlements. *Recent Innovations in International Banking,* 1986.

Board of Governors of the Federal Reserve System. *Country Exposure Lending Survey,* Washington, D.C., March 1991.

Compton, Eric. *The New World of Commercial Banking,* Lexington Books, Lexington, Massachusetts, 1987.

Dale, Richard. *The Regulation of International Banking,* Prentice-Hall, Englewood Cliffs, New Jersey, 1986.

Federal Deposit Insurance Corporation. *Statistics on Banking 1989,* Washington, D.C., 1990.

Foreign Economic Policy Subcommittee, Committee on Foreign Relations, U.S. Senate. *International Debt, the Banks, and U.S. Foreign Policy,* U.S. Government Printing Office, Washington, D.C., 1977.

Hulbert, Mark. *Interlock; The Untold Story of American Banks, Oil Interests, the Shah's Money, Debts, and the Astounding Connections between Them,* Richardson and Snyder, New York, 1982.

International Monetary Fund. *International Capital Markets; Developments and Prospects,* Washington, D.C., April 1990.

International Monetary Fund. *International Financial Statistics,* Washington, D.C., May 1991 and Yearbook 1990.

Johns, Richard Anthony. *Tax Havens and Offshore Finance,* St. Martin's Press, New York, 1983.

Johnson, G. G., Matthew Fisher, and Elliott Harris. *Officially Supported Export Credits; Developments and Prospects,* International Monetary Fund, Washington, D.C., May 1990.

Kim, Seung H., and Steven W. Miller. *Competitive Structure of the International Banking Industry,* Lexington Books, Lexington, Massachusetts, 1983.

Kraar, Louis. "How Americans Win in Asia," *Fortune,* vol. 124, no. 8 (October 7, 1991), p. 140.

Lorch, Donatella. "Banks Follow Immigrants to Flushing," *New York Times,* August 7, 1991, pp. B1–B2.

Mathis, F. John, Editor. *Offshore Lending by U.S. Commercial Banks,* 2d ed., Bankers' Association for Foreign Trade, Washington, D.C., and Robert Morris Associates, Philadelphia, 1981.

Mullineux, Andrew. *International Banking and Financial Systems: A Comparison,* Graham and Trotman, London, 1987.

Pastre', Oliver. *Multinationals: Bank and Corporation Relationships,* JAI Press, Inc., Greenwich, Connecticut, 1981.

Pauly, Louis W. *Regulatory Politics in Japan: The Case of Foreign Banking,* China-Japan Program, Cornell University, Ithaca, New York, 1987.

———. *Opening Financial Markets; Banking Politics on the Pacific Rim,* Cornell University Press, Ithaca, New York, 1988.

Reynolds, Paul D. *China's International Banking and Financial System,* Praeger Publishers, New York, 1982.

Seidman, Ann. *Money, Banking and Public Finance in Africa,* Zed Books, Ltd., London, 1986.

Spendlei, J. Andrew. *The Politics of International Credit; Private Finance and Foreign Policy in Germany and Japan,* The Brookings Institution, Washington, D.C., 1984.

Subcommittee on Financial Institutions Supervision, Regulation, and Insurance. *Task Force Report on the International Competitiveness of U.S. Financial Institutions,* Committee on Banking, Finance, and Urban Affairs, U.S. House of Representatives, Washington, D.C., 1990.

United Nations Centre on Transnational Corporations. *International Income Taxation and Developing Countries,* United Nations, New York, 1988.

United Nation Centre on Transnational Corporations. *Transnational Banks and the International Debt Crisis,* United Nations, New York, 1991.

United Nations. *World Economic Survey 1989,* New York, 1989.

Viner, Aron. *Inside Japanese Financial Markets,* Dow Jones–Irwin, Homewood, Illinois, 1988.

Walter, Ingo. *Global Competition in Financial Services; Liberalization,* Ballinger Publishing Company, Cambridge, Massachusetts, 1988.

Wilson, J. S. G. *Banking Policy and Structure; A Comparative Analysis,* Croom Helm, London, 1986.

Wriston, Walter, B. *Risk and Other Four Letter Words,* Harper & Row, New York, 1986.

31 MILK ST
TELEPHONE WORKERS'
CREDIT UNION
31
31

PART FIVE

NONBANK DEPOSITORY INSTITUTIONS

CHAPTER 19

SAVINGS AND LOAN ASSOCIATIONS AND MUTUAL SAVINGS BANKS

CHAPTER OUTLINE

CHAPTER OVERVIEW

This chapter:

- Outlines the nature of the crisis in the U.S. thrift industry
- Traces the origins of savings and loan associations and mutual savings banks
- Identifies the regulatory restrictions under which thrifts operated originally
- Lists the recent expansion of thrift powers
- Discusses the causes of the thrift industry crisis
- Highlights changes in asset and liability mix over time

The thrift industry in the United States is composed of savings and loan associations and mutual savings banks. These institutions were originally intended to provide residential mortgage financing and consumer loans. They also provided a safe investment for small savers. What started as an industry to serve the American family has turned into one of the worst financial scandals in U.S. history. Thrifts have failed at record rates. Federal deposit insurance guarantees have exposed the U.S. government and, ultimately, U.S. taxpayers to bailout costs that have been estimated in the range of $500 billion. This is roughly $2000 for every man, woman, and child in the United States. In addition, the enormous inventory of foreclosed real estate that once belonged to the failed thrifts has seriously weakened the real estate market. Thus, the crisis in the thrift industry has already negatively affected individual families and financial institutions (such as banks and insurance companies) that have substantial investments in real estate or real estate–based loans.

The causes of the crisis are varied. One of the primary causes is the historical mismatch of asset and liability maturities. The consequence of this mismatch became painfully obvious during the 1970s and early 1980s when long-term, low-yielding mortgage loans failed to produce sufficient income to offset the rising cost of deposits and short-term borrowings. Deregulation gave thrifts the power to invest in higher-yielding assets. But regulatory oversight of these expanded powers was grossly inadequate. This situation was further complicated by a lack of commitment on the part of the U.S. Congress to maintain safety and soundness within the industry. The net effect has been virtually a death blow to the thrift industry in the United States.

THE SAVINGS AND LOAN CRISIS IN THE UNITED STATES

Early Regulatory Structure

Created in 1932, the Federal Home Loan Bank Board regulated the savings and loan industry. Its stated purpose was to promote home ownership, and its structure was similar to the Federal Reserve System. Twelve regional Federal Home Loan Banks provided quasi-central bank services to member savings and loan associations (S&Ls). In 1934, the Federal Savings and Loan Insurance Corporation (FSLIC) was created to insure S&L deposits, as the FDIC insured commercial bank deposits. In 1978, the Federal Home Loan Bank Board received the power to grant federal charters to mutual savings banks. Before 1978, all mutual savings banks had been chartered by state banking authorities.

Over time, the same competitive forces that challenged commercial banks generated an even greater "profit squeeze" for savings and loan associations. Deposit rate deregulation and expanded asset powers followed but did not save the industry from further devastation.

Massive Losses and Thrift Failures

As shown in Exhibit 19-1, assets of federally insured thrift institutions rose from $170.6 billion in 1970 to $1.35 trillion by 1988, or at an average annual rate of 12.2 percent [($1350.5 billion/$170.6 billion)$^{1/18}$ − 1]. Over the same period, operating income grew at 14.7 percent annually. However, expenses grew even faster.

	1970*	1988*
Operating income	$10.7	$126.2
Operating expense	1.9	26.3
Interest on savings deposits	6.9	75.2
Interest on borrowed money	.8	27.8

*$ Billions.

Operating expenses increased an average of 15.7 percent per year. Interest on savings deposits and borrowed money grew at annual rates of 14.2 and 21.8 percent, respectively.

These disproportionate changes in income and expense caused net income to shift

EXHIBIT 19-1 STRUCTURE AND PROFITABILITY OF FSLIC/SAIF-INSURED THRIFTS FOR SELECTED YEARS, 1970–1989

	Number of institutions			Total assets ($ billions)			
	S&Ls	Mutual savings banks*	Total	S&Ls	Mutual savings banks*	Total	Net income ($ billions)
1970	4365	—	4365	170.6	—	170.6	.9
1975	4078	—	4078	330.3	—	330.3	1.4
1980	4002	3	4005	618.5	2.2	620.7	.8
1981	3779	6	3785	651.0	7.5	658.5	(4.6)
1982	3343	6	3349	692.7	6.9	699.6	(4.1)
1983	3040	143	3183	754.2	65.0	819.2	1.9
1984	2938	198	3136	879.1	98.4	977.5	1.0
1985	2907	339	3246	938.4	131.6	1070.0	3.7
1986	2817	403	3220	953.6	210.3	1163.9	.1
1987	2648	499	3147	966.6	284.3	1250.9	(7.8)
1988	2328	621	2949	924.5	426.0	1350.5	(13.4)
1989	2099	770	2869	753.2	498.5	1251.7	(17.4)

*Federally chartered mutual savings banks were not permitted until 1978.
Source: U.S. League of Savings Institutions, *Savings Institutions Sourcebook,* 1990, p. 28.

from the roughly $1 billion per year level in 1970 to a more erratic pattern. In 1981 and 1982, federally insured thrifts lost over $4 billion. Profits rebounded in 1983 only to decline again in 1984. The $3.7 billion net income of 1985 was followed by only $100 million the following year. Conditions continued to deteriorate, and the industry lost almost $8 billion in 1987. In 1988 and 1989, the losses were $13 billion and $17 billion, respectively.

The number of institutions declined from 4365 in 1970 to 2869 in 1989, a 34 percent decline. Many of the institutions that ceased operations required FSLIC assistance to pay off depositors and/or to be assumed by another, healthier institution. The FSLIC fund had held $6.5 billion in reserves in 1980, or 1.04 percent of assets of insured institutions. Even with the failures of the early 1980s, FSLIC reserves remained relatively stable. However, in 1984, reserves dropped to $5.6 billion, or .6 percent of insured institutions' assets. In a 1987 opinion rendered by the U.S. General Accounting Office, FSLIC was declared insolvent as of year-end 1986.

To increase the resources of FSLIC, in 1987, Congress authorized the agency to issue up to $10.8 billion in bonds through a funding corporation.[1] However, the legislation limited bond issuance to $3.75 billion per year. Even at this relatively modest level, the financial community did not receive the bonds enthusiastically. The first issue of $500 million in September 1987 was sold at a yield that exceeded the comparable Treasury bond rate by 90 basis points.

Regulatory Reorganization

The resources that were available to close insolvent thrifts (bond proceeds and FSLIC insurance premiums) were not sufficient. Estimates of the actual cost of "cleaning up the industry" grew from $10 billion to over $100 billion and are currently $500 billion or more. In August 1989, the Financial Institutions Reform, Recovery, and Enforcement Act (FIRREA) was passed, abolishing the Federal Home Loan Bank Board and the Federal Savings and Loan Deposit Insurance Corporation.

[1]The Financial Institutions Competitive Equality Act of 1987 also provided a 3-year "grace" period for well-managed insolvent thrifts (little or no capital base) in economically depressed areas and authorized acquisition of large thrifts (those with assets greater than $500 million) by nondepository institutions.

The Office of Thrift Supervision (OTS) assumed examination and supervisory functions. The OTS itself was placed under the supervision of the Treasury Department. The Federal Finance Housing Board was assigned to oversee credit functions of the twelve Federal Home Loan district banks. A new insurance fund, the Savings Association Insurance Fund (SAIF), was placed under the direction of FDIC. Responsibility for closing and managing failed institutions fell to a newly created Resolution Trust Corporation (RTC). The Secretary of the Treasury, the Chairman of the Federal Reserve Board, the Secretary of Housing and Urban Development, and two presidential appointees formed the RTC Oversight Board.

The intent of these regulatory changes was to discipline a federally insured industry that was clearly out of control. Stricter capital requirements were also imposed, and certain risky activities were restricted, especially for undercapitalized thrifts. To raise the money needed to close failed institutions, FIRREA authorized RTC to issue $30 billion in bonds through the Resolution Fund Corporation (REFCORP).

The Financial Drain of Insolvent Thrifts

Neither the provisions of FIRREA nor the $30 billion authorized for bond issuance have corrected the problems of the thrift industry. The assets of the closed thrifts have not been efficiently liquidated. Many of the thrifts that should be closed have not been because the RTC has insufficient funds to pay off depositors or to arrange a satisfactory transfer of assets to another healthier institution. As long as such institutions are permitted to continue to operate, the entire industry is threatened.

According to generally accepted accounting principles (GAAP), an institution is *solvent* as long as capital (the difference between assets and liabilities) exceeds zero. The GAAP capital does not include subordinated debentures and other liabilities that are classified as capital according to regulatory accounting principles (RAP).

Exhibit 19-2 illustrates the financial drain created by insolvent thrifts in 1988 and 1989. During these 2 years the total number of insured institutions continued to decline as it had in earlier years (see Exhibit 19-1). By the end of 1989 only 2869 remained. Of these, 1789 were GAAP solvent and profitable, down from 1971 the prior year-end. These thrifts generated approximately $5 billion in net income during each of the 2 years shown. The number of unprofitable, but solvent, institutions grew by 7.7 percent to 653 at the end of 1989. Their losses almost exactly offset the net income of the solvent, profitable counterparts during 1989.

Though smaller in number, insolvent thrifts are primarily responsible for industry losses. For example, in 1988, those that were insolvent and unprofitable (11 percent of the total number) lost $16.1 billion, an amount that more than offset the net profits earned by other institutions, bringing the industry to a $13.4 billion loss for the year. In 1989, these same insolvent thrifts represented 14 percent of the total number of institutions and almost 100 percent of the industry's $17.4 billion net loss, as the other institutions, as a group, only broke even.

To the extent that closings of insolvent thrifts are delayed, the ultimate cost of resolving the crisis escalates. As losses continue to mount, capital is further depleted, federally insured deposits (liabilities) increasingly exceed the value of underlying assets, and the cost of the thrift bailout continues to grow. Obviously, serious errors in management and regulation have occurred. In order to understand why these errors have occurred, it is necessary to examine:

- The origins and growth of the industry
- Changes in the economic environment
- Responses by regulators
- Influence of the U.S. Congress

EXHIBIT 19-2 SOLVENT VS. INSOLVENT FSLIC/SAIF-INSURED THRIFT INSTITUTIONS, 1988 AND 1989

Date/ quarter*	GAAP solvent		GAAP insolvent		
	Profitable	Unprofitable	Profitable	Unprofitable	Total
Number of Institutions					
Dec. 31, 1988	1,971	606	42	330	2,949
Dec. 31, 1989	1,789	653	19	408	2,869
Total Assets ($ billions)					
Dec. 31, 1988	893.4	336.9	11.2	109.0	1,350.5
Dec. 31, 1989	737.9	327.0	6.1	171.0	1,242.0
Net income ($ millions)					
1988: 1Q	1,267	(517)	56	(4,746)	(3,940)
2Q	1,422	(663)	44	(4,878)	(3,940)
3Q	1,402	(685)	18	(2,579)	(1,844)
4Q	1,353	(1,043)	22	(3,914)	(3,582)
Total 1988	5,444	(2,908)	140	(16,117)	(13,441)
1989: 1Q	1,276	(984)	21	(3,691)	(3,378)
2Q	1,221	(888)	13	(4,036)	(3,690)
3Q	1,228	(1,979)	10	(3,082)	(3,823)
4Q	1,247	(1,299)	11	(6,454)	(6,495)
Total 1989	4,972	(5,150)	55	(17,263)	(17,386)

*Breakdown of net income for first quarter 1989 has been approximated.
Source: Office of Thrift Supervision, Washington, D.C., unpublished data.

ORIGINS OF THE THRIFT INDUSTRY

Savings and Loan Associations

United States The first thrift in the United States was formed in 1831 in Frankfort, Pennsylvania. The objective of the Oxford Provident Building Association was to enable its shareholders to secure housing finance. Most shareholders worked in the textile industry as wage earners. The amounts that wage earners contributed were not deposits but, instead, equity investments. Thus, the first thrift was a *mutual organization* and the precursor of modern savings and loan associations.

Mutual depository organization:
Noncorporate financial institution in which individual contributions are considered equity investments even though they closely resemble deposits in most other aspects (stated interest rate, variability of amount invested, and ease of withdrawal, relative to other equity investments).

Each shareholder was entitled to a loan. However, no loan could be used to build a home more than 5 miles away from Frankfort. Oxford Provident, and other associations similar to Oxford, provided loans to buy land and to build homes and were called *building societies.*

Building society:
A mutual organization that uses its financial resources to make loans for the purpose of buying land and constructing homes.

Later, shareholders borrowed money to build on land that they already owned and to purchase existing homes. At this point, the organizations became *building and loan societies.* Originally, the societies *terminated* when each shareholder had obtained a loan and all loans had been repaid.

Terminating building society:
A mutual organization with the purpose of providing each member with a loan to construct a home. When each member has received and repaid the loan, the society ceases operations.

These early organizations served two purposes:

- Providing mortgage loans
- Providing investment vehicles for small-balance powers

If shareholders wished to withdraw their savings, they were required to give a month's notice. Early withdrawal resulted in a penalty. With this structure, the societies promoted thrift, savings, and mortgage financing for residential property. The thrifts' balance sheets reflected large amounts of mortgage loan investments that were funded by savings shares.

Thrift institution:
A financial institution that encourages moderate-income workers to save money on a regular basis. Likewise, the institution invests in loans to these savers, especially mortgage loans. In the United States, savings and loan associations and mutual savings banks are classified as thrift institutions.

At the time, building societies were necessary because commercial banks did not actively seek small savings deposits or solicit mortgage loan business. Essentially, commercial banks made commercial loans and accepted demand deposits. In fact, before 1816, there was little need for building societies in the United States. Most individuals were farmers, fishermen, traders, and merchants who routinely reinvested any operational surpluses in new equipment, increased merchandise inventories, or additional land.

It was not until the Napoleonic wars, during which trade between the United States and Europe was interrupted, that domestic manufacturing became a significant factor in the U.S. economy. Protective tariffs of the early 1800s also gave U.S. firms a competitive advantage. As the manufacturing sector grew, the population of cities in which these enterprises were located also grew. However, since the new wage earners spent most of their time working, little time remained to build their own homes. Building societies helped wage earners have their homes constructed by others.

United Kingdom Building societies were patterned after the same institution in Britain. The industrial revolution in England led to an unsatisfied demand for housing comparable to that which later developed in the United States. The first documented building society originated in 1781 in Birmingham, England.

The Birmingham Building Society was a mutual organization with overseers who were elected from within the ranks of the society and served without compensation. Each member was required to make a monthly contribution until all members had received a loan. The society terminated when all outstanding loans had been repaid.

Building societies spread throughout continental Europe and, later, to the United States, Canada, Australia, New Zealand, and other countries. The form of the building society evolved from a terminating plan to a permanent plan, that is, one that was not self-liquidating. Under a permanent plan, it was not necessary for all members to obtain a mortgage loan. Instead, the savings by those who did not wish to purchase homes were pooled to provide loans for members who *did* desire mortgage financing. An added advantage was that shares could be purchased in any amount at any time with no withdrawal penalties. Building societies and their successors have provided an important service in many countries.

Mutual Savings Banks

While the precursors of savings and loan associations were cooperative organizations of middle-class wage earners, mutual savings banks were motivated by philanthropic concerns. Eighteenth-century commercial banks neither satisfied the needs for residential mortgage finance nor provided depository services for wage earners. Mutual savings banks filled this gap.

The first prototype of a mutual savings bank was formed in Hamburg, Germany, in 1765. However, the first institution that was structurally similar to the modern savings bank began operations in Ruthwell, Scotland, in 1810. Unlike building societies, early mutual savings banks were not financed entirely by wage-earner contributions. The early institutions were benevolent organizations in the sense that wealthy individuals contributed necessary capital to establish them. The mutual banks then accepted small deposits from laborers. The founders' objective was to encourage thrift, virtue, industriousness, and prosperity.

The first U.S. savings bank, the Philadelphia Savings Fund Society, started in 1816 as a voluntary association and was not chartered until 1819. The Provident Institution for Savings in Boston was the first to be incorporated, receiving its charter in 1816. These early institutions frequently used the term "society" or "institution" in their titles because of the early distrust of banks in the United States.[2]

Mutual savings banks had no stockholders. In this sense, they were similar to early savings and loan associations. Depositors owned the assets, and any profits from operation were credited to their accounts. Bank trustees were not allowed to profit from the banks or to accept any form of compensation. However, as the banks successfully expanded, it became necessary for trustees to appoint salaried management personnel.

Also, like early savings and loan associations, mutual savings banks were largely funded by savings deposits. However, unlike S&Ls, savings banks invested in consumer loans as well as mortgage loans. In addition, savings banks gave depositors more flexibility in terms of denomination, maturity, and withdrawal.

It is clear that thrifts evolved because of unmet financial needs. Wage earners required an outlet for small savings and a source of mortgage and consumer finance. At the time, commercial banks did not satisfy these needs.

EVOLUTION OF THE THRIFT INDUSTRY

The Early Years

After the first thrift was established in the United States, the movement enjoyed considerable growth. Savings and loan associations appeared next in New York in 1836 and in South Carolina in 1843. By 1890, S&Ls could be found in every state. Until the late 1880s, all S&Ls had purely local operations. A brief experiment with nationwide fundraising and lending ended in failure for most of the associations that were involved. (See Exhibit 19-3.)

Initially, government oversight of the thrift industry was limited to the periodic reports of thrifts to state authorities in the late 1800s. Later, associations were subject first to voluntary, then to mandatory, regulatory examinations. By the early 1900s, state supervisors exercised significant power over thrifts' balance sheets and expansion. Authorities generally expressed disfavor for loans that were not intended to finance single-family residences. In addition, new charters were denied if the need for an additional savings and loan association could not be demonstrated. Thus, early government intervention placed some constraints on industry growth.

Nevertheless, the savings and loan industry continued to grow. As shown in Exhibit

[2]See Chapter 10 for a description of banking in the early years of the United States.

EXHIBIT 19-3 THE NATIONAL BUILDING AND LOAN ASSOCIATIONS

In the late 1880s, "nationals," or national building and loan associations appeared. These organizations solicited contributions nationwide and made loans through the mail. In an environment of widespread speculative investments, some nationals became "get-rich-quick" schemes for their organizers. Others made questionable loans over widely dispersed geographic areas. A sharply depressed real estate market during the 1890s, together with poor business practices and more restrictive legislation that followed later, caused most nationals to fail.

As early as the turn of the century, the savings and loan industry experienced the consequences of investment. As is true today, the well-publicized experiences of these "high-flying" associations hurt the public acceptance of safer, more conservatively run local associations.

Reference: Ornstein, Franklin H., *Savings Banking; An Industry in Change,* 1985, p. 10.

19-4, by 1900 savings and loan associations and mutual savings banks numbered 5356 and 626, respectively. During the next 25 years, the number of S&Ls more than doubled, and total assets increased by a factor of almost ten to $5.5 billion. This growth pattern compares favorably with that of commercial banks. In 1900, over 12,000 banks held $9 billion in assets. By 1925, the numbers had grown to 28,000 banks with $54 billion in assets. Although the number of commercial banks also more than doubled, bank asset growth was more modest than S&Ls asset growth.

EXHIBIT 19-4 NUMBER OF INSTITUTIONS AND ASSETS OF THE THRIFT INDUSTRY IN THE UNITED STATES, 1900–1989

	S&Ls		Mutual savings banks	
Year	Institutions*	Assets†	Institutions*	Assets†
1900	5,356	571	626	2,328
1905	5,264	629	615	2,969
1910	5,869	932	637	3,598
1915	6,806	1,484	627	4,257
1920	8,633	2,520	618	5,586
1925	12,403	5,509	610	7,831
1930	11,777	8,829	594	10,164
1935	10,266	5,875	559	11,046
1940	7,521	5,733	542	11,925
1945	6,149	8,747	534	15,924
1950	5,992	16,893	530	22,252
1955	6,071	37,656	528	30,383
1960	5,320	71,476	516	39,598
1965	6,185	129,580	505	56,383
1970	5,669	176,183	497	76,373
1975	4,931	338,200	476	121,100
1980	4,613	629,800	460	166,600
1985	3,246	1,069,547	403	157,400
1986	2,817	953,570	403	210,281
1987	2,648	966,585	499	284,270
1988	2,328	924,534	621	425,966
1989	2,099	753,175	770	498,522

*Includes insured and uninsured institutions from 1900 through 1985 and federally insured institutions only from 1986 through 1989.

†Millions of dollars.

Sources: Brumbaugh, R. Dan, Jr., *Thrifts under Seige; Restoring Order to American Banking,* 1988, p. 7 [1900–1985], and U.S. League of Savings Institutions, *Savings Institutions Sourcebook,* 1990 [1986–1989].

At the same time, the growth of mutual savings banks was not as strong. By the 1860s, these institutions had a significant presence in the northeast. Unlike S&Ls, however, mutual savings banks did not spread to other parts of the country in any meaningful way. This is partially due to the establishment of incorporated, or stock, savings banks in the west and partially to differing regional economic conditions. As the west was settled, industry and wage earners did not move into these regions as rapidly as the settlers themselves. The philanthropists that financed mutual savings banks were not a major segment of the frontier pioneers.

The Great Depression of the 1930s led to a number of failures in the thrift industry, primarily savings and loan associations. From 1930 through 1939, 1700 savings and loan associations, or 14 percent of all S&Ls in existence in 1925, failed. Consolidations within the industry explain the remaining reduction in numbers. By 1940, S&Ls and mutual savings banks numbered 7521 and 542 respectively.

After the Great Depression

In the post-Depression era, the number of thrift institutions continued to decline primarily through industry consolidation. At the same time, total assets grew substantially, and S&Ls, in particular, began to control a greater percentage of total financial assets. For example, in 1945, savings and loan associations held 3 percent of all financial assets of intermediaries. By 1975, this number had grown to 16 percent.[3]

However, high and volatile interest rates of the late 1970s placed considerable pressure on the thrift industry because of its substantial investment in residential mortgages. While the relatively short term cost of funds climbed, the yield on much longer term assets lagged behind.

Referring to Exhibit 19-5, notice that in 1976 the Treasury bill rate averaged approximately 5 percent and that new mortgages yielded just over 9 percent. Both savings and loan associations and mutual savings banks enjoyed a relatively comfortable spread between asset yield and cost of funds.

In the 6 years that followed, Treasury and new mortgage yields both increased by approximately 6 percentage points. As a result, the costs of funds for savings and loan associations and mutual savings banks grew by 5 and 3.7 percentage points, respectively. At the same time, the asset yields of the thrifts only increased by 2.6 and 2.5 percentage points, respectively.

In 1981, the cost of funds for S&Ls exceeded asset yields by 81 basis points. The following year, the difference was 56 basis points. It is, therefore, not surprising that the industry sustained substantial losses during this period.[4] Nor should it be surprising that 252 S&Ls failed during 1982. In fact, from 1980 through 1984 a total of 511 S&Ls failed.

These early 1980s failures were due to a severely mismatched balance sheet for the industry as a whole. A heavy concentration of fixed-rate mortgage loans left little opportunity to adjust asset portfolios in response to the rising cost of funds. To further complicate the situation, traditional savings deposits were being withdrawn in massive waves of disintermediation to be reinvested in more attractively priced money market mutual funds.

To remedy these structural problems in the industry, laws were enacted both to give thrifts greater investment flexibility and to make it easier for other healthy firms to acquire ailing institutions. Some of this legislative relief was misused, bringing the industry even more financial difficulty than it experienced in the early 1980s.

[3]Over the same period, holdings of financial assets by mutual savings banks were relatively stable at 7 percent in 1945 and 6 percent in 1975.

[4]The FSLIC-insured thrifts lost over $4 billion per year in 1981 and 1982.

EXHIBIT 19-5 SELECTED YIELDS, 1976–1989 (PERCENTAGES)

			Yields			
			S&Ls		Mutual savings banks	
Year	Rate on new mortgages	3-month T-bills	Assets	Funds	Assets	Funds
1976	9.10	4.99	8.18	6.38	7.23	5.98
1977	9.02	5.27	8.44	6.44	7.43	6.03
1978	9.61	7.22	8.73	6.67	7.73	6.14
1979	10.89	10.04	9.29	7.47	8.26	6.80
1980	12.90	11.51	9.72	8.94	8.79	7.96
1981	15.00	14.08	10.11	10.92	9.42	9.48
1982	15.38	10.69	10.82	11.38	9.71	9.64
1983	12.57	8.62	10.99	8.82	10.04	7.31
1984	12.38	9.57	11.34	9.08	10.62	7.57
1985	11.55	7.49	11.46	8.60	11.17	6.83
1986	10.17	5.97	10.54	7.51	11.08	6.77
1987	9.31	5.83	9.53	6.69	10.57	6.38
1988	9.19	6.67	9.31	6.90	10.44	6.60
1989	10.13	8.11	11.14	8.40	11.39	7.60

Source: Carron, Andrew S., *The Rescue of the Thrift Industry,* 1983, p. 5 [1976–1982]; calculations based on data from U.S. League of Savings Institutions, *Savings Institutions Sourcebook,* 1990 [1983–1989 yields]. U.S. League of Savings Institutions, *Savings Institutions Sourcebook,* 1990, p. 11 [1983–1989 rate on new mortgages]; and International Monetary Fund, *International Financial Statistics,* Yearbook 1990, p. 731 [1983–1989 3-month T-bills].

REGULATION AND DEREGULATION

Before the Great Depression

Before the late 1800s, the federal government had virtually no interest in the operation of thrifts. Even though these institutions accepted savings deposits, they were not involved in issuing currency or demand deposits. That is, thrifts did not affect the money supply. Further, virtually no thrifts had failed.

With the creation and failure of a number of national thrifts, local thrifts in 1892 formed the U.S. League of Local Building and Loan Associations (now the U.S. League of Savings Institutions). The league lobbied state legislatures for laws restricting nationals (see Exhibit 19-3). The measures that resulted helped protect the locals from territorial infringement by their peers (other local associations) and their competitors.

However, rising income levels brought the thrift and banking industries into direct competition. In the early 1900s, national banks were permitted to offer savings deposits, and the Federal Reserve placed lower reserve requirements on these deposits than on demand deposits. Thrifts did retain a competitive advantage, however, in that they were exempt from federal income taxation.

Federal Regulation since the 1930s

Federal Charters The widespread failures of the Great Depression attracted the attention of the federal government. After the Great Depression, the federal government began to also regulate the savings and loan industry. The Federal Home Loan Bank Board was established in 1932 to charter federal S&Ls and to provide advances to members. State S&Ls were entitled to join; federal S&Ls were obligated to do so. So as not to compete unfairly with their state-chartered counterparts, federal S&Ls were to be chartered only when the number of existing state institutions was insufficient to service the community adequately. Further, federal S&Ls were to be mutual organizations with a local focus.

Deposit Insurance The FSLIC was established in 1934 to provide deposit insurance to Federal Home Loan Bank members. For many years, insurance premiums were the same as for FDIC-insured institutions, 1⁄12 percent. Beginning in 1985, a special assessment of 1⁄8 percent was levied to help cover the large and mounting costs of the thrift industry bailout. This brought the total assessment to .2083 percent, or $0.2083 per $100 deposit. At the same time, the assessment for banks was only 1⁄12 percent, or $0.083 per $100 deposit. The higher cost of doing business has motivated some S&Ls to convert to bank charters in order to avoid the special assessment. Exhibit 19-4 reflects the impact of these conversions. The number of mutual savings banks stopped its previous decline in 1986 and began to grow. The number of savings and loan associations continued to decline.

In 1989, FIRREA increased the premiums even more. The law specified that insurance premiums would increase to $0.23 per $100 deposit but then be reduced to the same level as bank insurance premiums by 1998. But the FDIC was also given the power to increase the premiums for either fund (Savings Institution Insurance Fund or Bank Insurance Fund). The maximum was set at $0.325 per $100 deposit with a maximum increase in 1 year of no more than $0.075.

Deposit Interest Rates The Federal Home Loan Bank Board received the power to establish savings deposit interest rate ceilings in 1966. To encourage the accumulation of funds for residential housing finance, the savings deposit ceiling for thrifts was set at ½ percent above that for commercial banks. This differential was subsequently lowered to 25 basis points. Of course, all such ceilings were eliminated under provisions of the federal legislation of 1980.

Investment Powers In 1964, federal thrifts were allowed to diversify their asset portfolios.

1 The geographic limit for mortgage loans was expanded from 50 to 100 miles.
2 Personal loans were permitted for covering the cost of college and educational expenses.
3 Federal thrifts were given the power to:
   a Issue mortgages and buy real estate in urban renewal areas.
   b Purchase federal, state, and municipal securities.
   c Acquire and operate service corporations in nontraditional areas of business, such as stock brokerage and insurance brokerage activities, up to 1 percent of assets.

In 1968, powers were extended to loans for mobile homes, second homes, and housing fixtures, services which, up to that point, had been offered exclusively by commercial banks.

The measures empowered thrifts to protect their asset portfolios more effectively from the effects of holding large amounts of low-interest, fixed-rate, long-term mortgages. However, these new investment powers were followed by even greater changes in the industry, as new asset and liability combinations dramatically altered the nature of thrift business in the United States.

Deregulation of the 1970s and 1980s

Deposits The high interest rates of the 1970s, noted in Exhibit 19-5, led to substantial growth in money market mutual funds. Even with the savings deposit interest rate differential over commercial banks, thrift accounts became unattractive alternatives for small investors. Federal regulators responded in 1978 by authorizing money market certificate accounts with minimum denominations of $10,000. These instruments offered competitive, market rates of interest. Only 1 year later, the highly rate-competitive certificates constituted 20 percent of thrift deposits. While the new deposits halted the threat of massive disintermediation, money market certificates also placed significant pressure on thrift profitability.

The N.O.W. account, first introduced in Massachusetts in 1972, became another interest-bearing deposit, in large measure replacing the interest-free demand deposit account after its nationwide legalization in 1980. However, these and other liability innovations were not sufficient to stem the flow of funds out of savings and loan associations and mutual savings banks. Specifically, in 1981 and 1982, deposit withdrawals exceeded new deposits by $32 billion. Nevertheless, because of interest credited to those accounts that *did* remain, deposit balances actually increased by $52 billion.

Assets It was apparent that the historical purpose of thrift institutions had been, at least partially, compromised by competition for savings deposits from banks and nonbanks. The regulatory reaction to this phenomenon was to relieve thrifts of many of their historical *investment* restrictions. The logic was that greater asset powers should augment earnings and help offset the higher cost of funds. New powers were conferred by both regulators and legislators.

Exhibit 19-6 highlights the most significant regulatory changes in the thrift industry since 1980. Thrift regulators and federal law gave these institutions the power to invest in a wide variety of enterprises in which they had never engaged: commercial real estate, business loans, and corporate bonds. They were even allowed to engage in financial options trading. The intention was that thrifts would be able to "grow" their way out of industry collapse. The new activities would generate income at higher rates of return to help offset the high and increasing cost of funds. To take full advantage of these new powers, thrifts were permitted to make loans nationwide.

Regulatory Excesses The move toward deregulation went too far. At the same time that federal deposit insurance increased from $40,000 to $100,000 (1980), the safeguards that limited exposure to excessive risks were being dismantled.

Savings and loan associations that in 1979 had 68 percent of financial assets invested in home mortgages and derived 82 percent of financial liabilities from small time and savings deposits were permitted to engage in much riskier activities during the 1980s:

- Mutual fund investments
- Futures and options trading
- Retail securities repurchase agreements without limit
- Mortgage loans without restrictions as to the value of underlying collateral
- Security issuance for parent company through a finance subsidiary
- Commercial loans up to 55 percent of assets
- Corporate bonds up to 20 percent of assets

At the same time, deposit interest rates were deregulated, and the deposit insurance limit was raised to $100,000 per account. In essence, funds could easily be attracted by raising the rate on certificates of deposit (CDs) of $100,000 or more. These deposits could then be marketed through securities brokers to become *brokered deposits.*

Brokered deposits:
Deposits placed with an institution through a securities broker, who, in turn, earns a commission on the sale. Such deposits were most often sold in $100,000 increments to retain full federal deposit insurance.

EXHIBIT 19-6 DEREGULATION OF THE THRIFT INDUSTRY

Year	Regulatory changes
1980	Federal associations may open branch offices and operate mobile facilities statewide (100-mile restriction dropped). FSLIC members may borrow up to 50% of *assets* (was 50% of *savings)* and increase liabilities maturing in 90 days or less. FSLIC members may offer real estate loans for property in any geographic location, and a loan for one- to four-family residential property may exceed 90% of property value. Reserve requirement is reduced from 5 to 4%.
1981	Federal Home Loan Bank Board liberalizes the regulations with respect to conversion from a mutual form of business organization to a stock form. Adjustable-rate mortgages are authorized. Federal association service corporations receive permission to conduct a broader range of activities without prior approval, to serve a broader range of customers, and borrow (nondeposit funds) with even fewer restrictions.
1982	FSLIC members permitted to buy financial options and write call options without limitation, to write put options up to specified limit.
1983	California legislature passes a law permitting state-chartered thrifts to broaden their investment activities. State savings banks that convert to federal savings institution charters may retain the powers they had under state law. Thrifts permitted to make loans nationwide.
1984	Federal associations may operate finance subsidiaries to issue securities for the parent.

Year	Federal legislative changes
1980	Depository Institutions Deregulation and Monetary Control Act: 1. Federal savings and loan associations given expanded asset powers. a. Credit card issuance. b. Trustee service and trust departments. c. Up to 20% of assets in consumer loans, commercial paper, and corporate debt. d. Up to 3% of assets in service corporations. e. Up to 20% of assets in commercial real estate loans. 2. Federal mutual savings banks permitted to: a. Make business loans. b. Accept demand deposits from business clients. 3. Authorized all depository institutions to offer checking account services and to pay interest on individual transactions accounts. 4. Deposit insurance limit raised from $40,000 to $100,000.
1982	Garn–St Germain Depository Institutions Act: 1. Federal savings and loan associations given expanded asset and liability powers: a. Up to 55% of assets in commercial loans (up to 5% secured or unsecured, up to 10% of lease financing, and up to 40% secured by commercial real estate). b. Up to 30% of assets in consumer loans (up from 20%), including inventory and floor-planning loans. c. Investment in state and local revenue bonds (had been only general obligation bonds). d. Demand deposits permitted from persons or organizations that have a business loan relationship with the association or that wish to receive payments from non business clients. 2. All depository institutions allowed to offer money market deposit accounts with no interest rate ceiling and to offer interest-bearing transaction accounts to federal, state, and local governments.

Source: Brumbaugh, R. Dan, Jr., *Thrifts under Seige; Restoring Order to American Banking,* 1988, pp. 152–153, 196; Cooper, S. Kerry, and Donald R. Fraser, *Banking Deregulation and the New Competition in Financial Services,* 1984, pp. 134–136, 116–119, and Kane, Edward J., *The S&L Insurance Mess; How Did It Happen?* 1989, pp. 34–47.

Before FIRREA (1989) restricted their issuance, brokered deposits enabled an S&L to raise funds easily. In some cases, these deposits were invested in high-yielding corporate bonds of less than investment grade, that is, junk bonds. These bonds provided a positive spread over the high cost of brokered funds. Brokered deposits ensured a steady inflow of funds even if the institution was financially unsound.

Regulatory excesses went further. To encourage the purchase of dying thrifts, the ownership criteria were relaxed.

- Instead of 400 owners with no individual owner holding more than 25 percent of ownership interest, a single owner could purchase a thrift.
- Instead of investing cash to obtain ownership interest, land and other noncash assets were accepted.

Thus, a land developer with idle land could invest the land in exchange for control of a savings and loan association. Using brokered deposits, funds could then be attracted to invest in almost anything. This was particularly true for state-chartered S&Ls. In California, for example, a law enacted in 1983 allowed almost anyone to own a thrift, attract as much in brokered deposits as desired, and invest the proceeds in almost anything. Of course, the operation was fully backed by the federal government.

U.S. Congressional Action Savings and loan association fraud occurred frequently, especially in those states with liberalized thrift laws. The industry became even more unstable. Capital adequacy became a real concern. But because of the enormity of the problem and the lack of resources in the federal insurance fund, the 1982 Garn–St Germain Act also included a measure to conceal the degree of capital inadequacy. Those institutions with insufficient capital were permitted to issue *net worth certificates.*

Net worth certificate:
A claim issued by a capital-deficit S&L for the purpose of increasing regulatory capital. Its issuance is *not* accompanied by the infusion of real capital.

The net worth certificates were then exchanged for promissory notes issued by FSLIC. The FSLIC promissory notes were included in the computation of regulatory capital. Of course, the true capital of the institution was not enhanced by these exchanges because the FSLIC itself would soon be declared insolvent.

It was not until 1989 when FIRREA was enacted that many of these excesses were corrected. Specifically, FIRREA:

- Prohibited state-chartered, federally insured savings institutions from engaging in any activity not permitted federally chartered institutions
- Prohibited all savings associations from investing in junk bonds and required divestment of existing junk bond portfolios no later than 1994
- Required thrifts to invest 70 percent (up from 60 percent) of assets in residential mortgage assets
- Prohibited any depository institution with insufficient capital from accepting brokered deposits
- Established a federal subcommittee to monitor and oversee real estate appraisal practices
- Increased criminal and civil penalties for fraudulent practices
- Required that savings associations meet the same risk-based capital requirement as national commercial banks by 1992

The turmoil of the 1970s and 1980s has left the thrift industry very much transformed and weakened. Whether the industry will survive as originally structured is debatable.

THRIFT ASSETS AND LIABILITIES

Savings and Loan Associations

Financial assets of savings and loan associations (Exhibit 19-7) grew at an average annual rate of 10.3 percent to $1.4 trillion during the 25 years ended 1989. By 1991, this total was down to $1.1 trillion. Home mortgages represented 72.4 percent of S&L assets in 1964. By 1989, their share had dropped to 42.6 percent, with the greatest decline noted after 1979, that is, after the major deregulatory movement of the early 1980s. Two years after FIRREA this percentage had increased somewhat to 45.5 percent.

Government agency securities and corporate and foreign bonds constituted .5 percent of financial assets in 1964 and 19.7 percent in 1989. This percentage declined to 18.8 percent by 1991, with all the reduction in corporate bonds. At the same time, government agency bonds became even more important. The greater emphasis on government agency securities is due primarily to their relatively higher yields vis-à-vis Treasury securities. Indeed, Treasury security investment declined substantially over the period. Corporate and foreign bonds have been permissible investments for federal S&Ls only since the

EXHIBIT 19-7 FINANCIAL ASSETS OF U.S. SAVINGS AND LOAN ASSOCIATIONS, 1964–1991 (PERCENTAGES)

	1964	1969	1974	1979	1984	1989	1991
Financial assets (billions)	$117.1	$159.7	$292.3	$569.4	$989.6	$1,351.2	$1,056.2
Checkable deposits and currency	2.4%	.9%	.3%	.4%	1.1%	.9%	.7%
Time deposits	—	.1	1.2	.9	1.0	.5	.5
Federal funds and security repos	—	—	1.6	2.0	2.8	2.0	.1
Investment securities:							
Treasury	6.0	5.1	.6	.6	2.5	.9	1.7
Government agency	.5	1.4	4.5	5.4	12.2	15.7	16.2
Tax-exempt	—	.1	.2	.2	—*	.1	.1
Corporate & foreign bonds	—	—	—	—	1.6	4.0	2.6
Total securities	6.5	6.6	5.3	6.2	16.3	20.7	20.6
Loans:							
Mortgages:							
Home	72.4	72.4	67.6	67.6	46.5	42.6	45.5
Multifamily	6.1	7.3	8.2	6.6	6.2	6.6	6.4
Commercial	6.1	6.6	8.4	7.7	8.7	8.0	6.8
Total mortgages	84.6	86.3	84.2	81.9	61.4	57.2	58.7
Consumer:							
Installment	.5	.7	1.5	1.5	2.9	4.3	3.4
Noninstallment	1.3	1.2	1.1	1.1	0.6	.3	.1
Business	—	—	—	—	1.2	1.9	2.1
Total loans	86.4	88.2	86.8	84.5	66.1	63.7	64.3
Commercial paper and bankers' acceptances	—	.2	.6	.6	1.5	2.2	0.5
Miscellaneous	4.7	4.0	4.2	5.4	11.2	10.0	13.3
	100.0%	100.0%	100.0%	100.0%	100.0%	100.0%	100.0%

*Less than .1%.

Source: Board of Governors of the Federal Reserve System, *Flow of Funds Accounts, Financial Assets and Liabilities,* various issues.

1980 DIDMCA (Depository Institutions Deregulations and Monetary Control Act), but were restricted by the 1989 FIRREA.

Consumer and business loans have had less impact. Nevertheless, their 1.8 percent share grew to 5.6 percent by 1991. Again, note that business loans are a new addition to S&L portfolios.

Financial liabilities of savings and loan associations grew at 10.5 percent from 1964 to 1989, a rate roughly equivalent to that of asset growth (Exhibit 19-8), but declined substantially by 1991. Also, similar to the observed trend of home mortgages on the asset side, small time and savings deposits contributed 93.2 percentage points to financial liabilities in 1964 but only 61.8 percentage points in 1989. Most of the difference is explained by greater use of large time deposits (8.1 percentage points higher), Federal Home Loan Bank loans (7.6 percentage points higher), federal funds purchased and repurchase agreements (7.5 percentage points higher), and other bank loans (3.5 percentage points higher). Since FIRREA, all these provide much less funding for the S&L industry.

Mutual Savings Banks

The financial assets of mutual savings banks (Exhibit 19-9) grew over the same 25-year period at a slower annual rate of 6.6 percent to $269.9 billion by 1989 with a smaller contraction noted by 1991. In 1964, savings banks were more liquid than S&Ls with 74.8 percent invested in loans, as compared with 86.4 percent for S&Ls. Almost all the difference was connected with the mortgage loan portfolios. Savings banks maintained larger investment securities portfolios than savings and loan associations.

However, by 1991, some of these differences had been eliminated. Securities represented 21.4 and 20.6 percent of the financial assets of savings banks and S&Ls, respectively. Mortgage loans were 60.1 and 58.7 percent, respectively. Total loans were 62.9 and 64.3 percent, respectively.

Even more than S&Ls, mutual savings banks sustained an enormous loss of low-cost funding (Exhibit 19-10). In 1964, small time and savings deposits constituted 97.6 per-

EXHIBIT 19-8 FINANCIAL LIABILITIES OF U.S. SAVINGS AND LOAN ASSOCIATIONS, 1964–1991 (PERCENTAGES)

	1964	1969	1974	1979	1984	1989	1991
Financial liabilities (billions)	$109.2	$148.5	$273.9	$536.8	$966.0	$1,315.8	$1,057.5
Deposits:							
Checkable	.1%	.1%	.1%	.2%	2.6%	2.9%	2.2%
Small time & savings	93.2	91.2	87.0	82.1	66.3	61.8	70.5
Large time	—	—	1.6	5.3	13.6	8.1	3.9
Total deposits	93.3	91.3	88.7	87.6	82.5	72.8	76.6
Federal funds and security repos	—	—	.7	1.2	4.8	7.5	3.2
Federal Home Loan Bank loans	4.8	6.3	8.0	7.8	7.7	12.4	8.5
Bonds	—	—	—	.7	.5	1.3	1.1
Other bank loans	.3	.3	.5	.9	1.4	3.8	.1
Taxes payable	.1	.1	.1	.1	—	—*	.1
Miscellaneous	1.5	2.0	2.0	1.7	3.1	2.2	10.4
	100.0%	100.0%	100.0%	100.0%	100.0%	100.0%	100.0%

*Less than .1%.
Source: Board of Governors of the Federal Reserve System, *Flow of Funds Accounts, Financial Assets and Liabilities,* various issues.

EXHIBIT 19-9 FINANCIAL ASSETS OF U.S. MUTUAL SAVINGS BANKS, 1964–1991 (PERCENTAGES)

	1964	1969	1974	1979	1984	1989	1991
Financial assets (billions)	$55.0	$74.5	$109.1	$163.3	$204.7	$269.9	$264.0
Checkable deposits and currency	1.5%	1.2%	1.0%	1.7%	2.2%	2.2%	2.2%
Time deposits	.4	.1	.9	.2	.2	—*	—
Federal funds and security repos	—	.4	1.1	1.9	2.9	2.2	2.3
Investment securities:							
Treasury	10.5	4.3	2.4	2.9	4.7	3.2	3.5
Agency	1.4	2.4	4.0	9.0	11.8	12.1	9.6
Tax-exempt	.7	.3	.8	1.8	1.0	.7	.7
Corporate & foreign bonds	5.6	9.3	12.7	12.6	10.0	4.9	3.9
Corporate equities	3.6	3.4	4.0	2.9	2.0	3.2	3.7
Total securities	21.8	19.7	23.9	29.2	29.5	42.1	21.4
Loans:							
Mortgages:							
Home	55.8	55.2	44.8	40.5	34.9	37.4	41.9
Multifamily	10.3	10.2	11.8	10.2	6.5	7.5	7.0
Commercial	7.3	9.8	11.6	9.9	8.9	10.9	11.2
Farm	.2	.1	.1	—	—	—	—
Total mortgages	73.6	75.3	68.3	60.6	50.3	55.8	60.1
Consumer:							
Installment	.5	1.1	1.4	1.7	3.9	2.5	2.4
Noninstallment	.7	.5	.5	.7	1.0	.1	.4
Total loans	74.8	76.9	70.2	63.0	55.2	58.4	62.9
Commercial paper and banker's acceptances	.2	.4	.5	1.3	4.4	6.7	4.8
Miscellaneous	1.3	1.3	2.4	2.7	5.6	6.4	6.4
	100.0%	100.0%	100.0%	100.0%	100.0%	100.0%	100.0%

*Less than 0.1%.

Source: Board of Governors of the Federal Reserve System, *Flow of Funds Accounts, Financial Assets and Liabilities,* various issues.

EXHIBIT 19-10 FINANCIAL LIABILITIES OF U.S. MUTUAL SAVINGS BANKS 1964–1991 (PERCENTAGES)

	1964	1969	1974	1979	1984	1989	1991
Financial liabilities (billions)	$49.8	$68.7	$101.6	$151.9	$193.3	$245.5	$244.0
Deposits:							
Checkable	.4%	.5%	.6%	1.8%	5.2%	13.4%	17.8
Small time & savings	97.6	97.2	95.7	92.1	79.0	43.0	41.4
Large time	—	—	.8	2.2	9.3	27.9	28.7
Total deposits	98.0	97.7	97.1	96.1	93.5	84.3	87.9
Security repos	—	—	0.9	1.2	1.2	3.5	2.6
Federal Home Loan Bank loans	—	—	—	1.2	1.5	6.7	6.7
Miscellaneous	2.0	2.3	2.0	1.5	3.8	5.5	2.8
	100.0%	100.0%	100.0%	100.0%	100.0%	100.0%	100.0%

Source: Board of Governors of the Federal Reserve System, *Flow of Funds Accounts, Financial Assets and Liabilities,* various issues.

cent of financial liabilities. By 1991, this source provided only 41.4 percent of the total and large (rate-sensitive) time deposits, 28.7 percent. After the nationwide introduction of interest-bearing transaction accounts, checkable deposits rose from 1.8 percent of financial liabilities (in 1979) to 17.8 percent.

These exhibits suggest that, in many ways, the differences between savings and loan associations and mutual savings banks have been reduced. In the same sense, differences between thrifts and commercial banks are now also less pronounced.

Comparisons with Commercial Banks

Exhibit 19-11 illustrates the major asset categories of commercial banks, savings and loan associations, and mutual savings banks in 1964 and 1991. In 1964, banks held a much greater proportion of assets in securities and a much smaller one in mortgages. Business loans were offered only by commercial banks, and banks were also more liquid.

By 1991, some of the differences were much less pronounced. Securities portfolios and cash holdings were roughly equivalent among the three, and the difference in mortgage loan investment was reduced.

EXHIBIT 19-11 ASSET COMPOSITION OF COMMERCIAL BANKS, SAVINGS AND LOAN ASSOCIATIONS, AND MUTUAL SAVINGS BANKS, 1964 AND 1991

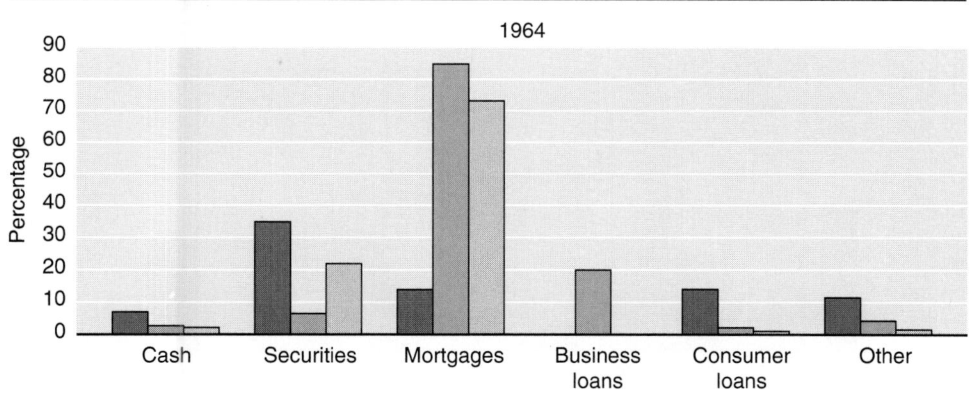

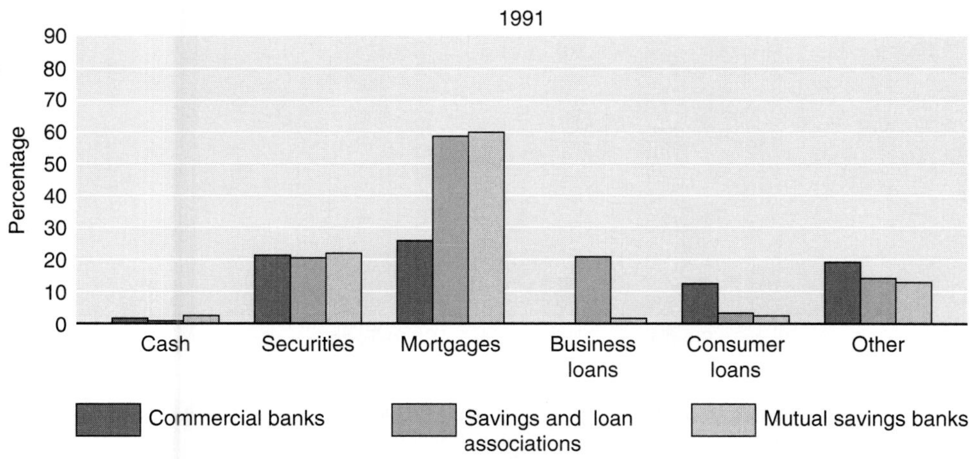

Source: Data from Board of Governors of the Federal Reserve System, *Flow of Funds Accounts, Assets and Liabilities,* various issues.

On the liability side, in 1964, transaction accounts provided half of banks and virtually no thrift funding. (See Exhibit 19-12.) Small time and savings accounts dominated the liability composition of thrifts. Large time deposits made no contribution to thrift funding and were less than 10 percent of bank funding.

By 1991, transaction accounts had declined in importance to commercial banks but were roughly equivalent to the levels maintained at mutual savings banks. This close correspondence is also noted for small time deposits. Large time deposits had become even more important for mutual savings banks than for commercial banks.

In most cases, the differences between commercial banks and thrifts are not as noticeable today as they were in the past. To the extent that thrifts begin to look and perform more and more like commercial banks, the greater the competitive pressures under which thrifts operate.

Share of the Mortgage Market

Exhibit 19-13 underscores an even greater threat to the thrift industry. These institutions developed primarily to provide mortgage finance. As recently as 1964, almost half (45.7 percent) of all mortgages were held by thrifts. This share was maintained through 1977 (45.9 percent). Thereafter the share declined substantially. By 1991, savings and loan associations and mutual savings banks held only 20 percent of all mortgages.

EXHIBIT 19-12 LIABILITY COMPOSITION OF COMMERCIAL BANKS, SAVINGS AND LOAN ASSOCIATIONS, AND MUTUAL SAVINGS BANKS, 1964 AND 1991

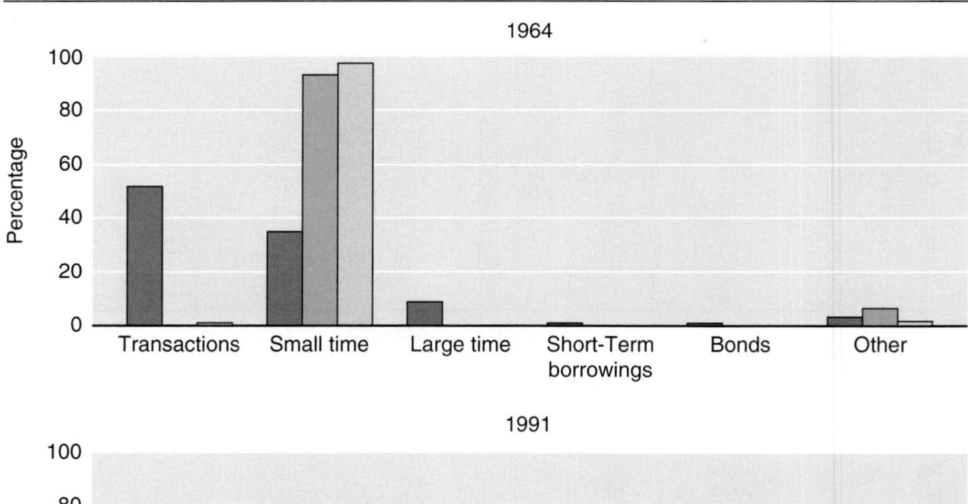

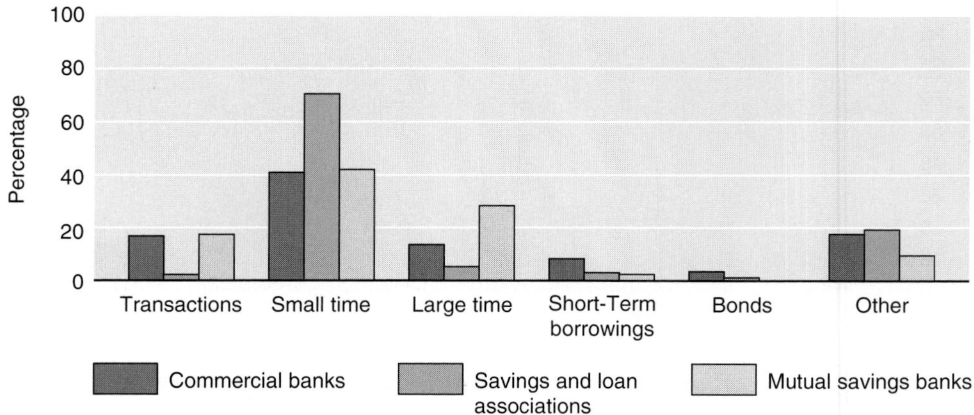

Source: Data from Board of Governors of the Federal Reserve System, *Flow of Funds Accounts, Assets and Liabilities,* various issues.

EXHIBIT 19-13 THRIFTS' SHARE OF THE MORTGAGE MARKET, 1961–1991

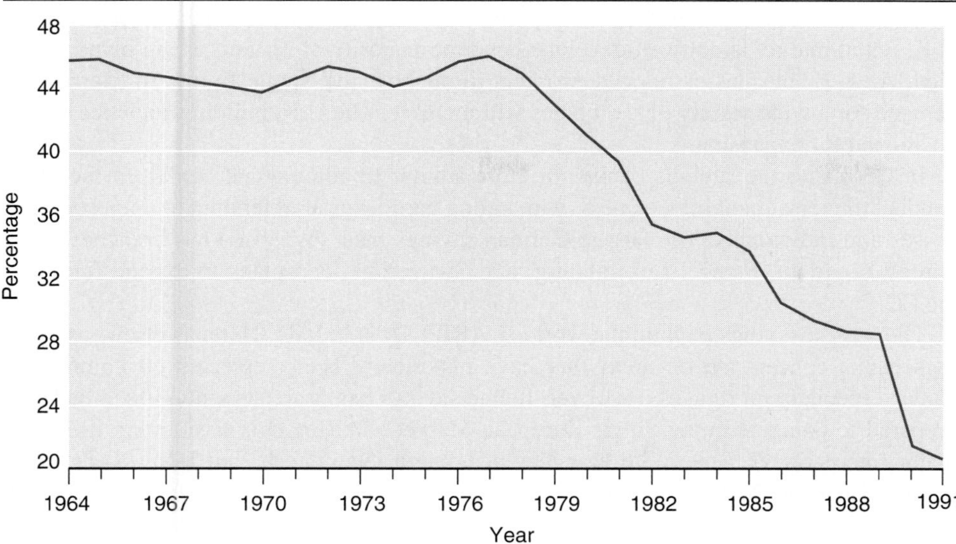

Source: Data from Board of Governors of the Federal Reserve System, *Flow of Funds Accounts, Financial Assets and Liabilities,* various issues.

This is the dilemma. Because of the excesses of the 1980s, regulators expect thrifts to concentrate more of their assets in mortgages. At the same time, thrifts are losing ground in the mortgage market. When this dilemma is considered together with the blurring of distinctions between thrifts and commercial banks, a real question arises as to whether the industry can compete. When the high failure rate of savings institutions is considered, the answer appears to be negative. Perhaps thrifts, as originally conceived, have become obsolete.

THRIFTS IN OTHER COUNTRIES

There is a sharp contrast between the thrift industry in the United States and those in other countries. A few examples follow.

United Kingdom

Thrifts in the United Kingdom also face competitive pressure from clearing (commercial) banks, but are nowhere near the point of extinction. In fact, United Kingdom building societies hold more deposits than the banks and are second only to insurance companies and pension funds.

Part of the reason for this is that building societies are still nonprofit organizations. As such, there is much trust in their management. As a result, deposits and mutual shares remain on deposit with the institution. Thus, disintermediation has not been a significant problem in the United Kingdom.

Nevertheless, the lines of demarcation between banks and building societies are blurring as is true in the United States. The industry is also consolidating as is true in the United States. In fact, the largest fifteen societies represent 85 percent of industry assets. Unlike the U.S. case, however, the future is much brighter for U.K. building societies.

European Community

In the Single European Market, U.K. building societies will have certain advantages. The U.K. mortgage market is more active than in other EC countries. For example, the German real estate market is much more oriented toward rental property. Even affluent Germans often do not seek home ownership until they are close to retirement. In contrast, the U.K. rental market is not well-developed and the majority of residences are owner-occupied. As U.K. businesses relocate workers throughout the Single European Market, the demand for a wide variety of mortgages will increase. The U.K. building societies will be positioned for expansion.

In Germany, the savings banks are more similar to commercial banks. In fact, they conduct universal banking business, with strong participation in lending to domestic businesses and individuals. The largest German savings bank (WestLB) has branches in the United Kingdom, France, Luxembourg, and Switzerland and plans to expand further in the EC.

The largest savings bank in the world (CARIPLO) is in Italy. Here, as elsewhere, savings banks concentrate on areas that have historically been neglected by commercial banks, especially mortgages. However, Italian savings banks are also merging to be better prepared to compete in the Single European Market. CARIPLO is positioning itself as a major international bank. With branches in London, New York, and Hong Kong, it already has the capability to operate on a 24-hour basis because of overlapping time zones.

Canada

In Canada, building societies have evolved into mortgage loan companies. Many are wholly owned subsidiaries of chartered (commercial) banks. Like the U.K. system the Canadian system is highly concentrated. Further, the chartered bank subsidiaries represent the largest share of mortgage loan company assets (over 50 percent).

Unlike the U.K. system, however, Canadian mortgage loan companies are for-profit operations. The problem of mismatched maturity of assets and liabilities is not solved through public trust and stable deposits. Instead, the term of mortgage loans is shorter. Prior to 1969, the average term of a mortgage loan was 25 years. However, in 1969 federal legislation was passed that introduced a 5-year renewable mortgage. This permitted institutions to better match the maturities of loans to term (long-term) deposits. Since the late 1970s, open mortgages have allowed borrowers to repay mortgages before maturity with no penalty. Three-year, one-year, and six-month renewable mortgage loans are now available.

Japan

In Japan, the Housing Loan Corporation is the major provider of mortgages, holding over 35 percent of all mortgage loans. This government agency is financed primarily by postal savings deposits (see Chapter 17) and by operating surpluses of other government agencies.

Ordinary (commercial) banks and insurance companies have also provided mortgage finance. However, until 1971, there were no private companies geared specifically to mortgage borrowers. There are now eight private housing finance companies funded by banks. The companies hold less than 10 percent of all mortgage loans outstanding but also act as lending agents for private insurance companies and the public Housing Loan Corporation.

In general, the organizations that provide housing finance in other industrialized countries have not undergone the stress that has been experienced in the United States. But with the possible exception of Japan (where all forms of consumer finance have been relatively slow to develop), thrifts or other institutions that primarily provide mortgage loans are evolving into commercial bank-like institutions or are already affiliated with commercial banks.

SUMMARY

The thrift industry in the United States filled a vital need in housing finance in its early years. Also, there was no outlet for small savings at the time. As long as both asset and liability portfolios conformed with this initial arrangement, thrifts were viable institutions. However, competition from commercial banks was but the first attack on the industry.

The inflation that began in the 1960s was a particularly troublesome development for thrifts. Except for a brief period of "national" thrifts, these institutions served a limited geographic region. Thus, overseas operations and Euromarket participation were not viable alternatives, as they were for commercial banks. Deregulation of the 1970s and 1980s opened the floodgates of innovation. The powers of thrifts were expanded to make them more competitive. However, regulatory overseers failed to monitor the thrifts for evidence of power abuse, and Congress was slow to react.

In 1989, FIRREA was enacted. The legislation took major steps to reverse the abuses and clean up the industry. However, the estimated cost to close all the troubled thrifts and to liquidate the asset inventory that the government now controls has been estimated at $500 billion or more. The impact of this failed experiment in deregulation will be felt for decades to come.

KEY TERMS

brokered deposit
building society
Federal Home Loan banks
FIRREA
generally accepted accounting principles (GAAP)
mutual savings bank
mutual depository organization
net worth certificate
Office of Thrift Supervision
regulatory accounting principles (RAP)
savings and loan association
Savings Association Insurance Fund (SAIF)
terminating building society
thrift institution
U.S. League of Savings Institutions

END-OF-CHAPTER QUESTIONS

1. The Federal Home Loan Bank System was designed in the 1930s to be roughly comparable to the Federal Reserve System. The Federal Savings and Loan Insurance Corporation was similarly intended to parallel the Federal Deposit Insurance Corporation. Explain how this thrift regulatory structure was dismantled by legislation in 1989.
2. How did early building societies differ from commercial banks?
3. What is a mutual depository organization?
4. What factors contributed to the need for thrifts in the 1800s?
5. How did the early mutual savings banks differ from savings and loan associations (building societies)?
6. Explain the effect of rising interest rates on the profitability of thrifts in the late 1970s and early 1980s. Be specific.
7. Summarize the scope of activities that were permitted for thrifts during the 1980s.
8. In previous years, savings and loan associations and mutual savings banks relied heavily on savings deposits as a source of funds. Currently, how has the mix of liabilities changed?
9. Differentiate between GAAP net worth and RAP net worth.
10. In light of recent, devastating losses in the thrift industry, assess the prospect of future viability of thrifts, in particular with respect to their original justification for existence.
11. If thrifts cease to exist, would you have any concerns about the mortgage services available to consumers?
12. Describe the potential impact of the Resolution Trust Corporation liquidating large holdings of foreclosed real estate for the rest of the economy.

13. What were the major mistakes that were made in regulating the thrift industry during the 1980s?
14. In theory, higher deposit insurance premiums will help cover the cost of the thrift bailout. Are there any possible negative implications?

SELECTED REFERENCES

Binhammer, H. H. *Money, Banking, and the Canadian Banking System,* 4th ed., Methuen Publications, Agincourt, Ontario, 1982.

Board of Governors of the Federal Reserve System, *Flow of Funds Accounts, Financial Assets and Liabilities,* various issues.

Brumbaugh, R. Dan, Jr. *Thrifts under Siege; Restoring Order to American Banking,* Ballinger Publishing Company, Cambridge, Massachusetts, 1988.

Carron, Andrew S. *The Rescue of the Thrift Industry,* The Brookings Institution, Washington, D.C., 1983.

Carter, H., and I. Partington. *Applied Economics in Banking and Finance,* 3d ed., Oxford University Press, Oxford, U.K., 1984.

Chant, John F. *The Market for Financial Services; Deposit-Taking Institutions,* The Fraser Institute, Vancouver, 1988.

Cooper, S. Kerry, and Donald R. Fraser. *Banking Deregulation and the New Competition in Financial Services,* Ballinger Publishing Company, Cambridge, Massachusetts, 1984.

Kane, Edward J. *The S&L Insurance Mess: How Did It Happen?* The Urban Institute Press, Washington, D.C., 1989.

Meyer, Dianne A., and Sandra A. Ballard. "Issues in Lending; A Practical Guide to FIRREA," *Journal of Commercial Bank Lending,* vol. 72 (Jan. 1990), pp. 11–23.

Office of Thrift Supervision, Washington, D.C., unpublished quarterly data.

Ornstein, Franklin H. *Savings Banking; An Industry in Change,* Reston Publishing Company, Inc., Reston, Virginia, 1985.

Pizzo, Stephen, Mary Fricker, and Paul Muolo. *Inside Job; The Looting of America's Savings and Loans,* Harper Perennial, New York, 1991.

Suzuki, Yoshio. *The Japanese Financial System,* Clarendon Press, Oxford, U.K., 1987.

United States Department of Commerce, Bureau of the Census. *Statistical Abstract of the United States* 1989, 109th ed., Washington, D.C.

U.S. League of Savings Institutions. *Savings Institutions Sourcebook,* Washington, D.C., 1990.

CHAPTER 20

CREDIT UNIONS

CHAPTER OUTLINE

CREDIT UNIONS AS COMPARED WITH THRIFTS

UNIQUE CHARACTERISTICS
- The Common Bond
- Other Characteristics

DEVELOPMENT OF CREDIT UNIONS
- Origins in Germany
- The Early Credit Union Movement in North America
  - Canada, United States
- Trade Associations
- Credit Union Growth

CREDIT UNION REGULATION

ASSETS AND LIABILITIES
- Assets
- Liabilities
- Comparison of Growth Rates of Thrift Institutions
- Comparison to Commercial Banks

CREDIT UNIONS AROUND THE WORLD

INTERNATIONAL COMPARISONS:
- Africa
- Asia
- Canada
- Europe
- Latin America and the Caribbean

CHAPTER OVERVIEW

This chapter:

- Compares and contrasts credit unions and thrifts
- Examines the first credit unions in Germany
- Highlights the important role that trade associations have played in the industry's development
- Describes credit union regulation
- Studies the industry balance sheet
- Illustrates differing structural aspects of credit unions in other regions of the world

Credit unions grew from the same spirit that motivated thrift institutions. Through a credit union formed on the basis of a common bond, members were able to obtain consumer financing that was not available from commercial banks. But while thrifts evolved into profit-seeking enterprises, credit unions never departed from their self-help, volunteer-worker mode of operation. As such, they have maintained their tax-free status.

At the same time, credit unions *have evolved* in terms of service. At one point, credit unions were funded almost exclusively by savings accounts and offered consumer loans. Today, credit unions also offer transactions accounts, credit cards, and home mortgages. Deposits are federally insured, and members have access to their accounts through automated teller machines (ATMs). A modern credit union offers consumers the same type of service available from a commercial bank. In fact, credit unions are so much like commercial banks that commercial banks often point to credit unions' exemption from income taxation as an unfair competitive advantage. This debate will continue as long as credit unions evolve more and more into banklike financial institutions.

CREDIT UNIONS AS COMPARED WITH THRIFTS

The primary difference between credit unions and other depository institutions is their emphasis on service. They are neither profit-oriented nor motivated by philanthropy. In fact, the industry motto has been:

Not for profit,

Not for charity,

But for service.

In terms of business structure, credit unions are tax-exempt, *mutual organizations* in which deposits are considered *shares* and interest paid is considered *dividend payment.*

Credit union share account:
An ownership claim on a credit union, similar in form to a common stock interest. Payments to owners are called dividend payments. In substance, share accounts are equivalent to deposits.

With the exception of the treasurer, most officers of credit unions are unpaid volunteers. While savings and loans and savings banks are also frequently mutual organizations, they *may* convert to a corporate form. Since credit unions *may not* convert to a corporate form, they represent the best example of a cooperative financial institution in the United States today.

More specifically, there are three other characteristics that distinguish credit unions from thrifts.

1. Mutual savings banks were first established to encourage *thrift* among members. The original savings and loan associations restricted operations to the provision of *mortgage finance* for members. Credit unions originated to provide reasonably priced *consumer finance.*
2. Early savings banks were started by wealthy individuals out of a sense of *philanthropy.* Credit unions are based on the concept of *self-help.* While early S&Ls also espoused a self-help philosophy, modern associations are more often *profit-oriented* than not.
3. Credit union members share a *common bond* that has never applied to savings banks. In the case of savings and loan associations, the only common characteristic originally shared by members was that property purchased with loan proceeds was restricted to a given geographic area. In a modern context, S&L loans are restricted neither to a specific geographic area nor to the association members (or depositors).

UNIQUE CHARACTERISTICS

The Common Bond

From the start, credit union members have shared a *common bond.*

Common bond:

An attribute that describes all members of a credit union. The common bond distinguishes credit unions from all other mutual financial institutions.

Common bonds are either *associational, occupational,* or *residential.* Examples of associational bonds are religious, fraternal, professional, and labor union groups. Occupational bonds most often describe a common employer. Residential bonds describe a common geographic location and have been less important in quantitative terms than associational and occupational bonds.

Credit unions with a residential common bond have recently accounted for less than 5 percent of all U.S. organizations; associational credit unions represent between 15 and 20 percent. By far, the largest category is occupational. Within this latter group, the manufacturing sector has dominated with as much as 34 percent of the total, and government and educational service make up approximately 15 and 9 percent, respectively.

Common bonds define a credit union's *field of membership.*

Field of membership:

The group of people who have a particular common bond and may join a particular credit union.

Over time, bonds have been loosely interpreted in many cases. For example, it is not unusual for the immediate family of a member also to be eligible for membership. When permitted by state law, those who leave the field of membership may retain their credit union membership. In some cases, the common bond defines a nontraditional field, such as owners of Arabian horses.

Other Characteristics

The common bond and other features give credit unions certain advantages.

- Members of occupational (job-related) credit unions often make contributions through payroll deduction. This process streamlines operations and reduces default risk of loans.
- Credit union income is *exempt from income taxation.* This reduces the cost of funds.
- Many of the employees of credit unions are *volunteer personnel.* This feature reduces the operating expense.

These cost advantages make it easier for credit unions to offer competitively priced loans. However, before interest rate deregulation, these cost advantages were partially offset by the higher interest rates that could be paid on share accounts. Federal Reserve Regulation Q (which limited deposit rates of banks and thrifts until the 1980s) did not apply to credit unions.

DEVELOPMENT OF CREDIT UNIONS

The credit union industry was established as the result of the efforts of a few individuals who had strong beliefs in its underlying principle: People should pool their money and make loans to each other. The movement started in Germany and then moved to North America and other regions of the world.

Origins in Germany

Victor Huber began to advocate the virtues of cooperative endeavors in Germany as early as 1844. His belief was that those most affected by depressed economic conditions of the

1840s could be best served through self-help, rather than charity. Huber's writings were widely read, and he established two associations.

Hermann Schulze founded a credit cooperative in Germany in 1850. This early urban credit union was not intended to provide consumer credit. Instead, loans were for productive purposes. Each member paid an entrance fee and proved capacity to pay for one share. Members also deposited their savings. Loans were endorsed by two members and usually had a term that was no longer than 3 months. Only members could borrow, and the character of the borrower (willingness to repay) was important because the money was borrowed from the group of friends.

Schulze began to travel to various urban areas in order to advocate the large-scale establishment of credit unions in 1853. By 1859, 183 credit unions existed with total membership of 18,000 members. Next, he worked to affiliate the organizations. In 1859, the existing credit unions formed a central office to coordinate business transactions and the exchange of information. Schulze was the first manager of this central office. By 1912, 1002 German urban credit unions boasted 641,000 members.

During roughly the same period, Friedrich Raiffeisen initiated rural credit unions, again in Germany. The first two, in 1849 and 1853, were funded by wealthy citizens. These early rural credit unions differed from those organized by Schulze (with more of a self-help focus). However, as the wealthy benefactors were excluded from participating, many lost interest. Raiffeisen then turned to the member-financed form of capitalization, even though most of the original capital was borrowed by the members, who shared responsibility for its repayment.

Rural credit unions initially did not grow as fast as the urban unions. There were six in 1862 and only 425 by 1888. But with the establishment of a central facility, the numbers increased significantly. Rural credit unions in Germany totaled 25,576 by 1913.

The credit union movement also spread to other European countries. The People's Bank of Milan, Italy, opened in 1866. By 1909, there were 25,000 members. Most members were small merchants and craftsmen. Rural credit unions also prospered, numbering 2000 by 1909. In addition, the number of Austrian urban and rural organizations grew to 3599 and 8000, respectively, by 1913.

The Early Credit Union Movement in North America

Canada The first credit union in North America was founded in Quebec, Canada. Alphonse Desjardins was a journalist who became particularly disturbed by the effects on poor people of the practices of "loan sharks," who charged annual interest rates up to 1200 percent on small loans. When he learned of the credit cooperatives of Europe, Desjardins found out more by corresponding with the people involved in the French and Italian credit unions.

In 1900, Alphonse Desjardins and twelve of his friends considered starting a credit union in Quebec. They decided to eliminate the distinction between urban and rural organizations. Later that year, eighty investors signed the charter of the *Caisse Populaire de Levis.* Collecting no salary, Desjardins operated the credit union out of his home. After 6 years of operation, the association rented space in the business district of Levis and hired a manager.

Desjardins organized the second and third credit unions in Canada in 1901 and 1905, respectively. By 1914, 150 *caisse populaires* served urban wage earners, farmers, and miners.

United States In the early years of credit unions in most countries, one or two individuals assumed primary responsibility. Boston merchant Edward Filene fulfilled this function in the United States. Filene first became familiar with the concept while visiting

India, during a world tour in 1907. His first impression was that credit cooperatives could be used to alleviate widespread poverty in developing countries.

At the same time, the new commissioner of banks in Massachusetts, Pierre Jay, became interested in cooperative banks. After corresponding with Desjardins in Quebec and other people in Europe, Jay decided to pursue the idea. Largely through his efforts, the Massachusetts Credit Union Act was passed in 1909. New York enacted similar legislation in 1913.

During 1910, two credit unions began operating in Massachusetts, with an additional seventeen the following year. Formation slowed during the next 2 years. In New York, only nineteen were operating by 1915, with eleven of these in New York City. This rate of formation was significantly slower than in Europe or Canada.

In order to stimulate the organization of more associations, Filene and other advocates founded the Massachusetts Credit Union (MCU) in 1914. While the MCU was a functioning credit union, its objectives also included encouraging the formation of additional associations and providing support for individual credit unions and the industry as a whole. Through its activities, the MCU evolved into a kind of central facility.

With the help of Roy Burgengren, the original MCU was eventually reorganized as the *Credit Union National Extension Bureau (CUNEB)* in 1921. The CUNEB would promote the movement on a national scale, while the Massachusetts Credit Union League would represent associations within the state.

Trade Associations

The CUNEB worked to have credit union laws passed in every state. Primarily through the efforts of Filene and Burgengren, Virginia and Kentucky enacted credit union legislation in 1922, followed by Tennessee and Indiana in 1923. Most of the financing for these lobbying efforts came from the Twentieth Century Fund, established and funded in 1919 by Filene.

While a number of states subsequently enacted credit union legislation, advocates sometimes faced strong opposition by banking and savings and loan representatives that did not welcome the competition. Nevertheless, in spite of this resistance and the Great Depression, by 1933 only ten states had failed to enact credit union legislation. Those states that had credit union laws represented 80 percent of the nation's population.

The *Credit Union National Association (CUNA)* replaced the CUNEB in 1935. The new structure was intended to serve state *leagues* that elected to affiliate with it. In turn, CUNA encouraged individual credit unions to affiliate with their state leagues. Membership dues, rather than outside financing, financed CUNA operations.

As early as the first meeting of CUNA's board of directors, the issue of mutual life insurance arose. *CUNA Mutual Insurance Group* began operation in 1935 to provide credit life insurance. In the event of death of a borrower prior to full repayment, CUNA Mutual guaranteed repayment. Today, seven companies (not owned by CUNA) constitute CUNA Mutual.

The *CUNA Service Group* is a profit-making affiliate that plays a support role and supplies new products to credit unions. The CUNA Service Group is owned by CUNA and by credit union leagues. Members of the group provide specific services:

- *CUNA Supply, Inc.,* makes wholesale purchases of operational and promotional supplies for distribution to CUNA members.
- *CUNA Internet* makes it possible for individual credit unions to be linked to an online telecommunications network.
- *ICU Services, Inc.,* provides U.S. government securities investment vehicles, automated payment mechanisms, debit and credit card programs, and individual retirement account or Keogh account plans.

EXHIBIT 20-1 U.S. CREDIT UNION SYSTEM

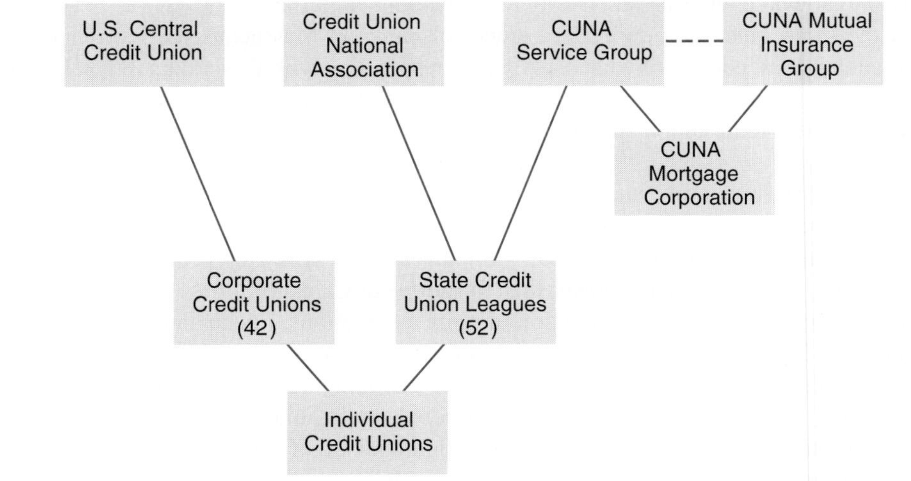

The *CUNA Mortgage Corporation* is jointly owned by CUNA Service Group and by CUNA Mutual Insurance Group. This mortgage corporation provides a liquidity facility for mortgage lending by purchasing mortgage loans that have been originated by credit unions, packaging them into mortgage pools, and selling the securitized mortgages on the secondary market. Taken together, the research and development activities of the CUNA Service Group help member credit unions realize economies of scale and maintain competitiveness in the provision of financial services.

In 1974, the *U.S. Central Credit Union* began operations. The corporation, capitalized at 1 percent of assets by member credit unions, acts as a *credit union for credit unions.* It is a private liquidity facility and provider of investment advice, settlement, and payment services. Its operations are funded with commercial paper issuances that have historically earned high ratings from rating services.

The U.S. Central Credit Union and the forty-two state corporate central facilities form the *CUNA Corporate Credit Union Network.* Through the network, individual credit unions may invest in a large portfolio of securities managed by U.S. Central and obtain services normally available only through a correspondent relationship with commercial banks. These services include wire transfers, share draft settlements, provision of currency and coin, and federal funds trading. (See also Exhibit 20-1).

Credit Union Growth

After a slow start following the 1909 Massachusetts credit union legislation, the number of associations grew more rapidly beginning in the early 1930s. Despite the adversity of the Great Depression, the number of credit unions grew 107 percent between 1929 and 1933. Over the same period, membership grew 35.9 percent. In 1933, 359,600 members belonged to 2016 associations. (See Exhibit 20-2.) During the same period, the number of commercial banks declined drastically from a high of 30,000 in 1920 to 15,000 in 1933. Credit unions prospered because of reduced confidence in the banking system.

State laws, federal credit union legislation in 1934, and restructuring of the national association provided a strong push for the industry. During the 3 years ended 1936, membership and the number of organizations more than doubled. Growth continued through 1941, at which time 9891 credit unions had 3.3 million members.

This trend reversed in 1941 when the United States became involved in World War II (1941–1945). The uncertainties of war resulted in more reductions in membership than had been witnessed during the Great Depression. By 1942, the number of credit unions dropped from 9891 to 9767, and membership fell back to 3.1 million. In the next 3 years, the reductions in organizations and membership were 11.1 and 9.6 percent of their 1942 levels.

After the war, membership gains resumed and remained strong. However, the growth in the number of associations has been mixed. From 1945 through 1960, there was double-digit growth in each 3-year period. From 1960, growth in the number of credit unions slowed to 5 or 6 percent during the next few 3-year periods.[1] At 23,776 credit unions in 1969, the industry reached its peak. Thereafter, numbers began to decline.

Liquidations and *mergers* have been responsible for most of the reduction. This is not to suggest that liquidations occurred only after 1969. In fact, between 1934 and 1970, 6000 federal credit unions alone were liquidated. Although these liquidated associations controlled $135.3 million in assets, members realized losses of only $1.8 million. This loss containment was primarily attributable to cooperation between other credit unions, state leagues, and central facilities. Attempts were made to transfer loan and savings accounts to other associations. Generally, such attempts have been successful.

Liquidations most often occur in connection with smaller credit unions. From 1970 through the early 1980s, less than 15 percent of liquidating associations controlled more

[1]From 1945 through 1960, average *annual* compound rates of growth in number of credit unions ranged from 3.5 (3 years ended 1960) to 10.1 percent (3 years ended 1954). From 1960 through 1969, average annual rates were on the order of 2 percent.

EXHIBIT 20-2 GROWTH IN NUMBERS AND MEMBERSHIP OF U.S. CREDIT UNIONS, 1929–1989

	Active credit unions		Membership	
Year		% change	Thousands	% change
1929	974		264.9	
1933	2,016	107.0	359.6	35.9
1936	5,241	160.0	1,170.4	225.5
1939	7,964	52.0	2,309.2	97.3
1942	9,767	22.6	3,144.6	36.2
1945	8,683	(11.1)	2,842.9	(9.6)
1948	9,924	14.3	4,090.7	43.9
1951	11,279	13.7	5,169.4	26.4
1954	15,041	33.4	7,355.6	43.3
1957	18,198	21.0	9,861.5	34.1
1960	20,148	10.7	12,059.2	22.3
1963	21,382	6.1	14,579.3	20.9
1966	22,684	6.1	17,922.6	22.9
1969	23,776	4.8	21,628.3	20.7
1972	23,070	(3.0)	25,690.3	18.8
1975	22,611	(2.0)	31,262.8	21.7
1978	22,202	(1.8)	40,720.0	30.3
1981	20,697	(6.8)	45,069.0	10.7
1985	15,045	(27.3)	45,265.0	0.4
1987	14,335	(4.7)	50,066.0	10.6
1989	13,371	(6.7)	60,400.0	20.6

Source: Pugh, Olin S., and F. Jerry Ingram, *Credit Unions: A Movement Becomes an Industry,* pp. 8–9 [1929–1978, unions and membership], U.S. Department of Commerce, Bureau of the Census, *Statistical Abstract of the United States,* 1989 [1981–1987, unions and membership].

than $100,000 in savings. Frequently, the organization was affiliated with a manufacturing plant that had been closed. In this respect, the credit union industry has been affected by the strong consolidation trend evident in other areas of financial services. The consolidation in the credit union industry during the 1970s and 1980s has resulted in fewer institutions that control more financial resources, that is, larger credit unions. This consolidation is now evident in the commercial banking industry.

CREDIT UNION REGULATION

Since 1934, federal charters for credit unions have been permitted. The Federal Credit Union Act of that year contained the following provisions:

- At least seven persons were required as founding members.
- Funds were to be invested only for provident (prudent) and productive purposes.
- Credit unions formed under the act were exempt from income taxation.
- Charters would be granted by the Farm Credit Administration.

In 1942, the Federal Credit Union Program was transferred to the Federal Deposit Insurance Corporation as the Credit Union Section. Six years later, the Federal Security Agency assumed responsibility. When this agency was liquidated in 1953, a newly reorganized Bureau of Federal Credit Unions was assigned to the Department of Health, Education, and Welfare. (See also Exhibit 20-3).

The Federal Credit Union Act was amended in 1970 to create the *National Credit Union Administration (NCUA)* and the *National Credit Union Share Insurance Fund (NCUSIF),* to be controlled by the administrator of NCUA. The NCUA is organized into six regions with headquarters in Albany, New York; Washington, DC; Atlanta, Georgia;

EXHIBIT 20-3 CONGRESSMAN STEAGALL AND THE FEDERAL CREDIT UNION ACT

Ray Burgengren (head of the predecessor of CUNA) helped draft the Federal Credit Union Act early in 1934. However, he knew that he needed the support of President Franklin Roosevelt (1933–1945) and of the chairman of the House Banking Committee, Henry Steagall, coauthor of the major banking legislation of 1933.

In early June 1934, the President endorsed the bill and encouraged Steagall to see to it that the legislation moved quickly through his committee before Congress adjourned near the middle of the month. On June 13, Burgengren and a close associate were called to Steagall's office to defend the measure. Satisfied that the legislation was sound, Steagall presided the next day when the Banking Committee rendered a favorable report.

At that point, adjournment seemed imminent. On the morning of June 16, predictions were that Congress would adjourn that evening. After 7 P.M., Steagall asked that the bill be considered. Only 30 minutes were allotted for debate. Chairman Steagall persuasively argued that the bill had received unanimous support in the Senate and in the House Banking Committee and that the President had endorsed it.

There was no opposition to the creation of federally chartered, tax-exempt credit unions that would later compete vigorously with the country's commercial banks. Even before the allotted 30 minutes had elapsed, the House passed the Federal Credit Union Act with only two dissenting votes.

Source: Moody, J. Carroll, and Gilbert C. Fite, *The Credit Union Movement, Origins and Development, 1850–1970,* 1971, pp. 160–165

Itasca, Illinois; Austin, Texas; and Concord, California. Since 1970, NCUA has acted as the primary federal regulator of credit unions, issuing charters, supervising operations, conducting examinations, and insuring shares and deposits.

From 1970 through the early 1980s, the NCUSIF insurance premium paid by member credit unions was 1⁄12 percent, or $0.083 per $100 of share account balance. The high interest rates of the early 1980s, together with numerous industrial plant closings, drained the insurance fund. Premiums were increased to $0.17 per $100 of share account balance to rebuild the fund. In 1984, the U.S. Congress authorized the recapitalization of NCUSIF. As a result of this legislation, member credit unions must place 1 percent of insured share balances on deposit at NCUSIF. This amount is not expensed but is recorded as an asset on the books of member credit unions. Income earned on these funds is used by NCUSIF to cover losses. An annual insurance premium up to 1⁄12 percent may be assessed if necessary.

The investment and lending powers of federal credit unions were liberalized in the 1977 amendment of the Federal Credit Union Act.

The amendment:

- Allowed federal credit unions to offer 30-year residential mortgages and 15-year mobile home and home-improvement loans
- Extended the maximum maturity for nonresidential loans from 10 to 12 years
- Permitted other new product offerings, such as government-insured loans, lines of credit, and share certificates (similar to certificates of deposit)

The *Financial Institutions Reform Act of 1978* reorganized the NCUA and helped make the shrinking numbers of credit unions more competitive financial institutions. A three-member board, appointed by the President and confirmed by the Senate, replaced the administrator and the credit union board. Members of the new board served staggered 6-year terms. In addition, the separate fees assessed for chartering, supervision, and examination were replaced by one fee.

Permissible products and activities were expanded to include:

- Six-month, $10,000 share certificates
- Share certificates in excess of $100,000 to carry market interest rates
- Small share certificates with interest rates up to 8 percent
- Sale of mortgages to Federal National Mortgage Association, Federal Home Loan Mortgage Corporation, and Government National Mortgage Association

The 1978 act also created a federal source of liquidity, or lender of last resort. The *Central Liquidity Facility (CLF)* was formed to fulfill this function for credit unions as the Federal Reserve did for commercial banks. By subscribing .5 percent of capital, federal- and state-chartered associations may join the CLF and receive short-term loans for temporary liquidity needs. The National Credit Union Share Insurance Fund may now also borrow from the CLF. Most of the funds of the CLF are borrowed from the federal government.

The *Depository Institutions Deregulation and Monetary Control Act (DIDMCA) of 1980* legalized share drafts (interest-bearing transactions accounts) and other interest-bearing transactions accounts. Credit unions were also brought under the control of the Federal Reserve System, along with thrifts (savings and loan associations and mutual savings banks) with respect to a uniform system of reserve requirements. As is true for other depository institutions, DIDMCA raised the federal insurance limit to $100,000, deregulated deposit interest rates, and superseded state usury laws. The previous credit union loan interest rate ceiling of 1 percent per month (12 percent per year) was increased to 15 percent per year. Subsequently, the NCUA gave individual credit union boards rate-setting authority.

The Garn–St Germain Act of 1982 gave credit unions additional flexibility. Federal credit unions were allowed to determine both the par value of shares and internal organizational structure. Provisions also included further liberalization of mortgage lending. Limits on the size and maturity of mortgage loans were lifted, first mortgages were allowed to be refinanced, and the limit on maturity of second mortgages was expanded. The suspension of reserve requirements for the first $2 million in reservable deposits exempted virtually all credit unions from reserve requirements since the account balances of the typical association fall well below this cutoff point.

In addition, the National Credit Union Administration interpreted the 1982 legislation in such a way as to provide more autonomy for credit union management. Individual credit unions may determine both the types of shares and the dividend rates to be paid. The NCUA has also allowed associations to join in shared activities with other credit unions.

ASSETS AND LIABILITIES

Assets

Compared with banks and thrifts, the balance sheet of credit unions is relatively simple. Member loans, time deposits, and government securities dominate the asset section, as can be seen in Exhibit 20-4. From 1964 through 1991, financial assets of credit unions increased from $9.9 billion to $222.0 billion, or at an average annual rate of 12.2 percent.

The relative small size of the industry is readily apparent when the corresponding data for savings and loan associations and mutual savings banks are examined. Recall from Exhibit 19-7 that the financial assets of S&Ls totaled $1.06 trillion in 1991. With approximately 2000 institutions in the industry, the average size is $530 million.

In 1991, financial assets of mutual savings banks (MSBs) amounted to $264 billion (Exhibit 19-9). However, the numbers of MSBs and credit unions are approximately 800 and 13,000, respectively. The average assets of MSBs and credit unions are, therefore, $330 million and $17 million, respectively. Credit unions are much smaller than thrifts.

Even the $17 million average is somewhat misleading. Over 80 percent of all credit unions currently control total assets of less than $5 million.

EXHIBIT 20-4 FINANCIAL ASSETS OF U.S. CREDIT UNIONS, 1964–1991

	1964	1969	1974	1979	1984	1989	1991
Financial assets (billions)	$9.9	$16.1	$31.1	$63.1	$113.0	$200.5	$222.0
Checkable deposits and currency	5.1%	3.8%	3.2%	1.7%	2.3%	2.6%	2.3%
Time deposits:							
At banks	11.2	5.1	6.1	4.0	7.1	6.1	6.4
At S&Ls	11.2	5.0	6.1	3.3	6.1	5.4	5.2
Total time deposits	22.4	10.1	12.2	7.3	13.2	11.5	11.6
Federal funds sold and repos	—	—	—	—	4.1	5.1	7.5
Investment securities:							
U.S. Treasury	3.1	3.1	2.6	1.0	3.0	7.1	4.0
Agency	—	3.1	6.8	4.3	5.2	3.7	6.7
Total securities	3.1	6.2	9.4	5.3	8.2	10.8	10.7
Loans:							
Consumer	64.3	75.5	70.4	73.7	58.6	43.6	40.9
Home mortgages	5.1	4.4	4.8	6.3	8.2	20.2	22.1
Total loans	69.4	79.9	75.2	80.0	66.8	63.8	63.0
Miscellaneous	—	—	—	5.7	5.4	6.2	4.9
	100.0%	100.0%	100.0%	100.0%	100.0%	100.0%	100.0%

Source: Board of Governors of the Federal Reserve System, *Flow of Funds Accounts, Financial Assets and Liabilities,* various issues.

The mix of assets has changed over time, as is true of other depository institutions. In 1964, over 22 percent was invested in time deposits, 5 percent in checkable deposits and currency, and only 3 percent in securities. Consumer loans represented over 64 percent, while home mortgages were only 5 percent of total financial assets. Essentially, credit unions were highly liquid with almost 28 percent of assets in cash or cash equivalents. Consistent with the original purpose, consumer installment credit absorbed well over half of investable funds.

The emphasis on consumer credit was sustained through 1979. After federal credit unions were permitted to offer residential mortgages in 1977, these loans became an increasingly important component of the industry's balance sheet. The 1982 Garn–St Germain Act again enhanced mortgage market participation. As a result, by 1991, mortgage loans represented over 20 percent of the asset portfolio, up from 5 percent in 1964.

Nevertheless, total loans actually declined in proportional terms from a high of 80 percent of financial assets in 1980 to 63 percent in 1991, lower than the 1964 level. Time deposits and cash represented only 14 percent in 1991 as the industry has become significantly less liquid. The reduction in loans (6 percentage) and liquid assets (14 percentage) has been largely offset by higher proportional investments in money and capital market instruments. Federal funds and repurchase agreements constituted 7.5 percent in 1991, having played virtually no role through 1979. Investment securities (Treasury and government agency) represented almost 8 percentage points more in 1991 than in 1964. In this respect, credit union asset portfolio changes have mirrored those in the thrift industry, that is, lower investments in liquid assets and loans and higher investments in securities.

Liabilities

The liability section of the credit union industry balance sheet (Exhibit 20-5) has also reflected significant changes, though not as marked as those in the asset section. Unlike S&Ls and mutual savings banks, credit unions still have relatively little reliance on large time deposits. The most notable change is the increase in checkable shares and deposits making up 10 percent of the total in 1991 (there were no such facilities in 1964).

A *share account* is an equity claim on the assets of the credit union. However, the dividends paid on a share account are a stated percentage of the value of the account. Thus, a share account is more similar to a deposit than to a typical equity investment. In fact, according to generally accepted accounting principles (GAAP) share accounts are classified as liabilities, and the Internal Revenue Service considers share dividends received as interest income.

EXHIBIT 20-5 FINANCIAL LIABILITIES OF U.S. CREDIT UNIONS, 1964–1991

	1964	1969	1974	1979	1984	1989	1991
Financial liabilities (billions)	$9.9	$16.1	$31.1	$63.1	$113.0	$200.5	$222.0
Shares and deposits:							
Checkable	—	—	.3%	2.4%	8.4%	9.6%	10.1%
Small time and savings	82.8%	85.6%	88.2	88.1	81.7	80.0	79.2
Large time	—	—	—	.5	.7	1.3	1.4
Total shares and deposits	82.8	85.6	88.5	91.0	90.8	90.9	80.6
Miscellaneous	17.2	14.4	11.5	9.0	9.2	9.1	9.3
	100.0%	100.0%	100.0%	100.0%	100.0%	100.0%	100.0%

Source: Board of Governors of the Federal Reserve System, *Flow of Funds Accounts, Financial Assets and Liabilities,* various issues.

EXHIBIT 20-6 GROWTH RATES OF FINANCIAL ASSETS AND LIABILITIES OF THRIFTS AND CREDIT UNIONS, 1964–1991 (%)

	Assets			Liabilities		
Period	S&Ls	MSBs	CUs*	S&Ls	MSBs	CUs*
1964–1969	6.4	6.3	10.2	6.3	6.6	10.2
1969–1974	12.9	7.9	14.1	13.0	8.1	14.1
1974–1979	14.3	8.4	15.2	14.4	8.4	15.2
1979–1984	11.7	4.6	12.3	12.5	4.9	12.3
1984–1989	6.4	5.7	12.2	6.4	4.9	12.2
1989–1991	(11.6)	(1.1)	5.2	(10.4)	(0.3)	5.2

Abbreviations: S&Ls — savings and loan associations
MSBs — mutual savings banks
CUs — credit unions

*Since credit unions are purely mutual organizations, financial assets and liabilities are equal; i.e., there is no corporate equity.

Note: Calculations are average annual compound rates of growth implied by respective industry totals in this chapter and Chapter 19 for the years 1964, 1969, 1974, 1979, 1984, 1989, and 1991.

It is interesting to note that small time and savings accounts have not declined as dramatically in the credit union industry as in the thrift industry. In 1964, savings and loan associations (Exhibit 19-8) and mutual savings banks (Exhibit 19-10) funded 93 and 98 percent, respectively, of their operations with these instruments. By 1991 these proportions were down to 70 and 41 percent, respectively. On the other hand, credit unions have managed to finance from 79 (1991) to 88 percent (1974 and 1979) of assets with small time and savings deposits for the years shown. Further, reliance on small time and savings accounts does not appear to have hampered the growth of the industry.

Comparison of Growth Rates of Thrift Institutions

In fact, over the 27-year period ended 1991, financial assets of savings and loan associations and mutual savings banks increased at average annual rates of 8.5 and 6 percent, respectively.[2] As noted earlier, credit union assets grew at an average annual rate of 12.2 percent over the same period.

Exhibit 20-6 shows a comparison of industry growth rates for each of the 5-year periods from 1964 through 1989 and the 2-year period ended 1991. From 1969 through 1984, credit unions grew at double-digit rates roughly comparable to those in the savings and loan industry. However, while S&L asset and liability growth slowed to 6.4 percent in the 1984–1989 period, credit unions managed to sustain a 12.2 percent rate of growth. Average annual growth rates for mutual savings banks ranged from a low of 4.6 percent (assets, 1979–1984) to a high of 8.4 percent (1974–1979), consistently lower than either S&Ls or credit unions. In the 1989–1991 period, assets and liabilities of S&Ls and MSBs actually declined, while credit union assets grew 5 percent.

The credit union industry is growing in terms of assets and membership even as the number of institutions shrinks.

Comparison to Commercial Banks

Credit unions are also beginning to look more like commercial banks. Exhibits 20-7 and 20-8 compare the asset and liability composition of commercial banks and credit unions

[2]S&Ls: $(\$1{,}056.2\text{ bil.}/\$117.1\text{ bil.})^{1/27} - 1 = .0849$
MSBs: $(\$264.0\text{ bil.}/\$55.0\text{ bil.})^{1/27} - 1 = .0598$
See Exhibits 19-7 and 19-9.

EXHIBIT 20-7 ASSET COMPOSITION OF COMMERCIAL BANKS AND CREDIT UNIONS, 1964 AND 1991

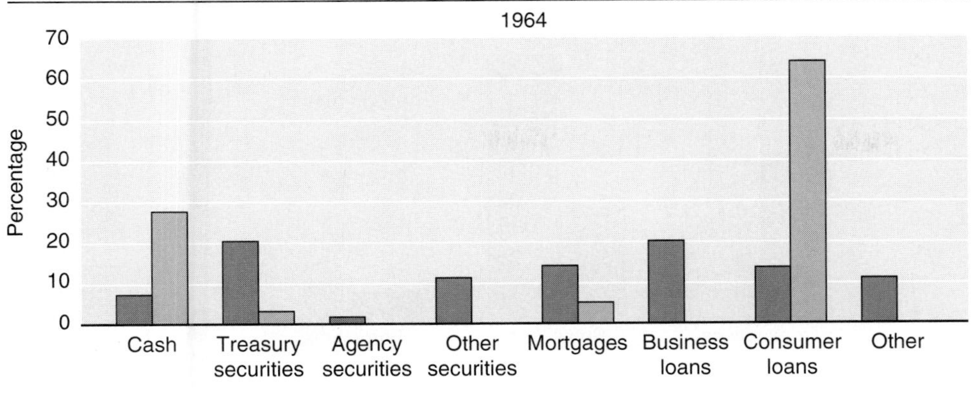

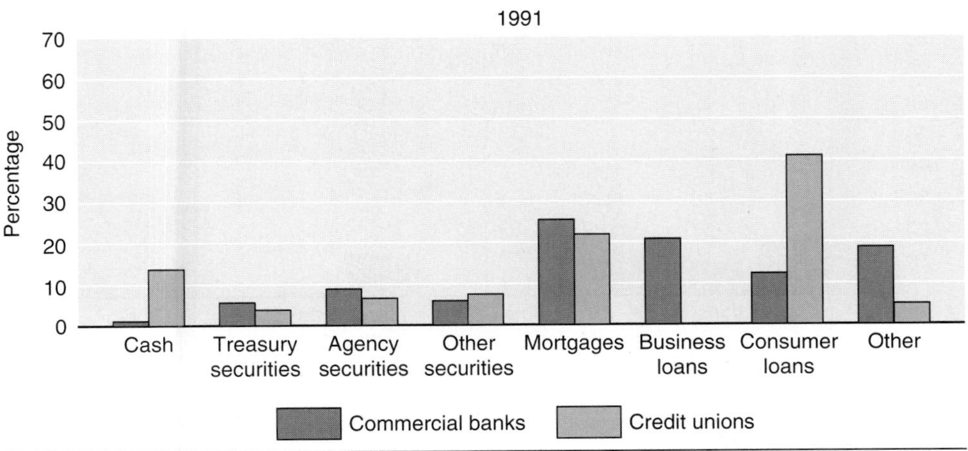

Source: Data from Board of Governors of the Federal Reserve System, *Flow of Funds Accounts, Assets and Liabilities,* various issues.

in 1964 and 1991. The biggest differences in asset mix are in the categories of cash holdings, business loans, and consumer loans. Credit unions are more liquid than commercial banks and, true to their tradition, concentrate more on consumer loans, with no business loans. However, the holdings of securities and mortgage loans are quite similar for the two institutions.

In the liability section of the balance sheet, the relative reliance on small time deposits has not changed significantly. Credit unions still have a greater reliance on them than banks. However, the transactions account balances (described below for credit unions) have converged in terms of share of total liabilities. Thus, when considering securities, mortgage loans, and transactions accounts, the industry balance sheet for credit unions is quite similar to that for commercial banks.

There are other similarities. Many credit unions (particularly the larger associations) now offer more advanced payment mechanisms, a development which has contributed to the industry's continued ability to attract and retain member funds. A *share draft* is a third-party payment mechanism, or transactions account. Since drafts are drawn on dividend-yielding membership shares, these accounts are analogous to N.O.W. accounts. In order to contain costs associated with share draft accounts, credit unions store drafts rather than return them to members.

EXHIBIT 20-8 LIABILITY COMPOSITION OF COMMERCIAL BANKS AND CREDIT UNIONS, 1964 AND 1991

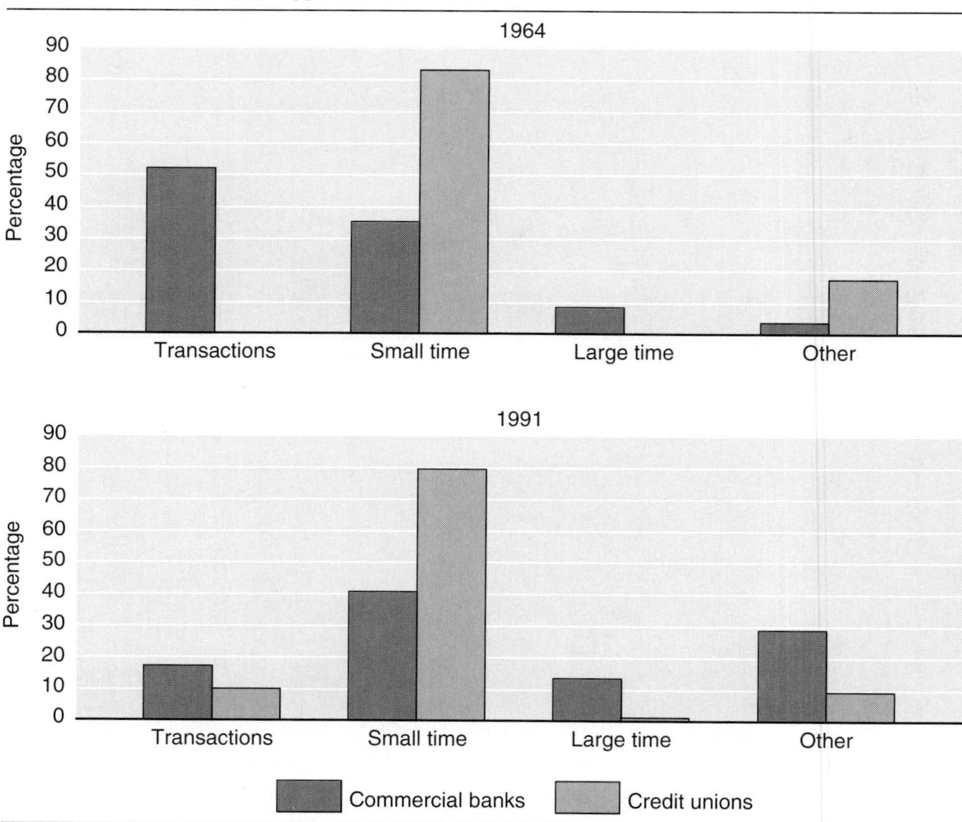

Source: Data from Board of Governors of the Federal Reserve System, *Flow of Funds Accounts, Assets and Liabilities,* various issues.

Automated teller machine (ATM) service is available through credit unions. As is true for other financial institutions, however, the feasibility of ATM service depends on the cost-benefit trade-off. To the extent that there are potentially large numbers of customers, ATMs can substantially enhance service at a modest cost on an average per-transaction basis. However, the small average size of credit unions can make the provision of this service particularly costly. Even the larger credit unions can realize significant economies of scale by participating in a shared ATM network.

CREDIT UNIONS AROUND THE WORLD

The credit union movement has reached every part of the world since Schulze and Raiffeisen began the experiment in the mid-1800s. As an illustration of the extent to which these associations have become established, consider the data for 1982 in Exhibit 20-9.

In 1982, over 175,000 credit unions operated worldwide with 153 million members. Asia accounted for approximately 71 percent of the organizations and 47 percent of members. Most of these were in India, where Boston merchant Edward Filene first learned of the movement. As of 1982, India accounted for 66 and 44 percent of all associations and members, respectively.

This implies that Indian credit unions, on average, are quite small with less than 600 members each in the early 1980s. Only African associations were smaller, with 140

EXHIBIT 20-9 CREDIT UNIONS AND MEMBERSHIP WORLDWIDE, 1982

	Credit unions		Membership	
Region/country	Number	%	Thousands	%
Asia*	125,832	70.8	71,937	47.0
United States	20,664	11.6	46,774	30.5
Europe	13,188	7.4	18,768	12.3
Canada	3,407	1.9	9,759	6.4
Africa	11,180	6.3	1,568	1.0
Latin America and the Caribbean	2,644	1.5	2,860	1.9
Australia and New Zealand	808	0.5	1,434	0.9
	177,723	100.0	153,100	100.0

*Of these totals for Asia, India represents 116,984 credit unions, or 65.8% of the worldwide total. Membership in India is 67.3 million, or 44% of the worldwide total.

Source: Dublin, Jack, and Selma M. Dublin, *Credit Unions in a Changing World; The Tanzania-Kenya Experience,* 1983, pp. 259–264.

members on average. Canadian and U.S. credit unions had much larger average memberships of 2864 and 2264, respectively. Average memberships in Europe, Latin America and the Caribbean, and Australia and New Zealand ranged from 1081 to 1775.

With respect to concentration of organizations, India, the United States, and Europe represented almost 85 percent of all associations and 87 percent of total membership. However, concentrations of shares and assets do not follow this pattern.

As shown in Exhibit 20-10, European credit unions held 58.2 percent of all shares and deposits, as well as 63.8 percent of total assets. Within Europe, Germany held 35 percent of worldwide resources. Given that Germany is the "home of the credit union," this is, perhaps, not a surprising result. With 3935 German associations in 1982, the average size in terms of total assets was $32.8 million,[3] much higher than the $3.6 million average in the United States.

The Netherlands, France, Austria, and Switzerland accounted for 25.6 percent of worldwide assets. In France and Switzerland, the average credit union controlled approxi-

[3]$129.18 billion/3935 credit unions = $32.8 million per credit union.

EXHIBIT 20-10 CREDIT UNION SHARES, LOANS, AND TOTAL ASSETS WORLDWIDE, 1982

	Shares/deposits		Loans		Total assets	
Region/country	Millions	%	Millions	%	Millions	%
Europe	$163,726.1	58.2	$146,200.0	62.2	$235,937.6	63.8
of which;						
Germany	104,117	37.0	85,816	36.5	129,180	34.9
Netherlands	21,068	7.5	31,205	13.3	44,747	12.1
France	12,926	4.6	7,544	3.2	18,189	4.9
Austria	9,431	3.3	9,479	4.0	24,349	6.6
Switzerland	6,213	2.2	4,436	1.9	7,511	2.0
Total*	153,755	54.6	138,480	58.9	222,976	60.5
United States	67,009.0	23.8	49,230.0	20.9	75,238.0	20.3
Canada	29,786.7	10.6	23,730.7	10.1	31,875.4	8.6
Asia	17,588.2	6.2	12,947.1	5.5	23,291.4	6.3
Australia and New Zealand	2,023.4	.7	1,773.8	.8	2,157.2	.6
Latin America and the Caribbean	1,062.5	.4	1,075.3	.5	1,326.8	.3
Africa	147.1	.1	101.8	—†	201.9	.1
	$281,343.0	100.0%	$235,058.7	100.0%	$370,028.3	100.0%

*These five countries represent the bulk of European credit union assets and liabilities.

†Less than 0.1%.

Source: Dublin, Jack, and Selma M. Dublin, *Credit Unions in a Changing World; The Tanzania-Kenya Experience,* 1983, pp. 259–264.

mately $6 million.[4] Austrian and Dutch associations were considerably larger. With 970 credit unions in the Netherlands, the average size was $46.1 million. The corresponding Austrian figures were 130 organizations and $187.3 million, respectively.

It is clear from the data above that the average European credit union, with $17.9 million in assets, is a larger organization than its U.S. counterpart. Also, in Canada, where credit unions were first introduced in North America, the average asset base was $9.4 million in 1982.

Excluding Africa, in the remaining regions, average assets ranged from $185,000 (Asia) to $2.7 million (Australia and New Zealand). Within Asia, the almost 117,000 Indian associations held assets totaling only $4.1 billion, yielding an average size of only $35,000. This low average is better understood when one considers the relatively low per-capita income levels in this part of the world.

In Africa, where income levels are the lowest in the world, we find even smaller associations. African countries operated 6.3 percent of all credit unions, but controlled only .1 percent of the movement's total assets. The average asset pool was $18,000. Unfortunately, as fragile as the African system is, the credit union is, in some cases, the only source of finance for its members in a relatively undeveloped economic environment.

SUMMARY

The credit union is a financial institution that began as a service organization for members, not unlike savings and loan associations and mutual savings banks. Over time, the latter have evolved into financial institutions that closely resemble commercial banks. They make business loans and invest in corporate securities. They market large time deposits in order to attract funds.

In contrast, credit unions have retained their service orientation and are the best example of cooperative banking in the United States. Their balance sheets are relatively simple, and small share accounts still dominate as the primary source of funds. While the industry is undergoing significant consolidation, assets under management have grown consistently since the early 1930s, with the exception of a brief period during World War II.

While credit unions are still small institutions when compared with banks and thrifts, the average size is growing as the number of institutions declines and total industry assets increase. And the competition between credit unions and banks is intensifying, because credit unions now offer consumers a wide variety of services including transactions accounts, retirement accounts, and mortgage loans. At the same time, credit unions have retained their volunteer work force and tax-exempt status, which has given them a significant cost advantage over commercial banks.

KEY TERMS

Central Liquidity Facility (CLF)
common bond
Credit Union National Association (CUNA)
CUNA Mutual Insurance Group
CUNA Service Group
Federal Credit Union Act of 1934
field of membership
Financial Institutions Reform Act of 1978
share account
U. S. Central Credit Union

END-OF-CHAPTER QUESTIONS

1. What is a common bond? In general, what are the three types of common bonds?
2. How do credit unions differ from savings and loan associations and mutual savings banks?

[4]In 1982, 3069 and 1207 credit unions operated in France and Switzerland, respectively.

3. In the mid-1800s, both Hermann Schulze and Friedrich Raiffeisen organized credit unions in Germany. Contrast the two types of associations.
4. In the United States, mutual savings banks and savings and loan associations were formed in the early 1800s. The first credit union was not organized until after the turn of the century. What events led to the introduction of credit unions in the United States?
5. Federal regulation of credit unions began in 1934, but there was no independent federal credit agency until 1970. Describe the private trade organizations that organized credit unions on a national basis in the face of this relative lack of federal involvement.
6. Compare the effects of the Great Depression on the credit union industry with those on the thrift industry. (Hint: Refer also to Chapter 19.)
7. In what ways did the federal legislation of 1980 and 1982 affect credit union operations?
8. Over time, credit unions have changed least among all depository institutions. Describe those changes that have occurred in the industry balance sheet.
9. In a global sense, where is the greatest concentration of resources held by credit unions?
10. Where are the largest credit unions in terms of average membership?
11. Present arguments for and against the continued exemption of credit unions from federal income taxation. Answer this question from the perspective first of the credit unions and then commercial banks.
12. In your opinion, why do you believe credit unions have enjoyed such a steady increase in membership over the years?

SELECTED REFERENCES

Board of Governors of the Federal Reserve System. *Flow of Funds Accounts, Financial Assets and Liabilities,* various issues.

Credit Union National Association Annual Report 1989, Madison, Wisconsin.

Dublin, Jack, and Selma M. Dublin. *Credit Unions in a Changing World, The Tanzania-Kenya Experience,* Wayne State University Press, Detroit, 1983.

Flannery, Mark J. *An Economic Evaluation of Credit Unions in the United States,* Federal Reserve Bank of Boston, 1974.

Friars, Eileen M., and Robert N. Gogel, Editors. *The Financial Services Handbook; Executive Insights and Solutions,* John Wiley and Sons, New York, 1987.

Havrilesky, Thomas, and Robert Schweitzer, Editors. *Contemporary Developments in Financial Institutions and Markets,* 2d ed., Harlan Davidson, Inc., Arlington Heights, Illinois, 1987.

Moody, J. Carroll, and Gilbert C. Fite. *The Credit Union Movement, Origins and Development, 1850–1970,* University of Nebraska Press, Lincoln, Nebraska, 1971.

Pugh, Olin S., and F. Jerry Ingram. *Credit Unions: A Movement Becomes an Industry,* Reston Publishing Company, Reston, Virginia, 1984.

U.S. Department of the Treasury. *Modernizing the Financial System; Recommendations for Safer, More Competitive Banks,* Washington, D.C., 1991.

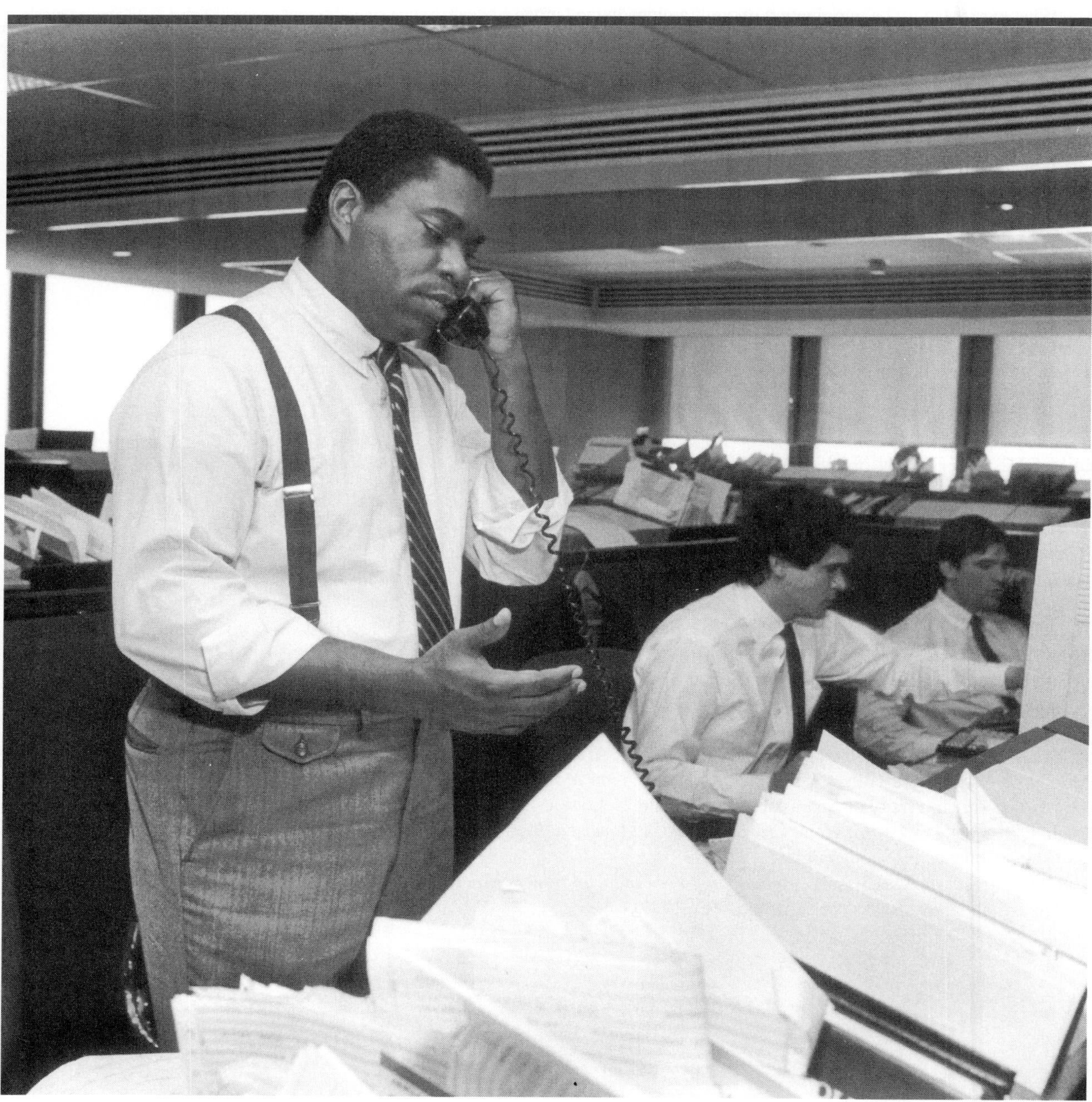

PART SIX

CONTRACTUAL NONBANK FINANCIAL INSTITUTIONS

CHAPTER 21

INVESTMENT COMPANIES

CHAPTER OUTLINE

THE NATURE OF INVESTMENT COMPANIES
- Closed-End Funds
- Mutual Funds
- Money Market Mutual Funds
- Growth of Mutual Funds

INVESTMENT COMPANY ORGANIZATION
- Financial Management
- Investors

SHARE PRICING
- Open-End Funds
  - Net asset value, sales charges, management fees, price volatility
- Closed-End Funds

INVESTMENT COMPANY REGULATION

MUTUAL FUND ASSETS
- Asset Mix
- Comparison to Commercial Banks

ORIGINS AND DEVELOPMENT OF INVESTMENT COMPANIES
- United Kingdom and United States
- Asia
- International Operations

INTERNATIONAL COMPARISONS:
- Italy
- Netherlands
- Australia
- Canada
- Germany
- France
- Japan
- Korea
- Hong Kong
- Singapore
- United Kingdom

CHAPTER OVERVIEW

This chapter:

- Compares and contrasts different forms of investment companies
- Describes investment company organizational structure
- Outlines regulatory issues
- Examines investment company asset composition
- Highlights development of investment companies in selected countries

Investment companies accept money (often small denominations) from individuals and others and invest these funds according to the company's investment philosophy.

Management and other fees have been deducted, profits from investing are passed through to the company's shareholders. During the 1970s and early 1980s, market rates of return increased sharply. These returns were passed through to owners of investment company shares, primarily money market mutual fund shares. During the same period, commercial banks and thrift institutions were unable to offer their small depositors the same market rates of return because of regulated deposit interest rate ceilings. Banks and thrifts suffered massive disintermediation. Assets of investment companies grew from $48 billion in 1969 to $1.1 trillion in 1991. In 22 years, the industry grew by more than twenty times its 1969 level. No other financial institutions have enjoyed this phenomenal growth. No other industry has been more of a threat to commercial banking.

THE NATURE OF INVESTMENT COMPANIES

An *investment company* is an organization through which individual investors purchase ownership interest in a well-diversified portfolio of securities.

Investment company:
A firm that is organized and operated for the exclusive purpose of purchasing the debt and/or equity of business organizations, government securities, municipal securities, or some combination of these.

When considering investing in the capital markets, an individual faces several potential problems:

- Knowledge of stocks and bonds may be limited.
- The amount of investable funds may be relatively small, enabling the purchase of relatively few issues.
- Each subsequent investment may require reevaluation of the holdings to ensure an appropriate mix.

To a large extent, investment companies offer viable solutions to these problems. An investment company portfolio is managed by professional investment advisers, who decide which securities to hold and in what proportions. Of course, these decisions must be consistent with the company's stated *investment philosophy.*

Investment philosophy:
An investment company's approach to investing in terms of types of securities, risk tolerance, average maturity of the portfolio, and emphasis on current income (interest or dividend income) or capital gains yield (change in market value of the securities).

Nevertheless, investors need not be concerned with day-to-day operations. Also, minimum investments may be as low as $250; that is, large amounts of investable funds are not necessary.

Because of this arrangement, the *control* of an investment company is even more likely to rest with management than is normally the case in a business organization. Further, the management team is often a relatively small group with considerable discretionary power over the firm's assets. Because of this power, state and federal regulations protect investors' funds.

Closed-End Funds

The shares of a *closed-end fund* are issued and exchanged much like the shares of other firms.

Closed-end fund:

An investment company that issues a fixed number of ownership claims, or shares. After these shares have been sold initially, investors who wish to purchase shares must buy them from other investors who own them.

That is, once issued, shares of a closed-end fund trade on secondary markets (where existing securities are exchanged among investors) at prices that are determined by factors of supply and demand.

The amount of capitalization (long-term financing) of closed-end funds is relatively fixed. New shares are sometimes issued to distribute capital gains, much like a stock dividend. Closed-end funds may also issue senior securities such as debentures or preferred stock, although these securities are now less common.

A few closed-end funds are *dual-purpose* companies in that one class of shares is entitled to all interest and dividend income of the portfolio and the other class of shares earns only capital gains. The former are *income shares* and the latter, *capital shares.*

Income shares:

Shares of a closed-end investment company that receive only the interest and dividend income from the fund's asset investments.

Capital shares:

Shares of a closed-end investment company that receive only the increase (or decrease) in market value of the fund's asset investments.

Income shares are comparable to preferred stock, with a minimum, cumulative dividend. Income shares are also entitled to any income that the portfolio earns (for example, premiums earned if the fund sells options on its securities). But income shares are callable after a number of years. In this sense, income shares are securities with a limited life. The capital shares of dual-purpose funds benefit from the use of leverage (fixed-rate debt), because the amount paid to debt holders does not increase even if assets earn a higher rate. However, capital shareholders must rely on increases in the market value of the portfolio for return.

With respect to portfolio composition, more than half the closed-end funds in the United States (less than 200 in total) are bond investment companies. The next largest group is composed of diversified funds that invest in a wide range of stocks and/or bonds. Other closed-end companies may specialize in a particular industry or in securities issued via private placement.[1] Total value of the asset portfolio is relatively stable. Managers of closed-end funds must make necessary adjustments within the essentially fixed portfolios to accommodate changing market conditions, required dividend payments, and other distributions to shareholers. (See Exhibit 21-1.)

A *real estate investment trust (REIT)* is a special type of closed-end fund that invests in real estate loans or in physical real estate. Shareholders in REITs receive the income attributable to these investments—interest or rental income. These investment companies originated during the late 1960s and reached their peak importance in 1974 with financial assets of $18 billion under management, much of it in the form of construction and development loans, that is, loans on incomplete projects. Then many of the borrowers default-

[1]An investment company may purchase private placement securities directly from the issuer or from another investor. In either case, the transaction is privately negotiated. Usually, a letter documents the transfer and stipulates that the securities are to be held as an investment and not sold for some specified period of time. An advantage of private placements is that the investment company may be able to make the purchase at a price below the market value of comparable, publicly traded securities.

EXHIBIT 21-1 SELECTED CLOSED-END U.S. INVESTMENT COMPANIES

Company	Year organized	Type of company	Net assets, 12/31/88*
Adams Express	1929	Diversified (common stock)	455.8
American Capital Bond Fund	1970	Bonds (nonconvertible corporate and government securities)	224.2
ASA Limited	1958	Specialized (common stock, South African mining)	481.3
Baker, Fentress & Co.	1960	Nondiversified (common stock)	406.3
Central Securities Corp.	1929	Diversified (common stock)	118.9
Fort Dearborn Income Securities	1972	Bonds (at least 75% in investment-grade debt securities)	101.0
Gabelli Equity Trust	1986	Nondiversified (common stock)	484.8
General American Investors	1929	Diversified (common stock)	301.8
John Hancock Income Securities	1973	Bonds (investment-grade debt securities, 75%, and income-producing preferred and common stock)	144.2
John Hancock Investors	1971	Bonds (up to 50% in direct placements)	142.2
Lehman Corporation	1929	Diversified (common stock)	885.4
Mass Mutual Corporate Investors	1971	Bonds (long-term debt securities issued through direct placement)	127.8
Montgomery Street Income Securities	1973	Bonds (at least 70% in investment-grade debt securities)	145.8
Niagara Share Corp.	1929	Diversified (common stock)	191.2
Petroleum & Resources Corp.	1929	Specialized (common stock and fixed-income securities of petroleum and energy-related companies)	278.3
Source Capital	1968	Diversified (primarily common stock and securities convertible into common stock)	285.0
Trans American Income Shares	1972	Bonds (at least 80% invested in fixed-income securities)	117.1
Tri-Continental Corp	1929	Diversified (common stock)	1301.5
Zweig Fund	1986	Diversified (common stock)	356.7

*Millions of dollars.
Source: Wiesenberger financial Services, *Investment Companies 1985* and *Investment Companies 1989.*

ed, and REITs became less popular, with financial assets for all REITs declining to $3 billion in the early 1980s. Stronger real estate markets in the mid-1980s helped spur interest in these funds. By 1991, financial assets of all REITs stood at $13 billion.

Mutual Funds

An investment company that makes new shares available on a continuous basis and *redeems* (buys back) outstanding shares at any time is an *open-end* investment company, or a *mutual fund.*

Mutual fund:
An open-end investment company, that is, one which issues new shares whenever investors wish to buy them. Likewise, a mutual fund redeems shares whenever investors wish to sell them.

Because of this arrangement, the capital of a mutual fund is not fixed. Instead, total capital will increase if more new shares are purchased than redeemed. Conversely, total capital declines when shareholders surrender more shares than are newly issued within a given period of time.

Even though easy redemption provides liquidity to an investor, a mutual fund investment should not be viewed as a bank deposit. As is also true with closed-end funds, there is no *guarantee* that the principal investment in a mutual fund will not decrease or that current income (interest and/or dividends) will be earned at a specified level.[2] In most cases, mutual fund investments should be considered medium- to long-term arrangements (5 to 10 years or more).

Investment philosophy varies from one fund to another. However, there are certain broad categories into which most funds can be placed.

Growth funds concentrate on appreciation of the value of the fund's portfolio. At the other end of the spectrum, *income funds* emphasize security investments with high periodic interest and dividend payments. Even within these categories, the investment philosophy can differ.

Some growth funds may seek *maximum capital gains* with little or no current income. Others may target *long-term price appreciation* with a *secondary focus* on periodic payments. The greater the emphasis on capital gains, however, the more risky the fund's investments are likely to be.

Income funds may invest primarily in stocks *or* bonds. Corporate stocks with consistent records of high dividend payments are selected for *common stock income funds. Senior securities income funds* invest in corporate bonds and preferred stock. If the income fund is permitted to invest in *either* stock or bonds, it is a *flexible income fund.*

Balanced funds hold roughly equivalent proportions of stocks and bonds. The rationale for a balanced fund is that shareholders may realize gains during periods of both economic expansion and contraction. Expansion is frequently accompanied by inflationary pressures that tend to be reflected in higher common stock prices in the long run. When the economy contracts, interest rates usually fall, boosting bond prices and, therefore, the value of the bond portfolio.[3]

Specialized mutual funds may target a particular sector for investment. For example, some hold only public utility stocks, others only high-technology stocks. International funds often select only the highest-quality stocks and bonds in the countries covered. Several specialized funds hold only U.S. government securities or tax-exempt bonds. Exhibit 21-2 contains twenty-two classifications of mutual funds and the number of each in 1990.

From management's perspective, a mutual fund portfolio is a more fluid pool of funds than a closed-end investment company. The size of a mutual fund is determined by shareholder purchases and redemptions. Management must invest large cash inflows as quickly as possible in a way that is consistent with the fund's investment philosophy. At the same time, the fund must always be liquid enough to meet unanticipated redemption requests. (See also Exhibit 21-3.)

Money Market Mutual Funds

Money market mutual funds are a subset of the broader category of open-end investment companies or mutual funds.

[2]This statement excludes income shares of dual-purpose funds discussed in the previous section.

[3]It should be noted that unanticipated inflation can *depress* stock prices in the short term. Also, as long as earnings forecasts are not adversely affected, the lower interest rates that are associated with slower economic activity can improve stock prices. See Chapter 4 for a discussion of stock and bond pricing.

EXHIBIT 21-2 TYPES AND NUMBER OF MUTUAL FUNDS 1990

Type	Objectives/composition	Number
Aggressive growth	Maximum capital gains	208
Balanced	1. Conserving initial principal 2. Paying current income 3. Promoting long-term growth of principal and income	66
Corporate bond	High income from corporate bonds	57
Flexible portfolio	Respond to economic conditions with no restrictions on investment	55
Ginnie Mae (GNMA)	Mortgage-backed securities	53
Global bond	Debt securities worldwide	37
Global equity	Equity securities worldwide	52
Growth	Common stock of well-established firms	368
Growth and income	Combining capital gains and current income	281
High-yield bond	At least ⅔ portfolio in below-investment-grade corporate bonds	106
Income bond	Obtaining high income from a combination of corporate and government bonds	114
Income, equity	Obtaining high income by investing in equities that provide a high-dividend yield	78
Income, mixed	Obtaining high income by investing in corporate bonds, government bonds, and high-dividend equities	88
International	At least ⅔ portfolio to be invested in equities of companies outside the United States	94
Long-term municipal bond	Long-term bonds issued by states and other political subdivisions for public purposes (interest income exempt from federal income taxation)	192
Money market	Investments in short-term, stable, money market instruments	508
Option, income	High income from high-dividend equities combined with option trading on those equities	8
Precious metals and gold	At least ⅔ in securities associated with gold, silver, and other precious metals	38
Short-term municipal bond	Short-term municipal securities, also called tax-exempt money market funds	135
State municipal bond (long-term)	Same as long-term municipal bond except that securities are issued by one state only	272
State municipal bond (short-term)	Same as short-term municipal bond except that securities are issued by one state only	103
U.S. government income	Combination of U.S. Treasury and government agency securities	195
		3108

Source: Investment Company Institute, *Mutual Fund Factbook 1991.*

Money market mutual fund:

An open-end investment company whose assets consist primarily of Treasury bills, negotiable certificates of deposit, Eurodollar deposits, commercial paper, and bankers' acceptances.

Several factors distinguish money market funds from other mutual funds:

- Average maturity of the asset portfolio
- Lower risk of the asset portfolio
- The relative importance of denomination intermediation in the growth of money market funds
- The rate of growth of money market mutual funds

EXHIBIT 21-3 SELECTED U.S. MUTUAL FUNDS

Fund	Year organized	Minimum initial investment	Investment*		Net assets, 12/31/88†
			Policy	Objective	
Affiliated Fund	1934	$250	CG	G, I	$3,267.0
American Capital Government Securities	1984	500	GS	I	5,238.1
Dean Witter U.S. Government Trust	1984	1000	GS	I	10,324.7
Drefus T/E Bond Fund	1976	2500	Bond	TF	3,346.6
Fidelity Equity Income Fund	1966	1000	Flex	I, G	4,064.9
Fidelity Magellan Fund	1962	1000	CS	MCG	8,971.1
Fidelity Puritan Fund	1946	1000	Flex	I, G	4,295.5
Franklin Calif. T/F Fund	1977	100	Bond	TF	8,434.0
Franklin Federal T/F Inc.	1983	100	Bond	TF	3,458.1
Franklin U.S. Government Series	1970	100	GS	I	11,649.9
IDS High Yield T/E Fund	1979	2000	Bond	TF	4,069.9
Investment Co. of America	1933	250	CS	G, I	4,119.0
Investment Port– Government Plus	1984	250	GS	I	6,247.3
Kemper U.S. Government Securities	1979	1000	GS	I	4,288.1
Lifetime Government Income Plus Tr.	1986	1000	GS	I	3,087.7
Merrill Lynch Federal Securities	1984	1000	GS	I	3,124.9
Pioneer II	1969	25	CS	G, I	3,762.0
Prudential Bache Government Plus	1983	1000	GS	I	3,913.1
Putnam High Income Government	1985	500	GS	I	8,824.7
Templeton World Fund, Inc.	1977	500	CS	G	3,921.5
Van Kampen Merritt U.S. Government	1984	1500	GS	I	3,820.3
Windsor Fund	1958	1500	CS	G, I	5,826.0

*Bond: primarily bonds
CG: capital gain
CS: primarily common stock
Flex: flexible; usually, but not necessarily, balanced
GS: primarily government securities
G: growth
I: income
MCG: maximum capital gain
TF: tax-free municipal bonds
†Millions of dollars.
Note: Money market mutual funds have been excluded.
Source: Wiesenburger Financial Services, *Investment Companies 1989,* pp. 88–136.

The average *maturity* of the investment portfolio is short. Money market fund assets are invested in short-term, highly liquid securities, such as Treasury securities, large-denomination bank deposits, and commercial paper.

Because these funds invest only in short-term, high-quality instruments, risk to shareholders is considerably lower as compared with common stock and long-term bond funds. This second distinguishing characteristic, *lower risk,* makes money market mutual funds a close substitute for bank deposits. While they are not federally insured, typical fund investments have historically low default rates.

Of course, it is true that individuals can invest directly in Treasury bills and other short-term instruments. However, the minimum denomination for a Treasury bill investment is $10,000. In the case of a negotiable certificate of deposit, the minimum is $100,000. Thus, *denomination intermediation* provided by money market funds is a particularly valuable attribute.[4]

In addition, money market fund balances can usually be withdrawn via check. Minimum check amounts are often $500 to discourage using the account as a transactions account. Nevertheless, the combination of convenient use, relatively safe fund investments, and high yield when compared with bank deposits leads to the third distinguishing characteristic. The money market fund industry has experienced phenomenal *growth* in recent years.

In fact, there was no money market mutual fund industry before the 1970s. Even in 1974, only $2.4 billion in assets were held in these investment companies. High and volatile market rates of interest during the late 1970s and early 1980s, together with low, regulated bank deposit interest rates, created enormous demand for small-denomination, higher-yielding investments. Before the 1980 Depository Institutions Deregulation and Monetary Control Act, small depositors could earn only 5 percent on savings, with *no interest* payable on demand deposits. A minimum of $100,000 was necessary in order to earn higher rates available on jumbo CDs.

At the same time, money market rates averaged 16 percent in 1981. Not surprising, investors poured billions of dollars into money market mutual funds. By 1982, industry assets totaled more than $200 billion. Legalization of the bank money market deposit account (with interest rates tied to money market rates) in 1982 attracted many investors back to commercial banks, and money market fund balances dropped below $200 billion. However, this was only a temporary setback. By 1991, the total was over $500 billion.

In the 17 years ended 1991, money market mutual fund assets grew at an average annual compound rate of 38 percent [($551.7 billion/$2.4 billion)$^{1/17}$ − 1]. Over the same period, bank deposits and other mutual fund investments increased at rates of 8 [($2299.5 billion/$650.6 billion)$^{1/17}$ − 1] and 19 percent [($643 billion/$35.2 billion)$^{1/17}$ − 1] respectively.[5]

Growth of Mutual Funds

Assets of mutual funds have grown faster than assets of commercial banks. While the commercial bank industry is consolidating in terms of the number of banks, the number of mutual funds grew substantially during the 1980s.

Exhibit 21-5 shows that the total number of funds grew from 564 in 1980 to 3108 by 1990. The majority of these are long-term funds, that is, stock, bond, and income funds. These increased from 458 to 2362 over the period shown in Exhibit 21-5. This is an annual increase of 18 percent [(2362/458)$^{1/10}$ − 1]. Short-term funds include regular money market funds and tax-exempt money market funds (short-term municipal bonds). The number of short-term funds grew even faster, from 106 (564–458) in 1980 to 746 (3108–2362) in 1990. This is an average growth rate of 22 percent [(746/106)$^{1/10}$ − 1].

No other financial institution has experienced these rates of growth. This trend reflects:

- More reliance on nonbank financial institutions by the investing public
- Increased sophistication of investors in terms of their knowledge of and appreciation for alternatives to commercial bank services

[4]See Chapter 1 for a discussion of intermediation functions.

[5]It should also be noted that the assets of closed-end investment companies have exhibited a somewhat different growth pattern. During the two 10-year periods ended 1974 and 1984, closed-end fund assets grew at average annual rates of 6 and 1.8 percent, respectively. However, from 1984 through 1988, the average annual increase was 57.2 percent, bringing the average growth rate for the 15 years ended 1988 to 12.5 percent.

EXHIBIT 21-4 SELECTED U.S. MONEY MARKET MUTUAL FUNDS

Fund	Year organized	Minimum initial investment	Net assets 12/31/88*
Cash Equivalent Fund: Money Market Portfolio	1979	$1,000	$5,658.6
CMA Money Fund	1977	20,000	19,615.8
Daily Cash Accumulated Fund	1978	500	3,133.0
Dean Witter/Sears Liquid Assets	1975	5,000	8,336.9
Dreyfus Liquid Assets	1974	2,500	7,304.1
Fidelity Cash Reserves	1979	1,000	10,550.6
Institutional Liquid Assets: Prime Obligations Portfolio	1976	50,000	3,800.1
Kemper Money Market Fund: Money Market Portfolio	1974	1,000	5,358.5
Merrill Lynch Ready Assets Trust	1975	5,000	9,130.3
Merrill Lynch Retirement Reserves	1982	—†	3,366.6
Paine Webber Cash Fund	1978	5,000	3,841.5
Prudential-Bache Money Mart Assets	1976	1,000	5,320.6
Shearson Lehman Hutton Daily Dividend	1979	2,500	11,516.3
Shearson Lehman Hutton Gov't & Agencies	1980	2,500	3,301.2
T. Rowe Price Prime Reserve Fund	1976	2,000	3,751.0
Temporary Investment Fund	1973	1,000	4,936.9
Trust for S/T U.S. Government Obligations	1975	100,000	4,095.5
Trust for U.S. Treasury Obligations	1979	100,000	5,399.1
Vanguard Money Market Trust: Prime Portfolio	1975	1,000	7,018.9

*Millions of dollars.
†No minimum initial investment.
Note: The investment objective of all these funds is income.
Source: Wiesenburger Financial Services, *Investment Companies 1989,* pp. 88–136.

As investors continue to become more involved in financial planning, they will continue to search for the combination of product and service that best suits their individual needs. As the mutual fund industry develops varied financial alternatives, it becomes more attractive. If commercial banks are constrained from competing in this way by law and regulation, they will become less attractive. The competition is intense, and the threat to commercial banks is real.

EXHIBIT 21-5 NUMBER OF MUTUAL FUNDS, 1980–1990

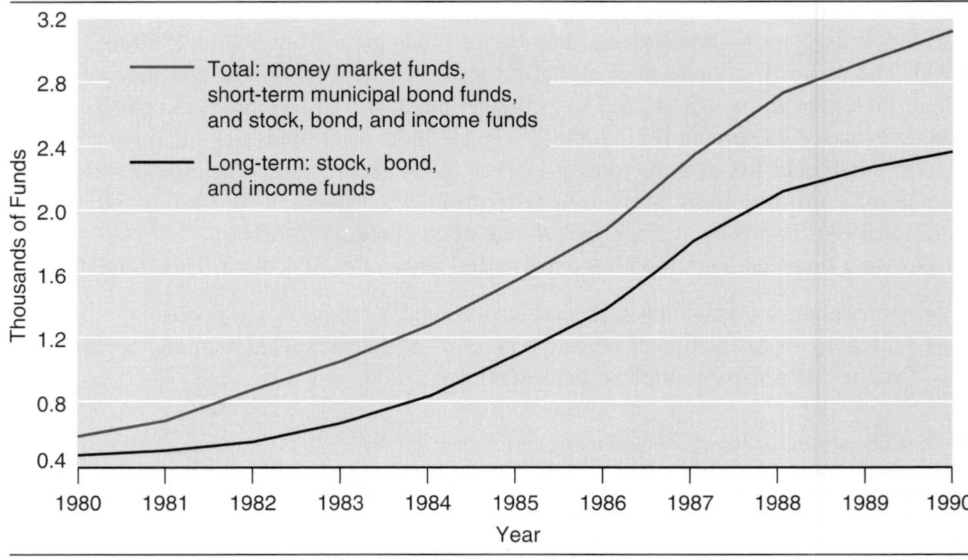

Source: Data from Investment Company Institute, *Mutual Fund Factbook 1991.*

Every investment company has an *investment adviser. Securities brokers* execute purchases and sales as directed by the investment adviser. *Investment company distributors* sell new shares to the public, in the case of open-end companies. *Shareholders* invest in the stock of the investment company.

Financial Management

Investment advisers may be individuals, partnerships, or corporations.

Investment adviser:
The party that makes asset investment decisions for an investment company. These decisions must conform with the company's stated investment philosophy.

An investment company is typically owned by a large number of shareholders with relatively little ownership control. The adviser, on the other hand, is likely to be a more closely held organization with significant ownership control. In addition, it is not uncommon for an adviser to provide physical facilities, clerical support, and bookkeeping service to its client investment company. Investment advisers are professional money managers. However, on average, the performance of investment companies is not better than the market as a whole. For example, for the 10 years ended 1990, the S&P 500, a broad-based stock index, rose an average of 13.9 percent per year. During the same period, stock mutual funds provided their investors an average annual return of 11.5 percent. Investment companies *do offer* diversification benefits along with denomination intermediation. At the same time, it has *not* been shown that mutual funds consistently "beat the market."

Securities broker:
In the context of an investment company, the party that executes the securities trades (purchases and sales) that have been initiated by the investment adviser.

Often, the *broker* selected to execute investment portfolio transactions is affiliated with the adviser. A bank or trust company is usually selected as custodian for portfolio securities. (See Exhibit 21-6.)

EXHIBIT 21-6 SELECTED U.S. INVESTMENT COMPANY ADVISERS-MANAGERS

Adviser-manager	Location
American Capital Management	Houston, Tex.
Capital Research & Management	Los Angeles, Calif.
Dean Witter Reynolds InterCapital, Inc.	New York, N.Y.
Dreyfus Corporation	New York, N.Y.
E.F. Hutton & Co.	New York, N.Y.
Fidelity Management & Research Co.	Boston, Mass.
Investors Diversified Services	Minneapolis, Minn.
Kemper Financial Services	Chicago, Ill.
Mass. Financial Services	Boston, Mass.
Merrill Lynch Asset Management	New York, N.Y.
Provident Institutional Management	Wilmington, Del.
Putnam Management Co.	Boston, Mass.
Standard Fire Insurance Co.	Pittsburgh, Pa.
T. Rowe Price Associates	Baltimore, Md.
Wellington Management	Boston, Mass.

Note: Each of these advisers-managers held at least $5 billion under management at year-end 1984.
Source: Weisenberger Financial Services, *Investment Companies 1985.*

EXHIBIT 21-7 MARKETING MUTUAL FUNDS THROUGH COMMERCIAL BANKS

The mutual fund industry has embarked on a number of ventures with commercial banks to facilitate share distribution. From their own perspective, commercial banks may offer their clients a wider range of services by also selling diversified investment instruments. Potential bank customers include individual retirement account or Keogh plan account owners and discount brokerage clients.

Since 1984, Fidelity Investments has offered a collaborative program for commercial banks through which more than fifty mutual funds are available. When a participatory bank has selected the products that it wishes to offer, the institution receives a complete marketing package from Fidelity with advertising material, press releases, brochures, and other promotional items. Alternatively, the bank may design its own marketing package. Through this arrangement, Fidelity gains access to a large customer base. The commercial bank enters a market in which it may earn significant fee income as a "middleman."

Unlike Fidelity, Dreyfus Corporation encourages its commercial bank "partners" to market funds with their own private labels. A typical arrangement is for the bank to form an investment management subsidiary that acts as investment adviser and manager. Because the 1933 Glass-Steagall Act prohibits banks from distributing mutual funds, Dreyfus provides the required disclosure material and executes the transactions.

As deregulation of financial services continues, it is likely that commercial banks will become more involved in the securities industry. Mutual funds are ideally suited for the small investors that constitute a significant share of retail banking clientele.

Source: Coler, Mark, and Ellis Ratner, *Financial Services—Insiders' Views of the Future,* 1988, pp. 46–48.

Distribution of new shares may be the responsibility of a separate organization or may be accomplished by the investment company itself.

Investment company distributor:
The party that markets the shares of an investment company to the public.

In general, larger investment companies employ their own sales force for new share distribution. Such a sales force is a *captive* or *dedicated* sales force. Alternatively, the investment company may avoid employing a distributor by advertising directly to the public through direct mail or other means. Most often, however, shares are distributed through *securities brokers* and *dealers* as are other securities. Distribution is a critical function since the sale of new shares is the primary source of asset growth for an open-end company. (See Exhibit 21-7.)

Investors

Since there are some 63 million mutual fund shareholder accounts, the average number of shareholders in an open-end investment company is approximately 20,000. The average account balance is just under $20,000. Thus, the average size of an open-end investment company is roughly $400 million. Specific mutual fund asset portfolios range from less than $1 million to over $10 billion.

Initially, individuals owned virtually all mutual fund shares. As can be seen in Exhibits 21-8 and 21-9, individuals still account for the vast majority of mutual fund holdings. Nevertheless, nonfinancial corporations, life insurance companies, and private pen-

EXHIBIT 21-8 INVESTORS IN U.S. MUTUAL FUNDS, 1964–1991*

	1964	1969	1974	1979	1984	1989	1991
Mutual fund financial liabilities (shares in billions of dollars)	$29.1	$47.6	$35.2	$51.8	$136.7	$486.3	$643.0
Investors:							
Households	97.6%	95.8%	90.6%	86.3%	86.1%	86.7%	84.6%
Nonfinancial corporations	1.0	1.5	2.3	2.1	5.3	3.7	2.5
Life insurance companies	.4	1.2	1.7	1.8	2.2	2.9	4.6
Private pension plans	1.0	1.5	5.4	9.8	6.4	6.7	8.3
	100.0%	100.0%	100.0%	100.0%	100.0%	100.0%	100.0%

*Excludes money market mutual funds.
Source: Board of Governors of the Federal Reserve System, *Flow of Funds Accounts, Financial Assets and Liabilities,* various issues.

sion plans held over 15 percent of non-money market mutual fund shares in 1991, or $99 billion. In addition, these firms held money market mutual fund investments amounting to 11 percent of industry shares, or $61 billion.

SHARE PRICING

Open-End Funds

Net Asset Value In an open-end investment company, the price of a share is dictated by the value of the investment portfolio. The *net asset value per share* is the basis for pricing.

Net asset value per share (NAV):
Market value of investment company assets *less* liabilities (net assets) *divided* by the number of shares outstanding.

Since asset market values change daily, so does the NAV. An investor who purchases (or redeems) shares pays (or receives) the NAV next computed after the order is received. Price determination occurs at least once a day, at the time that the New York Stock Exchange closes.

Price quotations are the *bid* and *asked* prices. The bid is the price at which shares may be redeemed and is usually the NAV. In some cases, a fund may charge a small redemption fee, which is reflected in the bid price. The asked, or purchase, price is the maximum amount that an investor would be required to pay for a mutual fund share.

EXHIBIT 21-9 INVESTORS IN U.S. MONEY MARKET MUTUAL FUNDS, 1974–1991*

	1974	1979	1984	1989	1991
Money market fund financial liabilities (shares in billions of dollars)	$2.4	$45.2	$233.6	$363.8	$551.7
Investors:					
Households	100.0%	88.5%	86.6%	89.5%	88.9%
Nonfinancial corporations	—	6.6	6.9	5.9	4.2
Life insurance companies	—	2.2	3.0	2.1	2.2
Private pension funds	—	2.7	3.5	2.5	4.7
	100.0%	100.0%	100.0%	100.0%	100.0%

*Prior to the 1970s, money market mutual funds did not exist.
Source: Board of Governors of the Federal Reserve System, *Flow of Funds Accounts, Financial Assets and Liabilities,* various issues.

Sales Charges The asked price includes a *sales charge,* or *load.*

Sales charge (load):
A sales commission that is paid by purchasers of mutual fund shares.

The load compensates the national distributor, the local firm, and the salesperson who executes the investor's order. Generally, this sales charge, or front-end load, ranges from 4.5 to 8.5 percent.

Also, some funds assess on *annual distribution fee.* This is called a *12b-1 fee,* named for the Securities and Exchange Commission (SEC) rule that permits it. The 12b-1 fee is 1.25 percent or less of the assets under management, spread proportionately among shareholders. This fee is used to pay for advertising or may substitute for the front-end load.

In addition, a *contingent deferred sales charge* may apply. Assessment of this sales charge occurs only if the investor redeems shares before a specified period elapses. Often, the contingent sales charge gradually declines after the specified period so that no fee is assessed for redemptions after a substantially longer period of time.

There are exceptions to these general rules. One exception is the group of investment companies that do not maintain a sales force and, therefore, assess little or no sales charge. Another exception is the practice of providing a quantity discount to investors for large purchases. For example, if an investor purchases shares worth less than $10,000, the sales charge may be 8 percent. Purchases equal to or greater than $10,000 but less than $25,000 may qualify for 7.5 percent sales charge. The sliding scale continues to decline to some minimum percentage which may be as low as 0 percent or as high as 1.25 percent. The minimums generally apply for purchases in excess of $250,000.

Management Fees In addition to sales charges when shares are purchased initially or redeemed, pricing is affected by *management fees.*

Management fee:
A annual fee charged to an investment company by its investment adviser for services rendered.

A management fee compensates the fund's adviser for making appropriate investment decisions, providing clerical and administrative support, and, generally, operating the company. The basis of the management fee is total net asset value. The typical fee is 1 percent or less of average net asset value per year. Management fees and other expenses are deducted from investment portfolio income before distributions are made to shareholder accounts.

Price Volatility With the exception of money market funds, price volatility will be linked to the average maturity of investment company assets. Assets held in money market funds are quite short term and, thus, not as sensitive to market interest rate changes. Further, the standard price for a money market share is $1. Long-term bond fund prices will be particularly sensitive to changes in market interest rates, just as the underlying bonds themselves are. In general, price volatility due to interest rate change declines as the average maturity of fund assets is reduced.

Closed-End Funds

Prices of closed-end investment companies can be above or below net asset value, since market forces of supply and demand determine price movement. However, more often than not, closed-end shares sell below NAV, that is, at a discount.

$$D = (\text{NAV} - \text{MV})/\text{NAV} \quad (1)$$

where D = discount from NAV
NAV = net asset value per share
MV = market value per share

Several possible reasons why closed-end investment company shares frequently sell at a discount have been proposed. They include:

- If the company were liquidated, substantial costs would be incurred, including severance packages for officers and market value dilution in the event of large asset sales.
- Management fees and expenses must be satisfied before investment income can be distributed to shareholders.
- The market for closed-end company shares may not be as large as the market for shares of the underlying companies.

While closed-end investment company shares *may* sell at a premium, *discounts* of 5 to 20 percent are not uncommon.

INVESTMENT COMPANY REGULATION

Investment companies are regulated at both state and federal levels. An investment company is incorporated at the state level. While a few companies are business trusts, most are corporations. However, as long as an investment company distributes at least 90 percent of its income during the year to shareholders, it is not subject to corporate income tax. "Blue sky" state laws protect investors who believe that they have received insufficient or inaccurate information with regard to a specific company. In some states, laws and regulations govern share pricing and commissions. These laws pertain to investment companies that operate within state borders.

The federal *Securities Act of 1933* governs the initial sales of securities to the public, including investment company shares. This law was enacted because of industry abuses during the 1920s that contributed to the stock market crash of 1929, which was then followed by the Great Depression. The SEC reviews the *registration statement* for accuracy and completeness. The registration statement details all pertinent management and financial data with respect to the securities offering. The SEC does not rule on the desirability of the new securities but determines the adequacy of disclosure. The *prospectus* is a shorter version of the registration statement and must be made available to every prospective purchaser. If it is later found that any material information was omitted or misrepresented, injured parties may pursue legal means to recover financial damages.

The *Investment Company Act of 1940* was enacted to further protect investors. The specific provisions cover the following aspects of investment company operation:

- Persons not affiliated with the company adviser must be included on the board of directors.
- Financial transactions between the investment company and advisers-managers (as principals) must be approved by the SEC.
- Shareholders must approve any change in the company's basic investment philosophy.
- Management contracts (for investment adviser, securities broker, and distributor) must be approved by a majority of shareholders, and the initial term of such contract may not exceed 2 years. Thereafter, the board of directors or a majority of shareholders must approve annual contract renewals.
- Redeemable shares must be sold at the price indicated in the prospectus.

The 1970 amendment to the Investment Company Act addressed the fairness of management fees and sales charges. Prior to 1970, a shareholder claim of excessive fees could not be upheld unless the amount was so large that it amounted to *corporate waste.* The 1970 amendment relaxed this criterion to *breach of fiduciary duty.* This change was motivated by a belief on the part of lawmakers that the normal .5 percent of net assets constituted excessive compensation, particularly in light of the rapid growth of the industry and the average size of the funds themselves. Recall that the average size of a mutual fund is $400 million. A management fee of .5 percent of net assets amounts to $2 million.

MUTUAL FUND ASSETS

Asset Mix

Exhibits 21-10 and 21-11 show the mix of mutual fund assets over the period from 1964 through 1991. Non-money-market mutual funds (Exhibit 21-10) held primarily corporate equities in 1964, with the percentage of total financial assets so invested approaching 90 percent. Treasury and corporate bonds made up another 10 percent. Over time, the equities share declined to 42 percent. With the exception of cash, every other asset category increased. In 1991, government securities represented 20 percent of the total; tax-exempt securities, 18 percent; and corporate and foreign bonds, 15 percent. This diversification of asset holdings in non-money-market mutual funds mirrors the increased variety of mutual funds, as indicated in Exhibit 21-2.

Exhibit 21-11 contains similar information for money market funds, beginning in 1974. (Before the mid-1970s, there were no such funds.) The early money market funds relied heavily on bank time deposits. Even before small deposit interest rate deregulation of the 1980s, the rate ceiling on large time deposit (CDs) over $100,000 had been removed (since 1970). It was through these CDs (67 percent of the industry's assets) and through commercial paper and bankers' acceptances (25 percent) that money market rates were first passed through to fund shareholders in 1974.

During the next 5 years, money market mutual fund assets grew from $2 billion to $45 billion. By then, the mix included more government securities (12 percent of industry assets) and even more commercial paper and banker's acceptances (43 percent). During the

EXHIBIT 21-10 FINANCIAL ASSETS OF U.S. MUTUAL FUNDS, 1964–1991*

	1964	1969	1974	1979	1984	1989	1991
Financial assets (billion)	$29.1	$47.6	$35.2	$51.8	$136.7	$486.3	$643.0
Demand deposits and currency	1.4%	1.5%	1.4%	1.4%	1.5%	1.5%	1.5%
Corporate equities	88.3	85.9	74.9	68.5	59.0	40.0	42.3
Debt instruments:							
U.S. government securities:							
Treasury issues	2.8	1.5	3.1	2.9	8.4	16.7	14.4
Agency issues	—	—	—	—	.3	6.7	6.0
Total U.S. government securities	2.8	1.5	3.1	2.9	8.7	23.4	20.4
Tax-exempt	—	—	—	7.7	14.0	16.9	17.8
Corporate and Foreign Bonds	7.2	6.1	14.0	13.9	12.1	13.9	14.8
Commercial paper and banker's acceptances	.3	5.0	6.6	5.6	4.7	4.3	3.2
Total debt instruments	10.3	12.6	23.7	30.1	39.5	58.5	56.2
	100.0%	100.0%	100.0%	100.0%	100.0%	100.0%	100.0%

*Excludes money market mutual funds.
Source: Board of Governors of the Federal Reserve System, *Flow of Funds Accounts, Financial Assets and Liabilities,* various issues.

EXHIBIT 21-11 FINANCIAL ASSETS OF U.S. MONEY MARKET MUTUAL FUNDS, 1974–1991*

	1974	1979	1984	1989	1991
Financial assets (billions)	\$2.4	\$45.2	\$233.6	\$363.8	\$551.7
Demand deposits and currency	—	.2%	(.5)%†	(.5)%†	(.3)†
Time deposits (domestic)	66.6%	26.5	10.1	9.7	5.0
Foreign deposits	—	1.3	9.1	8.0	5.9
Total currency & deposits	66.6	38.0	18.7	17.2	10.6
Security repos	4.2	5.3	9.8	13.1	13.3
Investment securities:					
U.S. government securities:					
Treasury issues	4.2	3.5	10.8	3.5	11.9
Agency issues	—	8.9	7.3	3.8	7.1
Total U.S. government	4.2	12.4	18.1	7.3	19.0
Tax Exempt	—	—	10.2	18.6	16.4
Commercial paper and bankers' acceptances	25.0	42.7	41.9	41.1	39.1
Total investment securities	29.2	55.1	70.2	67.0	74.5
Miscellaneous	—	1.6	1.3	2.7	1.6
	100.0%	100.0%	100.0%	100.0%	100.0%

*Prior to the 1970s, money market mutual funds did not exist.

†Aggressive cash management may involve considerable *payor float,* i.e., outstanding check disbursements that exceed actual bank balances. See also Chapter 17 for a description of payor float.

Source: Board of Governors of the Federal Reserve System, *Flow of Funds Accounts, Financial Assets and Lia-*

next 5 years (from 1979 to 1984), short-term municipal bonds (tax-exempts) became an important component. As reflected in the 1991 balance sheet, the industry asset mix is a well-diversified blend of short-term, liquid assets.

Comparison to Commercial Banks

While both commercial banks and investment companies have become more diversified over time, there are still significant differences in their asset holdings. Exhibit 21-12 highlights these differences. While bank asset portfolios contained a much higher proportion of government securities in 1964 than mutual funds, this relation had reversed by 1991. The same is true for other debt securities (excluding government securities, commercial paper, and banker's acceptances). Thus, mutual funds now invest a higher percentage of their portfolios in debt securities than do commercial banks. Also, non-money-market mutual funds invest large amounts in equities, a practice prohibited for commercial banks.

The large holdings of commercial paper by money market mutual funds have significant implications for commercial banks. Beginning in the 1970s, commercial paper was issued in greater quantities by large corporations in order to obtain short-term financing at lower interest rates than were charged for short-term bank loans. By 1991, money market funds held more commercial paper than any other sector of the economy, 36 percent of the total outstanding.

As noted earlier, money market funds threaten the *deposit base* of commercial banks by offering shares that pay a higher return than bank deposits. It is shown here that money market funds also threaten banks' *loan portfolio,* their core investment activity. Commercial paper makes it easier for large corporations to bypass the banking system. The large holdings of commercial paper by money market funds provide a ready market for its issuance. Thus, money market funds have attracted bank depositors and helped bank borrowers provide their own short-term finance.

EXHIBIT 21-12 ASSET COMPOSITION OF COMMERCIAL BANKS, MUTUAL FUNDS, AND MONEY MARKET MUTUAL FUNDS, 1964/1974 AND 1991*

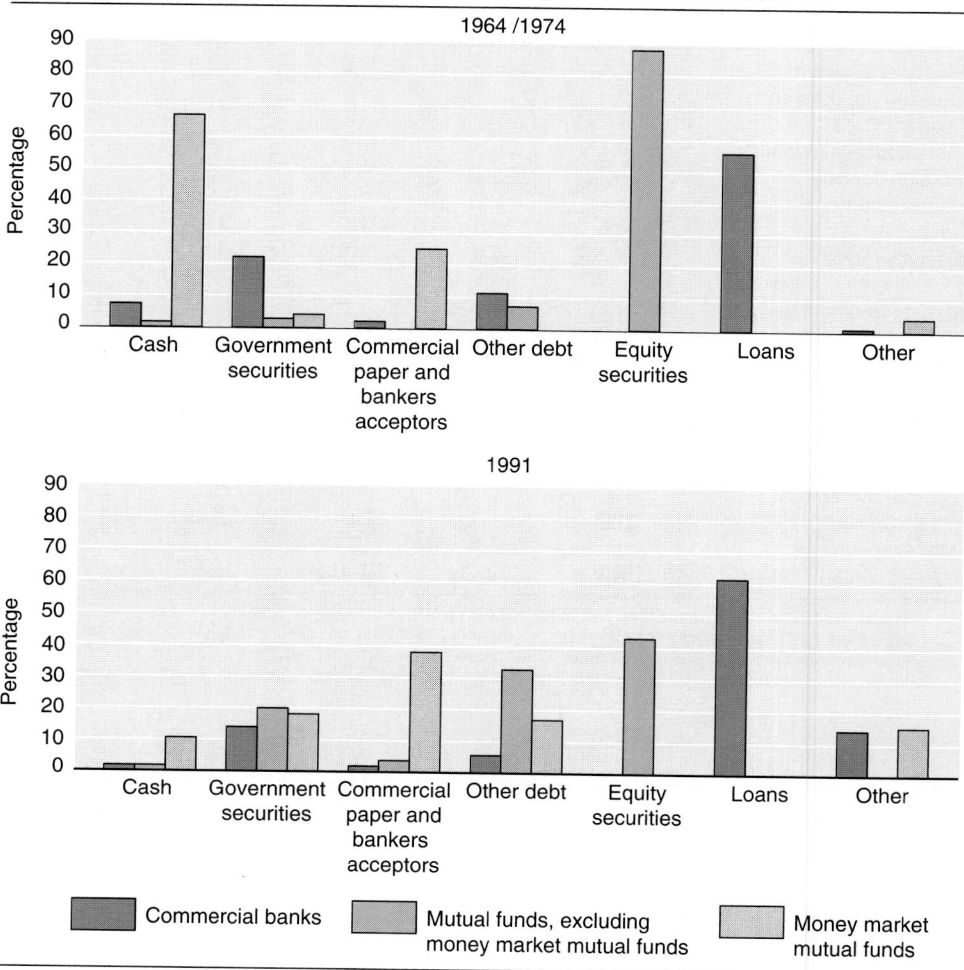

Source: Data from Board of Governors of the Federal Reserve System, *Flow of Funds Accounts, Financial Assets and Liabilities,* various issues.

ORIGINS AND DEVELOPMENT OF INVESTMENT COMPANIES

United Kingdom and United States

Although investment companies have had a profound impact on the U.S. financial system, the concept did not originate in the United States. The first investment company was organized in the United Kingdom in 1868. The Foreign and Colonial Government Trust was an *investment trust,* or closed-end fund, that was intended to provide higher returns to investors than were then available in British government securities. Portfolio investments included the government securities of eighteen foreign countries. The fund's 8 percent yield compared quite favorably to the 3 percent rate on British government securities.

In the following 7 years, sixteen similar trusts began operations. By 1914, the total number was approximately 100. The original companies appealed to wealthy individuals. It was not until some time later that they were considered appropriate investment vehicles for people of more modest means.

There has also been a shift away from the almost total concentration on foreign assets in British investment trusts. In 1914, foreign securities accounted for 90 percent of trust assets. In the mid-1930s, the proportion was 55 percent. By the 1940s, no more than 21 percent was represented by overseas assets. Recently, however, the foreign assets in British closed-end investment companies have increased in importance. In 1985, 48 percent of total assets were overseas securities, with the United States (27 percent) and Japan (11 percent) dominating.

In the United States, closed-end investment companies first evolved from other types of companies. The Boston Personal Property Trust began operations in 1893 and later began an investment company. Also in Boston, the Railway and Light Securities Company, formed in 1904, became the first American closed-end investment company to use leverage (debt) in its capital structure. However, it was not until 1921 that the Securities Trust of America emerged as a closed-end company from its inception. By 1929, there were 420 such companies in the United States.

Many of these companies were leveraged and suffered substantial losses during the 1929 stock market collapse. The closed-end company failures of that era were also frequently associated with fraudulent activities. These developments hurt the industry for several years thereafter. Even as the industry recovered, closed-end companies did not experience the same growth rates as open-end companies.

The first open-end company was the Massachusetts Investors Trust of 1924. The British counterpart, the *unit trust,* did not appear until 1931. The stock market crash had brought an end to the rapid expansion of closed-end companies. However, over the next 30 years, open-end companies would flourish, particularly in the United States. In 1960, U.S. and U.K. open-end investment companies numbered 330 and 51, respectively. These firms controlled assets of $23 billion and £200 million ($561 million), respectively.

However, this was only the beginning of rapid growth. By 1986, the 850 British (open-end) unit trusts controlled £23 billion ($34 billion). In contrast, the roughly 200 (closed-end) investment trusts held only £14 billion ($21 billion). Interestingly, money market unit trusts did not expand in the United Kingdom as did mutual funds in the United States. This is primarily due to the *absence* of interest rate restrictions. Of course, Regulation Q prevented depository institutions from offering competitive rates in the United States. There are only twenty money market trusts in the United Kingdom.

In 1990, 3108 investment companies in the United States held net assets of $1.1 trillion. A breakdown by general category and asset holdings follows:

Type of fund	Number of funds	Assets ($ billions)
Equity	1127	245.8
Bond and income	1235	325.0
Money market	508	414.7
Short-term municipal	238	83.6
	3108	1069.1

Asia

This is not to suggest that the United States and the United Kingdom are the only countries in which investment companies are significant financial institutions. After rather slow growth from 1950 to 1970, the assets of Japanese investment companies (investment trusts) increased from ¥1 trillion in 1970 to ¥6 trillion in 1980. By 1990, total Japanese funds amounted to one-third of the assets of U.S. mutual funds.

EXHIBIT 21-13 INTERNATIONAL COMPARISON OF MUTUAL FUND ASSETS, 1990

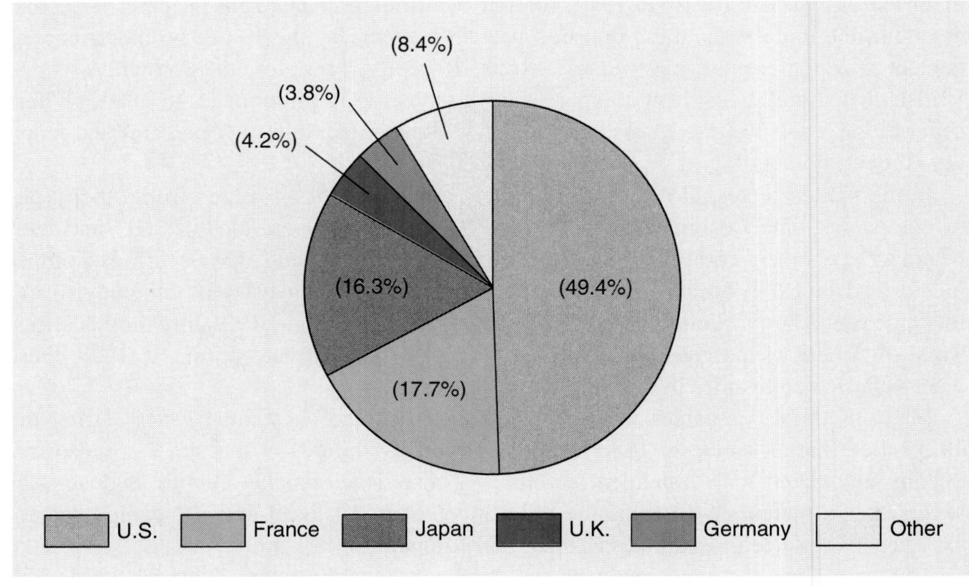

Source: Data from Investment Company Institute, *Mutual Fund Factbook 1991.*

In Korea, one of the four Asian (NICs), newly industrialized countries investment trusts are the largest stock market participants since there are few pension funds and little involvement of Korean insurance companies in the stock market. In Hong Kong, investment companies are less important in the stock market because individuals prefer to invest *directly* in the stock market. In Taiwan and Singapore, investment companies have little or no significant presence. (See also Exhibit 21-13.)

International Operations

Unlike commercial bank branches, investment companies have not spread across national boundaries to a great extent. The primary impediment has been securities laws that differ from one country to another. In the United States, a foreign company must obtain an "order" from the SEC permitting sale of the shares. However, before an order can be issued, the SEC must satisfy itself that it can enforce regulations with respect to the foreign company. Since U.S. laws usually require more disclosure and investor protection, the laws of the two countries are often incompatible. The advice of the SEC is frequently for the foreign entity to establish a "mirror fund," that is, an identical U.S. company.

The Single European Market will enable U.S. investment companies to market their products abroad more easily. The EC directive, Undertakings for Collective Investment in Transferable Securities, requires that registration in one EC country be recognized in the other EC countries. This eliminates the need for duplicate registrations.

From the perspective of the U.S. investor, buying shares of an investment company with international investments is becoming easier. In 1983, only twenty-one U.S. mutual funds held foreign securities. Three years later, the number was 114. By 1990, 183 mutual funds were specifically designated as global, or international, funds.

SUMMARY

Investment companies have enjoyed the most rapid growth among U.S. financial institutions during the last decade. This is particularly true of money market mutual funds. High and volatile interest rates of the 1970s and 1980s pushed up the yield on Treasury securities (minimum denomination of $10,000) and on large bank deposits (minimum $100,000) to over 13 percent. Small investors could do no better than 5 percent at commercial banks. When money market mutual funds offered market rates of interest to these small investors, the industry experienced explosive growth.

Now a wide variety of funds is available to investors. Some emphasize capital gains (increase in the market value of the fund's assets). Others concentrate on current income (interest and dividend income). Still others combine the two objectives. The newer generations specialize in tax-exempt securities or international investments.

Generally, these companies are not heavily regulated. Federal and state laws protect investors by requiring adequate disclosure of the funds' asset portfolio, management team, and operating expenses. Even though the shares in these companies are not insured (as are bank deposits), they are an attractive investment because of their variety, convenience, and competitive rates of return.

KEY TERMS

capital shares
closed-end fund
income shares
Investment Company Act of 1940
investment adviser
investment company
investment company distributor
investment philosophy
investment trust
money market mutual fund
mutual fund
net asset value
prospectus
sales charge
securities broker
unit trust

END-OF-CHAPTER QUESTIONS

1. How does an investment company differ from an industrial firm? from a depository institution?
2. What comparative disadvantages of a small investor are at least partially offset by mutual fund investment?
3. What is the difference between a closed-end fund and an open-end (mutual) fund?
4. Name the investment objectives that an investment company may adopt.
5. Describe a money market mutual fund.
6. What are the normal responsibilities of an investment company adviser-manager, and how is he or she compensated?
7. What is net asset value? Of what relevance is net asset value to an open-end company? a closed-end company?
8. What shareholder protections are incorporated into the Investment Company Act of 1940?
9. How do you explain the fact that the United Kingdom has only about twenty money market funds, while more than 500 operate in the United States?
10. Commercial banks have been granted limited rights to engage in the mutual fund business (see Chapter 17). How could less restricted activity in the industry (for example, managing a mutual fund) improve a bank's profits? Be as specific as possible.
11. Obtain a recent edition of the *Wall Street Journal.* Compare the 12-month rate of return on the S&P 500 with that of mutual funds also contained in that issue. Summarize your observations as to type of fund and rate-of-return variability among the funds.
12. Obtain the prospectus for a mutual fund. Pinpoint the sections of the prospectus that specify:
    - **a.** The fund management and investment adviser
    - **b.** The securities broker
    - **c.** The distributor
    - **d.** The fee arrangements
    - **e.** The investment philosophy
    - **f.** Total fund assets
    - **g.** Fund performance over the last 5 years

13. Suppose that you were contemplating the purchase of mutual fund shares. What characteristics would you look for if you were:

a. Twenty-five years from retirement?

b. Five years from retirement?

14. Refer to a recent edition of the *Wall Street Journal.*

a. How many of the closed-end funds listed in Exhibit 21-1 are included in the *Journal* price quotations?

b. On what exchanges are they listed?

SELECTED REFERENCES

Board of Governors of the Federal Reserve System. *Flow of Funds Accounts; Financial Assets and Liabilities,* Washington, D.C., various issues.

Goacher, D. J., and P. J. Curwen. *British Non-bank Financial Intermediaries,* Allen and Unwin, London, 1987.

Friars, Eileen M., and Robert N. Gogel. *The Financial Services Handbook; Executive Insights and Solutions,* John Wiley and Sons, New York, 1987.

Investment Company Institute. *Mutual Fund Factbook 1991; Industry Trends and Statistics for 1990,* Washington, D.C., 1991.

Investment Company Institute. *Reading the Mutual Fund Prospectus,* Washington, D.C., 1990.

Matatko, John, and David Stafford. *Key Developments in Personal Finance,* Basil Blackwell, Oxford, U.K., 1985.

Neufeld, E. P. *The Financial System of Canada,* St. Martin's Press, New York, 1972.

Rowley, Anthony. *Asian Stockmarkets; the Inside Story,* Far Eastern Economic Review, Hong Kong, 1987.

Securities and Exchange Commission. *Internationalization of the Securities Markets, Report of the Staff of the U.S. Securities and Exchange Commission to the Senate Committee on Banking, Housing, and Urban Affairs and the House Committee on Energy and Commerce,* Washington, D.C., 1987.

U.S. Department of Commerce. *Statistical Abstract of the United States, 1989,* 109th ed., Washington, D.C., 1989.

Wiesenberger Financial Services. *Investment Companies 1989,* New York, 1989.

CHAPTER 22

PENSION FUNDS

CHAPTER OUTLINE

TYPES OF PENSION FUNDS
- Classification by Sponsor
- Classification by Defined Attribute
  - Defined benefit plan, defined contribution plan
- Retirement Income in Selected Countries

GOVERNMENT PENSIONS
- Social Security
  - Coverage and contributions, trust fund assets and payments
- Other Federal Pensions
  - Civil service, military, railroad
- State and Local Government Pensions

PRIVATE PENSION FUNDS
- Defined Benefit Plans
  - Unit-benefit formula, flat-benefit formula
- Formation of Pension Plans by Year
- Defined Contribution Plans
- Formation of Pension Plans by Year and Industry
- Other Private Pension Plans
  - 401(k) plans, individual retirement accounts, Keogh accounts
- Pension Fund Performance
- Private Pension Plan Coverage in Selected Countries

REGULATION
- Funding
- Vesting and Coverage
- Fiduciary Responsibility

PENSION FUND ASSETS
- Trends over Time
- Comparison to Commercial Banks
- International Comparisons

INTERNATIONAL COMPARISONS:
- Canada
- France
- Germany
- Japan
- Netherlands
- Switzerland
- United Kingdom

CHAPTER OVERVIEW

This chapter:

- Outlines the classification of pension plans
- Describes coverage and funding of social security and other government pension plans
- Traces the patterns of formation of private pension plans
- Summarizes the regulations that govern private pension plans
- Examines aggregate pension fund asset composition and financial market involvement

During their working years, pension fund participants accumulate savings through employer and employee contributions. These savings then sustain participants during retirement. Today, pension funds control a large share of individual savings. In the process, pension funds have become major investors in financial markets.

As the pension fund industry grows in terms of assets under management, it is also changing in form and character. The employer-managed pension fund with relatively little set aside to meet future obligations (partially funded defined benefit pension plan) is decreasing in importance. The employee-managed pension fund with current contributions (fully funded defined contribution pension plan) is now becoming the industry standard. In this second type of pension plan, employees accept more risk in terms of future benefit payments because retirement income depends on the investment performance of the fund during the preretirement saving years. However, to the extent that there is more than one investment option, they also have more control and greater freedom of choice.

TYPES OF PENSION PLANS

Pension funds are asset pools that are accumulated over the working life of a participant for distribution at the time of or during retirement.

Pension fund:
A separate entity to which periodic (or, in some cases, lump-sum) contributions are made by or on behalf of covered participants. At the time of retirement, each participant receives a distribution from the fund in the form of an annuity or lump-sum payment.

A *pension plan* governs the operation of each pension fund. Pension plans may be classified by sponsor or by defined attribute.

Classification by Sponsor

Governments sponsor *public* pension plans. Individual corporations oversee *private* pension plans, while life insurance companies offer *insured* plans.

Public pension plan:
Pension plan sponsored by the federal government or by state or local governments.

At the federal level, the social security system covers virtually all nonfederal government employees. Other federal plans provide retirement benefits for federal civil and military personnel and for railroad employees. State and local governments sponsor similar pension plans for their employees. In 1991, assets held by federal and state and local government pension funds exceeded $1 trillion.

Private corporations may either administer their retirement programs or have a life insurance company perform this function.

Private pension plan:
Pension plan sponsored and administered by a private corporation.

Insured pension plan:
Pension plan sponsored by a private corporation but administered by an insurance company.

This distinction may derive more from the organizational form of the pension plan than from the type of administrator.

In an *insured* pension plan, there is no separate pool of assets. Instead, plan assets are held in the *general accounts* of a life insurance company.

General accounts:
The investment (asset) accounts of a life insurance company that appear in the firm's balance sheet.

The portion of the firm's assets that is devoted to pension plans appears as *pension fund reserves* in the liability section of the balance sheet. In 1991, these reserves totaled $827 billion, an amount just in excess of the total financial assets of state and local government pensions ($801 billion).

Private pension plans have separate legal entities, or *private pension funds,* associated with them. An insurance company may manage the private pension fund as a *separate account.*

Separate account:
Assets managed by an insurance company that do not appear on the insurance company balance sheet.

Alternatively, a bank trust department or an investment firm may manage and administer the fund. In other cases, large corporations maintain internal departments to oversee fund investments, participant accounting, and distributions. In 1991, the financial assets of all private pension funds amounted to $1.2 trillion, representing 37 and 117 percent of financial assets of commercial banks and savings and loan associations, respectively. (See Exhibit 22-1.)

Classification by Defined Attribute

Defined Benefit Plan A pension plan is either a *defined benefit plan* or a *defined contribution plan.*

Defined benefit plan:
A pension plan that entitles its participants, upon retirement, to specified cash *distributions,* based upon a formula that considers a number of variables, including years of service and salary during employment.

EXHIBIT 22-1 U.S. PENSION FUND RESERVES, 1991

	Total amount ($ billions)	% of total
Private reserves:		
Private pension funds	1,231.8	39.7
Life insurance companies	827.1	26.6
Total private reserves	2,058.8	66.3
Public reserves:		
U.S. government:		
Employee	236.3	7.6
Railroad	9.5	.3
Total U.S. government	245.8	7.9
State and local government	801.1	25.8
Total public reserves	1,046.9	33.7
Total pension reserves	3,105.7	100.0

Source: Board of Governors of the Federal Reserve System, *Flow of Funds Accounts, Financial Assets and Liabilities,* 1989.

A *defined benefit pension plan* fixes the level of retirement cash flow. It is a contract to provide future benefits. Since retirement benefits are based on factors such as salary and years of service, plan sponsors must manage the uncertainty of pension fund asset returns. Whether investment returns are strong or weak does not alter the level of retirement cash flows that are promised.

The method of providing these future payments varies.

Pension plan funding:
The extent to which assets are set aside currently to meet future pension plan obligations.

If assets are currently set aside in amounts equal to the *present value* of estimated retirement benefits, the plan is *fully funded.* If *no* assets are set aside currently, the plan is *unfunded.* If only some portion of the present value of future retirement benefits is funded, the plan is *partially funded.*

In addition to the formula for benefit determination, the present value of future benefits will also depend upon the plan's *vesting* provisions.

Vesting:
The process through which the right to receive cash distributions during retirement becomes a nonforfeitable right.

For example, if the pension plan provides for 10-year vesting, the plan sponsor is not obligated to provide retirement income to those participants who have less than 10 years of service. Any participant who leaves the plan (perhaps changes place of employment) before accumulating 10 years of service is not vested.

To the extent that participants *are* vested, the present value of their estimated future benefits is a *pension liability* for the plan sponsor.

Pension liability:
The amount of vested (nonforfeitable) pension benefits that a corporation or government organization is obligated to pay its current and retired employees.

In turn, it is this vested pension liability that is fully funded, partially funded, or unfunded. Unfunded pension liabilities of corporate plan sponsors can be substantial, and the amounts are disclosed in corporate financial statements.

Defined Contribution Plan In the case of *defined contribution pension plans,* the plan sponsor does *not* commit to provide participants a specified *retirement income.*

Defined contribution plan:
A pension plan that entitles its participants, during employment, to specified cash *contributions* to a pension fund.

Instead, the sponsor pays a specified *current amount* into a pension fund. The eventual retirement income of participants depends on the nature of the pension fund. If it is a *fixed-income* fund, a minimum rate of return is guaranteed with the possibility of higher returns if fund assets earn a return above the guaranteed minimum. A *variable-income* fund passes along to participants all investment income (or loss) in proportion to their holdings in the fund.[1] Often, participants have the option of choosing some combination of fixed and

[1]In principle, a variable-income pension fund operates like an investment company. (See Chapter 21.)

variable accounts. Because employers make the contributions to these plans currently, defined contribution plans are most often fully funded.

Upon retirement, a participant in a defined contribution plan receives benefits equal to the accumulated value in his or her account. The uncertainty of pension fund asset performance during the saving years is not managed by the fund sponsor but is assumed by the plan participant. The actual distribution may take the form of an annuity, as in a defined benefit plan. Alternatively, the participant may elect a lump-sum payment, an option almost universally available in defined contribution plans. If the latter option is chosen, the participant must then decide what combination of investment vehicles is best suited for his or her individual retirement needs. Again, this is a decision that must be made by the participant.

Retirement Income in Selected Countries

Exhibit 22-2 provides a breakdown of retirement income in several industrialized countries in 1981. In each case the largest source is social security, a public pension system. German retirees are more dependent on social security (82 percent of income) than their U.S. counterparts (50 percent). This is because of the relatively small size of private pension plans in Germany. The U.S. population is roughly three times that of Germany (including the residents of eastern Germany), but the amount of U.S. private pension fund assets is over twenty times the German total. As a result, the average benefit from German private plans is much smaller than in the United States.

Among the other countries shown in Exhibit 22-2, social security provides roughly one-half of retirement income. Private pensions represent another 16 to 22 percent. In addition, in the United States, Canada, and Switzerland, individual investment income contributes more than private pension plans. The importance of investment income reflects the extent to which retirees in these countries manage asset portfolios that are separate from their managed pension funds. These assets are either accumulated during working years as personal savings or received as lump-sum distributions of pension benefits at the time of retirement. Thus, in industrialized countries, retirement income is derived from a combination of individual savings, private pension plans, and government pensions.

GOVERNMENT PENSIONS

Social Security

Coverage and Contributions In the United States, almost everyone is insured by the federal social security system, the Old Age, Survivors, Disability, and Hospital Insur-

EXHIBIT 22-2 SOURCES OF INCOME OF RETIREES FROM THE AGES OF 65 THROUGH 74, 1981 (PERCENTAGES)

	U.S.	U.K.	Canada	Switzerland	Germany
Private pension benefits	20	22	16	18	14
Social security benefits	50	61	49	47	82
Investment income	25	11	29	32	2
Employment earnings	2	1	2	2	1
Means-tested public assistance	2	5	2	1	1
Other income	1	0	2	0	0
	100	100	100	100	100

Source: U.S. Department of Labor, Pension and Welfare Benefits Administration, *Trends in Pensions,* Washington, D.C., 1989, p. 328.

ance program (OASDHI). Exceptions are federal civilian employees and some employees of state and local governments and of nonprofit organizations. After working and paying social security contributions for forty quarters (3-month periods), an individual is insured for life. Contributions are a specified percentage of gross employee income, with matching employer contributions. Currently, the percentage is 7.65 percent—6.20 percent of earnings up to $53,400 for social security and 1.45 percent of earnings up to $125,000 for Medicare. Retirement benefits provide a "floor" for retirement income to ensure recipients of at least a subsistence standard of living.

Employees contribute through payroll deduction. Self-employed individuals make both the employee and employer contributions in quarterly payments, with an annual accounting in the federal income tax return.

In fact, the contributions themselves are commonly referred to as social security "tax" payments. Both the contribution percentages and the assessable income have increased over time in order to finance benefit payments to those already retired. Essentially, the social security pension system operates on a pay-as-you-go basis. This means that contributions collected from today's working population are the source of benefits for workers that have retired.

Trust Fund Assets and Payments Referring to Exhibit 22-3, note that the trust funds for the Old Age, Survivors, and Disability Insurance programs exceeded the $31.9 billion in disbursements (benefit payments) by only $6.2 billion in 1970. Without current contributions ($34.7 billion in 1970), the trust funds would soon be depleted. Thus, both the contribution rate (tax rate) and the amount of assessable income have increased over time in order to offset higher benefit payments.

Even with these increases, contributions have not always kept pace with benefits. Without extraordinary measures, the Old Age and Survivors Insurance trust fund (OASI) would have shrunk from $37 billion in assets in 1970 to less than $5 billion in the early 1980s. In 1982 and 1983 alone, OASI benefit payments exceeded contributions by $15

EXHIBIT 22-3 THE U.S. SOCIAL SECURITY SYSTEM: TRUST FUND ASSETS, CONTRIBUTIONS, AND DISBURSEMENTS, 1970–1987

		Contributions					
		Rate					
Year	Trust Fund Assets[a]	OASDI[b]	HI[c]	Total	Max. taxable earnings[d]	Total[e]	Disbursements[f]
1970	$38.1	4.20%	0.60%	4.80%	$7,800	$34.7	$31.9
1975	44.3	4.95[b]	0.90[c]	5.85	14,100	64.3	66.9
1980	26.5	5.08	1.05	6.13	25,900	116.7	120.5
1981	27.2[g]	5.35	1.30	6.65	29,700	139.4	141.0
1982	24.8	5.40	1.30	6.70	32,400	145.7	156.1
1983	24.9	5.40	1.30	6.70	35,700	156.3	167.0
1984	31.1	5.70	1.30	7.00	37,800	183.1	175.8
1985	42.2	5.70	1.35	7.05	39,600	197.6	186.2
1986	46.9	5.70	1.45	7.15	42,000	212.8	196.7
1987	68.8	5.70	1.45	7.15	43,800	225.6	204.2

[a]Represents the assets of two social security trust funds, i.e., Old Age and Survivors Insurance and Disability Insurance trust funds, in billions of dollars.
[b]Old Age, Survivors, and Disability Insurance.
[c]Hospital Insurance.
[d]Maximum taxable earnings per employee or self-employed person, per year.
[e]Represents contributions to the Old Age and Survivors Insurance and the Disability Insurance trust funds, in billions of dollars.
[f]Represents benefit payments under the Old Age, Survivors, and Disability Insurance programs, in billions of dollars.
[g]Represents balance at September 30.

Source: U.S. Department of Commerce Bureau of the Census, *Statistical Abstract of the United States, 1989,* 109th ed., Washington, D.C., 1989, pp. 352–354, and Office of Management and Budget, Executive Office of the President of the United States, *Historical Tables, Budget of the United States Government, Fiscal Year 1990,* pp. 312–313.

billion and $11 billion, respectively. An $18 billion transfer of assets from the Disability and Hospital Insurance trust funds saved the OASI fund from insolvency. Subsequently, the balance between contributions and payments has been restored, the OASI trust fund is growing once again, and the loans have been partially repaid.

However, required contributions have become increasingly burdensome for the average contributor. Referring to Exhibit 22-4, note that disbursements increased at an average annual rate of 11.5 percent from 1970 through 1987 [($204,156 million/$31,863 million)$^{1/17}$ − 1]. Over the same period, the number of contributors only grew by 1.9 percent per year [(115.5 million/83.6 million)$^{1/17}$ − 1]. Income increased faster than the number of contributors, but not as fast as social security disbursements. In 1970, wages, salaries, other labor income, and proprietor income totaled $664.2 billion. By 1987, the total was $2769.2 billion, representing a growth rate of 8.8 percent [($2769.2 billion/$664.2 billion)$^{1/17}$ − 1].

The result is that every contributor supports a higher average disbursement of old age, survivors, and disability insurance benefits each year. In 1970, the average disbursement per contributor was $381.14. By 1987, it had reached $1767.58. This is a 9.4 percent average annual increase, while personal income per contributor over the same period only grew an average of 6.7 percent a year.[2]

Further, as the "baby boom" generation (those U.S. citizens born during the years immediately following 1945, the end of World War II) continues to mature, the average age of the U.S. population will increase. When this generation reaches retirement age, it is projected that required contributions by those still in the work force will be even more

[2]Disbursements per contributor:

$$(\$1767.58/\$381.14)^{1/17} - 1 = .09444$$

Personal income per contributor:

$$1970: \frac{\$664.2 \text{ billion}}{.0836 \text{ billion}} = \$7944.98$$

$$1987: \frac{\$2769.2 \text{ billion}}{.1155 \text{ billion}} = \$23,975.76$$

$$(\$23,975.76/\$7944.98)^{1/17} - 1 = 0.06713$$

EXHIBIT 22-4 THE U.S. SOCIAL SECURITY SYSTEM: DISBURSEMENTS AND CONTRIBUTORS, 1970–1987

Year	Disbursements*	Contributors†	Ratio‡
1970	$31,863	83.6	$381.14
1975	66,923	88.9	752.79
1980	120,472	101.7	1184.58
1981	140,995	101.7	1386.38
1982	156,137	101.1	1544.38
1983	167,033	104.5	1598.40
1984	175,762	107.7	1631.96
1985	186,195	109.8	1695.77
1986	196,692	112.3	1751.49
1987	204,156	115.5	1767.58

*Represents benefit payments under the Old Age, Survivors, and Disability Insurance programs, in millions of dollars.
†Represents millions of employed workers under the social security system.
‡Represents average benefit payments per employed worker.
Source: U.S. Department of Commerce, Bureau of the Census, *Statistical Abstract of the United States,* 109th ed., Washington, D.C., 1989, pp. 351, 354.

burdensome. The additional burden could be serious enough to threaten the continued existence of the social security system.

Other Federal Pensions

Other federal pension plans have been established for particular segments of the work force. These include civil service, military, and railroad pension plans.

Civil Service ***Civil service*** plans cover federal employees who are not a part of the armed forces. These workers, generally, neither contribute to nor receive benefits from the social security system.

Contributions to the plan are made by participants and, to a much greater extent, the federal government. For example, in 1987, civilian pension contributions totaled $27.8 billion, of which $23.1 billion (83 percent) was appropriated by the federal government. In the same year, the $183 billion of financial assets in the retirement fund earned investment income of $16 billion, bringing total receipts to $43.8 billion. Benefit payments were only $24 billion.

The smaller social security trust fund acts as a reserve for payments to approximately 40 million beneficiaries. The federal employees retirement trust fund supports payments for only 2 million beneficiaries. Also, with only 3 million active employees, the federal civil service pension system should not face the kind of financial strain anticipated in the social security system in later years.

Military ***Military*** personnel pay social security taxes and are, therefore, eligible for social security benefits. In addition, after 20 years of service, career military personnel may retire with retirement benefits equal to 50 percent of final basic pay, regardless of age. After 30 years of service, the benefit increases to 75 percent. There are approximately 1.4 million military retirees. Their annual pension benefits amount to $20 billion and are paid by the federal government. In addition, a military retirement trust fund was originated in the mid-1980s.

Railroad The federal *railroad* pension system originated in the 1930s when the industry's private pension plans faced severe financial difficulty. Contributions to the railroad retirement trust are made by employers, employees, and the federal government. Just under 1 million beneficiaries receive approximately $6 billion under this pension plan each year. Like the social security system, the federal railroad pension was threatened with insolvency in the early 1980s. Trust fund financial assets dropped to a low of $500 million in 1982. Since that time, contributions have exceeded benefit payments in each year. Thus, the system was revived, and the fund balance stood at $9.5 billion by 1991.

State and Local Government Pensions

State and local governments sponsor pension plans that cover over 10 million full-time employees and pay benefits to almost 4 million retirees. Because of their funding arrangements (largely pay as you go), most federal government pension systems are defined benefit plans. Defined benefit plans also dominate in the state and local government category. Defined contribution plans cover only 8 to 13 percent of state and local government employees.[3]

[3]In 1987, 8 percent of teachers and 13 percent of police and firefighters were covered by defined contribution plans. Nine percent of all other full-time state and local government employees were also participants.

State and local governments have the option of not participating in the federal social security system. Further, the government of any political subdivision that *has* elected to participate in the social security system may give written notice of intent to withdraw after participating in social security for 5 years. Actual withdrawal is possible 2 years after the written notice.

In 1991, state and local pension funds held financial assets of $801 billion. Earnings on these investments constitute approximately 50 percent of annual fund receipts, with the remainder composed of employee and government contributions. In the late 1980s, total annual receipts from all sources and annual payments to beneficiaries were roughly $100 billion and $30 billion, respectively.

PRIVATE PENSION PLANS

Private pension funds grew substantially after World War II (1939–1945), when personal income and productivity rose consistently. Wages generally increased faster than prices, and most workers realized higher standards of living. An emphasis on postretirement income maintenance was a natural outgrowth of these circumstances. Saving for retirement was further encouraged by federal legislation. The 1921 Revenue Act permitted employers to deduct pension contributions from taxable corporate income. Employees received an income tax deferral on both contributed amounts and investment income until retirement. Defined benefit pension plans became the typical vehicle used to achieve the objective during the years immediately following the war, especially in larger organizations.

Defined Benefit Plans

As noted earlier, defined benefit plans promise a certain level of retirement income based upon the plan formula. The formula generally falls into one of two broad categories: *unit-benefit* and *flat-benefit* formulas.

Unit-Benefit Formula *Unit-benefit* formulas give beneficiaries a specified number of benefit units depending upon length of service with the plan sponsor. In those cases in which employees are paid on an hourly basis and there is little variation among wage rates, a set dollar amount of benefit often may be earned for each year of service. For example, an employee may earn $500 of annual retirement income for each year of service.

A more common unit-benefit formula is to award 1 to 2 percent of specified compensation for each year of service. For example, an employee who retires with 20 years of service may receive 40 percent of *specified compensation* as annual retirement income. The specified compensation may be average annual compensation over the participant's career or over the final years of his or her career. The final-average formula is, of course, the more generous of the two techniques because earnings are typically highest in the last years of a career.

Flat-Benefit Formula *Flat-benefit* formulas award a percentage of specified compensation that does not vary with length of service. The flat benefit usually ranges from 20 to 40 percent, and specified compensation may be either a career average or a final average. Generally, a minimum of 15 years of service is required in order to qualify for full benefits. Participants with insufficient years of service may receive a reduced level of benefits.

In the United States, the most common defined benefit pension formula is the final-average, unit-benefit formula. Further, until recent years, larger organizations have more frequently elected defined benefit pension plans than defined contribution alternatives.

Formation of Pension Plans by Year

Exhibit 22-5 shows the breakdown of the 805,405 pension plans operating in 1985 by type and period of formation. Of this total, only 48,636 plans covered 100 or more participants. The majority of these larger plans formed through 1970 were defined benefit pension plans. After that time, however, defined contribution plans became more important, representing 76 percent of all new plans with at least 100 participants between 1981 and 1985.

Among the smaller plans (those 756,769 with less than 100 participants in 1985), defined contribution arrangements have dominated almost all periods. The only exception to this was the period immediately after World War II when two-thirds of new, smaller plans were defined benefit.

From an administrative perspective, a defined benefit plan is more costly to administer. Determination of participant benefits depends on years of service and anticipated average compensation. The present value of the benefits (the pension liability) is a function of the anticipated future benefits and interest rate assumptions from the present time to the year of retirement. For a small company, maintaining adequate staff (or hiring an outside consultant) to administer a defined benefit plan can be prohibitively expensive.

Exhibit 22-6 illustrates the trend in average size of new defined benefit pension plans. Among the larger plans formed after 1960, the average number of participants in 1985 fell within the 600 to 800 range. Only those that began before 1950 have average

EXHIBIT 22-5 U.S. PRIVATE PENSION PLANS BY TYPE AND PERIOD OF FORMATION, THROUGH 1985

	Defined benefit		Defined contribution		
Time period	Number of plans formed	% of total*	Number of plans formed	% of total*	Total
Plans with less than 100 participants					
Prior to 1946	2,021	35.5	3,677	64.5%	5,698
1946–1950	1,941	67.1	950	32.9	2,891
1951–1955	2,325	43.4	3,030	56.6	5,355
1956–1960	4,018	40.1	5,994	59.9	10,012
1961–1965	9,367	42.4	12,732	57.6	22,099
1966–1970	15,753	26.8	42,967	73.2	58,720
1971–1975	27,559	19.6	113,263	80.4	140,822
1976–1980	54,567	24.4	169,352	75.6	223,919
1981–1985	79,360	29.1	193,397	70.9	272,757
Unallocated	2,820	19.5	11,676	80.5	14,496
Subtotal	199,731	26.4	557,038	73.6	756,769
Plans with 100 or more participants					
Prior to 1946	1,284	79.6	330	20.4	1,614
1946–1950	1,311	87.6	185	12.4	1,496
1951–1955	1,863	69.7	810	30.3	2,673
1956–1960	2,727	69.4	1,201	30.6	3,928
1961–1965	3,247	66.7	1,621	33.3	4,868
1966–1970	4,421	63.9	2,499	36.1	6,920
1971–1975	3,730	51.3	3,544	48.7	7,274
1976–1980	3,198	38.7	5,072	61.3	8,270
1981–1985	2,686	24.3	8,381	75.7	11,067
Unallocated	276	52.5	250	47.5	526
Subtotal	24,743	53.7	23,893	46.3	48,636
Total	224,474	27.9	580,931	72.1	805,405

*Represents the percentage of total private pension plans reflected in the relevant row.

Source: U.S. Department of Labor, Pension and Welfare Benefits Administration, *Trends in Pensions,* Washington, D.C., 1989, pp. 82–83.

EXHIBIT 22-6 ACTIVE PARTICIPANTS IN U.S. DEFINED BENEFIT PENSION PLANS BY PERIOD OF FORMATION, THROUGH 1985

Time period	Number of plans formed	Participants in 1985*	Average number of participants
	Plans with less than 100 participants		
Prior to 1946	2,021	38	19
1946–1950	1,941	39	20
1951–1955	2,325	59	25
1956–1960	4,018	114	28
1961–1965	9,367	179	19
1966–1970	15,753	266	17
1971–1975	27,559	336	12
1976–1980	54,567	401	7
1981–1985	79,360	427	5
Unallocated	2,820	21	7
	199,731	1,880	159
	Plans with 100 or more participants		
Prior to 1946	1,284	4,604	3,586
1946–1950	1,311	3,041	2,320
1951–1955	1,863	3,294	1,768
1956–1960	2,727	2,963	1,087
1961–1965	3,247	2,785	858
1966–1970	4,421	3,255	736
1971–1975	3,730	2,481	665
1976–1980	3,198	2,455	768
1981–1985	2,686	2,034	757
Unallocated	276	232	841
	24,743	27,144	1,097

*In thousands.
Source: U.S. Department of Labor, Pension and Welfare Benefits Administration, *Trends in Pensions,* Washington, D.C., 1989, pp. 82–85.

membership of over 2000 participants. The number of new plans is actually greater during the 5-year periods after 1950, but the corresponding numbers of active participants have declined.

Evidence of this trend is even more dramatic among defined benefit plans with less than 100 participants. Between 1971 and 1985, 161,486 of these organizations began operations, representing over 80 percent of the total of 199,731 smaller plans and over 70 percent of *all* defined benefit pension plans. However, their 1.16 million active participants account for only 4 percent of the total 29 million defined benefit plan participants in 1985. The net effect is that the average number of participants in the plans formed after 1970 is well below 20 in the smaller plans and less than 800 in the larger plans. That is, defined benefit pension plans are being formed by much smaller companies today than in the past.

Defined Contribution Plans

Defined contribution plans are essentially tax-deferred savings plans and, thus, are much simpler to administer than defined benefit plans. The actual pension fund to which contributions are made may be either an investment company with the objective of long-term growth or a family of funds with the option of transferring monies among them (see Chapter 21).

Alternatively, the pension fund may be a guaranteed investment contract or contracts with an insurance company. A conservative minimum rate of return is guaranteed by the insurance company. Contributions are placed either in the insurance company's general fund or in a separate account (separate legal entity). In turn, the insurance company invests in mortgages, private placements, or other long-term, fixed-income securities.

The convenience of these plans, together with more stringent federal regulation of defined benefit plans, has led to an explosive increase in the number of defined contribution plans. Referring once again to Exhibit 22-5, note that these plans represented 72 percent of all pension plans in 1985. As was true with defined benefit plans, the majority of them have less than 100 participants. Exhibit 22-7 shows that the average number of participants can be quite small. However, among the larger plans, there has not been as significant a decline in average number of participants as is the case with defined benefit plans. Generally, since 1946, the average has ranged from 1000 to 2000 participants. This means that since 1955, on average, larger firms have adopted defined contribution plans.

It should be noted that some of the new defined contribution plans supplement defined benefit plans. Nevertheless, the bulk of the new defined contribution plans are the primary retirement savings vehicle for their participants.

From the participants' perspective, most defined contribution plans offer *portability*.

Portability:

The right of an employee to retain the vested benefits of a pension plan when changing place of employment. The employee either receives a lump-sum distribution or transfers the amount to another pension fund.[4]

[4]Lump-sum distributions before the age of 59.5 that are not reinvested in a qualified pension plan are subject to the normal income tax rate plus a 10 percent penalty.

EXHIBIT 22-7 ACTIVE PARTICIPANTS IN U.S. DEFINED CONTRIBUTION PENSION PLANS BY PERIOD OF FORMATION, THROUGH 1985

Time period	Numer of plans formed	Participants in 1985*	Average number of participants
	Plans with less than 100 participants		
Prior to 1946	3,677	36	10
1946–1950	950	12	13
1951–1955	3,030	81	27
1956–1960	5,994	144	24
1961–1965	12,732	271	21
1966–1970	42,967	578	13
1971–1975	113,263	1,054	9
1976–1980	169,352	1,479	9
1981–1985	193,397	1,618	8
Unallocated	11,676	75	6
	557,038	5,348	10
	Plans with 100 or more participants		
Prior to 1946	330	776	2,352
1946–1950	185	359	1,941
1951–1955	810	1,078	1,331
1956–1960	1,201	1,419	1,182
1961–1965	1,621	1,424	878
1966–1970	2,499	2,140	856
1971–1975	3,544	3,110	878
1976–1980	5,072	6,272	1,237
1981–1985	8,381	11,063	1,320
Unallocated	250	255	1,020
	23,893	27,896	1,168

*In thousands.

Source: U.S. Department of Labor, Pension and Welfare Benefits Administration, *Trends in Pensions,* Washington, D.C., 1989, pp. 82–85.

When benefits are portable, they are not lost when the participant changes employment. Commonly, there is immediate vesting, and the plan sponsor (employer) has little or no involvement after the contributions are made.

Formation of Pension Plans by Year and Industry

The changing nature of the U.S. economy has affected mix and composition of pension plans. Among the pension plans formed before 1946, the manufacturing sector accounts for 16 percent of the total. Exhibit 22-8 shows that of the 7312 plans formed in this period, 1175 were affiliated with manufacturing firms. This share peaked at 32 percent during the 10 years ended 1955, then declined steadily to 9 percent during the 1976–1985 period. As of 1985, manufacturing pension plans constituted 11 percent of the total.

The service sector has more than made up the difference. With only 4 percent of plan formations before 1946, these firms started 50 percent of new plans from 1976 through 1985. By 1985, fully 45 percent of all private pension plans were connected with the service sector. These companies are generally smaller than manufacturing firms. With a total of 26 million participants in 1985, the average manufacturing pension plan covered 281 participants. Since there were only 7.2 million service sector participants, the average plan in this sector covered only twenty participants.

Other Private Pension Plans

In addition to defined benefit and defined contribution plans, individuals may also participate in *401(k)* plans, *individual retirement accounts (IRAs),* and *Keogh* accounts. The first is an employer-sponsored plan; the second and third are not sponsored by employers.

401(k) Plans The 401(k) plans are employer-sponsored arrangements that are permitted by the Internal Revenue Service and that allow deferral of income tax until retirement.

401(k) plan
A tax-deferred savings plan that sometimes supplements the basic retirement plan and allows both employer and employee contributions.

EXHIBIT 22-8 U.S. PRIVATE PENSION PLANS BY PERIOD OF FORMATION AND INDUSTRY, THROUGH 1985

	Number of plans formed						
Industry	Prior to 1946	1946–1955	1956–1965	1966–1975	1976–1985	Unallocated	Total
Agriculture	74	117	296	6,132	7,605	544	14,768
Mining	45	159	284	1,269	4,354	89	6,200
Construction	76	502	2,415	11,642	31,933	649	47,217
Manufacturing	1,175	3,972	11,247	27,069	48,010	1,113	92,586
Transportation	35	210	907	2,342	5,642	55	9,191
Communications and utilities	132	356	722	1,552	3,035	163	5,960
Wholesale trade	320	1,355	4,466	18,318	33,682	787	58,928
Retail trade	182	482	3,490	19,028	36,197	689	60,068
Finance, insurance, and real estate	1,004	2,663	5,122	15,349	38,470	981	63,589
Services	305	603	5,862	88,539	260,635	5,681	361,625
Tax-exempt organizations	3,379	1,273	3,362	8,350	9,841	453	26,658
Other	585	723	2,734	14,146	36,609	3,818	58,615
Total	7,312	12,415	40,907	213,736	516,013	15,022	805,405

Source: U.S. Department of Labor, Pension and Welfare Benefits Administration, *Trends in Pensions,* Washington, D.C., 1989, p. 90.

The most common 401(k) plans are profit sharing or thrift-savings arrangements. In the profit sharing plans, employees may accept the profit sharing distribution as taxable income in the current year or have it set aside in a 401(k) account. The Tax Reform Act of 1986 placed some limitations on the amounts that may be tax-deferred. However, the plan remains a popular vehicle for tax-deferred saving. There are approximately forty thousand 401(k) plans with 10 million participants.[5]

Individual Retirement Accounts In 1981, individual retirement accounts (IRAs) were made available to all wage earners in addition to employer-sponsored retirement plans.

Individual retirement account:
An individually funded, self-directed retirement account that may be established by employees that are also covered by employer-sponsored pension plans.

Each worker could contribute up to $2000 to an IRA per year on a tax-deferred basis. The earnings on this account also accumulate tax-deferred.

In 1986, the tax-deferred contributions were limited for higher-income employees. Only employees (1) not covered by employer-sponsored pension plans (whose spouses are also not covered) or (2) earning adjusted gross income of $25,000 or less ($40,000 for married, filing joint tax returns) may contribute the full $2000 on a tax-deferred basis. Above this income level for covered employees, the permissible amount is reduced and then completely eliminated for incomes in excess of $40,000 ($50,000 for married, filing joint). However, in all cases, the investment income on the account may accrue tax-deferred. Approximately 20 million IRA accounts are maintained.

Keogh Accounts Keogh accounts are retirement accounts for the self-employed.

Keogh account:
A retirement account maintained by a self-employed individual. Contributions and investment income are tax-deferred until distributions are received by the individual after retirement.

Keogh plans are treated for tax purposes as corporate pension plans. Thus, the form of the plan may be either a regular pension or a profit sharing plan. However, because tax laws discourage plans that favor high-income employees at the expense of lower-income employees, there are limitations on contributions. The maximum annual contribution to a Keogh account is $30,000 per year or 25 percent of self-employment income, whichever is less. A total of roughly 1 million Keogh accounts are maintained.

Pension Fund Performance

The overwhelming popularity of defined contribution pension plans means that the retirement income of increasingly more workers will be dependent on the investment performance of pension funds. Exhibit 22-9 shows the stock and bond investment results of the largest pension funds in the United States during the 16-year period ended 1983. The number of funds included in each year ranges from 64 (bond returns, 1968) to 118 (stock returns, 1975).

In terms of equity (stock) investments, the pension funds outperformed the S&P 500 stock index in only 6 of the 16 years. Four of these occurred in the late 1970s and early

[5]For employees of nonprofit organizations, a 403(b) offers similar features.

EXHIBIT 22-9 PENSION FUND PERFORMANCE, 1968–1983

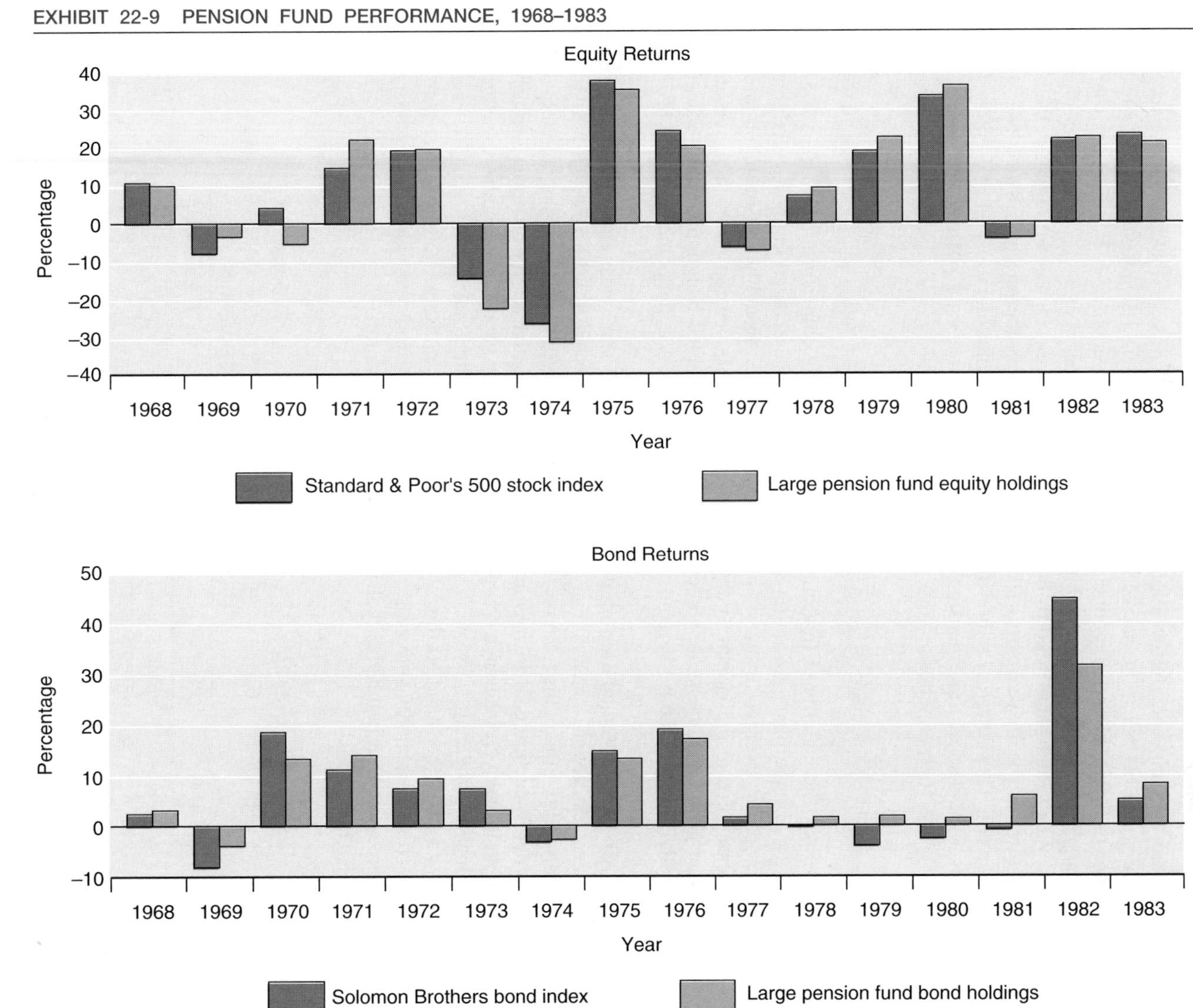

Source: Data from U.S. Department of Labor, Pension, and Welfare Benefits Administration, *Pension Policy: An International Perspective,* Washington, D.C., 1991, pp. 255, 256.

1980s, a more favorable stock market climate than the early and mid-1970s. For the entire period, the average annual return of the pension funds was 6.8 percent, while the S&P 500 gained 7.9 percent per year. It was noted in Chapter 21 that equity investment companies generally do not outperform the stock market. This is also true in the pension fund industry. Pension fund equity portfolios do not outperform the overall stock market.

The reverse is true for bond portfolios during this period. Exhibit 22-9 also shows that bond portfolios of large pension funds earned a higher rate of return in 11 of the 16 years than the Solomon Brothers long-term bond index. Five of these years are from 1977 through 1981 when the rate of inflation ranged from 7 (1977) to over 13 percent (1979). For the entire period, the bond index increased an average of 6.2 percent per year, while the pension fund bond portfolios gained 7.2 percent per year.

When total pension portfolios (stock and bond) are considered together, the average return for the 16-year period is 6.8 percent. However, the rate of inflation averaged 7.1 percent. Thus, the real return (nominal return *less* inflation rate) was −.3 percent. Overall, managers of these pension funds were unable to earn a positive real rate of return over the 16-year period.

Private Pension Plan Coverage in Selected Countries

Despite the inability of fund managers to consistently outperform the market as a whole, these private plans are quite common in many industrialized countries. Exhibit 22-10 compares coverage in several industrialized countries. Roughly half of the private-sector labor force in the United States is covered by private pension plans. In Japan and Germany the percentages are somewhat lower; in the United Kingdom and Canada substantially lower. In the Netherlands, Switzerland, and France, the percentages are 62, 92, and 100 percent, respectively.

In Canada, the administration of pension plans is somewhat complicated because the rules that govern pensions vary from one province (state) to the next. This complicates portability of benefits from one company to the next. In the United Kingdom, coverage is actually declining. British workers have always had the option of setting up a pension plan through an insurance company. Since 1988, they have also been able to set up a personal pension plan, very much like an IRA in the United States.

On the other hand, in the Netherlands, employer-sponsored pensions have come to be viewed as a moral obligation. The inclusion of pension plans in collective-bargaining agreements has helped boost the country's coverage ratio.

EXHIBIT 22-10 ACTIVE PARTICIPANTS IN PRIVATE PENSION PLANS AS % OF PRIVATE-SECTOR LABOR FORCE, 1988

Country	Percentage
United States	46*
United Kingdom	29*
Japan	38
Canada	28
Netherlands	62
Switzerland	92*
Germany	42*
France	100

*Data are for 1987.

Source: U.S. Department of Labor, Pension and Welfare Benefits Administration. *Pension Policy: An International Perspective,* Washington, D.C., 1991, p. 20.

In most countries, pension coverage is voluntary. However, in France and Switzerland, pensions are now mandatory. This explains the high coverage ratios noted for these two countries. The Swiss coverage is less than 100 percent because plans for workers under the age of 18 and part-time workers are not mandatory.

Exhibit 22-11 compares pension plan asset holdings and participants of the eight countries included. Most of the systems operate very much like the U.S. system. However, Japan and France have a low percentage of assets versus participants. This is because the pension plans of these two countries are run on a pay-as-you-go basis for the most part. Japanese pensions, once paid as lump sums upon retirement, are only now beginning to be funded.

REGULATION

Even with the mandatory pensions of France and Switzerland, the U.S. pension system is the most regulated pension system among industrialized countries. The Employee Retirement Income Security Act of 1974 (ERISA) is the major regulatory framework for private pension plans.

The ERISA created the Pension Benefit Guaranty Corporation (PBGC), and PBGC insures defined benefit pension plans. Premiums are based on the number of participants. Premiums are a combination of rates. Insured pensions pay both of the following:

- $19 per participant
- .6 percent of the plan's unfunded vested pension liability

The maximum premium is $72 per participant. The second of the two rates is a risk premium.

Within certain limits, pension payments are guaranteed to each participant.[6] In the event of plan termination *and* inadequate pension assets to provide benefits, PBGC may assess the plan sponsor (employer) for the lesser of the deficiency or 30 percent of the sponsor's net worth.

Unfortunately, PBGC itself has been plagued with financial difficulties since its founding. In 1991, PBGC held assets of $5.6 billion versus liabilities of $8.2 billion. This $2.6

[6]The maximum benefit coverage is $2352 per month.

EXHIBIT 22-11 SHARE OF ASSETS AND PARTICIPANTS IN PRIVATE PENSION PLANS IN SELECTED COUNTRIES, 1988

	Assets	Participants
United States	67.9%	43.7%
United Kingdom	10.1	6.1*
Japan	8.1	16.6
Canada	4.1	2.8
Netherlands	4.0	2.4
Switzerland	3.0*	2.4*
Germany	2.2*	9.6*
France	.6	16.4
	100.0%	100.0%

*Data are for 1987.

Source: calculations based on data from U.S. Department of Labor, Pension and Welfare Benefits Administration, *Pension Policy: An International Perspective,* Washington, D.C., 1991, pp. 19, 27.

billion deficit represents insured pension benefits of terminated pension plans for which insufficient funding existed at the time of plan termination. (See Exhibit 22-12.)

In addition to the creation of PBGC, the overall objective of ERISA is to ensure that pension benefits will be paid as promised. The specific areas addressed to accomplish this goal are pension plan *funding, vesting* of benefits, and *fiduciary responsibility.*

Funding

Before 1974, there was no statutory requirement that sponsors of defined benefit pension plans adequately fund the plans.[7] Thus, ERISA mandated a *minimum funding* arrangement and established a *penalty* for funding *deficiencies.* The penalty is a 5 percent excise tax on accumulated funding deficiencies (or 100 percent if not corrected promptly).

Minimum funding requirements for a given year involve both *normal cost* and *past service liabilities.*

Normal cost:
The present value of vested pension benefits earned by participants during the current year.

Past service liabilities:
The present value of vested pension benefits earned by participants before (1) 1974 or (2) plan adoption, whichever is later.

Plan sponsors must fund 100 percent of normal cost each year. However, ERISA permitted amortization of past service cost. For plans in existence in 1974, past service cost attributable to years before 1974 was amortizable over 40 years. If plans were upgraded after 1974 and additional past service liabilities generated as a result of such liberaliza-

[7]A 1946 IRS ruling required plan sponsors to fund plans in such a way that unfunded pension liabilities did not increase over time. However, this ruling was a regulation, rather than a law.

EXHIBIT 22-12 LARGEST PENSION BENEFIT GUARANTY CORPORATION CLAIMANTS, 1977–1987

Name of company	Amount of underfunding* (millions)	Year of claim	Number of plans
Wheeling-Pittsburgh	$498	1985	7
LTV	230	1986	1
Allis-Chalmers	175	1985	11
White Motor	74	1981	8
Rath Packing	66	1982	3
Wisconsin Steel	61	1980	2
Braniff Airlines	60	1982	3
Continental Steel	60	1986	3
White Farm Equipment	57	1982	4
McLoughlin Steel	51	1983	2
Phoenix Steel	43	1982	3
Alan Wood Steel	41	1977	3
	$1416		50

*Amount of underfunding represents the excess of pension plan liabilities over assets.
Source: U.S. Department of Labor, Pension and Welfare Benefits Administration, *Trends in Pensions,* Washington, D.C., 1989, p. 385.

tion, these were amortizable (could be written off) over 30 years. Should investment or mortality experience create unanticipated gains or losses, these differences were to be amortized over 15 years.

In 1987, the U.S. Congress updated ERISA funding requirements in order to prevent plan sponsors from inadequately funding their plans. *Minimum* funding for a given year became the sum of:

- Normal cost
- Investment and mortality experience gains and losses, amortized over 5 years
- Liabilities attributable to changes in actuarial assumptions, amortized over 10 years
- Required reduction of past funding deficits (as applicable)

Vesting and Coverage

While pension benefits begin to accumulate (or accrue) as soon as an individual is eligible to participate, benefits may not be *vested* until after some minimum period of time elapses. Whenever an *employee* contributes to his or her own plan, associated pension benefits are immediately vested. Frequently, *employer* contributions to defined contribution plans are also immediately vested. Approximately 90 percent of the participants in medium to large defined contribution plans in the United States have partially or fully vested pension benefits. The comparable statistic for defined benefit plans is roughly 50 percent.

With respect to vesting, ERISA provides a number of alternatives for employers. Under the 1974 act, a participant must be fully vested after 15 years and at least 50 percent vested—that is, entitled to at least 50 percent of accrued benefits—after 10 years. Specific vesting schemes were:

- 100 percent vesting after 10 years of service, with no vesting prior to 10 years' service. (This approach is also called *cliff* vesting.)
- *Gradual* vesting during a 15-year period:
  a. 25 percent after 5 years.
  b. 5 percent per year for years 6 through 10.
  c. 10 percent per year for years 11 through 15.
- The *rule of 45* requires 50 percent vesting whenever the sum of participant age and years of service equals 45. (The participant must have a minimum of 5 years of service.) An additional 10 percent per year is required during each of the next 5 years. A firm electing the rule of 45 is also subject to the 50 percent vesting minimum after 10 years, regardless of age.

The Tax Reform Act of 1986 reduced these alternatives to essentially two:

- 100 percent vesting after 5 years of service, with no vesting prior to the 5 years of service.
- Gradual vesting during a 7-year period:
  a. 20 percent after 3 years.
  b. 20 percent per year for years 4 through 7.

Multiemployer pension plans (such as the Teamsters Union) are also still permitted to use 100 percent vesting after 10 years.

Class-year pension plans in which each year's contribution vests separately are subject to a 100 percent vesting requirement after 5 years of service. Examples of these plans include defined contribution plans, such as profit sharing, stock bonus, and money purchase plans.[8] In addition to direct participant benefits, ERISA requires all pension plans to pay pension payments to surviving spouses when the participant dies (survivor benefits).

Generally, all employees must be covered by a sponsor's primary pension plan. Eligibility is required by ERISA for any employee, age 25 or older, after 1 year of service. A year of service is 12 consecutive months involving not less than 1000 hours of paid employment. New employees close to retirement age under the pension plan may be excluded. It is not mandatory that an employee who begins work within 5 years of retirement age be covered under a defined benefit plan. However, no such exclusion is possible under a defined contribution plan.

Fiduciary Responsibility

Each pension plan must provide for one or more persons with the authority to control the operation of the plan. Either the plan sponsor, participants, or both appoint these *fiduciaries.* The duties of a fiduciary may involve management of the plan or of pension fund assets. Accordingly, the designation applies to directors, officers, members of the investment committee, consultants, and advisers. In addition, any person that a fiduciary designates to fulfill some part of the latter's responsibilities also becomes a fiduciary.

An ethical standard for the conduct of a fiduciary was established by ERISA. The "prudent-man" rule, long used in the management of investment trusts, was applied. Under this standard, a fiduciary must act with the same diligence, skill, and prudence of a prudent person in like circumstances.

With respect to the investment of plan assets, subsequent rulings by the U.S. Department of Labor have interpreted the prudent-man rule from the perspective of total return. That is, every investment is not necessarily held to the prudent-man standard. Rather, the entire portfolio is considered. Relevant factors are, of course, diversification, short-term liquidity needs, and income requirements in order to satisfy plan obligations.

Nevertheless, there are certain activities that are strictly prohibited. A fiduciary may not:

- Manage the assets of the plan in order to benefit himself or herself.
- Accept compensation from any party that is involved in transactions that also involve plan assets.
- Act on behalf of any party with interests that conflict with those of the plan or its participants.
- Invest in assets that are not under the jurisdiction of U.S. district courts.

In general, a fiduciary is expected to fulfill his or her responsibilities to the plan in a way that neither compromises the interests of participants nor serves to promote the personal interests of the fiduciary. Plan assets are to be managed with the sole objective of providing benefits for participants and their beneficiaries. Those who perform plan asset transactions must be bonded (insured) for 10 percent of the aggregate dollar amount involved, with the maximum bond being $500,000. Last, each fiduciary must operate in accordance with the documents governing the plan.

PENSION FUND ASSETS

Trends over Time

As noted in Chapter 21, during the 17-year period ended 1991, the financial assets of open-end investment companies (excluding money market funds) and money market mu-

[8]Profit sharing plans involve contributions in cash based on sponsor profits. Stock bonus plans are similar except that contributions are in the form of the sponsor's (employer's) stock. Money purchase plans require cash contributions, usually a percentage of participant salary.

tual funds grew at average annual rates of 19 and 38 percent, respectively. Together, these firms outpaced all other financial institutions in terms of asset expansion for this 17-year period.

However, pension funds experienced the next highest growth rate. As indicated in Exhibits 22-13 and 22-14, financial assets of private and state and local pension funds grew by 13 [($1231.8 billion/$158.7 billion)$^{1/17}$ − 1] and 14 percent [$801.1 billion/$88 billion)$^{1/17}$ − 1] percent per year, respectively, from 1974 through 1991. Over the 27-year period ended 1991, the growth of pension fund assets was roughly equivalent to that of mutual funds; private plans grew 11.5% [($1231.8 billion/$64.9 billion)$^{1/27}$ − 1], state and local government plans 12.9% [($801.1 billion/$30.6 billion)$^{1/27}$ − 1]. Over the same period, mutual funds grew at an annual rate of 12.1 percent; money market funds did not exist before the 1970s.

Over time, the mix of pension fund assets has changed in some respects. Time deposits represented a substantial percentage of fund assets in 1989—8.1 percent in the case of private pension funds and 3.3 percent in the case of state and local government funds. These percentages had declined by 1991, but pension funds were still large purchasers of these instruments.[9]

[9]It should be noted that these instruments were not available in high-yielding, negotiable form until after 1960.

EXHIBIT 22-13 FINANCIAL ASSETS OF U.S. PRIVATE PENSION FUNDS, 1964–1991

	1964	1969	1974	1979	1984	1989	1991
Financial assets (billions)	$64.9	$103.8	$158.7	$386.1	$713.9	$1205.6	$1231.8
Checkable deposits and currency	1.4%	.9%	2.2%	1.3%	.7%	1.0%	.4%
Time deposits	—	.6	2.5	6.5	6.2	8.1	3.2
Money market fund shares	—	—	—	.3	1.1	.8	2.1
Cash & cash equivalents	1.4	1.5	4.7	8.1	8.0	9.9	5.7
Equity investments:							
Mutual fund shares	.5	.7	1.2	1.3	1.2	2.7	4.3
Other corporate equities	51.9	59.2	47.1	45.4	43.2	45.2	60.0
Total equities	52.4	59.9	48.3	46.7	44.4	47.9	64.3
Debt instruments:							
Government:							
Treasury issues	4.1	2.1	5.4	6.7	7.4	7.8	8.3
Agency issues	.8	.6	2.7	3.3	6.1	4.5	4.2
Total government	4.9	2.7	8.1	10.0	13.5	12.3	12.5
Corporate and foreign bonds	32.7	26.6	22.0	16.5	15.5	15.4	12.1
Mortgages:							
Home	2.0	1.7	.5	.3	.4	.1	1.1
Multifamily	1.2	1.2	.3	.1	.1	.1	.1
Commercial	1.1	1.2	.7	.4	.5	.3	1.1
Total mortgages	4.3	4.1	1.5	.8	1.0	.5	2.3
Commercial paper & banker's acceptances	—	—	3.4	4.0	5.9	8.1	3.1
Total debt instruments	41.9	33.4	35.0	31.3	35.9	36.3	30.0
Miscellaneous	4.3	5.2	12.0	13.9	11.7	5.9	—
	100.0%	100.0%	100.0%	100.0%	100.0%	100.0%	100.0%

Source: Board of Governors of the Federal Reserve System, *Flow of Funds Accounts, Financial Assets and Liabilities,* various issues.

EXHIBIT 22-14 FINANCIAL ASSETS OF STATE AND LOCAL GOVERNMENT PENSION FUNDS IN THE UNITED STATES, 1964–1991

	1964	1969	1974	1979	1984	1989	1991
Financial assets (billions)	$30.6	$53.2	$88.0	$169.7	$356.6	$633.4	$801.1
Checkable deposits and currency	1.0%	.6%	.4%	.3%	.6%	.4%	.4%
Time deposits	—	.4	1.7	2.1	3.4	3.3	2.6
Cash & cash equivalents	1.0	1.0	2.1	2.4	4.0	3.7	3.0
Corporate equities	6.5	13.7	18.7	21.8	27.1	37.6	39.9
Debt instruments:							
U.S. government:							
Treasury issues	22.9	10.1	1.8	8.7	19.0	21.8	17.7
Agency issues	1.3	3.0	5.2	9.1	12.1	9.3	10.2
Total U.S. government	24.2	13.1	7.0	17.8	31.1	31.1	27.9
Tax-exempt	9.5	4.3	1.1	2.3	.4	.1	.1
Corporate and foreign bonds	48.7	57.3	62.5	50.1	33.1	25.0	28.4
Mortgages:							
Home	5.2	5.2	3.6	1.8	1.1	.5	.2
Multifamily	3.3	3.5	2.5	1.9	1.7	.9	.1
Commercial	1.3	1.3	2.3	1.9	1.5	1.1	.4
Farm	.3	.6	.2	—	—	—	—
Total mortgages	10.1	10.6	8.6	5.6	4.3	2.5	.7
Total debt instruments	92.5	85.3	79.2	75.8	68.9	58.7	57.1
	100.0%	100.0%	100.0%	100.0%	100.0%	100.0%	100.0%

Source: Board of Governors of the Federal Reserve System, *Flow of Funds Accounts, Financial Assets and Liabilities,* various issues.

EXHIBIT 22-15 INVESTORS IN LARGE TIME DEPOSITS IN THE UNITED STATES, 1964–1991

	1964	1969	1974	1979	1984	1989	1991
Large time deposits* (billions)	$25.1	$30.5	$167.1	$256.9	$469.7	$615.3	$552.9
Households	7.2%	10.1%	33.2%	28.1%	27.5%	19.4%	32.8%
Business sector	26.7	12.1	16.9	21.2	32.3	37.5	36.3
State and local gov't.	39.0	42.8	29.1	22.2	10.9	6.5	3.5
Foreign sector	21.9	28.8	12.6	9.6	8.5	8.5	8.0
Depository institutions:							
S&Ls	.8	.6	2.2	1.9	2.0	1.1	.9
Mutual savings banks	4.4	.3	.6	.2	.1	—†	—
Credit unions	—	2.6	1.1	1.0	1.7	2.0	2.5
Total depository institutions	5.2	3.5	3.9	3.1	3.8	3.1	3.4
Pension funds:							
Private	—	2.0	2.4	9.8	9.4	15.9	7.2
State & local gov't.	—	.7	.9	1.3	2.6	3.4	3.8
Total pension funds	—	2.7	3.3	11.1	12.0	19.3	11.0
Money market funds	—	—	1.0	4.7	5.0	5.7	5.0
	100.0%	100.0%	100.0%	100.0%	100.0%	100.0%	100.0%

*Includes negotiable and nonnegotiable time deposits of $100,000 or more.
†Less than .1%.
Source: Board of Governors of the Federal Reserve System, *Flow of Funds Accounts, Financial Assets and Liabilities,* various issues.

Exhibit 22-15 illustrates the importance of pension funds in the large time deposit market. In 1969, pension funds held less than 3 percent of all large time deposits outstanding. By 1989, the percentage was closer to 20 percent, then declined to 11 percent in 1991. Nevertheless, with the exception of the nonfinancial business sector, no other sector increased its proportional share of large time deposits outstanding as much as pension funds over the 22 years ended 1991.

Corporate stock (excluding mutual fund shares) constituted over 50 percent of private pension fund assets in 1964 but only 6.5 percent of state and local government funds. By 1991, the percentages were up to 64 and 40 percent, respectively. In the market for corporate equities (Exhibit 22-16), this translates into a significant presence. Pension funds held less than 6 percent of corporate stock in 1964. Their 27 percent share in 1991 made pension funds the largest institutional investor in the stock market. Over the same period, the part held by individuals declined from almost 85 to just under 54 percent. In a real sense, institutional investing on behalf of individuals now substitutes for previously direct stock market involvement.[10]

United States Treasury and government agency securities held more prominent positions in pension fund portfolios in 1991 than in 1964, particularly in private funds. As Exhibits 22-17 and 22-18 show, the role of pension funds in the government securities market has expanded as a result. In 1991, these institutions held 9.5 and 9 percent of all U.S. Treasury and government agency securities, respectively.

The net effect of these changes is that pension funds have become major participants in today's money and capital markets. With the current growth in plans, particularly defined contribution plans, the role of pension funds in financial markets will not soon diminish.

[10]Of course, the same can be said to a lesser extent about mutual funds.

EXHIBIT 22-16 INVESTORS IN CORPORATE EQUITIES IN THE UNITED STATES, 1964–1991

	1964	1969	1974	1979	1984	1989	1991
Corporate equities* (billions)	$633.0	$866.4	$641.7	$1179.5	$2021.5	$3246.0	$3907.2
Households	84.7%	80.7%	71.7%	68.9%	65.4%	57.3%	53.8%
Foreign sector	2.2	3.1	3.8	4.1	4.7	6.3	6.4
Mutual savings banks	.3	.3	.6	.4	.2	.3	.2
Pension funds:							
Private	5.3	7.1	11.6	14.9	15.3	16.8	18.9
State and local gov't.	.3	.9	2.6	3.1	4.8	7.3	8.2
Total pension funds	5.6	8.0	14.2	18.0	20.1	24.1	27.1
Insurance companies:							
LIfe insurance	1.2	1.5	3.3	3.3	3.0	3.2	2.6
Other insurance	1.8	1.5	2.0	2.1	2.2	2.4	2.7
Total insurance:	3.0	3.0	5.3	5.4	5.2	5.6	5.3
Mutual funds†	4.1	4.7	4.1	3.0	4.0	6.0	7.0
Brokers & dealers	.1	.2	.3	.2	.4	.4	.2
	100.0%	100.0%	100.0%	100.0%	100.0%	100.0%	100.0%

*Represents the market value of corporate equities excluding mutual fund shares.
†Excludes money market mutual funds.
Source: Board of Governors of the Federal Reserve System, *Flow of Funds Accounts, Financial Assets and Liabilities,* various issues.

EXHIBIT 22-17 INVESTORS IN U.S. TREASURY SECURITIES 1964–1991 (PERCENTAGES)

	1964	1969	1974	1979	1984	1989	1991
Treasury issues (billions)	$256.6	$278.4	$351.5	$658.0	$1373.4	$2133.4	$2598.4
Sponsored credit agencies*	.7%	.7%	.4%	.2%	.3%	1.2%	1.8%
Monetary authority†	14.2	20.5	22.8	17.7	11.6	10.7	9.3
Households	29.5	34.2	28.7	30.8	31.1	26.5	28.6
Business sector	5.6	2.2	1.0	2.2	4.1	4.0	2.9
State and local gov't.	5.9	7.9	7.3	6.8	5.1	8.8	7.2
Foreign sector	5.2	3.6	16.6	17.7	14.1	17.0	16.2
Depository institutions:							
Commercial banks	24.8	19.9	16.0	15.1	13.5	9.5	7.5
S&Ls	2.7	3.4	.5	.5	1.8	.5	.7
Mutual savings banks	2.3	1.1	.7	.7	.7	.4	.4
Credit unions	.1	.2	.2	.1	.2	.7	.3
Total depository institutions	29.9	24.6	17.4	16.4	16.2	11.1	8.9
Pension funds:							
Private	1.1	.8	2.5	4.0	3.9	4.4	4.0
State and local gov't.	2.7	1.9	.5	2.2	4.9	6.5	5.5
Total pension funds	3.8	2.7	3.0	6.2	8.8	10.9	9.5
Insurance companies:							
Life insurance	2.2	1.5	1.0	.8	3.0	2.9	2.2
Other insurance	2.2	1.2	.8	1.6	1.7	2.4	3.4
Total insurance	4.4	2.7	1.8	2.4	4.7	5.3	5.7
Investment companies:							
Mutual funds‡	.3	.3	.3	.2	.8	3.8	3.6
Money market funds	—	—	—§	.3	1.9	.6	2.5
Total investment companies	.3	.3	.3	.5	2.7	4.4	6.1
Brokers and dealers	.5	.6	.7	(.9)¶	1.3	.1	3.8
	100.0%	100.0%	100.0%	100.0%	100.0%	100.0%	100.0%

*Includes: Federal Home Loan Banks, Federal National Mortgage Association, Federal Home Loan Mortgage Corporation, Student Loan Marketing Association, Federal Land Banks, Federal Intermediate Credit Banks, Banks for Cooperatives, and the Financing Corporation. (See Chapters 4 and 5.)

†Federal Reserve System.

‡Excludes money market mutual funds.

§Less than .1%.

¶Represents security repurchase agreements, net. (See Chapter 3.)

Source: Board of Governors of the Federal Reserve System, *Flow of Funds Accounts, Financial Assets and Liabilities,* various issues.

Comparison to Commercial Banks

The industry balance sheet for commercial banks differs from those of the pension fund industries is several ways. As shown in Exhibit 22-19, equity securities dominate the asset portfolios of pension funds. Mortgage loans and other debt (commercial paper, banker's acceptances, and other loans) comprise the largest share of bank assets. As pension funds have increased their proportional holdings of government bonds over time (including agency bonds that have been substituted for mortgage loans), commercial banks have curtailed theirs.

The large concentration of loans combined with reduced holdings of government securities has caused commercial banks to become much less liquid than in 1964. On the other hand, pension funds have increased their holdings of readily marketable government securities and marketable equity securities. These factors indicate that pension

EXHIBIT 22-18 INVESTORS IN U.S. GOVERNMENT AGENCY SECURITIES, 1964–1991

	1964	1969	1974	1979	1984	1989	1991
Government agency issues (billions)	$14.8	$42.9	$106.1	$235.2	$529.4	$1226.3	$1476.7
Sponsored credit agencies*	.7%	.5%	.4%	.3%	.1%	—†	.7%
Monetary authority‡	—	—	4.4	3.5	1.6	.6%	.4
Households	11.4	27.5	13.8	15.0	10.2	20.9	23.9
Business sector	6.7	4.0	2.8	.6	.3	.1	0.1
State and local gov't.	19.5	17.7	14.2	14.9	10.4	7.3	1.9
Foreign sector	6.7	6.3	2.6	3.3	2.3	3.1	3.8
Depository institutions:							
Commercial banks	34.9	23.5	31.3	21.7	14.7	14.3	20.1
S&Ls	4.7	5.4	12.4	13.3	22.9	17.3	11.6
Mutual savings banks	5.4	4.2	4.2	6.2	4.6	2.7	1.7
Credit unions	—	1.2	2.0	1.1	1.1	.6	1.0
Total depository institutions	45.0	34.3	49.9	42.3	43.3	34.9	34.4
Pension funds:							
Private	3.3	1.4	4.1	5.4	8.2	4.5	3.5
State and local gov't.	2.7	3.7	4.3	6.5	8.2	4.8	5.5
Total pension funds	6.0	5.1	8.4	11.9	16.4	9.3	9.0
Insurance companies:							
Life insurance	.7	.9	1.0	4.0	7.0	6.2	8.4
Other insurance	3.3	3.7	2.5	2.5	2.6	2.5	1.8
Total insurance	4.0	4.6	3.5	6.5	9.6	8.7	10.2
Investment companies:							
Mutual funds§	—	—	—	—	.1	2.7	2.6
Money market funds	—	—	—	.17	3.2	1.1	2.7
Total investment companies	—	—	—	1.7	3.3	3.8	5.3
CMOs¶	—	—	—	—	2.5	11.3	10.3
	100.0%	100.0%	100.0%	100.0%	100.0%	100.0%	100.0%

*Includes Federal Home Loan Banks, Federal National Mortgage Association, Federal Home Loan Mortgage Corporation, Student Loan Marketing Association, Federal Land Banks, Federal Intermediate Credit Banks, Banks for Cooperatives, and the Financing Corporation. (See Chapters 4 and 5.)

†Less than .1%.

‡Federal Reserve System.

§Excludes money market mutual funds.

¶Collateralized mortgage obligation. (See Chapters 4 and 5.)

Source: Board of Governors of the Federal Reserve System. *Flow of Funds Accounts, Financial Assets and Liabilities,* various issues.

funds should generally be considered much more liquid than commercial banks. When the nature of the two institutions' liabilities are considered, this is particularly true. Commercial bank liabilities are short-term and due on demand for the most part. Pension fund liabilities are much more long term and much more predictable.

International Comparisons

Heavy concentrations of stock and bond investments are also typical in other countries, as shown by Exhibit 22-20. This pattern is noted in the United Kingdom, Japan, Canada, Germany, and France. In the Netherlands and Switzerland, the combinations of loans plus private placements and real estate plus mortgages make up 55 and 42 percent of pension fund asset portfolios, respectively. In this sense, the pension funds in these countries are invested more like U.S. commercial bank assets.

EXHIBIT 22-19 ASSET COMPOSITION OF COMMERCIAL BANKS, PRIVATE PENSION FUNDS, AND STATE AND LOCAL GOVERNMENT PENSION FUNDS, 1964 AND 1991

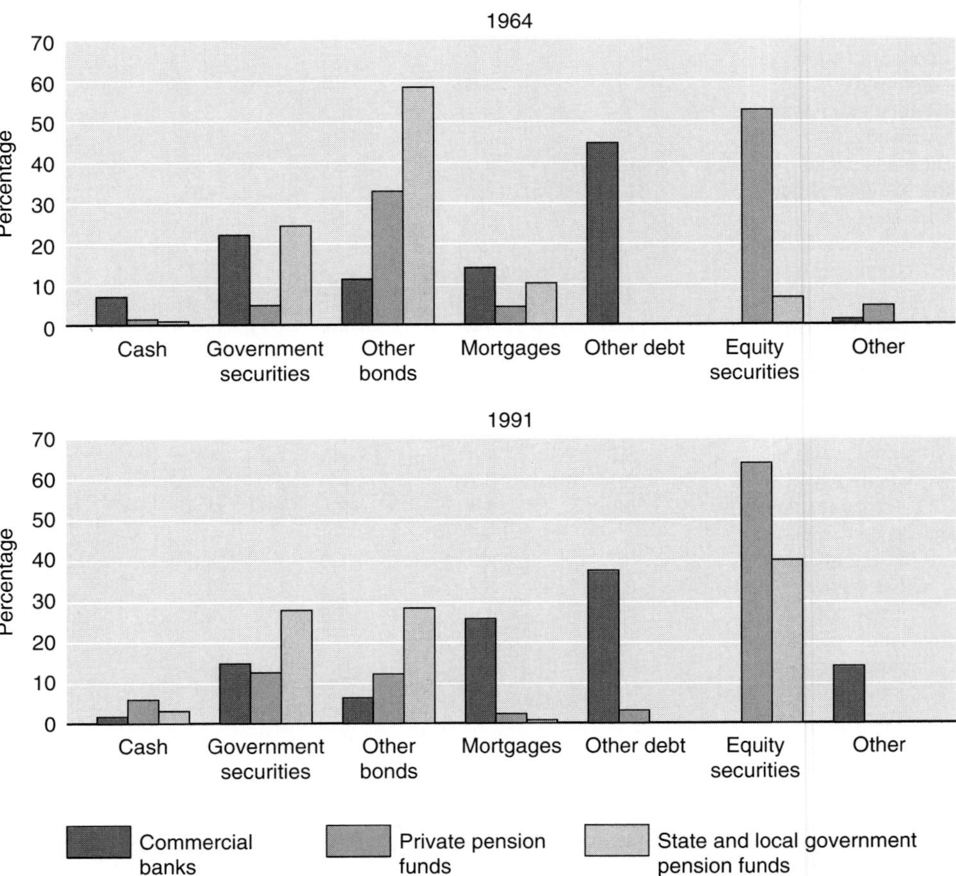

Source: Data from Board of Governors of the Federal Reserve System, *Flow of Funds Accounts, Financial Assets and Liabilities,* various issues.

EXHIBIT 22-20 ASSET MIX OF PRIVATE PENSION FUNDS IN SELECTED COUNTRIES, 1988 (PERCENTAGES)

	U.K.	Japan	Canada	Netherlands	Switzerland	Germany	France
Cash and short-term assets	5	—	12	—	10	2	—
Stocks	69	42	34	14	7	44	—
Bonds	13	38	32	21	30	37	80%
Loans and private placements	—	16	4	40	17	—	—
Real estate and mortgages	10	—	6	15	25	16	—
Pooled funds*	2	—	10	—	7	—	—
Other assets	1	4	2	10	4	1	20
	100	100	100	100	100	100	100

*Includes mutual funds, investment trusts, and insurance company managed funds.

Source: U.S. Department of Labor, Pension and Welfare Benefits Administration. *Pension Policy: An International Perspective,* Washington, D.C., 1990, p. 32.

SUMMARY

Pension plans grew in importance as personal income levels increased. The defined benefit plan was the most frequently adopted type of pension initially, especially among the larger plans. In recent years, however, far more defined contribution plans have been formed than defined benefit. In the public sector, government employees have pension coverage at both the federal and state and local levels. In addition, virtually all workers in the United States are protected by the social security system, a pay-as-you-go, minimum-income maintenance arrangement.

In addition to basic employer-sponsored pension plans, individuals may save for retirement through 401(k) plans, individual retirement accounts, and Keogh accounts. Many of these accounts are invested in investment company shares (mutual funds).

Pension funds in other major industrialized countries operate much as U.S. plans, except that the U.S. market is more highly regulated. Regulations cover plan funding, participant vesting, and the responsibilities of fiduciaries. Another difference is that the private pension plans in Japan (until recently) and France are almost entirely pay-as-you-go systems. This is not true in the United States. Among eight major industrialized countries, the United States accounts for 44 percent of participants and 68 percent of pension fund assets.

With its large number of plans, both public and private, U.S. pension funds controlled over $3 trillion in 1991. As a result, these funds are currently the most important institutional investors in a number of U.S. financial markets.

KEY TERMS

defined benefit pension plan
defined contribution pension plan
ERISA
fiduciary responsibility
401(k) plan
general accounts
individual retirement account (IRA)
insured pension plan
Keogh account
normal cost
past service liabilities
pension liability
pension plan funding
plan termination
portability
private pension fund
public pension fund
separate accounts
social security
vesting

END-OF-CHAPTER QUESTIONS

1. Differentiate public, private, and insured pension plans in general terms.
2. What distinguishes a defined benefit pension plan from a defined contribution plan?
3. Why are social security contributions commonly considered taxes rather than pension contributions?
4. Is the federal civil service pension plan operated in the same manner as the social security system from a financial standpoint?
5. With respect to defined benefit plans, what is the difference between unit-benefit and flat-benefit formulas?
6. What are some of the contributing factors to the increasing numbers of defined contribution plans?
7. Summarize the regulatory provisions of ERISA in the areas of pension funding, vesting of benefits, and fiduciary responsibility, in general terms.
8. More specifically, enumerate the vesting options available to plan sponsors under ERISA.
9. Relate the "prudent-man" rule to the responsibilities of a pension plan asset manager.
10. In which financial markets have pension funds become particularly important? Be specific in your answer.

11. Investigate the provisions of the pension plan to which you (or a member of your family) belong(s).
  a. Is it a defined benefit or defined contribution plan?
  b. What are the vesting requirements?

12. Contributions to the social security system in the United States are counted as revenues in the federal fiscal budget. The current excess of contributions over disbursements reduces the federal budget deficit. What will be the effect of this accounting when the "baby boomers" begin to retire?

13. More jobs have been created in the nation's service sector in recent years than in the manufacturing sector. What impact might this have on future retiree benefits that accrue to workers?

14. As corporate America restructures and downsizes, what type of pension plan will best protect workers?

15. If an overfunded defined benefit pension plan is terminated, converted to a defined contribution plan, and the vested pension liability satisfied by purchasing pension annuity contracts from an insurance company, what risk is faced by the pension plan participants?

16. In what ways is the exposure of Pension Benefit Guaranty Corporation similar to that of the Federal Deposit Insurance Corporation?

SELECTED REFERENCES

Board of Governors of the Federal Reserve System. *Flow of Funds Accounts, Financial Assets and Liabilities,* various issues.

Coleman, Barbara J. *Primer on ERISA,* the Bureau of National Affairs, Inc., Washington, D.C., 1985.

Investment Company Institute. *Mutual Fund Factbook 1990; Industry Trends and Statistics for 1990,* Washington, D.C., 1991.

Ippolito, Richard A. *Pensions, Economics, and Public Policy,* Dow Jones–Irwin, Homewood, Illinois, 1986.

Lynn, Robert J. *The Pension Crisis,* Lexington Books, Lexington, Massachusetts, 1983.

Office of Management and Budget, Executive Office of the President of the United States. *Historical Tables; Budget of the United States Government; Fiscal Year 1990,* Washington, D.C., 1990.

Slimmon, Robert F. *Successful Pension Design for Small- to Medium-Sized Businesses,* Prentice-Hall, Inc., Englewood Cliffs, New Jersey, 1985.

U.S. Department of Commerce, Bureau of the Census. *Statistical Abstract of the United States, 1989,* 109th ed., Washington, D.C., 1989.

U.S. Department of Labor, Pension and Welfare Benefits Administration. *Trends in Pensions,* Washington, D.C., 1989.

U.S. Department of Labor, Pension and Welfare Benefits Administration. *Pension Policy: An International Perspective,* Washington, D.C., 1991.

CHAPTER 23

INSURANCE COMPANIES

CHAPTER OUTLINE

CHAPTER OVERVIEW

This chapter:

- Defines the concepts and classifications of insurance
- Examines components and trends of industry profitability
- Discusses regulation of insurance companies
- Describes traditional insurance products
- Outlines recent economic and social factors and their impact on the industry
- Analyzes investment trends

Insuring risks is an activity that is almost as old as commercial banking. Insurance companies offer a wide range of products including life, health, property, and liability insurance. In 1991, the industry controlled financial assets of almost $2 trillion. After commercial banks and pension funds, insurance companies control more resources than any other financial industry in the United States.

Yet, insurance companies have not been immune to the challenges posed by volatile interest rates, deregulation of other financial institutions, and the economic distress caused by "junk" bonds and collapsing real estate values. After several well-publicized failures, policyholders have begun to wonder whether state regulators are adequately protecting their interests. In some circles, there are calls for greater federal regulation of these firms. In what was once considered a safe, conservative industry, there is now a crisis of confidence.

THE NATURE OF INSURANCE

Confidence in the insurance industry is of utmost importance because *insurance policies* protect individuals and businesses from the effects of unfavorable events.

Insurance policy:
A contract that provides a party (the insured) with protection against the financial loss associated with an undesirable event.

To obtain this protection, the insured pays *insurance premiums.*

Insurance premiums:
Either periodic or lump-sum payments to an insurer in exchange for protection against a specified risk.

Should the undesirable event occur, the insured receives monetary compensation from the insurer in accordance with the contract between the two parties. By purchasing the protection, the insured reduces exposure to potential loss. Should no claim arise—that is, should the undesirable event not occur—the insurer earns profits by the following equation:

$$\begin{aligned}\text{Profits} = {} & \text{premiums collected} \\ & + \text{income from the investment of premiums} \\ & - \text{operating expenses}\end{aligned}$$

An insurer cannot be certain whether an undesirable event will occur with respect to a particular insured party. However, by selling insurance policies to a large number of parties, the insurer establishes a fund from which future losses, or claims, are paid. The amount of an individual premium will depend on:

- The insurer's past experience
- The probability of loss
- The amount of compensation that is contractually agreed upon in the event of loss

Insurance Classifications

Insurance coverage is classified by the type of undesirable event against which the insured seeks protection. The two main classifications are *life* insurance and *property and casualty* insurance.

Life Insurance If the undesirable event is premature loss of life, the insurance contract is a *long-term* arrangement. The uncertainty for the insured is *when* loss of life occurs. *Life insurance* protects the beneficiary of the insured from an *unexpected* loss of income. Unless the policy is for a specified period of time (term) and the insured outlives that period, a claim is eventually paid. Thus, a life insurance policy is a kind of savings vehicle with protection against an unanticipated event. Over time, life insurance companies have offered more products that provide benefits to the insured after his or her productive years. Functionally, these products are similar to pension funds.

Life insurers set premiums that are based on:

- Age of the insured
- Average life expectancy
- Anticipated investment returns on the insurance fund
- Operating expenses
- A reasonable profit margin

Within a large group of policyholders, the percentage that will give rise to claims within a particular year may be fairly accurately estimated. Operating expenses are also reasonably predictable. Thus, life insurers must carefully evaluate their investment income assumptions in setting appropriate premiums.

Property and Casualty Insurance When the undesirable event is *not* associated with unexpected loss of life or livelihood, the insurance is referred to as *property and casualty insurance.* Examples are automobile, fire, homeowner's, and liability insurance. While these policies cover a wide variety of risks, they also share certain common features. First, the policies are essentially *short-term* contracts, subject to frequent renewal; that is, the insurer may cancel coverage after a relatively brief period of time. Second, there is *no savings component* associated with property and casualty insurance. If the event against which protection is provided does not occur, the insured is not entitled to cash payment. Last, because of the first two factors, a property and casualty insurer must rely more on *risk evaluation* in setting premiums than a life insurer.

Basic Principles of Insurance

A few basic concepts are helpful in order to understand the nature of the products that insurance companies offer and the operation of the firms themselves.

- *Insurable interest.* There must be a relationship between the insured and the subject covered by the insurance. Further, potential harm to the subject must represent a corresponding financial loss for the insured.
- *Utmost good faith.* Full disclosures on both sides of the transactions are expected. The insurer must inform the insured of all contractual terms. The insured must provide all information that is relevant for the assessment of risk.
- *Indemnity.* The insured is entitled to recover the amount of actual loss in connection with a property and casualty insurance claim, but may not profit as a result.
- *Right of subrogation.* If the insured receives remedy for a loss from a third party, which is responsible for the loss, the insurer is entitled to be reimbursed up to the amount of the claim actually paid by insurer.
- *Contribution.* With respect to an indemnity policy, if more than one insurer is involved, the insurer that actually pays a claim may collect a proportional share of such payment from the remaining insurers.

These principles are designed to maintain the integrity of the insurance process. The insurable interest principle is intended to discourage "gambling," for example, buying life insurance policies that cover strangers or well-known personalities with whom the insured has no financial relationship. The principle of utmost good faith protects both sides of the insurance transaction. The remaining concepts of indemnity, subrogation, and contribution essentially protect insurance companies from overpayment of claims.

INSURANCE COMPANIES

In terms of organizational form, insurance companies may be *mutual* or *stock* companies. The former are owned by policyholders, the latter by stockholders. In the United States, the largest and oldest insurers maintain the mutual form of business organization. Firms that have been established more recently have adopted the stock form. In total, there are over 6000 insurance companies in the United States.[1]

The Number of Firms in Selected Countries

Among industrialized countries, the number of U.S. insurance companies is relatively high, as illustrated in Exhibit 23-1. Only the number of German firms exceeds the U.S. total. Exhibit 23-1 also analyzes the populations that these companies serve. A relatively high population per company means that there are relatively few insurance companies. In the United States, the population per insurance company is approximately 43,000. The average company in New Zealand, Hong Kong, or Singapore serves somewhat fewer people, on average, while the number is slightly higher in Canada, the United Kingdom, and Australia.[2]

The population per insurance company in Switzerland is considerably higher at 88,000. This is primarily because of the historically limited role of foreign firms in the

[1]In 1990, life insurance companies and property and casualty insurance companies numbered 2200 and 3900, respectively.

[2]It should be emphasized that these are *averages.* In fact, in virtually all countries, a small number of firms dominate the insurance industry.

EXHIBIT 23-1 POPULATION PER INSURANCE COMPANY IN SELECTED COUNTRIES

Country	Number of Companies*	Population† (thousands)	Population per company (thousands)
United States	5665	246,043	43.4
Canada	391	20,882	53.4
Japan	47	122,626	2609.1
United Kingdom	852	56,936	66.8
Switzerland	68	5984	88.0
Germany	6500	60,646	9.3
France	182	55,798	306.6
Australia	246	16,260	66.1
New Zealand	88	3,343	38.0
South Korea	19	42,773	2251.2
Taiwan	23	20,004	879.3
Hong Kong	182	5,651	31.0
Singapore	82	2,645	32.3

*Represents the number of life and non-life insurance companies operating at various dates during the 1980s, with three exceptions. The relevant years for Canada and Switzerland are 1969 and 1967, respectively. In the case of Germany, the number shown applies to the mid-1970s.

†Represents 1988 populations with three exceptions. The populations shown for Canada and Switzerland are as of 1969 and 1967, respectively. The West German population is as of 1975.

Source: U.S. Department of Commerce, Bureau of the Census, *Statistical Abstract of the United States,* 1989, pp. 813–815, and World Bank, *World Development Report, 1989,* pp. 214–215.

Swiss insurance market. On the other hand, the more numerous companies in Germany serve only 9000 people, on average.

These figures are best used for general, comparative purposes in order to assess the overall structure of the insurance industry in the countries that are included. Along these lines, it is interesting to note that a Taiwanese insurance company serves an average of almost 1 million people. In Japan and South Korea, the number is in excess of 2 million.

In the case of Taiwan, this may be explained by government restrictions on the formation of new insurance companies after World War II (1939–1945). Only two firms operated in Taiwan until 1949, when the Communists took over Beijing and the Chinese Nationalist government moved from the mainland to the island. A total of seven insurance operations served the entire population until the restrictions were lifted in 1961. The governments of South Korea and Japan also tightly control their respective insurance industries, causing the relatively high averages noted in these cases.

Life Insurance in Force in Selected Countries

Another measure of the relative impact of the insurance industry in a country is the relationship between insurance in force (value of insurance policies) and the country's gross national product (GNP). Exhibit 23-2 contains countries for which this ratio exceeds 100 percent. The most notable among these is Japan, where life insurance in force is almost 400 percent of GNP. In the United States, the ratio is less than 200 percent. When the population per company is considered with this ratio, it becomes clear that the Japanese insurance industry is a major factor in that country's economy and that there are relatively few firms involved. While the U.S. industry is large and concentrated, the Japanese is even more so.

In South Korea, the population per company is quite large, but life insurance in force is approximately the same percentage as in the United States. Thus, a smaller number of Korean companies controls roughly the same share of GNP.

Compared with the United States, the insurance industries in Canada, Ireland, and South Africa command a greater share of GNP, that is, are more important in these

EXHIBIT 23-2 LIFE INSURANCE IN FORCE AS A PERCENTAGE OF GNP FOR SELECTED COUNTRIES, 1988

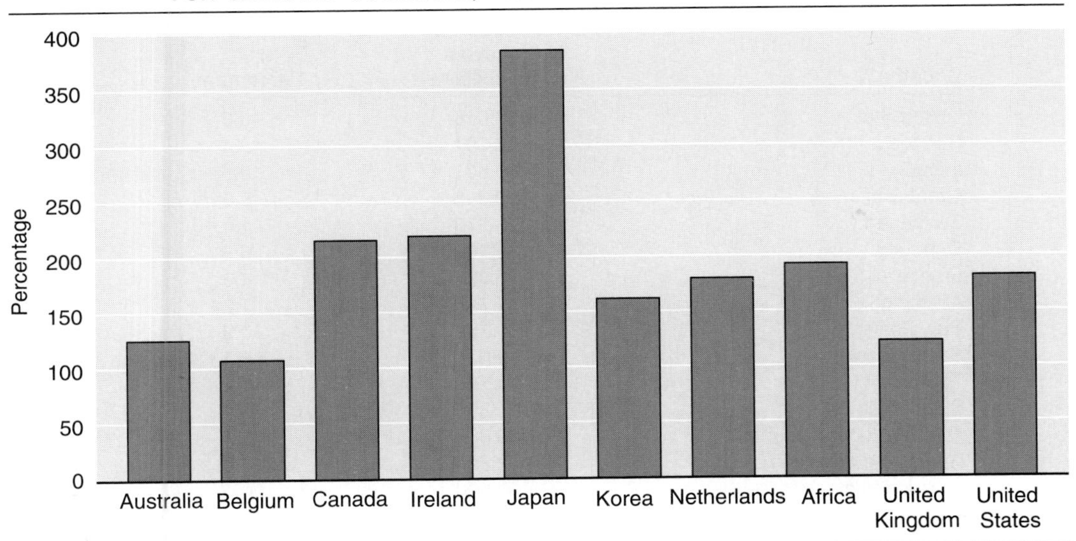

Source: Data from American Council of Life Insurance, *1990 Life Insurance Fact Book,* p. 117.

economies. In the other countries shown, the industry is not quite as dominant as in the United States.

Income and Expense

International Premium Comparisons The primary sources of income for an insurance company are *premiums* and *investment earnings.* The level of premiums depends on the policies that are written, or *underwriting* activities.[3] Investment earnings are tied to the management of insurance fund assets. Of these two sources, premium income accounts for the largest share of total income. Exhibit 23-3 contains a comparison of premiums written worldwide. From this perspective, the major markets are the United States, Japan, Germany, Great Britain, France, and Canada.

Profitability in the United States ***Benefit payments*** are the largest expense for an insurance company.

Benefit payments:
Payments by insurers to insureds that satisfy the terms of an insurance contract.

In addition, life insurance companies deduct *additions to policy reserves* to cover future payments to policyholders.

Policy reserves:
Profits set aside by insurance companies to enable them to make future benefit payments. These are the equivalent of capital or retained earnings in other industries.

Commissions and *administrative expense* apply to both life and property and casualty companies.

[3]The next section explains the underwriting function.

EXHIBIT 23-3 WORLD DISTRIBUTION OF INSURANCE PREMIUMS, 1981

Country	Total premiums (U.S.$ millions)	Percentage
United States	207,016	46.0
Canada	15,294	3.4
Japan	60,521	13.5
Great Britain	29,352	6.5
Switzerland	6,375	1.4
Germany	38,406	8.5
France	20,806	4.6
Australia	7,746	1.7
New Zealand	769	0.2
South Korea	2,024	0.4
Taiwan	752	0.2
Singapore	351	0.1
Other European countries*	38,064	8.5
Remaining countries	22,524	5.0
World total	450,000	100.0

*Includes the Netherlands, Italy, Belgium, Denmark, Ireland, Greece, Luxembourg, Sweden, Spain, Austria, Finland, Norway, Portugal, and Turkey.

Source: Wasow, Bernard, and Raymond D. Hill, Editors, *The Insurance Industry in Economics Development,* 1986, pp. 36–37.

EXHIBIT 23-4 U.S. LIFE INSURANCE COMPANY PREMIUMS, INVESTMENT INCOME, AND BENEFIT PAYMENTS, 1970–1989 ($ BILLIONS)*

	1970	1975	1980	1985	1989
Premiums	36.8	58.6	92.6	155.8	244.4
	—	(9.8%)	(9.6%)	(11.0%)	(11.9%)
Investment income	12.3	19.4	38.3	78.2	123.0
	—	(9.5%)	(14.6%)	(15.3%)	(12.0%)
Benefit payments	16.4	22.5	38.0	66.5	80.2
	—	(6.5%)	(11.1%)	(11.8%)	(4.8%)

*The numbers in parentheses are average annual growth rates over each 4- or 5-year period.
Source: American Council of Life Insurance, *1990 Life Insurance Fact Book,* pp. 42, 68.

As shown in Exhibit 23-4, total U.S. life insurance premiums in 1970 exceeded benefit payments by $20 billion, resulting in a net underwriting gain before administrative expense and commissions. After deducting these, there was still a positive underwriting cash flow of $10 billion.[4] In addition, the industry earned $12.3 billion in investment income. Thus, a total positive cash flow of $22.3 billion was realized in 1970. A $9.3 billion noncash addition to policy reserves resulted in net income before taxes of $13 billion.[5]

Since 1970, premium income has exceeded benefit payments, causing the industry to realize gains in underwriting income over the 19-year period ended 1989. In addition, investment income grew considerably faster than premiums from 1975 through 1989. Thus, the life insurance industry has maintained a strong earnings pattern in recent years. This is not to suggest that these companies have been unaffected by the forces of change that we have observed in the commercial banking, thrift, and investment company industries. Those companies that have invested in lower-quality corporate bonds, "junk bonds," have seen the value of their asset portfolios decline precipitously since the collapse of the junk bond market in the late 1980s.

Exhibit 23-5 shows similar information for property and casualty insurance companies. In 1970, premium income exceeded the sum of benefit payments and administrative expense by only $100 million. Over the next 19 years, benefit payments and administrative expense grew faster than premium income. As a result, by 1989 the non–life insurance industry sustained a pretax underwriting loss of $19.6 billion.[6]

[4]Administrative expenses, commissions, and additions to policy reserves are not shown in Exhibit 23-4.

[5]The addition to policy reserves is a noncash expense. At least in this respect, it is similar to depreciation expense or provision for possible loan loss.

[6]1989 underwriting loss (billions):

Premium income	$206.7
Benefit payments and administrative expense	(226.3)
Underwriting loss	$(19.6)

EXHIBIT 23-5 U.S. PROPERTY AND CASUALTY INSURANCE COMPANY PREMIUMS, INVESTMENT INCOME, AND TOTAL EXPENSE, 1970–1989 ($ BILLIONS)*

	1970	1975	1980	1985	1989
Premiums	32.9	50.0	95.6	144.2	206.7
	—	(8.7%)	(13.8%)	(8.6%)	(9.4%)
Investment income	2.0	4.2	11.1	19.5	35.9
	—	(16.0%)	(21.5%)	11.9%)	(16.5%)
Benefit payments and administrative expenses	32.8	53.0	97.3	166.8	226.3
	—	(10.3%)	(12.3%)	(11.4%)	(7.9%)

*The numbers in parentheses are average annual growth rates over each respective 5-year period.
Source: U.S. Department of Commerce, Bureau of the Census, *Statistical Abstract of the United States, 1989,* p. 510 [1970–1985], and Insurance Information Institute, *Data Base Reports,* April 1991, p. 3 [1989].

Even though investment income growth outpaced increases in premiums and in benefits, it was not sufficient to prevent net operating losses in the mid-1980s. The industry lost $9 billion, pretax, over the 2-year period ended 1985. It was not until the late 1980s that investment income was sufficient to offset underwriting losses which continued even then. The factors leading to these results have included both social and economic circumstances. A later section examines the impact of these factors on the insurance industry.

Insurance Industry Participants

Insurance policies are written by *underwriters.*

Insurance underwriter:
The party that assumes the risk associated with an insurance contract and agrees to pay claims arising from the policy.

In most cases, insurance companies fill the role of underwriters. (See Exhibit 23-6.)
The companies employ *insurance agents* to solicit business.

Insurance agent:
A party who conducts transactions on behalf of an insurance underwriter but takes no personal responsibility to honor the insurance contract.

An agent may have the authority to bind the insurance policy, that is, to legally commit the company to provide insurance coverage. The agent may also be permitted to accept premium payments and issue receipts for these payments. Generally, agents receive commissions, a percentage of premiums, as compensation for their services.

EXHIBIT 23-6 EARLY INSURANCE UNDERWRITERS

Almost 5000 years ago, Chinese merchants insured each other's cargo shipments by sharing the risk among themselves. Instead of placing cargo exclusively on his own boat, each merchant distributed his goods among the boats of his collaborators. They, in turn, did the same. In the event that one boat sank, no one merchant lost an entire shipment.

However, it was not until 1688 that insurance contracts were constructed in monetary terms. Once again, cargo shipments were the subject of the arrangement. At that time, England enjoyed prosperous commercial activity. Most of the goods involved were transported by sea. Lloyd's Coffee House in London became the primarily location for intelligence gathering with regard to the safe passage of specific vessels.

Since some merchants chose not to insure their ships until they were late in arriving back in London, most insurance activity began to gravitate to Lloyd's where the most up-to-date information was available.

For each insured voyage, the name of the ship was written on a piece of paper, together with all relevant details about the shipment. A person wishing to partially insure the vessel and cargo wrote his name and the portion of the risk that he was willing to assume under the details. These insurers, therefore, became known as *underwriters.* The coffee house was later known as Lloyd's of London.

Source: Falkena, H. B., L. J. Fourie, and W. J. Kok. *The Mechanics of the South African Financial System; Financial Institutions, Instruments, and Markets,* 1984, p. 121, and Davison, Ian Hay, *A View of the Room; Lloyds; Change and Disclosure,* 1987, pp. 20–21.

An *insurance broker* is self-employed and acts as a middleman between the insured and the insurer.

Insurance broker:
A party who conducts insurance transactions as an independent third party who brings together the insurer and the insured.

A broker generally negotiates on behalf of the insured to obtain the most competitively priced insurance product. However, the broker's compensation is, again, a commission that is paid by the insurer.

Regulation

United States Compared with commercial banks, thrift institutions, investment companies, and pension funds, insurance companies are subject to relatively little federal regulation in the United States. The Internal Revenue Service (IRS) is the industry's primary federal regulator.

In general, special taxation rules apply to *life insurance* companies. While an insurance company's taxable income is currently defined as gross income *less* deductions, an additional deduction of 20 percent of taxable income is permitted. This provision was granted in the 1984 Tax Reform Act to effectively exclude investment income from taxation. The rationale is that life insurance investment income is income primarily from policyholder savings and, therefore, should not be taxed at the corporate level.[7] This provision does not apply to *property and casualty* companies.

Most insurance company regulation occurs at the state level. The focus of regulation is to protect policyholders from company insolvency. Accordingly, asset portfolio composition is regulated as well as the premium-to-capital ratio. In addition, states stipulate minimum absolute capital requirements in order for a firm to be permitted to conduct insurance business.

For example, regulators in the state of New York have adopted a rule of thumb that *non–life* insurance premiums should not exceed an amount equal to twice the company's surplus. Limiting the amount of premiums that can be accepted is intended to ensure adequate resources for claims that may arise. In all U.S. states, it is not uncommon for *life* insurance company investments in common stock to be limited in some way. Such provisions attempt to protect policyholder savings from the extreme volatility associated with equity securities.

Life insurance firms have been able to avoid a certain amount of restriction with respect to asset composition, however. In most states, *separate accounts* have fewer investment guidelines than *general accounts*. Separate accounts are functionally similar to investment companies and are commonly offered as retirement savings vehicles, managed by a sponsoring insurance company. General accounts are legally assets of the insurance company, as well as associated liabilities.

Insurance companies are also exempted from antitrust law at the federal level. This means that insurance companies have the legal right to share information about their loss experience and to cooperate with other companies to set their premium rates. This is essentially legalized price-fixing. The McCarran-Ferguson Act of 1945 permitted this practice in order to avoid premium wars that would lead, it was felt, to the failure of many insurance companies. The only restriction in the law is that companies are prohibited from setting excessive, inadequate, or unfairly discriminatory rates.

[7]Investment companies that distribute the majority of investment earnings to shareholders receive similar tax relief.

Canada, Europe, and Japan Canadian insurance companies are licensed, or "registered," at the federal or the provincial (state) level. However, federally registered firms dominate the life and non–life insurance industries. Federal law limits common stock and mortgage investments of life insurance firms.

Elsewhere, laws governing the industry can vary significantly. For example, in France, thirty-four insurance companies that controlled over 55 percent of the market in 1945 were nationalized. The French insurance industry is now composed of ten restructured state-owned firms and 172 smaller, private companies.

German insurance companies are subject to regulation by the Federal Supervisory Office with respect to accounting and investment practices. Further, this regulator imposes minimum equity-to-loan ratios (borrower equity to insurance company loan amount) that must be satisfied before an insurance firm may lend directly to an industrial company. Often, these requirements are difficult to satisfy. As a result, the insurance company may lend to a bank that will, in turn, lend to the industrial firm.

The diversity of rules and regulations makes it somewhat difficult for firms to operate across national borders in Europe. Nevertheless, the Single European Market (after 1992) will also affect insurance companies. Member countries have adopted several directives aimed at harmonizing (coordinating) company requirements and insurance coverage throughout the EC. Essentially, a license to conduct insurance business in one country will enable the firm to operate throughout Europe.

The Ministry of Finance regulates Japanese insurance companies, imposing limits on common stock, real estate, and single-lender investments. Single-lender investments are particularly important in Japan. Long-term, fixed-rate loans to private industrial firms constitute as much as 60 and 23 percent of life insurance and non–life insurance asset portfolios, respectively.

In light of the large international trade surpluses generated by Japanese industrial companies during the late 1970s, the Ministry of Finance acknowledged the inability of domestic markets to absorb the increased level of assets controlled by insurance companies. *Samurai* loans (yen-denominated loans to foreigners) were permitted, and the limit on holdings of foreign currency securities was relaxed. Between 1975 and 1980, total insurance company investments attributable to these two categories rose from ¥13 billion to ¥1161 billion.[8]

INSURANCE SERVICES

Traditional Products

While companies compete to offer a differentiated product, certain standard types of insurance have evolved over time. In general, these products can be found in insurance markets around the world.

Life Insurance ***Term*** insurance covers the life of the insured for a specified period of time. This is the most basic form of life insurance and the least costly per dollar of coverage. If the insured dies during the term of the policy, the designated beneficiary receives the face value of the policy. Should the insured live beyond the policy term, the insurance company retains all premiums and no benefits accrue to the insured or the beneficiary.

Whole life insurance guarantees a benefit payment whenever death of the insured occurs. In exchange, the insured agrees to pay premiums for the remainder of his or her life. The benefit is composed of a specified face value, at a minimum. If the policy is profit-

[8]The average exchange rates in 1975 and 1980 were ¥296.78 and ¥226.63 to the dollar, respectively. Thus, the dollar value of insurance company foreign investments rose from approximately $43.8 million to $5.1 billion, an average annual growth rate of 159 percent in U.S. dollar terms.

participating, the benefit may also include the proportional share of investment profits that have accumulated while the policy was in force. A variation on this basic contract is the option of converting the policy into another, paid-up policy, requiring no further premiums. In any event, after a minimum number of years, it is usually possible to surrender the policy for some amount of cash that is less than the face value.

An *endowment* policy combines insurance and savings. The insured agrees to pay premiums until the policy's predetermined maturity date. Should death occur prior to that date, the beneficiary receives the face amount of the policy. If still living at the maturity date, the insured receives the face value. Thus, an endowment policy can provide both protection against premature death and savings for retirement or other purposes.

Group life insurance covers the employees of a single company or the members of a particular group under one policy. It is usually term insurance that is renewed each year. Policyholders remain eligible for coverage as long as they are members of the covered group. Commonly, coverage may be converted to an individual policy even after one leaves the group.

An *annuity* policy pays the policyholder a specified series of payments over some period of time. The choice of premium payment schedules may include a lump-sum payment or periodic payments. Generally, the time interval over which premiums are paid is called the *accumulation* period and that over which benefit payments are received, the *annuity* period.

Property and Casualty Insurance ***Marine*** insurance is the oldest form of insurance, predating even basic life insurance. This category has evolved over time to include commercial transportation over land as well. *Ocean marine* insurance covers ships and their cargo, while *inland marine* is available for ground transportation.

Fire insurance is also a traditional form of property insurance, covering hazards of fire and lightning. A commercial policy may protect the insured from loss of income during the repair of covered buildings or equipment. Residential fire insurance policies are also available.

Liability insurance provides protection in those cases in which the insured has injured a third party through negligence or other circumstances. The covered injuries may be associated with real estate owned by insured or with performance of the insured's professional activities.

Automobile insurance is of more recent vintage than those noted above but is currently the most important category of property and casualty insurance. Provisions covering damage to the insured's automobile and medical payments for the insured and passengers are common features. In addition, third-party liability insurance pays claims to other injured parties when the insured causes an auto accident. In fact, liability insurance for vehicle ownership is required in most U.S. states. Further, financial institutions that make automobile loans require that the vehicle be insured.

Multiperil insurance is also a more recent form of coverage. Through such policies, the insured is indemnified against losses from fire, theft and burglary, and liability claims. Because premiums for a multiperil policy are generally more price-competitive than the sum of premiums for more narrow coverage, multiperil insurance has enjoyed substantial growth in its share of total premiums.

Like automobile liability insurance, *workers' compensation* is required in most states. This coverage protects employees from loss of wages attributable to job-related injuries or provides death benefits for beneficiaries. Employers purchase and maintain the policies.

Other forms of insurance protect against more specific hazards. Boiler and machinery, glass, and crop insurance are examples. Also, fidelity insurance is available for those who handle large sums of money or securities and for those expected to appear in a court of law at a future date. (See Exhibit 23-7.)

EXHIBIT 23-7 PREMIUM INCOME OF U.S. PROPERTY AND CASUALTY COMPANIES, 1970 AND 1987

		1970		1987
Property and casualty premiums (billions)		$32.9		$193.2
Automobile:				
Liability	27.3%		25.5%	
Physical damage	14.7		16.6	
Total automobile		42.0%		42.1%
Liability*		6.5		12.9
Fire		9.6		4.0
Multiperil:				
Homeowners	7.8		8.6	
Commercial	4.0		8.9	
Total multiperil		11.8		17.5
Workers compensation		10.6		12.1
Marine:				
Inland	2.5		2.1	
Ocean	1.4		.7	
Total marine		3.9		2.8
Surety, fidelity, & financial guaranty		1.7		1.6
Burglary & theft		.4		.1
Crop, hail		.4		.2
Glass, boiler, and machinery		.5		.3
Other		12.6		6.4
		100.0%		100.00%

*Excludes automobile liability premiums.
Source: U.S. Department of Commerce, Bureau of the Census, *Statistical Abstract of the United States, 1989*, 109th ed., p. 510.

Recent Social and Economic Factors Affecting the Insurance Industry

Property and Casualty Insurance Litigation in U.S. courts has resulted in large settlements in liability cases in recent years. As new car prices have increased, the cost of repairs has risen with them. These and other factors led to higher benefit payments and to the underwriting losses (noted earlier) in the property and casualty industry. These losses, in turn, led to higher premiums. In light of these higher premiums, many large firms have elected to self-insure, or underwrite their own risks. As part of this new arrangement, a self-insuring organization may continue to use an insurance company to perform related administrative tasks.

Individuals and firms that cannot self-insure are resisting the higher premiums being charged. The rate-fixing privilege allowed by the McCarron-Ferguson Act is being challenged. The feeling is that this special treatment is no longer justified and that consumers are being overcharged as a result of it. In recognition of these sentiments, the insurance industry (through trade associations such as the American Insurance Association) has agreed in principle to no longer share loss experience and benefit payment information. The likely outcome of this is that the small firms that cannot afford to gather the necessary information to set rates properly will either raise their rates (to cover the additional cost) or be absorbed by larger companies.

Life Insurance In the life insurance industry, high and volatile interest rates during the late 1970s and early 1980s made the savings component of whole life policies unattractive to policyholders. As a result, new purchases of whole life insurance slowed, many existing policyholders voluntarily terminated their policies, and policy loans rose. After terminating a whole life policy, individuals sometimes purchase less expensive term insurance and invest the difference in premium cost in higher-yielding market securities (for example, mutual funds). Alternatively, policyholders may borrow against the cash value of the policy, the savings component, and invest the borrowed funds. A policy loan at 5 or 6 percent enables the policyholder to invest at higher market interest rates.

Life insurance premiums are now a declining portion of industry revenues. To counteract these trends, new products have been offered. *Variable premium life* insurance changes the required premium depending on the current rate of inflation. When inflation is high and investment income is also high, the required premium decreases. *Universal life* insurance offers a policyholder the option of varying the timing and amount of premium payments and even the ability to vary the amount of death benefit. *Universal variable life* insurance (offered for the first time in 1984) gives the policyholder a choice of investment vehicle for the savings component. Of course, the policyholder also shares the risks and rewards associated with these investments. This means that the death benefit varies with the investment performance of the underlying assets. In 1983, variable premium and universal life insurance in force totaled $145 billion. Six years later in 1989, the total for variable premium, universal, and universal variable was $1.6 trillion dollars, representing an average annual growth rate of 49 percent.

Also to offset declining life premiums, insurance companies have begun to market *annuity* contracts more actively. Growth in this area is linked to the increased number of defined contribution pension plans.[9] Such contracts offer either fixed returns or variable returns in which the policyholder shares investment gains and losses. As shown in Exhibit 23-8, annuities accounted for 10 percent of total life company premiums in 1970. By 1989, the percentage had increased to over 47 percent. All these innovations have helped life insurance companies offer rate-competitive products to an increasingly sophisticated consumer.

Problems in the Life Insurance Industry At the same time, the pressure to compete with mutual funds and money market funds motivated life insurance companies to invest in higher-yielding assets. One of these assets is real estate. Exhibit 23-9 illustrates the increase in life insurance real estate holdings. From 1965 to 1989, direct holdings of real estate increased from $4.7 billion to $39.9 billion, an average of 16.5 percent a year. Most of these were office buildings, shopping malls, and other commercial projects. It was the nationwide overbuilding of such projects in the United States that led to the collapse of real estate values in the late 1980s and early 1990s. Deteriorated real estate values hurt the financial standing of many life insurance companies and caused policyholders to become concerned about the safety of their life policies and annuities. Large-scale

[9]See Chapter 22.

EXHIBIT 23-8 PREMIUM INCOME OF U.S. LIFE INSURANCE COMPANIES, 1970 AND 1989

	1970	1989
Life insurance premiums (billions)	$36.8	$244.4
Life insurance	59.0%	30.0%
Annuities	10.1	47.1
Health insurance	30.9	22.9
	100.0%	100.0%

Source: American Council of Life Insurance, *1990 Life Insurance Fact Book*, p. 68.

EXHIBIT 23-9 LIFE INSURANCE COMPANY REAL ESTATE HOLDINGS, 1965–1989

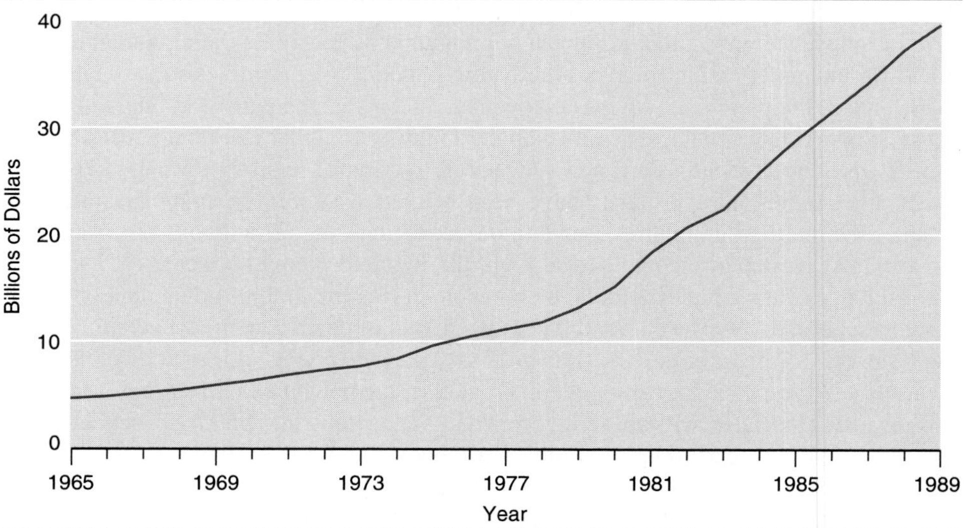

Source: Data from American Council on Life Insurance, *1990 Life Insurance Fact Book,* p. 98.

policy redemptions began once again. These redemptions have threatened industry solvency. Thirty small companies were absorbed by larger companies during 1990. In 1991, Equitable Life Assurance, the third-largest U.S. insurer with $60 billion in assets, publicly admitted that it needed as much as $1 billion in new capital.

Another form of high-yielding asset that became attractive for some insurance portfolio managers was the "junk bond." Industrywide, these bonds were less than 5 percent of life insurance company assets, and the defaulted bonds amounted to less than 1 percent. However, the averages are deceiving. Some companies never invested in the below-grade bonds, while others invested very heavily. The combination of large real estate and junk bond investments brought down several firms during 1991. Most notable among these are Executive Life and Mutual Benefit Life with assets of $15 billion and $14 billion, respectively.

These developments have stimulated discussion of more federal regulation of insurance companies. The fear is that state regulators are not adequately monitoring the activities of the firms with which they are charged. In this sense, the problems could mushroom into another S&L-type crisis. However, this is not likely to happen because of the size and strength of the largest firms that have not been as severely affected by the real estate slump and the junk bond collapse. What is likely to occur is an even greater concentration of assets among fewer firms.

ASSETS AND LIABILITIES

Life Insurance Companies

Changes in the mix of life insurance business have affected the industry's balance sheet (Exhibits 23-10 and 23-11). Equity investments are an increasingly larger part of the general accounts but represented less than 10 percent of financial assets in 1991. Corporate and foreign bonds have consistently commanded as much as 42 percent of financial assets. Of course, most of these are high-quality corporate bonds. As noted earlier, only a small share is composed of junk bonds. As holdings of real estate (which are real assets, not financial assets) have increased, mortgage loans have become less important. However, within the

EXHIBIT 23-10 FINANCIAL ASSETS OF U.S. LIFE INSURANCE COMPANIES, 1964–1991

	1964	1969	1974	1979	1984	1989	1991
Financial assets (billions)	$144.9	$191.3	$255.0	$419.3	$692.9	$1138.6	$1383.5
Checkable deposits and currency	1.0%	.8%	.8%	.6%	.7%	.3%	.4%
Money market fund shares	—	—	—	.2	1.0	.7	.9
Cash & cash equivalents	1.0	.8	.8	.8	1.7	1.0	1.3
Equity investments:							
Mutual fund shares	.1	.3	.2	.2	.4	1.2	2.1
Other corporate equities	5.4	6.9	8.3	9.3	8.7	9.0	7.3
Total equities	5.5	7.2	8.5	9.5	9.1	10.2	9.4
Debt instruments:							
Federal government:							
Treasury issues	3.9	2.2	1.3	1.2	6.0	5.4	4.3
Agency issues	.1	.2	.4	2.3	5.3	6.6	9.0
Total government	4.0	2.4	1.7	3.5	11.3	12.0	13.3
Tax-exempt	2.6	1.7	1.5	1.5	1.3	1.0	.9
Corporate & foreign bonds	40.2	38.0	37.8	40.6	35.0	39.1	41.8
Mortgages:							
Home	19.7	14.4	7.4	3.8	2.0	1.4	.8
Multifamily	5.0	7.4	7.7	4.6	2.7	2.1	2.1
Commercial	10.4	12.8	16.2	16.9	16.1	16.3	15.3
Farm	2.9	3.0	2.5	2.9	1.8	.9	.8
Total mortgages	38.0	37.6	33.8	28.2	22.6	20.7	19.0
Commercial paper and banker's acceptances	.1	.7	1.6	1.7	3.2	3.6	2.5
Policy loans	4.9	7.2	9.0	8.3	7.9	4.7	4.5
Total debt instruments	89.8	87.6	85.4	83.8	81.3	81.1	82.0
Miscellaneous	3.7	4.4	5.3	5.9	7.9	7.7	7.3
	100.0%	100.0%	100.0%	100.0%	100.0%	100.0%	100.0%

Source: Board of Governors of the Federal Reserve System, *Flow of Funds Accounts, Financial Assets and Liabilities,* various issues.

mortgage category, the share of assets devoted to home mortgages has declined most (96 percent), while commercial mortgages have increased by over 47 percent. In many cases, commercial mortgages are currently as much at risk as are the actual real estate holdings. These mortgages only intensify the industry's exposure to a weak real estate market.

In the liability section, the shift in industry emphasis is even clearer. In 1964, life insurance and pension reserves represented 70 and 19 percent of liabilities, respectively. By 1991, their relative positions were almost exactly reversed, with life insurance and pension reserves constituting 28 and 62 percent of liabilities, respectively.

EXHIBIT 23-11 FINANCIAL LIABILITIES OF U.S. LIFE INSURANCE COMPANIES, 1964–1991

	1964	1969	1974	1979	1984	1989	1991
Financial liabilities (billions)	$134.0	$177.5	$243.9	$396.9	$665.3	$1069.5	$1335.3
Life insurance reserves	70.0%	66.5%	61.7%	49.8	35.5%	28.3%	28.4%
Pension fund reserves	18.9	21.2	24.8	36.2	49.8	61.0	61.9
Taxes payable	.4	.4	.3	.4	.1	.1	.1
Miscellaneous	10.4	11.9	13.2	13.6	14.6	10.6	9.6
	100.00%	100.00%	100.00%	100.00%	100.00%	100.00%	100.00%

Source: Board of Governors of the Federal Reserve System, *Flow of Funds Accounts, Financial Assets and Liabilities,* various issues.

In search of higher returns, property and casualty companies have reduced their proportional holdings of equities in favor of corporate and foreign bonds. As can also be seen in Exhibit 23-12, the share of financial assets devoted to Treasury securities declined and then increased, but repurchase agreements and government agency securities have generally become more important over time. These changes reflect efforts to continually improve investment income results, efforts also observed in the case of other financial institutions.

Financial Market Participation

In total, insurance companies controlled financial assets amounting to $1.9 trillion in 1991. As a result, insurance companies, like pension funds, are major participants in U.S. financial markets. Recall from Chapter 22 that insurance company holdings of government securities and corporate equities in 1989 constituted significant shares of total outstanding issues.[10]

Life and non–life insurance firms hold even larger shares of other debt securities (Exhibit 23-13). In the tax-exempt securities market, households and commercial banks have historically been the largest investors. By 1991, insurance companies held 18 percent of outstanding municipals, more than all depository institutions combined. However, because of their rapid growth, investment companies have overtaken insurance companies in the tax-exempt market, controlling 24 percent of the market in 1991.

In the market for corporate bonds (Exhibit 23-14), no other sector has a stronger influence. In 1964, insurance company bond portfolios represented 53 percent of total bonds. This share declined to 40 percent by 1991. The greatest shift otherwise is noted in foreign holdings, with smaller increases by households, commercial banks, savings and loan as-

[10]In 1991, insurance companies held 5.7 and 10.2 percent of all Treasury (Exhibit 22-17) and government agency (Exhibit 22-18) securities, respectively, and 5.3 percent of corporate equities (Exhibit 22-16) excluding mutual fund shares.

EXHIBIT 23-12 FINANCIAL ASSETS OF U.S. PROPERTY AND CASUALTY INSURANCE COMPANIES, 1964–1991

	1964	1969	1974	1979	1984	1989	1991
Financial assets (billions)	$34.9	$45.5	$67.9	$155.1	$241.0	$460.1	$540.0
Checkable deposits and currency	4.0%	2.9%	2.4%	1.9%	1.3%	1.3%	1.2%
Security repos	—	—	—	—	7.4	6.1	4.8
Cash and short-term investments	4.0	2.9	2.4	1.9	8.7	7.4	6.0
Corporate equities*	32.7	29.2	18.8	16.0	18.5	17.2	19.2
Debt instruments:							
Federal government:							
Treasury issues	16.0	7.5	4.3	6.9	9.7	11.1	16.5
Agency issues	1.4	2.9	2.4	1.9	8.7	7.4	4.8
Total government	17.4	11.0	8.3	10.8	15.5	17.7	21.3
Tax-exempt	31.5	34.1	45.2	46.9	35.1	34.0	25.5
Corporate & foreign bonds	6.9	13.8	14.7	15.2	10.7	14.0	17.6
Commercial mortgages	.3	.4	.3	.4	1.1	1.0	1.2
Total debt instruments	56.1	59.3	68.5	73.3	62.4	66.7	65.6
Trade credit	7.2	8.6	10.3	8.8	10.4	8.7	9.2
	100.0%	100.0%	100.0%	100.0%	100.0%	100.0%	100.0%

*Does not include mutual fund shares.

Source: Board of Governors of the Federal Reserve System, *Flow of Funds Accounts, Financial Assets and Liabilities,* various issues.

EXHIBIT 23-13 INVESTORS IN U.S. TAX-EXEMPT SECURITIES, 1964–1991

	1964	1969	1974	1979	1984	1989	1991
Tax-exempt securities (billions)	$92.9	$133.1	$207.7	$320.1	$522.1	$764.9	$839.6
Households	37.4%	35.2%	29.8%	25.2%	35.1%	35.6%	39.7%
Business sector	4.0	2.1	2.3	1.2	.8	1.3	1.5
State and local government	2.3	1.6	1.2	2.1	1.7	1.3	1.8
Depository institutions:							
Commercial banks	36.1	44.7	48.7	42.4	33.4	19.6	13.5
S&Ls	—	.1	.2	.4	.1	.2	.1
Mutual savings banks	.4	.2	.4	.9	.4	.2	.2
Total depository institutions	36.5	45.1	49.3	43.7	33.9	20.0	13.8
State and local gov't. pension funds	3.1	1.7	.5	1.2	.3	.1	.1
Insurance companies:							
Life insurance	4.1	2.4	1.8	2.0	1.7	1.4	1.5
Other insurance	11.9	11.6	14.8	22.7	16.2	20.5	16.3
Total insurance	16.0	14.0	16.6	24.7	17.9	21.9	17.8
Investment companies:							
Mutual funds*	—	—	—	1.2	3.6	10.8	13.6
Money market funds	—	—	—	—	4.6	8.8	10.8
Total investment companies	—	—	—	1.2	8.2	19.6	24.4
Brokers and dealers	.7	.3	.3	.7	2.1	.2	.9
	100.0%	100.0%	100.0%	100.0%	100.0%	100.0%	100.0%

*Excludes money market mutual funds.
Source: Board of Governors of the Federal Reserve System, *Flow of Fund Accounts, Financial Assets and Liabilities,* various issues.

sociations, and mutual funds. Nevertheless, insurance companies are the single most important investor in the bond market. Of course, this only complicates the difficulties in the junk bond market. For the largest investor in any financial instrument to divest itself of the security can only encourage instability in that market. This, too, suggests that the required restructuring (absorption and liquidation) of troubled insurers will almost necessarily be done within the industry.

EXHIBIT 23-14 INVESTORS IN CORPORATE AND FOREIGN BONDS IN THE UNITED STATES, 1964–1991

	1964	1969	1974	1979	1984	1989	1991
Corporate and foreign bonds (billions)	$113.9	$177.4	$286.4	$464.9	$686.0	$1365.2	$1673.1
Households	7.9%	14.0%	20.5%	15.6%	6.5%	5.9%	10.2%
Foreign sector	.9	1.1	1.4	3.0	8.8	13.9	11.9
Depository institutions:							
Commercial banks	1.2	1.1	2.3	1.5	2.6	5.8	5.5
S&Ls	—	—	—	—	2.3	4.0	1.7
Mutual savings banks	2.7	3.9	4.9	4.4	3.0	1.0	.6
Total depository institutions	3.9	5.0	7.2	5.9	7.9	10.8	7.8
Pension funds:							
Private	18.6	15.6	12.2	13.7	16.1	13.6	8.9
State & local gov't.	13.1	17.2	19.2	18.3	17.2	11.6	13.6
Total pension funds	31.7	32.8	31.4	32.0	33.3	25.2	22.5
Insurance companies:							
Life insurance	51.1	41.0	33.7	36.6	35.4	32.6	34.5
Other insurance	2.1	3.6	3.5	5.1	3.7	4.7	5.7
Total insurance	53.2	44.6	37.2	41.7	39.1	37.3	40.2
Mutual funds*	1.9	1.6	1.7	1.5	2.4	4.9	5.7
Brokers and dealers	.5	.9	.6	.3	2.0	2.0	1.7
	100.0%	100.0%	100.0%	100.0%	100.0%	100.0%	100.0%

*Excludes money market mutual funds.
Source: Board of Governors of the Federal Reserve System, *Flow of Fund Accounts, Financial Assets and Liabilities,* various issues.

EXHIBIT 23-15 ASSET COMPOSITION OF COMMERCIAL BANKS AND INSURANCE COMPANIES, 1964 AND 1991

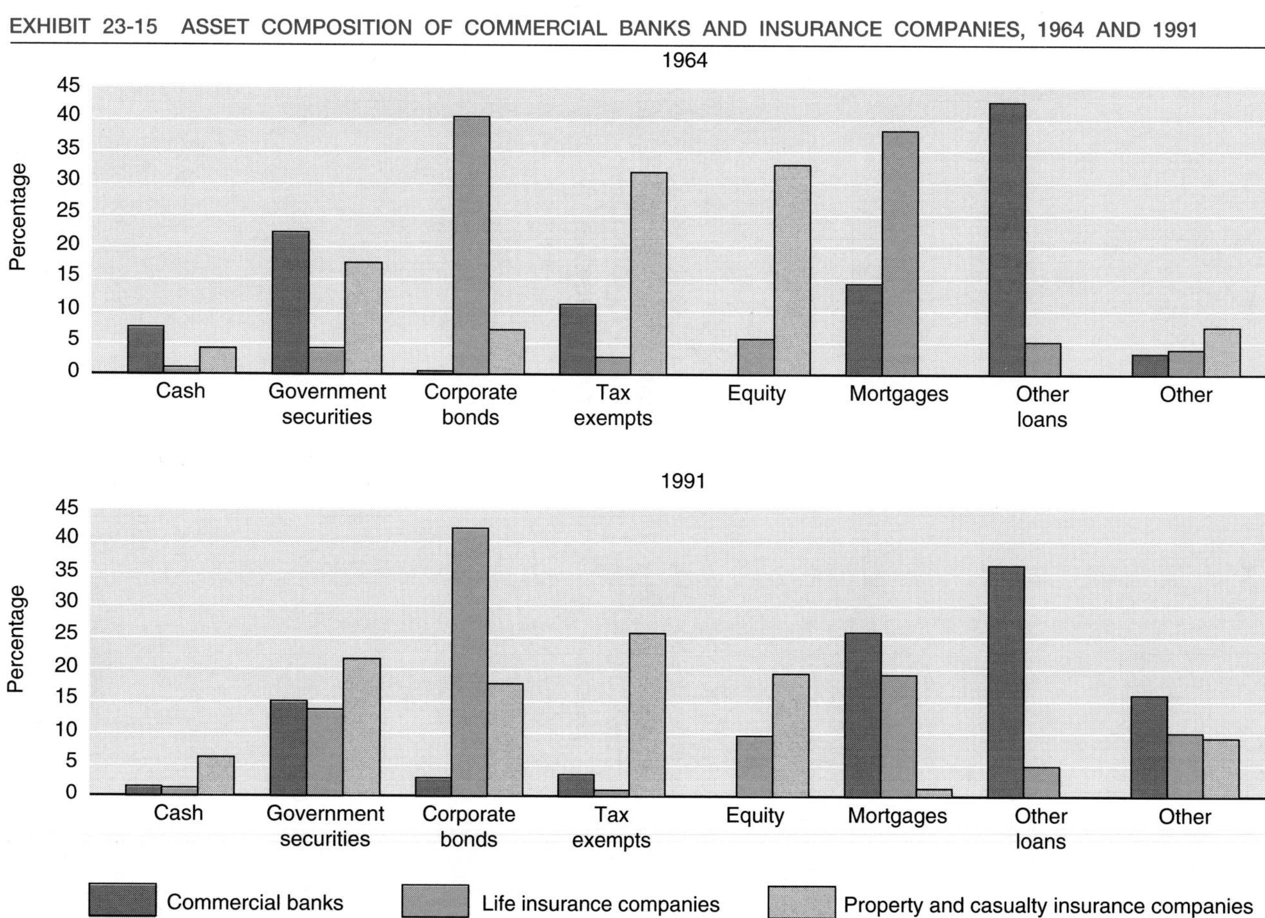

Source: Data from Board of Governors of the Federal Reserve System, *Flow of Fund Accounts, Financial Assets and Liabilities,* various issues.

The dominant position of insurance companies is also observed outside the United States. For example, the United Kingdom insurance sector is the largest institutional investor in that country. In fact, the Bank of England routinely consults with Prudential Insurance Company with respect to corporate investment policy. Insurance firms are also the largest institutional investors in Japan, providing long-term loans to the industrial sector and investing in more common stock than other groups of nonbank financial institutions.

In general, however, the extent to which insurance companies play a major role in domestic financial markets depends on the development of those markets. Investment choices are less numerous where markets are less mature. In less developed countries, bonds and common stocks may be relatively illiquid assets. As a result, cash and deposits will be the primary investment outlet for insurance company funds, resulting in less significant capital market impact.

Comparison to Commercial Banks

Exhibit 23-15 compares assets of commercial banks, life insurance, and property and casualty insurance companies in 1964 and 1991. The major differences are in corporate bonds, tax-exempt securities, and equities. Life insurance companies hold a much higher percentage of assets in corporate bonds, and banks hold no equities. Property and casualty companies concentrate more on tax-exempts. Also, loans other than mortgages have consistently represented the largest category for banks but have not been significant for insurance companies.

However, the areas in which the industries are converging are government securities and mortgage loans. Banks and life insurance companies now devote roughly the same share to government securities. Property and casualty firms are somewhat more heavily invested in them. In 1964, life insurance companies held more than twice the proportion in mortgages that commercial banks held. By 1991, banks actually devoted more to mortgage loans than life insurance companies. Of course, as noted earlier, some of the decrease in life insurance company mortgages has been offset by direct real estate investments (not shown in Exhibit 23-15). Overall, while the balance sheets are not as dissimilar as they were in 1964, insurance companies have much more involvement in stock and bond markets than is allowed for commercial banks.

SUMMARY

Insurance companies in the United States have traditionally performed the function of risk sharing (property and casualty firms) and savings (life companies). The industry underwent few changes until the 1970s and 1980s when inflation pushed the cost of claims beyond the level of premium receipts in the non–life insurance industry and prompted disintermediation in the life insurance industry.

The result has been restructuring of premium schedules and the introduction of new product lines and services. There has been a shift away from conventional life insurance products to more flexible, higher-yielding policies and to annuities designed to provide retirement income. These changes have been accomplished primarily at the state level since there is little federal regulation of insurance companies in the United States. The U.S. regulatory framework contrasts sharply with other industrialized countries where central government oversight is the rule rather than the exception.

But the situation could change in the United States. Investments in junk bonds and commercial real estate have weakened the balance sheets of companies even as premiums have risen. Some sort of federal regulation seems likely to prevent a reoccurrence of the situation. In the meantime, the industry will almost certainly consolidate further with larger firms capturing even more market share.

KEY TERMS

annuity
automobile insurance
benefit payments
general accounts
insurance agent
insurance broker
insurance premiums
insurance underwriter
liability insurance
life insurance
marine insurance
multiperil insurance
policy reserves
principles of insurance
property and casualty insurance
separate account
term insurance
whole life insurance

END-OF-CHAPTER QUESTIONS

1. For a particular insurance policy, explain why the sum of premiums paid is less than the face value of the protection that is provided. Include a discussion of both life and non–life insurance coverage.
2. Describe three common attributes of property and casualty insurance.
3. What are the basic principles of insurance?
4. Identify the primary components of insurance company income and expense.
5. Why are life insurance policies commonly considered savings vehicles? Why are non–life insurance policies not so classified?
6. How does U.S. regulation of insurance companies differ from that of other countries?
7. Describe traditional life insurance products.
8. In the property and casualty industry, marine and fire protection are the oldest form of coverage. However, these categories represent declining percentages of U.S. premiums written each year. Name some of the factors that have contributed to this phenomenon.
9. Why have life insurance premiums declined in importance in recent years and how have life insurance companies responded to this change?
10. Why have mortgage loans become a smaller share of life insurance company asset portfolios?
11. What is the McCarran-Ferguson Act, and why might it be reversed?
12. As compared with commercial banks, why is there relatively little public disclosure of insurance company financial performance?
13. Why is life insurance company investment income effectively not taxed?
14. Even though life insurance policies are not insured by the federal government, why do you think there has been so much public confidence in these policies until recently?
15. How will the Single European Market of 1992 change the way insurance business in Europe is conducted?
16. Many of the annuity policies that have been sold to the public in recent years have been purchased in order to provide retirement income for millions of people. As insurance companies fail, what role do you think the federal government should play in this restructuring?

SELECTED REFERENCES

Adams, T. F. M., and Iwao Hoshii. *A Financial History of the New Japan,* Kodansha International, Ltd., Tokyo, 1972.

American Council of Life Insurance. *1990 Life Insurance Fact Book,* Washington, D.C., 1990.

Bank of Japan. *Japan Economic Journal,* 1989.

Bayliss, B. T., and A. A. S. Butt Philip. *Capital Markets and Industrial Investment in Germany and France,* Saxon House, Westmead, England, 1980.

Board of Governors of the Federal Reserve System. *Flow of Funds Accounts; Financial Assets and Liabilities,* various issues.

Bronte, Stephen. *Japanese Finance: Markets and Institutions,* Euromoney Publications, London, 1982.

Clarke, William M. *How the City of London Works; An Introduction to Its Financial Markets,* Waterloo Publishers, London, 1986.

Davison, Ian Hay. *A View of the Room; Lloyd's; Change and Disclosure,* St. Martin's Press, New York, 1987.

Driscoll, Lisa. "Insurers Are Giving a Little to Avoid Giving a Lot, Congress Is Zeroing in on Their Antitrust Exemptions," *Business Week,* June 3, 1991, p. 27.

Falkena, H. B., L. J. Fourie, and W. J. Kok. *The Mechanics of the South African Financial System; Financial Institutions, Instruments, and Markets,* Macmillan South Africa, Johannesburg, 1984.

Friars, Eileen M., and Robert N. Gogel, Editors. *The Financial Services Handbook; Executive Insights and Solutions,* John Wiley and Sons, New York, 1987.

Goacher, D. J., and P. J. Curwen. *British Non-bank Financial Intermediaries,* Allen and Unwin, London, 1987.

Havrilesky, Thomas M., and Robert Schweitzer, Editors. *Contemporary Developments in Financial Institutions,* 2d ed., Harlan Davidson, Inc., Arlington Heights, Illinois, 1987.

Huat, Tan Chwee. *Financial Institutions in Singapore,* Singapore University Press, Singapore, 1981.

Iklé, Max. *Switzerland: An International Banking and Finance Center,* Dewden, Hutchinson, and Ross, Inc., Stroudsburg, Pennsylvania, 1972.

Light, Larry, Christopher Farrell, Michele Galen, Suzanne Woolley, Lisa Driscoll, and Susan Gardland. "Are You Really Insured? Questions You Should Ask about Your Coverage and Benefits," *Business Week,* August 5, 1991, pp. 42–48.

MacAvoy, Paul, Editor. *Federal-State Regulation of the Pricing and Marketing of Insurance,* American Enterprise Institute for Public Policy Research, Washington, D.C., 1977.

McRae, Hamish, and Frances Cairncross. *Capital City; London as a Financial Centre,* Methuen, London, 1984.

Neave, Edwin H. *Canada's Financial System,* John Wiley and Sons Canada, Ltd., Toronto, 1981.

Neufeld, E. P. *The Financial System of Canada,* St. Martin's Press, New York, 1972.

Sametz, Arnold, W. *The Emerging Financial Industry; Implications for Insurance Products, Portfolios, and Planning,* Lexington Books, Lexington, Massachusetts, 1984.

Scott, Robert Haney, K. A. Wong, and Yan Ki Ho, Editors. *Hong Kong's Financial Institutions and Markets,* Oxford University Press, Hong Kong, 1986.

Seidman, Ann. *Money, Banking and Public Finance in Africa,* Zed Books, Ltd., London, 1986.

Sheng-Yi, Lee. *The Monetary and Banking Development of Singapore and Malaysia;* Singapore University Press, Singapore, 1974.

Skully, Michael T. *Financial Institutions and Markets in the Far East, A Study of China, Hong Kong, Japan, South Korea and Taiwan,* St. Martin's Press, New York, 1982.

———. *Financial Institutions and Markets in the Southwest Pacific, A Study of Australia, Fiji, New Zealand, and Papua New Guinea,* Macmillan, London, 1985.

Struthers, J., and H. Speight. *Money; Institutions, Theory and Policy,* Longman, London, 1986.

U.S. Department of Commerce, Bureau of the Census. *Statistical Abstract of the United States, 1989,* 109th ed., Washington, D.C., 1989.

Wasow, Bernard, and Raymond D. Hill, Editors. *The Insurance Industry in Economic Developments,* New York University Press, New York, 1986.

Wiesenberger Financial Services. *Investment Companies, 1989,* New York, 1989.

World Bank. *World Development Report, 1989, Financial Systems and Development; World Development Indicators,* Oxford University Press, New York, 1989.

CHAPTER 24

FINANCE COMPANIES

CHAPTER OUTLINE

CHAPTER OVERVIEW

This chapter:

- Describes the origins of finance companies
- Explains the services that finance companies offer consumers and industrial firms
- Examines the participation of finance companies in the mortgage market
- Analyzes consumer and mortgage loans of finance companies

Finance companies have evolved from modest, one-location operations to multibillion-dollar enterprises. Some of the largest now offer banklike services to industry, while others remain focused on the consumer market. The services available from finance companies include consumer installment loans, consumer second mortgage loans, business inventory and mortgage financing, and money market accounts. Freedom from federal regulation enables finance companies to have this wide scope of operation and to avoid the expense of regulatory compliance. As a result, finance companies now compete vigorously with the nation's commercial banks.

For 100 years, finance companies have offered services to fill the gap between the needs of industrial and consumer clients and the services provided by commercial banks. At the inception of the finance company industry, three types of firms emerged:

- commercial finance companies
- sales finance companies
- consumer finance companies.

Commercial Finance Companies

Early in the twentieth century commercial banks did not offer loans to industrial firms using their accounts receivable as collateral, because the Federal Reserve only discounted, or bought, promissory notes that were related to productive purposes. A firm's receivables frequently arose from retail sales, that is, consumer purchases rather than industrial investment.

Commercial finance companies filled this void by making loans to industrial firms on the basis of accounts receivable. In exchange for the loan, the borrowing firm signed over its right to the receivables to the finance company and, upon collecting the receivables, turned over all proceeds to the finance company. Since the borrowing firm's original customer was not aware of this arrangement, the technique became known as *nonnotification accounts receivable financing.*

Nonnotification accounts receivable financing:
Method of obtaining a loan by assigning the future collection of accounts receivable to a financial institution without advising the customers (that gave rise to the receivables) of the arrangement.

Commercial banks did not begin to participate in this form of financing until the Great Depression in the 1930s and then only in those cases that the borrower's ability to repay was questionable. Thus, commercial banks associated accounts receivable financing with financial distress and did not adopt it as a standard method of banking. At the same time, commercial finance companies expanded their use of collateralized lending to accommodate their industrial customers. Soon finance companies were offering loans collateralized by equipment and inventory and gaining the reputation of finding innovative ways to finance small businesses.

Sales Finance Companies

When mass production of automobiles began in the early twentieth century, banks did not offer automobile loans again because the auto purchases were considered consumer purchases, not productive investment. Commercial finance companies started sales finance departments or subsidiaries that offered installment loans. Soon firms exclusively involved in sales finance sprang up and were so successful that they began to finance also the retail purchases of radios, refrigerators, washing machines, dryers, furniture, vacuum cleaners, and other consumer durables.

Automobile manufacturers expected their dealers to accept an even flow of car shipments to keep the factories running smoothly year-round. The pattern of consumer auto purchases, however, was subject to seasonal peaks and valleys, giving rise to the need for inventory financing during the slow-selling seasons. Sales finance companies arranged "floor plans," wholesale financing that involved placing a lien on each automobile in the showroom or warehouse, with the arrangement documented in a trust receipt. Effectively, the sales finance company owned the autos until they were sold to the dealers' customers, at which time the finance company received wholesale cost plus accrued interest. It was not long before the floor plans and the consumer installment financing were being handled by the same sales finance company. This process was then replicated in the sales of other consumer durables, such as washing machines, dryers, and television sets.

Some sales finance companies operated as *captive finance companies.*

Captive finance company:

A finance company that is wholly owned by a manufacturing firm and handles the retail and wholesale financing of only that manufacturer.

The first captive finance company, formed in 1919, was General Motors Acceptance Corporation (GMAC), currently the largest finance company in the United States. Similar institutions were formed by Ford, Chrysler, and General Electric a few years later. Over time, many others followed.

Consumer Finance Companies

Other consumer finance companies, which developed in the early 1900s, were not involved exclusively in sales finance. These companies made loans available to wage earners on the basis of their gainful employment for purposes including medical expense and emergency needs. Household furnishings were commonly used as collateral. Customers of these firms were generally considered to be high credit risks and unable to obtain financing from commercial banks.

THE INDUSTRY TODAY

As is true in the financial services industry in general, previous distinctions between commercial, sales, and consumer finance companies have blurred, and each now offers a wider range of services. In the late 1960s there was another important addition to the list of services—second mortgage loans, introduced in California by Beneficial Finance, one of the earliest consumer finance companies. Since then, second mortgage lending has become a fast-growing segment of the market. In other cases, services such as highly leveraged transactions (or leveraged buyout loans) have been added.

Exhibit 24-1 shows the breakdown of all finance company loans in 1991. Personal, or consumer, loans represent 31.3 percent and second mortgages 11.2 percent. The largest category of loans is business loans, representing 57.5 percent of the total.

To illustrate the expanding scope of finance company operations in these areas, six major firms will be discussed. The firms (and their 1990 total assets) are:

- General Motors Acceptance Corporation (GMAC, $105 billion)
- Ford Motor Credit Company (Ford, $59 billion)
- Toyota Motor Credit Corporation (Toyota, $6 billion)
- General Electric Capital Corporation (GECC, $70 billion)
- Household International (Household, $29 billion)
- Beneficial Corporation (Beneficial, $9 billion)

General Motors Acceptance Corporation, Ford, and Toyota are captive sales finance companies, wholly owned by their automobile-manufacturing parent companies. Ford is one of the members of the Ford Financial Group that also includes First Nationwide Financial Corporation, a thrift holding company, and Associates Corporation of North America, a consumer finance company. General Electric Capital Corporation is also a captive finance

EXHIBIT 24-1 MIX OF TOTAL LOANS, FINANCE COMPANIES, 1991

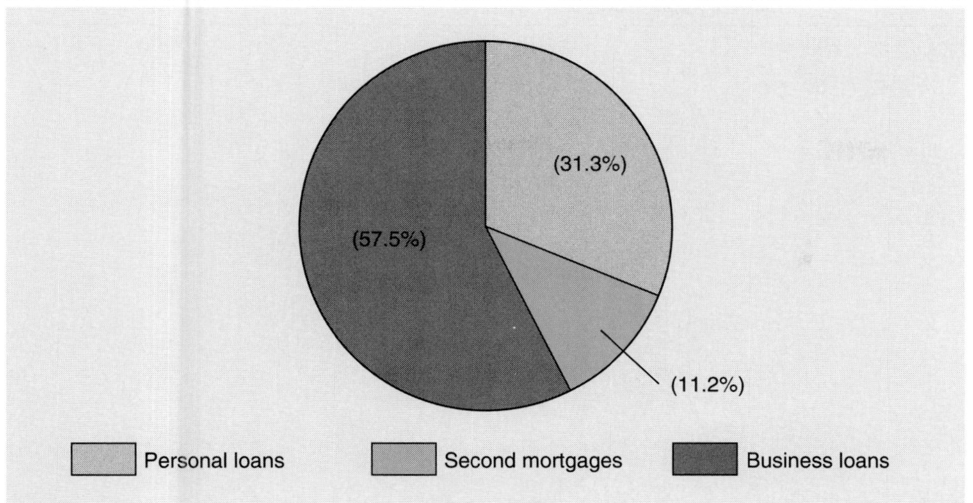

Source: Calculations and graphic based on data from *Federal Reserve Statistical Release, Finance Companies, June 1991.*

company owned by its manufacturing parent, but has diversified far beyond its original purpose. Household and Beneficial are consumer finance companies that have also become more widely diversified.

Consumer Services

Automobile financing was the cornerstone of the consumer finance industry and remains its most important category, representing in 1991 almost 60 percent of all consumer loans excluding mortgages as indicated in Exhibit 24-2. Loans to purchase other consumer durables and cash loans shared equal percentages of the total at 18 percent each.

Traditionally, finance companies have charged interest rates that have been higher than commercial bank rates because their clientele has had greater credit risk than banks' clientele. Excluding automobile loans, this is still generally true, with unsecured loan interest rates at finance companies going as high as 36 percent. Automobile loan interest rates, however, are more competitive. Exhibit 24-3 compares the new car loan rates of banks and finance companies from 1980 to 1991. In 5 of the 12 years (1981 to 1983 and 1985 to 1986), bank interest rates were actually higher than finance company rates.

This is an indication of the competition between the two industries. In 1991, finance companies held 26 percent of total car loans outstanding and banks 44 percent. As recently as 1987, however, finance companies held 38 percent and banks 41 percent. Commercial banks have now become successful competitors in a market that once belonged exclusively to finance companies. Nevertheless, finance companies remain strong in most of their traditional markets and are making significant inroads into other consumer finance areas, such as credit cards, savings bank activities, and money market accounts.

GMAC, Ford, and Toyota purchase *closed-end retail installment contracts* from affiliated vehicle dealers as the core of their operations.

Closed-end retail installment contract:
A contract that obligates a consumer purchasing goods to pay the lender specified installments for a specified period of time.

EXHIBIT 24-2 MIX OF CONSUMER LOANS (OTHER THAN MORTGAGES), FINANCE COMPANIES, 1991

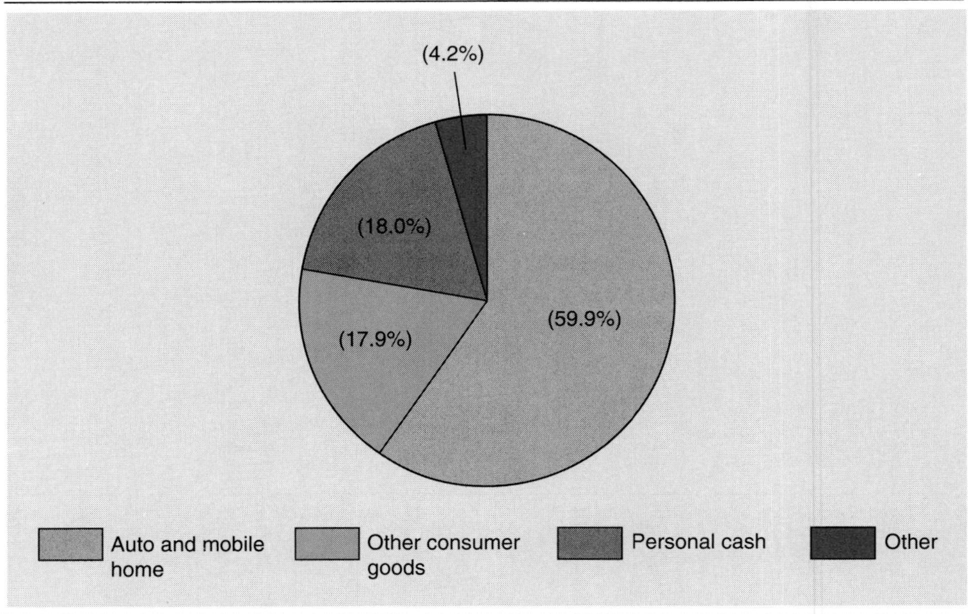

Source: Calculations and graphic based on data from *Federal Reserve Statistical Release, Finance Companies,* June 1991.

Recently, the three companies have added leasing plans to their consumer offerings through dealers. The marine division of GMAC extends installment and lease financing to several boat dealers. For GMAC, installment and lease transactions are the basis for 80 percent of its loans outstanding. Consumer vehicle financing loans are 70 percent of Ford loans and 94 percent of Toyota's.[1]

GECC purchases closed-end consumer installment contracts from a wide variety of retail establishments, including those that sell General Electric products. Leasing plans are offered through dealers of automobiles, manufactured housing, recreational vehicles, and boats. In addition, GECC issues credit cards directly to consumers through a *credit card bank* called Monogram Bank USA.

Credit card bank:
A bank designated to conduct primarily credit card business and is thus not subject to the same regulatory constraints as commercial banks.

Total consumer receivables for GECC are 34 percent of outstanding loans.

Household and Beneficial also purchase closed-end retail installment contracts from a large number of retailers. In addition, Household issues credit cards directly to consumers through its credit card bank, Household Bank, N.A., operating throughout the United States. Beneficial sold its credit card operation, as well as insurance and mail-order divisions, in 1986 in order to focus more on its traditional consumer business. Consumer receivables, excluding mortgage loans, are 35 percent of Household's total loans and 27 percent of Beneficial's.

[1]In 1991, the loans of Ford Consumer Finance, a division of Ford Motor Credit and specializing in nonautomotive lending, were transferred to Associates Corporation, an affiliated firm, leaving Ford to concentrate on vehicle financing.

EXHIBIT 24-3 INTEREST RATES OF NEW CAR LOANS, COMMERCIAL BANKS, AND FINANCE COMPANIES, 1980–1991

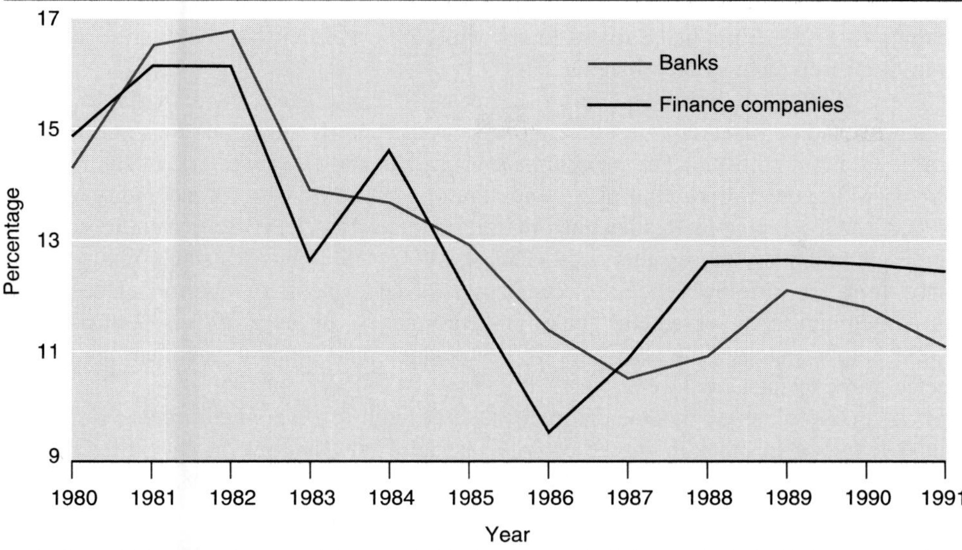

Source: Data from *Federal Reserve Bulletin,* various issues.

Three of these finance companies are also involved in the banking industry through acquisitions of thrift institutions. Ford is affiliated with California-based First Nationwide in the Ford Financial Group. Beneficial Savings Bank is based in Florida, and Household Bank, F.S.B., is headquartered in California with operations in several other states. These holdings represent the industrial ownership of banking concerns, allowed on a case-by-case basis to rescue failing thrifts. As these cases illustrate, the extent of finance company diversification is substantial.

Another area into which finance companies have expanded is money market accounts, technically only permitted for regulated depository institutions and money market mutual funds. Both GMAC and Ford offer money market accounts to employees and their families, and GMAC makes them available to shareholders. The cost of these funds is as much as 50 basis points lower than the commercial paper rate, making these accounts economical sources of short-term financing for the companies. At the same time, the rates are competitive with other money market accounts, making them attractive investments for employees and shareholders. Finance company money market accounts are not assessed management fees, as are money market funds, nor reserve requirements and insurance premiums, as are bank money market deposit accounts, and these savings are passed along to the investors.

The range of consumer services available through finance companies is extensive:

- Competitive automobile loans
- Other convenient retail installment contracts
- Cash loans
- Leasing
- Credit cards
- Other bank services
- Money market accounts

The lack of federal regulation as compared with banks gives these companies a competitive edge.

Mortgages

Residential and commercial mortgages are now a major component of finance company operations. Some firms make direct loans, while others solicit the mortgages, package them, and resell them as securitized assets.[2]

The GMAC Mortgage Corporation originates first mortgages on both single-family residences and commercial real estate throughout the United States but does not hold the mortgages in its portfolio. The loans are securitized and sold to investors. In some states, GMAC Mortgage Corporation also issues home equity loans or second mortgages. In 1990, GMAC purchased Residential Funding Corporation (RFC) to act entirely in the wholesale secondary mortgage market. Thus, GMAC RFC purchases single-family mortgages from the original lenders, securitizes, and sells them to investors. Once sold, GMAC continues to service the underlying mortgages. Because of these transactions, GMAC's mortgage activity is essentially "off balance sheet"; that is, the loans are not reflected as receivables by the company.

Ford makes loans on commercial real estate through its diversified financing division and is involved in other mortgage activity through First Nationwide, its thrift affiliate. Toyota, a participant in the U.S. finance company market only since 1983, extends mortgage loans to dealers only.

On the other hand, GECC has extensive holdings in real estate. The company provides financing for the acquisition, development, refinancing, and renovation of primarily commercial property. Most of the loans are in the form of intermediate-term, senior or subordinated floating-rate loans secured by existing income-producing commercial property, such as office buildings, rental apartments, shopping centers, hotels, industrial buildings, and warehouses. Over 90 percent of the loans are senior mortgages, receiving first priority in any liquidation. Also, GECC makes loans for the construction of commercial projects and for the acquisition and development of large parcels of land for single-family homes. Most of these loans also have senior status. The slump in real estate values in the late 1980s and early 1990s did not adversely affect GECC, because most of its real estate loans were for existing projects with established rental income. The loans on existing property and the construction loans make up 31 percent of GECC's total loans.

The mortgage subsidiary, Household Mortgage Services, provides first mortgages on residential and income-producing property. This is in addition to the mortgage loans provided by the savings bank, Household Bank, N.A. These loans represent 28 percent of the company's receivables. Home equity loans, that is, second mortgages, are available through Household's consumer division and constitute 17 percent of total company loans, bringing the total share of real estate loans to 45 percent.

Beneficial is even more committed to real estate. Sixty-two percent of the firm's loans are second mortgages. Beneficial Mortgage Corporation solicits, packages, and then sells first mortgages to investors, but the second mortgages stay on the books.

In general, home equity loans have become a lucrative business for finance companies, because the bad debt expense and administrative costs on these loans are much lower than those on unsecured loans. The borrowers essentially must qualify for the loans on the basis of their income, or ability to repay, so that the real estate collateral essentially becomes an additional assurance of repayment.

Business Services

Finance companies provide comprehensive services for industrial firms. As shown in Exhibit 24-4, the major categories are retail, wholesale, and leasing services with the largest

[2]See Chapter 4 for a description of mortgages and securitization.

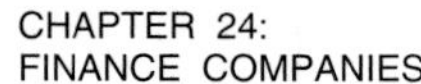

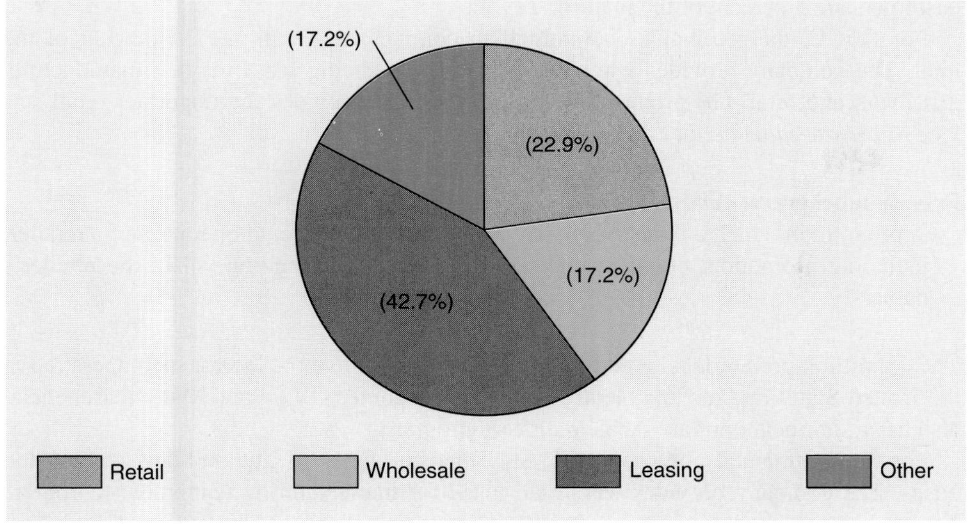

Source: Calculations and graphic based on data from *Federal Reserve Statistical Release, Finance Companies,* June 1991.

category being leasing, 43 percent of all finance company business receivables in 1991. Retail financing services are 23 percent of the total and wholesale 17 percent. *Retail financing* facilitates transactions between a retail seller of goods and the ultimate consumer. *Wholesale financing* accommodates transactions between parties other than the consuming public, for example, between a manufacturer and a distributor. The provision of securitized financing for industrial firms was the industry's strongest contribution as it developed years ago, and this is still its competitive advantage. The principle now applies to many classifications of collateral—inventory, transportation equipment, and industrial goods.

General Motors Acceptance Corporation provides wholesale financing to GM dealers for inventory floor plans and to firms that lease, rather than sell, GM vehicles. Several boat dealers are also entitled to these services. The wholesale leasing activities of GMAC extend to industrial equipment, with GMAC either owning and leasing the equipment directly to its industrial customer or providing the financial backing for a leveraged lease, that is, one in which the customer leases the equipment from another party with money borrowed from GMAC. The GM dealers may also receive from GMAC working capital cash loans and loans to purchase or remodel their dealership locations. Loans for commercial customers are 19 percent of GMAC's loan portfolio.

Ford offers much the same type of wholesale inventory, working capital, real estate, and capital improvement loans to dealers as GMAC. Furthermore, in its diversified financing division, the company invests in corporate preferred stock and other equity. Under a special program, Ford dealers can purchase used cars at auctions throughout the country and merely sign for them instead of having to pay for them on the spot. Last, an electronic funds transfer system between Ford and the dealers makes payment delivery to the dealers as expedient as possible. Commercial receivables constitute 31 percent of Ford's loan portfolio.

Toyota provides many of the same wholesale services to its dealers despite its relatively recent entry into the U.S. market. Dealers may obtain inventory, capital, and real estate loans from Toyota. Those dealers that operate daily rental fleets of company vehicles may also finance them through Toyota. Companies selling industrial equipment manufactured by affiliated firms are also eligible for inventory financing at Toyota. Loans to all these customers are 5 percent of the total for Toyota.

For GECC, the receivables committed to commercial clients are 34 percent of the total. The company provides wholesale inventory financing for firms that manufacture, distribute, and retail GE products. In addition, GECC provides the important retail service of *private-label credit card programs.*

Private-label credit card program:

A program in which a finance company manages the credit card operation of a retailer, including promotion, credit evaluations, billing, and accounting, all in the retailer's name.

The 35 million private-label credit cards of GECC constitute the largest such operation in the United States and include the accounts of Montgomery Ward and Macy's. Beneficial also has a significant private-label credit card program.

For its commercial clients, GECC also finances fleets of automobiles, trucks, and buses. The company provides wholesale loans for manufacturing equipment, corporate aircraft, construction equipment, business communications equipment, and high-tech equipment, including computers and scientific equipment. One of the largest leasing companies in the country, GECC owns over 250 commercial airplanes and 500,000 containers used for cargo transport and leases them to commercial airlines and shipping lines.

One of GECC's most innovative commercial services is used-automobile auctions.[3] Companies with corporate fleets to sell, rental car companies expecting new cars, and new car dealers with trade-ins that they have trouble selling bring their cars to these auctions to be sold quickly. On average, GECC earns $200 per car for repairs, cleanup, and sales commission. Because the firm auctions approximately 600,000 units per year, revenues from this enterprise are in excess of $100 million.

Even more lucrative, the corporate finance division of GECC has financed over 100 leveraged buyouts. General Electric Capital Corporation's highly leveraged transactions (HLTs), the loan equivalent of a junk bond, are usually senior obligations of the borrowing firm for an amount between 25 million and several hundred million dollars, with an original maturity of 5 to 10 years. As always, the loans are secured by borrower assets—accounts receivable or property, plant, and equipment. This division of the firm and its $8 billion in loans provided 28 percent of GECC's profits in 1989. A downturn in the economy and several troubled deals, however, caused its 1990 contribution to profits to shrink to 2 percent. Heavy write-offs in excess of $400 million were required, and other HLTs may necessitate more write-offs. Nevertheless, the corporate finance division of GECC has been one of the most aggressive in the industry.

Finance companies, in general, have been aggressive in the provision of commercial services. Their interest rates and fees are competitive, and they are comfortable with using asset-based lending. In 1990, the amount of loans made to industry by finance companies totaled twice the amount made by commercial banks.

The commercial services available from finance companies include:

- Inventory floor plans for company products
- Wholesale purchase and lease financing for other equipment
- Transportation fleet financing
- Real estate loans
- Working capital loans
- Private-label credit cards

[3]In 1986, Ford Motor Company became a 20 percent partner in GECC's auto auction enterprise.

- Highly leveraged transaction loans
- Auto auction financing

CONSUMER AND MORTGAGE LOAN CHARACTERISTICS

Although a wide range of commercial services is available from finance companies, most offices provide primarily consumer loans and mortgage finance. Each year the American Financial Services Association surveys the industry with respect to the characteristics of loans and borrowers. This section highlights some of the results from the survey for 1989, specifically, the purpose, maturity, and size of consumer and mortgage loans.

Purpose

Exhibit 24-5 shows that over 45 percent of consumer loans made in 1989 were for purposes other than those listed, suggesting that the purposes are quite varied. Among those purposes listed, however, bill consolidation loans represented 24 percent of the total. A bill consolidation loan enables the borrower to pay off a number of small financial obligations, usually reducing the total monthly cash outflow that is required. Loans for travel,

EXHIBIT 24-5 PURPOSE OF CONSUMER AND MORTGAGE LOANS, FINANCE COMPANIES, 1989

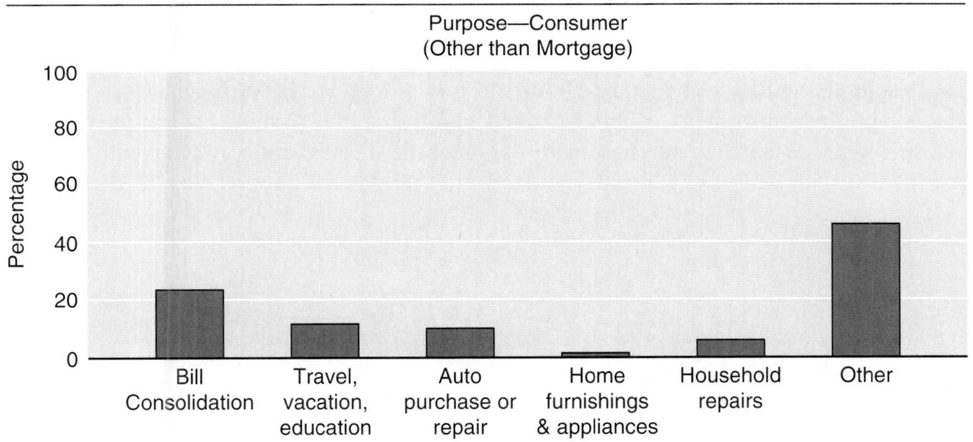

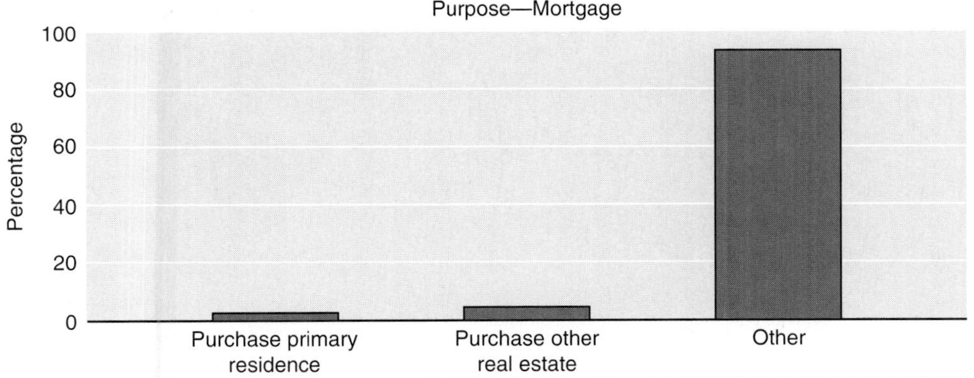

Source: Calculations and graphics based on data from *American Financial Services Association Research Report and Second Mortgage Lending Report,* 1989.

vacation, and education were the next most important at 12 percent. Only 8 percent of the loans were to pay for home furnishings, appliances, or household repairs.

Notably, despite the fact that auto loans are roughly 60 percent of consumer loans outstanding, auto purchase and repair was identified as the purpose for only 10 percent of the 1989 loans. This reflects the effect of the Tax Reform Act of 1986, which eliminated the tax deductibility of interest expense on all individual loans other than mortgages.

The breakdown of mortgage loans, also shown in Exhibit 24-5, is even more skewed with 93 percent of mortgage loans being obtained neither to purchase a primary residence nor to purchase other real estate. Those borrowers with equity in their homes are now obtaining second mortgage loans to pay for other major purchases, including automobiles, because the interest on mortgage loans remains tax-deductible. Tax deductibility will continue to make second mortgage loans an attractive alternative to meet personal financial needs.

Maturity

Exhibit 24-6 illustrates another reason why second mortgage loans will continue to be attractive as alternatives for personal finance—longer maturity. The most common maturity of personal loans in 1989 is between 2 and 5 years, with 71 percent of the total; 25 percent are for 2 years or less. On the other hand, 81 percent of second mortgages are for terms in excess of 5 years, enabling the borrower to reduce substantially the required monthly payment. The term of over half the second mortgage loans is between 10 and 15 years; 15 percent range from 7 to 10 years. An added advantage of second mortgage loans is that the interest rate is lower than on most personal loans obtained from finance companies.

Despite these attractive features, however, it is not advisable for finance companies to encourage their customers to obtain second mortgages that have a longer maturity than the life of the assets they purchase with the proceeds. For example, if a car with a useful

EXHIBIT 24-6 MATURITY OF CONSUMER AND MORTGAGE LOANS, FINANCE COMPANIES, 1989

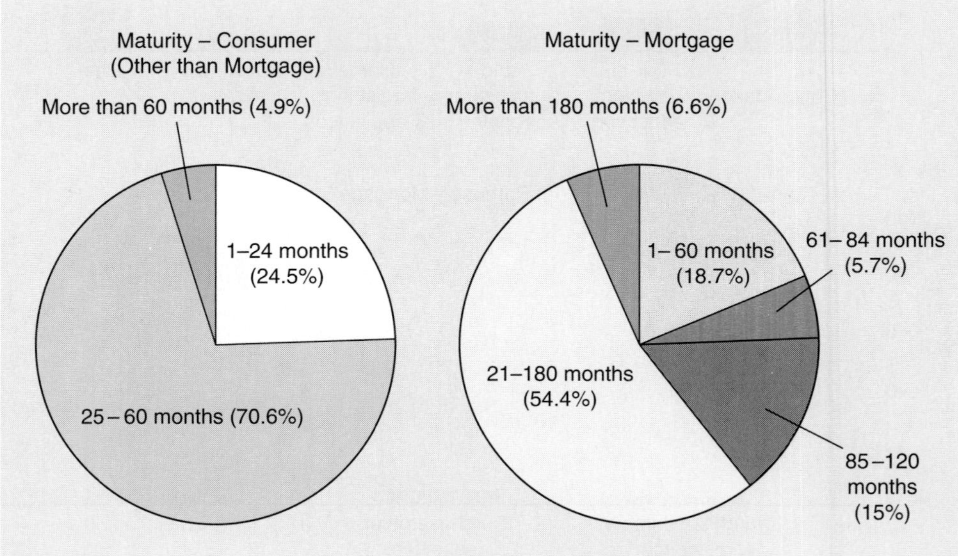

Source: Calculations and graphics based on data from *American Financial Services Association Research Report and Second Mortgage Lending Report,* 1989.

life of 4 years is purchased with a 10-year second mortgage, a second automobile will be needed before the loan is repaid. If the second mortgage loan is increased to pay for the second automobile, the borrower's total debt will increase. This cycle of piling new debt onto old can cause the borrower to become first overextended and then insolvent, forcing the finance company to foreclose on the borrower's home. Thus, the popular second mortgage should not be viewed by the finance company or the borrower as the solution to every financing need.

Size

Exhibit 24-7 shows the size breakdown of finance company loans. Almost half the consumer loans are for amounts between \$2000 and \$5000. Another 21 percent are between \$5000 and \$10,000. Mortgage loans are larger: 39 percent over \$50,000 and 31 percent between \$25,000 and \$50,000. The larger average transaction size of mortgage loans is a plus for finance company management, because the same amount of administrative expense may be incurred for a personal loan or a mortgage loan but the expense per dollar will be lower for the larger mortgage loan. This difference effectively increases loan of-

EXHIBIT 24-7 SIZE OF CONSUMER AND MORTGAGE LOANS, FINANCE COMPANIES, 1989

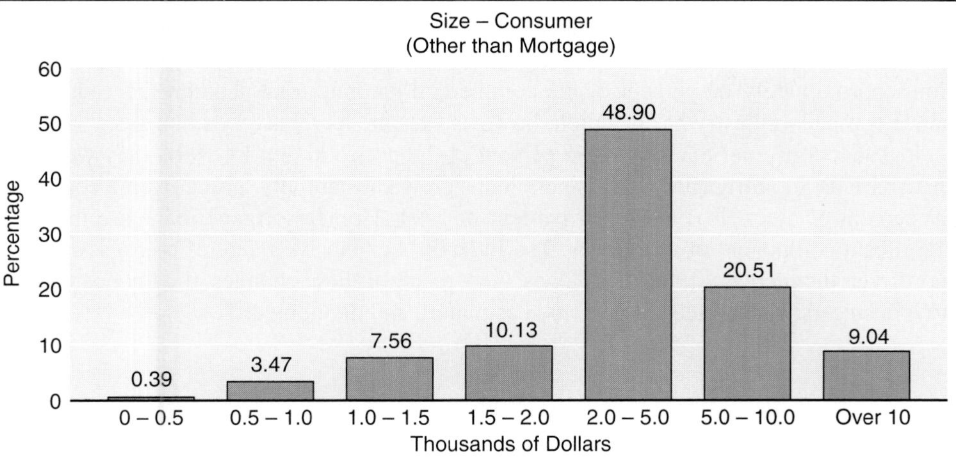

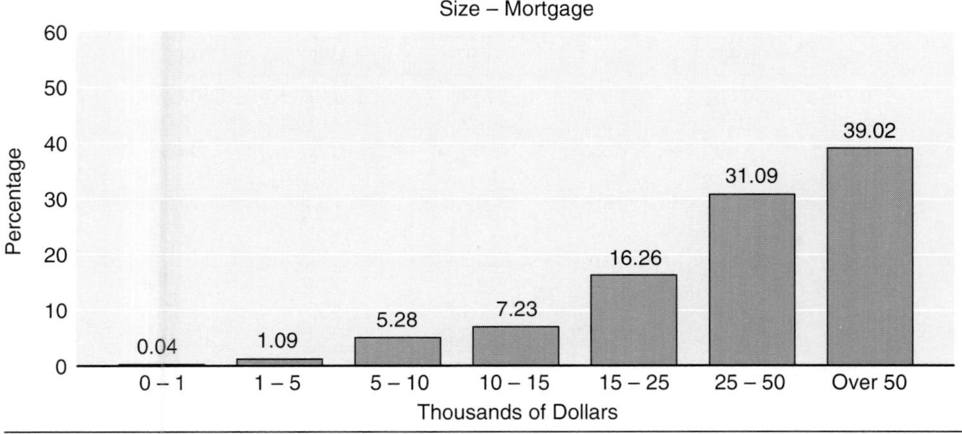

Source: Calculations and graphics based on data from *American Financial Services Association Research and Second Mortgage Lending Report,* 1989.

fice productivity. For this reason, mortgage loans are attractive to finance company management.

With respect to personal finance company loans, most are:

- From 2 to 5 years in duration
- Relatively small in amount, less than $5000

Most mortgage loans are:

- Over 10 years in duration
- Larger in amount, over $25,000

ASSETS AND LIABILITIES

Finance companies have grown rapidly in the last 2 decades. The asset mix has changed over time to reflect the industry's diversification, and much of its growth has been financed in the commercial paper market.

Assets

Exhibit 24-8 includes both the dollar amount of total financial assets and the major categories. The average annual compound rate of growth of finance company assets from 1964 to 1991 was 10.8 percent, higher than the rate of 9.2 percent for commercial banks over the same period. Total financial assets in the industry in 1991 amounted to $633 billion, approximately 20 percent of the commercial banking total. The presence of the finance company industry has been felt, however, despite its relatively small size.

In 1964, consumer loans were 56 percent of the portfolio, but by 1991, they were half that share. Both mortgages and business loans grew substantially, going from a combined 39 percent of assets in 1964 to 74 percent in 1991. Home mortgage loans are the most significant component of mortgages. The industry's expansive range of business services has driven the increase in business loans. As a result of these changes, the finance company industry may accurately be described as mature and diversified.

EXHIBIT 24-8 FINANCIAL ASSETS OF FINANCE COMPANIES, 1964–1991*

	1964	1969	1974	1979	1984	1989	1991
Financial assets (billion)	$39.7	$61.6	$98.5	$189.1	$301.6	$502.4	$633.0
Demand deposits and currency	4.5%	3.9%	3.8%	2.4%	1.5%	2.0%	1.9%
Consumer loans	56.4	51.9	45.2	38.1	37.8	36.5	24.4
Mortgages:							
Home	8.6	7.9	8.9	12.3	13.1	12.2	25.5
Multifamily	1.0	1.1	2.5	1.0	.6	.3	.4
Commercial	.3	.3	1.9	1.5	1.3	.9	1.5
Total mortgages	9.9	9.3	13.3	14.8	15.0	13.4	27.4
Business loans	29.2	34.9	37.7	44.7	45.7	48.1	46.3
	100.0%	100.0%	100.0%	100.0%	100.0%	100.0%	100.0%

*The percentage breakdown of assets in this exhibit, based on Federal Reserve Flow of Funds data, differs from that in Exhibit 24-1, based on Federal Reserve Statistical Release for finance companies. The statistical release provides a detailed breakdown of consumer and commercial categories, while the Flow of Funds data are consistent with other exhibits in the text that analyze financial institution trends over time.

Source: Calculations based on data from Board of Governors of the Federal Reserve System, *Flow of Funds Accounts; Financial Assets and Liabilities,* various issues.

Exhibit 24-9 illustrates how the industry has been financed. In 1964, finance companies depended on bond issues and commercial bank loans for 64 percent of their funding. In the next 27 years, the use of bond financing continued to be an important source of funds, remaining a fairly stable percentage of total liabilities after 1969. The use of bank financing, however, declined dramatically from 28 percent in 1964 to less than 5 percent in 1991.

Finance companies have successfully substituted commercial paper for bank loans, thereby becoming independent of the banking system as a source of funds. The first commercial paper in fact was issued by GMAC. Commercial paper began in the 1960s essentially as a viable alternative to bank loans for finance companies, institutions that had earned the reputation of devising innovative and imaginative ways to fund other companies. In 1964, finance companies issued 87 percent of all commercial paper outstanding. Their use of the instrument accelerated at an average rate of 15 percent per year through 1991. The use of the new method of direct short-term financing by other firms grew even faster—17 percent per year. By 1991, the other firms, including nonfinancial corporations and bank holding companies, represented 40 percent of outstanding commercial paper. Even in devising a short-term alternative for its own use, the finance company industry brought innovation to industrial and banking firms.

COMPARISON TO COMMERCIAL BANKS

The comparison of finance companies to commercial banks is natural, given the extent to which their areas of service overlap. In some ways the portfolios of the two types of financial institutions have become more similar.

Exhibit 24-10 compares the asset composition of banks and finance companies in 1964 and again in 1991. In 1964 bank portfolios contained more securities, which were 33 percent of financial assets, than business loans, 20 percent of assets, and consumer loans were the third most important asset at 14 percent.

Finance company portfolios were dominated by consumer loans, which were 56 percent of assets. Business loans constituted 29 percent. Both had 9 percent invested in home mortgages, while other mortgages were more important for banks, 5 percent, than for finance companies, 1 percent.

By 1991 bank assets were composed of a lower percentage of securities, but roughly the same percentage of business and consumer loans. The share of mortgage loans was significantly higher at 26 percent of total financial assets, up from 14 percent in 1964. The breakdown of these mortgages was 14 percent in home mortgages and 12 percent in other mortgages.

EXHIBIT 24-9 LIABILITIES OF FINANCE COMPANIES, 1964–1991*

	1964	1969	1974	1979	1984	1989	1991
Liabilities (billion)	$34.2	$57.1	$96.6	$193.9	$291.5	$574.0	$667.2
Commercial paper	21.3%	40.3%	28.3%	31.3%	34.6%	49.9%	49.6%
Bonds	35.4	26.4	29.0	27.0	26.5	27.0	27.7
Bank loans	28.4	16.8	19.5	11.2	5.2	−3.7*	4.7
Taxes payable	.6	0.4	0.3	0.2	—	.1	.1
Miscellaneous	14.3	16.1	17.7	17.9	17.8	5.4	9.6
Funds from parent company	—	—	5.2	12.4	15.9	21.3	8.3
	100.0%	100.0%	100.0%	100.0%	100.0%	100.0%	100.0%

*In 1989, finance companies were net creditors of commercial banks by providing loans to banks of 3.7% of finance company total liabilities.

Source: Calculations based on data from Board of Governors of the Federal Reserve System, *Flow of Funds Accounts; Financial Assets and Liabilities,* various issues.

EXHIBIT 24-10 ASSET COMPOSITION OF COMMERCIAL BANKS AND FINANCE COMPANIES, 1964 AND 1991

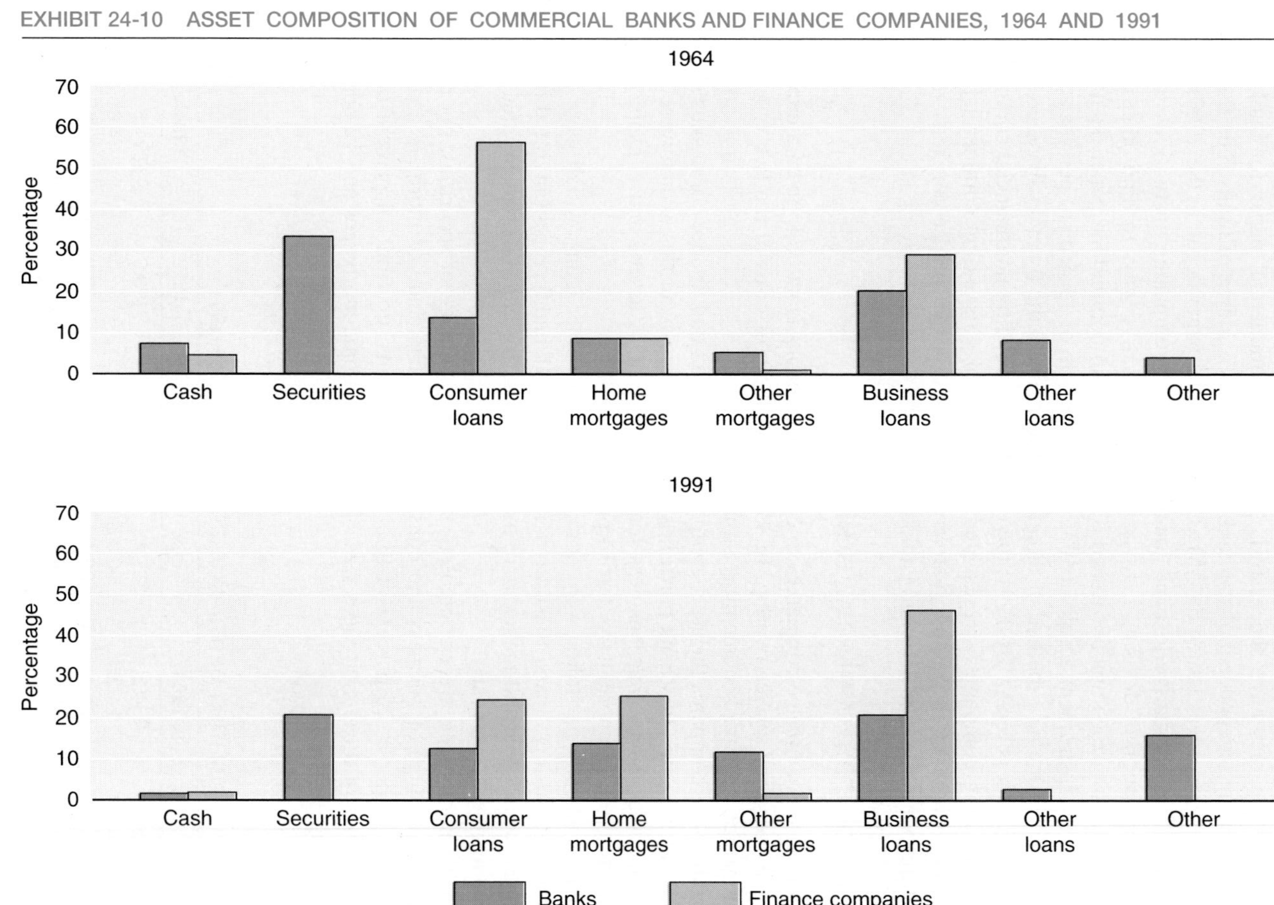

Source: Calculations and graphics based on data from Board of Governors of the Federal Reserve System, *Flow of Funds Accounts, Financial Assets and Liabilities,* various issues.

For finance companies, the 56 percent share of consumer loans plummeted to 24 percent by 1991, a difference of 32 percentage points. An increase in business loans offset part of this decrease, from 29 to 46 percent, an increase of 17 percentage points. There was also a 17 percentage points increase in total mortgage loans, from 10 percent to 27 percent. Total mortgages in 1991 were approximately the same share in finance company portfolios as in bank portfolios. The breakdown of the mortgages was not similar, however. Finance companies invested 25.5 percent in home mortgages alone, constituting that industry's largest commitment to the mortgage market.

There has been an increasing trend in home mortgages and business loans as a share of total assets in the finance company industry vis-à-vis the banking industry. This indicates that finance companies are now and will continue to be serious competition for commercial banks. The difference in regulation between the two industries puts banks at a competitive disadvantage. Banks are allowed neither to open offices nationwide nor to take equity positions in industrial firms. Moreover, the administrative expense of regulatory compliance is much greater for banks than for finance companies.

The difference in regulatory treatment is justified, of course, by the difference in the way the two industries are financed. Commercial bank deposits are federally insured, while finance company liabilities are not. Exhibit 24-11 compares the composition of their liabilities in 1964 and in 1991. In 1964, 97 percent of bank liabilities were insured

EXHIBIT 24-11 LIABILITY COMPOSITION OF COMMERCIAL BANKS AND FINANCE COMPANIES, 1964 AND 1991

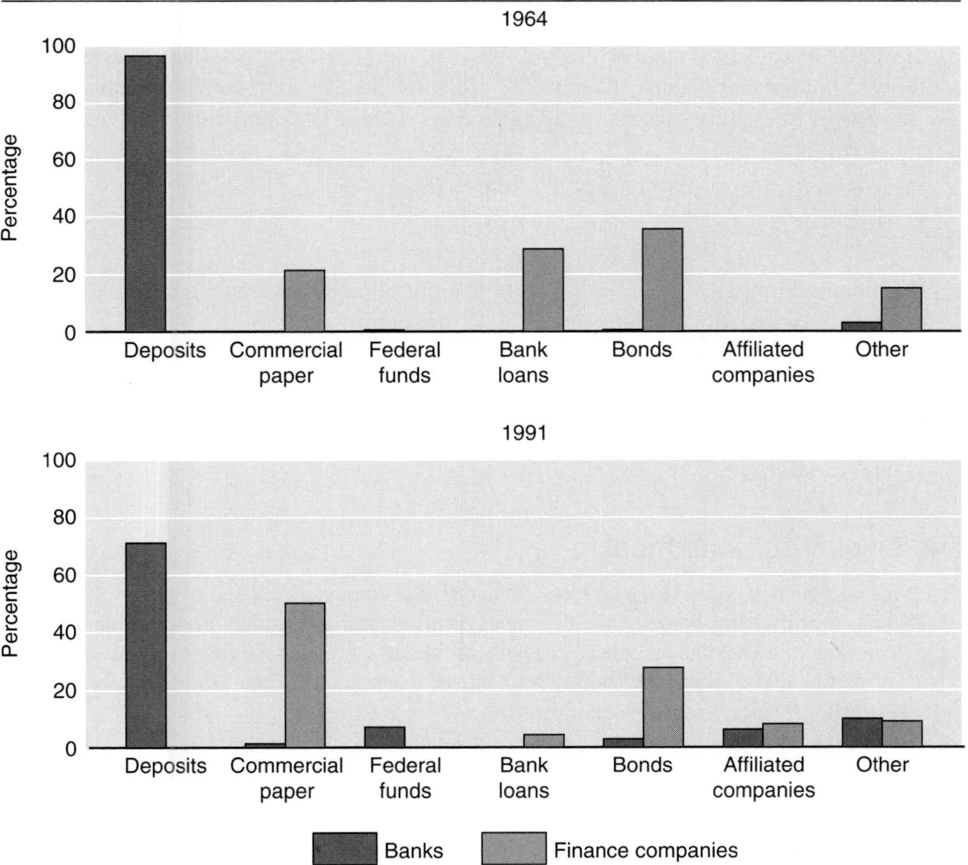

Source: Calculations and graphics based on data from Board of Governors of the Federal Reserve System, *Flow of Funds Accounts, Financial Assets and Liabilities,* various issues.

deposits. Finance company funding was derived primarily from a combination of commercial paper, bank loans, and bonds.

By 1991, commercial banks were less dependent on deposits and obtained more funds from the federal funds and bond markets, but deposits were still 72 percent of total liabilities. The shift in finance company financing was decidedly toward commercial paper, 50 percent of liabilities, and, to a lesser extent, bonds. Thus both industries use short-term sources of funds, deposits and commercial paper.

The competition between banks and finance companies extends beyond supplying business, consumer, and mortgage services. It also includes competition to attract short-term funds. Commercial banks and finance companies are now more similar than ever.

SUMMARY

The early finance companies provided services that commercial banks did not, pioneering the field of asset-based lending for industrial firms and consumers. Major manufacturers of vehicles and other products developed well-functioning captive finance companies.

Today consumers may obtain small loans for a wide variety of purposes and larger second mortgage loans. Through finance companies, consumers also may purchase high-ticket items and arrange financing with retail installment contracts. Some finance companies issue credit cards and own savings banks. Industrial firms have an even greater selection of services, including inventory floor plans, working capital loans, lease financing, highly leveraged transaction loans, and private-label credit cards.

Finance companies represent a significant challenge for commercial banks because banks also provide many of these services. There are some indications that finance companies have overtaken banks in the provision of financial services to industrial firms. Moreover, finance companies, like banks, are funded with short-term obligations. The two industries frequently operate in the same markets, and the competition between them no doubt will intensify.

KEY TERMS

captive finance company
closed-end retail installment contract
commercial finance company
consumer finance company
credit card bank
nonnotification accounts receivable financing
private-label credit cards
retail financing
sales finance company
wholesale financing

END-OF-CHAPTER QUESTIONS

1. What was the first type of financial service that finance companies offered industrial firms?
2. What is the difference between a sales finance company and a consumer finance company?
3. Given what you know about consumer loans (excluding mortgages) in finance companies, why do you think that commercial banks did not pursue this segment of the loan market in the early 1900s when finance companies developed?
4. What single factor contributed most to the popularity of second mortgages?
5. Can you provide any evidence that finance companies and commercial banks compete vigorously in the new-car loan market?
6. How did nonnotification accounts receivable financing help establish finance companies in industrial finance?
7. How does a closed-end retail installment contract differ from a credit card account?

8. Why is the interest rate for an unsecured consumer loan at a finance company higher than at a commercial bank?
9. Why do you think automobile loans represent such a large share of total consumer loans outstanding (excluding mortgage loans) in the finance company industry?
10. Given that finance company unsecured personal loans carry a higher interest rate than second mortgages, why have finance companies so actively pursued the second mortgage market?
11. General Motors Acceptance Corporation actively originates single-family and commercial mortgages. Why then do you think that the company packages and sells them instead of holding them in its own portfolio? [Hint: Consider the firm's balance sheet composition.]
12. Why might a retailer prefer to participate in a private-label credit card program available through a finance company rather than develop its own program?
13. Why might a finance company be more comfortable offering a highly leveraged transaction loan backed by the client's assets than a commercial bank?
14. What advantage accrued to finance companies when they started to issue commercial paper to finance their operations?
15. Obtain the annual reports of a major bank and a major finance company. Compare and contrast their credit operations and funding bases.
16. What advantages and disadvantages would you foresee if banks were allowed to operate in the same way as finance companies.
17. Should finance companies be allowed to own commercial banks? Why or why not?

SELECTED REFERENCES

Beneficial Corporation Annual Report 1990, Peapack, New Jersey.

Braitman, Ellen. "Ford Unit Tries to Mollify Banks; Denies It Would Muscle Them out of Auto Lending," *American Banker,* March 22, 1991, p. 7.

Captive Finance Companies; The Why and How of Credit Subsidiaries, American Management Association, Finance Division, 1966.

Chapman, John M., and Frederick W. Jones. *Finance Companies: How and Where They Obtain Their Funds,* Graduate School of Business, Columbia University, New York, 1959.

Egan, Jack. "The Bank of the Future; GE's Financing Unit Does Everything Except Make Traditional Loans," *U.S. News & World Report,* April, 29, 1991, pp. 51–54.

Federal Reserve Statistical Release; Finance Companies, Board of Governors of the Federal Reserve System, monthly series.

Ford Credit Annual Report 1990, Dearborn, Michigan.

Garsson, Robert M. "No Bank-Buying Rush Seen If Barriers Fall," *American Banker,* February 21, 1991, pp. 1, 10.

General Electric Capital Corporation Annual Report 1990, Stamford, Connecticut.

General Motors Acceptance Corporation Annual Report 1990, Detroit, Michigan.

Household International Annual Report 1990, Prospect Heights, Illinois.

Kantrow, Yvette D. "Finance Companies Are Thriving While Retail Loans Worry Banks," *American Banker,* March 1, 1990.

Lazere, Monroe R., Editor. *Commercial Lending,* The Ronald Press Company, New York, 1968.

McAleer, Ysabel Burns. *Finance Companies in 1989; American Financial Services Association Research Report and Second Mortgage Lending Report,* American Financial Services Association, Washington, D.C., 1990.

Mitchell, Russell. "How GE Is Electrifying the Auto-Auction Business," *Business Week,* May 16, 1988.

Nathans, Leah. "Beneficial Could Give Lending a Good Name Again; The Consumer Finance Giant's Self-Discipline Is Paying Off," *Business Week,* October 22, 1990, p. 102.

Pare, Terence. "Tough Birds That Quack Like Banks; George Bush Wants to Let Industrial Companies Own Banks. Should That Frighten Borrowers? Look at How IBM, GE, and Other Giants Run Huge Finance Operations Now," *Fortune,* March 11, 1991, pp. 79–84.

Phalan, Richard. "Eliminating the Middleman; General Motors Acceptance Corp.'s Money Market Account Offers High Yields to Investors and a Low Cost of Money to GMAC," *Forbes,* August 6, 1990, p. 122.

Tice, David. "Cruisin' for a Bruisin'? GE May Not Escape the Woes Affecting Other Big Lenders," *Barron's,* October 22, 1990, pp. 10–11, 32–35.

"Top 100 Finance Companies in the U.S." *American Banker,* October 26, 1989, p. 8.

Toyota Motor Credit Corporation, Form 10-K, 1990, Torrance, California.

Vogel, Todd. "GE's Finance Arm Is Showing Some Bruises; Despite an Elaborate Monitoring System, a Number of Corporate Loans Have Become Embarrassments," *Business Week,* March 18, 1991, pp. 112–114.

APPENDIXES

APPENDIX A-1

PRESENT VALUE OF $1

FVIF = $(1/(1+k)^n)$

Periods	1%	2%	3%	4%	5%	6%	7%	8%	9%
1	0.9901	0.9804	0.9709	0.9615	0.9524	0.9434	0.9346	0.9259	0.9174
2	0.9803	0.9612	0.9426	0.9246	0.9070	0.8900	0.8735	0.8573	0.8417
3	0.9706	0.9423	0.9151	0.8890	0.8638	0.8396	0.8163	0.7938	0.7722
4	0.9610	0.9238	0.8885	0.8548	0.8227	0.7921	0.7629	0.7350	0.7084
5	0.9515	0.9057	0.8626	0.8219	0.7835	0.7473	0.7130	0.6806	0.6499
6	0.9420	0.8880	0.8375	0.7903	0.7462	0.7050	0.6663	0.6302	0.5963
7	0.9327	0.8706	0.8131	0.7599	0.7107	0.6651	0.6227	0.5835	0.5470
8	0.9235	0.8535	0.7894	0.7307	0.6768	0.6271	0.5820	0.5403	0.5019
9	0.9143	0.8368	0.7664	0.7026	0.6446	0.5919	0.5439	0.5002	0.4604
10	0.9053	0.8203	0.7441	0.6756	0.6139	0.5584	0.5083	0.4632	0.4224
11	0.8963	0.8043	0.7224	0.6496	0.5847	0.5268	0.4751	0.4289	0.3875
12	0.8874	0.7885	0.7014	0.6246	0.5568	0.4970	0.4440	0.3971	0.3555
13	0.8787	0.7730	0.6710	0.6006	0.5303	0.4688	0.4150	0.3677	0.3262
14	0.8700	0.7579	0.6611	0.5775	0.5051	0.4423	0.3878	0.3405	0.2992
15	0.8613	0.7430	0.6419	0.5553	0.4810	0.4173	0.3624	0.3152	0.2745
16	0.8528	0.7284	0.6232	0.5339	0.4581	0.3936	0.3387	0.2919	0.2519
17	0.8444	0.7142	0.6050	0.5134	0.4363	0.3714	0.3166	0.2703	0.2311
18	0.8360	0.7002	0.5874	0.4936	0.4155	0.3503	0.2959	0.2502	0.2120
19	0.8277	0.6864	0.5703	0.4746	0.3957	0.3305	0.2765	0.2317	0.1945
20	0.8195	0.6730	0.5537	0.4564	0.3769	0.3118	0.2584	0.2145	0.1784
25	0.7798	0.6095	0.4776	0.3751	0.2953	0.2330	0.1842	0.1460	0.1160
30	0.7419	0.5521	0.4120	0.3083	0.2314	0.1741	0.1314	0.0994	0.0754
35	0.7059	0.5000	0.3554	0.2534	0.1813	0.1301	0.0937	0.0676	0.0490
40	0.6717	0.4529	0.3066	0.2083	0.1420	0.0972	0.0668	0.0460	0.0318
45	0.6391	0.4102	0.2644	0.1712	0.1113	0.0727	0.0476	0.0313	0.0207
50	1.0000	0.3715	0.2281	0.1407	0.0872	0.0543	0.0339	0.0213	0.0134

10%	11%	12%	13%	14%	15%	16%	17%	18%	19%	20%
0.9091	0.9009	0.8929	0.8850	0.8772	0.8696	0.8621	0.8547	0.8475	0.8403	0.8333
0.8264	0.8116	0.7972	0.7831	0.7695	0.7561	0.7432	0.7305	0.7182	0.7062	0.6944
0.7513	0.7312	0.7118	0.6931	0.6750	0.6575	0.6407	0.6244	0.6086	0.5934	0.5787
0.6830	0.6587	0.6355	0.6133	0.5921	0.5718	0.5523	0.5337	0.5158	0.4987	0.4823
0.6209	0.5935	0.5674	0.5428	0.5194	0.4972	0.4761	0.4561	0.4371	0.4190	0.4019
0.5645	0.5346	0.5066	0.4803	0.4556	0.4323	0.4104	0.3898	0.3704	0.3521	0.3349
0.5132	0.4817	0.4523	0.4251	0.3996	0.3759	0.3538	0.3332	0.3139	0.2959	0.2791
0.4665	0.4339	0.4036	0.3762	0.3506	0.3269	0.3050	0.2848	0.2660	0.2487	0.2326
0.4241	0.3909	0.3606	0.3329	0.3075	0.2843	0.2630	0.2434	0.2255	0.2090	0.1938
0.3855	0.3522	0.3220	0.2946	0.2697	0.2472	0.2267	0.2080	0.1911	0.1756	0.1615
0.3505	0.3173	0.2875	0.2607	0.2366	0.2149	0.1954	0.1778	0.1619	0.1476	0.1346
0.3186	0.2858	0.2567	0.2307	0.2076	0.1869	0.1685	0.1520	0.1375	0.1240	0.1122
0.2897	0.2575	0.2292	0.2042	0.1821	0.1625	0.1452	0.1299	0.1163	0.1042	0.0935
0.2633	0.2320	0.2046	0.1807	0.1597	0.1413	0.1252	0.1110	0.0985	0.0876	0.0779
0.2394	0.2090	0.1824	0.1599	0.1401	0.1229	0.1079	0.0949	0.0835	0.0736	0.0649
0.2176	0.1883	0.1631	0.1415	0.1229	0.1069	0.0930	0.0811	0.0708	0.0618	0.0541
0.1978	0.1696	0.1456	0.1252	0.1078	0.0929	0.0802	0.0693	0.0600	0.0520	0.0451
0.1799	0.1528	0.1300	0.1108	0.0946	0.0808	0.0691	0.0592	0.0508	0.0437	0.0376
0.1635	0.1377	0.1161	0.0981	0.0829	0.0703	0.0596	0.0506	0.0431	0.0367	0.0313
0.1486	0.1240	0.1037	0.0868	0.0728	0.0611	0.0514	0.0433	0.0365	0.0308	0.0261
0.0923	0.0736	0.0588	0.0471	0.0378	0.0304	0.0245	0.0197	0.0160	0.0129	0.0105
0.0573	0.0437	0.0334	0.0256	0.0196	0.0151	0.0116	0.0090	0.0070	0.0054	0.0042
0.0356	0.0259	0.0189	0.0139	0.0102	0.0075	0.0055	0.0041	0.0030	0.0023	0.0017
0.0221	0.0154	0.0107	0.0075	0.0053	0.0037	0.0026	0.0019	0.0013	0.0010	0.0007
0.0137	0.0091	0.0061	0.0041	0.0027	0.0019	0.0013	0.0009	0.0006	0.0004	0.0003
0.0085	0.0054	0.0035	0.0022	0.0014	0.0009	0.0006	0.0004	0.0003	0.0002	0.0001

APPENDIX A-2

PRESENT VALUE OF AN ANNUITY OF $1

$PVIFA = (1-1/(1+k)^n)/k$

Periods	1%	2%	3%	4%	5%	6%	7%	8%	9%
1	0.9901	0.9804	0.9709	0.9615	0.9524	0.9434	0.9346	0.9259	0.9174
2	1.9704	1.9416	1.9135	1.8861	1.8594	1.8334	1.8080	1.7833	1.7591
3	2.9410	2.8839	2.8286	2.7751	2.7232	2.6730	2.6243	2.5771	2.5313
4	3.9020	3.8077	3.7171	3.6299	3.5460	3.4651	3.3872	3.3121	3.2397
5	4.8534	4.7135	4.5797	4.4518	4.3295	4.2124	4.1002	3.9927	3.8897
6	5.7955	5.6014	5.4172	5.2421	5.0757	4.9173	4.7665	4.6229	4.4859
7	6.7282	6.4720	6.2303	6.0021	5.7864	5.5824	5.3893	5.2064	5.0330
8	7.6517	7.3255	7.0197	6.7327	6.4632	6.2098	5.9713	5.7466	5.5348
9	8.5660	8.1622	7.7861	7.4353	7.1078	6.8017	6.5152	6.2469	5.9952
10	9.4713	8.9826	8.5302	8.1109	7.7217	7.3601	7.0236	6.7101	6.4177
11	10.3676	9.7868	9.2526	8.7605	8.3064	7.8869	7.4987	7.1390	6.8052
12	11.2551	10.5753	9.9540	9.3851	8.8633	8.3838	7.9427	7.5361	7.1607
13	12.1337	11.3484	10.6350	9.9856	9.3936	8.8527	8.3577	7.9038	7.4869
14	13.0037	12.1062	11.2961	10.5631	9.8986	9.2950	8.7455	8.2442	7.7862
15	13.8651	12.8493	11.9379	11.1184	10.3797	9.7122	9.1079	8.5595	8.0607
16	14.7179	13.5777	12.5611	11.6523	10.8378	10.1059	9.4466	8.8514	8.3126
17	15.5623	14.2919	13.1661	12.1657	11.2741	10.4773	9.7632	9.1216	8.5436
18	16.3983	14.9920	13.7535	12.6593	11.6896	10.8276	10.0591	9.3719	8.7556
19	17.2260	15.6785	14.3238	13.1339	12.0853	11.1581	10.3356	9.6036	8.9501
20	18.0456	16.3514	14.8775	13.5903	12.4622	11.4699	10.5940	9.8181	9.1285
25	22.0232	19.5235	17.4131	15.6221	14.0939	12.7834	11.6536	10.6748	9.8226
30	25.8077	22.3965	19.6004	17.2920	15.3725	13.7648	12.4090	11.2578	10.2737
35	29.4086	24.9986	21.4872	18.6646	16.3742	14.4982	12.9477	11.6546	10.5668
40	32.8347	27.3555	23.1148	19.7928	17.1591	15.0463	13.3317	11.9246	10.7574
45	36.0945	29.4902	24.5187	20.7200	17.7741	15.4558	13.6055	12.1084	10.8812
50	39.1961	31.4236	25.7298	21.4822	18.2559	15.7619	13.8007	12.2335	10.9617

10%	11%	12%	13%	14%	15%	16%	17%	18%	19%	20%
0.9091	0.9009	0.8929	0.8850	1.8772	0.8696	0.8621	0.8547	0.8475	0.8403	0.8333
1.7355	1.7125	1.6901	1.6681	1.6467	1.6257	1.6052	1.5852	1.5656	1.5465	1.5278
2.4869	2.4437	2.4018	2.3612	2.3216	2.2832	2.2459	2.2096	2.1743	2.1399	2.1065
3.1699	3.1024	3.0373	2.9745	2.9137	2.8550	2.7982	2.7432	2.6901	2.6386	2.5887
3.7908	3.6959	3.6048	3.5172	3.4331	3.3522	3.2743	3.1993	3.1272	3.0576	2.9906
4.3553	4.2305	4.1114	3.9975	3.8887	3.7845	3.6847	3.5892	3.4976	3.4098	3.3255
4.8684	4.7122	4.5638	4.4226	4.2883	4.1604	4.0386	3.9224	3.8115	3.7057	3.6046
5.3349	5.1461	4.9676	4.7988	4.6389	4.4873	4.3436	4.2072	4.0776	3.9544	3.8372
5.7590	5.5370	5.3282	5.1317	4.9464	4.7716	4.6065	4.4506	4.3030	4.1633	4.0310
6.4116	5.8892	5.6502	5.4262	5.2161	5.0188	4.8332	4.6586	4.4941	4.3389	4.1925
6.4951	6.2065	5.9377	5.6869	5.4527	5.2337	5.0286	4.8364	4.5660	4.4865	4.3271
6.8137	6.4924	6.1944	5.9176	5.6603	5.4206	5.1971	4.9884	4.7932	4.6105	4.4392
7.1034	6.7499	6.4235	6.1218	5.8424	5.5831	5.3423	5.1183	4.9095	4.7147	4.5327
7.3667	6.9819	6.6282	6.3025	6.0021	5.7245	5.4675	5.2293	5.0081	4.8023	4.6106
7.6061	7.1909	6.8109	6.4624	6.1422	5.8474	5.5755	5.3242	5.0916	4.8759	4.6755
7.8237	7.3792	6.9740	6.6039	6.2651	5.9542	5.6685	5.4053	5.1624	4.9377	4.7296
8.0216	7.5488	7.1196	6.7291	6.3729	6.0472	5.7487	5.4746	5.2223	4.9897	4.7746
8.2014	7.7016	7.2497	6.8399	6.4674	6.1280	5.8178	5.5339	5.2732	5.0333	4.8122
8.3649	7.8393	7.3658	6.9380	6.5504	6.1982	5.8775	5.5845	5.3162	5.0700	4.8435
8.5136	7.9633	7.4694	7.0248	6.6231	6.2593	5.9288	5.6278	5.3527	5.1009	4.8696
9.0770	8.4217	7.8431	7.3300	6.8729	6.4641	6.0971	5.7662	5.4669	5.1951	1.9476
9.4269	8.6938	8.0552	7.4957	7.0027	6.5660	6.1772	5.8294	5.5168	5.2347	4.9789
9.6442	8.8552	8.1755	7.5856	7.0700	6.6166	6.2153	5.8582	5.5386	5.2512	4.9915
9.7791	8.9511	8.2438	7.6344	7.1050	6.6418	6.2335	5.8713	5.5482	5.2582	4.9966
9.8628	9.0079	8.2825	7.6609	7.1232	6.6543	6.2421	5.8773	5.5523	5.2611	4.9986
9.9148	9.0417	8.3045	7.6752	7.1327	6.6605	6.2463	5.8801	5.5541	5.2623	4.9995

APPENDIX A-3

FUTURE VALUE OF $1
FVIF = $(1+k)^n$

Periods	1%	2%	3%	4%	5%	6%	7%	8%	9%	10%
1	1.0100	1.0200	1.0300	1.0400	1.0500	1.0600	1.0700	1.0800	1.0900	1.1000
2	1.0201	1.0404	1.0609	1.0816	1.1025	1.1236	1.1449	1.1664	1.1881	1.2100
3	1.0303	1.0612	1.0927	1.1249	1.1576	1.1910	1.2250	1.2597	1.2950	1.3310
4	1.0406	1.0824	1.1255	1.1699	1.2155	1.2625	1.3108	1.3605	1.4116	1.4641
5	1.0510	1.1041	1.1593	1.2167	1.2763	1.3382	1.4026	1.4693	1.5386	1.6105
6	1.0615	1.1262	1.1941	1.2653	1.3401	1.4185	1.5007	1.5869	1.6771	1.7716
7	1.0721	1.1487	1.2299	1.3159	1.4071	1.5036	1.6058	1.7138	1.8280	1.9487
8	1.0829	1.1717	1.2668	1.3686	1.4775	1.5938	1.7182	1.8509	1.9926	2.1436
9	1.0937	1.1951	1.3048	1.4233	1.5513	1.6895	1.8385	1.9990	2.1719	2.3579
10	1.1046	1.2190	1.3439	1.4802	1.6289	1.7908	1.9672	2.1589	2.3674	2.5937
11	1.1157	1.2434	1.3842	1.5395	1.7103	1.8983	2.1049	2.3316	2.5804	2.8531
12	1.1268	1.2682	1.4258	1.6010	1.7959	2.0122	2.2522	2.5182	2.8127	3.1384
13	1.1381	1.2936	1.4685	1.6651	1.8856	2.1329	5.4098	2.7196	3.0658	3.4523
14	1.1495	1.3195	1.5126	1.7317	1.9799	2.2609	2.5785	2.9372	3.3417	3.7975
15	1.1610	1.3459	1.5580	1.8009	2.0789	2.3966	2.7590	3.1722	3.6425	4.1772
16	1.1726	1.3728	1.6047	1.8730	2.1829	2.5404	2.9522	3.4259	3.9703	4.5950
17	1.1843	1.4002	1.6528	1.9479	2.2920	2.6928	3.1588	3.7000	4.3276	5.0545
18	1.1961	1.4282	1.7024	2.0258	2.4066	2.8543	3.3799	3.9960	4.7171	5.5599
19	1.2081	1.4568	1.7535	2.1068	2.5270	3.0256	3.6165	4.3157	5.1417	6.1159
20	1.2202	1.4859	1.8061	2.1911	2.6533	3.2071	3.8697	4.6610	5.6044	6.7275
25	1.2824	1.6406	2.0938	2.6658	3.3864	4.2919	5.4274	6.8485	8.6231	10.8347
30	1.3478	1.8115	2.4273	3.2434	4.3219	5.7435	7.6123	10.0627	13.2677	17.4494
35	1.4166	1.9999	2.8139	3.9461	5.5160	7.6861	10.6766	14.7853	20.4140	28.1024
40	1.4889	2.2080	3.2620	4.8010	7.0400	10.2857	14.9745	21.7245	31.4094	45.2593
45	1.5648	2.4379	3.7816	5.8412	8.9850	13.7646	21.0025	31.9204	48.3273	72.8905
50	1.6446	2.6916	4.3839	7.1067	11.4674	18.4202	29.4570	46.9016	74.3575	117.3909

Note: FACTORS IN EXCESS OF 1000 ARE SHOWN IN SCIENTIFIC NOTATION WITH BASE 10. FOR EXAMPLE, 9.10E+03 MEANS 9.10 MULTIPLIED BY 10 RAISED TO THE POWER OF 3, OR 9100.

11%	12%	13%	14%	15%	16%	17%	18%	19%	20%
1.1100	1.1200	1.1300	1.1400	1.1500	1.1600	1.1700	1.1800	1.1900	1.2000
1.2321	1.2544	1.2769	1.2996	1.3225	1.3456	1.3689	1.3924	1.4161	1.4400
1.3676	1.4049	1.4429	1.4815	1.5209	1.5609	1.6016	1.6430	1.6852	1.7280
1.5181	1.5735	1.6305	1.6890	1.7490	1.8106	1.8739	1.9388	2.0053	2.0736
1.6851	1.7623	1.8424	1.9254	2.0114	2.1003	2.1924	2.2878	2.3864	2.4883
1.8704	1.9738	2.0820	2.1950	2.3131	2.4364	2.5652	2.6996	2.8398	2.9860
2.0762	2.2107	2.3526	2.5023	2.6600	2.8262	3.0012	3.1855	3.3793	3.5832
2.3045	2.4760	2.6584	2.8526	3.0590	3.2784	3.5115	3.7589	4.0214	4.2998
2.5580	2.7731	3.0040	3.2519	3.5179	3.8030	4.1084	4.4355	4.7854	5.1598
2.8394	3.1058	3.3946	3.7072	4.0456	1.4114	4.8068	5.2338	5.6947	6.1917
3.1518	3.4785	3.8359	4.2262	4.6524	5.1173	5.6240	6.1759	6.7767	7.4301
3.4985	3.8960	4.3345	4.8179	5.3503	5.9360	6.5801	7.2876	8.0642	8.9161
3.8833	4.3635	4.8980	5.4924	6.1528	6.8858	7.6987	8.5994	9.5964	10.6993
4.3104	4.8871	5.5348	6.2613	7.0757	7.9875	9.0075	10.1472	11.4198	12.8392
4.7846	5.4736	6.2543	7.1379	8.1371	9.2655	10.5387	11.9737	13.5895	15.4070
5.3109	6.1304	7.0673	8.1372	9.3576	10.7480	12.3303	14.1290	16.1715	18.4884
5.8951	6.8660	7.9861	9.2765	10.7613	12.4677	14.4265	16.6722	19.2441	22.1861
6.5436	7.6900	9.0243	10.5752	12.3755	14.4625	16.8790	19.6733	22.9005	26.6233
7.2633	8.6128	10.1974	12.0557	14.2318	16.7765	19.7484	23.2144	27.2516	31.9480
8.0623	9.6463	11.5231	13.7435	16.3665	19.4608	23.1056	27.3930	32.4294	38.3376
13.5855	17.0001	21.2305	26.4619	32.9190	40.8742	50.6578	62.6686	77.3881	95.3962
22.8923	29.9599	39.1159	50.9502	66.2118	85.8499	111.0647	143.3706	184.6753	237.3763
38.5749	52.7996	72.0685	98.1002	133.1755	180.3141	243.5035	327.9973	440.7006	590.6682
65.0009	93.0510	132.7816	188.8835	267.8635	378.7212	533.8687	750.3783	1.05+03	1.47E+03
109.5302	163.9876	244.6414	363.6791	538.7693	795.4438	1.17E+03	1.72E+03	2.51E+03	3.66E+03
184.5648	289.0022	450.7359	700.2330	1.08E+03	1.67E+03	2.57E+03	3.93+03	5.99E+03	9.10E+03

APPENDIX A-4

FUTURE VALUE OF ANNUITY OF $1

$FVIF = ((1+k)^n - 1)/k$

Periods	1%	2%	3%	4%	5%	6%	7%	8%	9%	10%
1	1.0000	1.0000	1.0000	1.0000	1.0000	1.0000	1.0000	1.0000	1.0000	1.0000
2	2.0100	2.0200	2.0300	2.0400	2.0500	2.0600	2.0700	2.0800	2.0900	2.1000
3	3.0301	3.0604	3.0909	3.1216	3.1525	3.1836	3.2149	3.2464	3.2781	3.3100
4	4.0604	4.1216	4.1836	4.2465	4.3101	4.3746	4.4399	4.5061	4.5731	4.6410
5	5.1010	5.2040	5.3091	5.4163	5.5256	5.6371	5.7507	5.8666	5.9847	6.1051
6	6.1520	6.3081	6.4684	6.6330	6.8019	6.9753	7.1533	7.3359	7.5233	7.7156
7	7.2135	7.4343	7.6625	7.8983	8.1420	8.3938	8.6540	8.9228	9.2004	9.4872
8	8.2857	8.5830	8.8923	9.2142	9.5491	9.8975	10.2598	10.6366	11.0285	11.4359
9	9.3685	9.7546	10.1591	10.5828	11.0266	11.4913	11.9780	12.4876	13.0210	13.5795
10	10.4622	10.9497	11.4639	12.0061	12.5779	13.1808	13.8164	14.4866	15.1929	15.9374
11	11.5668	12.1687	12.8078	13.4864	14.2068	14.9716	15.7836	16.6455	17.5603	18.5312
12	12.6825	13.4121	14.1920	15.0258	15.9171	16.8699	17.8885	18.9771	20.1407	21.3843
13	13.8093	14.6803	15.6178	16.6268	17.7130	18.8821	20.4106	21.4953	22.9534	24.5227
14	14.9474	15.9739	17.0863	18.2919	19.5986	21.0151	22.5505	24.2149	56.0192	27.9750
15	16.0969	17.2934	18.5989	20.0236	21.5786	23.2760	25.1290	27.1521	29.3609	31.7725
16	17.2579	18.6393	20.1569	21.8245	23.6575	25.6725	27.8881	30.3243	33.0034	35.9497
17	18.4304	20.0121	21.7616	23.6975	25.8404	28.2129	30.8402	33.7502	36.9737	40.5447
18	19.6147	21.4123	23.4144	25.6454	28.1324	30.9057	33.9990	37.4502	41.3013	45.5992
19	20.8109	22.8406	25.1169	27.6712	30.5390	22.7600	37.3790	41.4463	46.0185	51.1591
20	22.0190	24.2974	26.8704	29.7781	33.0660	36.7856	40.9955	45.7620	51.1601	57.2750
25	28.2432	32.0303	36.4593	41.6459	47.7271	54.8645	63.2490	73.1059	84.7009	98.3471
30	34.7849	40.5681	47.5754	56.0849	66.4388	79.0582	94.4608	113.2832	136.3075	164.4940
35	41.6603	49.9945	60.4621	73.6522	90.3203	111.4348	138.2369	172.3168	215.7108	271.0244
40	48.8864	60.4020	75.4013	95.0255	120.7998	154.7620	199.6351	259.0565	337.8824	442.5926
45	56.4811	71.8927	92.7199	121.0294	159.7002	212.7435	285.7493	386.5056	525.8587	718.9048
50	64.4632	84.5794	112.7969	152.6671	209.3480	290.3359	406.5289	573.7702	815.0836	1.16E+03

Note: FACTORS IN EXCESS OF 1000 ARE SHOWN IN SCIENTIFIC NOTATION WITH BASE 10. FOR EXAMPLE, 4.55E+04 MEANS 4.55 MULTIPLIED BY 10 RAISED TO THE POWER OF 4, OR 45,500.

11%	12%	13%	14%	15%	16%	17%	18%	19%	20%
1.0000	1.0000	1.0000	1.0000	1.0000	1.0000	1.0000	1.0000	1.0000	1.0000
2.1100	2.1200	2.1300	2.1400	2.1500	2.1600	2.1700	2.1800	2.1900	2.200
3.3421	3.3744	3.4069	3.4396	3.4725	3.5056	3.5389	3.5724	3.6061	3.6400
4.7097	4.7793	4.8498	4.9211	4.9934	5.0665	5.1405	5.2154	5.2913	5.3680
6.2278	6.3528	6.4803	6.6101	6.7424	6.8771	7.0144	7.1542	7.2966	7.4416
7.9129	8.1152	8.3227	8.5355	8.7537	8.9775	9.2068	9.4420	9.6830	9.9299
9.7833	10.0890	10.4047	10.7305	11.0668	11.4139	11.7720	12.1415	12.5227	12.9159
11.8594	12.1997	12.7573	13.2328	13.7268	14.2401	14.7733	15.3270	15.9020	16.4991
14.1640	14.7757	15.4157	16.0853	16.7858	17.5185	18.2847	19.0859	19.9234	20.7989
16.7220	17.5487	18.4197	19.3373	20.3037	21.3215	22.3931	23.5213	24.7089	25.9587
19.5614	20.6546	21.8143	23.0445	24.3493	25.7329	27.1999	28.7551	30.4035	32.1504
22.7132	24.1331	25.6502	27.2707	29.0017	30.8502	32.8239	34.9311	37.1802	39.5805
26.2116	28.0291	29.9847	32.0887	34.3519	36.7862	39.4040	42.2187	45.2445	48.4966
30.0949	32.3926	34.8827	37.5811	40.5047	43.6720	47.1027	50.8180	54.8409	59.1959
34.4054	37.2797	40.4175	43.8424	47.5804	51.6595	56.1101	60.9653	66.2607	72.0351
39.1899	42.7533	46.6717	50.9804	55.7175	60.9250	66.6488	72.9390	79.8502	87.4421
44.5008	48.8837	53.7391	59.1176	65.0751	71.6730	78.9792	87.0680	96.0218	105.9306
50.3959	55.7497	61.7251	68.3941	75.8364	84.1407	93.4056	103.7403	115.2659	128.1167
56.9395	63.4397	70.7494	78.9692	88.2118	98.6032	110.2846	123.4135	138.1664	154.7400
64.2028	72.0524	80.9468	91.0249	102.4436	115.3797	130.0329	146.6280	165.4180	186.6880
114.4133	133.3339	155.6196	181.8708	212.7930	249.2140	292.1049	342.6035	402.0425	471.9811
199.0209	241.3327	293.1992	356.7868	434.7451	530.3117	647.4391	790.9480	966.7122	1.18E+03
341.5896	431.6635	546.6808	693.5727	881.1702	1.12E+03	1.43E+03	1.82E+03	2.31E+03	2.95E+03
581.8261	767.0914	1.01E+03	1.34E+03	1.78E+03	2.36E+03	3.13E+03	4.16E+03	5.53E+03	7.34E+03
986.6386	1.36E+03	1.87E+03	2.59E+03	3.59E+03	4.97E+03	6.88E+03	9.53E+03	1.32E+04	1.83E+04
1.67E+03	2.40E+03	3.46E+03	4.99E+03	7.22E+03	1.04E+04	1.51E+04	2.18E+04	3.15E+04	4.55E+04

APPENDIX B-1

GLOSSARY

asked price The price at which a dealer will sell a security or foreign currency.

asset liquidity The extent to which an asset may quickly be converted to cash without realizing a loss on the transaction.

asset portfolio A combination of assets assembled to achieve certain investment objectives.

available balance That portion of an account balance that may be withdrawn immediately.

balance of payments The description of financial transactions between a country and its trading partners. The categories include goods (merchandise), services, and investment capital.

bank holding company A corporation whose primary function is to own other corporations, specifically, one or more commercial banks.

bank liquidity The ability of a bank to meet its current obligations for cash outflow and to respond to changes in customer demand for loans and cash withdrawals *without* selling assets at a substantial loss. Bank assets are liquid to the extent that they may be easily converted into cash without loss.

bank syndicate Group of banks that together contribute the necessary financing for a transaction (deposit withdrawal or loan).

banker's acceptance A time draft (postdated instrument) payable to a seller of goods with payment guaranteed by a bank.

basis point One hundredth of one percent.

benefit payments Payments by insurers to insureds that satisfy the terms of an insurance contract.

bid-asked spread Dealer profit in a securities transaction; the difference between the purchase and sales prices that a dealer will accept.

bid or tender system A predetermined quantity of securities that is offered for sale and sold or "tendered" to the highest bidders.

bid price The price that a dealer is willing to pay to purchase a security or foreign currency.

bill discounting Receiving payment on a bill of exchange prior to the bill's maturity by surrendering the bill for face value *less* applicable interest for the time remaining to maturity.

bill of exchange An order written by the seller of goods instructing the purchaser to pay the seller (or bearer of the bill) a specified amount on a specified future date.

Bond Theorem 1 When the coupon rate equals the required rate of return, a bond will sell at par.

Bond Theorem 2 When the coupon rate is less than (greater than) the required rate of return, a bond sells at a discount (premium).

Bond Theorem 3 All other things being equal, the price of a bond approaches its par value as its maturity date approaches.

Bond Theorem 4 There is an inverse relationship between bond price movements and changes in required rate of return.

Bond Theorem 5 Longer-term bonds are more price-sensitive to a given change in yield to maturity than are shorter-term bonds.

bonds Contractual liabilities that obligate the issuer to pay a specified amount (the par, face, or maturity value) at a given date in the future (maturity date), generally with periodic interest payments in the interim at a fixed rate (coupon rate).

brokered deposits Deposits placed with an institution through a securities broker, who, in turn, earns a commission on the sale. Such deposits were most often sold in $100,000 increments to retain full federal deposit insurance.

building society A mutual organization that uses its financial resources to make loans for the purpose of buying land and constructing homes.

call money Loaned funds that are repayable upon the request of either party.

call provision A feature of a bond that entitles the issuer to retire the bond before maturity.

capital gain The difference between the price that is originally paid for a security and cash proceeds at the time of maturity (face value of a bond) or at the time of sale (selling price of a bond or stock).

capital gains yield Capital gain as a percentage of the value of a security at the beginning of the time period.

capital markets Markets in which financial instruments with maturities greater than 1 year are bought and sold.

capital ratio Capital as a percentage of assets.

capital shares Shares of a closed-end investment company that receive only the increase (or decrease) in market value of the fund's asset investment.

captive finance company A finance company that is wholly owned by a manufacturing firm and handles the retail and wholesale financing of only that manufacturer.

central bank A financial institution that carries out the financial transactions of the federal government, controls and regulates the money supply, maintains order in financial markets, promotes favorable economic conditions, and/or acts as a lender of last resort for other financial institutions.

check float The time that elapses between the payee's receipt of a check and the corresponding reduction in the payor's account.

closed-end fund An investment company that issues a fixed number of ownership claims, or shares. After these shares have been sold initially, investors who wish to purchase shares must buy them from other investors who own them.

closed-end retail installment contract A contract that obligates a consumer purchasing goods to pay a lender specified installments for a specified period of time.

commercial paper Unsecured promissory notes, issued by corporations with an original maturity of 270 days or less.

commitment fee The rate charged to a bank customer for the unused portion of a line of credit.

common bond An attribute that describes all members of a credit union. The common bond distinguishes credit unions from all other mutual financial institutions.

corporate stock Financial claims on a corporation held by the owners of the firm.

correlation coefficient A measure of the degree to which the returns of two assets move together.

country risk Risk associated with the creditworthiness of a borrower with residence outside the home country of the lending institution.

credit card bank A bank designated to conduct primarily credit card business and is thus not subject to the same regulatory constraints as commercial banks.

credit card draft The sales slip created in a credit card transaction, showing amount, payee, payor, credit card issuer, and payor signature.

credit union share account An ownership claim on a credit union, similar in form to a common stock interest. Payments to owners are called *dividend payments.* In substance, share accounts are equivalent to deposits.

debit card A card whose use results in reduction of the payor's bank account balance, that is, a "debit" to the deposit account of that payor. The offsetting "credit" is to the payee's deposit account, or, alternatively, to the deposit account of the payee's bank.

default risk The risk that a borrower may not repay principal and/or interest as originally agreed.

default risk premium The component of a required interest rate that is based on the borrower's perceived risk of default. All other things being equal, it is the difference between the required rate of return and the risk-free (government security) rate.

deficit savings unit (DSU) An economic unit whose current income is less than current expenditures.

defined benefit plan A pension plan that entitles its participants, upon retirement, to specified cash *distributions,* based upon a formula that considers a number of variables, including years of service and salary during employment.

defined contribution plan A pension plan that entitles its participants, during employment, to specified cash *contributions* to a pension fund.

demand deposit Depository institution account that may be withdrawn upon demand via check or other means.

direct financing The provision of funds for investment to the ultimate user of the funds (deficit savings unit) by an ultimate investor (surplus savings unit).

discount pricing Setting the price of a financial instrument at the face value *less* the amount of interest that will be earned through the maturity date.

discount rate The interest rate at which a depository institution borrows directly from the Federal Reserve bank in its district.

disintermediation The withdrawal of funds from depository institutions for the purpose of investing in other vehicles.

diversification The combination of assets with the objective of reducing portfolio variability.

dividends Periodic cash flows paid to the owners of corporate stock (frequently paid on a quarterly basis).

double coincidence of want The situation in which each of two parties seeks to obtain the product or commodity that the other possesses, making it possible for them to engage in barter.

dual banking system Banking system in which a bank may obtain either a federal charter (from the Office of the Comptroller of the Currency) or a state charter (from state banking authorities).

Eurobonds Bonds issued by parties outside their domestic capital markets, underwritten by an international investment banking syndicate, placed in at least two countries, and, perhaps, issued in more than one currency.

Eurocommercial paper Short-term unsecured notes issued by firms in markets outside their domestic markets.

Eurodollars Deposits denominated in U.S. dollars issued by banks outside the United States. Even if the bank's home office is in the United States, the deposit is considered a Eurodollar deposit.

Euroequities Common and preferred stocks offered outside the issuer's domestic capital market in one or more foreign markets and underwritten by an international syndicate.

excess reserves The amount by which actual reserve assets exceed required reserves.

exchange rate risk The risk that changes in currency exchange rates may have an unfavorable impact on costs or revenues.

expected rate of return (k') The rate that causes an asset's present value of future cash flows to equal its market price. The expected rate of return is determined by substituting all known (or estimated) values into the asset's valuation formula and solving for k.

federal funds Immediately available short-term funds transferred (loaned or borrowed) between financial institutions, usually for a period of 1 day.

Federal Reserve System A system of twelve regional banks, coordinated by the Federal Reserve Board in Washington, D.C. This was the first system in the United States designed to perform all the functions of a central bank.

field of membership The group of people who have a particular common bond and may join a particular credit union.

financial intermediation The process of facilitating the flow of funds from surplus savings units (SSUs) to deficit savings units (DSUs), with primary securities (issued by DSUs) held by financial institutions and secondary securities (issued by financial institutions) held by SSUs.

fiscal policy The policy of government with respect to government revenues and expenditures.

foreign bonds Bonds issued by entities outside their domestic capital markets in a foreign market, underwritten by a firm that is domestic to that foreign market, usually denominated in the currency of the market in which they are issued, but occasionally denominated in another currency.

foreign currency exchange futures contract A contract, traded on organized exchanges in standard units, to exchange two currencies at some specified future date. The party purchasing the contract agrees to purchase foreign currency on the specified date. The party selling the contract agrees to sell the currency at that date.

foreign currency exchange options A contract that confers the right to buy or sell foreign currency at a specified price through some future date. The right is exercisable at the discretion of the option buyer.

foreign currency swap An exchange of foreign currency in the spot market with a simultaneous agreement to reverse the transactions in the forward market. Both exchange rates and timing of the forward market transaction are specified at the time of the swap.

foreign exchange hedging Using financial contracts to protect against adverse changes in foreign exchange rates.

forward foreign currency exchange contract An agreement between two parties to exchange foreign currencies at a predetermined rate on a specific date in the future. Two days before the specified date, the forward contract becomes a spot contract.

401(k) plan A tax-deferred savings plan that sometimes supplements the basic retirement plan and allows both employer and employee contributions.

full-bodied money Money (medium of exchange) with an intrinsic value that is equal to its value as a unit of account. Many commodities have been used as full-bodied money, but the most common have been precious metals.

futures contract An agreement to exchange a standard quantity of an asset at a specified date in the future at a predetermined price.

gap The difference between rate-sensitive assets and liabilities.

general accounts The investment (asset) accounts of a life insurance company that appears in the firm's balance sheet.

gilt-edged market The market for medium- and long-term government securities in the United Kingdom.

giro system A nonbank payments system (frequently at the post office) that transfers funds from one account to another on a same-day basis.

government agency securities Securities issued by an agency of the U.S. federal government, with implicit backing of the federal government.

greenbacks National currency printed by the federal government but not backed by gold.

hedging Using one or more financial innovations to protect the market value of specific assets and liabilities (microhedge) or of equity (macrohedge) from adverse effects of interest rate changes.

immediately available funds Funds on deposit in a commercial bank or other depository institution that may be withdrawn with no delay.

income shares Shares of a closed-end investment company that receive only the interest and dividend income from the fund's asset investments.

indifference tax rate That rate which produces an after-tax yield on taxable securities that is equal to the municipal yield, causing an investor to be indifferent between the two types of securities.

indirect financing The process by which entrepreneurs obtain money for investment from a financial intermediary who, in turn, has accumulated the funds from ultimate investors.

individual retirement account An individually funded, self-directed retirement account that may be established by employees also covered by employer-sponsored pension plans.

inflation rate The percentage increase in prices of goods and services that results from the loss of purchasing power of a nation's currency.

insurance agent A party who conducts transactions on behalf of an insurance underwriter but takes no personal responsibility to honor the insurance company.

insurance broker A party who conducts insurance transactions as an independent third party who brings together the insurer and the insured.

insurance policy A contract that provides a party (the insured) with protection against financial loss associated with an undesirable event.

insurance premiums Either periodic or lump-sum payments to an insurer in exchange for protection against a specified risk.

insurance underwriter The party that assumes the risk associated with an insurance contract and agrees to pay claims arising from the policy.

insured pension plan Pension plan sponsored by a private corporation but administered by an insurance company.

interbank market Money market transactions (short-term exchange of liquid assets) between banks with no intermediary.

interest rate parity A concept indicating that interest rate differentials are reflected in the forward exchange rate of two countries.

interest rate risk The risk that the market value of a fixed-income security will decline when interest rates increase.

interest rate spread The difference between the rate of return from earning assets and the rate paid on interest-bearing liabilities.

investment adviser The party that makes asset investment decisions for an investment company. These decisions must conform with the company's stated investment philosophy.

investment banks Securities firms that are retained to advise issuing entities on stock and bond offerings and that take an active role in the distribution of the securities to ultimate investors.

investment company A firm that is organized and operated for the exclusive purpose of purchasing the debt and/or equity of other business organizations, government securities, municipal securities, or some combination of these.

investment company distributor The party that markets the shares of an investment company to the public.

investment philosophy An investment company's approach to investing in terms of types of securities, risk tolerance, average maturity of the portfolio, and emphasis on current income (interest or dividend income) or capital gains yield (change in market value of the securities).

keiretsu A Japanese system of joint corporate ownership without a formal holding company. Each member of the group owns a small portion of stock in all the other members so that as much as 80 percent of the stock of each is held by affiliated companies.

Keogh account A retirement account maintained by a self-employed individual. Contributions and investment income are tax-deferred until distributions are received by the individual after retirement.

lender of last resort The financial institution from which other financial institutions may ultimately receive assistance during a liquidity crisis.

letter of credit A letter issued by a bank or other firm indicating that a company has arranged to obtain financing up to a specified amount.

leveraged buyout (LBO) The purchase of the common stock of a firm with borrowed funds.

LIBOR London Interbank Offered Rate, the rate of interest at which short-term funds are exchanged between banks in London.

line of credit A preapproved credit facility (usually for 1 year), enabling a bank customer to borrow up to the specified maximum amount at any time during the relevant period of time.

liquid assets Assets that may be converted into cash quickly, without significant loss of value.

liquidity The extent to which an asset may quickly be converted into cash without realizing a loss on the transaction.

M_1 Currency and coin in circulation, demand deposits in commercial banks, transactions accounts at other depository institutions, and traveler's checks.

M_2 M_1 plus savings accounts, money market deposit accounts at depository institutions, certificates of deposit and repurchase agreements in amounts under $100,000, overnight repurchase agreements of commercial banks, overnight Eurodollars issued to U.S. residents (excluding financial institutions), and retail money market fund balances.

M_3 M_2 plus certificates of deposit and repurchase agreements in denominations greater than $100,000, institutional money market fund balances, and term Eurodollars issued to U.S. residents (excluding financial institutions).

management fee An annual fee charged to an investment company by its investment adviser for services rendered.

medium of exchange The function of money that permits its universal exchange for other commodities.

merchant bank A bank that serves the needs of commercial enterprises by giving advice on financial alternatives and corporate mergers and by underwriting new issues, as well as accepting bills of exchange, providing foreign currency exchange facilities, and operating in the money markets.

monetary base Claims against a central bank that serve as money (currency) and the reserves held by a central bank that form the basis for creation of money (reserves of depository institutions).

monetary policy The policy of government with respect to its money supply.

money market A market in which financial instruments with maturities up to 1 year are bought and sold.

money market mutual fund An open-end investment company whose assets consist primarily of Treasury bills, negotiable certificates of deposit, Eurodollar deposits, commercial paper, and banker's acceptances.

money panic Rapid withdrawal of deposits from a commercial bank precipitated by fear that the bank will fail.

mortgages Long-term liabilities collateralized by real property. Commonly, monthly payments are made that fully repay both principal and interest over the term of the loan.

mutual depository organization Noncorporate financial institution in which individual contributions are considered equity investments even though they closely resemble deposits in most other aspects (stated interest rate, variability of amount invested, and ease of withdrawal, relative to other equity investments).

mutual fund An open-end investment company, that is, one which issues new shares whenever investors wish to buy them. Likewise, a mutual fund redeems shares whenever investors wish to sell them.

negotiable certificate of deposit (CD) A financial instrument issued by a bank documenting a deposit, with principal and interest repayable to the bearer at a specified future date.

net asset value per share (NAV) Market value of mutual fund assets *less* liabilities (net assets) *divided* by the number of shares outstanding.

net interest income The difference between interest earned on time deposits, investment securities, loans, and other earning assets and interest paid on deposits and other interest-bearing liabilities.

net interest margin The difference between the average rate earned on earning assets and the average rate paid on interest-bearing liabilities.

net worth The difference between the *market values* of assets and liabilities. In this context, net worth is to be distinguished from GAAP-defined (generally accepted accounting principles) shareholders' equity and from RAP-defined (regulatory accounting principles) capital.

net worth certificate A claim issued by a capital-deficit S&L for the purpose of increasing regulatory capital. Its issuance is *not* accompanied by the infusion of real capital.

nonnotification accounts receivable financing Method of obtaining a loan by assigning the future collection of accounts receivable to a financial institution without advising the customers (that gave rise to the receivables) of the arrangement.

normal cost The present value of vested pension benefits earned by participants during the current year.

off–balance sheet activity An activity or service that does not appear on a bank's financial statements, that is, a contingent obligation or an obligation to provide service in the future.

open-market operations The purchase and sale of government securities by the Federal Reserve in the public securities market.

operating cycle The length of time that it takes for a firm to produce its final product, sell to its customers, and collect proceeds of the sale in cash.

opportunity cost of holding cash The rate of return that could be earned if the next best alternative to cash were held by an investor, that is, the rate of return that is forgone when an investor holds cash.

option contract An agreement that confers the right to buy or sell an asset at a set price through some future date. The right is exercisable at the discretion of the option buyer.

organized stock exchange A specific location where stocks (and some bonds) are traded by exchange members who specialize in particular securities. These specialists match buyers and sellers and maintain an orderly market by trading for their own account whenever there is an imbalance of buyers and sellers.

overdraft A check written for which there are insufficient bank funds that the bank honors, effectively granting the check writer a short-term loan.

overlending The situation in which a bank's loan demand consistently exceeds available deposits and capital.

past service liabilities The present value of vested pension benefits earned by participants before (1) 1974 or (2) plan adoption, whichever is later.

pension fund A separate entity to which periodic (or in some cases, lump-sum) contributions are made by or on behalf of covered pension plan participants. At the time of retirement, each participant receives a distribution from the fund in the form of an annuity or a lump-sum payment.

pension liability The amount of vested (nonforfeitable) pension benefits that a corporation or government organization is obligated to pay its current and retired employees.

pension plan funding The extent to which assets are set aside currently to meet future pension plan obligations.

policy reserves Profits set aside by insurance companies to enable them to make future benefit payments. These are the equivalent of capital or retained earnings in other industries.

portability The right of an employee to retain the vested benefits of a pension plan when changing place of employment. The employee either receives a lump-sum distribution or transfers the amount to another pension fund.

price index The standardized value of a basket of goods and/or services.

price risk The risk that the market value of a fixed-income security will decline when interest rates increase.

primary markets Markets that bring surplus savings units together with deficit savings units in the process of financing productive activities. Securities are sold for the first time in primary markets.

primary security A financial claim issued by the ultimate user of the funds, the DSU.

private-label credit card program A program in which a finance company manages the credit card operation of a retailer, including promotion, credit evaluations, billing, and accounting, all in the retailer's name.

private pension plan Pension plan sponsored and administered by a private corporation.

public pension plan Pension plan sponsored by the federal government and by state and local governments.

purchasing power parity The concept that homogeneous goods cannot have more than one price measured in any one currency. If the price increases domestically, the domestic currency will depreciate so that the price denominated in foreign currency remains the same. This is the *law of one price.*

quota The minimum subscription (contribution) that a country must pay in order to become a member of the International Monetary Fund.

rate-sensitive assets and liabilities Assets and liabilities whose rates earned and paid change with market interest rates. They have floating interest rates instead of fixed rates.

redlining The systematic withholding of bank loans from low- to moderate-income communities while still accepting deposits in them, particularly communities with a significant minority population.

reinvestment risk The risk that it may not be possible to reinvest the proceeds of maturing fixed-income securities at rates equivalent to those of the maturing securities because of generally declining interest rates.

repurchase agreement (repo) An agreement between buyer and seller in the sale of securities to reverse the transaction in the future at a specified date and price.

reserve assets Assets (cash and other liquid assets) held for the satisfaction of future requests for cash (withdrawals) that are related to specific liabilities (deposits).

reserve requirement Minimum reserve assets that by law a depository financial institution must maintain. Reserve requirements are expressed in terms of a percentage of relevant bank deposits.

reserve tranche The excess of a country's International Monetary Fund quota over the holdings by IMF of its own currency.

return on assets (ROA) Net income as a percentage of average total assets.

return on equity (ROE) Net income as a percentage of average total shareholders' equity.

sales charge (load) A sales commission that is paid by purchasers of mutual fund shares.

secondary markets Markets in which already existing securities change hands. In effect, securities are transferred from one surplus savings unit to another.

secondary security A financial claim issued by a financial intermediary.

securities broker In the context of an investment company, the party that executes the securities trades (purchases and sales) that have been initiated by the investment adviser.

securitization The pooling of a group of loans with similar characteristics and the subsequent sale of interests in the resulting pool to investors.

separate account Assets managed by an insurance company that do not appear on the insurance company balance sheet.

solvency The financial condition of a bank in which the value of its assets exceeds the values of liabilities.

spot foreign currency exchange market transaction The immediate exchange of currencies in the form of bank deposits, bank notes (money), or traveler's checks. Transactions are over-the-counter (immediate), unless they involve bank deposits, in which case both parties in the exchange have 2 days to deliver.

stagflation Inflation that occurs simultaneously with stagnant economic growth (recession).

standard for deferred payments The function of money that allows future commitments to be denominated in financial terms rather than in terms of other nonmonetary commodities.

sterling money market Short-term market for funds denominated in British pounds.

store of value The function of money that prevents its value from declining over time.

surplus savings unit (SSU) An economic entity whose income for the applicable period exceeds expenditures.

swap contract An agreement between two parties (counterparties) to exchange assets or a series of cash flows for a specified period of time at predetermined intervals.

syndicate Group of banks that together contribute the necessary financing for a transaction (deposit withdrawal or loan).

tap system The system by which the government sells only those securities that the public requests.

taxable-equivalent amount The amount of before-tax income from a taxable source that is equivalent to a corresponding amount of tax-exempt income, once applicable taxes have been considered.

term structure of interest rates The relationship between time (term) and interest rates.

terminating building society A mutual organization with the purpose of providing each member with a loan to construct a home. When each member has received and repaid the loan, the society ceases operations.

thrift institution A financial institution that encourages moderate-income workers to save money on a regular basis. Likewise, the institution invests in loans to these savers, especially mortgage loans. In the United States, savings and loans associations and mutual savings banks are classified as thrift institutions.

tiered custodial system System that segments ownership records of Treasury securities. The Treasury Department records ownership by the relevant Federal Reserve bank. The particular Federal Reserve bank records ownership for a depository institution. Only the depository institution maintains records of ultimate ownership.

transaction account multiplier The potential increase in transactions accounts for a $1 change in depository institution reserves; the inverse of the reserve requirement for transactions accounts.

Treasury bills Short-term obligations of the U.S. Treasury Department with original maturities of 1 year or less.

underwriting The initial distribution of securities by an entity other than the issuer, with the risk of price fluctuations borne to some extent by the distributor(s).

unit of account The function of money that results in the pricing of other commodities in terms of units of an economy's money.

universal bank A bank that has the legal authority to offer all financial services and may, thus, be engaged in securities and insurance underwriting as well as the full range of more traditional banking services.

vesting The process through which the right to receive cash distributions during retirement becomes a nonforfeitable right.

window guidance Persuasion used by the Bank of Japan to convince commercial banks to support those industries deemed important for the country's growth and development.

yield curve A graphic description of the relationship between time to maturity and yields to maturity for a given risk class of securities.

yield to maturity (YTM) The average annual rate of return to a bond investor who buys a bond today and holds it until it matures. The YTM is that rate of return that causes the market price to equal exactly the present value of the future cash flows (interest payments and maturity value).

zaibatsu A Japanese holding company with a wide variety of subsidiary firms, a form of business organization that existed after the Meiji Restoration of 1868 until the end of World War II.

INDEX